NOTES

ON THE

OLD TESTAMENT

EXPLANATORY AND PRACTICAL

BY

ALBERT BARNES

ENLARGED TYPE EDITION

EDITED BY

ROBERT FREW, D.D.

PSALMS
VOL. III

BAKER BOOK HOUSE
GRAND RAPIDS, MICHIGAN

Library of Congress Catalog Card Number: 55-11630

ISBN: 0-8010-0542-6

First Printing, April 1950
Second Printing, December 1956
Third Printing, May 1959
Fourth Printing, June 1961
Fifth Printing, November 1963
Sixth Printing, January 1966
Seventh Printing, August 1968
Eighth Printing, June 1970
Ninth Printing, June 1971
Tenth Printing, August 1973

PRINTED IN U.S.A.

THE BOOK OF PSALMS.

PSALM XC.

THIS psalm is one of the most remarkable in the whole collection. It is said, in the title, to be " A Prayer of Moses, the man of God ;" or, as it is in the margin, " being a Psalm of Moses." The original word—תְּפִלָּה, *tephillah*—means properly (1) intercession, supplication for any one ; (2) prayer or supplication in general ; (3) a hymn or inspired song. Gesenius, *Lex.* In Ps. lxxii. 20, the word is applied to the whole preceding part of the Book of Psalms,—" The *prayers* of David, the son of Jesse, are ended." The word *prayer* would better represent the nature of the contents of this psalm than the word *psalm*, or *hymn*.

If the author was Moses, then this is the only one of his compositions which we have in the Book of Psalms. We know, from not a few places in the Pentateuch, that Moses was a poet as well as a lawgiver and statesman ; and it would not be improbable that there might have been some compositions of his of this nature which were not incorporated in the five books that he wrote, and which would be likely to be preserved by tradition. This psalm bears internal evidence that it may have been such a composition. There is no local allusion which would make it necessary to suppose that it was written at a later period ; there is nothing inconsistent with the sentiments and style of Moses in the Pentateuch'; there is much that is in accordance with his style and manner ; and there were numerous occasions when the sentiments of the psalm would be exceedingly suitable to the circumstances in which he was, and to the train of thoughts which we may suppose to have passed through his mind. The following remarks of Prof. Alexander seem to me to be eminently just and appropriate : — " The correctness of the title which ascribes the psalm to Moses is confirmed by its unique simplicity and grandeur ; its appropriateness to his times and circumstances ; its resemblance to the law in urging the connexion between sin and death ; its similarity of diction to the poetical portions of the Pentateuch, without the slightest trace of imitation or quotation ; its marked unlikeness to the Psalms of David, and still more to those of later date ; and finally the proved impossibility of plausibly assigning it to any other age or author." As a relic thus of most ancient times,—as coming down from the most remarkable man in the Jewish history, if not in the world, — as well as for its own instructive beauty and appropriateness to all times and lands,—it is a composition of great interest and value.

This psalm is placed at the beginning of the fourth book of the Psalter, according to the ancient traditional division of the Psalms. Or, perhaps, the author of the arrangement— probably Ezra—designed to place this *by itself* between the two great divisions of the book, containing respectively the earlier and the later psalms. It may be regarded, therefore, as " the heart or centre of the whole collection," suggesting thoughts appropriate to the entire current of thought in the book.

The phrase, " the man of God," in the title, is given to Moses in Deut. xxxiii. 1; Josh. xiv. 6 ; Ezra iii. 2, as a title especially appropriate to him, denoting that he was faithful to God ; that he was a man approved by God. The title is indeed given to others, Judges xiii. 6, 8; 1 Sam. ii. 27 ; ix. 6-8; 1 Kings xii. 22, *et al. ;* but there was a peculiar appropriateness in the title as given to Moses on account of his character, his eminent rank, and his influence in founding the Hebrew commonwealth.

It is impossible, of course, now to determine the time when the psalm was composed, but it may not improbably be supposed to have been near the close of the wanderings in the wilderness. The Hebrew people were about to enter the promised land ; the generation that came out of Egypt was passing away ; Moses himself felt that he was near the end of his course, for he had been apprized that he could not enter the land of promise to

B

PSALM XC.

A Prayer [1] of Moses, the man [a] of God.

LORD, thou hast been our

[1] Or, being a Psalm *of*.
[a] Deut. xxxiii. 1.

dwelling-place [b] in [2] all generations.

[b] Ps. lxxi. 3 ; Ez. xi. 16.
[2] *generation and generation.*

the borders of which he had conducted the people. These things were eminently fitted to suggest such views of the shortness of human life, and of its frailty, as are here presented. At the same time, all these circumstances were fitted to suggest the reference to the future, and the prayer in respect to that future, with which the psalm so beautifully closes. It seems, then, not improper to regard this psalm as one of the last utterances of Moses, when the wanderings of the Hebrew people were about to cease ; when an entire generation had been swept off; and when his own labours were soon to close.

The main subject of the psalm is the brevity—the transitory nature—of human life ; the reflections on which seem designed to lead the soul up to God, who does not die. The races of men are cut down like grass, but God remains the same from age to age. One generation finds him the same as the previous generation had found him—unchanged, and as worthy of confidence as ever. None of those changes can affect him, and there is in each age the comforting assurance that he will be found to be the refuge, the support, the "dwelling-place" of his people.

The psalm consists of the following parts :—

I. The fact that God is unchanging; that he *is* the refuge of his people, and always *has been ;* that from the eternity past to the eternity to come, he is the same,—he alone is God, vers. 1, 2.

II. The frailty of man—the brevity of human life—as contrasted with this unchanging nature— this eternity—of God, vers. 3–11. Man is turned to destruction ; he is carried away as with a flood ; his life is like a night's sleep ; the human race is like grass which is green in the morning and is cut down at evening ;—human existence is like a tale that is told—brief as a meditation—and narrowed down to threescore years and ten.

III. A prayer that the living might be able so to number their days—to take such an account of life as to apply the heart to wisdom ;—to make the most of life, or to be truly wise, ver. 12.

IV. A prayer for those who were to follow—for the coming generation—that God would continue his favours ; that though the present generation must die, yet that God, who is unchanging and eternal, would meet the next generation, and all the generations to come, with the same mercies and blessings, enjoyed by those who went before them,—prolonging these to all future time, vers. 13–17.

The psalm, therefore, has a universal applicability. Its sentiments and its petitions are as appropriate now as they were in the time of Moses. The generations of men pass away as certainly and as rapidly now as they did then ; but it is as true now as it was then, that God is unchanging, and that he is the "dwelling-place"—the home—of his people.

1. *Lord.* Not here *Jehovah,* but *Adonai*—אֲדֹנָי. The word is properly rendered *Lord,* but it is a term which is often applied to God. It indicates, however, nothing in regard to his character or attributes except that he is a *Ruler* or *Governor.* ¶ *Thou hast been our dwelling-place.* The LXX. render this, *refuge*—καταφυγή. So the Latin Vulgate, *refugium ;* and Luther, *Zuflucht.* The Hebrew word —מָעֽוֹן, *maon*—means properly a habitation, a dwelling, as of God in his temple, Ps. xxvi. 8 ; heaven, Ps. lxviii. 5 ; Deut. xxvi. 15. It also means a den or lair for wild beasts, Nah. ii. 12 ; Jer. ix. 11. But here the idea seems to be, as in the Septuagint, Vulgate, and Luther, *a refuge ;* a place to which one may come *as* to his home, as one does from a journey ; from wandering ; from toil ; from danger :—a place to which such a one naturally resorts, which he loves, and where he feels that he may rest secure. The idea is, that a friend of God has that feeling in respect to Him, which one has towards his own home—his abode—the place which he loves and calls his own. ¶ *In all*

2 Before ^{c} the mountains were brought forth, or ever thou hadst formed the earth and the world, even from everlasting to ever-

c Prov. viii. 25, 26.

lasting, thou *art* God.
3 Thou turnest man to destruction; and sayest, Return, ^{d} ye children of men.

d Gen. iii. 19.

---

generations. Marg., *generation and generation.* That is, A succeeding generation has found him to be the same as the previous generation had. *He* was unchanged, though the successive generations of men passed away.

2. *Before the mountains were brought forth.* Before the earth brought forth or produced the mountains. In the description of the creation it would be natural to represent the mountains as the first objects that appeared, as emerging from the waters; and, therefore, as the *first* or *most ancient* of created objects. The phrase, therefore, is equivalent to saying, Before the earth was created. The literal meaning of the expression, "were brought forth," is, in the Hebrew, "were born." The mountains are mentioned as the most ancient things in creation, in Deut. xxxiii. 15. Comp. Gen. xlix. 26; Hab. iii. 6. ¶ *Or ever thou hadst formed.* Literally, "hadst brought forth." Comp. Job xxxix. 1. ¶ *The earth and the world.* The word *earth* here is used to denote the world as distinguished either from heaven (Gen. i. 1), or from the sea (Gen. i. 10). The term *world* in the original is commonly employed to denote the earth considered as *inhabited*, or as capable of being inhabited,—a dwelling-place for living beings. ¶ *Even from everlasting to everlasting.* From duration stretching backward without limit to duration stretching forward without limit; that is, from eternal ages to eternal ages; or, for ever. ¶ *Thou* art *God.* Or, "Thou, O God." The idea is, that he was always, and ever will be, *God* :—the God; the true God; the only God; the unchangeable God. At any period in the past, during the existence of the earth, or the heavens, or before either

was formed, he existed, with all the attributes essential to Deity; at any period in the future — during the existence of the earth and the heavens, or beyond—far as the mind can reach into the future, and even beyond that—he will still exist unchanged, with all the attributes of Deity. The creation of the universe made no change in him; its destruction would not vary the mode of his existence, or make him in any respect a different being. There could not be a more absolute and unambiguous declaration, as there could not be one more sublime, of the eternity of God. The mind cannot take in a grander thought than that there is one eternal and immutable Being.

3. *Thou turnest man to destruction.* In contradistinction from his own unchangeableness and eternity. Man passes away; God continues ever the same. The word rendered *destruction*—אכד, *dakka*—means properly anything beaten or broken small or very fine, and hence *dust.* The idea here is, that God causes man to return to *dust ;* that is, the elements which compose the body return to their original condition, or seem to mingle with the earth. Gen. iii. 19 : "Dust thou art, and unto dust shalt thou return." The word *man* here, of course, refers to man in general,—all men. It is the great law of our being. Individual man, classes of men, generations of men, races of men, pass away; but God remains the same. The Septuagint and the Latin Vulgate render this, "Thou turnest man to *humiliation ;*" which, though not the sense of the original, is a true idea, for there is nothing more humiliating than that a human body, once so beautiful, should turn back to dust; nothing more humbling than the grave. ¶ *And sayest, Return,*

4 For a thousand years in thy sight *are but* as yesterday when ¹ it is past, and *as* a watch in the night.

5 Thou carriest them away as

¹ Or, *he hath passed* them.

ye children of men. Return to your dust; go back to the earth from which you came. Return, all of you without exception;—kings, princes, nobles, warriors, conquerors; mighty men, captains, and counsellors; ye learned and great, ye honoured and flattered, ye beautiful and gay, ye youthful and vigorous, and ye aged and venerable; whatever is your rank, whatever are your possessions, whatever are your honours, whatever you have to make you lovely, to charm, to please, to be admired; or whatever there is to make you loathsome and detestable; ye vicious, ye profane, low, grovelling, sensual, debased; go all of you alike to *dust!* Oh, how affecting the thought that this is the lot of man; how much should it do to abase the pride of the race; how much should it do to make *any* man sober and humble, that he himself is soon to turn back *to dust*—unhonoured, undistinguished, and undistinguishable dust!

4. *For a thousand years in thy sight.* Heb., " In thy eyes;" that is, It so appears to thee,—or, a thousand years so seem to thee, however long they may appear to man. The utmost length to which the life of man has reached—in the case of Methuselah—was nearly a thousand years (Gen. v. 27); and the idea here is, that the longest human life, even if it should be lengthened out to a thousand years, would be in the sight of God, or in comparison with his years, but as a single day. ¶ *Are but as yesterday when it is past.* Marg., " *he hath passed* them." The translation in the text, however, best expresses the sense. The reference is to a single day, when we call it to remembrance. However long it may have appeared to us when it was passing, yet when it is gone, and we look back to it, it seems short. So the longest period of human existence appears to God.

¶ *And* as *a watch in the night.* This refers to a portion of the night,—the original idea having been derived from the practice of dividing the night into portions, during which a watch was placed in a camp. These watches were, of course, relieved at intervals, and the night came to be divided, in accordance with this arrangement, into parts corresponding with these changes. Among the ancient Hebrews there were only three night-watches; the first, mentioned in Lam. ii. 19; the middle, mentioned in Judges vii. 19; and the third, mentioned in Ex. xiv. 24; 1 Sam. xi. 11. In later times—the times referred to in the New Testament—there were four such watches, after the manner of the Romans, Mark xiii. 35. The idea here is not that such a watch in the night would seem to pass quickly, or that it would seem short when it was gone, but that a thousand years seemed to God not only short *as a day* when it was past, but even as the *parts* of a day, or the divisions of a night when it was gone.

5. *Thou carriest them away as with a flood.* The original here is a single verb with the suffix—זְרַמְתָּם. The verb—זָרַם, *zaram*—means, to flow, to pour; then, to pour upon, to overwhelm, to wash away. The idea is, that they were swept off as if a torrent bore them from the earth, carrying them away without regard to order, rank, age, or condition. So death makes no discrimination. Every day that passes, multitudes of every age, sex, condition, rank, are swept away and consigned to the grave,—as they *would be* if a raging flood should sweep over a land. ¶ *They are as a sleep.* The original here is, *a sleep they are.* The whole sentence is exceedingly graphic and abrupt: " Thou sweepest them away;—a sleep they are,—in the morning,—like grass

with a flood; they are *as* a sleep : in the morning *they are* like grass *e which* 1 groweth up.

6 In *f* the morning it flourish- eth, and groweth up; in the

e Isa. xl. 6.   1 *is changed.*

—it passes away." The idea is that human life resembles *a sleep*, because it seems to pass so swiftly; to accom- plish so little; to be so filled with dreams and visions, none of which remain or become permanent. ¶ *In the morning* they are *like grass*, which *groweth up*. A better translation of this would be to attach the words " in the morning" to the previous member of the sentence, "They are like sleep in the morning;" that is, They are as sleep *appears* to us in the morning, when we wake from it— rapid, unreal, full of empty dreams. The other part of the sentence then would be, " Like grass, it passeth away." The word rendered *groweth up*, is in the margin translated *is changed*. The Hebrew word—חָלַף, *hhalaph*—means to pass, to pass along, to pass by; to pass on, to come on; also, to revive or flourish as a plant; and then, to change. It may be ren- dered here, *pass away;* and the idea then would be that they are like grass in the fields, or like flowers, which soon *change* by passing away. There is nothing more permanent in man than there is in the grass or in the flowers of the field.

6. *In the morning it flourisheth.* This does not mean that it grows with any special vigour or rapidity in the morning, as if that were illus- trative of the rapid growth of the young; but merely that, in fact, in the morning it is green and vigorous, and is cut down in the short course of a day, or before evening. The re- ference here is to grass as an emblem of man. ¶ *And groweth up.* The same word in the Hebrew which is used in the close of the previous verse. ¶ *In the evening it is cut down, and withereth.* In the short period of a

evening it is cut down, and withereth.

7 For we are consumed by thine anger, and by thy wrath are we troubled.

8 Thou *g* hast set our iniquities

f Job xiv. 2.   *g* Jer. ii. 22.

day. What was so green and flourish- ing in the morning, is, at the close of the day, dried up. Life has been arrested, and death, with its con- sequences, has ensued. So with man. How often is this *literally* true, that those who are strong, healthy, vigor- ous, hopeful, in the morning, are at night pale, cold, and speechless in death! How striking is this as an emblem of man in general:—so soon cut down; so soon numbered with the dead. Comp. Notes on Isa. xl. 6–8; 1 Pet. i. 24, 25.

7. *For we are consumed by thine anger.* That is, Death—the cutting off of the race of man—may be re- garded as an expression of thy dis- pleasure against mankind as a race of sinners. The death of man would not have occurred but for sin (Gen. iii. 3, 19; Rom. v. 12); and all the circumstances connected with it,— the fact of death, the dread of death, the pain that precedes death, the paleness and coldness and rigidity of the dead, and the slow and offensive returning to dust in the grave,— all are adapted to be, and seem de- signed to be, illustrations of the anger of God against sin. We cannot, in- deed, always say that death in a spe- cific case is proof of the direct and special anger of God *in that case;* but we can say that death always, and death in its general features, may and should be regarded as an evidence of the Divine displeasure against the sins of men. ¶ *And by thy wrath.* As expressed in death. ¶ *Are we troubled.* Are our plans confounded and broken up; our minds made sad and sorrowful; our habita- tions made abodes of grief.

8. *Thou hast set our iniquities before thee.* Thou hast arrayed

before thee, our secret *sins* in the light of thy countenance.

9 For all our days are [1] passed away in thy wrath; we spend

[1] *turned.*   [2] Or, *meditation.*

---

our years as a [2] tale *that is told.*

10 [3] The days of our years *are* threescore years and ten; and if

[3] As for *the days of our years, in them* are *seventy years.*

---

them, or brought them forth to view, as a *reason* in thy mind for cutting us down. Death may be regarded as proof that God has brought before his mind the evidence of man's guilt, and has passed sentence accordingly. The fact of death at all; the fact that any one of the race dies; the fact that human life has been made so brief, is to be explained on the supposition that God has arrayed before his own mind the reality of human depravity, and has adopted this as an illustration of his sense of the evil of guilt. ¶ *Our secret* sins. Literally, "our secret;" or, that which was concealed or unknown. This may refer to the secret or hidden things of our lives, or to what has been concealed in our own bosoms; and the meaning may be, that God has judged in the case not by external appearances, or by what is seen by the world, but by what *he* has seen in the heart, and that he deals with us according to our real character. The reference is, indeed, to sin, but sin as concealed, hidden, forgotten; the sin of the heart; the sin which we have endeavoured to hide from the world; the sin which has passed away from our own recollection. ¶ *In the light of thy countenance.* Directly before thee; in full view; so that thou canst see them all. In accordance with these, thou judgest man,—and hence his death.

9. *For all our days are passed away in thy wrath.* Marg., *turned.* The Hebrew word—פָּנָה, *panah*—means *to turn;* then, to turn *to* or *from* any one; and hence, to turn away as if to flee or depart. Here it means that our days seem to turn from us; to give the back to us; to be unwilling to remain with us; to leave us. This seems to be the fruit or result of the anger of God, as if he

were unwilling that our days should *attend* us any longer. Or, it is as if he *took away* our days, or caused them to *turn away,* because he was angry and was unwilling that we should any longer enjoy them. The cutting off of life in any manner is a proof of the Divine displeasure; and in every instance death should be regarded as a new illustration of the fact that the race is guilty. ¶ *We spend our years as a tale* that is told. Marg., *meditation.* The Hebrew word —הֶגֶה, *hegeh*—means properly (*a*) a muttering, or growling, as of thunder; (*b*) a sighing or moaning; (*c*) a meditation, thought. It means here, evidently, *thought;* that is, life passes away as rapidly as *thought.* It has no permanency. It makes no impression. Thought is no sooner come than it is gone. So rapid, so fleeting, so unsubstantial is *life.* The Septuagint and the Latin Vulgate in some unaccountable way render this "*as a spider.*" The translation in our common version, "as a tale that is told," is equally unauthorized, as there is nothing corresponding to this in the Hebrew. The image in the original is very striking and beautiful. Life passes with the rapidity of thought!

10. *The days of our years.* Marg., "As for *the days of our years, in them* are *seventy years.*" Perhaps the language would better be translated: "The days of our years! In them are seventy years;" or, they amount to seventy years. Thus the psalmist is represented as reflecting on human life—on the days that make up the years of life;—as fixing his thought *on* those days and years, and taking the sum of them. The days of our years—what are they? ¶ Are *threescore years and ten.* Not as life originally was, but as it has been narrowed down to about that period;

by reason of strength *they be* fourscore years, yet *is* their strength labour and sorrow : for

h it is soon cut off, and we fly away.

or, this is the ordinary limit of life. This passage proves that the psalm was written when the life of man *had* been shortened, and had been reduced to about what it is *at present;* for this description will apply to man now. It is probable that human life was gradually diminished until it became fixed at the limit which now bounds it, and which is to remain as the great law in regard to its duration upon the earth. All animals, as the horse, the mule, the elephant, the eagle, the raven, the bee, the butterfly, have each a fixed limit of life, wisely adapted undoubtedly to the design for which they were made, and to the highest happiness of the whole. So of man. There can be no doubt that there are good reasons—some of which could be easily suggested—why his term of life is no longer. But, at any rate, it *is* no longer; and *in* that brief period he must accomplish all that he is to do in reference to this world, and all that is to be done to prepare him for the world to come. It is obvious to remark that man has enough to do to fill up the time of his life; that life to man is too precious to be wasted. ¶ *And if by reason of strength,* etc. If there be unusual strength or vigour of natural constitution; or if the constitution has not been impaired or broken by toil, affliction, or vicious indulgence; or if the great laws of health have been understood and observed. Any of these causes may contribute to lengthen out life,—or they may all be combined; and under these, separately or combined, life *is* sometimes extended beyond its ordinary limits. Yet the period of seventy *is* the ordinary limit beyond which few can go; the great mass fall long before they reach that. ¶ *Yet* is *their strength.* Heb., "Their *pride."* That of which a man who has reached that period

might be disposed to boast—as if it were owing to himself. There is, at that time of life, as well as at other times, great danger lest that which we have received from God, and which is in no manner to be traced to ourselves, may be an occasion of *pride,* as if it were our own, or as if it were secured by our own prudence, wisdom, or merit. May it not, also, be implied here that a man who *has* reached that period of life,—who has survived so many others,—who has seen so many fall by imprudence, or vice, or intemperance,—will be in special danger of being proud, as if it were by some special virtue of his own that *his* life had been thus lengthened out? Perhaps in no circumstances will the danger of pride be *more* imminent than when one has thus passed safely through dangers where others have fallen, and practised temperance while others have yielded to habits of intemperance, and taken care of his own health while others have neglected theirs. The tendency to pride in man does not die out *because* a man grows old. ¶ *Labour and sorrow.* The word rendered *labour* —עָמָל, *amál*—means properly *toil;* that is, wearisome labour. The idea here is, that toil then becomes burdensome; that the body is oppressed with it, and soon grows weary and exhausted; that life itself is *like* labour or wearisome toil. The old man is constantly in the condition of one who is weary; whose powers are exhausted; and who feels the need of repose. The word rendered *sorrow*—אָוֶן, *aven*— means properly *nothingness, vanity;* Isa. xli. 29; Zech. x. 2; then, nothingness as to worth, unworthiness, iniquity—which is its usual meaning; Num. xxiii. 21; Job xxxvi. 21; Isa. i. 13; and then, evil, adversity, calamity; Prov. xxii. 8; Gen. xxxv. 18. This latter seems to be the meaning here. It is, that happiness cannot

11 Who knoweth the power of thine anger? even according to | thy fear, *so is* thy wrath.

ordinarily be found at that period of life; that to lengthen out life does not add materially to its enjoyment; that to do it, is but adding trouble and sorrow. The ordinary hopes and plans of life ended; the companions of other years departed; the offices and honours of the world in other hands; a new generation on the stage that cares little for the old one now departing; a family scattered or in the grave; the infirmities of advanced years on him; his faculties decayed; the buoyancy of life gone; and now in his second childhood dependent on others as he was in his first;—how little of happiness is there in such a condition! How appropriate is it to speak of it as a time of "*sorrow!*" How little desirable is it for a man to reach extreme old age! And how kind and merciful the arrangement by which man is ordinarily removed from the world before the time of "trouble and sorrow" thus comes! There are commonly just enough men of extreme old age upon the earth to show us impressively that it is not *desirable* to live to be very old; just enough to keep this lesson with salutary force before the minds of those in earlier life; just enough, if we saw it aright, to make us willing to die before that period comes! ¶ *For it is soon cut off,* etc. Prof. Alexander renders this, "For he drives us fast;" that is, God drives us,—or, *one* seems to drive, or to urge us on. The word here used—גָּז, *gaz*—is commonly supposed to be derived from גָּזַז, *gazaz,* to cut, as to cut grass, or to mow; and then, to shear, *sc.* a flock,—which is its usual meaning. Thus it would signify, as in our translation, to be cut off. This is the Jewish interpretation. The word, however, may be more properly regarded as derived from גּוּז, *gūz,* which occurs in but one other place, Num. xi. 31, where it is rendered *brought,* as applied to the quails which were *brought* or

driven forward by the east wind. This word means, to pass through, to pass over, to pass away; and then, to cause to pass over, as the quails were (Num. xi. 31) by the east wind. So it means here, that life is soon passed over, and that we flee away, *as if* driven by the wind; *as if* impelled or urged forward as chaff or any light substance is by a gale.

11. *Who knoweth the power of thine anger?* Who can measure it, or take a correct estimate of it, as it is manifest in cutting down the race of men? If the removal of men by death is to be traced to thine anger, —or is, in any proper sense, an expression of thy wrath,—who can measure it, or understand it? The cutting down of whole generations of men—of nations—of hundreds of millions of human beings—of the great, the powerful, the mighty, as well as the weak and the feeble, is an amazing exhibition of the *power*—of the might—of God; and who is there that can fully understand this? Who can estimate fully the wrath of God, if this is to be regarded as an expression of it? Who can comprehend what this *is?* Who can tell, after such an exhibition, what may be in reserve, or what further and more fearful displays of wrath there may yet be? ¶ *Even according to thy fear, so is thy wrath.* Literally, "And according to thy fear, thy wrath." The word rendered "*fear*" would here seem to refer to the *reverence* due to God, or to what there is in his character to inspire awe:—to wit, his power, his majesty, his greatness; and the sense seems to be that his wrath or anger as manifested in cutting down the race seems to be commensurate with all in God that is vast, wonderful, incomprehensible. As no one can understand or take in the one, so no one can understand or take in the other. God is great in all things; great in

12 So teach *us* to number our days, that we may [1] apply *our* hearts unto *i* wisdom.

13 Return, O LORD, how long? and let it repent thee concerning thy servants.

[1] *cause to come.*   *i* Prov. iv. 7.

14 O satisfy us early with thy mercy; that we may rejoice and be glad all our days.

15 Make us glad according to the days *wherein* thou hast afflicted us, *and* the years *wherein* we have seen evil.

---

himself; great in his power in cutting down the race; great in the expressions of his displeasure.

12. *So teach* us *to number our days.* Literally, "To number our days make us know, and we will bring a heart of wisdom." The prayer is, that God would instruct us to estimate our days aright:—their number; the rapidity with which they pass away; the liability to be cut down; the certainty that they must soon come to an end; their bearing on the future state of being. ¶ *That we may apply* our *hearts unto wisdom.* Marg., "*Cause to come.*" We will bring, or cause to come, a heart of wisdom. By taking a just account of life, that we may bring to it a heart truly wise, or act wisely in view of these facts. The prayer is, that God would enable us to form such an estimate of life, that we shall be truly wise; that we may be able to act as if we saw the whole of life, or as we should do if we saw its end. God sees the end—the time, the manner, the circumstances in which life will close; and although he has wisely hidden that from us, yet he can enable us to act *as if* we saw it for ourselves; to have the same objects before us, and to make as much of life, *as if* we saw when and how it would close. If any one knew when, and where, and how he was to die, it might be presumed that this would exert an important influence on him in forming his plans, and on his general manner of life. The prayer is, that God would enable us to act *as if* we had such a view.

13. *Return, O* LORD. Come back to thy people; show mercy by sparing them. It would seem probable from this that the psalm was composed in a time of pestilence, or raging sickness, which threatened to sweep all the people away—a supposition by no means improbable, as such times occurred in the days of Moses, and in the rebellions of the people when he was leading them to the promised land. ¶ *How long?* How long shall this continue? How long shall thy wrath rage? How long shall the people still fall under thy hand? This question is often asked in the Psalms. Ps. iv. 2; vi. 3; xiii. 1, 2; xxxv. 17; lxxix. 5, *et al.* ¶ *And let it repent thee.* That is, Withdraw thy judgments, and be merciful, as if thou didst repent. God cannot literally *repent,* in the sense that he is sorry for what he has done, but he may act *as if* he repented; that is, he may withdraw his judgments; he may arrest what has been begun; he may show mercy where it *seemed* that he would only show wrath. ¶ *Concerning thy servants.* In respect to thy people. Deal with them in mercy and not in wrath.

14. *O satisfy us early with thy mercy.* Literally, "In the morning;" as soon as the day dawns. Perhaps there is an allusion here to their affliction, represented as *night;* and the prayer is, that the morning—the morning of mercy and joy—might again dawn upon them. ¶ *That we may rejoice and be glad all our days.* All the remainder of our lives. That the memory of thy gracious interposition may go with us to the grave.

15. *Make us glad according to the days* wherein *thou hast afflicted us.* Let the one correspond with the other. Let our occasions of joy be measured by the sorrows which have come upon us. As our sufferings have been great, so let our joys and

16 Let thy work appear unto thy servants, and thy glory unto their children.

17 And let the beauty *ᵏ* of the

k Ps. cx. 3.

LORD our God be upon us : and establish thou the work of our hands upon us ; yea, the work of our hands establish *ˡ* thou it.

l Job xxii. 28 ; Prov. xvi. 3.

triumphs be. ¶ And *the years* wherein *we have seen evil.* Affliction and sorrow. They have been continued through many wearisome years; so let the years of peace and joy be many also.

16. *Let thy work appear unto thy servants.* That is, thy gracious work of interposition. Let us see thy power displayed in removing these calamities, and in restoring to us the days of health and prosperity. ¶ *And thy glory unto their children.* The manifestation of thy character; the display of thy goodness, of thy power, and thy grace. Let this spreading and wasting evil be checked and removed, so that our children may live, and may have occasion to celebrate thy goodness, and to record the wonders of thy love.

17. *And let the beauty of the* LORD *our God be upon us.* The word translated *beauty*—נֹעַם, *noam* —means properly *pleasantness ;* then, beauty, splendour; then grace or favour. The Septuagint renders it here, λαμπρότης, *splendour ;* and so the Latin Vulgate. The wish is clearly that all that there is, in the Divine character, which is *beautiful,* —which is fitted to win the hearts of men to admiration, gratitude, and love,—might be so manifested to them, or that they might so see the excellency of his character, and that his dealings with them might be such, as to keep the beauty, the loveliness, of that character constantly before them. ¶ *And establish thou the work of our hands upon us.* What we are endeavouring to do. Enable us to carry out our plans, and to accomplish our purposes. ¶ *Yea, the work of our hands establish thou it.* The repetition of the prayer here is emphatic. It indicates an intense desire that God would enable them

to carry out their plans. If this was written by Moses, we may suppose that it is expressive of an earnest desire that they might reach the promised land; that they might not all be cut down and perish by the way; that the great object of their march through the wilderness might be accomplished ; and that they might be permanently established in the land to which they were going. At the same time it is a prayer which it is proper to offer at any time, that God would enable us to carry out our purposes, and that we may be permanently established in his favour.

PSALM XCI.

The author of this psalm, and the occasion on which it was composed, are alike unknown. The psalm has no title ; and there are no internal marks by which we can ascertain when, or by whom, it was written. It is very general in its application, and may have been composed with no particular reference to any event occurring at the time, as it is evident that it had no special reference to the circumstances of the writer. Though it follows a psalm composed by Moses, yet there is no reason to suppose that it was written by him, nor is there any particular resemblance to that psalm.

From some things in the psalm, as vers. 3, 4, 5, 9, 11, it would appear to be not improbable that the psalm was composed with reference to some individual who was exposed to temptation, or to danger, either from secret enemies or from pestilence, and that it was intended to assure such an one that there was nothing to be feared if he put his trust in God. There is no evidence that it was designed to refer particularly to the Saviour. It is, indeed, applied to him by Satan in the temptation in the wilderness (Matt. iv. 6) ; but there is, in that case, no such recognition of its applicability to himself on the part of the Saviour as to justify us in the conclusion that it originally referred to him.

PSALM XCI.

HE that dwelleth ^m in the secret place of the Most High, shall

m Ps. xxvii. 5.

¹ abide under the shadow ⁿ of the Almighty.

¹ *lodge.*   *n* Ps. lvii. 1.

Its quotation by the tempter is no proof that this was the original reference of the psalm, and the quotation made is one which could be applied to him in the same way as *any* general premise in the Old Testament made to those who trusted in God might have been.

The most remarkable thing in the structure of the psalm is the frequent change of *persons*, leading some to suppose that it may have been composed with a view to its being sung by choirs in alternate responses, and Michaelis has suggested that there were probably *two* such choirs ; the one—as in vers. 1, 2—celebrating the praises of those who trusted in God ; the other—as in vers. 3 to 8—exciting and encouraging the people to put their trust in God, and suggesting reasons why they should do it. Such a thing is, undoubtedly, possible ; but the evidence that this was the intention of the author of the psalm is not clear.

Tholuck has divided the psalm, on the supposition that it was thus intended to be sung by alternate choirs, into portions arranged with that view :—ver. 1, the choir ; ver. 2, the response ; vers. 3-8, the choir ; ver. 9, the response ; vers. 10-13, the choir ; vers. 14-16, the response. This, however, is quite arbitrary, as it cannot be demonstrated to have been the original design.

This arrangement, however, suggests a good division of the psalm :

I. The general statement of the safety of those who put their trust in God, ver. 1.

II. A responsive declaration of the author of the psalm, that he would make the Lord his refuge, and the Most High his habitation, ver. 2.

III. A statement of the security or benefit of doing this, vers. 3-8.

IV. A responsive declaration — repeated—by the author of the psalm that he would do this ; that God *was* his refuge, ver. 9 (part first).

V. A further statement of the benefit of this, vers. 10–13.

VI. A general declaration embracing the sum of all that is said in the psalm, as coming from God himself, containing assurances of his protection to those who

thus put their trust in him, and confide in him, vers. 14–16.

This mode of division meets substantially all the changes of *persons* in the psalm, or arranges the different portions of it into parts belonging to the different speakers in the psalm. There is reason to believe that this was the line of thought in the mind of the psalmist, though it is not clear that this was designed to be so used in public responses in singing.

1. *He that dwelleth.* Every one that so dwells. The proposition is universal, and is designed to embrace all who are in this condition. It is true of one ; it is true of all. The word rendered *dwelleth* here is a participle from the verb to *sit,* and here means *sitting :* literally, *" sitting* in the secret place," etc. The idea is that of calm repose ; of resting ; of sitting down,—as one does in his dwelling. ¶ *In the secret place.* On the meaning of this see Notes on Ps. xxvii. 5. Comp. Ps. xxxi. 20 ; xxxii. 7. Abiding where God abides. The idea is that of having one's home or residence in the most holy place in the tabernacle or the temple, and of sitting with him *in* that sacred place. ¶ *Of the Most High.* Of God, represented as exalted above all ; over all the universe. ¶ *Shall abide.* Marg., as in Heb., *lodge.* That is his home,—his resting-place,—where he lodges, or passes the night. He takes up his lodging there ; he makes it his home. ¶ *Under the shadow of the Almighty.* Under his protection, as if under his wings. Comp. Notes on Ps. xvii. 8. This is a general statement, and is designed as an introduction to the whole psalm, or as expressing what the psalm is intended to illustrate, *the blessedness* of the man who thus dwells with God ; who makes him his friend ; who makes the home of God his home.

2 I will say of the LORD, *He is* my refuge, and my fortress : my God ; in him will I trust.

3 Surely *°* he shall deliver thee

o Ps. cxxiv. 7.

from the snare of the fowler, *and* from the noisome pestilence.

4 He shall cover thee with his feathers, and under his wings shalt thou trust : his truth *shall* be *thy* shield and buckler.

---

2. *I will say of the* LORD. I, the psalmist ; I will take this to myself ; I will endeavour to secure this blessedness ; I will thus abide with God. In view of the blessedness of this condition, and with the hope of securing it to myself ; I will adopt this resolution as the purpose of my life. It is what I need ; it is what my soul desires. ¶ *My refuge and my fortress.* "I will say of Jehovah, *My refuge and my fortress !*" I will address him as such ; I will regard him as such. On the meaning of these terms, see Notes on Ps. xviii. 2. ¶ *My God.* I will address him as *my* God ; as the God whom alone I worship ; as the only being to whom the name *God* can properly be applied ; as being to me all that is implied in the word *God.* ¶ *In him will I trust.* I will repose that confidence in him which is evinced by making my home with him, and seeking permanently to dwell with him.

3. *Surely he shall deliver thee from the snare of the fowler.* The snare or gin set for. catching birds ; meaning, here, that God would save him from the purposes of wicked men ; such purposes as might be compared with the devices employed to catch birds. On the meaning of the figure here used, see Notes on Ps. xviii. 5. ¶ And *from the noisome pestilence.* The *fatal* pestilence ; the pestilence that spreads death in its march. That is, he can prevent its coming upon you ; or, he can save you from its ravages, while others are dying around you. This promise is not to be understood as absolute, or as meaning that no one who fears God will ever fall by the pestilence,—for good men *do* die at such times as well as bad men ; but the idea is, that God *can* preserve us at such a time ;

and that, as a great law, he will be thus the protector of those who trust him. It is to be remembered that in times of pestilence (as was the case during the prevalence of the Asiatic cholera in 1832 and 1848), very many of the victims are the intemperate, the sensual, the debased, and that a life of this kind is a predisposing cause of death in such visitations of judgment. A large part of those who die are of that number. From the danger arising from *this* cause, of course the virtuous, the temperate, the pious are exempt ; and this is *one* of the methods by which God saves those who trust in him from the "noisome pestilence." Religion, therefore, to a considerable extent, constitutes a ground of security at such times ; nor is there any reason to doubt that, in many cases also, there may be a special interposition protecting the friends of God from danger, and sparing them for future usefulness. The promise here is substantially that general promise which we have in the Scriptures everywhere, that God is the Protector of his people, and that they may put their trust in him.

4. *He shall cover thee with his feathers,* etc. As the parent bird protects its young. See Notes on Ps. xvii. 8. Comp. Deut. xxxii. 11. ¶ *His truth.* His unfailing promise ; the certainty that what he has promised to do he will perform. ¶ *Shall* be thy *shield and buckler.* Literally, " Shield and buckler is his truth." The meaning is, that his pledge or promise would be unto them *as* the shield of the soldier is to him in battle. Comp. Ps. xxxv. 2. The word rendered *buckler* is derived from the verb *to surround,* and is given to

5 Thou shalt *p* not be afraid for the terror by night, *nor* for the arrow *that* flieth by day,

6 *Nor* for the pestilence *that* walketh in darkness, *nor* for the

destruction *that* wasteth at noonday.

7 A thousand shall fall at thy side, and ten thousand at thy right hand ; *but* it shall not come nigh thee.

---

the defensive armour here referred to, because it *surrounds,* and thus *protects* a person. It may apply to a coat of mail.

5. *Thou shalt not be afraid for the terror by night.* That which usually causes alarm at night — a sudden attack ; an unexpected incursion of enemies; sudden disease coming on by night; or the pestilence which seems to love night, and to " walk in darkness." Any one of these things seems to be aggravated by *night* and *darkness ;* and hence we most dread them then. We cannot see their approach ; we cannot measure their outlines ; we know not the extent of the danger, or what may be the calamity. ¶ Nor *for the arrow* that *flieth by day.* Whether shot from the bow of God—as pestilence and disease ; or from the hand of man in battle. The idea is, that he that trusts in God will be calm. Comp. Notes on Ps. lvi. 3.

6. Nor *for the pestilence.* The plague or pestilence was common in Oriental countries. ¶ That *walketh in darkness.* Not that it particularly comes in the night, but that it seems to creep along *as if* in the night; that is, where one cannot mark its progress, or anticipate when or whom it will strike. The laws of its movements are unknown, and it comes upon men as an enemy that suddenly attacks us in the night. ¶ Nor *for the destruction.* The word here used—קֶטֶב, *keteb*—means properly a cutting off, a destruction, as a destroying storm, Isa. xxviii. 2; and then, contagious pestilence, Deut. xxxii. 24. It may be applied here to anything that sweeps away men—whether storm, war, pestilence, or famine. ¶ That *wasteth at noonday.* It lays waste, or produces desolation, at noon ; that

is, visibly, openly. The meaning is, that whenever, or in whatever form, calamity comes which sweeps away the race,—whether at midnight or at noon,—whether in the form of pestilence, war, or famine,—he who trusts in God need not—will not—be afraid. He will feel either that he will be preserved from its ravages, or that if he is cut off he has nothing to fear. He is a friend of God, and he has a hope of a better life. In death, and in the future world, there is nothing of which he should be afraid. The Septuagint and the Latin Vulgate render this, strangely enough, " Nor of mischance and the demon of noonday."

7. *A thousand shall fall at thy side.* Though a thousand should fall at thy side, or close to thee. This alludes to the manner in which the pestilence often moves among men. ¶ *And ten thousand at thy right hand.* Comp. Ps. iii. 6. The word *myriad* would better represent the exact idea in the original, as the Hebrew word is different from that which is translated "a thousand." It is put here for any large number. No matter how many fall around thee, on the right hand and the left, you will have nothing to fear. ¶ But *it shall not come nigh thee.* You will be safe. You may feel assured of the Divine protection. Your mind may be calm through a sense of such guardianship, and your very calmness will conduce to your safety. This refers, as remarked above, to a *general* law in regard to the judgments of God. It is true that others, beside the dissipated, vicious, and debased, *may* be the victims; but the great law is that temperance, soberness, virtue, cleanliness, and that regard to comfort and health to which religion and virtue

8 Only ⁹ with thine eyes shalt thou behold and see the reward of the wicked.

9 Because thou hast made the

q Prov. iii. 25, 26.   *r* Prov. xii. 21.

LORD, *which is* my refuge, *even* the Most High, thy habitation,

10 There *r* shall no evil befall thee, neither shall any plague come nigh thy dwelling.

---

prompt, constitute a marked security, —so marked as to illustrate the *general* law referred to in the psalm before us.

8. *Only.* That is, This is *all* that will occur to you. The only thing which you have to anticipate is, that you will see how God punishes sinners. ¶ *With thine eyes shalt thou behold and see the reward of the wicked.* Your own eyes shall see it. See Notes on Ps. xxxvii. 34. You will see the just punishment of the ungodly, the vicious, the profane, the sensual. You will see what is the proper fruit of their conduct; what is the just expression of the views which *God* takes of their character. This undoubtedly refers to the general principle that there *is* a moral government on earth; that vice is often punished *as such;* that the general course of the Divine dealings is such as to show that God is favourable to virtue, and is opposed to vice. The system is not *complete* here, and there are many things which could not be reconciled with this, if the present world were all, and if there were no future state :—but the course of events indicates the general character of the Divine administration, and what is the tendency of things. The completion—the actual and perfect adjustment—is reserved for a future state. The facts as they occur on earth prove that there *is* an attribute of justice in God; the fact that his dealings here are not wholly and fully in accordance with what justice demands, proves that there will be a state where full justice *will* be done, and where the whole system will be adjusted.

9. *Because thou hast made the* LORD, which is *my refuge.* Literally, " For thou, O Jehovah, [art] my refuge." The Chaldee Paraphrase regards this as the language of Solomon,

who, according to that version, is one of the speakers in the psalm : " Solomon answered and said, ' Since thou, O Lord, art my refuge,' " etc. Tholuck regards this as the response of the choir. But this is unnecessary. The idea is, that the psalmist *himself* had made Jehovah his refuge, or his defence. The language is an expression of his own feeling—of his own experience— in having made God his refuge, and is designed here to be a ground of exhortation to others to do the same thing. He could say that he *had* made God his refuge; he could say that God was *now* his refuge; and he could appeal to this—to his own experience—when he exhorted others to do the same, and gave them assurance of safety in doing it. ¶ *Even the Most High thy habitation.* Literally, " The Most High hast thou made thy habitation;" or, thy home. On the word *habitation*, see Notes on Ps. xc. 1. The idea is, that he had, as it were, chosen to abide with God, or to dwell with him—to find his *home* with him as in a father's house. The consequence of this, or the security which would follow, he states in the following verses.

10. *There shall no evil befall thee.* The Chaldee Paraphrase has, " The Lord of the world answered and said, ' There shall no evil befall thee,' " etc. The sentiment, however, is that the psalmist could assure such an one, from his own personal experience, that he would be safe. He had himself made Jehovah his refuge, and could speak with confidence of the safety of doing so. This, of course, is to be understood as a *general* truth, in accordance with what has been said above. ¶ *Neither shall any plague come nigh thy dwelling.* On the word rendered *plague* here יָגַע, *naiga*— see Notes on Ps. xxxviii. 12; xxxix.

11 For *s* he shall give his angels charge over thee, to keep thee in all thy ways.

12 They shall bear thee up in *their* hands, lest thou dash thy foot against a stone.

s Matt. iv. 6.

13 Thou *t* shalt tread upon the lion and [1] adder; the young lion and the dragon shalt thou trample under feet.

14 Because he hath set his love upon me, therefore will I

t Job v. 23.   [1] Or, *asp.*

---

11. It is not the same word which is used in ver. 6, and translated *pestilence;* and it does not refer to what is technically called the *plague.* It may denote anything that would be expressive of the Divine displeasure, or that would be sent as a punishment. The word rendered "dwelling" here means a *tent;* and the idea is, that no such mark of displeasure would *abide* with him, or enter his tent as its home. Of course, this also must be understood as a *general* promise, or as meaning that religion would constitute a general ground of security.

11. *For he shall give his angels charge over thee.* Literally, "He will give *command* to his angels." That is, he would instruct them, or appoint them for this purpose. This passage (vers. 11, 12) was applied to the Saviour by the tempter. Matt. iv. 6. See Notes on that passage. This, however, does not prove that it had an original reference to the Messiah; for even if we should suppose that Satan was a correct and reliable expounder of the Scriptures, all that the passage would prove as used by him would be, that the righteous, or those who were the friends of God, might rely confidently on his protection, and that Jesus, if he was of God, might do this as others might. On the sentiment in the passage, to wit, that God employs his angels to protect his people, see Notes on Ps. xxxiv. 7; comp. Notes on Heb. i. 14. ¶ *To keep thee in all thy ways.* To preserve thee wheresoever thou goest.

12. *They shall bear thee up,* etc. As if they took hold of thee, and held thee up, when about to fall. ¶ *Lest thou dash thy foot,* etc. Lest you should stumble and fall. They will protect you so that you may walk safely.

13. *Thou shalt tread upon the lion and adder.* Thou shalt be safe among dangers, *as if* the rage of the lion were restrained, and he became like a lamb, and *as if* the poisonous tooth of the serpent were extracted. Comp. Mark xvi. 18. The word here used to denote the *lion* is a poetic term, not employed in prose. The word rendered *adder* is, in the margin, *asp.* The Hebrew word—פֶּתֶן, *pethen*—commonly means viper, asp, or adder. See Notes on Job xx. 14, 16; comp. Ps. lviii. 4; Isa. xi. 8. It may be applied to any venomous serpent. ¶ *The young lion.* The *young* lion is mentioned as particularly fierce and violent. See Ps. xvii. 12. ¶ *And the dragon,* etc. Heb., תַּנִּין, *tannin.* See Notes on Ps. lxxiv. 13; Job vii. 12; Isa. xxvii. 1. In Ex. vii. 9, 10, 12, the word is rendered serpent (and serpents);—in Gen. i. 21, and Job vii. 12, whale (and whales);—in Deut. xxxii. 33; Neh. ii. 13; Ps. lxxiv. 13; cxlviii. 7; Isa. xxvii. 1; li. 9; Jer. li. 34, as here, dragon (and dragons);—in Lam. iv. 3, sea-monsters. The word does not occur elsewhere. It would perhaps properly denote a sea-monster; yet it may be applied to a serpent. Thus applied, it would denote a serpent of the largest and most dangerous kind; and the idea is, that he who trusted in God would be safe amidst the most fearful dangers,—*as if* he should walk safely amidst venomous serpents.

14. *Because he hath set his love upon me.* Has become attached to me; has united himself with me; is my friend. The Hebrew word expresses the strongest attachment, and is equivalent to our expression—*to fall in love.* It refers here to the

deliver him : I will set him on high, because he hath known my name.

15 He *u* shall call upon me, and I will answer him : I *v will*

u Isa. lxv. 24.   v Isa. xliii. 2.

---

fact that God is the object of supreme affection on the part of his people; —and it also here implies, that this springs from their hearts: that they have seen such beauty in his character, and have such strong desire for him, that their hearts go out in warm affection towards him. ¶ *Therefore will I deliver him.* I will save him from trouble and from danger. ¶ *I will set him on high.* By acknowledging him as my own, and treating him accordingly. ¶ *Because he hath known my name.* He has known *me;* that is, he understands my true character, and has learned to love me.

15. *He shall call upon me.* He shall have the privilege of calling on me in prayer; and he will do it. ¶ *And I will answer him.* I will regard his supplications, and will grant his requests. There could be no greater privilege—no more precious promise—than this. ¶ *I* will be *with him in trouble.* I will stand by him; I will not forsake him. ¶ *I will deliver him, and honour him.* I will not only rescue him from danger, but I will exalt him to honour. I will recognize him as my friend, and will regard and treat him as such. On earth he shall be treated as my friend; in another world he shall be exalted to honour among the redeemed, and become the associate of holy beings for ever.

16. *With long life will I satisfy him.* The margin here, is "length of days;" that is, days lengthened out or multiplied. The meaning is, I will give him length of days as he desires, or until he is satisfied with life;—implying (1) that it is natural to desire long life; (2) that long life is to be regarded as a blessing (comp. Prov. iii. 2, 16; Ex. xx. 12); (3) that the tendency of religion is to lengthen

be with him in trouble; I will deliver him, and honour him.

16 With ¹ long life *w* will I satisfy him, and shew him my salvation.

¹ *length of days.*   w Prov. iii. 2; xxii. 4.

---

out life; since virtue, temperance, regular industry, calmness of mind, moderation in all things, freedom from excesses in eating and in drinking,—to all of which religion prompts, —contribute to health, and to length of days (see Notes on Ps. xxxiv. 12–14; xxxvii. 9; lv. 23); and (4) that a time will come, even under this promised blessing of length of days, when a man will be "satisfied" with living; when he will have no strong desire to live longer; when, under the infirmities of advanced years, and under his lonely feelings from the fact that his early friends have fallen, and under the influence of a bright hope of heaven, he will feel that he has had *enough* of life here, and that it is better to depart to another world. ¶ *And shew him my salvation.* In another life, after he shall be "satisfied" with this life. The promise extends beyond the grave : "Godliness is profitable unto all things, having promise of the life that now is, and of that which is to come." See Notes on 1 Tim. iv. 8. Thus, religion blesses man in this life, and blesses him for ever. In possession of this, it is a great thing to him to live long; and then it is a great thing to die—to go to be for ever with God.

PSALM XCII.

The author of this psalm is not indicated in the title, and it is impossible now to ascertain who he was. Nor can the occasion be determined *when* it was composed. It is of so general a character that it might have been written at any period of the Jewish history ; and, so far as the style and the contents are concerned, it may have been written by either of those whose names are attached to the other psalms. That it may have been composed by David, is

PSALM XCII.

A Psalm *or* Song for the sabbath-day.

*I*T *ˣ* is a good *thing* to give thanks unto the LORD, and

to sing praises unto thy name, O Most High:

2 To show forth thy loving-

x Ps. cxlvii. 1.

certainly possible, but of that there is no evidence.

In the title it is called "A Psalm or Song for the sabbath-day;" that is, to be used on the sabbath. The Chaldee Paraphrase has in the title, "Praise and a song which the first man spoke for the sabbath-day." This may indicate that there was an early tradition on this subject; but we have no proof of what would be so interesting a fact, that we have a genuine poetic composition of Adam. The contents are all such as might be properly used on the sabbath, though there is nothing in the psalm that has any *special* reference to the sabbath, or that is derived from the appointment of such a day. It is not improbable, however, that special psalms and hymns were composed with a view to be used on festal occasions; and this, as a psalm of praise, is well adapted still to the services of the sabbath.

The psalmist refers—

I. To the blessedness of praise, or to the propriety of celebrating the praise of God, vers. 1-4.

II. He refers to the works of God as laying the foundation of praise, vers. 5, 6.

III. He refers to the justice of God, or the fact that the wicked, however they may seem to be prospered, will be cut off, vers. 7-9.

IV. He refers to the prosperity and the security of the righteous; to the influence of religion and the favour of God on life, as making it prosperous and happy, and as preparing men to be useful and cheerful in old age, vers. 10-15.

1. It is a *good* thing *to give thanks unto the* LORD. Literally, "Good is it to give thanks unto Jehovah." That is, the act is appropriate; the effect is good. (1) The thing itself is appropriate; for there is much, under all circumstances, to be thankful for :—life, health, food, raiment, air, water, friends, recollections, hopes,— and, above all, the blessings of redemption, and the assurance that we may be happy for ever. Many of

these things may be found in the condition of all; but if all else fail, the hope of heaven—the assurance that the Redeemer died—the offer of salvation—cannot fail. That is ours, and cannot be taken away. (2) The effect is good. It is a desirable state of mind. It tends to happiness, contentment, peace. A gloomy mind makes all things around more gloomy; an unthankful mind is an unhappy mind; a murmuring, complaining, dissatisfied mind makes its possessor wretched, and all around him miserable. (3) It is good as it is due to God. For all his favour we should be thankful,—and all that we enjoy is his gift. (4) It tends much to lessen the real troubles and afflictions of life to dwell on those things for which we should be thankful. ¶ *And to sing praises unto thy name.* Unto thee. As this psalm was designed for the "Sabbath-day," this proves that one of the appropriate services of the Sabbath is "*praise.*" It is a day when it is fit to recall the mercies of God to our recollection; and the remembrance of those mercies, and their celebration by appropriate songs, tend to diffuse joy over all the coming days of the week. ·¶ *O Most High.* God exalted over all. The fact that he *is* exalted over all—over us—over our friends—over all worlds—is an appropriate thought when we come before him to praise him; appropriate at all times, and in all circumstances of life.

2. *To show forth thy loving-kindness.* To celebrate thy mercy; thy goodness; thy love. ¶ *In the morning.* That is, there is a fitness in doing this in the morning; or, there are special reasons why we should do this at that time. (*a*) We have been preserved through the dangers of the night; dangers when we were asleep, unconscious, and defenceless. (*b*) Life

C

kindness in the morning, *v* and
thy faithfulness [1] every night.

3 Upon an instrument of ten
strings, and upon the psaltery;
2 upon the harp with 3 a solemn
sound.

4 For thou, LORD, hast made
me glad through thy work; I
will triumph in the works of thy
hands.

y Lam. iii. 23.
[1] *in the nights.*

[2] Or, *upon the solemn sound with the harp.*
[3] *Higgaion,* Ps. ix. 16.

---

is then, as it were, a new gift,—for
we are raised from "the image of
death"—sleep,—and we should regard life then *as if* we had been raised
from the dead. (*c*) To praise God in
the morning will have a good influence
on us, in promoting cheerfulness; in
making us benignant and kind; in
preparing us for the toils and trials
of the day. There is no better preparation for a day, in view of its
burdens, cares, toils, and trials, than
a thankful, cheerful mind in the
morning. He who begins a day
with a sour, a morose, a murmuring,
an irritable spirit,—who has been
preserved through the night, and sees
nothing to be thankful for in the
morning,—will be a miserable man
through the day, and will make all
miserable around him. He who sees
nothing to be thankful for in the
morning will see nothing to hope for
in the day; he who has no gratitude
for the past, will have no bright
anticipations of the future. ¶ *And
thy faithfulness.* Faithfulness in the
laws of nature; in thy promises; in
thy character: in thy providential
dealings with men. ¶ *Every night.*
Marg., *in the nights.* The reference
is to the return of evening; and the
meaning is, that it is a good thing,
or that it is appropriate to contemplate the faithfulness of God at the
close of every day. (*a*) The mind is
then calm, after the toils of the day
are over. (*b*) The time—evening—
its stillness—its twilight—its approaching darkness,—all is favourable for reflection. (*c*) There is
much in every day to be thankful
for, and it is well to recall it at
night. (*d*) It has a happy effect on
the mind when we are about to lie
down to rest, to recall the mercies of

God; to reflect on what he has done
for us; to gather, from his kindness
in the past, lessons of confidence and
hope for the times to come. We lie
down at night more calmly in proportion as we are disposed at the
close of a day to think of the mercies
which we have received at the hand
of God; and the recalling of those
mercies to remembrance with the
voice, and with instruments of praise,
is always an appropriate mode of
closing a day.

3. *Upon an instrument of ten
strings.* The general idea in this
verse is, that instruments *of all
kinds* are to be employed in celebrating the praises of God. On the
instrument here referred to, see Notes
on Ps. xxxiii. 2. ¶ *And upon the
psaltery.* Or *lyre.* See Notes on
Isa. v. 12. The word is there translated *viol.* ¶ *Upon the harp with
a solemn sound.* Marg., *upon the
solemn sound with the harp.* Prof.
Alexander renders this, "On meditation with a harp." On the word
rendered *harp,* see Notes on Isa. v. 12.
The Hebrew word rendered *solemn
sound* is הִגָּיוֹן — *higgaion* — which
means properly *murmur;* then, the
sound of a harp; and then, meditation. See Notes on Ps. ix. 16. Here
the meaning seems to be, "*with
murmurs upon the harp;*" that is,
with the sound of the harp—its
murmuring tones. It does not denote here a distinct instrument of
music, but it refers to the tones of
the harp: not to the meditations
of the mind—of the worshipper—
but to the low and gentle sounds of
the instrument itself.

4. *For thou, LORD, hast made me
glad.* Thou hast made me happy;
thou hast given me such a state of

5 O Lord, how great are thy works! *and* thy thoughts *z* are very deep.

6 A brutish man knoweth not; neither doth a fool understand this.

z Isa. lv. 9; Rom. xi. 33.

7 When *a* the wicked spring as the grass, and when all the workers of iniquity do flourish, *it is* that they shall be destroyed for ever:

a Ps. lxxiii. 18—20; Mal. iv. 1.

feeling as finds an appropriate expression in *praise.* ¶ *Through thy work.* Either the work of *creation,* the finishing of which the Sabbath was designed particularly to commemorate; or the works of God in general,—the universe; or the general dealings of his providence; or some particular interpositions of Providence in his behalf that called for special praise. All these are appropriately combined in the celebrations —the praises—of the Sabbath; to these should be added, as among the most marvellous of his works, and that which furnishes special occasion for praise on the Christian Sabbath, the wonderful work of redemption— that which of all the "works" of God makes a heart rightly affected most "glad." ¶ *I will triumph.* I will exult or rejoice. ¶ *In the works of thy hands.* In all thy works; in all that thou hast done.

5. *O Lord, how great are thy works!* Comp. Ps. viii. 3; xl. 5. See also Notes on Job xi. 7. The meaning here is this:—The psalmist, on the Sabbath, in giving himself to meditation on the works of God, is overwhelmed with a sense of their vastness, their incomprehensible nature, and the depth of wisdom evinced, far beyond the grasp of man, in what God had done. How soon is man lost; how soon does he get beyond his depth; how soon does he feel that here is greatness which he cannot comprehend, and wisdom which he cannot fathom, and goodness which he cannot appreciate, when he sits down to meditate on the works of God! ¶ And *thy thoughts are very deep.* Comp. Isa. xxviii. 29; Rom. xi. 33, 34. The meaning is, that the plans or the purposes of God, as

evinced in the works of creation and providence, are too profound for man to understand them. Who but God himself *can* comprehend them?

6. *A brutish man knoweth not.* A man who is stupid, and who is like the beasts or brutes; that is, a man whose tastes and propensities are like the brutes, or who does not seem to act as if endowed with a rational nature. The idea evidently is, that there are many such men, and that it is not to be wondered at that they have no exalted idea of the greatness of God. As a matter of fact there are many in human form—many made in the image of God—who seem to have no more notion of God, and who see no more wisdom and goodness in his works, than the horse or the ox. Comp. Isa. i. 3. ¶ *Neither doth a fool understand this.* A fool, in the sense that he has been made foolish and stupid by sin; that he does not worship and honour God. He has no right understanding in regard to the Maker and the Governor of the universe.

7. *When the wicked spring as the grass.* When they grow up as plants do; when they seem to flourish and prosper. Comp. Ps. xc. 5, 6; xxxvii. 2, 35, 38. The word *grass* here refers to the vegetable creation generally, embracing plants and flowers of all kinds. ¶ *And when all the workers of iniquity do flourish.* As plants and flowers do. They are like vigorous plants; not like the stunted and dry shrubs of the desert. ¶ It is *that they shall be destroyed for ever.* The meaning here is, not that the *design* of their being thus made to flourish is that they should be destroyed, or that they are made to flourish *for* that purpose, but that

8 But thou, LORD, *art most* high for evermore.

9 For, lo, thine enemies, O LORD, for, lo, thine enemies shall perish: all *b* the workers of iniquity shall be scattered;

10 But my horn shalt thou exalt like *the horn of* an unicorn :

b Matt. vii. 23.

I shall be anointed *c* with fresh oil.

11 Mine eye also shall see *my desire* on mine enemies; *and* mine ears shall hear *my desire* of the wicked that rise up against me.

c 2 Cor. i. 21 ; 1 John ii. 20.

---

such *will be* the result. They will not be made happy in another world by their prosperous and prospered wickedness here, as if God approved of their course; but the end will be that they will be destroyed for ever. The design of the psalmist seems to be to turn the mind from the idea that mere external prosperity is necessarily connected with happiness; or that one who is prospered in this life is on that account safe. There is another world, and *there* ample justice will be done to all. See Ps. lxxiii. 16–20.

8. *But thou,* LORD, *art most high for evermore.* In the treatment of the righteous and the wicked, thou wilt maintain thine own exalted place as a sovereign. Whatever may occur to men, God will maintain this exalted position as supreme over all.

9. *For, lo, thine enemies, O* LORD, *for, lo, thine enemies shall perish.* The repetition of the word " lo " here —*behold !*—is emphatic. The attention of the psalmist was fixed on this as an event which would be sure to occur. It was certain that God would be exalted; it followed from this, that all his enemies would be subdued in order that he *might* be thus exalted. ¶ *All the workers of iniquity shall be scattered.* More literally, " shall scatter or disperse themselves;" implying eagerness and activity, as if they were in haste to flee away. The allusion is to an army that is discomfited, disorganized, " demoralized," and scattered; or to chaff that is dispersed by the wind. See Job xxi. 18; Isa. xvii. 13; xxix. 5; Hos. xiii. 3.

10. *But my horn shalt thou exalt.* The horn is a symbol of strength or power (see Notes on Ps. xviii. 2); and the meaning here is, that, while the wicked would be cut off, he would be prospered ; that is, he had such confidence that he was the friend of God, that he believed God would honour him and exalt him. The psalmist here speaks of himself not so much with reference to his own particular case, but as the *representative* of the righteous. The idea is, that God will thus exalt *a righteous man.* ¶ *Like* the horn of *an unicorn.* Supposed to be remarkable for the strength of its horn. On the animal here referred to, see Notes on Job xxxix. 9; comp. Ps. xxii. 21. ¶ *I shall be anointed with fresh oil.* Oil pure and sweet; not old and rancid. That is, he would be made happy, cheerful, bright, and prosperous. Anointing with oil in the East was the symbol of all this, or was equivalent to what we mean by putting on gay apparel—holiday apparel. Comp. Notes on Ps. xxiii. 5.

11. *Mine eye also shall see* my desire. That is, I shall be permitted to see the destruction of my foes ; I shall be gratified with seeing them overthrown. On the sentiment here expressed, see Notes on Ps. liv. 7 ; lix. 10. ¶ *On mine enemies.* The word here used—שׁוּרָי, *shur*—occurs nowhere else. It means, properly, a lier-in-wait; one who *watches;* one who is in ambush ; and refers to persons who *watched* his conduct; who *watched* for his ruin. ¶ And *mine ears,* etc. Literally, " Of those rising up against me, evil-doers, my ear shall hear." He would hear of their ruin ; he would hear what he desired to hear,

14 They shall still bring forth fruit in old age; they shall be fat and ¹ flourishing;

15 To shew that the LORD *is* upright: *he is* my rock, *e* and *there is* no unrighteousness *f* in him.

¹ *green.*   *e* Deut. xxxii. 4.   *f* Zeph. iii. 5.

14. *They shall still bring forth fruit in old age.* As a tree that is carefully planted and cultivated may be expected to live long, and to bear fruit even when it is old. It is true that such a tree may be cut down; or that it may be blown down by winds and tempests; or that it *may* be unproductive, but as a general rule, and as laying the foundation of a reasonable hope, such a tree may be expected to live long, and to produce fruit even when it is old. So of one devoted early to God, and trained up under the influences of religion. The care, the culture, the habits of temperance, of industry, of moderation, and of sobriety so formed, are favourable to length of days, and lay the foundation for usefulness when old age comes. An aged man should be useful. He should feel that whatever wisdom he may possess as the result of long study and experience, belongs to God and to truth; that one great reason for sparing him is that he may be useful; that the world needs the benefit of his counsel and his prayers; that his life is lengthened out not for his own ease or enjoyment, but that virtue and piety may be extended in the world by all the influence which he can bring to bear upon it in advanced years. It may be added that, as a matter of fact, those who are thus trained and are thus preserved, *are* useful in old age. No one thus spared need be useless; perhaps almost none are. There is something appropriate for old men to do, as there is for the young and the middle-aged; and it should be the object of an aged Christian to find out what that is, *and to do it.* The word rendered *old age* means literally *grey or hoary hair.* ¶ *They shall be fat.* The meaning is, that they shall be vigorous, or have the appearance of vigour and health. ¶ *And flourishing.* Marg., as in Heb., *green.* This image is taken from a tree, as if it were still green in old age, or gave no indications of decay.

15. *To shew that the* LORD *is upright.* That is, This will be a proof that God is faithful to his promises; that he is the true friend of his people. The fact that they live long,—that they are happy and useful even in old age, will be a demonstration that God is the friend of virtue, and that he deals with men according to their character. ¶ He is *my rock.* He is my defence; that which constitutes my security. See Notes on Ps. xviii. 2. This is language of strong confidence in view of all that is said in the psalm. ¶ And there is *no unrighteousness in him.* This is said in the most absolute form,—implying the most entire confidence. God is altogether to be trusted. There is *no* evil or wrong in his character or in his dealings. In all respects he is worthy of confidence :—*worthy* to be loved, trusted, adored, obeyed, by the inhabitants of all worlds. What a sublime thought is this! What a consolatory truth! What would the universe be if God, a Being of infinite POWER, were not a Being of perfect RIGHTEOUSNESS, and could *not* be trusted by the creatures which he has made!

PSALM XCIII.

The author of this psalm is unknown, and there is nothing by which we can determine this, or its date, or the occasion on which it was written. It seems, from ver. 5, to have been composed with some reference to the sanctuary, and to the service there :—" Holiness becometh thine *house*, O Lord," and it may have been designed, with the last psalm, to have been used in the place of public worship on the sabbath-day. It would appear, also, from the structure of the psalm, that it was composed in view of some danger which may have threatened the nation from some

PSALM XCIII.

THE *ᵍ* LORD reigneth; he is
clothed with majesty; the
LORD is clothed with strength,
wherewith he hath girded him-

g Isa. lii. 7; Rev. xix. 6.   *h* Ps. ᴀlv. 6.

hostile power (vers. 1–4), and that the
design was to impart confidence in God,
or to keep up the assurance in the mind
of the people that God presided over all,
and that his kingdom was safe. With
this view, it is adapted to inspire confidence in God in all ages, and in all
times of danger. In the Septuagint and
the Latin Vulgate, the title is, "The
praise of an ode by David, for the day
preceding the sabbath, when the earth
was founded." The origin of this title
is unknown, and it has no authority.
There is no evidence that it was composed by David, and the presumption
from ver. 5 is that it was composed after
the temple was built, and consequently
after the death of David.

1. *The* LORD *reigneth.* The same
commencement of a psalm occurs in
Ps. xcvii. and xcix. The same idea
is often found in the Scriptures.
1 Chron. xvi. 31; Ps. xlvii. 8; Isa.
lii. 7; Rev. xix. 6. The thought
seems abrupt here. It would appear
as if the psalmist had been meditating on the dark things which occur
in the world; the mysteries which
abound; the things which seem ir-
reconcilable with the idea that there
is a just government over the world,
and that suddenly the idea occurs, as
a flash of lightning in a storm, that
Jehovah reigns over all, and that all
must be right. Amidst all these
things God sits upon the throne; he
orders all events; he sways his
sceptre over all; he orders all things
according to his own will; he secures
the accomplishment of his own purposes. ¶ *He is clothed with majesty.*
That is, he puts on, or wears this;
he appears in this as a garb, or robe.
The word rendered "majesty" means
properly *loftiness,* and is applied to
the swelling of the sea (Ps. lxxxix.
9), or to a column of smoke, Isa. ix.
18. The idea here is, that God is

self: the world also is stablished, that it cannot be moved.
2 Thy throne *ʰ is* established
¹ of old: thou *art* from everlasting.

¹ *from then.*

exalted; and that he appears in such
a manner as to indicate his proper
dignity. See Notes on Isa. vi. 1.
¶ *The* LORD *is clothed with strength,*
wherewith *he hath girded himself.*
There is an allusion here to the mode
of dress among the Orientals—the
custom of girding the loins when one
laboured, or walked, or ran. See
Notes on Matt. v. 38–41. ¶ *The*
world also is stablished. Is firm; is
on a solid foundation. It cannot be
shaken or destroyed by natural convulsions, or by the power of man.
¶ *That it cannot be moved.* Moved
out of its place; overthrown; destroyed. This seems to have been
spoken in view of some impending
calamity, as if everything were to
be swept away. The psalmist con-
soles himself with the thought that
the world was firmly established;
that no storm or tempest could be so
violent as to remove it out of its
place. The ground of consolation is
the essential stability of what God
has ordained.
2. *Thy throne* is *established of old.*
Whatever might occur, the throne of
God was firm. That could not be
moved. It had been set up from all
eternity. It had stood through all
the convulsions and changes which
had occurred in the universe; and it
would stand firm for ever. Whatever might change, that was immovable; and as long as that *is* unchanged we have a ground of security
and hope. Should *that* be moved, all
would be gone. The margin here is,
as in Heb., *from then:*—but it means
of old; from the most ancient times;
that is, from the period indicated by
the next clause, "from everlasting."
¶ *Thou* art *from everlasting.* From
all eternity; thou hast always existed;
thou art ever the same (Ps. xc. 1).

3 The floods have lifted up, O
LORD, the floods have lifted up
their voice; the floods lift up
their waves.

4 The ^{i} LORD on high *is*
mightier than the noise of many

i Ps. lxxxix. 9.

waters, *yea, than* the mighty
waves of the sea.

5 Thy testimonies are very
sure : holiness ^{k} becometh thine
house, O LORD, ^{1} for ever.

k Heb. xii. 14; Rev. xxi. 27.
^{1} *to length of days*, Ps. xxiii. 6.

---

3. *The floods have lifted up, O*
LORD, *the floods have lifted up their*
voice. The word here rendered *floods*,
means properly *rivers*, and then it
may be applied to any waters. The
word *voice* here refers to the noise of
raging waters when they are agitated
by the winds, or when they dash on
the shore. See Notes on Ps. xlii. 7.
¶ *The floods lift up their waves.* As
if they would sweep everything
away. The allusion here is to some
calamity or danger which might, in
its strength and violence, be compared with the wild and raging waves
of the ocean. Or if it refers literally to the ocean in a storm, then
the psalm may have been the reflections of the author as he stood on the
shore of the sea, and saw the waves
beat and dash against the shore. To
one thus looking upon the billows as
they roll in towards the shore, it
seems as if they were angry; as if
they intended to sweep everything
away; as if the rocks of the shore
could not resist them. Yet they
have their bounds. They spend their
strength; they break, and retire as
if to recover their force, and then
they renew their attack with the
same result. But their power is
limited. The rocky shore is unmoved. The earth abides. God is
over all. His throne is unshaken.
No violence of the elements can
affect that ; and, under his dominion,
all is secure.

4. *The* LORD *on high* is *mightier*
than the noise of many waters. That
is, he is more powerful than those
waters; he is able to control them.
See Notes on Ps. lxv. 7; Job xxxviii.
11. The original here is more rapid
in the course of the thought ; more
emphatic and forcible :—" More than

the voice of waters—many—mighty
—the breakers of the sea—in the
high place is Jehovah." He is over
all those billows and breakers; more
mighty than they all. They can
proceed no farther than he permits ;
they will be stayed when and where
he commands. We can conceive of
few things which more illustrate the
power and the majesty of God than the
fact that he thus presides over, and controls, the waves of the ocean. ¶ Yea,
than *the mighty waves of the sea.*
The original word here corresponds
precisely with our word *breakers*—
the mighty waves that *break* on the
beach.

5. *Thy testimonies are very sure.*
All that thou hast borne *witness* to ;
all that thou hast affirmed or declared
to be true. This would embrace *all*
that God has spoken, whether his
law, his promises, his commands, his
prophecies, or his statements of what
has occurred and of what will occur.
See Notes on Ps. xix. 7. ¶ *Holiness*
becometh thine house, O LORD. The
psalm seems to have been intended to
be used in the sanctuary, as a part of
public worship, and the word *holi-*
ness here would seem to mean a proper respect for God ; confidence in
him ; a state of mind free from all
doubt, and from all that is impure.
Perhaps there may be here, also, the
idea that in all the convulsions of the
world ; in all that threatens to overthrow truth and righteousness ; in
all the attacks which are made on
the Divine government ; in all the
efforts of the defenders of error, and
in the midst of abounding iniquity,
the church *should* maintain a firm
adherence to the principles of *holi-*
ness, to that which is right and true.
There should be one place — the

church—where there would be no wavering in regard to truth and holiness;—one place, where the truth would be defended whatever commotions might be abroad. The main idea, therefore, in the psalm is, that, in view of the fact that God reigns, and that nothing can frustrate his plans, or disturb his throne, we should approach him with reverence, with humble trust, with sincere and pure hearts. In a larger sense, also,—in the largest sense conceivable,—it is true that *holiness*, purity, freedom from evil thoughts, from a wanton eye and a wanton imagination, from unholy plans and purposes, should prevail in the house of God, and should be regarded as indispensable to proper worship. As heaven is pure, and as there shall enter there nothing "that defileth, neither whatsoever worketh abomination or maketh a lie" (Rev. xxi. 27), so in the place where we seek to prepare for that holy world—the sanctuary of God,—nothing should be allowed to enter that is impure and polluting; nothing that tends to corrupt or defile the soul. It may be added, that attendance in a place of public worship is calculated to *make* the heart pure, and to banish unholy thoughts and purposes from the soul. A man who *feels* that he is in the presence of a holy God, will not be likely to welcome into his soul polluted images and unholy desires. ¶ *For ever.* Marg., as in Heb., *to length of days.* The idea is, that it is *always* appropriate. See Notes on Ps. xxiii. 6.

PSALM XCIV.

This psalm, in the Septuagint and the Latin Vulgate, is entitled "A Psalm of David, for the fourth day of the week." What is the origin of this title is unknown, as there is nothing corresponding to it in the Hebrew. In the original the psalm is without a title, nor is there anything in the contents of it which will enable us to determine who was the author, or to fix the date or the occasion of its composition. There is in it no-

thing necessarily inconsistent with the supposition that David was the author; and there were undoubtedly occasions in his life, when it would have been appropriate. There have been many conjectures as to the author, and as to the occasion on which it was composed. Rüdinger refers it to the times of David and the rebellion of Absalom; Venema supposes that it refers to the time of Antiochus Epiphanes, and the persecution under him; De Wette refers it to the time of the Babylonish exile; others suppose that it was written on the eve of the Babylonish captivity. Whatever may have been the occasion, the style and form of the psalm are so general that it may be made a vehicle of pious thought, and of the feelings of the people of God, in all ages.

From the psalm itself it is plain that it was composed during some impending or actual national calamity. This is evident from vers. 3, 4, 5, 14, 20. It would seem, also, from vers. 7-10, that it was probably some calamity which was brought upon the people by a foreign nation,—a nation that defied Jehovah, and proclaimed that he was unable to defend his friends, or that he would not interpose in their behalf: "They say, the Lord shall not see, neither shall the God of Jacob regard it." The object of the psalm is to show that God *is* the protector of his people; that he *does* regard them; that he *will* interpose in their behalf.

The psalm embraces the following subjects:—

(1) An appeal or prayer to God as the God of vengeance, or as a just God, vers. 1, 2.

(2) A statement of the character and purposes of the wicked who were bringing these calamities upon the nation, vers. 3-7.

(3) A direct appeal to these invaders themselves, — an appeal based on the ground that God could *not* be indifferent to the conduct of men; that he must hear their words, understand their thoughts, see their acts, and know all that they did, vers. 8-11.

(4) Consolation in the trouble derived from the fact that this was a deserved chastening of the Lord, and was not designed for their destruction, but for their good, vers. 12-15.

(5) The fact that God is a source of confidence, comfort, and support to his people, in all such times of trial, vers. 16-23.

PSALM XCIV.

O LORD God, [1] to whom [l] vengeance belongeth; O God, to whom vengeance belongeth, [2] shew thyself.

2 Lift up thyself, thou judge of the earth : render a reward to the proud.

[1] *God of revenges.*
[l] Deut. xxxii. 35 ; Nahum i. 2.

3 LORD, how long [m] shall the wicked, how long shall the wicked triumph ?

4 *How long* shall they utter *and* speak hard [n] things ? *and* all the workers of iniquity boast themselves ?

[2] *shine forth,* Ps. lxxx. 1.
[m] Job xx. 5; Jer. xii. 1, 2.
[n] Ps. lxxiii. 8, etc.; Jude 15.

---

1. O LORD God, *to whom vengeance belongeth,* etc. Marg., *God of revenges.* The idea is, that it pertains to God to take vengeance, or to punish for crimes. See Notes on Rom. xii. 19. The appeal here is made to God in view of the crimes committed by others, and which are referred to in the subsequent part of the psalm. God is addressed as having the right to restrain and punish wicked men, and he is asked to interpose and assert that right in a case which clearly demanded it. The appeal is repeated to make it emphatic, or to denote *earnestness* in the petition. ¶ *Show thyself.* Marg., as in Heb., *shine forth.* The meaning is, Manifest thyself; come forth *as* such a God ; prove thy right; display thy power, and show that thou *art* a God opposed to crime and wrong. The same Hebrew word is used here which is found in Ps. lxxx. 1, and which is there rendered *shine forth.* See Notes on that passage.

2. *Lift up thyself.* Be exalted or lifted up so as to be manifest in thy true character. The idea is that God was, as it were, sitting at his ease, or as if he were indifferent to what was occurring in the world. See Notes on Ps. iii. 7. ¶ *Thou Judge of the earth.* Ruler of the world ; to whom it appertains to exercise judgment over all classes of people, and in all circumstances. The meaning here is, that as he was the Ruler of the whole earth, this matter came without doubt under his jurisdiction. It was a case for his interposition. ¶ *Render a reward to the proud.* A just recompence to the men who

are confident in their own strength, and who are manifesting their pride in depriving others of their rights.

3. LORD, *how long shall the wicked,* etc. As if there were to be no end to their exaltation; their joy; their success. How long would God allow this ? How long would he sit by and see it done ? Was he disposed to let them go on for ever ? Would he never interpose, and arrest them in their career ? How often do we wonder that God does not interpose ! How often does it seem inexplicable that a Being of almighty power and infinite goodness does not interfere with respect to the wickedness, the oppression, the slavery, the wrong, the cruelty, the fraud, the violence of the world—and put an end to it ! Nay, how entirely are we overwhelmed at the thought that he does not put an end to iniquity in the universe altogether ; that he never *will* thus interpose, and put an end to sin and sorrow ! Such things are too high for us now ; perhaps will be always so. Things on earth are not as we should suppose they would be ; and we can only pause and adore where we cannot comprehend !

4. How long *shall they utter* and *speak hard things?* The word rendered *utter* means to pour forth—as water from a fountain ; to pour forth copiously. The meaning is, that they seemed to be full, and that they poured forth evil words as a fountain pours forth water. The phrase *hard things* means proud, unfeeling, insolent things ; things which are unjust, unkind, severe, harsh. ¶ And *all the workers of iniquity boast themselves?*

5 They break in pieces thy people, O LORD, and afflict thine heritage.

6 They slay the widow and the stranger, and murder the fatherless.

7 Yet they say, The LORD shall not see, neither shall the God of Jacob regard *it*.

8 Understand, *o* ye brutish among the people; and *ye* fools, when will ye be wise?

9 He *p* that planted the ear,

o Ps. xcii. 6; Rom. iii. 11.　　p Ex. iv. 11.

Boast of their power and their success. How long shall they be permitted to *have* such success as may seem to justify them in their exultation?

5. *They break in pieces thy people.* They tread down; they grind; they crush. The Hebrew word is often used as meaning to crush under foot; to trample on; and hence it means to oppress. Lam. iii. 34; Isa. iii. 15. ¶ *And afflict.* To wit, by oppression and wrong. If this refers to foreigners, it means that they did this by invasion and by the ravages of war. ¶ *Thine heritage.* Thy people, regarded as an inheritance or possession. See Notes on Ps. xxviii. 9; xxxiii. 12; lxviii. 9; lxxiv. 2; Isa. xix. 25; xlvii. 6; 1 Pet. v. 3.

6. *They slay the widow and the stranger, and murder the fatherless.* To do this is everywhere represented as a peculiar crime, and as peculiarly offensive to God from the fact that these classes are naturally feeble and unprotected. See Notes on Isa. i. 17; Ps. lxviii. 5; lxxxii. 3.

7. *Yet they say.* By their conduct; or, they seem to say. ¶ *The* LORD *shall not see.* In the original, יָהּ, *Jah.* This is an abbreviation of the word JEHOVAH. See Notes on Ps. lxviii. 4; lxxxiii. 18. On the impious sentiment here expressed, see Notes on Ps. x. 11. ¶ *Neither shall the God of Jacob regard* it. Implying that God was indifferent to the conduct of men; that he would not punish the wicked; that sinners have nothing to fear at his hand. This sentiment is very common still, either as an article in their creed, or as implied in their conduct. The doctrine of universal salvation is really founded on this opinion; and most

men *act* as if it were their belief that the wicked are in no danger of being punished, and that there is no such attribute in God as justice.

8. *Understand, ye brutish among the people.* See Ps. lxxiii. 22. The meaning here is, "You who are like the brutes; you who see and understand no more of the character and plans of God than the wild beasts of the desert." The meaning is, that they did not employ their reason in the case; they acted like beasts, regardless of the consequences of their conduct—*as if* God would treat men as he does the beasts; as if there were no retribution in the future world. ¶ *And* ye *fools, when will ye be wise?* How long is this stupidity to continue? When will you attend to the truth; when will you act as immortal beings; when will you suffer your rational nature to lead you up to just views of God? It is implied that this folly had been manifested for a long period, and that it was time they should arouse from this condition, and act like men. With what propriety may this language be addressed still to the great mass of mankind! What numbers of the human race are there now, who in respect to God, and to the purpose for which they were made, evince no more wisdom than the brutes that perish! Oh, if men were truly wise, what a beautiful world would this be;—how noble and elevated would be our now degraded race!

9. *He that planted the ear.* He that made the ear. The word here used in the original is a participle. "Shall not he *planting* the ear;" that is, the *planter* of the ear. The idea seems to have been taken from the act of making a *hole* in the

shall he not hear? he that formed the eye, shall he not see?

10 He that chastiseth the heathen, *q* shall not he correct? he

q Ez. xxxix. 21 ; Hab. iii. 12.
r Prov. ii. 6.

r that teacheth man knowledge, *shall not he know?*

11 The LORD knoweth the thoughts of man, that they *are* *s* vanity.

s 1 Cor. iii. 19, 20.

ground when we set out a plant,— as if, in like manner, a *hole* had been made in the side of the head to insert the ear. ¶ *Shall he not hear?* He could not have created the faculty of hearing, without possessing it himself. Or, it is reasonable to suppose that he who has made *man* capable of hearing, must be able to hear himself. We have nothing in our nature which is not possessed in an infinitely higher measure by God. ¶ *He that formed the eye.* This, too, is a participle: " He forming the eye;" that is, the Former of the eye. The word here used is frequently employed in reference to a *potter;* and the idea is that God has moulded or formed the eye as the potter fashions the clay. The more the eye is studied in its structure, the more deeply shall we be impressed with the wonderful skill and wisdom of God. See this beautifully illustrated in Paley's Natural Theology. ¶ *Shall he not see?* He that made the eye to see must himself be able to see. He must see all that the eye itself can see; he must see all that *all* eyes see; he must have the power of sight far beyond what there is in the mere *organ* which he has made.

10. *He that chastiseth the heathen.* More literally, "Shall not the Reprover of nations—shall he not chastise—he that teaches man knowledge?" The idea is, that God exercises a government over the nations of the earth; that he has them under his control; that he brings heavy judgments on them; that he thus conveys great lessons to man. And shall not such a Being, in individual cases, reprove and correct for sin? It is assumed here that God, in fact, brings judgments on nations; that he does this by fire, flood, famine, pesti-

lence; that these things are proofs that he presides over the nations of the earth; and the question here is, whether he that does this on the large scale must not be expected to do it in individual cases, so that the offender will not escape. ¶ *Shall not he correct?* Shall he not chastise, or bring judgments on offenders? ¶ *He that teacheth man knowledge,* etc. The idea in our translation, that he who imparts knowledge to mankind must himself possess intelligence, is a true one, but it is probably not that which is in the original. The sense is probably merely that God is the great Teacher, and this is the impression which it is intended should be impressed on the mind, leaving the consequences of this to be supplied by the reader : "He that teaches man all the knowledge that he has!"—reflect on the consequences of this, or what must follow from this! Such a Being cannot be ignorant; he must understand all things; he must, therefore, see human conduct everywhere as it is. The consequence —the result—of this is stated in the next verse, that he must see the *thoughts* of man, and understand his real character.

11. *The LORD knoweth the thoughts of man.* That is, He who teaches men all that they know (ver. 10), must understand all that there is in the mind. See Notes on 1 Cor. iii. 20. ¶ *That they* are *vanity.* That is, that they are foolish, vain, unwise, wicked. The knowledge of the thoughts themselves carries with it also the knowledge that they *are* vain and foolish,—for that is their character, and to know them truly is to know this of them. They do not appear to him as they do to men themselves. They are to his view

12 Blessed *t is* the man whom thou chastenest, O LORD, and teachest him out of thy law;

13 That thou mayest give him rest from the days of adversity, until the pit be digged for the wicked.

t Job v. 17; Prov. iii. 11; Heb. xii. 5, etc.

14 For *u* the LORD will not cast off his people, neither will he forsake his inheritance:

15 But judgment shall return unto righteousness; and all the upright in heart shall [1] follow it.

u 1 Sam. xii. 22; Rom. xi. 1, 2.
[1] be *after.*

stripped of all that is flattering and illusive, and are seen to be vain and foolish.

12. *Blessed* is *the man whom thou chastenest, O* LORD. "Happy the man;" or "Oh the blessedness of the man." See Notes on Ps. i. 1. The word here rendered *chastenest* does not mean to chasten in the sense of afflicting or punishing. It means here to instruct; to warn; to admonish; to exhort. So the word is employed in Prov. ix. 7; Job iv. 3; Ps. xvi. 7. The meaning here is, that the man is blessed or happy whom God so *instructs, warns,* or *teaches,* that he understands the principles of the Divine administration. Such a man will see reasons for confidence in him in trouble, and for calmness of mind until punishment is brought upon his enemies. ¶ *And teachest him out of thy law.* Causest him, from thy word, to understand the great principles of thy government.

13. *That thou mayest give him rest.* Mayest make his mind quiet and calm; mayest save him from murmuring, from despondency, from impatience, by just confidence in thee, and in thy government. ¶ *From the days of adversity.* Or, in the days of evil; the time of calamity and trouble. That his mind may then be composed and calm. ¶ *Until the pit be digged for the wicked.* Until the wicked be punished; that is, while the preparations are going on, or while God seems to delay punishment, and the wicked are suffered to live as if God did not notice them, or would not punish them. The idea is, that the mind should not be impatient as if their punishment would not come, or as if

God were unconcerned; and that just views of the Divine administration would tend to make the mind calm even when the wicked *seemed* to prosper and triumph. See Notes on Ps. lxxiii. 16–22. The phrase "until the pit be digged" is derived from the method of hunting wild beasts by digging a pit into which they might fall and be taken. See Notes on Ps. vii. 15.

14. *For the* LORD *will not cast off his people,* etc. He will interpose in their behalf though the wicked seem now to triumph. The certainty of this would give consolation; this would make the mind calm in the days of trouble. Comp. 1 Sam. xii. 22; 1 Kings vi. 13; Deut. xxxi. 6. See Notes on Rom. xi. 1, 2.

15. *But judgment shall return unto righteousness.* That is, The exercise of judgment shall be so manifest to the world,—as if it *returned* to it,— as to show that there is a righteous God. The truth here taught is, that the *results* of God's interposition in human affairs will be such as to show that he is on the side of righteousness, or such as to vindicate and maintain the cause of righteousness in the earth. ¶ *And all the upright in heart shall follow it.* Marg., *shall be after it.* The meaning is, that all who are upright in heart—all who are truly righteous—will follow on in the path of justice; that they will regard what God does as right, and will walk in that path. The fact that what occurs is done by God, will be to them a sufficient revelation of what *ought* to be done; and they will follow out the teachings properly suggested by the Divine dealings as their rules of life. In other words,

16 Who will rise up for me against the evil-doers? *or* who will stand up for me against the workers of iniquity?

17 Unless *v* the LORD *had been*

v Ps. cxxiv. 1, 2.   [1] Or, *quickly.*

the manifested laws of the Divine administration will be to them an indication of what is right; and they will embrace and follow the lessons thus made known to them by the dealings of Divine Providence as the rules of their own conduct.

16. *Who will rise up for me against the evil-doers?* etc. This is the language of the psalmist. It is what he *had* said in the circumstances referred to in the first part of the psalm, when the wicked seemed to triumph; when they had come in upon the land, and laid waste the heritage of God, vers. 3–6. At that time, full of anxiety and trouble, and deeply impressed with a sense of danger, he had anxiously looked around for help, and had asked with deep concern who would stand up for him and defend him. The following verses (17, 18) show what was then his reliance, and in what way confidence in God had kept him from falling into despair.

17. *Unless the* LORD *had been my help.* At the time referred to. If I had not had a God to whom I could have gone,—if my mind had not been directed to him,—if I had not actually found him a refuge and strength, I should have despaired altogether. There was no other one to whom I could go; there was nothing else but the help of God on which I could rely. ¶ *My soul had almost dwelt in silence.* Marg., *quickly.* The original is, "It was as it were but little;" that is, there was little wanting to bring this about; a little heavier pressure —a little added to what I was then suffering—a little longer time before relief was obtained — would have brought me down to the land of silence—to the grave. The Latin

VOL. III.

my help, my soul had [1] almost dwelt in silence.

18 When I said, My foot *w* slippeth; thy mercy, O LORD, held me up.

19 In the multitude of my

w Ps. xxxviii. 16.

Vulgate renders this, "My soul had dwelt *in inferno.*" The Septuagint, "in Hades"—τῷ ᾅδῃ. See Psalm xxxi. 17. The grave is represented as a place of silence, or as the land of silence: Ps. cxv. 17: "The dead praise not the Lord, neither any that go down into silence." Comp. Amos viii. 3.

18. *When I said, My foot slippeth.* I can no longer stand. My strength is gone; and I must sink into the grave. The original here is, "*If I say,* My foot slippeth," etc. The statement is general; that if at any time he had been, or should be, in such circumstances, then God would interpose. The general remark, however, is founded on his interposition on this particular occasion. His aid was then so marked and timely, that he felt that he could make the declaration general in regard to his whole life—to all circumstances in which he would ever be placed. ¶ *Thy mercy, O* LORD, *held me up.* By thy merciful interposition thou didst keep me from falling. It was strength put forth as the expression of *mercy;*—not strength to which he had any claim. How often in life may we say this of ourselves, that when just ready to sink; when our strength was almost gone; when a little severer pressure would have brought us to the grave, God by his mercy and his power interposed and saved us! Every such act of mercy—every new interposition in this manner—is a new gift of life, and lays us under obligation as if we had been just created,—for it is just so much more of life given us by God.

19. *In the multitude of my thoughts within me thy comforts delight my soul.* The Septuagint and the Latin

D

thoughts within me thy comforts *x* delight my soul.

20 Shall the throne of iniquity

x Ps. lxiii. 5, 6; 2 Cor. i. 3, 4.

have fellowship with thee, which *y* frameth mischief by a law?

21 They *z* gather themselves

y Isa. x. 1.   *z* Prov. i. 11, 16; Matt. xxvii. 1.

Vulgate render this, " In the multitude of my *griefs* within me," etc. De Wette renders it, " Bei meinen vielen Sorgen,"—*in my many cares.* The Hebrew word, however, properly means *thoughts;* and the idea seems to be that in the great number of thoughts which passed through his mind, so many of them perplexing, anxious, burdensome,—so many of them vain and profitless,—so many of them that seemed to come and go without any aim or object, there was *one* class that gave him comfort. They were those which pertained to God. In those thoughts he found calmness and peace. However much he might be disturbed by other thoughts, yet here he found rest and peace. In God,—in his character, in his law, in his government,—he had an unfailing source of consolation; and whatever trouble he might have from the cares of life, and from the evil imaginings in his own mind, yet here his soul found repose. God was an unfailing refuge; and meditation on him and his perfections made the mind calm. How many thoughts pass through our minds in a single day or a single hour! Who can tell whence they come, or by what laws they are linked together! How many of them *seem* to have no connexion with any that went before! How many of them seem to be thrown into our minds when we would avoid them! How many are vain and frivolous; how many are sceptical; how many are polluted and polluting! How many come into the mind which we would not for worlds disclose to our best friends! How few of us would walk abroad if we were conscious that all whom we meet could look into our bosoms, and see all that is passing there! What a consolation it is to us that they cannot see it! What a world of confusion and

blushes would this be if, in the streets of a crowded city, or when man meets his fellow man anywhere, all that is in his bosom were known! And yet, in this multitude of thoughts —so empty, so foolish, so sinful, so vexing, so sceptical, so polluting— there are others—there *are* thoughts of God, of Christ, of heaven, of hope, of faith, of love, of benevolence; thoughts within us, when the Divine promises come to the heart, and the prospect of heaven warms the soul. These give " comfort;" these fill the soul with " delight." Happy he who can find in his bosom, amidst the multitude of thoughts within him, those which pertain to God; to a higher life; to heaven!

20. *Shall the throne of iniquity.* The throne established in iniquity; or, sustaining iniquity. The allusion is probably to what was referred to in the former part of the psalm,— the powers that were spreading desolation through the land,—wicked princes or rulers, vers. 3–7. Their thrones were established on evil; they defended wickedness and wrong by their authority; they abused their power, and employed it to overthrow the rights of others. The *phrase* would be applicable to any unjust government, or to any laws that are designed to uphold that which is wrong. Such are all the laws which authorize or uphold slavery, gaming, lotteries, the traffic in intoxicating drinks, etc. ¶ *Have fellowship with thee.* With God. Shall they be united with thee; be sustained by thee; be regarded as a part of thine administration? Wilt thou sanction them? Wilt thou give to them thy patronage, as if they met with thine approbation? The Hebrew word means to be associated with, or allied to, and would be properly applied to a partnership, or anything where there is

together against the soul of the righteous, and condemn the innocent blood.

22 But the LORD is my defence; and my God *is* the rock of my refuge.

23 And he shall bring upon them their own iniquity, and shall cut them off in their own *a* wickedness; *yea,* the LORD our God shall cut them off.

a Prov. v. 22.

---

fellowship or alliance. The interrogative form here strongly implies that this *cannot be.* Such laws—such purposes—*cannot* be in accordance with the laws and authority of God; or, in other words, God does not sit on the same throne with those who authorize and by law sustain slavery, intemperance, and gambling. There can be no partnership here. ¶ *Which frameth mischief by a law.* The word rendered *mischief* usually means labour, toil; and then, trouble, vexation, sorrow. It may, however, be used to denote evil of any kind—crime, or wrong. The word rendered *frameth* means to form, to fashion, to make, as a potter does clay; Gen. ii. 7, 8, 19; or as a workman does statues, Isa. xliv. 9, 10, 12; or as one makes weapons, Isa. liv. 17. It is often applied to God as the Creator. See Notes on ver. 9 : "he that *formed* the eye." The word *law* here means a rule or statute; and the idea is, that the iniquity referred to was not the result of an irregular and fitful impulse; or of passion; of sudden excitement; or of mere *will* in a particular case; but was reduced to *statute,* and sustained by law. The expression would apply to all those cases where evil is upheld by the government or by civil authority, or where those who are engaged in it can plead in their defence the sanction of law. The statement here is, that such acts *cannot* have fellowship with God, or receive his approval. It is an insult to God to suppose that he has ever appointed legislators or magistrates for the purpose of making or upholding such enactments. Yet there are many such laws in the world; and a main reason why it is so difficult to remove such evils as have been above referred to is the

fact that they *are* sustained by law, and that they who hold slaves, or open gambling-houses, or sell intoxicating drinks, can plead the authority of the law; or, in other words, that the laws have done all they can to place such things on a level with those which *ought* to be protected by statute. Many a man in his business looks no farther than to the laws of the land, and if he has *their* sanction, in vain is the attempt to induce him to abandon a business that leads to oppression, or that scatters woe and sorrow through a community.

21. *They gather themselves together against the soul of the righteous.* Against the *life* of the righteous; that is, to take their lives. The Hebrew word rendered *gather together,* means to press or crowd upon any one; to rush in crowds or troops. It would refer particularly to a tumultuous gathering—*a mob*—intent on accomplishing its purpose. ¶ *And condemn the innocent blood.* Literally, *make guilty;* that is, they hold that blood to be guilty; or, they treat the innocent as if they were guilty.

22. *But the* LORD *is my defence,* etc. In all these purposes of the wicked; in all that they do,—whether under the form and sanction of law (ver. 20), or by the excitement of passion,—my trust is still in God. He is able to interpose in either case, and I may confidently commit my cause to him. On the language used here, as well as the sentiment, see Notes on Ps. xviii. 2.

23. *And he shall bring upon them their own iniquity.* The consequences of their sin. He shall punish them as they deserve. See Notes on Ps. vii. 16. ¶ *And shall cut them off in their own wickedness.* As the result

PSALM XCV.

O COME, let us sing unto the
LORD; let *b* us make a joyful

b Ps. c. 1.　　　*c* 2 Sam. xxii. 47.

noise to the rock *c* of our salvation.
2 Let us [1] come before his
presence with thanksgiving, and

[1] *prevent his face.*

---

of their wickedness, and while they
are engaged in perpetrating acts of
sin. ¶ Yea, *the* LORD *our God shall
cut them off.* Expressing, by the repetition of the sentiment, the utmost
confidence that this would be so.
This is in accordance with the prayer
with which the psalm opens, and is
expressive of entire faith that God
will deal justly with the children of
men. However the wicked may seem
to prosper and to triumph, yet the
day of vengeance is approaching, and
all which they have deserved will
come upon them.

PSALM XCV.

Of the author of this psalm nothing is
certainly known. It is, however, ascribed to David in the Latin Vulgate
and in the Septuagint; and in Heb. iv.
7, it is referred to as a psalm of David:
"Again, he limiteth a certain day, saying *in David,* 'To-day, if ye will hear
his voice,'" etc. This language may
refer in general to the Book of Psalms,
called from their chief author, the
Psalms of David; or it may mean that
David was the author of this particular
psalm. Either supposition would meet
all that is demanded by the quotation in
the Epistle to the Hebrews. There is,
however, no improbability in the supposition that the psalm was written by
David, as he doubtless composed many
songs to which his name was not attached.

Nothing is known of the *occasion* on
which the psalm was composed. It is a
general song of praise, and contains only
such language as might be proper in
any period of the Jewish history after
the people were established in the promised land. It is, indeed, a *Hebrew*
song; it has reference to the Hebrew
people; and it contains such arguments
and appeals as would be particularly
adapted to influence them.

The psalm consists of three parts:—
I. An exhortation to praise and wor-
ship God, vers. 1, 2.
II. Reasons for offering such praise,

vers. 3–7:—(*a*) He is a great God, ver.
3; (*b*) He has made all things, and all
things are under his control, vers. 4, 5;
(*c*) He is our Maker, ver. 6; (*d*) He is
our God, and we are his people, ver. 7.
III. An exhortation not to harden
the heart; not to be perverse and rebellious, vers. 7–11. This is enforced
by the example of the Israelites in the
wilderness, and by the results which
followed from their tempting God, and
provoking his wrath. The appeal is
founded on the fact that, in consequence
of their rebellion, they were shut out of
the promised land. On the same principle, if we are rebellious, we shall be
excluded from heaven.

1. *O come, let us sing unto the*
LORD. The word here rendered
come, means properly *go;* but it is
here used, as it often is, as a formula
of invitation, in calling on others to
share in what is done by the speaker.
It is here to be understood as used
by one portion of an assembly con-
vened for worship addressing the other
portion, and calling on them to unite
in the praise of God. ¶ *Let us make
a joyful noise.* The word here used
means commonly to make a loud
noise, to shout, Job xxx. 5. It is
especially used (*a*) of warlike shouts,
Josh. vi. 16; 1 Sam. xvii. 20; (*b*) of
the shout of triumph, Judges xv. 14;
(*c*) of the sound or clangour of a
trumpet, Num. x. 9; Joel ii. 1. It
may thus be used to denote any shout
of joy or praise. In public worship
it would denote praise of the most
animated kind. ¶ *To the Rock of
our salvation.* The strong ground
of our confidence; the basis of our
hope; our security. See Notes on
Ps. xviii. 2.

2. *Let us come before his presence.*
Marg., as in Heb., *prevent his face.*
The word in Hebrew means literally
to come before; to anticipate. It is
the word which is commonly rendered

make a joyful noise unto him with psalms.

3 For *d* the LORD *is* a great God, and a great King *e* above all gods.

4 In [1] his hand *are* the deep

d Ps. xcvii. 9. *e* Mal. i. 14.

places of the earth; the 2 strength of the hills *is* his also.

5 [3] The sea *is* his, and he made *f* it : and his hands formed the dry *land.*

[1] *whose.* [2] Or, *heights of the hills* are *his.*
[3] *Whose the sea is.* *f* Gen. i. 9, 10.

---

prevent. See Notes on Job iii. 12; Ps. xvii. 13; lix. 10; 1 Thess. iv. 15. Here it means to come before, in the sense of *in front of.* Let us stand before his face; that is, in his very presence. ¶ *With thanksgiving.* Expressing our thanks. ¶ *And make a joyful noise unto him.* The same word which occurs in ver. 1. ¶ *With psalms.* Songs of praise.

3. *For the* LORD *is a great God.* For *Jehovah* is a great God. The object is to exalt *Jehovah,* the true God, as distinguished from all who were worshipped as gods. The first idea is that he is "*great;*" that he is exalted over all the universe; that he rules over all, and that he is to be worshipped as such. ¶ *And a great King above all gods.* This does not mean that he is a great ruler of all other gods, as if they had a real existence, but that he is king or ruler far above all that were worshipped as gods, or to whom homage was paid. Whoever, or whatever was worshipped as God, Jehovah was supreme over all things. He occupied the throne; and all others must be beneath him, and under his dominion. If the sun, the moon, or the stars were worshipped,—if the mountains or the rivers,—if angels good or bad, —yet Jehovah was above all these. If imaginary beings were worshipped, yet Jehovah in his perfections was exalted far above all that was ascribed to them; for He was the true God, and the Ruler of the universe, while they were beings of the imagination only.

4. *In his hand.* In his power, or under his control as his own. That is, he so possesses all things that they can be claimed by no other. His right over them is absolute and entire. ¶ *Are the deep places of the*

earth. The word here used—מֶחְקְרֵי, *mehhkor*—means the interior, the inmost depth; that which is *searched out,* from חָקַר—*hhakar*—to search, search out, explore. The primary idea is that of searching by boring or digging; and the allusion here is to the parts of the earth which could be explored only by digging—as in mining, or sinking shafts in the earth. The meaning is, that all those places which lie beyond the ordinary power of observation in man are in the hand of God. He knows them as clearly as those which are most plain to human view; he possesses or owns them as his own as really as he does those which are on the surface of the ground. ¶ *The strength of the hills* is *his also.* Marg., *The heights of the hills are his.* The word rendered strength — תּוֹעֲפוֹת, *toăphoth* —means properly swiftness or speed in running; then, weariness, wearisome labour; and hence, wealth obtained by labour; *treasures.* Here the expression means *treasures of the mountains;* that is, treasures obtained out of the mountains, the precious metals, etc. Comp. Notes on Job xxii. 25, where the same word occurs. All this belongs to God. As he is the Maker of these hills, and of all that they contain, the absolute proprietorship is in him.

5. *The sea is his.* Marg., as in Heb., *Whose the sea is.* That is, The sea belongs to him, with all which it contains. ¶ *And he made it.* It is his, *because* he made it. The creation of anything gives the highest possible right over it. ¶ *And his hands formed the dry* land. He has a claim, therefore, that it should be recognised as his, and that all who

6 O come, let us worship and bow down : let us kneel *g* before the LORD our maker.

g Acts xxi. 5 ; Phil. ii. 10.   *h* Heb. iii. 7, 15.

7 For he *is* our God ; and we *are* the people of his pasture, and the sheep of his hand.   To-day, *h* if ye will hear his voice,

---

dwell upon it, and derive their support from it, should acknowledge him as its great Owner and Lord.

6. *O come, let us worship and bow down.* Let us worship him by bowing down ; by prostrating ourselves before him. The word here rendered "come" is not the same which is used in ver. 1. Its literal meaning is *come,* and it is an earnest exhortation *to* come and worship. It is not a particle merely calling *attention* to a subject, but it is an exhortation to approach—to enter—to engage in a thing. The word rendered *worship,* means properly to bow down ; to incline oneself ; and then, to bow or prostrate oneself before any one in order to do him homage, or reverence. Then it means to bow down before God in the attitude of worship. It would most naturally refer to an entire *prostration* on the ground, which was a common mode of worship ; but it would also express adoration in any form. The word rendered *bow down,* means properly to bend, to bow, spoken usually of the knees. Isa. xlv. 23 : "every knee shall bow." Comp. Judges vii. 5, 6 ; 1 Kings viii. 54 ; 2 Kings i. 13. The word *might* be applied, like the former word, to those who bow down with the whole person, or prostrate themselves on the ground. 2 Chron. vii. 3.   ¶ *Let us kneel before the* LORD *our Maker.* The usual attitude of prayer in the Scriptures. See Notes on Dan. vi. 10 ; comp. 2 Chron. vi. 13 ; Luke xxii. 41 ; Acts vii. 60 ; ix. 40 ; xx. 36 ; xxi. 5. All the expressions here employed denote a posture of profound reverence in worship, and the passage is a standing rebuke of all irreverent postures in prayer ; of such habits as often prevail in public worship where no *change* of posture is made in prayer, and where a congregation irreverently *sit* in the act of professedly worship-

ping God.   Men show to their fellow-men the respect indicated by rising up before them :—much more should they show respect to God—respect in a posture which will indicate profound reverence, and a deep sense of his presence and majesty. Reverently kneeling or standing *will* indicate this ; sitting does *not* indicate it.

7. *For he* is *our God.* Not only the God whom we worship as the true God, but One who has revealed himself to us as *our* God. We worship him as God—as entitled to praise and adoration *because* he is the true God ; we worship him also as sustaining the relation of God to us, or *because* we recognize him as our God, and *because* he has manifested himself as ours.   ¶ *And we* are *the people of his pasture.* Whom he has recognized as his flock ; to whom he sustains the relation of shepherd ; who feeds and protects us as the shepherd does his flock. See Notes on Ps. lxxix. 13 ; comp. Ps. xxiii. 1–3.   ¶ *And the sheep of his hand.* The flock that is guided and fed by his hand.   ¶ *To day if ye will hear his voice.* His voice calling you ; commanding you ; inviting you ; encouraging you. See this passage explained in the Notes on Heb. iii. 7–11. The word *to-day* here means *the present time ;* now. The idea is, that the purpose to obey should not be deferred till to-morrow ; should not be put off to the future. The commands of God should be obeyed at once ; the purpose should be executed immediately. All God's commands relate to the present. He gives us none for the future ; and a true purpose to obey God exists only where there is a willingness to obey *now,—to-day ;—* and can exist only then. A purpose to repent at some future time, to give up the world at some future time, to embrace the Gospel at some future time, is *no* obedience,—for there is *no*

8 Harden not your heart, as in the [1] provocation, *i and as in* the day of temptation in the wilderness:

9 When your fathers tempted *k* me, proved me, and saw my work

[1] *contention.*
i Ex. xvii. 2, 7; Num. xiv. 2, etc.; Deut. vi. 16.

10 Forty years long was I grieved with *this* generation, and said, It *is* a people that do err in their heart, and they have not known my ways:

11 Unto whom I sware *l* in my wrath, [2] that they should not enter into my rest.

k 1 Cor. x. 9. *l* Heb. iv. 3, 5. [2] *if they enter.*

such command addressed to us. A resolution to put off repentance and faith, to defer attention to religion till some future time, is real disobedience,—and often the worst form of disobedience,—for it is directly in the face of the command of God. " *If* ye will hear." That is, If there is a disposition or willingness to obey his voice at all ; or, to listen to his commands. See Notes on Heb. iii. 7.

8. *Harden not your heart.* See this verse explained in the Notes on Heb. iii. 8. ¶ *As in the provocation,* etc. Marg., *contention.* The original is *Meribah.* See Ex. xvii. 7, where the original words *Meribah,* rendered here *provocation,* and *Massah,* rendered here *temptation,* are retained in the translation.

9. *When your fathers.* Your ancestors. See this verse explained in the Notes on Heb. iii. 9. ¶ *Tempted me.* Tried me; tried my patience, to see how much I would bear. This does not mean, as it commonly does now with us, to place inducements before one to lead him into sin, but to *try* one—to put his patience to the test. This they did, in the case referred to, by their obduracy and evil conduct. ¶ *Proved me.* See Notes on Heb. iii. 9. *And saw my work.* Though they constantly saw my work ; saw my gracious interpositions ; saw what I was doing for their own good.

10. *Forty years long.* All the time that they were in the wilderness. During this long period their conduct was such as to try my patience and forbearance. ¶ *Was I grieved.* The word here used—קוּט, *kût*—means properly to loathe, to nauseate, to

be disgusted with. It is translated *loathe* in Ezek. vi. 9; xx. 43; xxxvi. 31; and *grieved* in Ps. cxix. 158; cxxxix. 21. It is here expressive of the strong abhorrence which God had of their conduct. Comp. Rev. iii. 16. ¶ *With* this *generation.* With the entire generation that came out of Egypt. They were all cut off in the wilderness, except Caleb and Joshua. ¶ *And said, It* is *a people.* It is a characteristic of the entire people, that they are disposed to wander from God. ¶ *That do err in their heart.* In the Epistle to the Hebrews (iii. 10) where this is quoted, it is, " They do always err in their heart." The sense is substantially the same. See Notes on that place. ¶ *And they have not known my ways.* See Notes on Heb. iii. 10.

11. *Unto whom I sware in my wrath.* See Notes on Heb. iii. 11. ¶ *That they should not enter into my rest.* Marg., as in Heb., *If they enter into my rest.* The *rest* here referred to was the land of Canaan. They were not permitted to enter there as a place of *rest* after their long and weary wanderings, but died in the wilderness. The meaning is not that none of them were saved (for we must hope that very many of them were brought to the heavenly Canaan), but that they did not come to the promised land. Unbelief shut them out ; and this fact is properly made use of here, and in Heb. iii., as furnishing a solemn warning to all not to be unbelieving and rebellious, since the consequence of unbelief and rebellion must be to exclude us from the kingdom of heaven, the true place of " rest."

PSALM XCVI.

O SING *m* unto the LORD a new

m 1 Chron. xvi. 23—33.

song; sing unto the LORD, all the earth.

2 Sing unto the LORD, bless

PSALM XCVI.

This psalm is similar in structure and design to Ps. xcv. It is an exhortation to universal praise, and was doubtless designed to be used in public worship,— in the service of the sanctuary.

The psalm has no title in the Hebrew, and its authorship cannot with any certainty be determined. There is, however, a very marked similarity between this psalm and a portion of that which was composed and sung at the removal of the ark by David, as recorded in 1 Chron. xvi., and of which it is said (1 Chron. xvi. 7), "Then on that day David delivered first this psalm to thank the Lord, into the hand of Asaph and his brethren." Of the original psalm, therefore, David was undoubtedly the author. The ninety-sixth psalm is merely an abridgment of that one, or more properly an *extract* from it, since it is essentially similar to one portion of it, and is taken from it with very slight variations, 1 Chron. xvi. 23–33. But by whom the *extract* and the slight alterations were made, and on what occasion this was done, we have no certain means of ascertaining. The title in the Septuagint is, "When the house was built after the captivity. An ode by David." The same is the title in the Latin Vulgate. According to this, it is supposed that on the dedication of the temple, when it was rebuilt after the Babylonish captivity, a portion of a psalm composed by David was selected and arranged for that purpose. Hence it might be properly called "A Psalm of David;" though not, of course, composed by him for that particular occasion. This seems to me to be a very probable account of the origin of the psalm, and of the reason why it has its present form. In the original psalm (1 Chron. xvi.) there were things which would not be particularly appropriate to the dedication of the temple, while the portion which is extracted is eminently fitted for such a service. De Wette doubts the genuineness of the psalm in 1 Chron. xvi.; and Hengstenberg supposes that that psalm was made up of parts taken from psalms which were then in common use. But it seems to me that the suggestion above is the most natural, and

sufficiently explains the origin of this psalm. It would be very appropriate to the re-dedication of the temple; and it is appropriate to be used in similar services at all times.

The structure of the psalm is very simple, and it does not admit of any particular analysis.

1. *O sing unto the* LORD *a new song.* See Notes on Ps. xxxiii. 3. This is the only addition made to the original form of the psalm. The word *new* here implies that there was some fresh occasion for celebrating the praises of God ; that some event had occurred, or that some truth relating to the Divine character had now been made known, which could not well be expressed in any psalm or hymn then in use. It is a call on all to celebrate the praises of the Lord in a "new" song—new, particularly, as it calls on *all the earth* to join in it; and possibly this was designed to suggest the idea that while that temple stood, a dispensation would commence, under which the distinction between the Jews and the Gentiles would be broken down, and all mankind would unite in the praise of God. ¶ *Sing unto the* LORD, *all the earth.* All nations. All people had occasion to bless his name ; to praise him. What he had done, what he was still doing, was of interest to all lands, and made an appeal to all people to praise him. The psalm is constructed on this supposition, that the occasion for praise referred to was one in which all people were interested; or, in other words, that Jehovah was the true God over all the nations, and that all people should acknowledge him.

2. *Sing unto the* LORD, *bless his name.* This verse is substantially the same as 1 Chron. xvi. 23 ; "Sing unto the Lord, all the earth; show forth from day to day his salvation." ¶ *Show forth his salvation.* His interposition; the fact that he has saved or delivered us. This may have re-

his name: shew forth his salvation from day to day.

3 Declare his glory among the heathen, his wonders among all people.

4 For the LORD *is* great, and

n greatly to be praised: he *is* to be feared above all gods.

5 For *o* all the gods of the nations *are* idols: but *p* the LORD made the heavens.

n Ps. xviii. 3.　*o* Jer. x. 11, 12.　*p* Isa. xlii. 5.

ferred originally in particular to what he had done to save the people in time of danger, but the language is such also as to express salvation in a higher sense—salvation from sin and death. As such it may be employed to express what God has done for mankind—for all men, Jews and Gentiles—in providing a way of salvation, and making it possible that they should reach heaven. For this all men have occasion for praise. ¶ *From day to day.* Continually; always. It is a fit subject for unceasing praise. Every man should praise God every day—on each returning morning, and on every evening—for the assurance that there is a way of salvation provided for him, and *that he may be happy for ever.* If we had right feelings, this would be the first thought which would burst upon the mind each morning, irradiating, as with sunbeams, all around us; and it would be the last thought which would linger in the soul as we lie down at night, and close our eyes in slumber—making us grateful, calm, happy, as we sink to rest, for whether we wake or not in this world we may be for ever happy.

3. *Declare his glory among the heathen.* Among the nations; the people who are not Hebrews. The meaning is, Let it be proclaimed in all lands, among all people. Let it not be confined to those who are professedly his people, but let it be announced everywhere. This is copied literally from 1 Chron. xvi. 24. ¶ *His wonders among all people.* His "marvellous works;" those things which are fitted to produce astonishment in the mind. The reference is to those works and doings of God which lie so far beyond the power of any created being, and which by their vastness,

their wisdom, and their benevolence, are fitted to produce a deep impression on the human mind.

4. *For the* LORD *is great.* Jehovah is great. See Notes on Ps. lxxvii. 13. This verse is taken literally from 1 Chron. xvi. 25. ¶ *And greatly to be praised.* Worthy of exalted praise and adoration. ¶ *He* is *to be feared above all gods.* He is to be reverenced and adored above all that are called gods. Higher honour is to be given him; more lofty praise is to be ascribed to him. He is Ruler over all the earth, and has a claim to universal praise. Even if it were admitted that they were real gods, yet it would still be true that they were local and inferior divinities; that they ruled only over the particular countries where they were worshipped and acknowledged as gods, and that they had no claim to *universal* adoration as Jehovah has.

5. *For all the gods of the nations are idols.* All the gods worshipped by the people of other lands are mere *idols.* None of them can claim to have a real existence *as* gods. The word here rendered *idols* is translated by the Septuagint δαιμόνια, *demons.* So the Latin Vulgate *dæmonia.* The Hebrew word —לֶּ֫א, *Elil*—means properly *of nothing, nought, empty, vain.* See Job xiii. 4. The meaning here is, that they were mere nothings; they had no real existence; they were the creations of the imagination; they could not in any sense be regarded as what it was pretended they were; they had no claim to reverence and worship *as* gods. Of most of them it was a fact that they had *no* existence at all, but were mere creatures of fancy. Of those that did really exist, as the sun, moon, stars, animals, or the spirits of departed men, though it was true that they had an actual ex-

6 Honour and majesty *are* before him : strength *q* and beauty *are* in his sanctuary.

q Ps. lxiii. 2.

7 Give *r* unto the LORD, O ye kindreds of the people, give unto the LORD glory and strength.

r Jude 25.

istence, yet it was also true that they had no existence *as gods,* or as entitled to worship ; and hence it was also true that the worship offered to them was as vain as that which was offered to mere beings of the imagination. This verse is extracted literally from 1 Chron. xvi. 26. The Hebrew is the same. ¶ *But the* LORD *made the heavens.* Jehovah *created* the heavenly hosts, and therefore he is the true God, and is entitled to worship. The power of *creation*—of causing anything to exist where there was nothing before—must pertain to God alone, and is the highest act of Divinity. No pretended heathen god has that power; no man has that power. The true God has reserved the exercise of that power to himself, and has never, in any instance, imparted it to a created being.

6. *Honour and majesty* are *before him.* This part of the verse is taken literally from 1 Chron. xvi. 27. The meaning is, that that which constitutes honour, glory, majesty, is *in his presence,* or wherever he is. Wherever he manifests himself, there are the exhibitions of honour and majesty. They are always the accompaniments of his presence. ¶ *Strength and beauty* are *in his sanctuary.* This is slightly varied from the parallel passage in 1 Chron. xvi. 27. The word rendered *strength* is in both places the same. The word rendered *beauty* here — תִּפְאָרֶת, *tiphereth* — is in 1 Chron. xvi. 27 הֶדְוָה, *hhedvah—joy* or *gladness.* The word here rendered *sanctuary* — מִקְדָּשׁ, *mikdosh,*—is in 1 Chron. xvi. 27—מָקוֹם, *makom,*— *place.* These variations are such as to show that the psalm is not a mere extract, but that it was altered of design, and adapted to the occasion on which it was to be employed,—confirming the supposition that it may have been used in the re-dedication of

the temple after the return from the captivity. The word *sanctuary* refers to the holy place where God dwells ; his sacred abode, whether his residence in heaven, or the temple on earth as the place of his earthly habitation. When it is said that "*strength*" is there, it means that the dwelling-place of God is the source of *power,* or that power emanates from thence; that is, from God himself. When it is said that "beauty" is there, the meaning is, that whatever is fitted to charm by loveliness ; whatever is a real ornament ; whatever makes the world attractive ; whatever beautifies and adorns creation, has its home in God ; it proceeds from him. It may be added that whatever there is of *power* to reform the world, and convert sinners ; whatever there is to turn men from their vicious and abandoned course of life ; whatever there is to make the world better and happier, proceeds from the "sanctuary"—the church of God. Whatever there is that truly adorns society, and makes it more lovely and attractive ; whatever there is that diffuses a charm over domestic and social life ; whatever there is that makes the world more lovely or more desirable to live in,—more courteous, more gentle, more humane, more kind, more forgiving,—has its home in the "sanctuary," or emanates from the church of God.

7. *Give unto the* LORD. Ascribe unto the Lord,—to Jehovah. This is extracted literally from 1 Chron. xvi. 28. ¶ *O ye kindreds of the people.* Heb., *Families* of the people :—people, *as* united by family ties. The idea is that of worship not merely as individuals, nor as a mere *aggregate* of individuals united by no common bonds, but as those united by strong ties ; bound by blood and affection ; constituted into communities. It is

8 Give unto the LORD the glory [1] *due unto* his name : bring an offering, [s] and come into his courts.

9 O worship the LORD in the [2] beauty of holiness: fear before him, all the earth.

[1] *of.*   [s] Heb. xiii. 15.

---

a call on such to worship God in their capacity *as* thus bound together; —to come *as* families and to worship God. In other words, it is a call *on* families *as such* to acknowledge God. A family is a proper place where to honour God. When the same joy pervades all hearts in prosperity, and when all are alike made sorrowful in adversity, there is an evident fitness that all should unite in the same worship of God; and that, as in all other things they have common interests, sympathies, and affections, so they should have in religion,—in the service of their Creator. ¶ *Give unto the* LORD *glory and strength*. That is, Proclaim that these belong to God; or, worship him as a God of glory and power.

8. *Give unto the* LORD *the glory* due unto *his name*. This also is literally taken from 1 Chron. xvi. (ver. 28). The margin here is, as in Hebrew, *of his name* :—the honour of his name. The idea is that which is expressed in our translation. Bring to God what is *due* to him ; or, render such an acknowledgment as he deserves and claims. Acknowledge him *as* God, and acknowledge him to be *such* a God as he is. Let the honour due to God as such be given him ; and let the honour due to him, for the *character* which he actually has, be ascribed to him. ¶ *Bring an offering*. This is language taken from the temple-worship, and means that God is to be worshipped, in the manner which he has prescribed, as a suitable expression of his majesty. The word here rendered *offering—*מִנְחָה, *min-hhah*—is that which is commonly used to denote a *bloodless* offering — a thank-offering. See Notes on Isa. i.

10 Say among the heathen, [t] *that* the LORD reigneth : [u] the world also shall be established, that it shall not be moved : he shall judge the people righteously.

[2] Or, *glorious sanctuary.*
[t] Ps. xlvi. 6, 10.   [u] Rev. xix. 6.

13. ¶ *And come into his courts*. The courts or areas around the tabernacle and the temple, where sacrifices were made, and where the people worshipped. See Notes on Matt. xxi. 12.

9. *O worship the* LORD *in the beauty of holiness*. This verse is literally taken from 1 Chron. xvi. 29, 30. The margin here is, *in the glorious sanctuary*. The Septuagint, ἐν αὐλῇ ἁγίᾳ—*in his holy court*. So the Latin Vulgate. On the meaning of the expression, see Notes on Ps. xxix. 2. ¶ *Fear before him, all the earth*. All lands ; all people. The word rendered *fear* means properly to writhe, to twist, to be in pain ; and then, to tremble, to quake, to be afraid. The word *tremble* would perhaps best express the idea here. It is that solemn awe produced by the sense of the Divine presence and majesty which causes trembling. It denotes profound reverence for God.

10. *Say among the heathen*. Among the nations; all nations. Make this proclamation everywhere. This is changed from the parallel passage in 1 Chron. xvi. The language there is, " Fear before him, all the earth ; the world also shall be stable, that it be not moved : let the heavens be glad, and let the earth rejoice : and let men say among the nations, The Lord reigneth." The sense is, however, essentially the same. The idea here is, " Make universal proclamation that Jehovah is King." ¶ That *the* LORD *reigneth*. See Notes on Ps. xciii. 1. ¶ *The world also shall be established*, etc. Under the reign of God. The meaning is, that the world is fixed or immovable. It has its place, and it cannot be moved out of it. The government of God is fixed

11 Let *v* the heavens rejoice, and let the earth be glad; let the sea roar, and the fulness thereof.

12 Let the field be joyful, and all that *is* therein: then shall all

v Ps. lxix. 34.

the trees of the wood rejoice

13 Before the LORD: for he cometh, for he cometh to judge the earth: he shall judge the world with righteousness, *w* and the people with his truth.

w Rev. xix. 11; xx. 13.

and stable. It is not temporary, changing, vacillating, like the dynasties of the earth, but is stedfast and abiding, and is well represented by the earth—so fixed and firm that nothing can move it from its place. ¶ *He shall judge the people righteously.* The people of all lands; the nations of the earth. See Notes on Ps. lxvii. 4.

11. *Let the heavens rejoice, and let the earth be glad.* Let all worlds be full of joy, as they are all interested in the fact here stated. The universe is one. It has been made by the same hand; it is under the control of the same mind; it is governed by the same laws. The God who reigns on earth reigns in heaven; and what affects one part of the universe affects all. Hence, in all the manifestation of the character of God, whether made in heaven or in the earth, it is proper to call on *all* the universe to partake in the general joy. ¶ *Let the sea roar.* In praise to God. It is not uncommon in the Scriptures to call on inanimate things to praise God. Comp. Ps. cxlviii. 7–9. The same thing is common in all poetry. ¶ *And the fulness thereof.* Its abundance. That which fills it. All that it contains. That is, Let all that dwell in the seas praise God. His reign is an occasion for universal gladness. All in the inanimate world;—all among the irrational tribes of being;—all in the air, in the waters, or on the earth, have occasion for praise, and would render praise if they could appreciate the wisdom and goodness evinced in their creation. Though unconscious, the lower creatures *seem* to celebrate his praise; but man only can give an intelligent utterance to thanksgiving.

12. *Let the field be joyful,* etc. This is taken—with the change of a single letter, not affecting the sense—from 1 Chron. xvi. 32, 33. It is a call on the fields—the cultivated portions of the earth—to rejoice in the reign of God. As if conscious of the beauty with which he clothes them, and of the happiness which they confer on man in their beauty and in the abundance of their productions, they are called on to praise God. ¶ *Then shall all the trees of the wood rejoice.* The forests—the oaks, the cedars, the pines, that wave with so much majesty. If they were conscious of their own magnificence and beauty,—if they could see how much wisdom and goodness God has lavished on them, in their forms, their branches, their leaves, their flowers, their fruit,—if they could know how much they are made to accomplish in rendering the world beautiful, and in contributing to the happiness of man,—if they understood what a bare, bleak, cold, desert world this would be but for them, they, too, would have abundant occasion for praise and joy.

13. *Before the* LORD. This is altered from 1 Chron. xvi. The language there is simply, "Then shall the trees of the wood sing out at the presence of the Lord, because he cometh to judge the earth." The meaning here is, that all these things have occasion to praise the Lord whenever he appears; to rejoice in the presence of Him who has made them what they are. ¶ *For he cometh.* That is, he will come. He will manifest himself as a righteous judge. He will come to reign over the world, and there will be in his reign universal occasion for joy. The allusion would seem to be to some future time when God

would come to reign among men; to dispense justice; to vindicate his people, and to establish truth. The *language* is such as would properly refer to the anticipated reign of the Messiah, as a reign of righteousness, and is such language as is frequently employed in the Old Testament to denote the character of his reign. There is no reason to doubt that this psalm may be *designed* to describe the reign of the Messiah, and that the psalmist in this language may have looked forward to that future kingdom of righteousness and peace. ¶ *For he cometh to judge the earth*, etc. See this language explained in the Notes on Ps. lxxii. 2–4; Isa. xi. 2–5. What is here stated occurs now, wherever the gospel reigns in the hearts of men; it will be fully accomplished when the Lord Jesus shall come again and judge the world.

PSALM XCVII.

The author of this psalm is unknown, and the occasion on which it was composed cannot be ascertained. Its structure is similar to that of the two preceding psalms, and it *may* have been written by the same author, and at the same time; but it is of so general a nature that it may be employed at all times, and in all lands. From the contents, it would seem not improbable that it may have been composed in view of some victory over the enemies of the Hebrew people, and especially over idolaters; but when this occurred, if the psalm had such an origin, it is impossible now to determine. Venema supposes that it had reference to the times of the Maccabees, but of that there is no proof. Many of the expressions in the psalm are taken from the older portions of the Scriptures; and it has been remarked (Hengstenberg) that none are taken from the writings after the return from the Babylonish captivity. From this it has been inferred that it must have been composed before the exile. Still, this inference is not certain, for a writer after the return from Babylon *may* have made his references solely to the more ancient writings of his country.

The author of the Septuagint version regarded this as a psalm of David, when the land was restored to peace. The title in that version is, Τῷ Δαυίδ, ὅτ' ἡ γῆ αὐτοῦ καθίσταται ;—" by David, when his land was restored," (or, was at peace). The same title occurs in the Latin Vulgate. Luther entitles it, " Of Christ and his kingdom." The general subject of the psalm is the sovereignty or the supremacy of God, and the manifestation of that sovereignty or supremacy in vindicating his people, and in bringing to pass events which gave them ground of confidence and rejoicing in him.

Perhaps the most that can be said now on the origin and design of the psalm is, that these *six* psalms (xcv.-c.) seem to have been composed with reference to the same occasion, and may have been designed to be used together. They are similar in their contents and structure; and they refer to the same thing—the sovereignty or the supremacy of God. Bishop Horsley regards these psalms as " one entire prophetic poem." " Each psalm," says he, " has its proper subject, which is some particular branch of the general argument, the establishment of the Messiah's kingdom. The xcvth Psalm asserts Jehovah's Godhead and power over all nature, and exhorts his people to serve him. In Psalm xcvith, all nations are exhorted to join in his service, because he cometh to judge all mankind, Jew and Gentile. In the xcviith Psalm, Jehovah reigns over all the world, the idols are deserted, and the Just One is glorified. In the xcviiith Psalm, Jehovah hath done wonders, and wrought deliverance for himself; he hath remembered his mercy towards the house of Israel; he comes to judge the whole world. . . . In the xcixth, Jehovah, seated between the cherubim in Zion [the visible church], reigns over all the world, to be praised for the justice of his government. . . . In the cth Psalm, all the world is called upon to praise Jehovah the Creator, whose mercy and truth are everlasting." There may be something fanciful in this supposition, but the views thus expressed indicate the general course of thought in this group of psalms.

In this psalm (the xcviith) the particular point, then, is, that Jehovah is supreme over all the world; that the idols are proved to be nought; and that the righteous are vindicated.

The psalm embraces the following points :—

I. A description of the majesty and glory of God as a sovereign, vers. 1–6.

PSALM XCVII.

THE *x* LORD reigneth, let the earth rejoice; *y* let the [1] multitude of isles *z* be glad *thereof.*

x Ps. xcix. 1.　　　*y* Ps. ii. 11.
[1] *many, or, great.*　*z* Isa. lx. 9.

2 Clouds *a* and darkness *are* round about him : righteousness *b* and judgment *are* the [2] habitation of his throne.

a 1 Kings viii. 12.　*b* Ps. lxxxix. 14.
[2] Or, *establishment.*

Clouds and darkness are around him ; fire goes before him ; the lightnings play, and the earth trembles ; the hills melt, and are dissolved ; the heavens in their splendour declare his righteousness.

II. In view of this, all idol images and gods are confounded, and are shown to be nothing ; and the friends of the true God have occasion for joy, vers. 7-9.

III. The prosperity and happiness of the righteous under the reign of God, vers. 10-12. God will deliver them; light is sown for them in darkness; gladness is their portion, and they are called on to rejoice and give thanks at the remembrance of his holiness.

1. *The* LORD *reigneth.* See Notes on Ps. xciii. 1. This is the general fact to be dwelt upon; this is the foundation of joy and praise. The universe is not without a sovereign. It is not the abode of anarchy. It is not the production of chance. It is not subject to mere physical laws. It is not under the control of evil. It is under the government of a GOD :—a wise, holy, intelligent, just, benevolent Being, who rules it well, and who presides over all its affairs. If there is anything for which we should rejoice, it is that there is One Mind, everlasting and most glorious, who presides over the universe, and conducts all things according to his own wise and eternal plan. ¶ *Let the earth rejoice.* The earth itself; all parts of it ; all that dwell upon it. As the earth everywhere derives whatever it has of fertility, beauty, grandeur, or stability, from God,— as order, beauty, productiveness are diffused everywhere over it,—as it has received so many proofs of the Divine beneficence towards it, it has occasion for universal joy. ¶ *Let the multitude of isles be glad* thereof.

Marg., *Many,* or *great isles.* The Hebrew is *many.* So the Septuagint, the Latin Vulgate, the Chaldee, and the Syriac. The eye of the psalmist is evidently on the many islands which are scattered over the sea. Not merely the continents—the extended countries where nations dwell—have occasion for joy, but the beautiful islands,—the spots of earth which have risen from the deep, and which are covered with fruits and flowers, —these, too, have occasion to rejoice : —to rejoice that God has raised them from the waters ; that he keeps them from being overflowed or washed away ; that he clothes them with beauty ; that he makes them the abode of happy life ; that he places them in the wastes of the ocean as he does the stars in the wastes of the sky, to beautify the universe. The *idea* in the verse is, that *all* the earth has cause to rejoice that Jehovah reigns.

2. *Clouds and darkness* are *round about him.* This is a description of the majesty of God, derived probably from the manner in which he manifested himself at Mount Sinai. Ex. xix. 16-19. God is often thus represented as encompassed with clouds. Ps. civ. 3 ; Dan. vii. 13 ; Matt. xxiv. 30 ; Rev. i. 7. See Notes on Ps. xviii. 7-15. The word rendered *clouds* is the common word to denote a cloud ; the word translated *darkness* means properly *thick clouds, cloudy darkness, gloom.* It would refer to a cloud considered as dark, and as casting a gloom over the world. There is no reference here to the fact that the dealings of God are dark, mysterious, and incomprehensible, *as if* he were surrounded by clouds and darkness. This is indeed often true ; but that is not the truth taught here.

3 A fire *c* goeth before him, and burneth up his enemies round about.

4 His lightnings enlightened the world: the earth saw, and trembled.

5 The hills melted *d* like wax at the presence of the LORD, at

c Dan. vii. 10; Heb. xii. 29.

the presence of the Lord of the whole earth.

6 The heavens declare his righteousness, and all the people see *e* his glory.

7 Confounded be all they that serve graven images, that boast

d Judges v. 5; Micah i. 4.
e Num. xiv. 21; Matt. xxv. 31.

The meaning here is, that the character of God is fitted to fill the mind with solemn awe, or with emotions of sublimity. ¶ *Righteousness and judgment.* He is a righteous God; he is a God who will execute just judgment. Though he is encompassed with clouds, yet he is a just God; and this is fitted to impress the mind with profound reverence. That he will do right we may be assured, even when he covers himself with clouds; the fact that he will thus do right is fitted to calm the minds of those who love and obey him, and at the same time to fill the minds of the wicked with alarm. ¶ Are *the habitation of his throne.* Marg., *establishment.* The Hebrew word means *place;*—the place where one stands, or where one abides; a habitation, or a dwelling. It then means a foundation or basis, Ps. lxxxix. 14; civ. 5. This would seem to be the idea here. His throne rests upon, or is sustained by, justice and righteousness. Nothing else would uphold the government of the universe; nothing else will sustain any government.

3. *A fire goeth before him.* See Notes on Ps. xviii. 13; l. 3. ¶ *And burneth up his enemies round about.* Is especially directed against his foes. That is, he manifests himself as a just God, inflicting vengeance on his enemies. He comes to reign, and in his reign all his foes will be destroyed.

4. *His lightnings enlightened the world,* etc. See Notes on Ps. lxxvii. 18. Comp. Ps. civ. 32; Hab. iii. 6–10.

5. *The hills melted like wax at the presence of the* LORD. They seemed to flow down as if they were like

melted wax:—that is, they could not stand before him. The most firm, solid, lofty things were as nothing in his presence. Comp. Rev. xx. 11; Judges v. 5; Micah i. 4; Nah. i. 5. The object here is to describe the sublimity, the greatness, the majesty of God, as if nothing could stand before him; as if everything fled away when he approached. There is perhaps a general allusion to his glory and power as manifested at Sinai. ¶ *At the presence of the Lord of the whole earth.* The Creator and Ruler of the entire world. The God who thus manifested himself is not a local Deity, or the God of a particular nation or country, but the God of the whole world, before whom all created things are as nothing.

6. *The heavens declare his righteousness.* See Notes on Ps. l. 6. Comp. Notes on Ps. xix. 1. ¶ *And all the people see his glory.* As manifested in the heavens, and in the power which he puts forth on the earth. That is, They have the opportunity of seeing it; it is made manifest in all his works. They see what in fact *is* a manifestation of his glory, to wit, his great and wondrous works. It is not affirmed that they *appreciate* all this, or that they see this *to be* a manifestation of his glory,—which would not be true,—but that they see what is *in fact* a revelation of his greatness, his wisdom, and his power.

7. *Confounded be all they that serve graven images.* Heb., "Let them be ashamed." The idea is, that they would be disappointed. They would find that these were not real gods; that their trust in them was vain; and that they had evinced

themselves of idols: worship
f him, all *ye* gods.

8 Zion heard, and was glad;
and the daughters of Judah rejoiced because of thy judgments,
O LORD.

9 For thou, LORD, *art* high

f Heb. i. 6.   *g* Prov. iii. 7; Rom. xii. 9.

above all the earth: thou art
exalted far above all gods.

10 Ye that love the LORD,
hate *g* evil: he preserveth the
souls of his saints; he delivereth
h them out of the hand of the
wicked.

h Dan. iii. 28.

great folly, in relying on that which
could not aid them in the day of
necessity. See Notes on Job vi. 20;
Ps. xxii. 5; xxv. 2. Comp. Isa. xx. 5.
What is here affirmed of the worshippers of idols will be found to be
true at last of all who put their trust
in anything but the true God. ¶ *That
boast themselves of idols.* That worship idols, and glory in them as if
they could save; or, that glory in
their own idol-gods as if they were
more powerful than those of other
people. It would not be unnatural
that nations which worshipped idols
should glory in them, or that one
people should boast of their gods as
more powerful—more worthy to be
trusted—than those which were worshipped in other lands. ¶ *Worship
him, all* ye *gods.* Heb., *Elohim.* The
Septuagint and the Vulgate render
this, "all his angels." The original
word *Elohim* is that which is commonly applied to the true God (Gen.
i. 1, *et sæpe*), though it may be applied to angels, or to magistrates.
See Notes on Ps. lxxxii. 1, 6. On
the general meaning of this passage,
and the question respecting its reference to the Messiah, see Notes on
Heb. i. 6. The reference here, according to the quotation in Heb. i. 6,
is to the angels. The original word
will admit of this interpretation, and
the entire structure of the psalm
will justify its application to the
Messiah.

8. *Zion heard, and was glad.* The
good news came to Zion that all the
idols of the heathen were confounded
or were overcome:—that is, that the
Lord reigned. There was joy in Zion
that the evils and abominations of
idolatry were at an end, and that the

worship of Jehovah had taken the
place of idol-worship. The idea is,
that the displacement of idols, or the
fact that they had ceased to be worshipped, was a cause of joy to the
worshippers of the true God. Whatever tends to remove the worship of
idols from the world, and to extend
and establish the worship of the
living God, is an occasion of gladness. ¶ *And the daughters of Judah
rejoiced,* etc. See Notes on Ps. xlviii.
11. Woman has special occasion to
rejoice in the spread of the true
religion. It is that only which has
lifted her from a state of deep degradation; which has elevated her to
be a companion instead of a slave;
which has made her the intelligent
wife and mother, rather than the
mere inmate of a harem.

9. *For thou,* LORD, art *high above
all the earth.* See Notes on Ps. lxxxiii.
18. ¶ *Thou art exalted far above all
gods.* See Notes on Ps. xcv. 3.

10. *Ye that love the* LORD, *hate
evil.* Show your love for the Lord
by hating all that is evil; that is, all
that he hates, or that is evil in his
sight. There can be no true love for
God where evil is not hated in all its
forms, since it is the object of the
Divine abhorrence. We cannot be
like God unless we love what he
loves, and hate what he hates. There
is nothing more clearly affirmed in
the Scriptures than that in order to
the love of God there must be the
hatred of all that is wrong, and that
where there is the love of sin in the
heart, there can be no true religion.
Comp. Notes on Isa. i. 16–20. ¶ *He
preserveth the souls of his saints.* The
lives of his saints, or his holy ones.
That is, he guards them from danger,

11 Light is sown for the righteous, and gladness for the upright in heart.

i Phil. iv. 4.

12 Rejoice *i* in the LORD, ye righteous; and give thanks [1] at the remembrance of his holiness.

[1] Or, *to the memorial.*

and watches over them with a careful eye. See Ps. iii. 8; xxxvii. 39. ¶ *He delivereth them out of the hand of the wicked.* That is, he often does this; they may expect that he will do it. He does not, indeed, always deliver them from the temporal calamities which wicked men bring upon them —for they are not unfrequently persecuted and wronged; but ultimately he will deliver them altogether from the power of the wicked. In heaven none of the machinations of wicked men can reach them. At the same time it is also true that God often interposes in behalf of his people, and delivers them *as such* from the designs of the wicked:—that is, he delivers them because they *are* righteous, or because they *are* his friends. Comp. Notes on Dan. iii. 16, 17, 24, 25; vi. 18–23.

11. *Light is sown for the righteous.* That is, There *is* light for the righteous; or, they shall be brought into light, though they may be for a time in darkness. The word rendered *sown* —זָרֻעַ, *zarua*—is from a verb which properly denotes to scatter, to disperse,—as seed is scattered or dispersed when sown in a field. It is hence used with reference to moral subjects, as to sow righteousness, Prov. xi. 18; to sow iniquity, Prov. xxii. 8; to sow mischief, Job iv. 8;— that is, these things are scattered or sown, as seed is in a field, and produce a corresponding harvest. Thus light is scattered abroad, and will produce an appropriate harvest—a harvest of joy. It will spring up around the righteous, and he shall reap that which light tends to produce — happiness, intelligence, and peace. The figure of *sowing* light is an unusual one, but the meaning is plain. It is, that the righteous will not always be in darkness; that there is in preparation for him a harvest of

joy; that it will as certainly be produced as a harvest will from grain that is sown; that though there may be present calamities, there will be ultimate peace and triumph. ¶ *And gladness for the upright in heart.* The word *gladness* here—joy, or rejoicing—is parallel to the word *light.* Joy or gladness is *sown* for the righteous; that is, arrangements are made for producing joy, as preparations are made by sowing seed for a harvest. The world is full of arrangements for conferring happiness on the righteous.

12. *Rejoice in the* LORD, *ye righteous.* See Notes on Ps. xxxiii. 1. ¶ *And give thanks at the remembrance of his holiness.* Marg., *to the memorial* (comp. Ps. xxx. 4). The idea is, *to the memory of his holiness;* that is, when his holiness comes before the mind; when it is remembered; when it is thought of. Give thanks or rejoice, (*a*) that God *is* holy; that he is of purer eyes than to behold iniquity; that there is One eternally pure who presides over the universe; that there is One who will always do what is right; (*b*) that such a Being is *our* God,—our covenant-keeping God; that we may look to him, trust in him, enjoy him. Wicked men do not rejoice that there is a God at all, and especially that God is a *holy* God; but it is one of the characteristics of true piety to rejoice in the thought that there *is* a God, and that he is perfectly holy,—and hence to feel conscious happiness whenever his name is mentioned, and whenever his attributes are referred to. The highest source of joy for man is that there *is* a God, and that God is exactly *what* he is, pure and holy. It would be a source of deepest sorrow if there were no God, or if God were in any respect, even the slightest, a different being from what he is.

E

PSALM XCVIII.

A Psalm

0 SING unto the LORD a new
song; for he hath done marvellous things: his right ^{k} hand,
and his holy arm, hath gotten
him the victory.

2 The ^{l} LORD hath made
known his salvation: his right-
.eousness hath he ^{1} openly shewed
in the sight of the heathen.

3 He ^{m} hath remembered his
mercy and his truth toward the

k Ex. xv. 6; Isa. lix. 16.   *l* Isa. lii. 10.
^{1} Or, *revealed.*   *m* Luke i. 54, 72.

PSALM XCVIII.

This is entitled simply "A Psalm."
But who is its author is unknown. It
is similar in its design and structure to
the group of Psalms (xcv.-c.) in which
it is found. Bishop Horsley, in accordance with the views which he has of
the design of the group (see the Introd.
to Ps. xcvii.), supposes that this psalm
refers to the restoration of the Jewish
people. It is a psalm which would have
been appropriate at the dedication of the
temple after the Babylonish captivity,
and may have been composed for that
occasion. It is of so general a character,
however, that it is appropriate to all
times in the church. The psalm does
not admit of a particular analysis.

1. *O sing unto the* LORD *a new
song.* Comp. Ps. xxxiii. 3; xcvi. 1.
¶ *For he hath done marvellous things.*
Things fitted to excite wonder, or to
fill the mind with astonishment. See
Ps. lxxvii. 14; lxxxvi. 10. ¶ *His
right hand.* The instrument by which
we execute any purpose. Comp. Isa.
lix. 16; lxiii. 5. ¶ *And his holy
arm.* The arm of his holiness; that
is, his arm put forth in a righteous
cause, or vindicating that which is
right. ¶ *Hath gotten him the victory.* Literally, *has wrought salvation for him :*—for himself, or in his
own cause. The victory—the salvation—was really in defence of his own
government; in maintaining his own
authority against those who set themselves in opposition to it. What is
here said may be applied to all that
God does. It is really in his own
cause, in order to maintain the principles of his own administration.

2. *The* LORD *hath made known his
salvation.* See Notes on Isa. lii. 10.
This does not mean that he had
merely *proclaimed* his salvation, or

his willingness to save, but that he
had *shown* his salvation—his power
to save—by some public act. What
the particular act referred to here
was, it is impossible now to ascertain.
Such acts, however, have been often
performed, as when he delivered his
people out of Egypt; when he restored
the Hebrews from the Babylonish captivity; and whenever he interposed
in their behalf in times of danger.
He has done it also in the gift of a
Saviour; he does it in every revival
of true religion; he does it in the
salvation of a single sinner. ¶ *His
righteousness.* His righteous character; his faithfulness to his people.
Whenever he interposes, it is in behalf
of that which is right; and such interposition, therefore, is an illustration of his character *as* just. It is in
this way we learn that his character
is that of a just God. ¶ *Hath he
openly showed.* Marg., as in Heb.,
revealed. He has disclosed it, or
made it manifest. ¶ *In the sight of
the heathen.* The nations; or, so that
the nations could see it:—that is, the
nations outside of Palestine. His acts
were so public—so remarkable—that
surrounding nations could learn what
was his true character. Thus it was
when he delivered his people from
Egyptian bondage; and thus also frequently in the history of his people.

3. *He hath remembered his mercy.*
Comp. Notes on Luke i. 54, 55, 72,
where this passage in the Psalms was
not improbably referred to by Mary
and Zacharias. The idea is, that God
had called to mind his promise of
mercy to his people; that he had not
suffered it to pass out of his recollection; that he had kept his word.
¶ *And his truth.* He has kept his

house of Israel : all the " ends of the earth have seen the salvation of our God.

4 Make a joyful noise unto the LORD, all the earth; make a loud noise, and rejoice, and sing praise.

5 Sing unto the LORD with the harp; with the harp, and the voice of a psalm.

6 With trumpets and sound of cornet, make a joyful noise before the LORD, the King.

n Rom. x. 12, 18.

promise; he has shown that he is a God of truth. ¶ *Toward the house of Israel.* Towards his people. ¶ *All the ends of the earth have seen the salvation of our God.* This appears to have been quoted from Isa. lii. 10. See Notes on that passage. The resemblance in the language is so strong as to make it probable that the psalm was composed after the times of Isaiah, and not improbably to be used (as remarked above) in the dedication of the temple after the captivity. The whole psalm would be appropriate to celebrate that deliverance; while, at the same time, like the language in Isaiah, it would be adapted to celebrate a higher deliverance—under the Messiah—of which that was an emblem.

4. *Make a joyful noise unto the* LORD. By singing; by instruments of music. See Notes on Ps. xcv. 1. ¶ *All the earth.* All lands. The event is of sufficient importance to be celebrated by all nations. It is a matter of universal exultation and joy. ¶ *Make a loud noise.* The word here used—פָּצַח—*patzahh,* means properly to break in pieces; then, to break forth, as a shout of triumph or joy, as if the joy could be no longer confined or repressed. See Notes on Isa. xiv. 7. The word occurs only in the following places (besides that which is before us), in all of which it is rendered *break forth.* Isa. xiv. 7; xliv. 23; xlix. 13; lii. 9; liv. 1; lv. 12,—(except in Micah iii. 3, where it is rendered *break*). It is expressive of irrepressible joy. ¶ *Rejoice and sing praise.* This very combination of the words, " Break forth into joy, sing together"—the same words in Hebrew as here—occurs in Isa. lii. 9, showing, as above remarked, that

the psalm was composed after the times of Isaiah, and probably had reference to the same event.

5. *Sing unto the* LORD *with the harp.* A song or psalm accompanied by the harp. On the harp. See Notes on Isa. v. 12. ¶ *And the voice of a psalm.* The voice in singing; a musical voice. Let it not be mere instrumental music, but let that be accompanied with the voice uttering intelligible sounds or words. The only proper use of instrumental music in the worship of God is to deepen the impression which the *words* are adapted to make; to secure a better influence of truth on the heart.

6. *With trumpets.* The word here used is uniformly rendered *trumpets* in the Scriptures. Num. x. 2, 8–10; xxxi. 6; *et al.* The trumpet was mainly employed for convening a public assembly for worship, or for assembling the hosts for battle. The original word—חֲצֹצְרָה, *hhatzotzerah* —is supposed to have been designed to imitate " the broken pulse-like sound of the trumpet, like the Latin *taratantara."* So the German *trarara,* and the Arabic *hadadera.* The word here used was given to the long, straight trumpet. ¶ *And sound of cornet,* etc. The word here translated *cornet* is also usually rendered *trumpet,* Ex. xix. 16, 19; xx. 18; Lev. xxv. 9; Josh. vi. 4–6, 8, 9, 13, 16, 20; *et sæpe.* It is rendered *cornet* in 1 Chron. xv. 28; 2 Chron. xv. 14; Hos. v. 8. In the Septuagint and the Latin Vulgate it is here rendered *horn*—the meaning of *cornet.* The name—שׁוֹפָר, *shophar*—is supposed to have been given to this instrument from its clear and shrill sound, like the English name *clarion.* It was either made *of* horn, or similar *to*

7 Let the sea roar, and the fulness thereof; the world, and they that dwell therein.

8 Let the floods clap *their* hands : let the hills be joyful together

9 Before the LORD: for *o* he cometh to judge the earth : with righteousness shall he judge the world, and the people with equity.

o Rev. i. 7.

---

a horn—an instrument curved *like a horn.* The instrument was in frequent use among the Hebrews.

7. *Let the sea roar, and the fulness thereof.* See Notes on Ps. xcvi. 11. ¶ *The world, and they that dwell therein.* The habitable world—the land—in contradistinction from the sea. Let there be universal praise on the water and the land.

8. *Let the floods clap* their *hands.* The rivers. Let them join in the universal praise. As if conscious of their beauty, their grandeur, their usefulness ;—as if sensible that all this was conferred by God; as if rejoicing in the goodness of God manifested to them, and through them,— let *them* unite in the universal praise. Comp. Notes on Isa. lv. 12. ¶ *Let the hills be joyful together.* The mountains—in view of the goodness of God towards them—crowning them with beauty — clothing them with sublimity and grandeur—let them also rejoice in God as *their* God. Let all nature thus join in praise.

9. *Before the* LORD, *for he cometh to judge the earth,* etc. This verse is essentially the same as Ps. xcvi. 13. See Notes on that verse. The psalm calls for universal praise. The very *reading* of the psalm—so joyous—so jubilant—so animated—so exulting—is fitted to awaken the mind to praise ; to rouse it to thankfulness; to fill it with joy. One cannot read the psalm without being a happier man ; without being lifted above the world ; without lofty views of God ; without a feeling that he is worthy of this universal praise ; without recognising that we are in a world where the mind should be joyful ; that we are under the dominion of a God whose reign should fill the mind with gladness.

PSALM XCIX.

This psalm is closely linked in its general character and design with those which have gone before (xcv.-xcviii.), and with the one following (c.),—forming a connected group or series. The general subject is the kingship of Jehovah, or the foundations of praise derived from the fact that he reigns, or is king. As the foundation of praise on this account, reference is made in this group of psalms to his attributes ; to what he has done in the works of creation ; to what he has done for his people ; and to the certainty that he will come ultimately to rule over all the earth, and to exercise just judgment among men.

This psalm consists of the following parts :—

I. A statement of the fact that Jehovah reigns, and that this should make a deep impression on the world ; that the people should tremble ; that the earth should be moved, ver. 1.

II. Reasons for this, or reasons why he should be reverenced and adored by mankind, vers. 2-9. These reasons are two :

(1) The first is derived from the fact that he is a holy and a righteous God, and is therefore worthy of universal adoration, vers. 2-5.

(2) The second is derived from what he has done for his people : for his merciful interposition in times of trouble, when Moses, and Aaron, and Samuel called upon his name ; and from the fact that he answered his people when they cried unto him ; and from the manner in which it was done, vers. 6-9. He had shown himself ready to hear prayer ; he had come for their protection in the cloudy pillar, he had answered their supplications, and had forgiven them. He had not swept them wholly away, or cut them off, but had spared them, and had shown mercy to them.

PSALM XCIX.

THE *p* LORD reigneth; let *q* the people tremble: he sitteth *between* the cherubims; let the earth ¹ be moved.

2 The LORD *is* great in Zion,

p Ps. xciii. 1.   *q* Jer. v. 22.   ¹ *stagger.*

and he *is* high above all the people.

3 Let them praise thy great *r* and terrible name; *for* it *is* holy.

4 The king's strength also loveth judgment: thou *s* dost

r Deut. xxviii. 58.   *s* Job xxxvi. 5—7.

---

1. *The* LORD *reigneth.* The Lord, Jehovah, is king. See Ps. xciii. 1. ¶ *Let the people tremble.* The Septuagint and the Latin Vulgate render this, "Let the people rage"—or, be angry:—as if the idea were that God reigned, *although* the people were enraged, and were opposed to him. The true meaning of the word used here, however, is *tremble,*—properly signifying to be moved, disturbed, disquieted, thrown into commotion; and then it may mean to be moved with anger, Prov. xxix. 9; Isa. xxviii. 21; or with grief, 2 Sam. xviii. 33: or with fear, Ps. iv. 4; or with joy, Jer. xxxiii. 9. Hence it means to be agitated or moved with fear or reverence; and it refers here to the reverence or awe which one has in the conscious presence of God. ¶ *He sitteth* between *the cherubims.* See Notes on Ps. lxxx. 1. ¶ *Let the earth be moved.* Marg., *stagger.* The word means to move or quake. It occurs nowhere else. Comp. Notes on Ps. xviii. 7. See also Hab. iii. 6, 10.

2. *The Lord* is *great in Zion.* Comp. Ps. xcv. 3. The meaning here is, not that God is *absolutely* great, —which is indeed true,—but that there is a sense in which he has shown himself great *in Zion;* that is, in his manifestations toward his own people. He has evinced power in their behalf; he has interposed for them in times of danger; he has so discomfited their enemies as to show that he is a great God—a God worthy to be adored. ¶ *And he* is *high above all the people.* Above all the nations. He has them under his control. He rules over all. The God who rules in Zion also rules all the

nations of the earth; and his people, therefore, have special occasion to praise him.

3. *Let them praise thy great and terrible name.* The word rendered *terrible* means *to be feared* or *reverenced;* that is, his name—his being —he himself—is fitted to inspire awe and reverence. The word *them* here refers to the nations over whom God reigns. It is a call on them to praise their king and their God. ¶ For *it* is *holy.* See Notes on Isa. vi. 3; Rev. iv. 8. The fact that God *is* holy —that he is pure and righteous— that he cannot look upon sin but with abhorrence—is a just foundation for universal praise. Who could worship or honour a God who was *not* pure and holy?

4. *The king's strength.* The word *king* here undoubtedly refers to God *as* a king, ver. 1. The word rendered *strength,* means power, force; and the reference here is to what constitutes the main strength or power of his character and government. It is rendered in the Septuagint τιμή— *honour.* So in the Latin Vulgate— *honor.* De Wette renders it, "The praise of the king who loves judgment." So Rosenmüller, "Let them praise the strength—the power—of the king who loves judgment." But perhaps our common version best expresses the sense, that whatever there is in the character of the "king," that is God, which constitutes strength, or gives power to his administration, is favourable to justice, or will be exerted in the cause of right. God's essential character; all the acts of his power; all the demonstrations of his authority, will be in favour of justice, and may be re-

establish equity, thou executest judgment and righteousness in Jacob.

5 Exalt ye the LORD our God,

t 1 Chron. xxviii. 2.　　¹ Or, *it.*

and worship at his footstool; *t for* ¹ he *is* holy.

6 Moses and Aaron among his priests, and Samuel among them that call upon his name: they

---

lied on as sustaining the righteous cause. It is not the *mere* exertion of power,—it is power that is always exercised in favour of right; and this lays the foundation of praise. We could not praise a being of mere *power*, or one who was merely *almighty*, without respect to his moral character. It is only when the character is such that power will be exerted in favour of that which is right and just that it becomes the proper subject of praise. ¶ *Loveth judgment.* Is always on the side of justice and right. He so loves justice that his power will be put forth only in behalf of that which is right. God shows this by his law, and by all the acts of his administration. ¶ *Thou dost establish equity.* That which is equal and just; alike by thy law, and by thine interpositions. All that thou doest, and all that thou dost appoint, is in favour of that which is equal and just. ¶ *Thou executest judgment and righteousness in Jacob.* That which is just; that which ought to be done. Thou doest this among thy people; thou doest it in their relation to the surrounding nations. All the acts of thy administration tend to the establishment of that which is right.

5. *Exalt ye the* LORD *our God.* See Notes on Ps. xxx. 1. The meaning is, Let his name be, as it were, lifted up on high, so as to be conspicuous or seen from afar. Let it be done with a lofty voice; let it be with ascriptions of praise. ¶ *And worship at his footstool.* By humble prostration at his feet. The footstool is that on which the feet rest when one is sitting, and the reference here is to the footstool on which the feet of a king rested when he sat on his throne or chair of state. To worship at his footstool—comp. 1 Chron.

xxviii. 2; Ps. cxxxii. 7—denotes the deepest humility and the profoundest prostration and reverence. It is as if we could not look on his face, or on his throne, or on his gorgeous and magnificent robes, but bowed our heads in lowly reverence, and deemed it sufficient honour to lie low before that on which his feet rested. To show the dignity and majesty of God, the earth itself is represented as being merely his footstool; as being, in comparison with the heaven —the place of his seat—his "throne," only as the footstool is as compared with the splendid chair of state. Isa. lxvi. 1; Matt. v. 34, 35. ¶ For *he* is *holy.* See ver. 3. Marg., *it is holy.* The translation in the text best expresses the sense. The fact that God is *holy* is a reason for lowly and profound prostration before him.

6. *Moses and Aaron among his priests.* Among the ministers of religion; or, as officiating in the service of God. Let them come as representatives of their order—as representing those who conduct the public worship of God, and join in his praise. The idea is, that all mankind should join in his praise, and those here mentioned as among the most eminent of those who were engaged in directing the public worship of God. Moses could be called a "priest" only in the most general sense of the term, as having been employed in directing and arranging for public worship, and as being of the original tribe of Levi, from whom the whole sacerdotal order sprang. ¶ *And Samuel among them that call upon his name.* Among those who are true worshippers, in distinction from the priests who were specially appointed to the public service of God. The idea is, that praise should be offered by *all* classes :—by priests

u called upon the LORD, and he answered them.

7 He spake unto them in *v* the cloudy pillar: they kept his testimonies, and the ordinance *that* he gave them.

u Ex. xv. 25; 1 Sam. vii. 9.

and by people. As Moses and Aaron were among the most eminent of the former class, so Samuel was among the most distinguished of those who were *not* of the priestly order. These were *representative men;* and the meaning is, that all who were of their order or rank—priests and people—should unite in the worship of God. ¶ *They called upon the* LORD. They *did* call upon the Lord; they worshipped Jehovah. They gave the influence of their names and of their position to his public service. They thus showed their sense of the propriety of praising God; they gave the countenance of their example to public worship and praise; and the benefits which they received in answer to prayer showed the propriety and advantage of thus publicly acknowledging God. ¶ *And he answered them.* They did not call upon him in vain. He heard their prayers. He bestowed blessings on them in connexion with their worship. It was not a useless thing to praise and worship him. The worship of God is thus commended to us not merely from the propriety of the act itself, but from its advantages. It is unnecessary to refer to particular instances in the history of these men when their prayers were answered. Their lives were full of such instances —as the lives of all who truly call upon God are now. If a man who prays could *see* all that comes to him every day in answer to prayer—all the things bestowed which he had *desired* in prayer, and which would not have been conferred on him if he had *not* prayed, there would no longer be any doubt on the question whether God answers prayer.

7. *He spake unto them in the cloudy*

8 Thou answeredst them, O LORD our God: thou *w* wast a God that forgavest them, though thou tookest vengeance of their inventions.

v Ex. xxxiii. 9.
w Neh. ix. 27—31; Ps. lxxxix. 33.

pillar. He spake to the men of other times; to those who called upon his name. It cannot be meant literally that he spake to *Samuel* from the "cloudy pillar"—the pillar which guided the Israelites in the wilderness, unless that term be understood in the general sense as denoting the *Shechinah*—the visible symbol of the Divine presence—the cloud that rested on the ark. The idea is, that God addressed his people in ancient times from the cloud—the symbol of his presence; that he communed with them; that he heard their prayers; that he gave them his commandments; that he interposed in their behalf, and that it was not a vain thing that they worshipped him. All this was as true of Samuel—it is as true now of those who call upon God —as it was of Moses and Aaron. ¶ *They kept his testimonies,* etc. They obeyed his laws, and he thus heard and answered them.

8. *Thou answeredst them, O* LORD *our God.* The reference here is to God as *"our"* God; that is, the language used by those who now worship him is designed to give encouragement in approaching his throne. The God that *we* worship is the same that *they* worshipped; and as he answered them, we may feel assured that he will answer us. ¶ *Thou wast a God that forgavest them.* They were not perfect; they were sinners; they often offended thee, and yet thou didst answer them, and show them mercy. ¶ *Though thou tookest vengeance.* Though thou didst manifest thy displeasure at their misconduct; though thou in thy judgments didst show that thou wast displeased with them; nevertheless thou didst answer them. Sinners as they were, and

9 Exalt the LORD our God.
and worship at his holy *x* hill:
for the LORD our God *is* holy.

x Ps. ii. 6.
[1] Or, *thanksgiving*, Ps. cxlv., *title.*
[2] *the earth.*

often as thou didst show thy displeasure
at their conduct, yet thou didst hear
their prayers and bless them. ¶ *Of
their inventions.* The Hebrew word
denotes work, deed, doing, conduct. It
means here what they *did :*—their
sins. There is no allusion to any special
art or *cunning* in what they did,—as
if they had *invented* or found out some
new form of sin.

9. *Exalt the* LORD *our God.* See
notes on ver. 5. ¶ *And worship at
his holy hill.* In ver. 5, this is, *at
his footstool.* The *holy hill* refers
to Zion, as the seat of the national
worship. ¶ *For the* LORD *our God*
is *holy.* See ver. 5. This appropriately closes the psalm, by a distinct
and solemn statement that the fact
that Jehovah is a holy God is a reason for worshipping him. This is at
all times the highest reason for adoration and praise.

PSALM C.

This psalm—so beautiful—so grand—
so often sung in all lands and languages
—completes this *group* of psalms respecting the reign of God, or the reasons
for praise as derived from the fact that
he reigns. In the previous psalms in
this group (xcv.-xcix.) the call to praise
had been in some respects local and particular; in this, it is universal. All
lands are called on to praise him; all
people to worship him as God. The
ground of this, as stated in the psalm, is
that he is their "Maker;" that he is
the Creator of all. As all have derived
their being from him, they are called on
to praise him as their common Creator
and Father. So far as the reason here
referred to is a ground for praise and
worship, it applies to all men now.
The nations—the people of the earth—
are one. However much they may differ
in complexion, in language, in customs,
in religion, they have all been formed
by the same God; they are all of one
family; they are all entitled to the

PSALM C.

A Psalm of [1] praise.

MAKE a joyful noise unto the
LORD, all [2] ye lands.
2 Serve the LORD with glad-

same privileges; they may all have the
same access to his throne. The races of
men are one; and all should gather
around the throne of their common
Creator, and render him united praise.
This psalm has been sung by millions
and hundreds of millions; it will continue to be sung to the end of time.

The psalm is entitled "A Psalm of
praise." In the margin, *thanksgiving.*
The Septuagint is, "A Psalm of Confession"—εἰς ἐξομολόγησιν. So the Latin
Vulgate, and the Chaldee. The Syriac
version is, "*anonymous,*" or, *without a
name;* "concerning Joshua the son of
Nun, when he subdued the Ammonites."
Luther: "A Psalm of Thanksgiving."

1. *Make a joyful noise unto the*
LORD. See Notes on Ps. xcv. 1.
¶ *All ye lands.* Marg., as in Heb.,
all the earth. The margin expresses
the sense. The idea in the psalm is,
that praise did not pertain to one
nation only; that it was not appropriate for one people merely; that it
should not be confined to the Hebrew
people, but that there was a proper
ground of praise for *all;* there was
that in which all nations, of all languages and conditions, could unite.
The ground of that was the fact that
they had one Creator, ver. 3. The
psalm is based on the unity of the
human race; on the fact that there
is one God and Father of all, and one
great family on earth.

2. *Serve the* LORD *with gladness.*
That is, In your worship, and in all
your acts of obedience. Let there
be joy in this service. Let it not be
with the fear of slaves; not as a matter of compulsion and force; not with
reluctance, moroseness, or gloom. Let
it be a cheerful, happy service; let it
be freely rendered, let it be an occasion of joy to the soul. The service
of God is a source of the highest joy
that man knows. ¶ *Come before his
presence with singing* As expressive

ness; come before his presence with singing.

3 Know ye that the LORD, he is God : *it is* he *v that* hath made us, and [1] not we ourselves : *we are* his people, *z* and the sheep *a* of

y Ps. cxlix. 2.　　　[1] Or, *his we* are.
z Isa. lxiii. 19.

his pasture.

4 Enter *b* into his gates with thanksgiving, *and* into his courts with praise : be thankful unto him, *and* bless his name.

5 For the LORD *is* good, his

a Ez. xxxiv. 11, etc.; 1 Pet. ii. 25.
b Ps. lxv. 1; Isa. xxxv. 10.

---

of joy. So the birds sing; so nature rejoices; so should man,—intelligent, redeemed, immortal man, be joyful.

3. *Know ye that the* LORD, *he* is *God.* That is, Let all the nations know that *Jehovah* is the true God. The idols are vanity. They have no claim to worship; but God is the Creator of all, and is entitled to universal adoration. ¶ It is *he* that *hath made us.* The Hebrew is, "He made us," and this expresses the exact idea. The fact that he is the Creator proves that he is God, since no one but God can perform the work of creation. The highest idea that we can form of power is that which is evinced in an act of creation; that is, in causing anything to exist where there was nothing before. Every created thing, therefore, is a proof of the existence of God; the immensity of the universe is an illustration of the greatness of his power. ¶ *And not we ourselves.* Marg., *And his we* are. The difference between the text and the margin is owing to a different reading in the Hebrew, varying only in a single letter. The reading in the text is, "And not (לֹא) we ;" in the margin, "And to him (לוֹ) we." These words would be pronounced in the same manner, and either of them would convey good sense. The weight of authority is in favour of the common reading, — "And not we ;" that is, We are not self-created; we derive our being from him. All that we have and are, we owe to him. ¶ We are *his people.* By virtue of creation. The highest *property* which can exist is that derived from an act of creation. He that has brought anything into existence has a right to it, and may dispose of it as

he pleases. It is on this idea essentially that *all* idea of *property* is founded. ¶ *And the sheep of his pasture.* As the shepherd owns the flock, so God is our owner; as the shepherd guards his flock and provides for it, so God guards us and provides for us. See Notes on Ps. xcv. 7.

4. *Enter into his gates,* etc. The gates which lead to his temple, or to the place of public worship. ¶ *Into his courts,* etc. The *courts* were literally the open spaces which surrounded the tabernacle or temple. It was in these that worship was celebrated, and not *in* the tabernacle or temple. See Notes on Ps. lxv. 4; lxxxiv. 2; xcii. 13. ¶ *Be thankful unto him.* That is, Offer thanksgiving and praise. Come before him with a grateful heart. See Notes on Ps. l. 14. ¶ *Bless his name.* Bless him; praise him; ascribe honour to him; acknowledge him as God.

5. *For the* LORD is *good.* For good is Jehovah. That is, He is not a being of mere *power;* he is not *merely* the Creator; but he is benevolent, and is, therefore, worthy of universal praise. In the former verses, his claim to adoration is founded on the fact that he is the *Creator,* and has, as such, a right to our service ; in this verse, the claim is asserted on account of his moral character : (1) his benevolence; (2) his mercy ; (3) his truth;—(a) the fact that he is a God of truth ; and (b) the fact that his truth endures, or that in all generations he shows himself to be faithful to his promises. The first of these is his *benevolence :* "The Lord is *good.*" As such, assuredly, God is worthy of praise and honour. A

mercy *is* everlasting; and his
¹ *generation and generation,* Ps. lxxxix. 1.

truth *endureth* to ¹ all generations.

---

being of mere *power* we could not
love or praise; a being whose power
was united with malignity or malevo-
lence, could only be the object of
hatred and terror; but a being whose
power is united with goodness or benevolence *ought* to be loved. ¶ *His
mercy* is *everlasting.* This is the
second reason, drawn from his moral
character, why he should be praised
and adored. A being of mere *justice*
may be feared and respected; but a
character of *mere* justice would be to
man an object of dread,—and may
be so anywhere. There are other
attributes than the one of *justice,*
high and valuable as that may be,
which are necessary to constitute a
perfect character; and man, in order
to find happiness and security, must
find some other attribute in God than
mere *justice,*—for man is a sinner,
and needs pardon; he is a sufferer,
and needs compassion; he is to die,
and needs support and consolation.
Besides, mere *justice* may drive its
decisions over some of the kindest
and tenderest feelings of human nature; for there *are* cases, under all
administrations, where pardon is desirable and mercy is proper. It is,
therefore, a ground of unspeakable
joy for man that God is not a Being
of *mere justice,* but that there is
mingled in his character the attribute
of mercy and kindness. But for this,
man could have no hope; for, as a
sinner, he has no claim on God, and
all his hope *must* be derived from
God's infinite compassion. To all
this as a ground of praise is to be
added the fact that this mercy of
God is "*everlasting.*" Its fruits—
its results—will extend to the vast
eternity before us; and in all that
eternity we shall never cease to enjoy
the benefits of that mercy; never be
suffered to fall back on the mere *justice*
of God. ¶ *And his truth* endureth *to
all generations.* Marg., as in Heb.,
to generation and generation. That

is, for ever. It is the same in every
generation of the world. This is the
third reason derived from the moral
character of God for praising him;
and this is a just ground of praise.
We could not love and honour a God
who was not true to his promises,
and who did not himself love the
truth; we could not honour one who
was changeable and flexible — who
loved one thing in one generation and
a different thing in the next; who in
one age was the friend of truth, and
in the next the patron of falsehood.
It is the just foundation for praise to
God—our God—that he is essentially
and always—in all worlds, and in all
the generations of men—towards all
in the universe—a Being of unchangeable benevolence, mercy, and truth.
Such a God is worthy to be had in
universal reverence; such a God is
worthy of universal praise.

PSALM CI.

This psalm purports to be a Psalm of
David, and there is no reason to doubt
that it was composed by him, though it
is not possible to ascertain why it did
not have a place in the collection of his
psalms in the early part of the book
(Ps. i.-lxxii.). There are several such,
however, scattered through the latter
part of the Book of Psalms, leading us to
suppose that this which may have been
an early collection or *edition* of his
psalms, became known *as* the Psalms of
David, and that miscellaneous psalms—
and among them not a few of his composition — perhaps later psalms — were
subsequently *added* to the volume.

The time when it was composed cannot
be ascertained with any certainty or
probability. It would *seem* to have been
written when he was entering on domestic life, as the psalm consists of *rules*
which he appears to have laid down for
himself as the head of a family, or as
indicating the course which he purposed
to pursue in the management of his
household. As such, the psalm has a
universal application, and may be useful
in all times and in all places. Few
questions are more important than those

PSALM CI.

A Psalm of David.

I WILL sing of mercy and judgment: unto thee, O LORD, will I sing.

2 I will behave *c* myself wisely in a perfect way. O when wilt

c 1 Sam. xviii. 14.

which occur to one entering on married life, in regard to his own conduct as the head of a family, to the principles which he shall maintain in his own dwelling, and to the rules by which he shall govern his own conduct. For one in such circumstances it is an inestimable advantage to have an inspired composition like this, indicating what is proper, and suggesting the rules which should guide one in such circumstances.

The psalm consists of the following parts:—

I. The introduction—the purpose to praise God with respect to "mercy and judgment;" that is, to make these the theme of his song, ver. 1.

II. His purpose to lead an upright life—a life characterised by wisdom—especially in his own family, vers. 2, 3. It is a purpose to *begin* life in this relation aright; *to be* an upright man in his family.

III. The *principles* on which he purposed to do this, especially in reference to those who should be in his employ as domestics, servants, or labourers, vers. 4-7 :—

(1) He would employ no "froward" person, ver. 4.

(2) He would employ no one who was a "slanderer," ver. 5.

(3) He would employ no one who had "a high look or a proud heart," ver. 5.

(4) He would seek out the faithful and the pious in the land to be in his service, ver. 6.

(5) He would employ no one who was deceitful; no one who could not be trusted; no one who was a liar, ver. 7.

IV. These same principles, he says, should govern him in a higher relation —as a sovereign and monarch; for they were principles which were as needful in administering the government of a nation, as in a family; they were principles which a good man *should* take with him to all the public duties of life, whatever might be his rank, ver. 8.

Thus understood, the psalm contains important principles applicable (*a*) to man or woman entering on the married life; (*b*) to those who are at the head of manufacturing establishments; (*c*) to farmers and mechanics; (*d*) to those who occupy official positions, and who administer the government of a land,—judges, rulers, princes, monarchs. No better rules could be given to guide those who have others under them or in their employ, in respect to their own conduct, or in respect to those who shall be employed, than such as the psalmist here says should guide him.

1. *I will sing of mercy and judgment.* That is, In the psalm which he was about to compose, he would make these the burden of his song; he would, in fact, by stating his views as to the regulation of his own conduct, commend these virtues—mercy and justice—to mankind, and celebrate their value. He who himself *adopts* the principles of mercy, kindness, truth, and justice, as his own guide, commends these virtues to mankind in the best way possible. No *language* can do it effectually, unless a man practises these virtues himself. ¶ *Unto thee, O* LORD, *will I sing.* As commending and approving these things; as having put it into my heart to practise them; as displaying them in thine own higher administration:—for a father of a family, or a magistrate, is but the representative of God.

2. *I will behave myself wisely.* In the choice of principles to guide me; in my conduct in my family; in my official relations. This expresses a *desire* to act wisely, and a *purpose* to do it. ¶ *In a perfect way.* In accordance with the perfect rules of right. I will make these my guide. I will *aim* to be perfect; I will have before me a perfect standard. ¶ *O when wilt thou come unto me?* Perhaps this would be better rendered, "When thou dost come unto me;" that is, When thou dost visit me and my dwelling, thou shalt find that these

thou come unto me ? I will walk
d within my house with a perfect
heart.

3 I will *e* set no ¹ wicked thing
before mine eyes: I hate the

d 1 Kings ix. 4.   *e* Isa. xxxiii. 15.
¹ *thing of Belial.*

work of them *f* that turn aside;
it shall not cleave to me.

4 A froward heart shall depart
from me; I will not know *g* a
wicked *person.*

f Ps. cxxv. 5.   *g* 1 Cor. xv. 33.

are the principles which regulate and
govern me in my house. The idea is
that God would come to visit his
habitation, and inspect his conduct;
and that whenever this should occur,
however often it might be, or however unexpectedly he might come, he
should *always* find these principles
governing him in his family. A man
should so live that *whenever* God
comes into his dwelling, or when any
one comes, or however narrow and
searching may be the inspection, these
principles shall be found to regulate
his conduct. ¶ *I will walk within
my house.* Before my family; in the
principles which shall govern me there.
¶ *With a perfect heart.* Always
aiming to do exactly that which is
right:—in my general conduct; in the
rules by which I live; in my treatment of all under my charge and in
my employ. The great principles of
right, in everything—in the smallest
matters—shall guide and govern me.

3. *I will set no wicked thing before
mine eyes.* That is, I will propose no
wicked thing to be done; I will have
no such object in view; I will employ
no one to do that which is wrong.
The marg., as the Heb., is, *thing of
Belial.* See Notes on Ps. xli. 8. It
here means that which is worthless,
bad, wicked. He would have no
wicked aim; he would not look upon
a wicked thing for a moment, or with
the least favour. ¶ *I hate the work
of them that turn aside.* All their
doings, motives, plans. The word
rendered *turn aside* means to turn
out of the way; out of the right path:
Wanderers — transgressors — those
who leave the path of truth and
honesty. ¶ It *shall not cleave to me.*
I will have nothing to do with it. It
shall not be allowed to attach itself to

me. A wicked plan or purpose is
thus represented as having a tendency
to fasten itself on a man, or to "*stick
to him*"—as pitch, or wax, or a *burn*
does.

4. *A froward heart shall depart
from me.* The word here rendered
froward means perverse, false, deceitful, depraved. See Notes on Ps. xviii.
26. The *idea* here is that of one who
is inclined to evil; who has some
wrong passion or inclination to indulge; who has an obstinate and perverse will; who does not listen to reason or the voice of wise persuasion;
who *will* do wrong, despite all the
means which may be employed to
induce him to do right. The language may either refer to the author
of the psalm himself, as regulating
his own conduct; or it may refer to
those in his employ. In the former
sense, it would mean that he would
not himself be perverse and froward;
in the latter sense, that he would not
have such persons in his employ. The
connexion seems to require that we
should understand it in the latter
sense, as referring to the class of persons that the psalmist would have
about him. ¶ *I will not know a
wicked* person. I will not countenance such a one; I will not recognize such a one among those who are
admitted into my house, or own him
as my friend; or, I will not have
such in my employ. Probably the
language embraces both these ideas,—
as it should in the case of all who are
at the head of a family:—(*a*) I will
not countenance or recognize as among
my friends, who are to be admitted to
my fireside and family, and who are
to be familiar with me and my children, those who are profligate, wicked,
and unprincipled, whatever may be

5 Whoso privily slandereth his neighbour, him will I cut off: him that hath an high look and a proud heart will not I suffer.

6 Mine eyes *shall be* upon the faithful of the land, that they may dwell with me: he that walketh ¹ in a perfect way, he shall serve me.

¹ Or, *perfect in the way*, Ps. cxix. 1.

---

their rank, their wealth, their accomplishments, their fascination of manner, or their power of conversation; (*b*) I will have in my employ no one who is not honest, temperate, virtuous, pure. The welfare of a family depends more on the former of these things than the latter; no family can be well ordered where both are not found.

5. *Whoso privily slandereth his neighbour.* Literally, "One who speaks concerning his neighbour in secret." If a man has any good to say of another, he will be likely to say it openly; if he has any evil to say, it will be likely to be said in secret. Hence to speak in secret of any one comes to mean the same thing as to slander him. ¶ *Him will I cut off.* That is, I will cut him off from me; I will not employ him. He would not have one in his house, or in his service, who did injustice to the character of others; who stabbed their reputation in the dark. This was alike indicative of the personal character of the author of the psalm, and of his purpose as the head of a family. It is hardly necessary to say that no one *should* employ another who is in the habit of slandering his neighbour. ¶ *Him that hath an high look.* That is proud,—as a proud man commonly carries his head high. ¶ *And a proud heart.* The Hebrew word here rendered *proud* commonly means wide, broad, large, as of the sea, or of an extended country, Job xi. 9; Ex. iii. 8. It is applied also to the law of God as comprehensive, and without limit, Ps. cxix. 96. Then it comes to mean swelled up —*made* large — inflated (Prov. xxviii. 25); and hence, proud and arrogant. ¶ *Will not I suffer.* I will not tolerate such a person near me. No one can have peace in his house who has such a class of servants or domestics; no one should counte-

nance such persons. Humility is the very foundation of all virtue.

6. *Mine eyes* shall be *upon the faithful of the land*, etc. I will look to them to be employed in my house, and in my service. The word rendered *faithful* means those who are worthy of belief or confidence. It does not *necessarily* mean those who are pious or religious—though it is often used to denote such persons, in reference to the principal trait in the character of the pious, *i. e.* confidence or faith in God. The essential meaning here is, that he would seek those who were trustworthy; on whom he could place reliance; whose truth, fidelity, and honesty he could confide in. This would be most certainly found in those who are "faithful" to God, and who would then be "faithful" to lower obligations. Undoubtedly, also, it is desirable, on some accounts, to have only such in our employ, if such can be found. But we are not to regard this passage as teaching the doctrine, even by the example of the psalmist, that we are to employ no persons but such as are truly religious. There are others who will be found faithful, honest, and reliable; and they have such a claim to our confidence as to impose on us a moral obligation to show them that confidence,—so far, at least, that we shall not, by any act of ours, declare them *not* worthy of trust *because* they are not religious. Besides, it may be desirable, on many accounts, that persons who are not religious should be brought under the influence of religion in pious families, and enjoy the advantages which may be connected with a religious household. In seeking our own interest, and what will be for our own welfare and happiness, we should not be unmindful of what may be for the good of

7 He that worketh deceit shall not dwell within my house; he that telleth lies [h] shall not [1] tarry in my sight.

[h] Rev. xxi. 27. [1] *be established.*

8 I [i] will early destroy all the wicked of the land, that I may cut off all wicked doers from the city of the LORD.

[i] Jer. xxi. 12.

---

others. Religion may extend itself much in the world by thus bringing into the service of religious households those who *may,* by example, instruction, and prayer, be led to the possession and practice of true religion. ¶ *He that walketh in a perfect way,* etc. Marg., *perfect in the way.* The translation in the text is the more correct. The phrase means an upright man; a man of integrity. It does not necessarily imply that he is absolutely holy, or free from all sin, but that he is upright, consistent, honest : a man whose moral character is developed in proper proportions, or is such that it may be relied on. See Notes on Job i. 1.

7. *He that worketh deceit.* The man who is dishonest,—who is full of tricks, false pretences, and devices,—who cannot be confided in as straightforward and sincere,—one whose word cannot be relied on,—one whose course is subterranean or serpentine. ¶ *Shall not dwell within my house.* Shall neither be employed in my service, nor be admitted as a guest and companion. I will not, in any way, patronise or countenance such a person. ¶ *He that telleth lies.* In any way :—by stating what is false; by promising what is not performed; by deceiving me in his professions. I will seek only those who love and speak the truth. ¶ *Shall not tarry in my sight.* Marg., *shall not be established.* The idea is that of being confirmed or established. The sense here seems to be, that though such a person *should* gain admittance to his house on any pretence or profession, he should not obtain a permanent residence there. As soon as his real character was known, he would be dismissed or discharged. The psalmist says that he would do nothing to show him countenance; he would not

give occasion to have it represented that he favoured liars or dishonest persons, or that such persons might find employment with him. As a universal rule, no man should have such plans to accomplish in his family, or in his business-transactions, that he cannot employ, in accomplishing those things, persons who are perfectly honest; or, in other words, no man should engage in any undertaking, or pursue any kind of business, that would require men of loose principles—the cunning, the crafty, the deceitful, the dishonest—to carry it out. Yet there *are* many such employments in the world; and there *are* men fitted for such employments, and who are willing to engage in such work. It may be a good test for a man in regard to the business in which he is engaged, to ask himself what kind of agents, clerks, or servants, it will be necessary for him to employ in carrying it out. If the business is such as to make it necessary to employ unprincipled men — men who have easy consciences—men who will violate the sabbath—men who have more skill than honesty—more cunning than principle—that very fact should determine him at once in regard to the propriety of the business.

8. *I will early destroy,* etc. Heb., "In the mornings I will destroy." That is, It shall be my first business as I enter upon the day. Possibly, also, by the use of the plural here—" in the *mornings*"—there may be the idea that this would be his constant rule of conduct :—he would do it every day; he would do it morning by morning. He would on no day— at no time—allow the wicked to be in his service. This rule would be unvarying. It would extend through his life. The word *destroy* here may refer not only to his conduct as a man,

and as the head of a family, but to the act of a magistrate; and the idea may be, that the rule which he prescribed for himself in his own house was a rule which he would carry with him into public:—that is, as the psalm was composed by David, that, as a king and sovereign, it should be his aim to carry those principles to the throne; that, in respect to the state, he would do what he purposed to do in his home-relations. The strict and stern regard for truth, sincerity, honesty, fidelity, which he would evince in the one case he would evince in the other; carrying to the high employments of public life, where there were so many temptations to a contrary course, the inflexible virtues which were needful for peace, for happiness, and for success in domestic life. ¶ *That I may cut off.* By discountenancing them; by punishing them if they are guilty. ¶ *All wicked doers.* All violators of law. ¶ *From the city of the* LORD. From Jerusalem, the place where God dwelt, and which was sacred to his service. See Notes on Ps. xlvi. 4; xlviii. 2, 8. Happy is the man at the head of a family—happy is the magistrate—who adopts for himself, and who faithfully carries out the principles laid down by the author of this psalm—divinely inspired to adopt such rules for himself, and to suggest them for others in all ages.

PSALM CII.

This psalm purports, in the title, to be a "Prayer of the afflicted, when he is overwhelmed, and poureth out his complaint before the Lord." It *is* a prayer, made up of earnest supplications, as of one who was in great affliction, whether he refers to his own individual sorrows, or whether he speaks as one of the people. The word "afflicted," means here a suffering one; one who is in trouble. The word is in the singular number, and is one which is often applied to a person who is in trouble—whatever may be the nature of that trouble. The word rendered *overwhelmed* means properly to cover as with a garment; to clothe; and then, to be covered with darkness,

affliction, grief, Ps. lxi. 2. This is the meaning here. It denotes a state where the soul was enshrouded in gloom and sorrow. The word rendered *complaint*, means properly meditation; then, moaning; then, the expression of sorrow. It does not necessarily mean, as the word does with us, *finding fault*, or expressing dissatisfaction, but it rather denotes that deep sorrow which finds utterance in low and plaintive sounds;—not in boisterous and loud outcry, but in subdued notes, —in sounds uttered not because one wishes to complain, but because the sorrow is such that it will find vent. Comp. 1 Sam. i. 16; 1 Kings xviii. 27; Job vii. 13; ix. 27; x. 1; xxi. 4; Ps. lv. 2; lxiv. 1 (*Heb.*).

On what occasion, or by whom, this psalm was composed, it is not possible now to ascertain. Hengstenberg and Prof. Alexander suppose that it was by David. It seems more probable, however, from vers. 13-21, that it was in the time of the captivity, and was in view of the troubles of that long and weary exile, and that the psalmist speaks not of individual and personal troubles, but speaks as one of the people—as one in exile with others who had been long held in captivity, and who sighed for deliverance, and for a restoration to their native land. In the midst of these troubles, which are so tenderly described in the first eleven verses, he saw encouraging evidences that the Lord was about to manifest his mercy, and to restore the people to their native land; and he pleads most earnestly with God, on the ground that he was faithful and unchanging, that he *would* thus interpose and accomplish the earnest desire of his afflicted people. The *language*, indeed, in the psalm, is that of an individual, and the author of the psalm speaks of his own personal sorrows, but it may be as one among many who were equally crushed and overwhelmed, so that the language used to represent his sorrow may describe the sorrows experienced by others in the same circumstances. Beyond all question, the language used in the psalm would express the feelings of many a pious Hebrew in the time of the exile,—the sorrow—the sadness—the cherished hopes—the prayers—of many a one in that prolonged and painful captivity.

The psalm may be divided into three parts :—

I. A description of the sorrows of the

PSALM CII.

A Prayer [1] of the afflicted, when *k* he is overwhelmed, and poureth *l* out his complaint
before the LORD.

HEAR *m* my prayer, O LORD,
and let my cry come unto
thee.

[1] Or, *for.*   *k* Ps. lxi. 2.   *l* Ps. lxii. 8.
m Ps. cxlv. 19.   *n* Isa. xliii. 2; 1 Cor. x. 13.

2 Hide *n* not thy face from me
in the day *when* I am in trouble;
incline thine ear unto me: in
the day *when* I call, answer me
speedily.

3 For my days are consumed
[2] like smoke, and my bones are
burned as an hearth.

[2] Or, (as some read) *into.*

---

author of the psalm, as representative of
the condition and feelings of the exiles,
vers. 1-11. In this, the language of
lamentation and complaint predomi-
nates.

II. The grounds of hope—the indications of deliverance—the evidences that
God was about to show favour to his
people, and to restore them to their own
country,—that the time, the set time, to
favour Zion was about to come, vers.
12-22.

III. The confidence of the psalmist
in God, on the ground of his unchangeableness:—on the fact that God is always
the same; that his promises must be
sure; that his purposes must be accomplished; that the very heavens and the
earth would change,—that the skies
would grow old like a garment and pass
away,—but that God did not, would not
change. All that he had spoken must
be true; all that he had purposed must
be accomplished; all that he had promised must come to pass, vers. 23-28.

1. *Hear my prayer, O* LORD. The
prayer which I offer in view of my
personal trials; the prayer which I
offer as one of an afflicted people.
Comp. Ps. iv. 1; xvii. 1; xviii. 6.
¶ *And let my cry come unto thee.*
My prayer, accompanied with an
outward expression of my earnestness.
It was not a silent, or a mental
prayer; it was a loud and earnest
cry. Ps. v. 2; xviii. 6, 41; xxx. 2;
lxxii. 12; Job xxxv. 9; xxxvi. 13.

2. *Hide not thy face from me.* The
Septuagint and the Latin Vulgate
render this, " Do not turn away thy
face from me." The sense is essentially the same. The prayer is, that
God would not refuse to look graciously
upon him; that he would turn his
attention to him; that he would regard his supplications. See Notes on

Ps. x. 1; comp. Ps. xiii. 1; xxvii. 9;
Job xiii. 24; xxxiv. 29; Deut. xxxi.
17. ¶ *In the day* when *I am in
trouble.* When sorrows come upon
me; when I need thy gracious help.
Literally, " When there is distress to
me." ¶ *Incline thine ear unto me.*
See Notes on Ps. v. 1; xvii. 6; comp.
Ps. xvii. 1; lv. 1; lxxxvi. 6; xxxix.
12. ¶ *In the day* when *I call, answer
me speedily.* Grant at once my requests; give me immediate evidence
that my prayer is heard. The psalmist
believed in an immediate answer to
prayer. He often had evidence that
his prayer was answered at once; his
mind became calm; he had comfort
and peace; he obtained the blessing
which he earnestly sought. No one
can doubt that prayer *may* be answered at once; no one who prays can
fail to find such answers in his own
case, in his peace, his calmness, his joy.
In multitudes of cases blessings are
granted in such a way that there can
be no doubt that they have come in
answer to prayer. Comp. Notes on
Dan. ix. 20—23.

3. *For my days are consumed like
smoke.* Marg., *into smoke.* Literally,
in smoke. That is, They vanish as
smoke; they pass away and become
nothing; they are spent in affliction,
and seem to accomplish nothing.
The idea is, that in his affliction he
seemed to accomplish none of the
ends of life. His life seemed to be
wasted. This is often the feeling in
trial:—and yet *in* trial a man may be
more useful, he may do more to accomplish the real ends of life, he may do
more to illustrate the power and excellence of religion, than he ever did
in the days of prosperity. ¶ *And my*

9 For I have eaten ashes like bread, and mingled my drink with weeping;

10 Because of thine indignation and thy wrath: for *p* thou hast lifted me up, and cast me down.

p Ps. xxx. 7.　　　*q* Eccles. vi. 12.

11 My days *are* like a shadow *q* that declineth; and I am withered *r* like grass.

12 But thou, *s* O Lord, shalt endure for ever, and thy remembrance unto all generations.

r James i. 10.　　　*s* Lam. v. 19.

harm. It is not the wrath of an individual that I am to meet, but the combined wrath of those who act under the solemnities of an oath. Comp. Acts xxiii. 12.

9. *For I have eaten ashes like bread.* I have seated myself in ashes in my grief (comp. Job ii. 8; xlii. 6; Isa. lviii. 5; lxi. 3; Jonah iii. 6; Dan. ix. 3; Matt. xi. 21); and ashes have become, as it were, my food. The ashes in which he sat had been mingled with his food. ¶ *And mingled my drink with weeping.* Tears have fallen into the cup from which I drank, and have become a part of my drink. The idea is, that he had shed copious tears; and that even when he took his food, there was no respite to his grief.

10. *Because of thine indignation and thy wrath.* Heb., " From the face of thine indignation," etc. That is,—he regarded all his sufferings as proof of the indignation and wrath of God against him. See Ps. xc. 7-9. ¶ *For thou hast lifted me up.* In former times. Thou hadst given me prosperity; thou hadst given me an elevated and honourable place among men. ¶ *And cast me down.* Thou hast brought me into a low condition, and I feel it all the more from the fact that I had enjoyed prosperity. Comp. Notes on Ps. xxx. 7. The passage, however, is susceptible of another interpretation: " Thou hast lifted me up, and cast me away." That is, Thou hast lifted me from the ground as a storm or tempest takes up a light thing, and hast whirled me away. This idea occurs in Isa. xxii. 18. See Notes on that passage. The former, however, seems to me to be the more correct interpretation.

11. *My days* are *like a shadow that declineth.* The shadow made by the gnomon on a sun-dial, which marks the hours as they pass. See 2 Kings xx. 10. The idea is that the shadow made by the descending sun was about to disappear altogether. It had become less distinct and clear, and it would soon vanish. It would seem from this, that the dial was so made that the shadow indicating the hour ascended when the sun ascended, and declined when the sun went down. See Notes on Isa. xxxviii. 8. ¶ *And I am withered like grass.* See Notes on ver. 4.

12. *But thou, O* Lord, *shalt endure for ever.* Though my condition has been changed, though I have been cast down from an exalted position, though kingdoms rise and fall, yet thou art unchanged. Thy purposes will abide. Thy promises will be fulfilled. Thy character is the same. As thou hast been the hearer of prayer in past times, so thou art now. As thou hast interposed in behalf of thy people in other ages, so thou wilt now. As thy people in affliction have been permitted to come to thee, so they may come to thee now. The psalmist here brings to his own mind, as an encouragement in trouble, as we may at all times, the fact that God is an unchanging God; that he always lives; that he is ever the same. We could have no ground of hope if God changed; if he formed purposes only to abandon them; if he made promises only to disregard them; if to-day he were a Being of mercy and goodness, and to-morrow would be merely a Being of justice and wrath. This argument is enlarged upon in vers. 25-28.

13 Thou shalt arise, *and* have mercy upon Zion: for the time *t* Isa. lx. 1, etc.; Zec. i. 12, 13. *u* Isa. xl. 2.

t to favour her, yea, the set *u* time, is come.

14 For thy servants take plea-

¶ *And thy remembrance unto all generations.* Thy memory; or, the remembrance of thee. *My* days are like a shadow. I shall pass away, and be forgotten. No one will recollect me; no one will feel any interest in remembering that I have ever lived (see Notes on Ps. xxxi. 12). But while one knows that this must be so in regard to himself and to all other men—that he and they are alike to be forgotten—he may also feel that there is One who will *never* be forgotten. God will never pass away. He will be always the same. All the hopes of the church—of the world—are based on this. It is not on man—on any one man—on any number of men—for they will all alike pass away and be forgotten; but one generation of men after another, to the end of time, may call on God, and find him an ever-living, an unchanged and unchangeable protector and friend.

13. *Thou shalt arise.* Thou wilt come forth—as if God had been inattentive or inactive. ¶ *And have mercy upon Zion.* That is, Upon Jerusalem—represented as in a state of desolation. God would at length pity her, and interpose in her behalf. ¶ *For the time to favour her.* Implying that there was an appointed time to favour her, or to bring her troubles to an end. ¶ *Yea, the set time is come.* The word here used—מוֹעֵד, *moaid*—means properly an appointed season—a designated moment. It refers to some purpose or appointment in regard to anything that is to be done, as in 1 Sam. xiii. 8, 11; 2 Sam. xx. 5; Gen. xvii. 21; or to a fixed period, as when certain things are to be done, certain festivals to be held regularly at a certain season of the year, Lam. i. 4; ii. 6; Hos. ix. 5; xii. 9; Lev. xxiii. 2, 4, 37, 44. Here it means that there was some period fixed in the Divine Mind when this

was to occur, or a definite time when it had been predicted or promised that it would occur. The language is such as would be applicable to the captivity in Babylon, concerning which there was a promise that it should continue but seventy years. If the psalm refers to that, then the meaning is that there were indications in the course of events that that period was about to arrive. Comp. Notes on Dan. ix. 2. What those indications were in this case, the psalmist immediately states, ver. 14. It may be remarked here, that there are usually some previous intimations or indications of what God is about to do. "Coming events cast their shadows before." Even the Divine purposes are accomplished usually in connexion with human agency, and in the regular course of events; and it is frequently possible to anticipate that God is about to appear for the fulfilment of his promises. So it was in the coming of the Saviour. So it was in the destruction of Jerusalem by the Romans. So it is when God is about to revive religion in a church. So it is, and will be, in regard to the conversion of the world.

14. *For thy servants take pleasure in her stones.* Those who profess to be thy servants; thy friends. This was the *evidence* to the mind of the psalmist that God was about to visit his people, and to rebuild Jerusalem. It was an *awakened interest* among the professed people of God, leading them to manifest their love for Zion, and for all that pertained to her,—a love for the very stones that lay in undistinguished heaps where the city once stood,—the piles of rubbish where the walls and dwellings had once been. The people of God in their captivity began to look with strong interest on these very ruins, and with an earnest wish that from

sure in her stones, and favour the dust thereof.

15 So the heathen shall fear the name of the LORD, and all

the kings of the earth thy glory.

16 When the LORD shall build up Zion, he shall appear in his glory.

---

these ruins the city may again arise, and the walls be rebuilt. ¶ *And favour the dust thereof.* Literally, *pity*—or, show compassion for. They no longer look with indifference on these ruins of Zion. They look with a tender heart on the very dust of those ruins. They feel that a wrong has been done to Zion; they ardently desire its restoration to its former splendour and glory. They long for a return to it as to their home. They are weary with their captivity, and they are anxiously waiting for the time when they may revisit their native land. This would seem to refer to an awakened interest on the subject, caused perhaps in part by the fact that it could be ascertained (see Dan. ix. 2) that the period of the captivity *was* about to end, and partly by an influence on their hearts from on high, awakening in them a deeper love for Zion—a revival of pure religion. The practical truth taught here is, that an indication of a coming revival of religion is often manifested by the increased attention to the subject among its professed friends; by the desire in their hearts that it may be so; by tenderness, pity, compassion among them in view of abounding desolations, the coldness of the church, and the prevalence of iniquity; by their looking with interest on that which had before been neglected, like shapeless ruins — the prayer-meeting, the communion, the sanctuary; by a conscious returning love in their hearts for all that pertains to religion, however unimportant it may be in the eyes of the world, or however it may be despised. A surrounding world would look with unconcern on the ruins of Jerusalem; a friend of God, in whose heart religion was revived, would look with the most tender concern even on that rubbish, and those ruins. So it is

in a revival of religion, when God is about to visit his church in mercy. Everything in regard to the church becomes an object of deep interest.

15. *So the heathen.* The nations. That is, The surrounding people, who hear what thou hast done for thy people, will see the evidence that thou art God, and learn to love and worship thee. ¶ *Shall fear the name of the* LORD. Shall reverence and honour thee. ¶ *And all the kings of the earth thy glory.* The sovereigns of the earth will be especially affected and impressed with thy majesty. If this refers to the return from the captivity at Babylon, then it means that that event would be particularly fitted to impress the minds of the rulers of the world, as showing that God had all nations under his control; that he could deliver a captive people from the grasp of the mighty; that he was the friend of those who worshipped him, and that he would frown on oppression and wrong.

16. *When the* LORD *shall build up Zion.* The Septuagint, the Latin Vulgate, and Luther, render this, " Because the Lord hath built up Zion." This also is the most natural and correct translation of the Hebrew. The reference, however, may be to the future. The psalmist may throw himself into the future, and—standing there — he may describe things as they will appear then,—as already done. ¶ *He shall appear in his glory.* The idea is that the building up of Zion would be an occasion in which God would manifest his glory. In reference to the restoration of his people from bondage; in rebuilding Zion, then in ruins; in restoring the splendour of the place where he had been so long worshipped, he would display his true character as a God of glory, truth, power, and goodness. As applied to the

17 He *v* will regard the prayer of the destitute, and not despise their prayer.

18 This *w* shall be written for

v Neh. i. 6, 11; ii. 1—8.

the generation to come; and the people which shall be created shall praise the LORD.

19 For he hath looked down

w Rom. xv. 4; 1 Cor. x. 11.

church in general, this would mean that when God comes to revive religion, to visit his people, to recover them from their backslidings, to convert and save sinners, he appears in his appropriate character *as* the God of his people,—*as* a glorious God. Then the perfections of his nature are most illustriously displayed; then he appears in his true character, as a God of mercy, grace, and salvation. There is no scene on earth where the character of God is more gloriously exhibited than in a revival of true religion.

17. *He will regard the prayer.* Literally, "He looks upon," or "he *turns himself* to their prayer." He does not any longer seem to turn away from them and disregard them. He shows by thus building up Zion that he *does* regard prayer; that he hears the supplications of his people. There is no higher proof that prayer is heard than that which is often furnished in a revival of pure religion. All such revivals, like that on the day of Pentecost (Acts ii. 1, *et seq.*), are usually preceded, as that was (Acts i. 13, 14), by special prayer; *in* those revivals there are often most manifest and clear answers to prayer for the conversion of individuals; to prayer for a blessing on a preached gospel; to prayer for particular relatives and friends. ¶ *Of the destitute.* Literally, *of the poor.* The word— עֲרָר, *arâr*—occurs only here and in Jer. xvii. 6, where it is rendered *heath:* "He shall be like the *heath* in the desert." The word, according to its etymology, means *naked;* then, poor, stripped of everything, impoverished, wholly destitute. It would thus be eminently applicable to the poor exiles in Babylon; it is *as* applicable to sinners pleading with God, and to the people of God themselves,

destitute of everything like self-righteousness, and feeling that they have nothing in themselves, but that they are wholly dependent on the mercy of God. Comp. Rev. iii. 17. ¶ *And not despise their prayer.* Not treat it with contempt; not pass it by unheard. This is stated as one of the reasons why the nations would be struck with awe,—that God, the infinite God, would hear the prayers of those who were so poor, so powerless, so friendless. There is, in fact, nothing more fitted to excite wonder than that God *does* hear the prayer of poor, lost, sinful man.

18. *This shall be written for the generation to come.* It shall be recorded for the instruction and encouragement of future ages. The fact that God has heard the prayer of his people in a time of trial shall be so recorded and remembered that it may be referred to in similar circumstances in all time to come, for he is an unchanging God. What he has done now, he will always be willing to do hereafter. ¶ *And the people which shall be created.* Future generations. Each successive generation is in fact a new creation; each individual is also; for the essential idea in *creation* is that of bringing something into existence where there was nothing before. There is a *beginning* of existence in every human being. Man is not in any proper sense a *development* from former being, nor is his life merely a *continuance* of something which existed before. ¶ *Shall praise the* LORD. Shall praise the Lord for what he has now done; shall learn, from the great principles now illustrated in regard to his administration, to praise him.

19. *For he hath looked down from the height of his sanctuary.* From his high and holy dwelling-place, in

from the height of his sanctuary; from heaven did the LORD behold the earth;

20 To ^x hear the groaning of the prisoner; to loose ¹ those that are appointed to death;

21 To ^y declare the name of

x Ps. cxlvi. 7.
¹ *the children of death.*

the LORD in Zion, and his praise in Jerusalem;

22 When the people are gathered together, and the kingdoms to serve the LORD.

23 He ² weakened my strength in the way; he shortened my days.

y 1 Pet. ii. 9.   ² *afflicted.*

heaven. The word here rendered *looked down*, means, in Kal, to lay upon or over; then, in Niphil, to lie out over anything, to project; and then, to bend forward. It then means to bend or incline forward with an intention to look at anything, as from a window, Gen. xxvi. 8. Comp. Ps. xiv. 2. See also Notes on Ps. lxxxv. 12; 1 Pet. i. 12. ¶ *From heaven did the* LORD *behold the earth.* Did he look abroad over all the world.

20. *To hear the groaning of the prisoner.* Meaning here, probably, the captives in Babylon; those who were held as prisoners there, and who were subjected to such hardships in their long captivity. See Notes on Ps. lxxix. 11. ¶ *To loose those that are appointed to death.* Marg., as in Heb., *the children of death.* Comp. Notes on Matt. i. 1. This may mean either those who were sentenced to death; those who were sick and ready to die; or those who, in their captivity, were in such a state of privation and suffering that death appeared inevitable. The word rendered *loose* means, properly, to *open*,—applied to the mouth, for eating, Ezek. iii. 2; or in song, Ps. lxxviii. 2; or for speaking, Job iii. 1;—or the ear, Isa. l. 5;—or the hand, Deut. xv. 8;—or the gates of a city, a door, etc., Deut. xx. 11. Then it means to set free, as by opening the doors of a prison, Isa. xiv. 17; Job xii. 14. Here it means to *set free*, to *deliver*. Comp. Isa. lxi. 1.

21. *To declare the name of the* LORD *in Zion,* etc. That his name might be declared in Zion, or that his praise might be set up in Jerusalem again. That is, that his people might be re-

turned there, and his praise be celebrated again in the holy city.

22. *When the people are gathered together.* When they shall be brought from their dispersion in distant lands; when they shall assemble again in the city of their fathers, and when public worship shall be celebrated there as in former ages. ¶ *And the kingdoms, to serve the* LORD. The Septuagint and the Latin Vulgate render this, *kings.* The reference must be to the time when those of other lands—kings and their people — would be converted to the true religion; when the Gentiles as well as the Jews, then one undistinguished people, would be brought to the knowledge of the true God, and would unite in his worship. See Notes on Isa. lx. All, of all lands, will yet praise the Lord *as if* they were one great congregation, assembled in one place. Thus, though separate, they will with united feeling recount the mercy and goodness of God to his people in past times.

23. *He weakened my strength in the way.* Marg., as in Heb., *afflicted.* The idea is, that God had taken his strength away; he had weakened him,—humbled him,—brought him low by sorrow. The word *way* refers to the course which he was pursuing. In his journey of life God had thus afflicted—humbled—prostrated him. The psalmist here turns from the exulting view which he had of the future (vers. 21, 22), and resumes his complaint,—the remembrance of his troubles and sorrows (vers. 3–11). He speaks, doubtless, in the name of his people, and describes troubles which were common to them all. Perhaps the allusion to his troubles

24 I *z* said, O my God, take
me not away in the midst of my
days: thy years *are* throughout
all generations.

25 Of *a* old hast thou laid the
foundation of the earth; and the
heavens *are* the work of thy
hands.

z Ps. xxxix. 13; Isa. xxxviii. 10.

26 They shall perish, but thou
shalt [1] endure; yea, all of them
shall wax old like a garment; as
a vesture shalt thou change them,
and they shall be changed:

27 But *b* thou *art* the same,
and thy years shall have no end.

28 The children of thy ser-

a Heb. i. 10—12.   [1] *stand.*
b Mal. iii. 6; Heb. xiii. 8.

here may be designed, as such a recollection should do, to heighten his
sense of the goodness and mercy of
God in the anticipated blessings of
the future. ¶ *He shortened my days.*
Comp. Job xxi. 21; Ps. lxxxix. 45.
That is, He seemed to be about to
cut me off from life, and to bring me
to the grave. The psalmist felt so
confident that he would die,—that he
could not endure these troubles, but
must sink under them, that he spoke
as if it were already done. Comp.
Ps. vi. 4, 5.

24. *I said, O my God, take me not
away in the midst of my days.* This
was the burden of my prayer; for
this I earnestly pleaded. See Ps.
xxx. 9; Isa. xxxviii. 1-3, 9-18. The
word here used means *to cause to
ascend* or *go up,* and the expression
might have been translated, "Cause
me not to ascend." The Septuagint
and the Latin Vulgate render it,
"Call me not away." Bishop Horsley, "Carry me not off." In the
word there *may* be an allusion—an
obscure one, it is to be admitted —
to the idea that the soul *ascends* to
God when the body dies. The common idea in the Old Testament is
that it would *descend* to the regions
of the departed spirits—to Sheol.
It is plain, however, that there *was*
another idea,—that the soul would
ascend at once to God when death
occurred. Comp. Eccl. iii. 21; xii.
7. The word rendered "in the
midst" means properly *in the half;*
as if life were divided into two portions. Comp. Ps. lv. 23. ¶ *Thy
years* are *throughout all generations.*
Thou dost not die; thou art ever the

same, though the generations of men
are cut off. This seems to have been
said here for two reasons: (1) As a
ground of consolation, that God was
ever the same; that whatever might
happen to men, to the psalmist himself, or to any other man, God was
unchanged, and that his great plans
would be carried forward and accomplished; (2) As a reason for the
prayer. God was eternal. He had an
immortal existence. He could not
die. He knew, in its perfection, the
blessedness of *life*—life as such; life
continued; life unending. The psalmist appeals to what God himself enjoyed—as a reason why life—so great
a blessing—should be granted to him
a little longer. By all that there was
of blessedness in the life of God, the
psalmist prays that that which was
in itself—even in the case of God—
so valuable, might yet a little longer
be continued to *him.*

25-27. *Of old.* See this passage
fully explained in the Notes on Heb.
i. 10-12. In the beginning; at the
first. The phrase here used means
literally *to the face;* then, *before* in
the order of time. It means here,
long ago; of olden time; at the
beginning. The meaning is, that the
years of God had stretched through
all the generations of men, and all
the changes which had occurred upon
the earth; that at the very beginning
he existed, and that he would continue to exist to the very close,
unchangeably the same.

28. *The children of thy servants
shall continue.* The descendants of
those that serve and obey thee. This
represents the confident expectation

vants shall continue, and their seed shall be established before thee.

of the psalmist that, as God was unchangeable, all his promises toward his people would be fulfilled, even though the heavens and the earth should pass away. God was the same. His word would not fail. His promises were sure. Comp. Matt. v. 18; xxiv. 35. The word rendered *continue*, means to dwell, as in a habitation; then, to abide. It stands opposed to a wandering, nomadic life, and indicates permanency. ¶ *And their seed shall be established before thee.* The word here used means properly to stand erect; then to set up, to erect, to place, to found, to make firm, as a city, Ps. cvii. 36; the earth, Ps. xxiv. 2; the heavens, Prov. iii. 19. It means here that they would be firmly and permanently established:—that is, the church of God would be permanent in the earth. It would not be like the generations of men that pass away. It would not be like the nomadic tribes of the desert that have no fixed habitation, and that wander from place to place. It would not be even like the heavens that might put on new forms, or wholly pass away:—it would be as enduring and changeless as God himself; it would, in its proper form, endure for ever. As God is eternal and unchangeable, so would the safety and welfare of his people be.

PSALM CIII.

This very beautiful psalm is entitled "A Psalm of David." Nothing in the psalm forbids the supposition that he was its author, although nothing in the psalm or elsewhere enables us to ascertain the precise occasion on which it was written.

It seems to have been composed after some signal manifestation of the mercy of God, or some striking proof of his compassion and loving-kindness; after some danger which threatened life, and was regarded as evidence of the Divine

PSALM CIII.
A Psalm of David.

BLESS the LORD, O my soul;

displeasure, but had now passed by; after God had interposed, and checked and arrested judgments which threatened ruin, and had manifested himself again as a loving Father. This merciful interposition filled the heart of the psalmist with emotions of gratitude and praise, and led him to call on his own soul (vers. 1, 2), and all the angels (ver. 20), and the hosts of heaven (ver. 21), and all the works of God everywhere (ver. 22) to unite in celebrating his praise. The psalm is exceedingly regular in its structure and composition; beautiful in its language and conceptions; adapted to all times and ages; fitted to express the feelings of gratitude to God for deliverance from trouble, and for the manifestation of his mercy; fitted to elevate the soul, and to fill it with cheerful views. These circumstances have made it a favourite psalm as a vehicle of praise in all ages. It is, moreover, eminently fitted to express the feelings of the soul in view of the redeeming love and mercy of God; the goodness of God in the forgiveness of sin through a Saviour; and his tender compassion for his people as a Father; and it is, therefore, one to which the Christian oftener turns than to almost any other of the psalms as expressive of the deep and grateful feelings of his heart.

1. *Bless the* LORD, *O my soul.* The word *bless,* as applied to God, means to praise, implying always a strong affection for him as well as a sense of gratitude. As used with reference to men, the word implies a *wish* that they may be blessed or happy, accompanied often with a *prayer* that they may be so. Such is the purport of the "blessing" addressed to a congregation of worshippers. Comp. Num. vi. 23–27. The word *soul* here is equivalent to mind or heart:—my mental and moral powers, as capable of understanding and appreciating his favours. The soul of man was *made* to praise and bless God; to enjoy his friendship; to delight in his favour; to contemplate his perfections. It can never

and all that is within mê, *bless* his holy name.

2 Bless the LORD, O my soul, and forget not all his benefits :

3 Who forgiveth *c* all thine iniquities ; who healeth *d* all thy diseases ;

c Matt. ix. 2—6 ; Eph. i. 7.   *d* Ex. xv. 26.

---

be employed in a more appropriate or a more elevated act than when engaged in his praise. ¶ *And all that is within me,* etc. All my powers and faculties; all that can be employed in his praise:—the heart, the will, the affections, the emotions. The idea is, that God is worthy of all the praise and adoration which the entire *man* can render. No one of his faculties or powers should be exempt from the duty and the privilege of praise.

2. *Bless the* LORD, *O my soul.* The repetition here denotes the intensity or earnestness of the wish or desire of the psalmist. It is an emphatic calling upon his soul, that is, himself, never to forget the many favours which God was continually conferring upon him. ¶ *And forget not all his benefits. Any* of his favours. This refers not to those favours in the aggregate, but it is a call to remember them in particular. The word rendered *benefits*—בְמוּל, *gemūl*—means properly an act, work, doing, whether good or evil, Ps. cxxxvii. 8 ; and then, *desert,* or what a man deserves *for* his act ; *recompence.* It is rendered *deserving* in Judges ix. 16 ;—*benefit,* as here, in 2 Chron. xxxii. 25 ; — *desert,* Ps. xxviii. 4 ;—*reward,* Ps. xciv. 2 ; Isa. iii. 11 ; Obad. 15 ;—*recompence,* Prov. xii. 14 ; Isa. xxxv. 4 ; lix. 18 ; lxvi. 6 ; Jer. li. 6 ; Lam. iii. 64 ; Joel iii. 4, 7. The proper reference here is to the Divine *dealings,*—to what God had *done,*—as a reason for blessing his name. His *dealings* with the psalmist had been such as to call for praise and gratitude. What those *dealings* particularly were he specifies in the following verses. The call here on 'his soul is not to forget these Divine dealings, as laying the foundation for praise. We shall find, when we reach the end of life, that *all* which God has done, however dark

and mysterious it may have appeared at the time, was so connected with our good as to make it a proper subject of praise and thanksgiving.

3. *Who forgiveth all thine iniquities.* Pardoning all thy sins. That is, It is a characteristic of God to pardon sin, and I have evidence that he has done it in my own case, and this is a ground for praise. It is observable that this is the *first* thing in view of the psalmist—the first of the "benefits" which he had received from God, or the first thing in importance among his acts or his dealings, which called for praise. Properly considered, this *is* the first thing which calls for praise. That God is a merciful God,—that he has declared his willingness to pardon sin,—that he has devised and revealed a way by which this can be done,—and that he has actually done it in our own case, is the most important matter for which we should praise him. When we understand all the things which most affect our welfare, and which enter most deeply into our happiness here and hereafter, we shall find that this is a blessing compared with which all other favours are comparative trifles. ¶ *Who healeth all thy diseases.* Perhaps, in the case of the psalmist, referring to some particular instance in which he had been recovered from dangerous sickness. The word rendered *diseases*-תַּחֲלֻאֵי, *tahhalūim*—occurs only in the plural form. It is translated *sicknesses,* in Deut. xxix. 22 ; *diseases,* as here, in 2 Chron. xxi. 19 ; *them that are sick,* in Jer. xiv. 18 ; and "*grievous* [deaths]" in Jer. xvi. 4. It does not elsewhere occur. It is applicable to all forms of sickness ; or in this place it may refer to some particular diseases with which David had been afflicted. We have several allusions in the Psalms to times when the authors of the psalms were afflicted with sickness.

4 Who redeemeth thy life from destruction; who crowneth thee with loving-kindness and tender mercies;

5 Who satisfieth thy mouth with good *things; so that* thy

youth is *e* renewed like the eagle's.

6 The LORD executeth righteousness and judgment for all that are oppressed.

e Isa. xl. 31.

So in the Psalms of David. Comp. Ps. vi. 2; xxxviii. 7; xli. 8. The thought here is, that it is a proper ground of praise to God that he has the power of healing disease. All instances of restoration to health are illustrations of this, for whatever may be the skill of physicians, or the wise adaptation of means, healing virtue comes from God alone.

4. *Who redeemeth thy life from destruction.* That is, who saves it from death when exposed to danger, or when attacked by disease. The word "destruction" or *corruption* here is equivalent to the grave, since it is there that the body returns to corruption. Comp. Notes on Ps. xvi. 10. ¶ *Who crowneth thee.* The idea here is not merely that God is the source of these blessings, but that there is something of beauty, of dignity, of honour, as in the conferring of a crown or garland on any one. Comp. Notes on Ps. lxv. 11. ¶ *With loving-kindness and tender mercies.* Mercy and compassions. God showed mercy to him,—evinced compassion,—and these were so abundant that they might be said to be the crown or ornament of his life.

5. *Who satisfieth thy mouth with good* things. The word translated *thy mouth* here is rendered in the Chaldee *thy age;* in the Arabic, the Septuagint, and the Latin Vulgate, *thy desire;* in the Syriac, *thy body;* De Wette renders it, *thy age.* So also Tholuck. The Hebrew word—עֶדְיֵךְ, *adi*—is rendered *ornaments* in Ex. xxxiii. 4—6; 2 Sam. i. 24; Isa. xlix. 18; Jer. ii. 32; iv. 30; Ezek. vii. 20; xvi. 11, 17 (marg.); xxiii. 40; and *mouth* in Ps. xxxii. 9, as here. These are the only places in which it occurs. Gesenius renders it here *age*, and supposes that it stands in con-

trast with the word *youth* in the other part of the verse. The connexion would seem to demand this, though it is difficult to make it out from any usage of the Hebrew word. Professor Alexander renders it *thy soul*—from the supposition that the Hebrew word *ornament* is used as if in reference to the idea that the *soul* is the chief glory or ornament of man. This seems, however, to be a very forced explanation. I confess myself unable to determine the meaning. ¶ So that *thy youth is renewed like the eagle's.* Comp. Isa. xl. 31. The allusion, to which there is supposed to be a reference here, is explained in the Notes on that passage. Whatever may be true in regard to the supposed fact pertaining to the eagle, about its renewing its strength and vigour in old age, the meaning here is simply that the strength of the psalmist in old age *became* like the strength of the eagle. Sustained by the bounty of God in his old age he became, as it were, young again.

6. *The* LORD *executeth righteousness and judgment.* That is, *justice.* He sees that justice is done to the oppressed. He is on their side. His law, his commands, his judicial decisions, his providential interpositions, are in their favour. This does not mean that it will be done at once; or that there will never be any delay; or that they may not suffer even for a long time,—for this occurs in fact; but the meaning is, that God has their true interest at heart; that at proper times, and whenever and wherever there are any dealings of his in the case, his acts are in favour of those that are oppressed; and that there will be sooner or later such interpositions in their behalf as shall entirely vindicate their cause. ¶ *For all that*

7 He made known his ways unto Moses, his acts unto the children of Israel.

8 The LORD *is* merciful and gracious, slow to anger, and [1] plenteous in mercy.

[1] *great of.*

9 He *f* will not always chide; neither will he keep *his anger* for ever.

10 He hath not dealt with us after our sins, nor rewarded us according to our iniquities.

f Isa. lvii. 16; Micah vii. 18, 19.

---

are oppressed. By harsh laws; by unjust governments; by slavery; by unrighteous decisions in courts; by the pride and power of wicked men. Comp. Notes on Isa. i. 17, 23–27.

7. *He made known his ways unto Moses.* This is another ground of praise,—that God had *revealed his will;* that this had been done in an indubitable manner to Moses; and that these revelations had been recorded by him for the instruction and guidance of his people. The word "*ways*" here means his laws; his methods of administration; the principles on which he governs mankind, and the conditions on which he will save men. There is no higher ground of gratitude to God than the fact that he has given a revelation to mankind. ¶ *His acts unto the children of Israel.* His methods of doing things have been made known to them; and his acts—his interpositions—have been in their favour.

8. *The* LORD is *merciful and gracious.* See Notes on Ps. lxxviii. 38. The idea here is derived evidently from Ex. xxxiv. 6, 7—that great and glorious statement of God himself in regard to his own character. Our world is a different world under that statement from what it would be if that and kindred declarations had not been made. There is here a *progression* of thought; an *advance* on the previous statements. At first the psalmist referred to his own individual experience (vers. 3–5); then he referred to the dealings of God towards the Hebrew people (vers. 6, 7); and now he rises to the general contemplation of his character as it relates to all mankind. It was a characteristic of God in respect to all, that he was kind, compassionate, and forbearing.

¶ *Slow to anger.* That is, patient; not soon excited; bearing much, and bearing it long. See James v. 11; comp. Ex. xxxiv. 6, 7. ¶ *And plenteous in mercy.* Marg., *great of mercy.* The Hebrew word means *much,* or *great;* and the idea is, that mercy is not manifested by him in small or stinted measure. It is rich; full; abundant; overflowing; free.

9. *He will not always chide.* Rebuke; contend; strive;—for so the Hebrew word means. He will not always contend with men, or manifest his displeasure. See Notes on Isa. lvii. 16; Ps. lxxviii. 38, 39. This implies that he *may* chide or rebuke his people, but that this will not be for ever. He will punish them; he will manifest his displeasure at their sins; he will show that he does not approve of their course, but he will show that he *loves them,* and does not seek their ruin. ¶ *Neither will he keep* his anger *for ever.* The words *his anger* are supplied by the translators, but not improperly. The meaning is the same as in the former member of the sentence. He will not cherish hatred when the object of the chastisement is accomplished. It is not his character to retain anger for its own sake, or for any personal gratification.

10. *He hath not dealt with us after our sins.* All may say this, and this *is* a ground of thanksgiving and praise. It is a matter for which we *should* render unceasing praise that God has not done to us as our sins deserved. Who of us can fail to stand in awe and to tremble when we think what God *might* have justly done to us; what sufferings he *might* have brought upon us, which would have been no more than we have

11 For [1] as the heaven is high above the earth, *so* great is his mercy toward them that fear him.

12 As far as the east is from the west, *so* far hath he removed

[1] *according to the height of heaven.*
g Jer. 1. 20.

g our transgressions from us.

13 Like as a father pitieth *his* children, *so* the LORD pitieth them that fear him.

14 For he knoweth our frame; he remembereth that we *are* dust.[h]

[h] Gen. iii. 19.

deserved; what pain of body, what distress of mind, what anguish of bereavement—what sorrow, danger, sickness, losses—we *might* have suffered before the point would be reached at which it could be said that we were suffering more than a holy and just God might properly inflict on us. ¶ *Nor rewarded us according to our iniquities.* That is, he has not inflicted suffering on us that could be regarded in any proper sense as a just retribution for what we have done; or, so that it could properly be said that the one fairly *measured* the other.

11. *For as the heaven is high above the earth.* See Notes on Ps. lvii. 10. Comp. Notes on Isa. lv. 9. The literal translation of the phrase here would be, *For like the height of the heavens above the earth.* The heavens—the starry heavens—are the highest objects of which we have any knowledge; and hence the comparison is used to denote the great mercy of God,—meaning that it is as great as can be conceived; that there is nothing beyond it; that we cannot imagine that it could be greater—as we can imagine nothing higher than the heavens. ¶ So *great is his mercy toward them that fear him.* To those who reverence and serve him. That is, His mercy is thus great in forgiving their offences; in imparting grace; in giving them support and consolation.

12. *As far as the east is from the west.* As far as possible; as far as we can imagine. These are the points in our apprehension most distant from each other, and as we can conceive nothing beyond them, so the meaning is, that we cannot imagine our sins could be more effectually removed

than they are. The literal meaning of the Hebrew is, *like the distance of the east from the west;* or, *like its being far.* ¶ So *far hath he removed our transgressions from us.* That is, he has put them entirely away. They are so removed that they cannot affect us any more. We are safe from all condemnation for our sins, as if they had not been committed at all. Comp. Notes on Isa. xliii. 25; xliv. 22.

13. *Like as a father pitieth* his *children.* Heb., *Like the compassion of a father for his children.* See Notes on Matt. vii. 9–11. God often compares himself with a father, and it is by carrying out our ideas of what enters into the parental character that we get our best conceptions of the character of God. See Notes on Matt. vi. 9. That which is referred to here, is the natural affection of the parent for the child; the tender love which is borne by the parent for his offspring; the disposition to care for its wants; the readiness to forgive when an offence has been committed. Comp. Luke xv. 22–24. Such, in an infinitely higher degree, is the compassion—the kindness—which God has for those that love him. ¶ So *the* LORD *pitieth them that fear him.* He has compassion on them. He exercises towards them the paternal feeling.

14. *For he knoweth our frame.* Our formation; of what we are made; how we are made. That is, he knows that we are made of dust; that we are frail; that we are subject to decay; that we soon sink under a heavy load. This is given as a reason why he pities us—that we *are* so frail and feeble, and that we are so easily broken down by a pressure of trial. ¶ *He remembereth that we* are *dust.* Made

15 *As for* man, his days *are* as grass; as a *i* flower of the field, so he flourisheth.

16 For the wind passeth over

i Isa. xl. 6—8 ; James i. 10, 11.

it, and it is [1] gone; and the place *k* thereof shall know it no more.

17 But the mercy of the LORD *is* from everlasting to everlasting

[1] *not.*   *k* Job xx. 9.

---

of the earth. Gen. ii. 7 ; iii. 19. In his dealings with us he does not forget of what frail materials he made us, and how little our frames can bear. He tempers his dealings to the weakness and frailty of our nature, and his compassion interposes when the weight of sorrows would crush us. Remembering, too, our weakness, he interposes by his power to sustain us, and to enable us to bear what our frame could not otherwise endure. Comp. Notes on Isa. lvii. 16.

15. As for *man.* Literally, "Man; like the grass are his days!" The thought is fixed on *man :*—man so frail and weak; man, not only made originally of earth, but man delicate, feeble, soon to pass away like the springing grass, or like the fading flower. ¶ *His days* are *as grass.* See Notes on Ps. xc. Notes on Isa. xl. 6—8; 1 Pet. i. 24. ¶ *As a flower of the field.* As a blossom. It opens with beauty and fragrance, but soon fades and perishes. ¶ *So he flourisheth.* Rather, "So he blossoms." That is, he is like a flower that is fresh and beautiful, and that soon withers away.

16. *For the wind passeth over it, and it is gone.* Marg., as in Heb., *it is not.* The reference is either to a hot and burning wind, that dries up the flower; or to a furious wind that tears it from its stem; or to a gentle breeze that takes off its petals as they loosen their hold, and are ready to fall. So man falls,—as if a breath — a breeze — came over him, and he is gone. How easily is man swept off! How little force, apparently, does it require to remove the most beautiful and blooming youth of either sex from the earth! How speedily does beauty vanish; how soon, like a fading flower, does such a one pass away! ¶ *And the place*

thereof shall know it no more. That is, It shall no more appear in the place where it was seen and known. The "place" is here personified as if capable of recognizing the objects which are present, and as if it missed the things which were once there. They are gone. So it will soon be in all the places where *we* have been; where we have been seen; where we have been known. In our dwellings; at our tables; in our places of business; in our offices, counting-rooms, studies, laboratories; in the streets where we have walked from day to day; in the pulpit, the court-room, the legislation-hall; in the place of revelry or festivity; in the prayer-room, the Sabbath-school, the sanctuary — we shall be seen no longer. We shall be GONE :—and the impression on those who *are* there, and with whom we have been associated, will be best expressed by the language, *he is gone!* Gone;—where? No one that survives can tell. All that they whom we leave will know will be that we are absent—that we are *gone.* But to us now, how momentous the inquiry, *Where shall we be, when we are gone from among the living?* Other places *will* "know" us; will it be in heaven, or hell?

17. *But the mercy of the* LORD. The favour of the Lord; or, his loving-kindness. ¶ *Is from everlasting to everlasting.* Is from the eternity past to the eternity to come. It had its foundation in the eternal decrees of God; it has its security in his purpose that where it is conferred, it shall not be withdrawn. It had no beginning; it will have no end. There never was a period in the past when it was not the purpose of God to save his people; there never will be a period in the future when it will be said that his saving mercy has

upon them that fear him, and his righteousness unto children's children:

18 To *l* such as keep his covenant, and to those that remember his commandments to do them.

l Ex. xx. 6 ; Deut. vii. 9.

19 The LORD hath prepared his *m* throne in the heavens; and his kingdom *n* ruleth over all.

20 Bless the LORD, ye his angels, [1] that excel in strength, *o* that do his commandments,

m Ps. xi. 4.   *n* Dan. iv. 34, 35.
[1] *mighty in.*   *o* Joel ii. 11.

---

ceased. It would be difficult to think of a statement which would at the same time, in so few words, confirm at once the doctrine of the Divine decrees, and the doctrine of the perseverance of the saints. If either of these doctrines is denied, then what is here stated by the psalmist is not true:—if the doctrine of the Divine decrees is denied, then his purpose of mercy had a beginning, and is not "*from* everlasting;" if the doctrine of the perseverance of the saints is denied, then his mercy has an end, and is not "*to* everlasting." ¶ *Upon them that fear him.* In respect to those who are his true worshippers, or his true people. ¶ *And his righteousness.* His righteous purpose; or, his purpose in regard to their *becoming* righteous. ¶ *Unto children's children.* Literally, *sons of sons.* That is, his purposes embrace the children and children's children of the righteous; or, they are included in the covenant of mercy. See Notes on Acts ii. 39. Comp. Ex. xx. 6.

18. *To such as keep his covenant.* To such as adhere to the arrangements of his covenant, or who are faithful on their part. God will be faithful to his part of the covenant; and where there is fidelity on the part of his people, the blessings implied in the covenant will be conferred on them and on their children. The promise is ample, and the fidelity of God is certain, but still it is true that *in* those promises, and *in* that fidelity, it is implied that his people on their part must be faithful also, or the blessings will not be bestowed. There are no promises of blessings to the unfaithful, nor have those who are unfaithful any reason to hope that

they or theirs will be partakers of the blessings of the covenant of mercy. Our only hope that we or our children will be partakers of the blessings of the covenant is to be found in the fact that we ourselves are faithful to God. ¶ *And to those that remember his commandments to do them.* Who do not *forget* his law. If they *do* forget it, they have no right to expect the blessing. Obedience and fidelity are our only reasonable grounds of expectation of the blessing of God.

19. *The LORD hath prepared his throne in the heavens.* He has *fixed* his throne there. This is the ground of the security that his blessing will be imparted to those who fear him, and to their children's children, or that it will be transmitted to coming generations. God is a Sovereign. His throne is fixed and firm. His dominion is not vacillating and changing. His reign is not, like the reign of earthly monarchs, dependent on the capriciousness of a changeable will, or on passion ; nor is it liable to be altered by death, by revolution, or a new dynasty. The throne of God is ever the same, and nothing can shake or overthrow it. Comp. Notes on Ps. xi. 4. ¶ *And his kingdom ruleth over all.* He reigns over all the universe—the heavens and the earth; and he can, therefore, execute all his purposes. Comp. Ps. xlvii. 2.

20. *Bless the* LORD. The psalm began (vers. 1, 2) with an exhortation to "bless the Lord." That exhortation was, however, then addressed by the psalmist to his own soul, and was especially founded on the benefits which he had himself received. The psalm closes also with

hearkening unto the voice of his word.

21 Bless ye the LORD, all *ye* his hosts; *ye* ministers *ᵖ* of his, that do his pleasure.

22 Bless the LORD, all *q* his works, in all places of his dominion : bless the LORD, O my soul.

p Dan. vii. 10; Heb. i. 14.   *q* Ps. cxlv. 10.

an exhortation to "bless the Lord," yet on a much wider scale. The psalmist feels that there is not only occasion for *him* to do it, but that the reason for it extends to the whole universe. The meaning is, that God is worthy of universal praise; and all ranks of beings—all worlds—should join in that praise. Man, feeble, frail, dying, could not come up to the fulness of the praise required. Praise such as was appropriate to God—such as his perfections and works deserved — demanded loftier powers than those of man;—the loftiest powers in the universe. ¶ *Ye his angels.* All beings higher than man; beings around and before his throne. ¶ *That excel in strength.* Marg., as in Heb., *mighty in strength,* and therefore more *able* to offer adequate praise. ¶ *That do his commandments.* Who perfectly obey his law, and who, therefore, can render more acceptable praise than can ever come from human lips. ¶ *Hearkening unto the voice of his word.* Who always listen to his voice; who never are disobedient; and who can, therefore, approach him *as* holy beings, and more appropriately worship him.

21. *Bless ye the* LORD, *all* ye *his hosts.* His armies; the vast multitudes of holy beings, arranged and marshalled as hosts for battle, in all parts of the universe. Comp. Notes on Isa. i. 9; Eph. i. 21. ¶ Ye *ministers of his.* The same beings referred to by the word "hosts," and all others who may be employed in executing his will. The "hosts" or armies of the Lord are thus marshalled that they *may* "do his pleasure," or that they may execute his purposes. ¶ *That do his pleasure.* What is agreeable to him; that is, who perform his will. Employed in his service, and appointed

to execute his will, they are called on to bless his name. The fact of *being* employed in his service is a sufficient reason for praise. It is implied here that those "ministers of his" actually *do* his will. They are obedient to his commands; they regard themselves *as* employed for him.

22. *Bless the* LORD, *all his works.* All that he has made, animate and inanimate, intelligent and brute. It is not uncommon to call on the inanimate creation to join with intelligent beings in praising God. Comp. Ps. cxlviii. The same thing is often found in the "Paradise Lost," and in fact occurs in all poetry. ¶ *In all places of his dominion.* Wherever he reigns, on earth, or in heaven; here or in distant worlds. ¶ *Bless the* LORD, *O my soul.* Ending the psalm as it began, and with the additional reason derived from the fact that the *universe* is called on to do it. As one of the creatures of God; as a part of that vast universe, the psalmist now calls on his own soul to unite with all others—to be one of them—in praising and blessing the Creator. He *desired* thus to unite with all others. His heart was full; and in a universe thus joyous—thus vocal with praise—he wished to be one among the immense multitudes that lifted their voices in adoration of the great Jehovah.

PSALM CIV.

This psalm in the Syriac, the Arabic, the Greek. and the Latin versions, is ascribed to David, but on what authority is now unknown. That it *may* have been composed by him cannot be doubted, but there is no certain evidence that he was the author. In the Hebrew, it has no title, and there is nothing in the psalm itself which would furnish any indication as to its authorship.

The occasion on which the psalm was

composed is unknown, and cannot now be ascertained. Rosenmüller and Hengstenberg suppose that it was at the time of the return from the Babylonish exile, and that it was intended to be used at the re-dedication of the temple. But it has no special applicability to such a service; it has no such local references as would fix it to that time; it has nothing which would make it inappropriate at *any* time, or in *any* public service. It is such a psalm as might be composed at any period of the world, or in any country, where there was an intelligent view and a careful observation of the works of God. It implies, indeed, such a knowledge of the fact that God made the world as could be obtained only by revelation; but it evinces also a power of close observation; a large acquaintance with the creation around us; a relish for the scenes of nature; as well as a rich poetic faculty, and a power of description, adapted to place such scenes before the mind as realities, and to make us feel, in reading it, that we are in the very midst of the things which are described,—so that they seem to live and move before our eyes.

The psalm was probably founded on the record of the creation in Gen. i., with a design to show that the order of the creation, as there described, *was adapted to the purposes which were intended, and was carried out in the providential arrangements now existing on the earth;* or, that, taking the order of the creation as described there, the existing state of things furnished an illustration of the wisdom and benevolence of that order. Accordingly, in the psalm, it was convenient for the writer to follow substantially the *order* observed in Gen. i. in narrating the creation of the world; and he states, under each part, the *acting out* of that order in existing things;—creation in its being actually carried out, or in its results—the creation *developing itself* in the varied and wonderful forms of being—of vegetable and animal life—of beauty, of harmonious movement, of ceaseless activity,—on the land, in the air, and in the waters. Accordingly there is in the psalm,—

I. An allusion to the work of the *first* day, vers. 2-5 (comp. Gen. i. 1-5): —to the stretching out of the heavens as a curtain; to the source of light,— "who coverest thyself with light as

with a garment;"—to the laying of the foundations of the earth to abide for ever;—to God as Creator of all things, with the additional ideas of his being clothed with honour and majesty; making the clouds his chariot; walking upon the wings of the wind; making the winds his messengers, and flames of fire his ministers.

II. An allusion to the work of the *second* day, vers. 6-9 (comp. Gen. i. 6-8). Here it is the separation of the waters—the power exerted on the waters of the earth;—in Genesis, the dividing of the waters above from those on the earth; in the psalm, the poetic images of the deep covering the earth as with a garment; the waters climbing up the mountains, and rolling down into the valleys, until they found the place appointed for them, a boundary which they could not pass so as to return again and cover the earth.

III. An allusion to the work of the *third* day, vers. 10-18 (comp. Gen. i. 9-13). In Genesis, the waters gathering together; the dry land appearing, and the earth yielding grass, and herbs, and fruit trees,—the creation of vegetables; in the psalm, the springs running into the valleys, and winding among the hills,—giving drink to the beasts, and quenching the thirst of wild asses,—furnishing a place for the fowls to build their nests, causing the grass to grow for the cattle, and herbs for the service of man,—supplying him wine to make him glad, and oil to make his face shine, and bread to strengthen his heart,—bringing forth the trees of the Lord, the cedars of Lebanon for the birds to make their nests, and the fir trees for the stork,—making the hills a refuge for the wild goats, and the rocks for the conies:—that is, the work of creation on the third day is seen by the eye of the psalmist not *as* mere *creation*, but in the *result*,—as enlivened and animated by all these varied forms of life, activity, and beauty, which had been spread over the earth as the *consequence* of this part of the work of creation.

IV. An allusion to the work of the *fourth* day, vers. 19-23 (comp. Gen. i. 14-19). Here, as in the previous divisions of the psalm, it is not a reference to the mere *creation*—to the power evinced—but to the creation of the sun and moon *as seen in the effects* produced by them—the living world as it is influenced by the sun and moon:—the sea-

PSALM CIV.

BLESS the LORD, O my soul.
O LORD, my God, thou art
very great; thou *r* art clothed
with honour and majesty:
  2 Who coverest *thyself* with

r Rev. i. 13, etc.

light *s* as *with* a garment; who
t stretchest out the heavens like
a curtain;
  3 Who *u* layeth the beams of
his chambers in the waters; who
maketh the clouds *v* his chariot;

s Dan. vii. 9; 1 Tim. vi. 16.
t Isa. xl. 22. u Amos ix. 6. v Isa. xix. 1.

---

sons—the alternations of day and night.
Thus (ver. 20), at night, when the sun
has gone down, all the beasts of the
forest are seen creeping forth; the lions
roar after their prey, and seek their
meat from God; and again when the
sun arises (vers. 22, 23), they are seen
gathering themselves together, and retiring to their dens, and *man* is seen
going forth to *his* work and to his labour
until the evening. It is thus not the
original act of creation which is before
the mind of the psalmist, but that act in
its development, or when it is seen what
God contemplated by it, or what he
intended that in this respect the world
should be when he made the sun, the
moon, and the stars.

  V. An allusion to the work of the *fifth*
day, vers. 24-30 (comp. Gen. i. 20-23);
the creation of *life* in the waters, and
in the air; as the fowls of heaven—the
whales, etc. Here, too, the psalmist
sees all this as it *is*,—or developed on
the sea, and in the air. *In* the sea
there are things creeping innumerable,
small and great; there are the ships;
there is leviathan; there is everywhere
animated life; there are beings innumerable all dependent on God; there
are the processes of renewing, creating,
destroying, continually going on — a
moving scene, showing the *effect* of *life*
as it is produced by God.

  VI. It is remarkable, however, that
the allusion to the successive days of
the work of creation, so obvious in the
other parts of the psalm, seems to close
here, and there is no distinct reference
to the sixth day, or the seventh,—to the
creation of *man* as the crowning work,
and to the *rest* provided for man in the
appointment of the Sabbath. The purpose of the psalmist seems to have been
to celebrate the praises of God in the
varied scene — the panorama passing
before the eye in the works of *nature*.
The purpose did not seem to be to contemplate *man*—his creation,—his history,—but *nature*, as seen around us.
The remainder of the psalm, therefore,

is occupied with a description of the
glory of the Lord *as thus manifested*;
the works of God as fitted to fill the
mind with exalted views of his greatness, and with a desire that his reign
may be universal and perpetual, vers.
31-35.

  1. *Bless the* LORD, *O my soul.* See
Ps. ciii. 1. ¶ *O* LORD *my God,
thou art very great.* This is a reason
why the psalmist calls on his soul to
bless God; viz., for the fact that he is
so exalted; so vast in his perfections;
so powerful, so wise, so great. ¶ *Thou
art clothed with honour and majesty.*
That is, with the emblems of honour
and majesty, as a king is arrayed in
royal robes. Creation is the garment
with which God has invested himself.
Comp. Notes on Ps. xciii. 1.

  2. *Who coverest* thyself *with light*
as with *a garment.* Referring to the
first work of creation (Gen. i. 3),
"And God said, Let there be light,
and there was light." He *seemed* to
put on light as a garment; he himself appeared as if invested with
light. It was the first *manifestation*
of God. He seemed at once to have
put on light as his robe. ¶ *Who
stretchest out the heavens like a curtain.* As an expanse spread over us.
The word here used means a curtain
or hanging, so called from its tremu-
lous motion, from a word meaning to
tremble. Thus it is applied to a curtain before a door; to a tent, etc.
It is applied here to the heavens, as
they seem to be *spread out* like the
curtains of a tent, as if God had
spread them out for a tent for himself to dwell in. See Notes on Isa.
xl. 22.

  3. *Who layeth the beams of his
chambers in the waters.* The word

who ^w walketh upon the wings of the wind;

4 Who ^x maketh his angels spirits; his ministers a flaming fire;^y

w Ps. xviii. 10.   x Heb. i. 7.
    y 2 Kings ii. 11; vi. 17.

here rendered *layeth* — from קָרָה, *karah*—means properly to meet; then, in Hiphil, to cause to meet, or to fit into each other, as beams or joists do in a dwelling. It is a word which would be properly applied to the construction of a house, and to the right adjustment of the different materials employed in building it. The word rendered *beams*—עֲלִיָּה, *aliyah*—means an upper chamber, a loft, such as rises, in Oriental houses, above the flat roof; in the New Testament, the ὑπερῷον, rendered *upper room*, Acts i. 13; ix. 37, 39; xx. 8. It refers here to the chamber—the exalted abode of God—as if raised *above* all other edifices, or *above* the world. The word *waters* here refers to the description of the creation in Gen. i. 6, 7,—the waters " above the firmament," and the waters " below the firmament." The allusion here is to the waters *above* the firmament; and the meaning is, that God had constructed the place of his own abode —the room where he dwelt—*in* those waters; that is, in the most exalted place in the universe. It does not mean that he made it *of* the waters, but that his home—his dwelling-place —was *in* or *above* those waters, *as if* he had built his dwelling not on solid earth or rock, but in the waters, giving stability to that which seems to have no stability, and making the very waters a foundation for the structure of his abode. ¶ *Who maketh the clouds his chariot.* Who rides on the clouds as in a chariot. See Notes on Isa. xix. 1. Comp. Notes on Ps. xviii. 11. ¶ *Who walketh upon the wings of the wind.* See Notes on Ps. xviii. 10.

4. *Who maketh his angels spirits.* The meaning here literally would be,

5 1 *Who* laid the foundations of the earth, *that* it should not be removed for ever.

6 Thou ^z coveredst it with the

1 *He hath founded the earth upon her bases.*
        z Gen. i. 9.

" Who makes the winds his messengers," or " his angels;" that is, who employs them to execute his purpose; who sends them out *as* messengers or angels to do his will. ¶ *His ministers a flaming fire.* That is, Fire is employed by him—in lightnings—to accomplish his purpose as his ministers or his servants. They are entirely under his command. They are sent by him to do his will; to carry out his designs. This is intended to describe the majesty and the power of God,—that he can employ wind and lightning—tempest and storm— to go on errands such as he commands; to fulfil his plans; to do his bidding. For the application of this to the angels, and as employed by the apostle Paul to prove the inferiority of the angels to the Messiah, see Notes on Heb. i. 7.

5. Who *laid the foundations of the earth.* Referring still to the creation of the earth. The margin is, *He hath founded the earth upon her bases.* The Hebrew word rendered in the margin *her bases* means properly a place; then a basis or foundation. The idea is, that there was something, as it were, placed *under* the earth to support it. The idea is not uncommon in the Scriptures. Comp. Notes on Job xxxviii. 4. ¶ *That it should not be removed for ever.* So that it cannot be shaken out of its place. That is, It is fixed, permanent, solid. Its foundations do not give way, as edifices reared by man, but it abides the same from age to age—the most fixed and stable object of which we have any knowledge. Comp. Notes on Ps. lxxviii. 69.

6. *Thou coveredst it with the deep as* with *a garment.* Comp. Notes on Job xxxviii. 9. The meaning is, that

deep as *with* a garment: the waters stood above the " mountains.

7 At thy rebuke they fled; at the voice of thy thunder they hasted away.

8 ¹ They go up by the moun-

a Ps. xxxiii. 7, 9.
¹ Or, *the mountains ascend, the valleys descend.*

tains; they go down by the valleys unto the place which thou hast founded for them.

9 Thou ᵇ hast set a bound that they may not pass over, that they turn not again to cover the earth.

b Job xxxviii. 10, 11.

God covered the earth with the sea—the waters—the abyss—as if a garment had been spread over it. The reference is to Gen. i. 2, where, in the account of the work of creation, what is there called " *the deep* "—the abyss—(the same Hebrew word as here—תְּהוֹם, *tehom*)—covered the earth, or was what *appeared*, or was manifest, before the waters were collected into seas, and the dry land was seen. ¶ *The waters stood above the mountains.* Above what are now the mountains. As yet no dry land appeared. It seemed to be one wide waste of waters. This does not refer to the Deluge, but to the appearance of the earth at the time of the creation, before the gathering of the waters into seas and oceans, Gen. i. 9. At that stage in the work, all that appeared was a wide waste of waters.

7. *At thy rebuke they fled.* At thy command; or when thou didst speak to them. The Hebrew word also implies the notion of *rebuke*, or *reproof*, as if there were some displeasure or dissatisfaction. Prov. xiii. 1; xvii. 10; Eccl. vii. 5; Isa. xxx. 17; Ps. lxxvi. 6. It is *as if* God had been displeased that the waters prevented the appearing or the rising of the dry land, and had commanded them to *hasten* to their beds and channels, and no longer to cover the earth. The allusion is to Gen. i. 9, and there is nowhere to be found a more sublime expression than this. Even the command, " And God said, Let there be light; and there was light," so much commended by Longinus as an instance of sublimity, does not surpass this in grandeur. ¶ *At the voice of thy thunder they hasted*

away. They fled in dismay. The Hebrew word—יֵחָפֵזוּן, *hhaphaz*—contains the idea of haste, trepidation, consternation, alarm, *as if* they were frightened; Ps. xxxi. 22. God spake in tones of thunder, and they fled. It is impossible to conceive anything more sublime than this.

8. *They go up by the mountains,* etc. That is, when they were gathered together into seas. They seemed to roll and tumble over hills and mountains, and to run down in valleys, until they found the deep hollows which had been formed for seas, and where they were permanently collected together. The margin here is, *The mountains ascend, the valleys descend.* So it is translated in the Septuagint, in the Latin Vulgate, by Luther, and by De Wette. The more natural idea, however, is that in our translation: " They [the waters] go up mountains; they descend valleys." ¶ *Unto the place.* The deep hollows of the earth, which seem to have been scooped out to make a place for them. ¶ *Which thou hast founded for them.* Where thou hast laid a permanent foundation for them on which to rest; that is, which thou hast prepared for them.

9. *Thou hast set a bound that they may not pass over.* See Notes on Job xxvi. 10; xxxviii. 10, 11. ¶ *That they turn not again to cover the earth.* As it was before the dry land appeared; or as the earth was when " darkness was upon the face of the deep" (Gen. i. 2), and when all was mingled earth and water. It is *possible* that in connexion with this, the psalmist may also have had his eye

10 [1] He sendeth the springs into the valleys, which [2] run among the hills.

11 They give drink to every beast of the field : the wild asses [3] quench their thirst.

[1] Who.   [2] walk.

12 By them shall the fowls of the heaven have their habitation, which [4] sing among the branches.

13 He watereth the hills from his chambers : the earth is satisfied with the fruit of thy works.

[3] break.   [4] give a voice.

on the facts connected with the deluge in the time of Noah, and the promise then made that the world should no more be destroyed by a flood, Gen. ix. 11, 15.

10. *He sendeth the springs into the valleys.* Though the waters are gathered together into seas, yet God has taken care that the earth shall not be dry, parched, and barren. He has made provision for watering it, and by a most wise, wonderful, and benevolent arrangement, he has formed springs among the valleys and the hills. It is now animated nature which comes before the eye of the psalmist; and all this he traces to the fact that the earth is *watered*, and that it is not a waste of rocks and sands. The allusion in this part of the psalm (see the Introd.) is to the earth as covered with vegetation,—or, to the third day of the week of creation (Gen. i. 9–13), which, in Genesis, is connected with the gathering of the waters into seas. This description continues to vers. 18. The literal rendering here would be, "sending springs into the valleys." He conducts the waters from the great reservoirs—lakes and seas—in such a way that they form springs in the valleys. The way in which this is done is among the most wonderful and the most benevolent in nature,—by that power, derived from heat, by which the waters of the ocean, contrary to the natural law of gravitation, are lifted up in small particles—in vapour—and carried by the clouds where they are needed, and let fall upon the earth, to water the plants, and to form fountains, rivulets, and streams,—and borne thus to the highest mountains, to be filtered through the ground to form springs and

streams below. ¶ Which *run among the hills.* Marg., *walk.* That is, they go between the hills. The streams of water flow along in the natural valleys which have been made for them.

11. *They give drink to every beast of the field.* All are thus kept alive. The wild beasts that roam at large, find water thus provided for them. ¶ *The wild asses quench their thirst.* Marg., as in Heb., *break.* The meaning is, that the most wild and ungovernable of beasts—those which are farthest from the habits of domesticated animals, and the most independent of any aid derived from man, find abundance everywhere. On the word rendered *wild asses,* and on the habits of the animals here referred to, see Notes on Job xi. 12.

12. *By them shall the fowls of the heaven have their habitation.* Among them the fowls of the air dwell. That is, among the trees which spring up by the fountains and water-courses. The whole picture is full of animation and beauty. ¶ Which *sing among the branches.* Marg., as in Heb., *give a voice.* Their voice is heard— their sweet music—in the foliage of the trees which grow on the margin of the streams and by the fountains. There is scarcely to be found a more beautiful poetic image than this.

13. *He watereth the hills from his chambers.* The waters, as stated before, run in the valleys—in the natural channels made for them among the hills, ver. 10. But still, it was a fact that the hills themselves were watered; that there were springs far up their heights; and that vegetation was sustained above the reach of the fountains and streams below; and it was a proof of the Divine skill and beneficence

14 He causeth *c* the grass to grow for the cattle, and herb for the service of man, that he may bring forth food out of the earth; 15 And wine *that* maketh

c Ps. lxv. 9, 10.

glad the heart of man, *and* [1] oil to make *his* face to shine, and bread *which* strengtheneth man's heart.

[1] *to make* his *face shine with oil,* or, *more than oil.*

---

that, in some way, water was furnished on the summits and sides of the hills themselves. This was caused, the psalmist says, by God's pouring water on them, as it were, from his own "chambers"—his abode on high. The allusion is, doubtless, to rain, which seems to be poured down from the very abode of God. The word rendered *chambers* means *upper rooms,* (see Notes on ver. 3); and the reference is to the dwelling-place of God, as far above the earth. ¶ *The earth is satisfied with the fruit of thy works.* Thy doings; with what thou hast done. All the wants of the earth seem to be met and "satisfied;" all that it could desire to make it fertile and beautiful; and the proper abode of man, of beast, and of fowl, has been granted. It has no cause of complaint; nothing has been left undone, in the valleys or on the hills, on the dry land or in the waters, that was needful to be done to carry out the purpose for which it has been called into being.

14. *He causeth the grass to grow for the cattle.* Out of the earth there is caused to grow every variety of food necessary for the various orders of beings that are placed upon it. The idea here is not merely that of *abundance;* it is also that of *variety:*—the wants and tastes of all have been consulted in the productions of the earth. The one earth—the same earth—has been made to produce the endless varieties of food required for the creatures that have been placed on it. The word *grass* here refers to all the vegetable productions needful for cattle. ¶ *And herb for the service of man.* Gen. i. 29. The word *herb* here would include every green plant or vegetable; or all that the earth produces for the food of man. This, of

course, refers to the earth as it came from the hand of God, and to the original arrangement, before permission was given to man to eat the flesh of animals, Gen. ix. 3. The word translated *service* might be rendered *culture,*—as if man was to cultivate it for his use, not that it was to be produced, as the food for cattle, spontaneously. ¶ *That he may bring forth food out of the earth.* Heb., *bread.* That is, that by culture he may bring forth that which would make bread.

15. *And wine* that *maketh glad the heart of man,* etc. Literally, "And wine [it] gladdens the heart of man to make his face to shine more than oil." Marg., *to make his face shine with oil,* or *more than oil.* The latter expresses the idea most accurately. So De Wette renders it. The meaning is, that the earth is made to produce wine (or grapes which produce wine), and this exhilarates the heart, so that the effect is seen on the countenance, making it more bright and cheerful than it is when anointed with oil. On the use of oil, see Notes on Ps. xxiii. 5. The reference here, in the original, is not to wine *and* oil as produced by the earth, as would seem to be implied in our translation, but to wine that makes the heart glad, and the face brighter than if anointed with oil. The psalmist here states a *fact* about the use of wine—a well-known fact that it exhilarates the heart, and brightens the countenance; and he states it merely *as* a fact. He says nothing on the question whether the use of wine as a beverage is, or is not, proper and safe. Comp. Notes on John ii. 10. ¶ *And bread* which *strengtheneth man's heart.* That is, Which sustains the heart, — that being regarded as the seat of life. Comp. Gen. xviii. 5.

16 The trees of the LORD are full *of sap :* the cedars *d* of Lebanon, which he hath planted ;

17 Where the birds make

d Ps. xcii. 12.

their nests : *as for* the stork, the fir-trees *are* her house.

18 The high hills *are* a refuge for the wild goats, *and* the rocks for the conies.

16. *The trees of the* LORD. From the grass, from the herb, from the vine, and from bread, as adapted to sustain the living beings upon the earth, the psalmist passes to the more lofty and grand productions of the vegetable world—to those which display more manifestly the power of God, and which furnish abodes and retreats for the various orders of living beings. The phrase "the trees of the Lord" means great and magnificent trees—as the expression "mountains of God" means great and lofty mountains—as if they seemed to *approach* God, or as if no appellation would so well describe their nature as that which was derived from the Infinite One. See Notes on Ps. xxxvi. 6; lxv. 9; lxxx. 10. ¶ *Are full* of sap. The word so rendered means merely to be full, to be saturated,—the words "of sap" being supplied by the translators. The idea is, that, lofty as they are, they are abundantly supplied with that which is necessary to their growth. There is no want—no lack—of that which is needful to supply them. They flourish, sustained abundantly by that which is derived from the earth and the waters. ¶ *The cedars of Lebanon.* As among the loftiest and most magnificent productions of the earth. See Notes on Ps. xxix. 5; xcii. 12; Isa. ii. 13. ¶ *Which he hath planted.* So lofty and large, that it would seem as if none *could* plant them but the Almighty.

17. *Where the birds make their nests.* Furnishing a home for the birds where they may breed their young. In ver. 12, the birds are introduced as singing among the foliage of trees and shrubs by the watercourses ; here they are introduced as having their home in the lofty cedars in places which God had made for them. The word rendered *birds* here

is the word which in Ps. lxxxiv. 3 is translated *sparrow,* and which is commonly used to denote *small* birds. Comp. Lev. xiv. 4 (margin), and 5–7, 49–53. It is used, however, to denote birds of any kind. See Gen. vii. 14 ; Ps. viii. 8; xi. 1; cxlviii. 10. ¶ As for *the stork.* See Notes on Job xxxix. 13. ¶ *The fir trees* are *her house.* Her retreat ; her abode. The *stork* here is used to represent the larger class of birds. The meaning is, that they build their nests among the fir-trees or cypresses. See Notes on Isa. xiv. 8; xli. 19. So Milton says,—

> "The eagle and the *stork*
> On cliffs and cedar-tops their eyries build."

They build their nests, however, not only on fir and pine trees, but on houses and castles. Dr. Thomson ("Land and the Book," vol. i. p. 504), says of them, "These singular birds do not breed in Syria, but pass over it to Asia Minor, and into Northwestern Europe, where they not only build in fir and pine trees upon the mountains, but also enter cities and villages, and make their nests on houses, castles, and minarets."

18. *The high hills* are *a refuge for the wild goats.* Still keeping up the description of animated nature—the carrying out of the work of creation. The idea is, that nature is full of life. Even the most inaccessible places— the rocks—the high hills—have their inhabitants. Where man cannot climb or dwell, there are abodes of animals which God has made to dwell there, and which find there a refuge—a shelter— a home. On the word here used, and rendered *wild goats,* see Notes on Job xxxix. 1. The word occurs elsewhere only in 1 Sam. xxiv. 2. ¶ *And the rocks for the conies.* The word here employed—שָׁפָן, *Shaphan*—denotes a quadruped that chews the cud, in the manner of a hare (Lev. xi. 5 ; Deut.

19 He appointed the moon for seasons: the sun knoweth his going down.

20 Thou makest darkness, and it is night, wherein all the beasts [1] of the forest do creep *forth.*

21 The young lions *e* roar

[1] *thereof do trample on the forest.*
e Job xxxviii. 39.

---

xiv. 7), and living in flocks. The Rabbins render it the *coney,* or rabbit, as our translators have done. The habits of the rabbit accord with this description. The word occurs nowhere else, except in Prov. xxx. 26, where it is rendered, as here, *conies.*

19. *He appointed the moon for seasons.* Gen. i. 14—18. That is, The moon, as well as the sun, is appointed to divide time; to determine its progress; to indicate the return of festival occasions, or appointed times to be observed in any manner. It is, in fact, the foundation of the division of the year into *months,* and consequently the indication of all that is to be observed in the *months* of the year. But for this, there would be no natural divisions of time except those of day and night, and of the year. How great an advantage it is for the purpose of life, to have time broken up into brief intervals or periods which can be marked and remembered, both in our private life and in history, it is not necessary to say. God has been pleased to *add* to the natural divisions of time into days, and years, and months, an *artificial* division—the *fourth* part of the moon's course—*a week,* indicated by the Sabbath, thus greatly facilitating the plans of life in regard to stated times or "seasons," and especially in regard to religious observances. The idea in the passage before us is, that the whole arrangement is one of benevolence, promoting the comfort of man, and bringing the ideas of succession, variety, and beauty into the system. ¶ *The sun knoweth his going down.* As if conscious of what he is doing, he knows the exact time of setting, and never varies, but always obeys the Divine command; never sets *before* his time—unexpectedly shortening the day, and leaving man in sudden darkness in the midst of his toil; and never lingers above the horizon *after* the moment has come for his setting, but withdraws at the exact time, enabling man to close his toil, and seek repose, and giving an opportunity for another class of creatures to come forth on the animated scene. Their good is regarded as well as that of man; and the operations of nature are so arranged as to promote the welfare of all.

20. *Thou makest darkness, and it is night.* Thou hast made arrangements for the return of night—for the alternations of day and night. The Hebrew word rendered *makest,* means *to place;* and the idea is, that God constitutes the darkness, or so disposes things that it occurs. ¶ *Wherein all the beasts of the forest.* The margin is, *the beasts thereof do trample on the forest.* The reference is to the beasts which seek their prey at night. ¶ *Do creep* forth. The Hebrew word here used means properly *to creep,* as the smaller animals do, which have feet, as mice, lizards, crabs, or as those do which glide or drag themselves upon the ground, having no feet, as worms and serpents. Gen. i. 21, 26, 28, 30; ix. 2. The allusion here is to the quiet and noiseless manner in which the animals come forth at night in search of their prey, or seem to crawl out of their hiding-places—the places where they conceal themselves in the day-time. The idea is, that the arrangements which God has made in regard to day and night are wisely adapted to the animals which he has placed on the earth. The earth is full of animated beings, accomplishing by day and night the purposes of their existence.

21. *The young lions roar after their prey.* This is a continuation of the description in the previous verse. At night the beasts which had been hidden in the day-time crawl forth, and seek their food.

after their prey, and seek their meat from God.

22 The sun ariseth, they gather themselves together, and lay them down in their dens.

23 Man *f* goeth forth unto his

f Gen. iii. 19.

work and to his labour, until the evening.

24 O Lord, how manifold are thy works! in wisdom *g* hast thou made them all: the earth is full of thy riches.

g Prov. iii. 19.

The lion is particularly specified as one of the beasts that in a general survey would attract attention. The psalmist hears his "roar" as he goes forth in the forest in pursuit of his prey. ¶ *And seek their meat from God.* Their food. That is, God bestows it on them, and they act *as if* they sought it at his hand. They seek it where he has placed it; they are dependent on him for it. It is a beautiful idea that even the brute creation act as if they called on God, and sought the supply of their wants at his hands.

22. *The sun ariseth.* A new scene in this endless variety of incidents in a world full of life and beauty. The psalmist sees the light break in the east, and the sun appear above the horizon, — and the whole scene is changed. The animals that had gone forth at night are seen to return again to their hiding-places, and man in *his* turn (ver. 23) is seen to go forth to his daily toil. ¶ *They gather themselves together.* Though scattered in the night, when light returns, they all bend their steps to the places where they are accustomed to repose in the daytime. The scene is most beautiful. At night they sally forth for their prey; when the morning light returns, they all retrace their steps to the places in dens and caverns where they pass the day, and there they repose in silence until night returns again.

23. *Man goeth forth,* etc. Man is now seen to go forth from his dwelling, and he appears on the stage to perform his daily toil, until evening comes, and then again he gives way for the beasts of night. Thus the scene is ever varying,—showing how full of animated existence the earth

is; how varied are the occupations of its different inhabitants; and how the varieties of being are adapted to its own varied condition in the alternations of day and night.

24. *O Lord, how manifold are thy works!* Literally, *how many.* The reference is to the *number* and the *variety* of the works of God, and to the wisdom displayed in them all. The earth is not fitted up merely for one class of inhabitants, but for an almost endless variety; and the wisdom of God is manifested alike in the number *and* in the variety. No one can estimate the *number* of beings God has made on the earth; no one can comprehend the richness of the variety. By day the air, the earth, the waters swarm with life,—life struggling everywhere as if no place was to be left unoccupied; even for the dark scenes of night countless numbers of beings have been created; and, in all this immensity of numbers, there is an endless variety. No two are alike. Individuality is everywhere preserved, and the mind is astonished and confounded alike at the numbers and the variety. ¶ *In wisdom hast thou made them all.* That is, Thou hast adapted each and all to the different ends contemplated in their creation. Any one of these beings shows the wisdom of God in its formation, and in its adaptations to the ends of its existence; how much more is that wisdom displayed in these countless numbers, and in this endless variety! ¶ *The earth is full of thy riches.* Heb., *possessions.* So the LXX. and the Vulgate. That is, these various objects thus created are regarded as the *possession* of God; or, they *belong* to him, as the property of a man belongs to himself. The psalmist says

25 *So is* this great and wide
h sea, wherein *are* things creeping innumerable, both small and
great beasts.

26 There go the ships; *there is*
that leviathan, *i whom* thou hast
1 made to play therein.

h Ps. xcv. 5.   *i* Job xli. 1, etc.

27 These wait all upon thee,
that thou mayest give *them* their
meat in due season.

28 *That* thou givest them they
gather : thou *k* openest thine
hand, they are filled with good.

1 formed.   *k* Ps. cxlv. 16.

---

that this wealth or property abounds
everywhere; the earth is full of it.
25. So is *this great and wide sea,*
etc. Our translation here does not
quite express the beauty and the
force of the original;—"This sea!
Great and broad of hands! There
is the creeping thing,—and there is
no number; animals,—the little with
the great." The reference here is,
undoubtedly to the Mediterranean
Sea, which not improbably was in
sight when the psalm was composed,
—as it is in sight not only along the
coast, but from many of the elevations in Palestine. The phrase "wide
of hands" applied to the sea, means
that it seems to stretch out in all
directions.   Comp.   Notes on Isa.
xxxiii. 21. The *creeping things* refer
to the variety of inhabitants of the
deep that glide along *as if* they crept.
See Notes on ver. 20. The word
beasts refers to any of the inhabitants of the deep, and the idea is that
there is an endless variety *there.*
This reflection cannot but impress
itself on the mind of any one when
looking on the ocean : What a countless *number,* and what a vast *variety* of
inhabitants are there in these waters
—all created by God; all provided
for by his bounty !
26. *There go the ships.* There the
vessels move along — objects that
would, of course, attract the attention of one looking at the sea, and
admiring its wonders. The psalmist
is describing the active scenes on the
surface of the globe, and, of course,
on looking at the ocean, these would
be among the objects that would
particularly attract his attention.
¶ There is *that leviathan.* The Septuagint and the Vulgate render this,

dragon. On the meaning of the word
leviathan, see Notes on Job xli. 1.
¶ Whom *thou hast made.* Marg., as
in Heb., *formed.* The idea of *creation* is implied in the word. ¶ *To
play therein.* As his native element.
To move about therein; to make
quick and rapid motions, as if in
sport.
27. *These wait all upon thee.* That
is, These are all dependent on thee.
It does not, of course, mean that
they "wait" in the sense that they
are conscious of their dependence on
God, but that they are *actually* dependent. The original word implies
the idea of *expecting* or *hoping,* and
is so rendered in the Septuagint and
Vulgate. They have no other ground
of expectation or hope but in thee.
¶ *That thou mayest give* them *their
meat in due season.* Their food at
the proper time. That is, They are
constantly dependent on thee, that
thou mayest give them food from day
to day. Perhaps there is also the
idea that they do not lay up or hoard
anything; or that they cannot anticipate their own wants, but must
receive from one day to another all
that they want directly from God.
28. That *thou givest them they
gather.* What thou dost place before
them they collect. They have no
resources of their own. They can in-
vent nothing; they cannot vary their
food by art, as man does; they cannot make use of reason, as man does,
or of skill, in preparing it, to suit and
pamper the appetite. It comes prepared for them direct from the hand
of God. ¶ *Thou openest thine hand.*
As one does who bestows a gift on
another. The point in the passage
is, that they receive it immediately

29 Thou hidest thy face, they are troubled; thou takest away their breath, they die, and return to their dust.

30 Thou *l* sendest forth thy

l Gen. ii. 7; Job xxxiii. 4.
[1] *be.*

spirit, they are created; and thou renewest the face of the earth.

31 The glory of the LORD shall [1] endure for ever: the LORD shall rejoice *m* in his works.

m Gen. i. 31; Isa. lxii. 5.

---

from God, and that they are wholly dependent on him for it. They have not to labour to prepare it, but it is made ready for them, and they have only to gather it up. The allusion in the *language* may be to the gathering of manna in the wilderness, when it was provided by God, and men had only to collect it for their use. So it is with the brute creation on land and in the waters. ¶ *They are filled with good.* They are *satisfied* with good; that is, They are satisfied with what to them is good, or with what supplies their wants.

29. *Thou hidest thy face.* As if God turned away from them; as if he was displeased with them; as if he withdrew from them the tokens of his friendship and favour. ¶ *They are troubled.* They are confounded; they are overwhelmed with terror and amazement. The word *troubled* by no means conveys the sense of the original word—בָּהַל, *bahal*—which means properly to tremble; to be in trepidation; to be filled with terror; to be amazed; to be confounded. It is that kind of consternation which one has when all support and protection are withdrawn, and when inevitable ruin stares one in the face. So when God turns away, all their support is gone; all their resources fail, *and they must die.* They are represented as conscious of this; or, this is what would occur if they *were* conscious. ¶ *Thou takest away their breath.* Withdrawing that which thou gavest to them. ¶ *They die, and return to their dust.* Life ends when thou dost leave them, and they return again to earth. So it is also with man. When God withdraws from him, nothing remains for him *but to die.*

30. *Thou sendest forth thy spirit,*

they are created. That is, New races are created in their place, or start up as if they were created directly by God. They derive their being from him as really as those did which were first formed by his hand, and the work of creation is constantly going on. ¶ *And thou renewest the face of the earth.* The earth is not suffered to become desolate. Though one generation passes off, yet a new one is made in its place, and the face of the earth constantly puts on the aspect of freshness and newness.

31. *The glory of the LORD shall endure for ever.* Marg., as in Heb., *shall be.* It might be rendered, "Let the glory of the Lord be for ever," implying a strong desire that it should be so. But the language may denote a strong conviction that it *would* be so. The mind of the writer was filled with wonder at the beauty and variety of the works of God on the land, in the air, and in the waters; and he exclaims, with a heart full of admiration, that the glory of a Being who had made all these things could never cease, but must endure for ever. All the glory of man would pass away; all the monuments that he would rear would be destroyed; all the works of art executed by him must perish; but the glory of One who had made the earth, and filled it with such wonders, could not but endure for ever and ever. ¶ *The LORD shall rejoice in his works.* See Gen. i. 31. The idea here is, that God finds pleasure in the contemplation of his own works; in the beauty and order of creation; and in the happiness which he sees as the result of his work of creation. There is no impropriety in supposing that God finds pleasure in the mani-

32 He looketh on the earth, and it trembleth; [n] he toucheth the hills, and they smoke.[o]

33 I will sing unto the LORD as long as I live; I will sing praise to my God while I have

n Hab. iii. 10.   *o* Ex. xix. 18.

festation of the wisdom, the power, the goodness, the mercy, and the love of his own glorious nature.

32. *He looketh on the earth, and it trembleth.* There is great sublimity in this expression, as indicating the power and the majesty of God. He has only to *look* upon his works, and they stand in awe and tremble. The most mighty and fearful convulsions of nature occur *as if* they were the mere effect of God's *looking* on the earth. Comp. Hab. iii. 10,—"The mountains saw thee, and they trembled." ¶ *He toucheth the hills, and they smoke.* That is, as Mount Sinai did when God came down upon it. Ex. xix. 18. It is as if the hills were conscious of his presence, and were awed.

33. *I will sing unto the* LORD *as long as I live.* That is, I will continue to praise him ; I will never cease to adore him. The result of the psalmist's meditations on the wonderful works of God is to awaken in his mind a desire to praise God for ever. He is so filled with a sense of his greatness and glory that he sees that there would be occasion for eternal praise; or that the reason for praise could never be exhausted. He who has any proper sense of the greatness, the majesty, and the glory of God *intends* to praise him for ever. He sees that there is enough in the character of God to demand eternal praise, and he does not anticipate that a period can ever occur in all the future when he will feel that the causes for praise have come to an end, or when his heart will be indisposed to celebrate that praise.

34. *My meditation of him shall be sweet.* That is, I will find pleasure in meditating on his character and works.

my being.

34 My [p] meditation of him shall be sweet: I will be glad [q] in the LORD.

35 Let [r] the sinners be consumed out of the earth, and let

p Ps. lxiii. 5, 6.   *q* Ps. xxxii. 11.   *r* Prov. ii. 22.

See Notes on Ps. i. 2. It is one of the characteristics of true piety that there is a *disposition* to think about God; that the mind is *naturally* drawn to that subject ; that it does not turn away from it, when it is suggested ; that this fills up the intervals of business in the day-time, and that it occupies the mind when wakeful at night. Ps. lxiii. 6. It is also a characteristic of true piety that there is *pleasure* in such meditations ; happiness in thinking of God. The sinner has no such pleasure. The thought of God is painful to him ; he does not desire to have it suggested to him; he turns away from it, and avoids it. Comp. Notes on Isa. xxx. 11. It is one of the evidences of true piety when a man *begins* to find pleasure in thinking about God ; when the subject, instead of being unpleasant to him, becomes pleasant ; when he no longer turns away from it, but is sensible of a desire to cherish the thought of God, and to know more of him. ¶ *I will be glad in the* LORD. That is, I will rejoice that there *is* such a Being ; I will seek my happiness *in* him as my God.

35. *Let the sinners be consumed out of the earth.* Comp. Ps. xxxvii. 38. This might with propriety be rendered, "Consumed are the sinners out of the earth,"—expressing a *fact* and not a *desire;* and it may have been prompted by the feeling of the psalmist that such an event *would* occur; that is, that the time would come when sin would no more abound, but when the world would be filled with righteousness, and all the dwellers on the earth *would* praise God. The word translated *consumed*—from םמַתָּ, *tamam*—means properly to complete, to perfect, to finish, to cease. It

the wicked ^s be no more. Bless

s Ps. i. 4.

thou the LORD, O my soul.
Praise ye the LORD.

does not mean *consume* in the sense of being burned up—as our word means —or destroyed, but merely to come to an end, to cease, to pass away :—that is, Let the time soon come,—or, the time will soon come,—when there will be no sinners on the earth, but when all the inhabitants of the earth will worship and honour God. The *con-nexion* here seems to be this : The psalmist was himself so filled with the love of God, and with admiration of his works, that he desired that *all* might partake of the same feeling ; and he looked forward, therefore, as those who love God must do, to the time when all the dwellers on earth would see his glory, and when there should be none who did not adore and love him. All that is *fairly* implied in the wish of the psalmist here would be accomplished if all sinners were converted, and if, in that sense, there were to be no more transgressors in the world. ¶ *And let the wicked be no more.* Let there not be any more wicked persons ; let the time come when there shall be no bad men on the earth, but when all shall be righ-teous. In this prayer all persons could properly unite. ¶ *Bless thou the* LORD, *O my soul.* The psalm closes (as Ps. ciii. does) as it began. The psalmist commenced with the ex-pression of a purpose to bless God ; it closes with the same purpose, con-firmed by a survey of the wonderful works of God. ¶ *Praise ye the* LORD. Heb., *Hallelu-jah.* The psalmist ex-presses the earnest desire of a truly pious heart (in looking upon a world so beautiful, so varied in its works, so full of the expressions of the wisdom and goodness of God—a world where all the inferior creation so completely carries out the purpose of the Creator), that *man*, the noblest of all the works of God, might unite with the world around and beneath him in carrying out the great purpose of the creation, —so that he might, in his own proper

place, and according to the powers with which he is endowed, acknow-ledge God. How beautiful—how sub-lime—would be the spectacle on earth, if *man* accomplished the purpose of *his* creation, and filled *his* place, as well as the springs, the hills, the trees, the fowls, the wild goats, the moon, the sun, the young lions, and the inhabitants of the " great and wide sea " do in their spheres ! Oh, come the time when on earth there shall be harmony in all the works of God, and when all creatures here shall carry out the purpose which was contemplated when God called the earth into exist-ence.

PSALM CV.

The author of this psalm is unknown, as is the occasion on which it was com-posed. It resembles the seventy-eighth psalm in the fact that both are of an his-torical nature, recounting the dealings of God with his people in their deliver-ance from the bondage in Egypt. The object of the former psalm, however, seems to have been *to recall the nation from their sins,* and to vindicate the dealings of God with the Hebrews in his arrangements for their government, or in the change of the administration, by giving the government to the tribe of Judah under David, rather than to Ephraim ; the object of this psalm is *to excite the people to gratitude* by the re-membrance of the goodness of God to the people in former times. Accordingly this psalm is occupied with recounting the mercies of God—his various acts of intervention in their history—all ap-pealing to the nation to cherish a grate-ful remembrance of those acts, and to love and praise him.

The first sixteen verses of the psalm are substantially the same as the first part of the psalm composed by David when he brought up the ark, as recorded in 1 Chron. xvi. 8-22. But at that point the resemblance ceases. Probably the author of this psalm found in the one composed by David what was suit-able to the occasion on which this was composed, and adopted it without any material change. In the remainder of

PSALM CV.

O *t* GIVE thanks unto the LORD; call upon his name; make *u* known his deeds among the people.

t 1 Chron. xvi. 8—22.   *u* Isa. xii. 4.

2 Sing unto him, sing psalms unto him: talk ye of all his wondrous works.

3 Glory ye in his holy name: let the heart of them rejoice that seek the LORD.

---

the psalm, he has simply carried out in the history of the Jews what was suggested by David in the psalm in 1 Chron. xvi., and has applied the idea to the other events of the Jewish history, as furnishing a ground of praise. The psalm is a mere summary of the principal events of that history to the time when the people entered the promised land,—as laying the foundation of praise to God.

1. *O give thanks unto the* LORD. The design here is to show that thanks should be given to the Lord in view of his dealings with his people, as stated in the subsequent portions of the psalm. ¶ *Call upon his name.* More literally, "Call him *by* his name;" that is, Address him by his proper title; ascribe to him the attributes which properly belong to him; or, address him in a proper manner. ¶ *Make known his deeds among the people.* What he has done in former times. The allusion is to his acts in behalf of his people in delivering them from Egyptian bondage, and bringing them to the promised land. The word "people" here refers to the Hebrew people; and the exhortation is, that the knowledge of these deeds should be diffused and kept up among them. One of the ways of doing this was that proposed by the psalmist, to wit, by a psalm of praise—by recording and celebrating these acts in their devotions. One of the most effective modes of keeping up the knowledge of what God has done in our world is by songs of praise in worshipping assemblies.

2. *Sing unto him.* Sing before him; offer him praise. ¶ *Sing psalms unto him.* The word here rendered *sing psalms* means properly to *prune,* and then, to *cut off,* as a discourse at regular periods; or, to utter in rhyth-

mical numbers; and then it means to accompany such words with an instrument of music. The idea here is, that he is to be approached, not merely with *singing,* but with sentiments expressed in the form of regular composition—in musical numbers. ¶ *Talk ye.* The word here used very commonly means to meditate, to muse (comp. Notes on Ps. i. 2), but would here seem to be employed in the sense of *talking over,* to wit, in singing. That is, In the psalms used let there be a *narrative* of what God has done. Let his works be the subject of the words used in the psalm. ¶ *Of all his wondrous works.* Of what he has done that is fitted to excite wonder and admiration. Comp. Ps. lxxvii. 12.

3. *Glory ye in his holy name.* The original word rendered *glory* is the same word which is commonly used to denote *praise,* and it has that meaning here. The idea is, In your praises let the main subject be the name of God—that holy name by which he chooses to be known. The Hebrew is, "the name of his holiness." It implies (*a*) that we should rejoice in God—in his very name—in that by which he chooses to make himself known; (*b*) that it is a special subject of praise and rejoicing that his name is *holy;* that is, that he is a holy Being. This can be a subject of real rejoicing only to those who are themselves holy; but properly considered, one of the highest reasons for rejoicing in God is the fact that he *is* holy; that he cannot look upon sin but with abhorrence. There would be no ground of confidence in God if this were not so. ¶ *Let the heart of them rejoice that seek the* LORD. That desire to know him; that come to praise him. Let their hearts rejoice,—or, let them be happy, —(*a*) because they are *permitted* to

4 Seek *v* the LORD, and his strength; seek *w* his face evermore.

5 Remember his marvellous works that he hath done; his wonders, and the judgments of his mouth;

6 O ye seed of Abraham his

v Amos v. 4, 6.   *w* Ps. xxvii. 8.

servant, ye children of Jacob his chosen.

7 He *is* the LORD our God; his *x* judgments *are* in all the earth.

8 He *y* hath remembered his covenant for ever, the word *which* he commanded to a thousand generations:

x Isa. xxvi. 9.   *y* Luke i. 72, 73.

seek him; (*b*) because they are *inclined* to seek him; (*c*) because they have *such* a God to come to,—One so mighty, so holy, so good, so gracious.

4. *Seek the* LORD *and his strength.* Seek strength from him; seek that his strength may be imparted to you; seek him as a Being of almighty power; as One by whom you may be strengthened. The Septuagint and Vulgate render this, "Seek the Lord, and *be strengthened.*" Strength comes from God, and it is only by his strength that we can be strong; only by our making use of his omnipotence in our own behalf that we can discharge the duties, and bear the trials of this life. Comp. Notes on Isa. xl. 29–31. ¶ *Seek his face evermore.* His favour. His smiling upon us, his lifting up the light of his countenance, is synonymous with his favour. See Ps. xxiv. 6; xxvii. 8. Comp. Notes on Ps. iv. 6.

5. *Remember his marvellous works,* etc. The works fitted to excite wonder. Call them to remembrance in your psalm; seek the aid of music and song to impress the memory of them deeply on your hearts. ¶ *His wonders.* His miracles. See Notes on Ps. lxxviii. 43; Isa. viii. 18. ¶ *And the judgments of his mouth.* That is, properly, the judgments which he pronounced on his enemies, and which were followed by their overthrow. The word does not refer here, as it often does, to his statutes or commands.

6. *O ye seed of Abraham his servant, ye children of Jacob his chosen.* All you who are descendants of Abraham and Jacob;—the former being particularly mentioned here because

he was the great ancestor of the Hebrew people; the latter, because the events referred to were closely connected with the history of Jacob—with his going down into Egypt, and with the division of the tribes named after his sons. The word rendered "his chosen" would seem in our version to refer to Jacob. In the original, however, it is in the plural number, and must agree with the word rendered *children,*—"Ye chosen sons of Jacob" (comp. ver. 43). So it has been translated in 1 Chron. xvi. 13, "Ye children of Jacob, his chosen ones."

7. *He is the* LORD *our God.* His name is *Jehovah*—the true God; and this God is ours. See Notes on Ps. xcv. 7. ¶ *His judgments* are *in all the earth.* More properly "*in all the land;*" that is, in every part of the land he is honoured as our God. His institutions are established here; his laws are obeyed here; his worship is celebrated here. No other God is worshipped here; everywhere he is acknowledged as the nation's God.

8. *He hath remembered his covenant for ever.* That is, God has had it constantly in remembrance, or always. Comp. Notes on Luke i. 72. Though the covenant was made long since; though many generations of men have passed by; though great changes have occurred; though many calamities have come upon the nations, yet his ancient covenant and promise have never been forgotten. All his promises have been fulfilled; all ever will be. The "covenant" here referred to is that which was made with Abraham, and through him with the Hebrew

9 Which *covenant* he made with Abraham, [z] and his oath unto Isaac;[a]

10 And confirmed the same unto Jacob [b] for a law, *and* to Israel *for* an everlasting cove-, nant;

11 Saying, Unto thee will I give the land of Canaan, the [1] lot of your inheritance:

[z] Gen. xvii. 2.　　[a] Gen. xxvi. 3.

12 When they were *but* a few [c] men in number; yea, very few, and strangers in it.

13 When they went from one nation to another, from *one* kingdom to another people,

14 He suffered no man to do them wrong; yea, he reproved kings for their sakes;

[b] Gen. xxviii. 13—15.　　[1] *cord.*
[c] Deut. vii. 7.

people. ¶ *The word* which *he commanded.* The thing which he commanded; that is, *all* which he ordained and appointed. ¶ *To a thousand generations.* Very many generations; or, any number of generations:—that is, always. Comp. Ex. xx. 6. The experience of the people through all the generations of their history has shown that in what he has promised and directed he is unchanging.

9. *Which* covenant *he made with Abraham.* Which he *ratified* with Abraham. Literally, "which he *cut* with Abraham." Gen. xvii. 2–14. Comp. Notes on Ps. l. 5. ¶ *And his oath unto Isaac.* Confirming the promise made to Abraham. See Gen. xxvi. 2–5.

10. *And confirmed the same unto Jacob.* Literally, "caused it to stand;" that is, he made it fast or secure. He renewed it, commanding the same things; making the same promises; and pledging himself for its fulfilment in the same manner. Gen. xxviii. 10–15. ¶ *For a law.* For an established or settled ordinance; for a rule by which future things were to be regulated:—that is, they would occur *according to* that promise, and be conformed to it. It was, as it were, a rule which God prescribed for himself in regard to his own future conduct. ¶ And *to Israel*, etc. Another name for Jacob, Gen. xxxii. 28.

11. *Saying, Unto thee will I give the land of Canaan.* Gen. xiii. 14, 15. ¶ *The lot of your inheritance.* Or, that shall *be* the lot of your inheritance;—or, what you shall in-

herit. The margin is, *the cord.* The Hebrew word—חֶבֶל, *hhebel*—means properly a cord, a rope; and then, a measuring-line. Hence it means a portion *measured out* and assigned to any one as land, Josh. xvii. 14; xix. 9. Comp. Ps. xvi. 6. The meaning is, that the land of Canaan was given by promise to the patriarchs as their lot or portion of the earth; as that which they and their descendants were to possess as their own.

12. *When they were* but *a few men in number.* Literally, "In their being men of number, very little." That is, They could then be easily numbered, and they were so few that they could not take possession of it themselves. This is in contrast with the promise then made to them that they should be in number as the stars, and as the sand on the sea shore. ¶ *And strangers in it.* Foreigners. They were mere sojourners. They did not become incorporated with the people of the land. They did not acquire property there. They were regarded and treated as belonging to a foreign people. See Notes on Heb. xi. 9.

13. *When they went from one nation to another*, etc. Wandered about, as if they had no home and no fixed habitation. See Gen. xii. 6, 9, 10; xiii. 1; xx. 1; xxvi. 1, 17, 22, 23.

14. *He suffered no man to do them wrong.* He protected them as they wandered from place to place, and as they were exposed to dangers. See the history of Abraham, Isaac, and Jacob, in their wanderings, as it is recorded in the book of Genesis.

15 *Saying*, Touch not mine anointed, and do my prophets no harm.

16 Moreover, *d* he called for a famine upon the land : he brake the whole staff *e* of bread.

d Gen. xli. 5 k.　　*e* Isa. iii. 1.

¶ *Yea, he reproved kings for their sakes.* That he might protect them ; that he might keep them from danger and from sin. See the case of Pharaoh in the time of Abraham, Gen. xii. 17–20, and the case of Abimelech, Gen. xx. 3, 6.

15. Saying, *Touch not mine anointed.* That is, This was the language of his *providence.* It was *as though* God had said this. It is not meant that this was said in so many words, but this is the *poetic* form of representing the dealings of Providence. Comp. Gen. xxvi. 11. The word *anointed* here means that God had, as it were, set them apart to his service, or that they were to him as kings, and priests, and prophets,—sacred men, belonging to God. The *language* is not found in the Old Testament as applied to the patriarchs, but the *idea* is fairly implied there, that they belonged to God as sacred and holy men. ¶ *And do my prophets no harm.* As if God had thus spoken to them, and called them prophets. That is, they belonged to God as a sacred order :—they were separate from other men, and God regarded them as his own.

16. *Moreover, he called for a famine upon the land.* It was not by chance ; not by the mere operation of physical laws, but it was because God *ordered* it. The famine here referred to, as the connexion shows, was that which occurred in the time of Jacob, and which was the occasion of the migration into Egypt. There was also a famine in the time of Abraham (Gen. xii. 10) ; but the design of the psalmist here is to refer to that period of the Jewish history which pertained to their residence in Egypt, and to the dealings of God with the nation when there, as furnishing an occasion for

VOL. III.

17 He *f* sent a man before them, *even* Joseph, *who* was sold *g* for a servant ;

18 Whose feet they hurt with fetters : [1] he was laid in iron ;

f Gen. xlv. 5.　　*g* Gen. xxxix. 1, 20.
[1] *his soul came into.*

gratitude. Gen. xli ; xlii. ¶ *He brake the whole staff of bread.* That which supports life, as a staff does a feeble man. See Notes on Isa. iii. 1.

17. *He sent a man before them.* That is, He so ordered it by his providence that a man — Joseph — *was* sent before the family of Jacob into Egypt, that he might make arrangements for their reception and preservation. The whole matter was *as if* God had sent him, or had commanded him to go. And yet it was brought about as the result of a series of acts of the most wicked character ; —by the envy and the hatred of his brethren ; by their guilt and hardness of heart in proposing at first to put him to death, and then in their arrangements for selling him to hopeless slavery ; by their plan so to dispose of him that their father might never hear of him again, and that they might be troubled with him no more. God did not cause these acts. He did not command them ; he did not approve of them. And yet, since they *did* occur, and since Joseph's brethren *were* so wicked, God made use of these things to accomplish his own benevolent purposes, and to carry out his great designs. So he makes use of the passions of wicked men at all times to execute his plans (comp. Notes on Isa. x. 5–7 ; see also Ps. lxxvi. 10, and Gen. l. 20) ; and so he *will* do to the end of time. Men are free in their wickedness ; but God is equally free in frustrating their schemes, and overruling their designs for the accomplishment of his own purposes. ¶ Who *was sold for a servant.* For a slave ; Gen. xxxvii. 28, 36 ; xxxix. 1.

18. *Whose feet they hurt with fetters.* In Gen. xl. 3, it is said of

II

19 Until the time that his word came; the word of the LORD tried him.

20 The king *ʰ* sent and loosed him; *even* the ruler of the people, and let him go free.

ʰ Gen. xli. 14, 40.

21 He made him lord of his house, and ruler of all his [1] substance;

22 To bind his princes at his pleasure, and teach his senators wisdom.

[1] *possession.*

Joseph that he was *"bound"* in prison. It is not improbable that his *feet* were bound, as this is the usual way of confining prisoners. ¶ *He was laid in iron.* In the prison. The margin is, *his soul came into iron.* The version in the Prayer-Book of the Episcopal Church is, *the iron entered into his soul.* This is a more striking and beautiful rendering, though it may be doubted whether the Hebrew will permit it. De Wette renders it, "In iron lay his body."

19. *Until the time that his word came.* The word, or the communication from God. ¶ *The word of the* LORD *tried him.* That is, tested his skill in interpreting dreams, and his power to disclose the future. Gen. xli. This furnished a *trial* of his ability, and showed that he was truly the favourite of God, and was endowed with wisdom from on high. The word rendered *tried* is that which is commonly applied to metals in testing their genuineness and purity. Comp. Notes on Ps. xii. 6.

20. *The king sent and loosed him.* Released him from prison. Gen. xli. 14. The object was that he might interpret the dreams of Pharaoh. ¶ *The ruler of the people, and let him go free.* Heb., *peoples*, in the plural,—referring either to the fact that there were *many* people in the land, or that Pharaoh ruled over tributary nations as well as over the Egyptians.

21. *He made him lord of his house.* Gen. xli. 40. This implied that the administration of the affairs of the nation was virtually committed to him. ¶ *And ruler of all his substance.* Marg., as in Heb., *possession.* Of all he had. He placed all

at his disposal in the affairs of his kingdom.

22. *To bind his princes at pleasure.* Giving him absolute power. The power here referred to was that which was always claimed in despotic governments, and was, and is still, actually practised in Oriental nations. Literally, "to bind his princes *by his soul;*" that is, at his will; or, as he chose. ¶ *And teach his senators wisdom.* This is now an unhappy translation. The word *senator* in fact originally had reference to *age* (see Webster's Dic.), but it is now commonly applied to a body of men entrusted with a share in the administration of government,— usually a higher body in a government,—as the Senate of the United States. As these were usually *aged* men, the word has acquired its present meaning, and is now ordinarily used without reference to age. But there was no such constituted body in the government of Egypt,—for despotism does not admit of such an arrangement. The Hebrew word here means *aged men,* and is employed with reference to those who were connected with the administration, or whom the monarch would consult,—his counsellors. The meaning of the phrase "to teach them wisdom" is, that he would instruct them *what to do;*—literally, he would "make them *wise,*" that is, in reference to the administration. He had the right of commanding them, and directing them in the administration. At the same time, it is doubtless true that Joseph was endowed with practical wisdom in the affairs of government far beyond them, and that in instructing them what to *do,* he actually imparted *wisdom* to them.

23 Israel *i* also came into Egypt, and Jacob sojourned in the land of Ham.

24 And *k* he increased his people greatly, and made them stronger than their enemies.

25 He turned their heart to hate his people, to deal subtilly with his servants.

i Gen. xlvi. 6, 7.　　*k* Ex. i. 7, etc.
l Ex. iv. 12, etc.

26 He sent Moses *l* his servant, *and* Aaron whom he had chosen.

27 They shewed his *1* signs *m* among them, and wonders in the land of Ham.

28 He sent darkness, *n* and made it dark; and they rebelled not against his word.

1 *words of his signs.*
m Ex. vii.—xii.　　*n* Ex. x. 21—23

23. *Israel also came into Egypt.* Another name for Jacob; see ver. 10. ¶ *And Jacob sojourned in the land of Ham.* Not as a permanent abode, but as a temporary arrangement, until the time should come for the people to be removed to the land of promise. See Gen. xlvi. 6. The more literal rendering would be, "Jacob was a stranger—a foreigner—in the land of Ham." On the meaning of the word *Ham*, see Notes on Ps. lxxviii. 51.

24. *And he increased his people greatly*, etc. God caused them to multiply. Ex. i. 7, 9.

25. *He turned their heart to hate his people.* God turned their heart. That is, He so ordered things that they became the enemies of his people, and made it necessary that they should be removed into another land. It is not said that God did this by his direct *power;* or that he *compelled* them to hate his people; or that he in any way interfered with their *will;* or that he regarded this *as a good* in itself; or that he *approved* of it: —but this is said in accordance with the usual representations in the Bible, where God is spoken of as having all things under his control, and where it is constantly affirmed that nothing takes place without his own proper agency and government in the matter. Nothing—not even the human will— free as it is—is independent of God; and not even the worst passions of men are *outside of his plan*, or independent in such a sense that they does not afford the opportunity for their development and display. Comp. Notes on Isa. vi. 10; x. 5–7, 15.

¶ *To deal subtilly.* In a fraudulent, or deceitful manner. See Ex. i. 10.

26. *He sent Moses his servant.* He sent Moses to be his servant in delivering his people; that is, to accomplish the work which he had designed should be done. ¶ And *Aaron whom he had chosen.* Whom he had selected to perform an important work in delivering his people from bondage.

27. *They shewed his signs among them.* Literally, "They placed among them the words of his signs." So the margin. The reference is to the miracles wrought in Egypt in bringing calamities upon the Egyptians to induce them to permit the children of Israel to go out from their bondage. They were the agents in setting these wonders before the Egyptians. The term *words* is employed here—"the words of his signs"—to keep up the idea that it was by the command of God that this was done, or by his word. It was by no power of their own, but only by the authority of God. ¶ *And wonders in the land of Ham.* Miracles. Things fitted to produce astonishment. See ver. 5.

28. *He sent darkness, and made it dark.* Ex. x. 21–23. ¶ *And they rebelled not against his word.* More literally, *his words.* The reference is to Moses and Aaron; and the idea, as expressed here, is that they were obedient to the command of God; that they went and did what he ordered them; that, although he required them to go before a mighty and proud monarch, to denounce against him the vengeance of heaven, and to be the in-

29 He turned their waters *o* into blood, and slew their fish.

30 Their land brought forth frogs *p* in abundance, in the chambers of their kings.

31 He *q* spake, and there came divers sorts of flies, *and* lice in all their coasts.

32 He gave them ¹ hail *r* for rain, *and* flaming fire in their land.

33 He smote their vines also and their fig-trees; and brake the trees of their coasts.

34 He spake, and the locusts

o Ex. vii. 20, 21.   *p* Ex. viii. 5, 6.
q Ex. viii. 17, 24.   ¹ *their rain hail.*
r Ex. ix. 23—25.   *s* Ex. x. 12—14.

s came, and caterpillars, and that without number,

35 And did eat up all the herbs in their land, and devoured the fruit of their ground.

36 He smote also all the first-born *t* in their land, the chief *u* of all their strength.

37 He *v* brought them forth also with silver and gold; and *there was* not one feeble *person* among their tribes.

38 Egypt *w* was glad when they departed; for the fear of them fell upon them.

t Ex. xii. 29.   *u* Gen. xlix. 3.
v Ex. xii. 35.   *w* Ex. xii. 33.

struments of bringing upon the land unspeakably severe judgments, yet they did not shrink from what God commanded them to do. They were true to his appointment, and showed themselves to be faithful messengers of God. Others, however, suppose that this refers to the Egyptians, and that it is to be taken as a question: "And did they not rebel against his word?" The language might bear this, and the translators of the Septuagint seem to have so understood it, for they render it, "And they rebelled against his words." But the most natural construction is that in our common version, and the design is evidently to commend the boldness and the fidelity of Moses and Aaron.

29–36. See an account of these plagues in Ex. vi.-xi. Comp. Ps. lxxviii. 43–51. This is mostly a mere enumeration of the plagues in the order in which they occurred, but without, of course, the details of the circumstances attending them. There are no circumstances mentioned here which require particular explanation.

37. *He brought them forth also with silver and gold.* Which they had begged of the Egyptians. In Ex. xii. 35, it is said, in our translation, that they had "*borrowed*" this gold and silver, together with raiment, of the Egyptians. This is an unhappy trans-

lation, as our word *borrow* means to ask anything of another for the purpose of using it for a time, with an implied understanding that it shall be returned, if an article to be used, —or that as much money shall be repaid, if it is money that is borrowed, —and according to this there would have been dishonesty and fraud on the part of the Israelites in *borrowing* these things of the Egyptians, when not intending (as they evidently did not) to return them. The Hebrew word, however, in Ex. xii. 35— שָׁאַל *shaal*—means merely *to ask, to demand, to require, to request, to petition, to beg.* The idea of an obligation to *return* the things, as in our word *borrow,* is not attached to the Hebrew word. ¶ *And* there was *not one feeble* person, etc. Literally, Not one who was lame; or, who halted, or staggered. This, of course, is not necessarily to be understood literally. It is a general description of the capability of the people for travelling, or for war.

38. *Egypt was glad when they departed.* They had suffered so many plagues; the land was so utterly desolate, there was so much sorrow in their dwellings, from the calamities which had come upon them for refusing to let the Israelites go, that at last they were glad to have them de-

39 He *x* spread a cloud for a covering, and fire to give light in the night.

40 *The people* asked, *y* and he brought quails, *z* and satisfied them with the bread of heaven.

41 He *a* opened the rock, and the waters gushed out; they ran in the dry places *like* a river.

42 For he remembered his holy

x Ex. xiii. 21; Neh. ix. 12.
y Ps. lxxviii. 18.   z Ex. xvi. 13, 14.
a Ex. xvii. 6; Num. xx. 11; 1 Cor. x. 4.

promise, *b and* Abraham his servant.

43 And he brought forth his people with joy, *and* his chosen with [1] gladness;

44 And *c* gave them the lands of the heathen: and they inherited the labour of the people ;

45 That *d* they might observe his statutes, and keep his laws. [2] Praise ye the LORD.

b Gen. xv. 14.   1 *singing.*   c Jos. xxi. 43.
d Deut. iv. 1, 40; vi. 24, 25.   2 *Hallelujah.*

---

part, and they were willing to aid them that they might get rid of them. This will, in part, account for the fact that they were willing to give them what they asked,—even silver and gold,—if they might thus facilitate their departure. ¶ *For the fear of them fell upon them.* The fear of them, as being under the protection of God; and the fear of the judgments, which must follow if they continued to oppress them.

39. *He spread a cloud for a covering.* See Notes on Ps. lxxviii. 14. In Num. x. 34, it is said that "the cloud of the Lord was upon them by day," and from this seems to have been derived the idea of its *covering* them, as if it were a protection from the heat in the desert.

40. The people *asked, and he brought quails.* See Notes on Ps. lxxviii. 26–29. ¶ *And satisfied them with the bread of heaven.* Manna, sent down, as it were, from heaven. In Ps. lxxviii. 25, it is called "angels' food." See Notes on that verse.

41. *He opened the rock,* etc. See Notes on Ps. lxxviii. 15. ¶ *They ran in the dry places* like *a river.* Or, *a river.* They flowed along in the desert,—a river of waters. See Notes on 1 Cor. x. 4.

42. *For he remembered,* etc. He was faithful to his promise made to Abraham, and did not forget his descendants in the hour of need. This is the statement made in vers. 8, 9; and to illustrate and confirm the faithfulness of God, this reference is made

to the history of the Hebrew people. See Notes on those verses.

43. *And he brought forth his people with joy.* With joy at their deliverance from bondage, and for his merciful interposition. ¶ And *his chosen with gladness.* Marg., as in Heb., *singing.* See Ex. xv.

44. *And gave them the lands of the heathen.* Of the *nations* of the land of Palestine, according to his promise. See Notes on Ps. lxxviii. 55. ¶ *And they inherited the labour of the people.* The fruit of their labours. See Deut. vi. 10, 11; Josh. xiii. 7, *et seq.*

45. *That they might observe his statutes, and keep his laws.* The end —the design—of all this was that they might be an obedient people. This was the purpose of all his interventions in their behalf; and their obligation to obedience was enforced and measured by what he had done. The same is true in regard to his people now. ¶ *Praise ye the* LORD. Heb., Hallelu-jah. See Ps. civ. 35.

PSALM CVI.

The author of this psalm is unknown, and the occasion on which it was composed cannot now be ascertained. It belongs to the same *class* as Psalms lxxviii., and cv., as referring to the ancient history of the Hebrew people, and as deriving lessons of instruction, admonition, gratitude and praise from that history. The cvth Psalm referred to that history particularly as showing the mercy and favour of God to that people, and hence their obligation to love and serve him; this psalm is occupied

PSALM CVI.

PRAISE 1 ye the LORD. O
e give thanks unto the LORD;
for *he is* good: for his mercy
endureth for ever.

2 Who *f* can utter the mighty
acts of the LORD? *who* can shew

1 *Hallelujah.*　　　*e* 1 Chron. xvi. 34.

---

forth all his praise?

3 Blessed *g are* they that keep
judgment, *and* he that doeth
righteousness at all times.*h*

4 Remember *i* me, O LORD,
with the favour *that thou bearest*

f Ps. xl. 5.　　　*g* Ps. xv. 2.
h Gal. vi. 9.　　　*i* Ps. cxix. 132.

---

mainly with a confession, drawn from a
review of that history, that the nation
had *not* been mindful of those mercies,
but that they had rebelled against God,
and incurred his displeasure. The psalm
has a striking resemblance in many respects to the prayer in Daniel ix.; and,
like that, is a prayer that God would
now interpose and deliver the people as
in times that were past. It is *possible*
that the psalm may have been composed
in the time of the Babylonish captivity
(comp. ver. 47), and this is the opinion
of Hengstenberg; but it is impossible to
demonstrate this with any certainty. It
was evidently composed in some period
of public calamity, and there is no impropriety in supposing that it *may* have
been then.

The psalm consists essentially of three
parts:—

I. A brief introduction, setting forth
the duty of praising God, and referring
to his mercy, and expressing the desire
of the author of the psalm that he himself might participate in his mercy, and
share the happy lot of the "chosen" of
God, vers. 1–5.

II. A reference to the history of the
nation, and a confession of their sins in
all the periods of their history, and their
proneness as a people to disobey God,
referring particularly to their history in
Egypt, vers. 6–12; in the desert, vers.
13–33; and in the land of Canaan, vers.
34–43.

III. A prayer—founded on the fact
that God had often interposed in their
behalf—that he would now again interpose, and gather them from among the
heathen, that they might again sing his
praises, vers. 44–48.

1. *Praise ye the* LORD. Marg.,
Hallelu-jah. The two Hebrew words
mean, *praise ye the Lord.* They are
the same words with which the previous psalm closes, and are here designed to indicate the general duty
illustrated in the psalm. ¶ *O give*

thanks *unto the* LORD. See Notes
on Ps. cv. 1. ¶ *For* he is *good: for
his mercy* endureth *for ever.* See
Notes on Ps. c. 5, and cvii. 1, where
the language in the Hebrew is the
same.

2. *Who can utter the mighty acts
of the* LORD? Who can speak the
great things of God? Who can find
language which will suitably express
what he has done, or which will *come
up* in sublimity to his acts? In other
words, human language must fall im-
measurably short of adequately expressing the praises of Jehovah, or
conveying the fulness of what he has
wrought. Who has not felt this when
he has endeavoured to praise God in
a proper manner? Comp. Notes on
Ps. xl. 5. ¶ Who *can shew forth all
his praise?* Heb., *Cause to be heard.*
That is, Language cannot be found
which would *cause it to be heard* in a
suitable manner.

3. *Blessed* are *they that keep judgment.* They are blessed, for their conduct is right, and it leads to happiness. The Hebrew is, "the keepers
of judgment;" that is, they who observe the rules of justice in their conduct, or who are governed by the
principles of integrity. ¶ And *he
that doeth righteousness at all times.*
All who yield obedience to just law—
whether a nation or an individual.
The psalm is designed to illustrate
this *by contrast;* that is, by showing,
in the conduct of the Hebrew people,
the consequences of *disobedience,* and
thus impliedly what would have been,
and what always must be, the consequences of the opposite course. Comp.
Ps. xv.

4. *Remember me, O* LORD, *with the
favour* that thou bearest unto *thy*

unto thy people : O visit me with thy salvation ;

5 That I may see the good of thy chosen, *k* that I may rejoice in the gladness *l* of thy nation,

k Eph. i. 4.   *l* Isa. xxxv. 10; John xvi. 22.

that I may glory with thine inheritance."*m*

6 We *n* have sinned with our fathers, we have committed iniquity, we have done wickedly.

m Eph. i. 18.   *n* Dan. ix. 5.

people. Literally, "Remember me with the favour of thy people." This is the language of the author of the psalm:—a pious ejaculation such as will occur to the mind in recounting what God has done for his church; what are the advantages of being his friends; what blessings of peace, happiness, and joy are connected with true religion. Even the wicked sometimes have this feeling when they look on the happy life, and the peaceful death of the godly. So Balaam said, "Let me die the death of the righteous, and let my last end be like his!" Num. xxiii. 10. ¶ *O visit me with thy salvation.* Come to me with salvation; confer it upon me.

5. *That I may see the good of thy chosen.* Thy chosen people; or, thine elect. That I may possess and enjoy the same favour and happiness which they do. It is implied here that there *are* peculiar favours conferred on them; or, that happiness is found in the friendship of God which is *not* to be found elsewhere. It is a characteristic of true piety to *desire* to make that our own. A truly religious man more desires the happiness which results from being among the "chosen" of God than all that the world can confer. ¶ *That I may rejoice in the gladness of thy nation.* The happiness found in the *nation* that serves thee. True religion—the favour of God—not only confers happiness on the *individual* who possesses it, but on the *nation* or *people* where it prevails. It is just as much *fitted* to produce happiness there, and is just as *necessary* for happiness there, as in the case of an individual. ¶ *That I may glory with thine inheritance.* That I may share the honour of thy people. The word *inheritance* here is used to denote that

which is one's own, and is thus applied to the people of God considered as *his*. The meaning is, that the psalmist desired no other glory, honour, or distinction, than that which pertained to God's people as such. He sought not the "glory" connected with the distinctions of the world; the display of wealth; the triumph of genius, of conquest, of arms,—but the "glory" of being a friend of God, and of partaking of that which God confers on his people.

6. *We have sinned with our fathers.* We have sinned as *they* did; we have followed their example. The illustration of the manner in which the nation had sinned occupies a considerable part of the remainder of the psalm; and the idea here is, that, in the generation in which the psalmist lived, there had been the manifestation of the same rebellious spirit which had so remarkably characterised the entire nation. The *connexion* of this with the foregoing verses is not very apparent. It would seem to be that the psalmist was deeply impressed with a sense of the great blessings which follow from the friendship of God, and from keeping his commandments,—as stated, vers. 3–5; but he remembered that those blessings had *not* come upon the people as might have been expected, and his mind suddenly adverts to the *cause* of this, in the fact that the nation had *sinned.* It was not that God was not disposed to bestow that happiness; it was not that true religion *failed* to confer happiness; but it was that the nation had provoked God to displeasure, and that in fact the sins of the people had averted the blessings which would otherwise have come upon them. The psalmist, therefore, in

7 Our fathers understood not thy wonders in Egypt; they remembered not the multitude of thy mercies; but *o* provoked *him* at the sea, *even* at the Red sea.

8 Nevertheless, he saved them

o Ex. xiv. 11, 12.　　　*p* Ez. xx. 14.

for *p* his name's sake, that *q* he might make his mighty power to be known.

9 He *r* rebuked the Red sea also, and it was dried up : so he led them through the depths, as through the wilderness.

q Ex. ix. 16.　　　*r* Ex. xiv. 21, etc.

---

emphatic language, — repeating the confession in three forms, "we have sinned,—we have committed iniquity, —we have done wickedly,"—acknowledges that the failure was in them, not in God. The language here is substantially the same as in Daniel ix. 5, 6, and it would seem not improbable that the one was suggested by the other. Which was prior in the order of time, it is now impossible to determine. Comp. Notes on Dan. ix. 5, 6.

7. *Our fathers understood not.* They did not fully comprehend the design of the Divine dealings. They did not perceive the greatness of the favour shown to them, or the obligation to obey and serve God under which they were placed by these remarkable manifestations. ¶ *Thy wonders in Egypt.* The miracles wrought there in behalf of the Hebrew people. ¶ *They remembered not the multitude of thy mercies.* The great number of the Divine interpositions in their behalf. They did not allow them to influence their conduct as they should have done. The aggravation of their offence in the case here referred to was particularly in the *multitude* of the mercies. It would have been sinful to have forgotten even *one* act of the Divine favour; it was a great aggravation of their guilt that *so many* acts were forgotten, or that they failed to make an impression on them. So now. It is a great sin to be unmindful of a *single* favour conferred by God; it is a great aggravation of guilt that men live continually amidst so many proofs of the Divine goodness; that they are fed, and clothed, and protected; that they breathe the pure air, and look

upon the light of the sun; that they enjoy the comforts of domestic life, the blessings of liberty, and the offers of salvation; that they lie down and rise up; that their toils are crowned with success, and that the blessings of every land are made to come around them,—and yet *they forget or disregard all these proofs of the Divine mercy.* ¶ *But provoked* him *at the sea,* even *at the Red Sea.* Ex. xiv. 10–12. They *rebelled* against him. Even amidst the wonders there occurring, and after all the blessings which they had received at his hands, when they were in danger they doubted his power, and called in question his faithfulness.

8. *Nevertheless, he saved them for his name's sake.* For the promotion of his own honour and glory; that it might be seen that he is powerful and merciful. This is constantly given as the reason why God saves men; why he forgives sin ; why he redeems the soul; why he delivers from danger and from death. Comp. Ezek. xxxvi. 22, 32; Isa. xxxvii. 35; xliii. 25; xlviii. 9; Jer. xiv. 7 ; Ps. vi. 4; xxiii. 3; xxv. 11; xxxi. 16; xliv. 26. This is the highest reason which can be assigned for pardoning and saving sinners. ¶ *That he might make his mighty power to be known.* Ex. ix. 16. Comp. Notes on Rom. ix. 17.

9. *He rebuked the Red Sea also.* The word rendered *rebuke* commonly means to chide—as when one is angry with another for having done wrong. Here it is evidently a poetic term, meaning that he spake *as if* he were angry; or *as if* the Red Sea did wrong in presenting an obstacle or obstruction to the passage of his people. Comp. Ex. xiv. 21, 22. ¶ *So*

10 And he saved them from the hand of him that hated *them*, and redeemed them from the hand of the enemy.

11 And ˢ the waters covered their enemies: there was not one of them left.

12 Then believed they his words; they sang ᵗ his praise.

ˢ Ex. xv. 5.　ᵗ Ex. xv. 1, etc.
¹ *made haste, they forgat.*　ᵘ Ex. xv.—xvii.

13 They ¹ soon forgat ᵘ his works; they waited not for his counsel.

14 But ² lusted ᵛ exceedingly in the wilderness, and tempted God in the desert.

15 And he gave them their request; but sent leanness ʷ into their soul.

² *lusted a lust*　ᵛ Num. xi. 4, 33; Ps. lxxviii. 18.
ʷ Isa. x. 16.

he led them through the depths. Through what *had* been the abyss; what had *seemed* to be depths, being covered with water. ¶ *As through the wilderness.* As through a desert or dry place; as he afterwards led them through the wilderness. The waters parted asunder, and made a way for them.

10. *And he saved them from the hand of him that hated* them. From Pharaoh. By making a path through the waters, they were enabled to escape; by the overthrow of the Egyptians in the Red Sea, they were completely and for ever delivered from their oppressors. Ex. xiv. 30.

11. *And the waters covered their enemies*, etc. Ex. xiv. 27, 28; xv. 5.

12. *Then believed they his words.* In immediate view of his interpositions in their behalf in conducting them through the Red Sea, and in the destruction of their enemies. ¶ *They sang his praise.* In the song composed by Moses on the occasion of their deliverance. Ex. xv.

13. *They soon forgat his works.* On vers. 13–15, see Notes on Ps. lxxviii. 17–22. Literally here, as in the margin, *They made haste, they forgat.* They did it soon; did it without any delay. It was as if they were impatient to have it done. ¶ *They waited not for his counsel.* For the fulfilment of his promise; or for his command in regard to their future conduct. They did not look to him, but they depended on themselves, and followed their own desires and wishes.

14. *But lusted exceedingly in the*

wilderness. Marg., as in Heb., *lusted a lust.* The reference is to their desire of better food than the manna. ¶ *And tempted God in the desert.* Tried God, whether he *could* provide for them food and drink. Ps. lxxviii. 19, 20.

15. *And he gave them their request.* By sending great quantities of *quails.* Num. xi. 31, 32. ¶ *But sent leanness into their soul.* The word translated *leanness* is from a verb—רָזָה, *razah*—to make thin; to cause to waste away; to destroy. The radical idea is that of abrading or *scraping;* and hence it means to become lean, to waste away. It occurs only here and in Isa. x. 16, rendered *leanness,* and in Micah vi. 10, rendered *scant;* marg., *leanness.* It means here that the effect of all this on their souls was similar to the effect on the body when it wastes away by disease or want of food. This effect often occurs. In the gratification of their desires, in great temporal success and prosperity, individuals, churches, nations, often forget their dependence on God; lose their sense of the value of spiritual privileges and blessings: are satisfied with their condition; become self-confident and proud, and forfeit the favour of God. If we pray for temporal prosperity, we should also pray that we may at the same time have grace commensurate with it, that it may be a blessing and not a curse; if we are visited with prosperity when it has not been a direct object of our prayer,—if we inherit riches, or if our plans are successful beyond our expectations—or, in the

16 They [x] envied Moses also in the camp, *and* Aaron the saint of the LORD.

17 The earth opened and swallowed up Dathan, and covered the company of Abiram.

18 And a fire was kindled in their company; the flame burned up the wicked.

19 They made a calf [y] in Ho-

reb, and worshipped the molten image.

20 Thus [z] they changed their glory into the similitude of an ox that eateth grass.

21 They forgat God their saviour, which had done great things in Egypt;

22 Wondrous works in the land of Ham, *and* terrible things by the Red sea.

[x] Num. xvi. 1, etc.   [y] Ex. xxxii. 4.

[z] Jer. ii. 11.

language of the world, if "fortune smiles upon us," there should be special prayer on our part that it may not be a curse rather than a blessing; —that it may be so received and used as *not* to alienate our minds from God. Few are the Christian men who can bear continued success in life; few are those who are not injured by it; rare is it that growth in grace keeps pace with uninterrupted worldly prosperity; rare is it that the blessings of earth are so received and employed that they are seen to be a means of grace, and not a hindrance to growth in piety. A man does not know what is best for him when his heart is set on worldly prosperity; and God is more benevolent to men than they are to themselves, in withholding what is so often the object of their intense desire. "What is asked in passion, is often given in wrath."—*Henry.*

16. *They envied Moses also in the camp.* They were envious of him, or rebelled against him, as assuming too much authority. See Num. xvi. 1, 2. The reference here is rather to the *result* of that envy in producing rebellion than to the envy itself. It is true, however, that the foundation of their opposition to him *was* envy. ¶ And *Aaron the saint of the* LORD. That is, as set apart to the service of the Lord; or, as employed in holy things. The reference is to his *office*, not to his personal character.

17, 18. On these verses see Num. xvi. 31–35. This refers to the time when they rebelled against Moses.

19. *They made a calf in Horeb.* Ex. xxxii. 4. Probably in resemblance of the Egyptian god *Apis.* The image was made by Aaron out of materials furnished by the people, and at their request (Ex. xxxii. 1–3), so that it might be said to be the act of the people. ¶ *And worshipped the molten image.* The word rendered *molten* is from a verb—נָסַךְ, *nasach*—to pour, to pour out; hence, to cast, to found; and it means any thing that is made by fusion or casting. This image was *cast* (Ex. xxxii. 4), and hence this name is given to it.

20. *Thus they changed their glory.* Their true glory,—the proper object of worship—God. Comp. Notes on Rom. i. 23. They *exchanged* that as an object of worship for the image of an ox. ¶ *Into the similitude of an ox that eateth grass.* Into the likeness of an ox. That is, They worshipped God under that image. The circumstance of its "eating grass" is added to show the absurdity of the act. Instead of worshipping God—an independent Being, who does not need to be supported, but who himself sustains all things, and provides for all—they worshipped an animal that had need of constant sustenance, and would itself soon die if deprived of its proper nourishment. Comp. Notes on Isa. xl. 18–20; xli. 6, 7.

21, 22. *They forgat God their Saviour,* etc. The God who had saved, or delivered them, out of Egypt. The sentiment here is the same as in Ps. lxxviii. 11, 12. See Notes on that piece.

23 Therefore *ª* he said that he would destroy them, had not Moses his chosen stood before him in the breach, to turn away his wrath, lest he should destroy *them.*

24 Yea, they despised 1 the

a Ez. xx. 13.   1 *a land of desire.*   *b* Deut. viii. 7.

pleasant land; *b* they believed not his word;

25 But murmured in their tents, *and* hearkened not unto the voice of the LORD:

26 Therefore he lifted up his hand against them, to overthrow them in the wilderness:

---

23. *Therefore he said that he would destroy them.* See Ex. xxxii. 10-14. He threatened to destroy them, and he would have done it, if Moses had not interposed and pleaded for them. There was nothing strange or very unusual in this. Many a descending curse on guilty men is turned away by prayer, and by human intervention. We are constantly endeavouring to turn aside evils which would come upon others—by our intervention—by labour or by prayer. Thus, when we toil to provide food for our children, or give it in charity to the poor, we are endeavouring to avert the evil of starvation which would otherwise come upon them; when we provide for them clothing, we turn away the evils of nakedness and cold; when we give them medicine we turn away the evil of long-continued disease or of death; when we rush through the flames if a house is on fire, or venture out in a rough sea in a boat, to save others from devouring flame or from a watery grave, we seek to turn aside evils which would otherwise come upon them. So when we pray for others we *may* turn away evils which would otherwise descend on the guilty. No one can estimate the number or the amount of evils which are thus turned away from the guilty and the suffering by intervention and intercession; no one can tell how many of the blessings of his own life he owes to the intercessions and the toils of others. *All* the blessings that come upon sinners,—*all* that is done to turn away deserved wrath from men, — is owing to the fact that the one great Intercessor—greater than Moses—cast himself into the

"breach," and himself met and rolled back the woes which were coming upon a guilty world. ¶ *Had not Moses his chosen.* Chosen to lead and guide his people to the promised land. ¶ *Stood before him.* Presented himself before him. ¶ *In the breach.* Literally, *in the breaking.* The allusion is to a breach made in a wall (1 Kings xi. 27; Isa. xxx. 13; Amos iv. 3; Job xxx. 14), and to the force with which an army rushes through a breach that is thus made. So God seemed to be about to come forth to destroy the nation.

24. *Yea, they despised the pleasant land.* Marg., as in Heb., *land of desire.* That is, a country *to be* desired,—a country whose situation, climate, productions, made it desirable as a place of abode. Such Palestine was always represented to be to the children of Israel (Lev. xx. 24; Num. xiii. 27; xiv. 8; xvi. 14; Deut. vi. 3; xi. 9, *et al.;*) but this land had to them, at the time here referred to, no attractions, and they rather desired to return again to Egypt; Num. xi. 5. ¶ *They believed not his word.* His assurance in regard to the land to which they were going.

25. *But murmured in their tents,* etc. Num. xiv. 2, 27. They complained of Moses; they complained of their food; they complained of the hardships of their journey; they complained of God. They did this when "in their tents;" when they had a comfortable home; when safe; when provided for; when under the direct Divine protection and care. So men often complain: perhaps oftener when they have *many* comforts than when they have *few.*

26. *Therefore he lifted up his hand*

27 To [1] overthrow their seed
also among the nations, and to
scatter them in the lands.

28 They *c* joined themselves
also unto Baal-peor, and ate the
sacrifices of the dead.

29 Thus they provoked *him* to

[1] *make them fall.*   *c* Num. xxv. 2, etc.

anger with their inventions; and
the plague brake in upon them.

30 Then stood up Phinehas,
and executed judgment : and *so*
the plague was stayed.

31 And that was counted unto
him for righteousness, unto all
generations for evermore.

---

against them. Num. xiv. 27–33. He
resolved to cut them off, so that none
of them should reach the promised
land. ¶ *To overthrow them in the wilderness.* Literally, *to cause them to fall.*
27. *To overthrow their seed also
among the nations.* Marg., as in
Heb., *to make them fall;* to wit,
among the surrounding people. The
reference here is to the posterity
of those who murmured and fell
in the wilderness. The result of
their rebellion and murmuring would
not terminate with them. It would
extend to their posterity, and the rebellion of the fathers would be remembered in distant generations. The
overthrow of the nation, and its captivity in Babylon was thus one of
the remote consequences of their rebellion in the wilderness. ¶ *And to
scatter them in the lands.* In foreign
lands—as at Babylon. If this psalm
was written at the time of the Babylonish captivity, this allusion would
be most appropriate. It would remind the nation that its captivity
there had its origin in the ancient
and long-continued disposition of the
people to revolt from God.
28. *They joined themselves also
unto Baal-peor.* They joined in their
devotions, or, they shared in the rites
of idolatrous worship. This occurred
when they were in the regions of
Moab, and on the very borders of the
promised land. Num. xxv. Many
other instances of a similar kind are
passed over by the psalmist, and this
seems to have been selected because
of its peculiar aggravation, and to
show the general character of the
nation. Even after their long-continued enjoyment of the favour and
protection of God,—after he had con-

ducted them safely through the wilderness,—after he had brought them
to the very border of the land of
Canaan, and all his promises were
about to be fulfilled, they still showed
a disposition to depart from God.
Baal-peor was an idol of the Moabites, in whose worship females pros-
tituted themselves. Gesenius, *Lex.*
Comp. Num. xxv. 1–3. Baal was the
name of the idol; Peor was the
name of a mountain in Moab, where
the idol was worshipped. ¶ *And ate
the sacrifices of the dead.* Of false
gods, represented as *dead* or having
no life, in contradistinction from the
true and *living* God. They ate the
sacrifices offered to those idols; that
is, they participated in their worship.
Num. xxv. 2.
29. *Thus they provoked* him *to
anger with their inventions.* The
word rendered *inventions* means properly *works; deeds;* then it is used
in the sense of *evil* deeds, crimes.
¶ *And the plague brake in upon them.*
See Num. xxv. 8, 9. No less than
twenty-four thousand fell in the
plague. Num. xxv. 9.
30. *Then stood up Phinehas, and
executed judgment,* etc. Inflicted
summary punishment upon a principal offender. Num. xxv. 7, 8.
31. *And that was counted unto him
for righteousness.* See Num. xxv.
11–13. Comp. Notes on Rom. iv. 3.
The meaning here is, that this was
regarded as a *proof* or *demonstration*
that he was a righteous man—a man
fearing God. ¶ *Unto all generations
for evermore.* Heb., "To generation
and generation for ever." The record would be transmitted from one
generation to another, without any
intermission, and would be perma-

32 They ^d angered *him* also at the waters of strife, so that it went ill with Moses for their sakes :

33 Because they provoked his spirit, so that he spake unadvisedly with his lips.

34 They ^e did not destroy the nations, concerning whom the LORD commanded them :

35 But were mingled among the heathen, and learned their works.

d Num. xx. 3, etc.　　*e* Judges i. 21, etc.

---

nent. This is one of the illustrations of the statement so frequently made in the Scriptures (comp. Ex. xx. 6; Deut. vii. 9; Rom. xi. 28) that the blessings of religion will descend to a distant posterity. Such instances are constantly occurring, and there is no legacy which a man can leave his family so valuable as the fact that he himself fears God and keeps his laws.

32. *They angered* him *also at the waters of strife*. Num. xx. 3-13. They complained of the want of water. They wished that they had died as others had done. They murmured against God as if he could *not* supply their wants. They showed an unbelieving and rebellious spirit,—provoking God, and tempting Moses to an act of great impatience by their conduct. In Num. xx. 13, this is, "the waters of *Meribah;*"—marg., *strife.* This is the meaning of the Hebrew word. The place took its name from the fact that the people there *strove* against the Lord and against Moses. ¶ *So that it went ill with Moses for their sakes.* Evil came upon him. He was betrayed into impatience, and was tempted to use words which offended God, and prevented his being permitted to lead the people into the promised land. Num. xx. 12.

33. *Because they provoked his spirit.* Literally, "They made his spirit *bitter,*" or they embittered his soul. They threw him off his guard, so that instead of manifesting the meekness and gentleness which so eminently characterised him in general (see Num. xii. 3), he gave way to expressions of anger. See Num. xx. 10. ¶ *So that he spake unadvisedly with his lips.* Passionately ; in a

severe, harsh, and threatening manner. He did not bear with them as he should have done; he did not refer to God, to his power, and to his goodness as he should have done; he spake as if the whole thing depended on him and Aaron :—"Hear now, ye rebels ; must *we* fetch you water out of this rock ?" The word rendered "spake unadvisedly"—בָטָא, *bata*—means properly *to babble ;* and then, to talk idly, or unadvisedly ; to utter that which has no meaning, or an improper meaning. Let us not harshly blame Moses, till we are placed in circumstances similar to his, and see how we would ourselves act. Who is there that would *not* have been provoked as he was, or even to a greater degree ? If there *are* any such, let them "cast the first stone."

34. *They did not destroy the nations.* The Canaanites, Hivites, Jebusites, etc. ;—the nations that inhabited the land of Canaan. ¶ *Concerning whom the* LORD *commanded them.* The command on this subject was positive ; and it was to destroy them, to spare none of them. Num. xxxiii. 52 ; Deut. vii. 5, 16.

35. *But were mingled among the heathen.* Among the nations ; by intermarriage, and by commerce. They suffered them to remain in the land, contrary to the command of God, and thus greatly exposed and endangered the purity of their religion and their own morals. See Judges ii. 2 ; iii. 5, 6. ¶ *And learned their works.* Their practices ; their customs and habits :—learned to live as they did. This was an illustration of the danger of intercourse with the wicked and the worldly. What occurred in their case has often occurred since in the history of the people of God, that by

36 And *f* they served their idols; which were a snare unto them.

37 Yea, they sacrificed *g* their sons and their daughters unto devils,

38 And shed innocent blood, *even* the blood of their sons and

f Judges ii. 3, etc.   *g* Ez. xvi. 20.
    h Num. xxxv. 33.

of their daughters, whom they sacrificed unto the idols of Canaan: and the land *h* was polluted with blood.

39 Thus were they defiled *i* with their own works, and went a whoring *k* with their own inventions.

i Ez. xx. 18.
k Lev. xvii. 7; Jer. iii. 6—9.

"mingling" with the world they have learned to practise their "works;" have become conformed to their manner of living, and have thus lost their spirituality, and brought dishonour on the cause of religion. There is some proper sense in which the people of God are *not* to be conformed to the world; in which, though living among them, they are to be separate from them; in which, though they are parts of the same nation, and live under the same government and laws, they are to be a distinct and peculiar people, ruled supremely by higher laws, and having higher and nobler ends of life. Rom. xii. 2; 2 Cor. vi. 14–17.

36. *And they served their idols.* Judges ii. 12, 13, 17, 19; iii. 6, 7. ¶ *Which were a snare unto them.* Like the snares or toils by which birds and wild beasts are caught. That is, they were taken unawares; they were in danger when they did not perceive it; they fell when they thought themselves safe. The bird and the wild beast approach the snare, unconscious of danger; so the friend of God approaches the temptations which are spread out before him by the enemy of souls,—and, ere he is aware, he is a captive, and has fallen. Nothing could better describe the way in which the people of God are led into sin than the arts by which birds are caught by the fowler, and wild beasts by the hunter.

37. *Yea, they sacrificed their sons and their daughters.* See 2 Kings xvi. 3; Ezek. xvi. 20; xx. 31; Isa. lvii. 5. ¶ *Unto devils.* Heb., שֵׁדִים shaidim. The Septuagint, δαιμονίοις,

demons. So the Vulgate, *dæmoniis.* The word is used only in the plural number, and is applied to idols. It occurs only in this place, and in Deut. xxxii. 17. On the meaning of this, see Notes on 1 Cor. x. 20.

38. *And shed innocent blood,* etc. The blood of those who had committed no crime; who did not *deserve* the treatment which they received. That is, they were sacrificed *as* innocent persons, and *because* it was believed that they *were* innocent:—the pure for the impure; the holy for the unholy. It was on the general principle that a sacrifice for sin must be itself pure, or it could not be offered in the place of the guilty; that an offering made for one who had violated law must be by one who had *not* violated it. This was the principle on which *lambs* were offered in sacrifice. It is on this principle that the atonement for sin by the Lord Jesus was made; on this depend its efficacy and its value. ¶ *And the land was polluted with blood.* That is, Either so much blood was thus poured out, that it might be said that the very land was polluted with it; or, the sin itself was so great, that it seemed to defile and pollute the whole land.

39. *Thus were they defiled with their own works.* By their very attempts to deliver themselves from sin. They were corrupt, and the consciousness that they were sinners led them to the commission of even greater enormities in attempting to expiate their guilt, even by the sacrifice of their own sons and daughters. Thus all the religions of the heathen begin in sin, and end in sin. The consciousness of sin

40 Therefore *l* was the wrath of the LORD kindled against his people, insomuch that he abhorred *m* his own inheritance.

41 And he gave them into the hand of the heathen; and they that hated them ruled over them.

l Judges ii. 14, etc.; Neh. ix. 27, etc.; Ps. lxxviii. 59.

42 Their enemies also oppressed them, and they were brought into subjection under their hand.

43 Many times did he deliver them; but they provoked *him* with their counsel, and were ¹ brought low for their iniquity.

m Lam. ii. 7.
¹ Or, *impoverished*, or, *weakened*.

---

only leads to the commission of greater sin; to all the abominations of idol-worship; to the sacrifice—the murder—of the innocent, with the vain hope of thus making expiation for their crimes. Sinners have never yet been able to devise a way by which they may make themselves pure. It is only the great Sacrifice made on the cross which meets the case; which provides expiation; and which saves from future sin. ¶ *And went a whoring.* Apostacy from God and backsliding are often illustrated in the Scriptures by the violation of the marriage compact, as the relation between God and his people is often compared with the relation between a husband and wife. Comp. Isa. lxii. 5; Jer. iii. 14; vii. 9; xiii. 27; Ezek. xvi. 20, 22, 25, 33, 34; xxiii. 17. ¶ *With their own inventions.* More literally, With their own *works.* See Notes on ver. 29.

40. *Therefore was the wrath of the* LORD *kindled against his people.* Anger is often compared with a fire; as we say now, a man is *inflamed* with passion. See Esther i. 12; Lam. ii. 3; Ps. lxxix. 5; lxxxix. 46; Jer. iv. 4; Judges ii. 14. Of course, this must be taken in a manner appropriate to God. It means that his treatment of his offending people was *as if* he were burning with wrath against them. ¶ *Insomuch that he abhorred his own inheritance.* He was offended with his people; he treated them *as if* they were an abomination to him. He punished them; he cast them off; he left them to the just results of their own conduct. Were ever any writers more

candid and honest than the sacred penmen? There is no effort to vindicate the nation; there is no apology offered for them; there is no concealment of their guilt; there is no attempt to soften the statement in regard to the feelings of God towards them. Their conduct *was* abominable; they deserved the Divine displeasure; they were ungrateful, evil, and rebellious; and the sacred writers do not hesitate to admit the truth of this to the fullest extent.

41. *And he gave them into the hand of the heathen.* That is, of foreign nations. They were indeed *heathens,* in the sense in which that term is used now,—that is, they were ignorant of the true God, and worshipped idols; but that idea is not necessarily in the original word. The word *Gentiles* expresses all that the word implies. ¶ *And they that hated them ruled over them.* Had them in subjection.

42. *Their enemies also oppressed them.* Sept., *Afflicted them.* They invaded their country; they destroyed their vintages; they laid desolate their land; they made them captives. ¶ *And they were brought into subjection.* Heb., made to bow.

43. *Many times did he deliver them.* From danger of invasion; from foreign arms; from entire overthrow. Numerous instances of this are recorded in the history of the Hebrew people. ¶ *But they provoked* him *with their counsel.* This does not mean that they gave counsel or advice to God; but it refers to the counsel which they took among themselves; the plans which they formed. These were such as to offend God. ¶ *And were*

44 Nevertheless, [n] he regarded
their affliction, when he heard
their cry :
45 And he remembered for them
his covenant, and repented ac-

n Lev. xxvi. 40—42.

cording to the multitude of his
mercies.
46 He made them also to be
pitied [o] of all those that carried
them captives.

o Ezra ix. 9.

brought low for their iniquity. Marg.,
impoverished or weakened. The Hebrew word means to melt away, to
pine ; and hence to decay, to be
brought low. See Job xxiv. 24,
where it is rendered brought low, and
Eccl. x. 18, where it is rendered de-
cayeth. The word does not occur elsewhere. The meaning is, that they were
weakened ; their national strength
was exhausted as a punishment for
their sins.
  44. Nevertheless, he regarded their
affliction. Literally, "And he looked
upon the trouble that was upon them;"
or, "and he saw in the distress to
them." The meaning is, that he did
not turn away from it; he saw the
need of interposition, and he came to
them. ¶ When he heard their cry.
Literally, "In his hearing their cry."
Their cry for help came before him,
and he did not refuse to look upon
their affliction. The idea is, that he
was attracted to their case by their
loud cry for help ; and that when he
heard the cry, he did not refuse to
look upon their low and sad condition.
God assists us when we cry to him.
We ask his attention to our troubles ;
we pray for his help ; and when he
hears the cry, he comes and saves us.
He does not turn away, or treat our
case as unworthy of his notice.
  45. And he remembered for them
his covenant. His solemn promises
made to their fathers. He remembered that covenant in their behalf;
or, on account of that, he came and
blessed them. He had made gracious
promises to the patriarchs; he had
promised to be the God of their posterity; he had his own great purposes to accomplish through their
nation in the distant future; and on
these accounts, he came and blessed
them. ¶ And repented. He averted

impending judgments. He checked
and arrested the calamities which he
was bringing upon them for their sins.
He acted towards them as though his
mind had been changed; as though
he was sorry for what he was doing.
The word repent can be applied to
God in no other sense than this. It
cannot be applied to him in the sense
that he felt or admitted that he had
done wrong; or that he had made a
mistake; or that he had changed his
mind or purposes; or that he intended to enter on a new course of
conduct; but it may be applied to
him in the sense that his treatment
of men is as if he had changed his
mind, or as if he were sorry for what
he had done :—that is, a certain course
of things which had been commenced,
would be arrested and changed to
meet existing circumstances, because
they had changed,—though all must
have been foreseen and purposed in
his eternal counsels. ¶ According
to the multitude of his mercies. The
greatness of his mercy; the disposition of his nature to show mercy;
the repeated instances in which he
had shown mercy in similar circumstances.
  46. He made them also to be pitied
of all those that carried them captives. That is, he exercised such
control over the minds of the heathen
that they were willing to show them
mercy and to release them. It was
not by any native tenderness on the
part of the heathen; it was not because they were disposed of themselves to show them any favour; it
was not because they had any natural
relentings on the subject; but it was
because God had access to their hearts,
and inclined them to show compassion for their suffering prisoners.
This is a remarkable instance of the

47 Save ^{p} us, O LORD our God, and gather us from among the heathen, to give thanks unto thy holy name, *and* to triumph in thy praise.

p 1 Chron. xvi. 35.　*q* Ps. xli. 13.

48 Blessed *q be* the LORD God of Israel from everlasting to everlasting: and let all the people say, Amen. ^{1} Praise ye the LORD.

^{1} *Hallelujah.*

power of God over even the hardened minds and hearts of heathen men; and it shows that he holds this power, and can exercise it when he pleases. If he could excite in their hard hearts feelings of compassion towards his own people in bondage, what should prevent his having such access to the hearts of the heathen now as to lead them to repentance towards himself? On the exercise of this power the salvation of the heathen world—as of all sinners—must depend; and for the putting forth of this power we should most fervently pray. The *literal* rendering of this verse would be, "And he gave them to compassions before all those that made them captive." That is, he inclined them to show favour or compassion. Comp. Dan. i. 9; 1 Kings viii. 50.

47. *Save us, O* LORD *our God, and gather us from among the heathen.* From among the nations. From this it would seem that the psalm was composed when the nation was in captivity, or was dispersed among the nations that were hostile to them. The prayer is, that as God had, in former periods, recovered his people when they were in exile, or were scattered abroad, he would again graciously interpose and bring them to the land of their fathers, where they had been accustomed to worship God. ¶ *To give thanks unto thy holy name.* Unto thee; a holy God. That we may praise thee in the place where thou art accustomed to be worshipped—in the sanctuary. ¶ And *to triumph in thy praise.* To exult; to rejoice; to be glad in praising thee,—in thy worship.

48. *Blessed* be *the* LORD *God of Israel from everlasting to everlasting.* For ever. As he has been adored in the past—even from the beginning of the

VOL. III.

creation—so let him be adored and praised in all periods to come—for ever and for ever. See Notes on Ps. xli. 13. ¶ *And let all the people say, Amen.* In Ps. xli. 13, this is, "Amen and amen." The idea is, Let all the people join in this; let them all express and declare their assent to this:—let them all say, "Be it so." The word *Amen* is a word expressing assent — meaning *verily, truly, certainly.* ¶ *Praise ye the* LORD. Heb., *Hallelu-jah.* See Ps. civ. 35.

PSALM CVII.

This psalm is without a title, and its author is unknown. The occasion on which it was composed is not particularly designated, though from vers. 2, 3, it is probable that it was on a return from exile or captivity. There is nothing in the psalm to forbid the supposition that this was the return from the captivity at Babylon, and that the psalm was designed to be used at the re-dedication of the temple after the restoration. Every part of it would be appropriate to such an occasion, and it is every way probable that so important an event would be celebrated with appropriate songs of praise.

The *design* of the psalm, so far as it has a practical bearing, is indicated in vers. 8, 15, 21, 31, in the language repeated in those verses :—"Oh that men would praise the LORD for his goodness, and for his wonderful works to the children of men !" The purpose of the psalm is so to set forth these "works," or these *doings* of God, as to lead men to praise and adoration.

The psalm is very regular in its structure. The first three verses are introductory, intended to designate the people who were specially called on to praise God,—as those who had been redeemed from the hand of the enemy, and gathered out of the lands—east, west, north, and south.

I

PSALM CVII.

O GIVE thanks unto the LORD, for *he is* good; *r* for his mercy *endureth* for ever.

r Ps. cxix. 68; Matt. xix. 17.

2 Let the redeemed of the LORD say *so*, whom he hath redeemed *s* from the hand of the enemy;

s Ps. cvi. 10.

The remainder of the psalm is divided into portions marked by the above words, " Oh that men would praise the Lord for his goodness," etc., vers. 8, 15, 21, 31. These portions are of unequal length, and this language (with a few appropriate words added) is placed *at the close of each part*, as being that which was suggested by the previous thoughts. In the closing portion, however, (vers. 32-43,) this language is not employed, but the expression of *desire* in the other cases is changed into an *affirmation* that all who were wise *would* " observe these things," and *would* " understand the loving-kindness of the Lord."

The particular parts of the psalm are the following :—

I. A reference to the redeemed of the Lord as having wandered in the wilderness; as having been hungry and thirsty; as having no city to dwell in; and then, as calling upon the Lord in such a manner that he heard them, and led them in a right and safe way. For *this* the psalmist expresses the wish that " men would praise the Lord for his goodness," vers. 4-9.

II. A reference to God as displaying goodness towards those who sit in darkness and in the shadow of death, and who are bound in affliction and iron :— illustrated by a reference to the people of God in the times of bondage, as being cast down and punished for their sins, and as then calling upon the Lord in their trouble, so that he brought them out of that darkness and shadow of death, and brake their bands asunder. For *this* the psalmist expresses the wish that " men would praise the Lord for his goodness," vers. 10-16.

III. A reference to the deliverance wrought for the people of God. They had sinned; they had shown their folly; they had drawn near to the gates of death, and then they cried unto the Lord, and he sent his word and healed them. For *this* the psalmist expresses the desire that " men would praise the Lord for his goodness," vers. 17-22.

IV. A reference to the goodness of the Lord as manifested towards those who go down to the sea in ships, and do business in the great waters. They see the wonders of the Lord in the deep. They encounter storms and tempests. They are raised up to the heavens on the waves, and then sink to a corresponding depth. They reel to and fro and stagger like a drunkard ; and then they cry to the Lord, and he hears them, and makes the sea calm, and brings them to the desired haven. For *this* the psalmist expresses the wish that " men would praise the Lord for his goodness," vers. 23-32.

V. A reference to the goodness of the Lord in preparing a place for men to dwell in :—turning rivers into a wilderness, the water-springs into dry ground, the wilderness into standing water, and the dry ground into water-springs :— making arrangements for men to dwell upon the earth, so that they may sow the fields and plant vineyards—setting the poor on high from affliction, and making them families like a flock. In reference to *this*, and to *all* that God does, the psalmist says, in the conclusion of the psalm, that all who are " wise, and will observe these things, shall understand the loving-kindness of the Lord," vers. 33-43.

1. *O give thanks unto the* LORD, *for* he is *good*. See Notes on Ps. cvi. 1. ¶ *For his mercy* endureth *for ever*. He is unchanging in his mercy. It is an attribute of his very nature. He is constantly manifesting it. The word rendered *mercy* here, however—חֶסֶד, *hhesed*—is more general in its signification than our word *mercy*. Our word means *favour shown to the guilty ;* the Hebrew word means kindness, goodness, benignity in general. It is this which is celebrated in the psalm before us.

2. *Let the redeemed of the* LORD *say so*. They are peculiarly qualified to say so; they have special occasion to say so ; they can and will appreciate this trait in his character. The word rendered *redeemed* here—from

3 And gathered *t* them out of the lands from the east, and from the west, from the north, and from the ¹ south.

t Isa. xliii. 5, 6; Ez. xxxix. 25, etc.
¹ *sea.*

4 They wandered in the wilderness *u* in a solitary way; they found no city to dwell in.

5 Hungry and thirsty, their soul fainted in them.

u Deut. xxxii. 10.

גָּאַל, *gaal*—means *delivered, rescued,* without reference to any price paid for the deliverance. It refers here not to a ransom from *sin,* but to deliverance from *danger.* The probable allusion is to the deliverance from the captivity in Babylon. Comp. Notes on Isa. xliii. 3. ¶ *Whom he hath redeemed from the hand of the enemy.* The power of the enemy. That is, He has saved them from their enemies, and has not suffered them to be destroyed by them. What is here said is true in the most eminent sense of those who are redeemed by the blood of the Son of God, and who are made heirs of salvation. Every consideration makes it proper that *they* should praise the Lord. Of all on earth, they have most occasion for such praise; of all among men, it may be presumed that they will be best qualified to appreciate the goodness of the Lord.

3. *And gathered them out of the lands.* The countries where they were scattered. In the times of the captivity the people were not all taken to one place, or did not all abide in one place. In the long exile—of seventy years — in Babylon, they would naturally be much scattered in the different provinces; and the attempt to collect them together, to restore them again to their native land, might be attended with much difficulty. ¶ *From the east,* etc. From all quarters; from the places where they were scattered abroad. That is, one taking his position in Babylon would see them dispersed from that place as a centre into all the surrounding country. ¶ *And from the south.* Marg., as in Heb., *from the sea.* In general, in the Old Testament, the word *sea* is used for the *west,* because the western boundary of

the land of Palestine was the Mediterranean Sea. Comp. Ps. cxxxix. 9. But the supposed position of the speaker here is *Babylon,* and on that account the south might be fitly designated by the word *sea;* —as, on the south of Babylon, the Persian Gulf and the Indian Ocean would be soon reached.

4. *They wandered in the wilderness.* On their return from Babylon; or, when God was conducting them again to their own land. The word *wilderness* in the Scriptures means a desolate, barren, uninhabited region, usually destitute of trees, of springs, and of water-courses. It does not denote, as it does with us, a region of extensive *forests.* Comp. Notes on Matt. iv. 1. ¶ *In a solitary way.* Rather, in a *waste* way; a land that was desolate and uncultivated. ¶ *They found no city to dwell in.* In their journeyings. This was true of the region between Babylon and Palestine; — a wide, barren, desolate waste.

5. *Hungry and thirsty.* As they would be, when wandering in such a desert. A more literal and expressive rendering would be, "Hungry,—also thirsty." ¶ *Their soul fainted in them.* The word here used—עָטַף, *ataph*—means properly to cover, to clothe, as with a garment, Ps. lxxiii. 6; or a field with grain, Ps. lxv. 13; then, to hide oneself, Job xxiii. 9; then, to cover with darkness, Ps. lxxvii. 3; cii., *title;* thus it denotes the state of mind when darkness seems to be in the way—a way of calamity, trouble, sorrow; of weakness, faintness, feebleness. Here it would seem from the connexion to refer to the exhaustion produced by the want of food and drink.

6 Then *v* they cried unto the
LORD in their trouble, *and* he
delivered them out of their distresses.

7 And he led them forth by
the right *w* way, that they might
go to a city of habitation.

v vers. 13, 19, 28; Ps. l. 15; Hos. v. 15.

8 Oh that *men* would praise
the LORD *for* his goodness, and
for his wonderful works to the
children of men !

9 For *x* he satisfieth the longing soul, and filleth the hungry
soul with goodness.

w Ezra viii. 21; Isa. xxx. 21.   *x* Luke i. 53, 79.

6. *Then they cried unto the* LORD
in their trouble. The language in
this verse is repeated in this psalm
in vers. 13, 19, 28,—as if this were
the main subject of the psalm, that
when the people of God in different
circumstances, or under various forms
of trouble, call upon God, he hears
them and delivers them. ¶ *And he
delivered them out of their distresses.*
The verb from which the noun here
used is derived has the idea of being
narrow, straitened, compressed. Hence
the word comes to be used in the sense
of distress of any kind,—as if one were
pressed down, or compressed painfully
in a narrow space.

7. *And he led them forth by the
right way.* A literal version, if the
term necessary to express it might be
allowable, would be, " He *wayed* them
in a straight *way;*" he made a way
for them, and that was a straight
way. He conducted them in the
most direct path to the land to
which they were going. ¶ *That they
might go to a city of habitation.* A
city where they might permanently
dwell. The word *city* here seems to
be used in the sense of *abode;* and
the idea is, that he led them to a
land where they might cease to be
wanderers, and might find a settled
home.

8. *Oh that* men *would praise the*
LORD *for his goodness.* More literally, " Let such—or, let these—praise
the Lord for his goodness,"—the word
" *men* " having been supplied by our
translators. Yet it is not improper
to suppose that a wider range is intended than would be denoted if it
were confined to those who had then
been delivered. It was evidently designed to impress the minds of those

who might use this psalm in their
devotions; and the idea is, that the
deliverance then vouchsafed to the
people of God in their troubles should
lead all to praise and adore him. Such
a surprising interposition suggested
an important lesson in regard to God,
applicable to all men; and should lead
all to praise him in view of the trait
of character thus manifested, as that
of a God who hears prayer when his
people are in trouble, and who can
make a straight path before them
when they are in danger of being
lost, and who can conduct them
through the wilderness—the waste
places—of this world, as he did his
people across the pathless sands of
the desert. The true use of all history is to teach us lessons about God.
¶ *And* for *his wonderful works to the
children of men.* His doings as fitted
to excite wonder and admiration. His
dealings with his people in the desert
furnished one illustration of this; the
world is full of such illustrations. The
desire expressed in this verse suggests
the great lesson of the psalm.

9. *For he satisfieth the longing soul.*
This does not mean—what is indeed
true in itself—that God has made
provision for the *soul* of man, and
satisfies it when it longs or pants for
its needed supply, but the reference
is to the creatures of God—the living
things that he has made; and the
idea is, that he has made provision
for their wants. He gives them food
and drink, so that their wants are
met. The *particular* reference here,
however, in the word rendered *longing* is to *thirst,* as contradistinguished
from the other member of the verse,
where the reference is to *hunger.* So
the word is used in Isa. xxix. 8.

10 Such as sit in darkness and in the shadow of death, *being* bound *y* in affliction and iron ;

11 Because *z* they rebelled against the words of God, and contemned the counsel *a* of the Most High ;

12 Therefore he brought down their heart with labour ; they

y Job xxxvi. 8, 9.　　*z* Lam. iii. 42 ; v. 16, 17.

fell down, and *there was* none to *b* help.

13 Then they cried unto the LORD in their trouble, *and* he saved them out of their distresses.

14 He *c* brought them out of darkness and the shadow of

a Luke vii. 30.　　*b* Job ix. 13.
c Ps. cxlvi. 7.

¶ *And filleth the hungry soul with goodness.* Supplies the wants of the hungry with "good ;" that is, with that which is "good" for it ; which meets its wants, and imparts strength and happiness.

10. *Such as sit in darkness.* The reference in these verses (10–14) is evidently to the children of Israel, when in Babylon ; and the design is, to show the goodness of God to them in their trouble, and the occasion which they had for praising him on that account. To "sit in darkness" is significant of great ignorance (comp. Notes on Luke i. 79 ; Isa. ix. 2) ; or of affliction and trouble, as darkness is an emblem of calamity. ¶ *And in the shadow of death.* A dark, gloomy, chilly shade such as *Death* would cast if he stood between us and the light. See Notes on Job iii. 5 ; comp. Job x. 21 ; Ps. xxiii. 4 ; xliv. 19 ; Isa. ix. 2. The reference is to the sad and gloomy residence of the Hebrews in the land of captivity. ¶ *Being bound in affliction and iron.* Captives and slaves. Comp. Ps. cv. 18.

11. *Because they rebelled against the words of God.* The commands of God. They did not keep his commandments. Their captivity was produced by national disobedience. See Notes on Dan. ix. 5–8. ¶ *And contemned the counsel.* They despised the instructions of God. The law of God, at the same time that it *is* law, is of the nature of *counsel,* since it is indicative of what God regards as wise and good, and since it is the best *advice* that God can give to men. A just and righteous law, while it involves *obligation* to obey it, is also

the best counsel that can be given, and implies that the highest *wisdom* would be shown in being obedient to it. God will *command* nothing which he would not *advise,* and which it would not be *wisdom* to obey. ¶ *Of the Most High.* Of God, who, being supreme, has a right to rule over all, and to require that his laws shall be obeyed.

12. *Therefore he brought down their heart.* Their pride ; their self-sufficiency ; their self-complacency. They thought that they could do without God ; they relied on their own resources, and were self-satisfied ; but God showed them that all this was vain, and humbled them, as he often does the proud, in the dust. ¶ *With labour.* With trouble ; with affliction ; with disappointment ; with reverses ; with sorrow. The Hebrew word—עָמָל, *amal*—would include all this. Comp. Gen. xli. 51 ; Deut. xxvi. 7 ; Job iii. 10 ; xvi. 2. ¶ *They fell down.* They, as it were, *stumbled*— for so the Hebrew word means. They were walking along with a haughty air, and a high look, and suddenly they stumbled and fell. ¶ *And there was none to help.* No God to interpose ; no nation to befriend them ; no human arm to be stretched out for their deliverance. God gave them up, helpless, to the just consequences of their folly and wickedness.

13. *Then they cried unto the* LORD *in their trouble.* Comp. Dan. ix. This is repeated in the psalm in vers. 6, 13, 19, 28,—in all the divisions of the psalm except the last. See Notes on ver. 6.

14. *He brought them out of dark-*

death, and brake their bands in sunder.

15 Oh that *men* would praise the LORD *for* his goodness, and *for* his wonderful works to the children of men!

16 For *d* he hath broken the

d Isa. xlv. 2.   *e* Ps. xxxviii. 3, 5.

gates of brass, and cut the bars of iron in sunder.

17 Fools, because of *e* their transgression, and because of their iniquities, are afflicted.

18 Their soul abhorreth all manner of meat; and they draw near unto the gates of death.

---

ness and the shadow of death. From their captivity; from calamity which seemed to be as gloomy as the shadow of death. ¶ *And brake their bands in sunder.* Delivered them from their bondage, *as if* the bands of a prisoner or captive were suddenly broken.

15. *Oh that* men *would praise*, etc. See Notes on ver. 8. The idea here is that the things just referred to *should* call forth expressions of gratitude to God. The immediate reference is to those who had partaken of these proofs of the Divine goodness, but still the language is so general as to be applicable to all classes of men.

16. *For he hath broken the gates of brass.* The immediate *reason* here given for praising the Lord is that he had "broken the gates of brass," continuing the thought from vers. 10-14. In the previous part of the psalm, in giving a reason for praising the Lord, the fact that he feeds the hungry was selected (ver. 9) because in the preceding part the allusion was to the sufferings of hunger and thirst (vers. 4, 5); here the fact that he had broken the gates of brass is selected, because the allusion in the immediately preceding verses (12-14) was to their imprisonment. In the construction of the psalm there is great regularity. The "gates of brass" refer probably to Babylon; and the idea is, that their deliverance had been as if the brazen gates of that great city had been broken down to give them free egress from their captivity. Thus the conquest of Babylon by Cyrus is announced in similar language: "I will break in pieces the gates of brass, and cut in sunder the bars of iron," Isa. xlv. 2. See Notes on that passage.

17. *Fools, because of their trans-*

gression. Wicked men, considered as fools, because they *are* transgressors. Comp. Notes on Ps. xiv. 1; lxxiii. 3; lxxv. 4. The immediate allusion here, probably, is to the Jews, who had been so wicked and so supremely foolish in violating the commands of God, and making it necessary to bring upon them as a punishment the captivity at Babylon; but the language is made general because it will with equal propriety describe the conduct of *all* wicked men. There is nothing more foolish than an act of wickedness; there is no wisdom equal to that of obeying God. ¶ *And because of their iniquities, are afflicted.* A more literal rendering of this verse would be, "Fools from the way of their transgressions [that is, by their course of transgression], and by their iniquities, afflict themselves." The idea is, that it is *in the very line* of their transgressions; or, that they *bring it upon themselves.* All punishment is in fact in the line of the offence; that is, sin leads directly to it; or, in other words, if a man treads along in the path of sin, he will come to this result—to punishment. Punishment is not arbitrary on the part of God, and it is not of the nature of a mere direct infliction from *his* hand. It is what men mete out to themselves, and what they might have avoided if they had chosen to do so.

18. *Their soul abhorreth all manner of meat.* All food; all that is to be eaten. The word rendered *abhorreth* is a word which is used with reference to anything that is abominable or loathsome; that from which we turn away with disgust. The language is expressive of sickness, when

19 Then *f* they cry unto the LORD in their trouble; *and* he saveth them out of their distresses.

20 He sent his word *g* and healed them, *h* and delivered *them* from their destructions.

21 Oh that *men* would praise

f Job xxxiii. 19, etc.
g 2 Kings xx. 4, 5; Matt. viii. 8.

the LORD *for* his goodness, and *for* his wonderful works *i* to the children of men!

22 And let them sacrifice the sacrifices of thanksgiving, *k* and declare his works with *l* rejoicing.

h Ps. xxx. 2, 3.   *i* Ps. lxvi. 5.
k Lev. vii. 12; Heb. xiii. 15.
l *singing.*

we *loathe* all food. ¶ *And they draw near unto the gates of death.* They are sick, and are ready to die. The reference is to the under world—the world where the dead are supposed to dwell. This is represented here as a city which is entered through gates. See Notes on Ps. ix. 13.

19. *Then they cry unto the* LORD, etc. See Notes on vers. 6, 13. The meaning here is, that if the *sick* cry to the Lord, he hears them, and delivers them. This cannot mean that it *always* occurs, but it occurs *so often* as to show that God can and does interpose to save; *so often* as to encourage us thus to call upon him when we are sick; *so often* as to lay a proper foundation for praise. Many persons — very many — can recall such instances in their own lives, when they seemed to all human appearance to be drawing near to the gates of death, and when, in connexion with prayer, their disease took a favourable turn, and they were restored again to health. Comp. Notes on James v. 14, 15.

20. *He sent his word, and healed them.* He did it by a word; it was necessary for him merely to give a command, and the disease left them. So it was in the life of the Saviour, who often healed the sick by a "word" (Matt. viii. 8; Luke vii. 7); and so now restoration from disease often *seems* to be accomplished as if some *word* had been spoken by one who had power, commanding the disease to depart. In all cases, also, whatever means may be used, healing power comes from God, and is under his control. Comp. Ps. xxx. 2. ¶ *And*

delivered them *from their destructions.* From what would have destroyed them, if it had not been checked and removed.

21. *Oh that* men, etc. See Notes on ver. 8. Who can help joining in this wish, that those who have been restored from sickness, who have been raised up from the borders of the grave, *would* praise God for it! Who can help wishing that they had the feelings of Hezekiah when he was saved from the sickness which threatened his life—saved by the direct and manifest interposition of God—when he said (Isa. xxxviii. 20), "The Lord was ready to save me: therefore we will sing my songs to the stringed instruments, all the days of our life in the house of the Lord!" Who can help wishing that men everywhere would see in such interpositions the proof of the benevolence of God, and would thank him that he has not forgotten guilty and suffering men!

22. *And let them sacrifice.* As in the cases before (vers. 9, 16), this is connected with the preceding part of the psalm, or is a *continuation* of the thought which had been interrupted by the prayer, "Oh that men would praise the Lord." The particular idea here is, that they who have been sick, and who have been restored to health, *should* offer the sacrifice of thanksgiving; or, that they are the proper persons to praise the Lord. The word *sacrifice* here is used in a large sense to denote worship or adoration. Let them worship God with thanks or praises. ¶ *The sacrifices of thanksgiving.* Heb., *praise.* Let them offer praise. ¶ *And*

23 They that go down to the sea in ships, that do business in great waters;

24 These see the works of the LORD, and his wonders in the deep.

25 For *l* he commandeth, and 1 raiseth the stormy wind, which

l Jonah i. 4, etc.
1 *maketh to stand.*

lifteth up the waves thereof.

26 They mount up to the heaven, they go down again to the depths; their soul is melted *m* because of trouble.

27 They reel to and fro, and stagger like a drunken man, and 2 are at their wit's end.

m Nahum ii. 10.
2 *all their wisdom is swallowed up.*

declare *his works with rejoicing.* Marg., as in Heb., *singing.* Let them set forth his *doings* in songs. Comp. Ps. ix. 11.

23. *They that go down to the sea in ships.* The scene here changes again. From those that wander in the desert,—from those who are in prison,—from those who are sick,—the eye of the psalmist turns to those who encounter the perils of the ocean, and he finds there occasion for praise to God. The phrase "go down" or *descend* is employed here because the sea is lower than the land, and because we *descend* when we embark on board of a vessel. ¶ *That do business,* etc. Whose business or employment is on the ocean.

24. *These see the works of the Lord.* They—sailors—have a special opportunity to see the works of God. They see manifestations of his power which are not seen on the land. They see things which seem to come *directly* from God; which are *immediately* produced by him,—not as the things which occur on the land, which are the result of *growth,* and which are slowly developed. They seem in the solitariness and grandeur of the ocean to stand more directly in the presence of the great God. ¶ *And his wonders in the deep.* In the abyss; in that which is distinguished for its *depth,* as the mountains are for their height. Comp. Ps. cxlviii. 7.

25. *For he commandeth.* Heb., *he says;* that is, He speaks the word, and it is done. The mere expression of his will raises up the storm, and throws the sea into commotion. ¶ *And raiseth the stormy wind.*

Marg., as in Heb., *Maketh to stand.* The "stormy wind" is literally, *the wind of the tempest.* ¶ *Which lifteth up the waves thereof.* The waves of the ocean. The wind seems to take them up, and lift them on high.

26. *They mount up to the heaven.* The mariners. That it refers to the seamen, and not to the waves, is apparent from the close of the verse: "their soul is melted." ¶ *They go down again to the depths.* The word here is different from that used in ver. 24, and rendered *deep,* but the idea is essentially the same. It is the sea or ocean considered as *deep;* as bottomless. The idea here is, that they seem to descend into the very depths of the ocean. ¶ *Their soul is melted because of trouble.* It seems to dissolve; it loses all its vigour; it faints. The word used—מוּג, *mŭg* —means to melt; to flow down; to soften; and is then applied to the heart or mind that loses its courage or vigour by fear or terror. Ex. xv. 15; Josh. ii. 9, 24; Nah. i. 5. The *trouble* here referred to is that which arises from fear and danger.

27. *They reel to and fro.* The word here used — חָגַג, *hhagag —* means to dance as in a circle; then, to reel, or be giddy as drunkards are. ¶ *And stagger,* etc. This word means to move to and fro; to waver; to vacillate; and it is then applied to a man who cannot walk steadily—a drunkard. So the vessel, with the mariners on board, seems to stagger and reel in the storm. ¶ *And are at their wit's end.* Marg., as in Heb., *All their wisdom is swallowed up.* That is, They have no skill to guide

28 Then they cry unto the
LORD in their trouble, and he
bringeth them out of their distresses.
29 He ⁿ maketh the storm a

calm, so that the waves thereof
are still.
30 Then are they glad because
they be quiet; so he bringeth
them unto their desired haven.

---

the vessel. All that has been done
by the wisdom of naval architecture
in constructing it, and all that has
been derived from experience in navi-
gating the ocean, seems now to be
useless. They are at the mercy of
the winds and waves; they are dependent wholly on God; they can
now only cry to him to save them.
Often this occurs in a storm at sea,
when the most skilful and experienced seaman feels that he can do no
more.

28. *Then they cry unto the* LORD *in
their trouble*, etc. See vers. 6, 13, 19.
Sailors pray. If they do not pray
elsewhere, they often do in a storm,
when in danger of being wrecked and
lost. A storm at sea brings hundreds
on their knees who never prayed
before,—for they feel that their only
help is in God, and that it is a fearful
thing to die. Then they do *right*.
They do what *ought* to be done. But
they do then only what men ought
always to do; for it is as plain a duty
to pray when we are in safety as when
we are in danger; when sailing on a
smooth sea as in a storm; when on
the land as on the ocean. Men anywhere, and at any time may die; and
men everywhere and at all times
should, therefore, call upon God.
Storms, tempests, fire, disease, and
danger, only impel men to do what
they *should* do always from higher
motives, and when their motives will
be likely to be more disinterested and
pure.

29. *He maketh the storm a calm.*
God does this, and God only can do
it. The fact, therefore, that Jesus
did it (Matt. viii. 26), proves that
he was Divine. There can be no
more striking proof of Divine power
than the ability to calm the raging
waves of the ocean by a word.

This is literally, " He places the tempest to silence." ¶ *So that the waves
thereof are still.* Are lulled. The
ocean ceases to be agitated, and the
surface becomes smooth. Nothing
is more still than the ocean *in* a calm.
Not a breath of air seems to stir; not
a ripple agitates the surface of the
sea; the sails of the vessel hang loose,
and even the vessel seems to be perfectly at rest: " As idle as a painted
ship upon a painted ocean." So God
can calm down the tempest of the
soul. He can make the mind which
was heaving and tossed, like the ocean,
with anguish on account of guilt, and
which trembled in view of the coming
judgment, as calm as the ocean is
when in its state of perfect repose.
God can do *this*, and none *but* God
can do it; and as Jesus thus stills the
agitation of the guilty soul, as he did
the waves of the sea, *this* proves also
that he is Divine.

30. *Then are they glad because they
be quiet.* Because the storm subsides,
and they have the feeling of safety
from danger. ¶ *So he bringeth them.*
Rather, "*And* he guides them."
¶ *Unto their desired haven.* The word
translated *haven* occurs nowhere else.
By some it is rendered *shore*, but the
word *haven* or *port* seems best to express the sense of the passage: " the
haven of their desire." No one can
appreciate this fully who has not
been long at sea, and who has not experienced the intense desire once more
to see *land*. Even then no one experiences it fully who has not some
object there which he desires to see,
or to accomplish. If his business is
there, if it is his native land, if his
father, mother, wife, or children are
there, if it is the place of his father's
sepulchre, and the place where he was
born and reared, how intense becomes

31 Oh that *men* would praise
the LORD *for* his goodness, and
for his wonderful works to the
children of men!

32 Let them exalt him also in
o the congregation of the people,
and praise him in the assembly

o Ps. xxii. 22; lxvi. 16; cxi. 1.
p 1 Kings xvii. 1, 7.

of the elders.

33 He *p* turneth rivers into a
wilderness, and the water-springs
into dry ground;

34 A *q* fruitful land into [1] barrenness, for the wickedness of
them that dwell therein.

q Gen. xiii. 10, xix. 25.
[1] *saltness.*

---

the desire to see that land once more.
So God brings his people to rest in
heaven,—their haven, their home.
After being tossed by the tempests of
life, after encountering its storms and
dangers, after the fear and agitation
experienced, he stills the storms; the
way becomes smooth and calm; the
end of the voyage is serene; and death
is like the ship smoothly gliding into
port with its sails all set. The soul
enters heaven—the desired haven—
the port that was longed for; a safe
haven, beyond all storms or tempests;
an eternal home!

31. *Oh that* men, etc. See Notes on
vers. 8,15,21. Assuredly they who are
thus delivered from the dangers of the
sea should praise the Lord; they who
have seen the wonders of God on the
great ocean should *never* forget God.

32. *Let them exalt him also.* Let
them lift up his name on high; let
them make it conspicuous. The word
means *to lift up,* and is applied to
praise because we thus, as it were,
lift up God, or make him conspicuous.
¶ *In the congregation of the people.*
Not merely in private, but in public.
As his doings are public and conspicuous,—as they pertain to all,—
men should acknowledge him in their
public capacity, or when assembled
together. ¶ *And praise him in the
assembly of the elders.* The old men;
the men eminent for experience and
wisdom. Perhaps this refers to those
who occupied some official position in
public worship, as appointed to preside
over that worship, and to conduct it.
We know that the arrangement was
early made to appoint a body of aged
men to preside over the assemblies
for worship, and to direct the devo-

tions of the people. In the presence
of such venerable and venerated men,
they are here exhorted to give due
praise to God. The *reason* for this
seems to be partly drawn from what
had been referred to in the previous
verses,—the power of God as seen in
stilling the tempests of the ocean;
and partly from what is immediately
referred to—the blessing of God on
the labours of man in cultivating the
earth.

33. *He turneth rivers into a wilderness.* He makes great changes in the
earth; he shows that he has absolute
dominion over it. See Notes on Isa.
xliv. 26, 27. On the word *wilderness,*
see Notes on ver. 4. The point here
is, that God had such control over
nature that he could make the bed of
a river dry and barren as the rocky
or sandy desert. He could effectually
dry up the stream, and make it so
dry and parched that nothing would
grow but the most stunted shrubs,
such as were found in the waste and
sandy desert. ¶ *And the water-springs
into dry ground.* The very fountains
of the rivers: not only drying up the
river itself by leading it off into burning wastes where it would be evapo-
rated by the heat, or lost in the sand,
—but so directly affecting the *sources*
of the streams as to make *them* dry.

34. *A fruitful land.* Heb., A land
of fruit. That is, a land that would
produce abundance. The word *fruit*
here is not used in the limited sense
in which we now employ it, but
means *any* productions of the earth.
¶ *Into barrenness.* Marg., as in Heb.,
saltness. The word is used to denote
a barren soil, because where salt
abounds the soil *is* barren. Thus it

35 He [r] turneth the wilderness into a standing water, and dry ground into water-springs.

36 And there he maketh the hungry to dwell, that they may prepare a city for habitation;

37 And sow the fields, and plant vineyards, which may yield

r Ps. cxiv. 8; Isa. xli. 18.

fruits of increase.

38 He blesseth them also, so that they are multiplied greatly, and suffereth not their cattle to decrease.

39 Again, they are minished [s] and brought low through oppression, affliction, and sorrow.

s 2 Kings x. 32.

is around the Dead Sea. Comp. Job xxxix. 6; Jer. xvii. 6. See also Virg. Geor. II. 238, "Salsa...tellus—frugibus infelix;" Pliny, Hist. Nat. 31. 7; Bochart, Hieroz. t. i., p. 872. ¶ *For the wickedness of them that dwell therein.* As he overthrew Sodom and Gomorrah;—probably alluding to that.

35. *He turneth the wilderness into a standing water.* A pool; a lake. See Notes on Isa. xxxv. 6, 7. ¶ *And dry ground into water-springs.* Not merely watering it with rain from heaven, but causing gushing fountains to break forth, and to flow continually, diffusing fertility and beauty everywhere.

36. *And there he maketh the hungry to dwell.* Those who were in want; those who would have perished. It is not necessary to refer this to any particular case. It is a general statement, pertaining to changes which God makes upon the earth, as great as if he *should* thus convert a desert into a fruitful field—a barren waste into a land abounding in springs of water; as if he *should* conduct thither a company of famished men, and provide for them food in abundance. ¶ *That they may prepare a city for habitation.* A permanent dwelling-place for man.

37. *And sow the fields, and plant vineyards.* Cultivate the earth. The culture of the vine was an important feature in agriculture in Palestine, and hence it is made so prominent here. ¶ *Which may yield fruits of increase.* The fruits which the earth produces.

38. *He blesseth them also.* In the manner immediately specified. ¶ *So*

that they are multiplied greatly. This was regarded as one of the highest blessings which God could confer, and hence it was so often promised by him to the patriarchs, as a proof of his favour, that their seed should be as the stars of heaven, and as the sand upon the sea-shore. Gen. xiii. 16; xxii. 17; xxvi. 4; xxxii. 12. ¶ *And suffereth not their cattle to decrease.* The keeping of herds of cattle was also an important point in husbandry, and hence it was a blessing that they were made to increase, and that they were kept from the diseases to which cattle are subject.

39. *Again, they are minished,* etc. Literally, "And they are made to decrease." That is,—all is in the hand of God. He rules and directs all things. If there is prosperity, it comes from him; if there are reverses, they occur under his hand. Men are not always prosperous. There are changes, misfortunes, disappointments, sorrows. God so deals with the race as in the best manner to secure the recognition of himself: —not always sending prosperity, lest men should regard it as a thing of course, and forget that it comes from him;—and not making the course of life uniformly that of disappointment and sorrow, lest they should feel that there is no God presiding over human affairs. He visits now with prosperity, and now with adversity;— now with success, and now with reverses, showing that his agency is constant, and that men are wholly dependent on him. In existing circumstances—since man is what he is —it is better that there should be alternations, reverses, and changes,

40 He ' poureth contempt upon
princes, and causeth them to
wander in the [1] wilderness, *where
there is* no way.

41 Yet " setteth he the poor

t Job xii. 21, 24.   [1] Or, *void place*
u 1 Sam. ii. 5—8; Ps. cxiii. 7—9.

on high [2] from affliction, and
maketh *him* families like a flock.

42 The *v* righteous shall see *it*,
and rejoice; and all iniquity
shall stop her mouth.

[2] *after.*
v Job v. 15, 16; xxii. 19.

---

than that there should be a uni-
form course. ¶ *Through oppression.*
Anything that *presses* or *straitens.*
¶ *Affliction.* Evil;—here, in the
sense of calamity. ¶ *And sorrow.*
Anguish, pain:—of body or mind.

40. *He poureth contempt upon
princes.* He treats them as if they
were common men; he pays no regard in his providence to their station
and rank. They are subjected to the
same wants as others; they meet
with reverses like others; they become captives like others; they sicken
and die like others; they are laid in
the grave like others; and, with the
same offensiveness, they turn back to
dust. Between monarchs and their
subjects, masters and their slaves,
mistresses and their handmaidens,
rich men and poor men, beauty and
deformity, there is no distinction in
the pains of sickness, in the pangs of
dying, in the loathsomeness of the
grave. The process of corruption
goes on in the most splendid coffin,
and beneath the most costly monument which art and wealth can rear,
as well as in the plainest coffin, and
in the grave marked by no stone or
memorial. What can more strikingly
show *contempt* for the trappings of
royalty, for the adornings of wealth,
for the stars and garters of nobility,
for coronets and crowns, for the dia-
monds, the pearls, and the gold that
decorate beauty, than that which
occurs *in a grave!* The very language used here, alike in the Hebrew
and in our translation, is found in
Job xii. 21. The word rendered
princes properly means *willing, voluntary, prompt;* and is then applied to
the generous, to the noble-minded, to
those who give liberally. It then denotes one of noble rank, as the idea

of rank in the mind of the Orientals
was closely connected with the notion
of liberality in giving. Thus it comes
to denote one of noble birth, and
might be applied to any of exalted
rank. ¶ *And causeth them to wander
in the wilderness.* Marg., *void place.*
The Hebrew word — תֹהוּ, *tohu*—
means properly wasteness, desolate-
ness; emptiness, vanity. See Gen.
i. 2; Job xxvi. 7; Isa. xli. 29; xliv.
9; xlix. 4. Here it means an empty,
uninhabited place; a place where
there is no path to guide; a land of
desolation. The reference seems to
be to the world beyond the grave;
the land of shadows and night. Comp.
Notes on Job x. 21, 22. ¶ *Where
there is no way.* Literally "no way."
That is, no well-trodden path. All
must soon go to that pathless world.

41. *Yet setteth he the poor on high
from affliction.* Marg., *after.* The
sense is not materially different. The
idea is, that while he thus humbles
princes, bringing them down from
their lofty position, he has respect to
the poor in their condition of suffering and trial, and raises them from
that depressed state, and gives them
prosperity. Thus he orders the circumstances of men, and shows his
sovereignty. ¶ *And maketh* him
families like a flock. Numerous as a
flock. Large families were accounted
a blessing among the Hebrews. See
Notes on ver. 38.

42. *The righteous shall see it, and
rejoice.* Shall see all these changes;
shall see in their own case the proofs
of the Divine favour. They shall thus
have occasion for praise. ¶ *And all
iniquity shall stop her mouth.* The
wicked shall be silenced; they shall
be dumb. The righteous shall find,
in these varied scenes, occasion for

43 Whoso *w* *is* wise, and will observe these *things*, even they
w Jer. ix. 12; Hosea xiv. 9.

shall understand the loving-kindness of the LORD.

praise and joy; the wicked shall be able to find no occasion for complaining or murmuring. The Divine dealings shall be manifestly so just, and so worthy of universal approval, that, even though the wicked are disposed to complain against God, they will be able to find nothing which will justify them in such complaints.

43. *Whoso* is *wise*. All who are truly wise. That is, all who have a proper understanding of things, or who are disposed to look at them aright. ¶ *And will observe these* things. Will attentively consider them; will reason upon them correctly; will draw just conclusions from them; will allow them to produce their *proper* impression on the mind. The meaning is, that these things would not be understood at a glance, or by a hasty and cursory observation, but that all who would take time to study them would see in them such proofs of wisdom and goodness that they could not fail to come to the conclusion that God is worthy of confidence and love. ¶ *Even they shall understand the lovingkindness of the* LORD. They will perceive that God is a merciful Being; that he seeks the welfare of the universe; that he desires the good of all; that the whole system is so arranged as to be adapted to secure the greatest good in the universe. No one can study the works of God, or mark the events of his providence, without perceiving that there are *innumerable* arrangements which have no other end than to produce happiness; which can be explained only on the supposition that God is a benevolent Being; which would not exist under the government of a malevolent being. And, although there *are* things which *seem* to be arrangements to cause suffering, and although sin and misery have been allowed to come into the world, yet we are not in circumstances to

enable us to show that, in some way, these may *not* be consistent with a desire to promote the happiness of the universe, or that there may *not* be some explanation, at present too high for us, which will show that the principle of benevolence is applicable to *all* the works of God. Meantime, where we can—as we can in numberless cases—see the proofs of benevolence, let us praise God; where we cannot, let us silently trust him, and believe that there will yet be some way in which we may see this as the angels now see it, and, like them, praise him for what now seems to us to be dark and incomprehensible. There is an *eternity* before us in which to study the works of God, and it would not be strange if *in* that eternity we may learn things about God which we cannot understand now, or if in that eternity things now to us as dark as midnight may be made clear as noonday. How many things incomprehensible to us in childhood, become clear in riper years!

PSALM CVIII.

This psalm is ascribed to David, and there is no reason to doubt the correctness of the title in this respect. The psalm is not an original composition, but is made up, with slight alterations, of parts of two other psalms, Ps. lvii. 7–11; lx. 5–12.

When the psalm was so arranged, or why the parts of two former psalms were thus brought together to form a new composition, it is impossible now to determine. It *may* have been for a mere purpose of art; or it may, more probably, have occurred when the two parts of psalms already in use might be so combined as to be adapted to some new event. It may have been, also, that what had been expressed *on two different occasions* might now be fulfilled or accomplished *on some one occasion*, and that thoughts which had been expressed separately before might now be unitedly uttered in praise. Rosenmüller

PSALM CVIII.

A Song *or* Psalm of David.

O GOD, [x] my heart is fixed; I will sing and give praise, even with my glory.

2 Awake, psaltery and harp; I *myself* will awake early.

3 I will praise thee, O LORD, among the people: and I will sing praises unto thee among

x Ps. lvii. 7—11.

the nations.

4 For thy mercy *is* great above the heavens, and thy truth *reacheth* unto the [1] clouds.

5 Be thou exalted, O God, above the heavens; and thy glory above all the earth:

6 That *v* thy beloved may be delivered, save *with* thy right hand, and answer me.

1 Or, *skies.*   y Ps. lx. 5, etc.

supposes that the psalm in its present form was arranged on the return from the captivity at Babylon, and that the parts of the two separate psalms were found to be suitable for a national song at that time, and were therefore thus brought together. This supposition would have much probability if the psalm were not ascribed to David;—and perhaps this fact need not be an insuperable objection,— since, if the two psalms from which this is compiled were the work of David, the author of the arrangement might without impropriety attribute the composition itself to David.

There are some slight variations in the psalm, as here arranged, from the original psalms; but why these were made cannot now be determined. Substantially all that will be necessary in the exposition of the psalm will be to notice these variations.

1. *O God, my heart is fixed.* Prepared, fitted, ready. See Notes on Ps. lvii. 7. In Ps. lvii. 7, this is repeated :—" My heart is fixed; O God, my heart is fixed :"—indicating that there *might* have been some doubt or vacillation caused by the circumstances then existing, and the repetition would have respect to that, as if the psalmist had been unsettled and wavering for a time, but was at last firm. In such circumstances it would not be unnatural to *repeat* the assertion, as if there were no longer any doubt. In the beginning of a psalm, however, where there had been no previous expression or feeling of doubt so far as appears, there would be no propriety in repeating the assertion. ¶ *I will sing and give praise.* See Notes on Ps. lvii. 7. ¶ *Even with my*

glory. This is not in Ps. lvii. It is literally here, "*truly my glory.*" In Ps. lvii. 8, however, the expression, " Awake up, my glory," occurs, and this seems to correspond with that language. It means here that it was his glory—his honour—thus to be employed in giving praise to God. It was worthy of all that there was elevated in his nature; of all that constituted his glory; of his highest powers. At no time is man employed in a more noble and lofty work than praise.

2. *Awake, psaltery and harp,* etc. This is copied without change from Ps. lvii. 8.

3. *I will praise thee, O* LORD, etc. This is taken from Ps. lvii. 9. The only change is the substitution here of the name *Jehovah* for *Adonai. Why* that change was made is unknown.

4. *For thy mercy,* etc. This is taken from Ps. lvii. 10. The only change is in the expression "above the heavens," instead of "unto the heavens." The sense is essentially the same. The particular idea here, if it differs at all from the expression in Ps. lvii., is, that the mercy of God seems to *descend* from heaven upon man, or *comes down* from on high.

5. *Be thou exalted,* etc. This is taken from Ps. lvii. 11. The only change in the Hebrew is in the insertion of the word "and," " *and* thy glory above all the earth."

6. *That thy beloved may be delivered.* The word rendered *beloved,* and the verb rendered *may be delivered,* are both in the plural number,

7 God hath spoken in his holiness : I will rejoice ; I will divide Shechem, and mete out the valley of Succoth.

8 Gilead *is* mine ; Manasseh *is* mine ; Ephraim also *is* the strength of mine head ; Judah *z is* my law-giver ;

9 Moab *is* my wash-pot ; over Edom will I cast out my shoe ; over Philistia will I triumph.

10 Who will bring me into the

z Gen. xlix. 10. *a* Job xvi. 2 ; Isa. ii. 22.

strong city ? who will lead me into Edom ?

11 *Wilt* not *thou*, O God, *who* hast cast us off ? and wilt not thou, O God, go forth with our hosts ?

12 Give us help from trouble : for *a* vain *is* the help of man.

13 Through God *b* we shall do valiantly : for he *c it is that* shall tread down our enemies.

b 2 Chron. xx. 12 ; Isa. xlv. 24.
c Rom. xvi. 20 ; 2 Cor. ii. 14.

showing that it is not an individual that is referred to, but that the people of God are intended. This is taken without any alteration from Ps. lx. 5. In *that* psalm the prayer for deliverance is grounded on the afflictions of the people, and the fact that God had given them "a banner that it might be displayed because of the truth,"—or, in the cause of truth. See Notes on that psalm. In the psalm before us, while the prayer for deliverance is the same, the *reason* for that prayer is different. It is that God is exalted ; that his mercy is above the heavens ; that his glory is above all the earth, and that he is thus exalted that he *may* interpose and save his people. ¶ *Save* with *thy right hand, and answer me.* The Hebrew here is the same as in Ps. lx. 5, where it is rendered "and *hear* me."

7. *God hath spoken*, etc. This is taken, without change, from Ps. lx. 6. See Notes on that place.

8. *Gilead is mine*, etc. This is taken from Ps. lx. 7. The only change is the omission of the word *and* before "Manasseh."

9. *Moab*, etc. This is taken from Ps. lx. 8. The only change is in the close of the verse. Instead of "Philistia, triumph thou because of me" (Ps. lx. 8), it is here, "Over Philistia will I triumph." Why the change was made is unknown.

10. *Who will bring me*, etc. This is taken, without alteration, from Ps. lx. 9.

11. Wilt *not* thou, O God, etc.

This is taken from Ps. lx. 10, with no change in the Hebrew, except that the word *thou* (in the first member of the verse) is omitted.

12. *Give us help from trouble*, etc. This is copied from Ps. lx. 11.

13. *Through God we shall do*, etc. This also is taken from Ps. lx. 12, without change.

Thus the psalm, though made up of parts of two separate psalms, is complete and continuous in itself. There is no break or discrepancy in the current of thought, but the unity is as perfect as though it had been an original composition. It is to be remarked, also, that though in the original psalms the parts which are here used have a different connexion, and are separately complete there, yet as employed here, they seem to be exactly fitted to the new use which is made of the language ; and though the original *reasons* for the use of the language do not appear here, yet there is a sufficient reason for that language apparent in the psalm as rearranged. To an Israelite, also, there might be a new interest in the use of the language in the fact that words with which he was familiar, as employed for other purposes, *could* be thus combined, and made applicable to a new occasion in the national history.

PSALM CIX.

This psalm is ascribed to David, and there is nothing in the psalm to make us doubt the correctness of the title.

PSALM CIX.

To the chief Musician.   A Psalm of David.

HOLD *d* not thy peace, O God of my praise; *e*

2 For the mouth of the wicked and the mouth of [1] the deceit-

d Ps. lxxxiii. 1.   *e* Jer. xvii. 14.

ful [2] are opened against me: they have spoken against me with a lying *f* tongue.

3 They compassed me about also with words of hatred; and

[1] *deceit.*   [2] *have opened* themselves.
f Matt. xxvi. 60; Acts vi. 13.

Kimchi supposes that it refers to the enemies of David in the time of Saul. Grotius and Knapp suppose that it refers to Ahithophel; Dathe, to Shimei; De Wette, that it refers to national foes at a later period than the time of David. It is impossible now to ascertain the occasion on which it was composed. It would seem to have been one of the most trying in the life of David, when his enemies were most bitter against him. It is one of the "*imprecatory*" psalms, and one which is as difficult to reconcile with a kind and forgiving spirit as any other in the book.

In the New Testament (Acts i. 20) a part of the psalm is applied to Judas the traitor, but without its being necessary to conclude that it had any original reference to him. The conduct of Judas was *like* the conduct of the enemy of David; the language used in the one case might be properly used in the other.

The psalm consists of three parts:—

I. A description of the enemies of the psalmist (vers. 1–5), as (*a*) deceitful and lying; (*b*) as using words of hatred; (*c*) as fighting against him without cause; (*d*) as returning evil for good, and hatred for love. From this it would seem that the persons referred to were some who had been closely connected with the author; who had received important benefits from him; who had been the subjects of his prayer; and who pursued him from mere malice.

II. A prayer for the punishment of those who had thus wronged him—referring particularly to some *one* person who had been prominent, or who had instigated others, imploring the infliction of just punishment on *him* as if he were alone responsible, vers. 6–20. It is in this part of the psalm that the principal difficulty in the interpretation consists, as this is made up of severe and apparently harsh and revengeful imprecations. All is in fact invoked on him that any man could ever desire to see inflicted on an enemy.

III. A prayer for the sufferer's own

deliverance, with a promise of thanksgiving, vers. 21–31. The psalmist here describes his miserable and suffering condition, and prays that God would interpose,—expressing a willingness to suffer *any* thing at the hand of man if God would be his friend—a willingness that they should continue to "*curse,*" if God would "*bless.*" As the result of all, he says that he would find delight in praise—in the public acknowledgment of the goodness of God.

On the phrase in the title, "To the chief Musician," see Notes on the title to Ps. iv.

1. *Hold not thy peace.* That is, Speak for my defence,—as if God had looked with unconcern on the wrongs which were done to him. See Notes on Ps. lxxxiii. 1. ¶ *O God of my praise.* The God whom I praise; whom I worship and adore. It implies that he was accustomed to praise him, and desired still to praise him. He sought that God would interpose now that he might have new occasion for praise.

2. *For the mouth of the wicked and the mouth of the deceitful.* Literally, "The mouth of wickedness, and the mouth of deceit." This acquaints us with the nature of the wrong which had been done him. It was slander; —undeserved reproach. ¶ *Are opened against me.* Marg., *have opened;* that is, have opened themselves. ¶ *They have spoken against me with a lying tongue.* They have accused me of things which are not true; they have made false charges against me. David, as has not been uncommon with good men, was called repeatedly to this trial.

3. *They compassed me about also with words of hatred.* They attacked me on every side; they assailed me,

fought against me without g a
cause.

4 For my love they are my
adversaries : but h I *give myself
unto* prayer.

g John xv. 25. h Luke vi. 11, 12.
i Ps. xxxv. 7, 12.

---

not merely in one form and direction,
but in every form, and in every direction. I could turn no way—I could
go nowhere—where I did not encounter these slanderous reports. ¶
And fought against me without a cause.
Contended against me, or fought
against me, with *words.* They sought
to do me all the harm they could.
The phrase " without a cause " means
that he had given them no occasion
for this conduct; he had not wronged
them; it was mere malignity. See Ps.
xxxv. 7 ; lxix. 4. Comp. John xv. 25.

4. *For my love,* etc. As a recompence
for my love; or, this is the return
which I get for all the expressions
of my love to them. The enemies
referred to were those whom he had
treated kindly ; to whom he had done
good. This is not uncommon in the
world. It was illustrated in an eminent degree in the life of the Saviour.
¶ *But I* give myself unto *prayer.*
Literally, " I—prayer ;" that is, I am
all prayer; I continually pray. This
may mean, either, that he bore these
trials with a meek spirit, and did not
allow these things to disturb his devotions; or, more probably, that he
prayed constantly *for them ;* he desired their good, and sought it from
above.

5. *And they have rewarded me
evil for good.* Literally, " They have
placed against me." They have put
it in my way; it is what they had
to set before me. See Notes on Ps.
xxxv. 12, where the same expression
occurs. ¶ *And hatred for my love.*
Instead of loving me in return for
my love, they have met me with the
expressions of hatred. This often
occurred in the life of David; it was
constant in the life of the Saviour;
it is habitually manifested by men

5 And i they have rewarded
me evil for good, and hatred for
my love.

6 Set thou a wicked man over
him; and let l Satan stand at
his right hand.

l Or, *an adversary,* Zech. iii. 1.

---

towards God; it is often experienced
by good men now; it *may* occur in the
life of any man—and if it *does* occur
to us, we should not think that any
strange thing has happened to us.

6. *Set thou a wicked man over him.*
This commences the imprecatory part
of the psalm, extending to ver. 20.
The first thing that the psalmist asks
is, that his foe might be subjected to
the evil of having a man placed over
him like himself:—a man regardless
of justice, truth, and right; a man
who would respect character and propriety no more than he had himself
done. It is, in fact, a prayer that he
might be punished *in the line of his
offences.* It cannot be wrong that a
man should be treated as he treats
others ; and it cannot be in itself
wrong to desire that a man should be
treated according to his character and
deserts,—for this is the object of all
law, and this is what all magistrates
and legislators are endeavouring to
secure. ¶ *And let Satan stand at his
right hand.* As his counsellor and
adviser. The language would be properly applicable to one who had been
a counsellor or adviser to a king in
the administration of the government; and the prayer is, that he
might know what it was to *have* such
a one as *his* counsellor and adviser.
The language used would seem to
make it not improbable that David
here refers particularly to some one
who had occupied this position in
reference to himself, and who had
betrayed his trust; who had given
him crafty and malignant counsel ;
who had led him into bad measures;
who had used his position to promote
his own interests at the expense of
his master's. David *had* such counsellors, as any one in authority *may*

7 When he shall be judged,
let him [1] be condemned: and let
his prayer [k] become sin.

[1] *go out guilty,* or, *wicked.*

8 Let his days be few: *and* let
another take [l] his [2] office.

k Prov. xxviii. 9.   *l* Acts i. 20.
[2] Or, *charge.*

---

have. The prayer, then, would be,
that such a man might be punished
in his own line; that he might know
what it was to have a bad and wicked
adviser. The word rendered *Satan*—
שָׂטָן—is in the margin rendered
adversary. In the Septuagint it is
διάβολος; in the Vulgate, *diabolus.*
See Notes on Job i. 6, for its meaning. The prayer here seems not to
be that the devil or Satan might
stand near him as his counsellor; but
that a man—a real adversary—an
accuser—one with a malignant heart
—one who would make use of his
position to accomplish his own purposes, and to betray the interests of
his master, might give him counsel,
as seems to have been done in the
case of David.

7. *When he shall be judged,* etc. When
for his offences he shall be arraigned.
The psalmist supposes that he *might*
be put on trial; he seems to suppose
that this *would be.* Such wickedness
could not always escape detection,
and sooner or later he would be arrested and brought to trial. *When*
this should occur, the psalmist prays
that justice might be done; that he
might be condemned, as he *ought* to
be. Such a prayer could not in itself
be wrong, for assuredly it cannot be
proper for magistrates to pray that the
wicked man may escape, or that they
may themselves fail in the very object
for which they are appointed. See
General Introd. § 6. (5.) *e, f.* ¶ *And
let his prayer become sin.* Evidently
his prayer in reference to his *trial* for
crime; his prayer that he might be
acquitted and discharged. Let it be
seen in the result that such a prayer
was *wrong;* that it was, in fact, a
prayer for the discharge of a bad man
—a man who *ought* to be punished.
Let it be seen to be what a prayer
would be if offered for a murderer, or
violator of the law,—a prayer that

he might escape or not be punished.
All must see that *such* a prayer would
be wrong, or would be a " sin ;" and
so, in his own case, it would be
equally true that a prayer *for his
own escape* would be "sin." The
psalmist asks that, by the result of
the trial, such a prayer might be
seen to be in fact a prayer for the
protection and escape of a *bad man.*
A just sentence in the case would demonstrate this; and this is what the
psalmist prays for.

8. *Let his days be few.* Let him
be soon cut off; let his life be shortened. It cannot be wrong for an
officer of justice to aim at this; to
desire it; to pray for it. How strange
it would be for a magistrate to pray
*that a murderer or a traitor should be
long-lived!* ¶ And *let another take
his office.* So every man acts, and
practically prays, who seeks to remove a bad and corrupt man from
office. As such an office must be
filled by some one, all the efforts which
he puts forth to remove a wicked
man tend to bring it about that
" another should take his office;"
and for this it is *right* to labour and
pray. The act does not of itself
imply malignity or bad feeling, but
is consistent with the purest benevolence, the kindest feelings, the strict-
est integrity, the sternest patriotism,
and the highest form of piety. The
word rendered *office* here is in the
margin *charge.* It properly denotes
a mustering, an enumeration; then,
care, watch, oversight, charge, as in
an army, or in a civil office. In Acts
i. 20, this passage is applied to Judas,
and the word—the same word as in
the Septuagint here—is rendered in
the text *bishopric,*—in the margin,
office. See Notes on that passage.
It had no original reference to Judas,
but the language was exactly adapted
to him, and to the circumstances of

9 Let his children be fatherless, ^{m} and his wife a widow.

10 Let his children be continually vagabonds, and beg: let

m Ex. xxii. 24. n Job xviii. 9, 19.

them seek *their bread* also out of
their desolate places.

11 Let ^{n} the extortioner catch
all that he hath: and let the
strangers spoil his labour.

---

the case, as it is used by the apostle
in that passage.

9. *Let his children be fatherless.*
Heb., *his sons.* This is what *always*
occurs when a criminal who is a father
is executed. It is one of the consequences of crime; and if the officer
of justice does his duty, of course,
the sons of such a man *must* be made
fatherless. The prayer is, simply,
that justice may be done, and all this
is but an enumeration of what must
follow from the proper execution of
the laws. ¶ *And his wife a widow.*
This implies no malice against the
wife, but may be consistent with the
most tender compassion for her sufferings. It is simply *one* of the consequences which must follow from
the punishment of a bad man. The
enumeration of these things shows
the enormity of the crime—just as
the consequences which follow from
the execution of a murderer are an
illustration of the Divine sense of the
evil of the offence.

10. *Let his children be continually
vagabonds, and beg.* Let them continually wander about with no home
—no fixed habitation. Let them be
compelled to ask their daily food at
the hand of charity. Here we enter
on a part of the psalm which is more
difficult to be reconciled with a proper feeling than the portions which
have been considered. It is, indeed,
a frequent consequence of crime that
the children of those who are punished
are vagabonds and beggars, but this
is not a necessary consequence; and
there *seems* here, therefore, to be a
mixture of personal feeling, or a
feeling of revenge. This runs through
the remaining portion of the imprecatory part of the psalm. I confess
that it is difficult to explain this
without admitting that the expressions are a record only of what

actually occurred in the mind of a
man, truly pious, but not perfect,—a
man who thus, to illustrate the work-
ings of the mind even when the
general character was holy, was allowed to record his own feelings,
though wrong, just as he would record the conduct of another, or his
own conduct, though wrong, as a
simple matter of fact—a record ot
what actually was felt. The *record*
may be exactly correct; the sentiment recorded may have been wholly
incapable of vindication. See General
Introd. § 6 (6). ¶ *Let them seek
their bread also out of their desolate places.* In places uninhabited by
man; in barren regions; in deserts:
let them be compelled to live on the
scanty food which they may pick up
there,—the roots, or the wild fruits,
which will simply keep them alive.
See Notes on Job xxx. 4.

11. *Let the extortioner catch all
that he hath.* Literally, "Let the
extortioner cast a snare over all that
he hath;" that is, let him seize all
his property. The word rendered
catch — שׁקַנ, *nakash* — is a word
which means to lay a snare, as for
birds and wild animals, and hence it
means to ensnare, to entrap, to catch.
The word rendered "*extortioner*"
means literally one who lends or borrows money; a money-loaner; in our
times, *a broker.* Here it refers to
one who loaned money on interest;
or who took advantage of the necessities of others to lend money at
high rates — thus sooner or later
seizing upon and securing the property of another. The prayer here
is, that he might be in such circumstances as to make it necessary to
fall into the hands of those who
would thus come into possession of
all his property. ¶ *And let the
strangers spoil his labour.* Let

12 Let there be none to extend mercy unto him; neither let there be any to favour his fatherless children.

13 Let his posterity [o] be cut off; *and* in the generation following let their name be [p] blotted out.

14 Let the iniquity of his

o Ps. xxxvii. 28; Isa. xiv. 20.

fathers [q] be remembered with the LORD ; and let not the sin of his mother be blotted out.

15 Let them be before the LORD continually, that he may cut off the memory of them from the earth.

16 Because that he remembered not to shew mercy, [r] but

p Prov. x. 7.   q Ex. xx. 5.   r James ii. 13.

strangers *plunder* his labour ; that is, the fruit of his labour. Let them seize and possess what he has earned and gained to enjoy it themselves. The remarks made on ver. 10, will apply to this verse and the following. 12. *Let there be none to extend mercy unto him.* Let him find compassion and sympathy in no one. When he suffers, let him be left to bear it alone. Let there be none found to shed a tear of compassion over him, or to relieve him. Literally, " Let there be no one *to draw out* kindness to him." ¶ *Neither let there be any to favour his fatherless children.* To show them mercy or kindness. See Notes on ver. 10.

13. *Let his posterity be cut off.* To have a numerous posterity, to have the name and family perpetuated, was regarded among the Hebrews as one of the greatest and most desirable blessings. Hence to pray that all one's family might be cut off was one of the severest forms of malediction which could be employed. ¶ And *in the generation following.* The very next generation. Let not his family be perpetuated at all. ¶ *Let their name be blotted out.* As a name is erased from a catalogue or muster-roll when one dies.

14. *Let the iniquity of his fathers.* Of his ancestors. ¶ *Be remembered with the* LORD. Or, by the Lord. The doctrine of the Bible is, that God " visits the iniquities of the fathers upon the children unto the third and fourth generation of them that hate " him (Ex. xx. 5); the matter of fact is that children and children's children often suffer from the errors, the

crimes, and the follies of their parents, as in the case of intemperance, murder, and treason (comp. Notes on Rom. v. 12, *et seq.*) ; and the prayer here is, that this regular effect of sin might follow in this instance; that these consequences might not be arrested by Divine interposition. ¶ *And let not the sin of his mother be blotted out.* This is probably added to complete the parallelism ;—the sin of his father and his mother. There may, however, if this is a composition of David, be a similar allusion to that which occurs in Ps. li. 5, " Behold, I was shapen in iniquity, and in sin did my mother conceive me." The prayer is, that whatever effects might properly follow from the fact that his mother was a sinner —either in some peculiar sense, or in the general sense that all are sinners—might come upon him.

15. *Let them be before the* LORD *continually.* Let their sins never pass from the mind of God. Let him never so forget them as *not* to inflict punishment for them. ¶ *That he may cut off the memory of them from the earth.* That they may be wholly forgotten among men. Let their very name perish ; and let the offender in this case be in the condition of those who have no ancestors to whom they can refer with pride and pleasure. The idea here is drawn from the honour which is felt in being able to refer to ancestors worthy of being remembered for their virtues.

16. *Because that he remembered not to show mercy.* He had no compassion ; he was severe, harsh, unjust, unfeeling. ¶ *But persecuted the poor*

persecuted the poor and needy man, that he might even slay the broken in heart.

17 As [s] he loved cursing, so let it come unto him; as he delighted not in blessing, so let it be far from him.

18 As he clothed himself with cursing like as with a garment, so let it come [1] into his bowels

s Ez. xxxv. 6.　　1 within him.

like water, [t] and like oil into his bones.

19 Let it be unto him as the garment which covereth him, and for a girdle wherewith he is girded continually.

20 Let this be the reward of mine adversaries from the LORD, and of them that speak evil against my soul.

t Num. v. 22.

and needy man. The man that was destitute of friends; that was a wanderer and a beggar. There were times in the life of David when this would be strictly and literally applicable to him. ¶ That he might even slay the broken in heart. The man whose heart was crushed by sorrow,—that he might put "the finishing stroke" to all, and send him to the grave. Whatever might have been the feeling which prompted to this prayer, or however difficult it may be to vindicate the psalmist's expression of feeling, there can be no doubt as to the propriety of inflicting punishment on such a man. The sufferings invoked are none too severe to be inflicted on a man who persecutes the poor and needy, and seeks so to multiply sorrows that the man already crushed and broken in heart shall sink to the grave.

17. As he loved cursing, etc. As he loved to curse others; as he seemed to have a pleasure alike in the act of cursing and in the feeling which prompts to cursing, let him see what it is; let it come upon him in its fulness. He has chosen this as his portion; let it be his. This, in the original, is in the indicative mood, and not, as in our version, in the optative form: "He loved cursing, and it has come upon him; he did not delight in blessing, and it is far from him." Still, the connexion would rather seem to require that we should understand this as a prayer, and not as an affirmation, for the object of the whole seems not to be to state what had come upon him, but what the

psalmist wished might come upon him. ¶ As he delighted not in blessing, etc. As he had no pleasure in wishing that others might be happy, or in any measures which would tend to promote their happiness, so let everything that could be regarded as a blessing be put far from him;—let him know nothing of it.

18. As he clothed himself with cursing like as with a garment. Moral qualities are often compared with raiment—as that in which we appear to our fellow-men. See 1 Pet. v. 5; Job xxix. 14. ¶ So let it come into his bowels like water. Marg., within him. Heb., In his midst. Let it penetrate him through and through. Let no part of him be unaffected by it. ¶ And like oil into his bones. As if oil flowed through all his bones, so let the effects of cursing pervade his whole frame. The prayer is, that his entire nature might feel the effects of cursing; that he might know to the full what he was endeavouring to bring on others.

19. Let it be unto him as the garment which covereth him. He has chosen to put it on, to wear it, to appear in it; so let him constantly feel its consequences. As he is always obliged to wear clothing, so let this be as constantly with him and upon him as his mantle and his sash. ¶ And for a girdle wherewith he is girded continually. The belt or girdle which he constantly wears. See Notes on Matt. v. 38.

20. Let this be the reward of mine adversaries from the LORD, etc. The word rendered reward means usually

21 But do thou for me, O God the Lord, for thy name's *u* sake : because thy mercy *is* good, deliver thou me.

22 For I *am* poor and needy, and my heart is wounded within me.

23 I am gone like the shadow *v* when it declineth : I am tossed up and down as the locust.

24 My knees *w* are weak

u Ps. xxv. 11.　　*v* Ps. cii. 11 ; cxliv. 4.

through fasting, and my flesh faileth of fatness.

25 I became also a reproach *x* unto them : *when* they looked upon me *y* they shaked their heads.

26 Help me, O Lord my God : O save me according to thy mercy ;

27 That they may know that

w Heb. xii. 12.　　*x* Ps. xxii. 6, 7.
　　　　y Matt. xxvii. 39.

---

work, labour, occupation, business; then, what one earns by his work,—reward, recompence, Lev. xix. 13. The meaning here is, Let them constantly receive these things which I have prayed for (vers. 6–19); let them be constantly treated in this manner. This is a summing up of his entire wish—his whole desire. It cannot be proved that they did *not deserve* all this; it cannot be shown that if all this came upon them at the hand of God, it would be unjust; it cannot be denied that such things as these, either singly, in groups, or in succession, do actually come upon wicked men; and the prayer in the case *may* have been merely that *justice* might be done. Still, as before remarked, it is not easy wholly to vindicate the expressed feelings of the psalmist. See Notes on ver. 10.

21. *But do thou for me, O God the Lord, for thy name's sake.* That is, Interpose for me; exert thy power in my behalf. The phrase " for thy name's sake" implies that the motive which prompted him was a desire that God might be honoured. It was not primarily or mainly for his own happiness; it was that God might be glorified, that his character might be illustrated, that his plans might be accomplished. Comp. Notes on Dan. ix. 18, 19. ¶ *Because thy mercy is good.* That is, It is the characteristic of mercy to do good; to show kindness. ¶ *Deliver thou me.* He prays that God would *manifest* himself as he really *was*, as a God of mercy.

22. *For I* am *poor and needy.* I

am helpless and dependent. I am in a condition where I need thy gracious interposition. ¶ *And my heart is wounded within me.* I am as one that is prostrated by a weapon—as if my heart had been pierced. I have no courage, no strength. I am like one who lies wounded on a battle-field.

23. *I am gone like the shadow when it declineth.* See Notes on Ps. cii. 11. ¶ *I am tossed up and down as the locust.* Agitated, moved, driven about, as a cloud of locusts is by the wind. The meaning of the whole is, that he was frail and weak, and needed strength from on high.

24. *My knees are weak through fasting.* Hunger; want of food. Strength to stand is connected with firmness in the knee-joints, and hence weakness and feebleness are denoted by the giving way of the knees. Comp. Heb. xii. 12. ¶ *And my flesh faileth of fatness.* I am lean and weak. There is not the proper supply for my strength. The idea seems to have been that fatness (Heb., *oil*) was necessary to strength.

25. *I became also a reproach unto them.* They reproached or reviled me as a bad man. Comp. Notes on Ps. xxii. 6. The plural here — " unto *them*"—shows that there were more than one to whom the psalm had reference, though one of them was so prominent that a considerable part of the psalm might properly be spoken of him alone. ¶ *When they looked upon me, they shaked their heads.* In contempt. See Ps. xxii. 7. Comp. Matt. xxvii. 39.

this *is* thy hand; *z that* thou, LORD, hast done it.

28 Let *a* them curse, but bless thou : when they arise, let them be ashamed; but let thy servant *b* rejoice.

29 Let *c* mine adversaries be clothed with shame, and let them cover themselves with their own

z Ps. xvii. 13, 14.　　a 2 Sam. xvi. 11, 12.
b Isa. lxv. 14.　　c Ps. xxxv. 26.

confusion as with a mantle.

30 I will greatly praise the LORD with my mouth; yea, I *d* will praise him among the multitude.

31 For he shall stand at the right *e* hand of the poor, to save *him* from [1] those that condemn his soul.

d Ps. cxi. 1.　　e Ps. xvi. 8.
1 *the judges of.*

---

26. *Help me, O* LORD *my God,* etc. Stand by me; interpose.

27. *That they may know that this* is *thy hand.* That this has been done by thee; that it has all occurred under thy direction, or has been ordered by thee. The reference seems to be particularly to God's interposition :—" Let it be manifest to all that *thou* hast interposed in my behalf; that *thou* hast undertaken for me; that *thou* art my Friend." He desired an interposition from God that he might be vindicated before all his enemies. ¶ That *thou,* LORD, *hast done it.* Let it be such an interposition that it will be manifest to all that no other one *but* God could have done this.

28. *Let them curse, but bless thou.* See ver. 17. Let them continue to curse me, provided thou wilt bless me. I am willing to bear all these reproaches, if I may have thy favour. That favour I value infinitely more than I do theirs; and it is a small matter that I am reviled and cursed by men, if I may secure the favour and friendship of God. ¶ *When they arise.* When they rise up against me; when they attempt to persecute me. ¶ *Let them be ashamed,* etc. Let them be disappointed; let them not be successful in their designs against me. On the word *ashamed,* see Notes on Job vi. 20; Ps. xxv. 2, 3.

29. *Let mine adversaries be clothed with shame.* Let confusion and disappointment seem to cover them, so as to constitute a garment. See Notes on vers. 18, 19. They had "clothed themselves with cursing"

(ver. 18), and the prayer now is, that the covering of shame might be as complete and entire. ¶ *And let them cover themselves with their own confusion as with a mantle.* As with an outer garment,—the mantle or robe, —which they might wrap all round them. Let it be so abundant that they may entirely wrap their person in it. Let their confusion correspond with their sin in the fullest manner.

30. *I will greatly praise the* LORD *with my mouth.* I will sing abundant praises to him. Comp. Notes on Isa. xxxviii. 20. ¶ *Yea, I will praise him among the multitude.* In the great congregation. I will publicly acknowledge his goodness and mercy. See Notes on Ps. xxii. 25.

31. *For he shall stand at the right hand of the poor.* He will thus show that he befriends the poor and the helpless. ¶ *To save* him *from those that condemn his soul.* Marg., *from the judges of his soul.* The Hebrew is, " from those that judge his soul." The meaning is, from those that pronounce a harsh or unjust judgment; from those that condemn the innocent.

PSALM CX.

This psalm is entitled " A Psalm of David." It is also ascribed to David by the Saviour (Matt. xxii. 43) ; and by Peter (Acts ii. 34) ; and there is no reason to doubt the correctness of the title. There is nothing, however, in the title, or in the psalm, to determine at what period of David's life, or on what occasion it was written. Aben Ezra supposed that it was at the time referred to in 2 Sam. xxi. 15-17; and others have

PSALM CX.

A Psalm of David.

THE *f* LORD said unto my

f Matt. xxii. 44; Acts ii. 34; 1 Cor. xv. 25; Heb. i. 13.

Lord, Sit thou at my right

selected other occasions in the life of David. But all this is conjecture. The psalm has no particular reference to anything in his history, and as it is wholly prophetic of the Messiah, it might have been composed at any period of his life.

The psalm is repeatedly quoted in the New Testament as referring to the Messiah, and in such a manner as to show that this was the customary interpretation among the Jews, or that it might be referred to by way of *proof* in regard to the Messiah, so that the relevancy and pertinence of the argument would be at once admitted. Matt. xxii. 44 (comp. Mark xii. 36; Luke xx. 42); Acts ii. 34; Heb. v. 6; vii. 17, 21. The way in which it is quoted shows that this was the prevailing and received mode of interpreting the psalm.

Yet this belief has not been uniform. De Wette supposes that it refers to David himself. Jarchi supposed that it referred to Abraham; Borhek, to Solomon; Justin Martyr and Tertullian, to Hezekiah. See Rosenmüller.

The application of the psalm in the New Testament to the Messiah is so clear and unequivocal, that we are bound to defend the opinion that it was *designed* to refer to him; and the manner in which it is quoted shows that it was in no secondary sense, and in no way of "accommodation," but that it had an original and exclusive applicability to him. Every principle of honesty in interpretation demands this. There may be difficulties in the interpretation itself, but the fact that it refers to the Messiah involves no difficulty, if it be once admitted that there is such a thing as prophecy at all, and that *any* portion of the Old Testament has reference to a Messiah. There is no part of the Old Testament that is more clearly applied to him in the New Testament than this psalm; there is no part that more naturally suggests the Messiah; there is none that is more difficult of explanation if it be maintained that it does not refer to him; there is none that is made more plain *by* referring it to him. It will be assumed, therefore, in this exposition, that the psalm *had* an original and exclusive reference to the Messiah, and that the friends of revelation are bound to show that in him who claimed to be the Mes-

siah, and to whom it *is* applied in the New Testament—the Lord Jesus—there is a *fair* fulfilment of the predictions which are contained in it.

The idea in the psalm is that of the exaltation, the conquest, the priesthood, and the dominion of the Messiah. Two things—the kingship and the priesthood of the Messiah—are combined. The leading idea is that of the *priest-king* or the *king-priest*, as in the case of Melchizedek, in whom the two offices of priest and king were in a very unusual manner and form united in one person. Usually they were separate, even in the earliest ages of the world. In the case of Melchizedek they were *combined*, and hence he was selected as a proper representative of the Messiah—of one who should combine these offices, apparently incongruous, in one.

The psalm embraces the following points :—

I. The appointment of the Messiah—acknowledged by the author of the psalm as *his* " Lord "—to that high office, to be held until he should subdue all his enemies, ver. 1.

II. His being endowed with *power* needful for the accomplishment of the design for which he was appointed, ver. 2.

III. The assurance that his people would be made "*willing*" in the day when he should put forth his power, ver. 3.

IV. The peculiar characteristic of his reign, as that of a *priest-king*, after the order of Melchizedek; combining the two functions of king and priest in his own person and office, ver. 4.

V. His conquest and triumph, vers. 5 7.

1. *The* LORD *said unto my Lord.* In the Hebrew, "Spake Jehovah to my Lord." The word *Jehovah* is the incommunicable name of God. It is never given to a created being. The other word translated *Lord—Adonai* —means one who has rule or authority; one of high rank; one who has dominion; one who is the owner or possessor, etc. This word is applied frequently to a creature. It is ap-

hand, until I make thine enemies thy footstool.

2 The LORD shall send the rod of thy strength out of Zion :

g Ps. xlv. 5.

rule *g* thou in the midst of thine enemies.

3 Thy people *shall be* willing *h* in the day of thy power, in the

h Judges v. 2; Gal. i. 15, 16.

---

plied to kings, princes, rulers, masters. The phrase " *my* Lord " refers to some one who was superior in rank to the author of the psalm; one whom he could address as his superior. The psalm, therefore, cannot refer to David himself, as if Jehovah had said to *him*, " Sit thou at my right hand." Nor was there any one on earth in the time of David to whom it could be applicable; any one whom *he* would call his " Lord" or superior. If, therefore, the psalm was written by David, it must have reference to the Messiah—to one whom he owned as *his* superior—*his* Lord—*his* Sovereign. It cannot refer to God as if *he* were to have this rule over David, since God himself is referred to as *as speaking* to him whom David called his Lord :—" Jehovah said unto my Lord." The reasoning of the Saviour, therefore, in Matt. xxii. 43-45, was founded on a fair and just interpretation of the psalm, and was so plain and conclusive that the Pharisees did not attempt to reply to it. Matt. xxii. 46. See Notes on that passage. No other interpretation *can* be given to it, consistently with the proper rules of expounding language, unless it be shown that the psalm was not composed by David, and might, therefore, be applied to some one whom the author would acknowledge as his " Lord." But there is no evidence of this, and there is no one in the Old Testament history to whom the psalm would be applicable. ¶ *Sit thou at my right hand.* The position of honour and of rank. Comp. Notes on Ps. xvi. 8. See also Ps. xlv. 9; Mark xiv. 62; Luke xxii. 69; Acts vii. 55; Heb. i. 3; viii. 1. The phrase is properly applicable to the Messiah as exalted to the highest place in the universe — the right hand of God. ¶ *Until 1 make thine enemies thy*

footstool. Until they are entirely subdued under thee. See Notes on Matt. xxii. 44. The enemies here referred to are the enemies of the Messiah considered as King (see Ps. ii.); and the promise here is, that " he must reign till he shall have put all enemies under his feet." See Notes on 1 Cor. xv. 25.

2. *The LORD shall send the rod of thy strength out of Zion.* The sceptre of thy power; that with which thou shalt rule. It will be given to thee by Jehovah; and it will be given to thee, as it were, *out of Zion;* that is, as proceeding from the church, and as derived from that. It will be an appointment connected with the church, and will be *as if* the church had conferred it on thee. The idea is, that the Messiah would receive, as it were, his designation, authority, commission, power from the church. He would spring from it (Isa. xi. 1); would act for it; would do what was needful for its good; would wield the power which properly belongs to the church on the earth. Comp. Notes on Ps. ii. 9. ¶ *Rule thou in the midst of thine enemies.* Set up thy power over them, and reign in them. This is a commission to set up a kingdom *in the very midst* of those who were his enemies; in the hearts of those who had been and were rebellious. His kingdom is set up not by destroying them, but by *subduing* them so that they become his willing servants. They yield to him, and he rules over them. It is not here a commission to cut them off, but one much more difficult of execution,—to make them his friends, and to dispose them to submit to his authority. Mere *power* may crush men; it requires more than that to make rebels willingly submissive, and to dispose them voluntarily to obey.

beauties ; of holiness ¹ from the

i Ps. xcvi. 9.   ¹ *more than.*   ² *shalt have.*

3. *Thy people.* All who are given
to thee; all over whom thou art to
rule. This verse has been variously
translated. The LXX. render it,
"With thee is the beginning in the
day of thy power, in the splendour of
thy saints, from the womb, before the
light of the morning have I begotten
thee." So the Latin Vulgate. Luther
renders it, "After thy victory shall
thy people willingly bring an offering
to thee, in holy adorning : thy children shall be born to thee as the dew
of the morning." De Wette, "Willingly shall thy people show themselves to thee on the day of the assembling of thy host in holy adorning,
as from the womb of the morning, thy
youth [vigour] shall be as the dew."
Prof. Alexander, "Thy people (are)
free-will offerings in the day of thy
power, in holy decorations, from the
womb of the dawn, to thee (is) the
dew of thy youth." Every clause
of the verse is obscure, though the
general idea is not difficult to perceive;—that, in the day of Messiah's
power, his people would willingly
offer themselves to him, in holy robes
or adorning, like the glittering dew
of the morning;—or, in numbers that
might be compared with the drops of
the morning dew. The essential ideas
are (1) that he would have a "people ;"
(2) that their subjection to him would
be a "willing" subjection; (3) that
this would be accomplished by his
"power;" (4) that they would appear before him in great beauty—in
robes of holy adorning; (5) that they
would in some way resemble the dew
of the morning ; and (6) that to him
in thus subduing them there would
be the vigour of youth,—the ardour
of youthful hope.   ¶ Shall be *willing.*
Literally, "Thy people [are, or shall
be] willing-offerings." The word
rendered willing—נְדָבֹת, *nedaboth*—
is in the plural number;—"thy
people, *willingnesses.*" The singular
—נְדָבָה, *nedabah*—means voluntariness, spontaneousness : and hence it

womb of the morning : thou
² hast the dew of thy youth.

comes to mean spontaneously, voluntarily, of a willing mind. It is rendered *a willing offering,* in Ex. xxxv.
29; *free offering,* in Ex. xxxvi. 3;
voluntary offering, in Lev. vii. 16;
free-will offering, in Lev. xxii. 18,
21, 23; xxiii. 38; Num. xv. 3; xxix.
39; Deut. xii. 6, 17; xvi. 10; xxiii.
23; 2 Chron. xxxi. 14; Ezra i. 4;
iii. 5; viii. 28; Ps. cxix. 108; *willingly,* in 2 Chron. xxxv. 8; *plentiful,*
in Ps. lxviii. 9; *voluntary,* and *voluntarily,* in Ezek. xlvi. 12; *freely,* in
Hos. xiv. 4; and *free-offering,* in
Amos iv. 5. It does not occur elsewhere. The idea is that of *freeness ;*
of voluntariness; of doing it from
choice, doing it of their own will.
They did it in the exercise of freedom.
There was no compulsion; no constraint. Whatever "power" there
was in the case, was to make them
"willing," not to *compel* them to do
a thing *against* their will. That
which was *done,* or that which is
here intended to be described as
having been done, is evidently the
act of devoting themselves to him
who is here designated as their Ruler
—the Messiah. The allusion may be
either (*a*) to their devoting themselves to *him* in conversion, or becoming his; (*b*) to their devoting
themselves to his *service*—as soldiers
do in war; or (*c*) to their devoting
their time, wealth, talents, to him in
lives consecrated to him. *Whatever*
there is as the result of his dominion
over them is *voluntary* on their part.
There is no compulsion in his religion. Men are not constrained to do
what they are unwilling to do. All
the power that is exerted is on the
will, disposing men to do what is
right, and what is for their own interest. No man is forced to go to
heaven against his will; no man is
saved from hell against his will; no
man makes a sacrifice in religion
against his will; no man is compelled
to serve the Redeemer in any way
against his will. The acts of religion

are among the most free that men ever perform; and of all the hosts of the redeemed no one will ever say that the act of his becoming a follower of the Redeemer was not perfectly voluntary. He *chose*—he *professed* —to be a friend of God, and he never saw the time when he regretted the choice. ¶ *In the day of thy power.* The power given to the Messiah to accomplish the work of his mission; the power to convert men, and to save the world. Matt. xxviii. 18; xi. 27; John xvii. 2. This implies (*a*) that *power* would be employed in bringing men to submit to him; and (*b*) that there would be a fixed time when that power would be put forth. Still, it is power which is not inconsistent with freedom. It is power exerted in making men *willing*, not in *compelling* or *forcing* them to submit to him. There *is* a power which may be exerted over the will consistent with liberty, and that is the power which the Messiah employs in bringing men to himself. ¶ *In the beauties of holiness.* This power will be connected with the beauty of holiness; or, holiness will be manifested when that power is put forth. The object is to *secure* holiness; and there will be beauty *in* that holiness. The only power put forth in the case is to make men holy; and they will, in their lives and conduct, manifest all the beauty or attractiveness which there is in a holy and pure character. The word rendered *beauty* is in the plural number, and the allusion *may* be to the raiment of those who are referred to. They would appear in pure garments—in sacerdotal vestments—as priests of God. Comp. Lev. xvi. 4. The idea may be that they would be a "kingdom of priests," clad in priestly vestments (Ex. xix. 6; comp. Notes on 1 Pet. ii. 5, 9), and that they would be adorned with robes appropriate to that office. This *may* refer, however, to their actual, internal holiness, and may mean that they would, when they were subjugated to him, appear *as* a holy or a righteous people. ¶ *From the womb*

of the morning : thou hast the dew of thy youth. Marg., *more than the womb of the morning, thou shalt have,* etc. The expression here is evidently designed to refer to the source of the *dew*—the dew of the early dawn—as having its *birth* then, or as seeming to be *born* then. The morn is represented as the *mother* of the dew. The figure is highly poetic and beautiful. The ground of the comparison may be either (*a*) that the "beauty of holiness"—the beautiful array of the saints—is *more than* that produced in the womb of the morning; or (*b*) that the dew of youth is more beautiful than the dew produced in the morning. As the word *dew*, that on which the comparison must turn, occurs in the *last* member of the sentence, it is probable that the second of these interpretations is the true one, as indicated in the margin : "More than the womb of the morning (more than the morning produces) thou hast the dew of thy youth." That is, "as the young morning—the *youth* of the day —has its beauties in the abundance and lustre of the dew-drops, so shall the dew of *thy* youth be—the beginning of *thy* glorious day." May there not be here also an allusion to the *multitudes* that would be among his "people"—numerous as the dew-drops of the morning, and as beautiful as they—on his going forth to the world with all the beauty of a bright dawn? The meaning of the whole, I apprehend, is, "Thy reign shall be like the day—a long bright day. Thy coming—the morning of that day—shall be like the early dawn —so fresh, so beautiful, made so lovely by the drops of dew sparkling on every blade of grass. More beautiful by far—more lovely—shall be the beginning of the day of thy reign; more lovely to the world *thy* youth— thy appearing—the beginning of *thy* day." Thus understood, the verse is a most beautiful poetic description of the bright morning when the Messiah should come; the dawn of that glorious day when he should reign. Comp. Isa. ix. 1–3.

4 The LORD hath sworn, and will not repent, Thou *k art a priest for ever after the order of Melchizedek.

5 The Lord at thy right hand

k Heb. v. 6; vi. 20: vii. 17, 21.

shall strike through kings in the day *l* of his wrath.

6 He shall judge among the heathen, he shall fill *the places*

l Rom. ii. 5; Rev. vi. 17.

---

4. *The* LORD *hath sworn.* He has confirmed the appointment of the Messiah by a solemn oath, or *as* by an oath. That is, It is as sure and fixed *as if* he had taken an oath. Comp. Heb. vi. 13. The *time,* so to speak, if the word *time* can be applied to transactions in a past eternity, was that when he was designated in the Divine purpose as Messiah; in the eternal counsels of God. Comp. Ps. ii. 7. ¶ *And will not repent.* Will not change his purpose. ¶ *Thou* art *a priest for ever after the order of Melchizedek.* The word rendered *order* here means properly a word, a thing, a matter; hence, a way or manner. The meaning here is, that he would be a priest *after the manner* of Melchizedek; or, such a priest as he was. He would not be of the tribe of Levi; he would not be in the regular line of the priesthood, but he would resemble, in the characteristics of his office, this ancient priest-king, combining in himself the two functions of priest *and* king; as a priest, standing alone; not deriving his authority from any line of predecessors; and having no successors. See this verse explained at length, in its application to the Messiah, in the Notes on Heb. v. 6, 10; vii. 1–3. The passage as it stands here, and as looked at without any reference to the use made of it in the New Testament, would imply these things:—(1) That he who was spoken of would be, in a proper sense, a priest. (2) That he would have a perpetual or permanent priesthood, — "for ever." (3) That he would not be of the established line of priests in the tribe of Levi, but that his appointment would be unusual and extraordinary. (4) That the appointment would come directly from God, and would not be *derived*

from those who went before him. (5) That as a priest he would *resemble* Melchizedek, according to the record which was found of Melchizedek in Genesis. (6) That as Melchizedek was a priest of the Most High God, so *he* would be. (7) That as Melchizedek combined in himself the functions of both priest and king, so these would be found in *him.* (8) That as Melchizedek had no successors in office, so *he* would have none. How far these things were applicable to the Lord Jesus Christ, and with what propriety the passage might be applied to him, may be seen by examining the Epistle to the Hebrews, chap. v. vi. vii.

5. *The Lord at thy right hand.* See Notes on Ps. xvi. 8. ¶ *Shall strike through kings.* The Hebrew word here rendered *shall strike,*—from מָחַץ, *mahhatz*—means to shake, to agitate; and then, to shake in pieces, to dash in pieces, to crush; and here it has the sense of dashing in pieces, smiting, wounding, crushing. The "kings" referred to are the enemies of God and the Messiah, and the idea is that all would be subdued before him; that he would set up a universal dominion; that none would be able to stand before him; or, that he would reign over all the earth. The *language* is that which is derived from conquests in war; from the subjugation of enemies by force of arms. Comp. Notes on Ps. ii. 9–12; Isa. xi. 4. ¶ *In the day of his wrath.* Ps. ii. 12.

6. *He shall judge among the heathen.* Among the *nations.* That is, he shall set up a kingdom, or shall rule over the nations of the earth. He shall come to execute judgment and justice, and shall apportion to men what is due to them. See Notes on Isa. xi. 3–5. ¶ *He shall fill* the places *with*

with the dead bodies; he *m* shall wound the heads over [1] many countries.

m Hab. iii. 13.   [1] Or, *great.*

the dead bodies. He shall make a great slaughter,—indicative of conquest, and of the subjugation of the world to himself. It would be *as if* the bodies of the slain in battle strewed the ground, or filled the valleys of the earth. ¶ *He shall wound the heads.* The same word is used here that occurs in the previous verse, and that is there rendered *shall strike.* It is the language of *conquest*, as if the world was to be subdued to himself *by war.* ¶ *Over many countries.* Marg., *great.* Over vast and extensive regions,—carrying his conquests into distant lands. This will be fulfilled only when *all* the earth shall be subject to the reign of the Messiah. 1 Cor. xv. 24–28.

7. *He shall drink of the brook in the way.* The design here seems to be to represent the Messiah as a victorious king and conqueror pursuing his enemies. In the previous verse the psalmist had represented him under the image of one engaged in battle, and slaying his enemies with a great slaughter. He here represents him as pursuing those who should escape from the battle, and as pursuing them without fainting or exhaustion. He is like one who finds abundant springs and streams of water in his journeyings; who refreshes himself at those fountains and streams; who, therefore, is not faint and weary. He pursues his foes vigorously and with success. ¶ *Therefore shall he lift up the head.* Therefore shall he triumph, or be successful. The head falls when we are faint and exhausted, when we are disappointed and are ashamed, when we are conscious of guilt. It is lifted up in conscious rectitude, in success and triumph, in the exuberance of hope. The idea here is, that the Messiah would be triumphant. He would achieve the victory over all his foes;

7 He shall drink of the brook *n* in the way : therefore shall he lift up the head.

n Judges vii. 5, 6.

he would pursue, without exhaustion, his flying enemies, and he would return from the conquest joyous, exulting, triumphant. All this is under the image of a victorious hero; all this will be accomplished in the conquest of the world by the Gospel; in the subduing of the foes of God; in the final scene when the Redeemer shall deliver up the kingdom to God. 1 Cor. xv. 24–28.

PSALM CXI.

The author of this psalm is unknown, as is the occasion on which it was composed. It is one of the psalms, of which there are in all ten in number, that commence with the phrase *Hallelu-jah* in the Hebrew; in our version rendered, *Praise ye the Lord.* Those psalms are the cvi., cxi., cxii., cxiii., cxxxv., cxlvi., cxlvii., cxlviii., cxlix., cl. The use of this phrase shows that the psalms where it is found were designed for public worship. It is probable that this was one of the later psalms,—a fact that might be indicated by the very use of this phrase *Hallelujah.* Venema supposes that it was composed in the time of the Maccabees, but of this there is no evidence.

This is one of the alphabetical psalms. In that class of psalms there is considerable variety. In some a letter of the Hebrew alphabet commences each verse in the psalm; in others, the successive letters of the alphabet begin each two or three verses in succession, or, as in Ps. cxix., eight verses in succession; in others, the successive letters of the alphabet are used in the beginning of separate clauses of the *verses* of a psalm.

The peculiarity of this psalm is that the first eight verses of the psalm contain *two* clauses, beginning with the letters of the alphabet taken in their order, the last two verses, *three.* Why this arrangement was adopted, it is impossible now to determine,—as it is in regard to *many* things which are thought to be beauties in poetry. There is very much in the measure, the rhythm, the rhyme, of modern poetry, that is quite

PSALM CXI.

PRAISE [1] ye the LORD. I will praise the LORD with *my* whole heart, in the assembly *o* of the upright, and *in* the congregation.

[1] *Hallelujah.*   *o* Ps. cix. 30.

2 The works *p* of the LORD *are* great, sought out of all them that have pleasure therein.

3 His work *is* honourable and glorious: and his righteousness endureth for ever.

p Job xxxvi. 24; Ps. xcii. 5 ; Rev. xv. 3.

as artificial, and quite as inexplicable, as this.

The psalm is a call to the praise of God on account of his *works*, and is designed to suggest grounds of confidence in him as drawn *from* those works. It is, therefore, of universal applicability; and may be used in any nation, at any time, and among any people. It is a psalm which may be translated into all the languages of the world, and whatever language men may speak, it would express in their own tongue what they have occasion to give thanks for in the various lands where they dwell.

1. *Praise ye the* LORD. Marg., *Hallelujah.* See Ps. cvi. 1. ¶ *I will praise the* LORD *with* my *whole heart.* With undivided affections; holding back nothing. I will allow nothing to be in my heart that would interfere with the fulness of praise ; no coldness or dividedness of affection; no love for other things that would deaden my love for God; no suspicion respecting him that would chill my ardour; no unbelief that would drag me down to earth, while the language of my lips ascended to God. See Notes on Ps. lxxxvi. 12. ¶ *In the assembly of the upright.* With the righteous when they are gathered together for public worship. ¶ *And* in *the congregation.* See Ps. xxii. 22, 25 ; lxvi. 13 ; lxxxix. 5.

2. *The works of the* LORD are *great.* They are great in number; great in magnitude ; great in wisdom; great in goodness. This language was appropriate in the time of the psalmist, when men looked upon the heavens with the naked eye alone, and when they had very imperfect views of the real magnitude of the universe as it is now disclosed by the telescope. It is entirely appropriate now, and conveys a more solemn and sublime impression

than it would in the time of the psalmist. It will still be appropriate under the larger views which may yet be obtained of the universe by more perfect instruments, by more accurate observation, and by more profound study. And it will be appropriate when men shall survey the greatness of the universe from the heights of heaven. ¶ *Sought out of all them.* Studied by all such. ¶ *That have pleasure therein.* More literally, "Sought to all their wishes." Perhaps the meaning is, that they would find all their desires gratified in those works; they would find in them all that they would *wish* to find respecting the power, wisdom, goodness, and majesty of God. Still it implies that they *have* a desire thus to study his works, or that they *do find* a pleasure in examining the proofs of the being and attributes of God *in* his works. A man who loves God will have real pleasure in studying his works as well as his word ; and it is as proper to find pleasure in the one as in the other,—as proper to wish to find the knowledge which the one imparts as that which the other bestows. One great error among the friends of God is the neglect to study his *works*. In doing this, men need not neglect or undervalue the Bible and the knowledge which it gives, for such studies would be among the best means of illustrating the Bible.

3. *His work* is *honourable and glorious.* Literally, " Honour and glory is his work;" that is, All that he *does* is honourable and glorious. The language would cover all that God does in the works of creation, providence, and redemption. There is honour—there is majesty—in *every-*

4 He hath made his wonderful works to be remembered: the LORD *is* gracious and full of compassion.

5 He *q* hath given [1] meat unto them that fear him: he will ever

q Matt. vi. 26, 33.

be mindful of his covenant.

6 He hath shewed his people the power of his works, that he may give them the heritage of the heathen.

7 The works of his hands *are*

[1] *prey.*

thing that he does. ¶ *And his righteousness endureth for ever.* That is, It will be found in all the investigations of his works, that he is unchangeably righteous or just. All that he has done, or that he now does, goes to demonstrate this. There are doings of men—even of good men —which will not bear investigation; but there are no such acts of God. There are things that men do which excite admiration only when there is no investigation in regard to them; but the works of God are admired the more, the more they are studied. There are things which appear beautiful, or appear sweet only when they are not shaken; a collection of perfumes will give out sweets the more it is stirred.

4. *He hath made his wonderful works.* In heaven and in earth. ¶ *To be remembered.* Literally, " Memory hath he made for his wonderful works." *They* are so made, that man may remember them; the memory of man, also, is so made, that it may retain them. The highest and most appropriate exercise of memory is to retain the lessons which the works of God inculcate; to treasure up for gratitude and for use what he teaches his intelligent creation through those works. Memory can never be better employed than in treasuring up the truths which the Creator teaches in his providential dealings with us, and in his word. How much better would it be for man if he laboured more to *remember* these things; if he sought to *forget* many of those things which he is so careful now to retain in his recollection. ¶ *The* LORD is *gracious,* etc. See Notes on Ps. lxxxvi. 5. This is stated here as the *result* of the careful study of the doings of God; as the conclusion to which all will

come who carefully study his works. *Illustrations* of what God has done that deserves to be remembered occupy the remainder of the psalm, except the last verse.

5. *He hath given meat unto them that fear him.* Marg., *prey.* The idea is, that he has supplied their wants. The Hebrew word is, *prey,* and the allusion is to the mode in which the wants of the beasts of the field are supplied. The meaning *may* be that they had obtained this from their enemies, as beasts of prey take their food by making war; or the word may be used in a general sense, as meaning that God had supplied their wants. ¶ *He will ever be mindful of his covenant.* He will never leave or forsake his people; he will be faithful to all the promises that he has made to them.

6. *He hath showed his people.* The Jewish people. He has made this known to them. The reference here is not to his *announcing* it, or *stating* it, but to his acts of interposition in their behalf in which he had manifested the greatness of his power. ¶ *The power of his works.* The power of his acts; the power involved in what he does. The power referred to here was that which was evinced in destroying the Egyptians, and in subduing the nations of Canaan. ¶ *That he may give them the heritage of the heathen.* The nations; to wit, the nations of Palestine. The word *heritage* is often used in the large sense of possessions; and the meaning here is, that God had shown the greatness of his power by giving all that they possessed into the hands of his people.

7. *The works of his hands.* All that he does in the works of creation and providence;—all in his

verity and judgment: all *r* his
commandments *are* sure.

8 They [1] stand fast for ever
and ever, *and are* done in truth
and uprightness.

r Ps. xix. 7.   [1] are *established.*

acts towards the children of men.
¶ *Are verity.* Truth. That is,
They tend to establish and confirm
the truth; they are done in the cause
or the defence of truth. Truth in any
case may be ascertained by what God
does,—for all that he defends and
protects is *truth,* and his acts, therefore, may be regarded as an expression
of what is true and right. ¶ *And
judgment.* In the cause of justice;
or, in maintaining the principles of
right. God never does anything to
vindicate wrong. None of his acts
can be fairly interpreted as having
been done to sustain injustice, fraud,
deceit, ambition, oppression, murder,
or licentiousness. That he suffers
free agents to do these things without interference is no evidence that
he approves of them. That he *dis-
approves* of them is shown (*a*) by his
declarations; (*b*) by his threatenings;
(*c*) by all that he does to punish the
wicked here. ¶ *All his commandments* are *sure.* His statutes; his
ordinances. They are *sure;* that is,
they are to be relied on; or, are
worthy of confidence.

8. *They stand fast for ever and
ever.* Marg., *established.* The Hebrew word means *sustained, supported.* They will not fail or fall.
Whatever else may be shaken, his
law, his word, and the principles of
his administration, will not fail. See
Notes on Matt. v. 18. Comp. Luke
xvi. 17; Matt. xxiv. 35. The great
principles of truth and righteousness
will stand, and whatever is founded
on those principles will endure for
ever. ¶ And are *done in truth and
uprightness.* Are based on truth, or
on a just view of things; they are
done in such a way that truth will
be maintained and promoted. The
word *uprightness* here means that all

9 He sent redemption unto
his people: he hath commanded
his covenant for ever; holy [s] and
reverend *is* his name.

10 The *t* fear of the LORD *is*

s Deut. xxviii. 58.
t Job xxviii. 28; Prov. i. 7; ix. 10; Ec. xii. 13.

this is done on the principles of
equity—of what *ought* to be done, or
what is *best* to be done. Comp. Ps.
xix. 9.

9. *He sent redemption unto his
people.* In their deliverance from
Egypt. He has now sent it in a
higher sense under the great Deliverer, the Saviour. ¶ *He hath commanded his covenant for ever.* He
has ordained or appointed it. The
covenant is here represented as if it
were obedient to the will of God, or
under his control. The covenant refers to his arrangements with his
people;—his assurances of favour,
with the terms on which that favour
will be shown. ¶ *Holy and reverend
is his name.* Holy and to be venerated; literally, "*to be feared.*" That
is, he has shown in all this that he is
holy, and that he is a Being who is
to be had in reverence.

10. *The fear of the* LORD. Reverence for God; respect for his law,
his will, his government, himself;
the fear of offending him, which will
lead us to do right. This fear is not
that of a slave; it is not mere dread;
it is not terror. It is consistent with
love, and springs from it. It is consistent with calmness of mind, and
promotes it. It does not produce
terror, but rather delivers from it,
and preserves the mind from alarms.
The word here rendered *fear* is a
noun of the same origin as the word
rendered *reverend* in the previous
verse. The suggestion to the mind
of the psalmist that the "name of
the Lord" was "*reverend,*" or was to
be venerated, introduced this thought
that such reverence is the very foundation of wisdom. ¶ Is *the beginning of wisdom.* The foundation, the
origin, the commencement of being
truly wise. It is so. There is no

the beginning of wisdom : [1] a good understanding have all they that do [2] *his commandments :* his praise endureth for ever.

[1] Or, *good success,* Prov. iii. 4.   [2] *them.*

true wisdom which does not recognize the being, the perfections, and the claims of God. The highest wisdom—the most lofty endowment of man—is that he *may* know and honour God. This, in capability, makes him wise above the brute creation ; this, in exercise, makes one man more wise than another ; this, when it springs up in the soul, makes a man more wise than he was before —or, is the *beginning* of true wisdom in the soul. Comp. Prov. i. 7 ; ix. 10 ; Deut. iv. 6 ; Job xxviii. 28 ; Ecc. xii. 13. ¶ *A good understanding,* etc. Marg., *good success.* The original word—שֵׂכֶל, *sēchěl*—is rendered *understanding* (as here) in 1 Sam. xxv. 3 ; Ezra viii. 18 ; Job xvii. 4 ; Prov. iii. 4 ; xiii. 15 ; xvi. 22 ; *wisdom* in 1 Chron. xxii. 12 ; Prov. xii. 8 ; xxiii. 9 ; *prudence,* 2 Chron. ii. 12 ; Prov. xix. 11 (marg.) ; *sense,* in Neh. viii. 8 ; *knowledge,* 2 Chron. xxx. 22 ; and *policy* in Dan. viii. 25. It *may* denote, therefore, understanding, wisdom, knowledge, success, prudence ; and it is true in regard to *all* of these, —for the fear of the Lord, or true religion, produces them *all.* It is not necessary, therefore, to endeavour to ascertain precisely which of these is the meaning here. ¶ *That do* his commandments. Marg., as in the Heb., *do them.* That do the things connected with the fear of the Lord ; that is, who obey God. ¶ *His praise endureth for ever.* That is, the foundation for his praise endures to all eternity ; or, is unchangeable. As God is always the same, so there is, as derived from his being and perfections, always the same foundation for praise. As there will always be created beings who can and will appreciate this, so it will be literally true, as it should be, that his praise *will* be celebrated for ever.

VOL. III.

PSALM CXII.

PRAISE [3] ye the LORD. Blessed *is* the man *that* feareth the

[3] *Hallelujah.*

PSALM CXII.

The author of this psalm, as of the preceding, is unknown, and equally with that it is impossible now to ascertain the time or the occasion of its composition. It is a psalm of the same structure as that, with the same number of verses ; like that, it is alphabetical in its form, and composed in the same manner,—the first eight verses with *two* clauses each, beginning with successive letters of the Hebrew alphabet,—and the last two verses with *three* clauses, beginning, in like manner, with three letters of the alphabet in succession. This peculiarity of structure makes it highly probable that it was composed by the same author.

It is further to be noticed that this psalm *begins* where the other *ends,* with the happiness or blessedness of " fearing God," and is designed to set forth that blessedness, or to show what are the advantages of true religion. This fact makes it further probable that the two psalms were composed by the same author.

This psalm is very simple in its structure. It sets forth the advantages or benefits of the fear of the Lord, or of religion in respect (*a*) to the posterity of the man, ver. 2 ; (*b*) in securing wealth, ver. 3 ; (*c*) in the light which springs up in darkness, ver. 4 ; (*d*) in the discretion with which such a man is enabled to manage his affairs, ver. 5 ; (*e*) in the firmness and composure of his mind in times of danger and trouble, vers. 6-8 ; (*f*) in his being so prosperous, and so exalted, that he will become an object of envy to the wicked, vers. 9, 10.

1. *Praise ye the* LORD. Marg., as in Heb., *Hallelujah.* See Notes on Ps. cvi. 1. ¶ *Blessed* is *the man.* Heb., *The blessings of the man.* See Notes on Ps. i. 1. That is, Blessed, or happy, is such a one. ¶ That *feareth the* LORD. In Ps. cxi. 10, the psalmist had referred to " the fear of the Lord " as " the beginning of wisdom," and had *alluded* to the success, prosperity, or happiness which

L

LORD, *that* delighteth " greatly in his commandments.

2 His seed shall be mighty upon earth: the generation of the upright shall be blessed.

3 Wealth and riches *shall be*

u Ps. i. 1—3; cxix. 16.

in his house; and his righteousness endureth for ever.

4 Unto the upright there ariseth ʳ light in the darkness: *he is* gracious, and full of compassion, and righteous.

v Ps xcvii. 11 ; Isa. lviii. 10.

attends the fear of the Lord, or true religion. This psalm is designed more fully to *illustrate* that thought. ¶ That *delighteth greatly in his commandments.* See Notes on Ps. i. 2. It is a characteristic of true piety to find pleasure in the commands of God;—in the commandments themselves, and in obedience to them.

2. *His seed shall be mighty upon earth.* His children; his posterity. That is, they shall be prospered; honoured; distinguished among men:—distinguished for their virtues, for their influence, for their success in life. This refers to what was regarded among the Hebrews as an object of great desire, and is in accordance with the promises everywhere found in their Scriptures. See Notes on Ps. xxv. 13; xxxvii. 25, 26. Comp. Gen. xii. 2; xvii. 6; Ex. xx. 6. It is in accordance, also, with a general fact in the course of events. The best security for the virtue and success of children is the virtue and the piety of parents; the surest inheritance as pertaining to happiness, respectability, and usefulness in life, is that which is derived from the example, the prayers, the counsel of a pious father and mother. ¶ *The generation of the upright shall be blessed.* The family; the children. Such promises are to be expected to be fulfilled *in general;* it is not required by any proper rules of interpreting language that this should be universally and always true.

3. *Wealth and riches* shall be *in his house.* The Septuagint and the Vulgate render this, *"glory* and riches shall be in his house."* The word, however, properly means riches or wealth, and the two terms are used apparently to convey the idea

that wealth or property in *varied forms* would be in his house; that is, not merely gold and silver, but all that was understood to constitute wealth—variety of garments, articles of furniture, etc. This promise is of the same nature as that of the previous verse. It pertains to a *general* truth in regard to the influence of religion in promoting prosperity. Comp. Notes on 1 Tim. iv. 8. ¶ *And his righteousness endureth for ever.* That is, The effects of it shall be transmitted from age to age in the prosperity, the respectability, the wealth, the happiness of his descendants. It travels on from age to age, and blesses distant generations.

4. *Unto the upright.* The just; the pious; the man who fears God. ¶ *There ariseth light in the darkness.* This is a new form of the blessing which follows the fear of the Lord, or another of the benefits which spring from true religion, and by which the pious man is distinguished from other men. The distinction is *not* that days of darkness will not come upon him as well as upon others; for he may be sick as others are, he may be bereaved as others are, he may lose his property as others do,—since there are general laws that affect mankind in these respects. God has not promised that he will interpose to save his people *from* these things, but that he will save them *in* them. The peculiarity in regard to those who fear God is, that these things will not always continue; that they shall not be overwhelmed by them; that it will not be uninterrupted and unmitigated gloom; that the sky shall not be always overcast. Comp. Notes on Ps. xcvii. 11; Job xi. 17. ¶ *He is gracious, and*

5 A good man sheweth favour, and lendeth : *w* he will guide his affairs [1] with discretion. *x*

w Luke vi. 35.   [1] *judgment.*

6 Surely he *y* shall not be moved for ever : the righteous

x Eph. v. 15.   *y* Ps. xv. 5.

full of compassion, and righteous. These words are designed to be applied to the " upright " man, and are intended more fully to designate his character, and to show *why* light shall spring up to him when he is in darkness. It is because his character is *really* pure and holy, so that whatever cloud may come over it for a time, however it may be temporarily obscured, however he may be calumniated by men, or however God may for a time seem to forsake him and to treat him as if he were a bad man, yet ultimately his character will appear as it really is. Light will come in upon the darkness. The clouds will break away. The prejudices against him will be dispersed. Full justice will be done to his character both by man and by God, and the world will see that he is a just and pious man. See Notes on Ps. xxxvii. 5, 6. Every man will ultimately be seen as he is ; every man will attain the position, and have the reputation which he *ought* to have.

5. *A good man sheweth favour.* He has the means to show favour to others, or to promote their welfare, and he is disposed to do this. It is the characteristic of a good man—of a heart that is truly pious—to do good to others ; to promote their welfare here, and to assist them in their endeavour to secure happiness in the world to come. ¶ *And lendeth.* The original word here—לָוָה, *lavah*—means to join oneself to any one ; to cleave to him ; then, to form the union which is constituted between debtor and creditor, borrower and lender. Here it is used in the latter sense, and it means that a good man will accommodate another—a neighbour—with money, or with articles to be used temporarily and returned again. A man who always *borrows* is not a desirable neighbour ; but a

man who never lends—who is never willing to accommodate—is a neighbour that no one would wish to live near—a crooked, perverse, bad man. True religion will always dispose a man to do acts of kindness in any and every way possible. ¶ *He will guide his affairs.* The word here used means literally to hold, contain ; to hold up, or sustain ; to nourish, to furnish the means of living. Gen. xlv. 11 ; xlvii. 12 ; l. 21. Here it means that he would uphold or *manage* his business. ¶ *With discretion.* Marg., *judgment;* so the Hebrew. He would do it prudently, sensibly, economically, wisely. This is, or should be, one of the characteristics of a good man. Religion prompts to this ; religion will aid a man in doing this ; religion will tend to check everything of a contrary nature. A man who neglects his "affairs," who pays no attention to his business, who is indifferent whether he is successful or fails, is a man who gives *just so much evidence* that he is a stranger to true religion.

6. *Surely he shall not be moved for ever.* Luther, " For he shall remain always." He shall be fixed, stable, firm, prosperous. He shall not be driven from place to place. He shall have a permanent home. He shall have a steady reputation. He shall have a constant influence. He shall be a firm, established, prosperous man. Of course this is to be taken in the general, and should not be pressed to mean that it will be, in the most literal sense, and always, true ; for a good man *may* be " unfortunate in business," and suffer with others ; he may be sick ; he may see reason to change his residence ; he will certainly die. But still it is true that religion *tends* to produce this permanency, and that in this respect there is a marked difference between men who

shall be in everlasting remembrance.

7 He ^z shall not be afraid of evil tidings: his heart is fixed, trusting in the LORD.

8 His heart *is* established, he shall not be afraid, until he see *his desire* upon his enemies.

9 He hath dispersed; he hath

z Prov. iii. 25, 26.

are truly pious, and those who are not. ¶ *The righteous shall be in everlasting remembrance.* In Prov. x. 7, it is said that "the name of the wicked shall rot;" and the meaning here is, that the way to secure a grateful remembrance among men after we are dead is to be righteous, —to do something that shall deserve to be remembered. It cannot mean that a man who is righteous will *never* be forgotten, or that his name and deeds will never pass from the recollection of mankind,—for that would not be true; but that men will delight to cherish the memory of the righteous; that they will be disposed to do justice to their character after they are dead; that the benevolent and the upright will be remembered when the names of the wicked shall be forgotten. The world has no interest in keeping up the memory of bad men, and as soon as it can be done hastens to forget them. Wicked men are remembered only when their deeds are enormous, and then their memory is cherished only to admonish and to warn. The world has no interest in keeping up the memory of Benedict Arnold, or Alexander VI., or Cæsar Borgia, except to warn future generations of the guilt and baseness of treason and profligacy; it *has* an interest in never suffering the names of Howard, of Wilberforce, of Henry Martyn, to die, for those names excite to noble feelings and to noble efforts wherever they are known. Such names are to be had "in everlasting remembrance."

7. *He shall not be afraid of evil tidings.* Of bad news; of reverses and losses; of the destruction of his ship at sea, or his property by land; of disaster by flood, by famine, by war. His heart will so fully confide in God that he can commit all calmly

into his hands. He will feel assured that all will be well; that nothing occurs but that which the wisest and the best Being in the universe sees it best should occur; and that in all which *does* take place he is able to sustain the sufferer. There is nothing so well fitted to make the mind calm as trust in God. What has a man to be afraid of who does trust in him? Comp. Ps. xxvii. 3; xlvi. 2; lvi. 3, 4; Heb. xiii. 6; Prov. i. 33. ¶ *His heart is fixed.* Is firm; is established. See Notes on Ps. lvii. 7. ¶ *Trusting in the* LORD. This is the reason *why* his heart is "fixed" or firm. It is not any native courage or resolution; it is not any firmness of his own; it is simply because he has confidence in God, and feels assured that all things will be well.

8. *His heart* is *established.* Sustained; upheld. This is the same idea, though somewhat varied in form. The word means to sustain; to support; and the idea is, that there is some basis of support—some strength —which is not his own. ¶ *He shall not be afraid.* When he is assailed by enemies. ¶ *Until he see* his desire *upon his enemies.* This implies that he had nothing really to fear. He would certainly overcome his foes; and in the mean time he might look calmly on all their efforts to destroy him, for those efforts would be vain. So the believer now looks calmly on all his spiritual foes. He has nothing to fear, for he will overcome them all; he will certainly triumph; he will trample them all under his feet. He may well, therefore, endure these conflicts for a brief period, for the issue is certain, and the conflict will soon come to an end.

9. *He hath dispersed,* etc. This is another characteristic of a righteous man, and another reason of the per-

given to the poor; his ^arighteous-
ness ^b endureth for ever: his horn
shall be exalted with honour.

10 The wicked shall see *it*, and

_a Deut. xxiv. 13.   _b Rev. xxii. 11.

be grieved; he shall gnash ^cwith
his teeth, and melt away; the
^d desire of the wicked shall perish.

_c Luke xiii. 28.   _d Prov. xi. 7.

manent honour which will be rendered to him. The meaning is, that he
is liberal; he freely scatters what he
has; he divides it with those who are
needy and unfortunate. One part of
mankind have an overplus — have
more than they need for themselves
and their families—and that overplus
is what is designed to meet the wants
of the unfortunate, the weak, the
aged, the imbecile, the infirm, who
have *not* enough. It is the *treasury*
of God—the *reservoir* where that is
gathered which is to be distributed
for the wants of the helpless and the
dependent. The righteous man is
one who enters fully into this arrangement, and who feels that all this
overplus belongs to God, and is to be
appropriated as he shall direct. ¶ *His
righteousness endureth for ever.* His
acts of charity are constant. His
piety is not fitful, spasmodic, uncertain; it is steady principle; it is firm
and solid; it may always be relied on.
See ver. 3. ¶ *His horn shall be exalted with honour.* See Notes on Ps.
lxxv. 10.

10. *The wicked shall see* it, *and be
grieved.* They shall see his prosperity; shall see the evidence that
God approves his character and his
conduct. The word rendered *grieved*
means rather to be angry or enraged.
Perhaps the word *fret* would best express the sense. ¶ *He shall gnash
with his teeth.* As indicative of hatred
and wrath. See Notes on Ps. xxxvii.
12. ¶ *And melt away.* Disappear,
—as snow does that melts; or as a
snail (see Notes on Ps. lviii. 8); or as
waters that run away (see Notes on
Ps. lviii. 7); or as wax (see Notes on
Ps. lxviii. 2). Their wrath shall be of
no avail, for they themselves shall
soon disappear. ¶ *The desire of the
wicked shall perish.* He shall not
be able to accomplish his desire, or to

carry out his purposes. He shall be
disappointed, and all his cherished
plans will come to nought. This is
in strong contrast with what is said
in the psalm would occur to the righteous. They would be prospered and
happy; they would be able to carry
out their plans; they would be respected while living, and remembered
when dead; they would find God interposing in their behalf in the darkest hours; they would be firm and
calm in the day of danger and of
trouble; they would put their trust
in the Lord, and all would be well.
Surely there is an advantage in our
world in being a friend of God.

PSALM CXIII.

The author of this psalm, as of those
which immediately precede it, is unknown. It is very general in its character, and has no allusion to any circumstances by which one could determine the name of the author, or the
occasion on which it was written. In
connexion with the five following psalms,
it constitutes what was known among
the Hebrews as the *Hallel;* that is, the
song of praise, sung on great occasions,
at the annual festivals, and especially at
the Passover and the Feast of Tabernacles. Buxtorf, *Lex. Tal.*, p. 613, *et seq.*

This psalm, which is expressive of the
majesty of God, as having a claim to
universal praise, consists essentially of
two parts:—

I. The general statement that God is
to be praised, and a call on all to engage
in that service, vers. 1-3.

II. Reasons why he should be praised,
vers. 4-9. (1.) He is exalted above all
nations, ver. 4; (2.) None can be compared with him, ver. 5; (3.) He is con-
descending, and looks with interest on
the things in heaven and on earth, ver.
6; (4.) He exalts the poor to positions
of honour and influence, vers. 7, 8;
(5.) He constitutes and appoints families,
with all that is tender and joyous in the
domestic relation, ver. 9.

PSALM CXIII.

PRAISE [1] ye the LORD. Praise,
O ye servants of the LORD,
praise the name of the LORD.

2 Blessed be the name of the
LORD, from this time forth and
for evermore.

3 From *c* the rising of the sun,

[1] *Hallelujah.*   *c* Isa. lix. 19; Mal. i. 11.

unto the going down of the
same, the LORD'S name *is* to be
praised.

4 The LORD *is* high above all
nations, *and* his glory above the
heavens.

5 Who *is* like unto the LORD
our God, who [2] dwelleth on high;

[2] *exalteth* himself *to dwell.*

1. *Praise ye the* LORD. Marg., as
in Heb., *Hallelujah.* See Notes on
Ps. cvi. 1. ¶ *Praise, O ye servants
of the* LORD. You who profess to
serve and obey him; who acknowledge him as your God. In the
original this is also the word *Hallelu,*
הַלְלוּ. ¶ *Praise the name of the*
LORD. Still the same word *Hallelu.*
The *name* of the Lord is put here, as
it is often, for the Lord himself.

2. *Blessed be the name of the* LORD.
Blessed be the Lord; or, *Let* the
name of the Lord be blessed. ¶ *From
this time forth and for evermore.*
Now and for ever. He is worthy of
praise now, and he ever will be.
What he is now, he will always continue to be; and as praise is proper
now, it will be for ever and ever.
An eternal God has claims to eternal
praise.

3. *From the rising of the sun,* etc.
From the farthest east to the farthest
west,—the sun in its rising and setting
being the remotest object that we see
in the horizon. ¶ *The* LORD'S *name*
is *to be praised.* This does not mean
that it *will* be—though that is true;
but that it *ought* to be,—that it is
worthy of universal praise. All men
in the east and in the west—everywhere—*should* praise and adore that
name.

4. *The* LORD is *high above all
nations.* Heb., Exalted above all
nations is Jehovah. That is, he
rules over all nations; he directs
their affairs; he is their sovereign
king As a matter of fact, and from
the necessity of the case, he is on a
throne which is elevated above all
the kings and kingdoms of the world.

He is the Sovereign not only of one
nation, but of all; and it is meet
that this should be acknowledged by
them all. ¶ And *his glory above the
heavens.* That which renders him
glorious. The manifestations of his
glorious character are not confined
to the earth; they extend to the
heavens;—they are not confined to
the visible heavens; they extend far
beyond, in the regions of illimitable
space. The universe—the earth and
the starry worlds—all are full of the
manifestations of his glory; and far
beyond the bounds of created things
(if they have a boundary), God is
there—without limit—the same God
—worthy there of universal praise!
Who can comprehend such a God?
Comp. Notes on Ps. viii. 1.

5. *Who* is *like unto the* LORD *our
God?* Who can be compared with
Jehovah our God? See Notes on
Isa. xl. 17–25. The meaning is, that
no creature—no idol—can be compared with Jehovah. The remark
here has special reference to his attributes as immediately specified—
his humbling himself to behold the
things in heaven and in earth; his
raising up the poor, etc. It is true
in general, in regard to God, that no
creature can be compared with him;
it is true, in regard to each one of
his attributes, that they are far above
all created excellence. ¶ *Who dwelleth
on high.* Marg., *exalteth himself to
dwell.* Literally, "The one making
high to sit." The language is applicable to one who is seated on a
lofty throne. Comp. Ps. viii. 1. He
has his dwelling—his throne—his
permanent seat—in the heavens :—

6 Who *f* humbleth *himself* to behold *the things that are* in heaven, and in the earth !

7 He *g* raiseth up the poor out of the dust, *and* lifteth the needy

f Isa. lvii. 15.   *g* 1 Sam. ii. 8.

out of the dunghill ;

8 That he may set *him* with princes, *even* with the princes *h* of his people.

9 He maketh the barren wo-

h Ps xlv. 16.

---

so high and exalted that it requires infinite condescension to look upon the earth, or even upon the heavens.

6. *Who humbleth* himself, etc. So high that it is necessary he *should* stoop even to behold the things which seem most lofty to us; and who actually *does* stoop thus to regard the things which he has made in heaven and on earth. ¶ *To behold* the things that are *in heaven, and in the earth!* More literally, "to look in heaven and in earth." Even to look on heaven, high as it is to us,— still more to look on earth, so insignificant as compared with the vast bodies in the heavens,—is condescension on the part of God. It requires him to stoop—even to look on the sun—the stars—the distant worlds! Yet he does this. There is not a world which he does not survey constantly; not a creature whose interests he does not regard; not an insect—a flower—an atom—that he does not regard with as much minute attention as though there were nothing else to demand his care.

7. *He raiseth up the poor out of the dust.* From the most humble condition in life. He exalts them to conditions of wealth, rank, honour. He has *power* to do this; he actually *does* it. This is not intended to be affirmed as a universal truth, or to assert that it is always done, but that it is among the things which show his majesty, his power, and his goodness, and which lay the foundation for praise. ¶ And *lifteth the needy out of the dunghill.* From the condition of lowest poverty. Instances are sufficiently abundant in which this is done, to justify such an assertion, and to show that it is a proper foundation of praise to God.

8. *That he may set* him *with princes.*

May give him a rank—a position— with nobles and great men upon the earth. Many instances of this nature have occurred in the history of the world. Not a few of the nobles of England, including several of its lord chancellors, have been raised thus from very humble life; and in every nation God shows that he has power to give to those of humblest rank a name and place which no hereditary titles and honours can bestow : thus Shakspeare was the son of a glover and woolstapler. God has power to come into the humblest cottage of poverty, and to bring forth those who shall stand foremost in their generation as men of genius and power. Nothing is more absolute than the power which God thus holds over the nations of the earth, and it is meet that a Being who has this power, and who exercises it, should be praised and honoured. ¶ Even *with the princes of his people.* Among those who are selected to preside over the people whom he has chosen for himself. It is implied here that this would be a higher honour than to be exalted to power among a heathen people—a people ignorant of the true God. It is a higher honour to be counted worthy to rule a Christian nation than a heathen people; it is a higher honour to be a ruler in the church—over those whom God has redeemed for himself—than it is to administer a secular government.

9. *He maketh the barren woman to keep house,* etc. Marg., as in Heb., *to dwell in a house.* That is, to be at the head of a family. See Notes on Ps. lxviii. 6. Comp. 1 Sam. ii. 5. This, too, is suggested as a reason why God should be praised and adored. In instances where all hope of posterity is cut off, he interposes, and diffuses

man to [1] keep house, *and to be*
a joyful mother of children.
Praise ye the LORD.

1 *dwell in an.*   i Ex. xii. 41.
k Ps. lxxxi. 5.   l Lev. xxvi. 11, 12.
              m Deut. xxxii. 9.

joy through a dwelling. We may
look abroad, and see abundant occasion for praising God,—in his condescension to human affairs,—in his
lifting up the poor from the humblest
condition,—in his exalting those of
lowly rank to places of honour, trust,
wealth, and power; but, after all, if
we wish to find occasions of praise
that will most tenderly affect the
heart, and be connected with the
warmest affections of the soul, they
will be most likely to be found in the
domestic circle—in the mutual love—
the common joy—the tender feelings
—which bind together the members
of a family. In such a family, the
words with which this psalm begins
and ends, "Hallelujah," "Hallelujah,"
are peculiarly appropriate; and if any
community on earth should apply
these words to itself it should be such
a family, called upon by everything
tender, holy, and lovely, to *praise the*
LORD.

PSALM CXIV.

This psalm, a part of the Hallel (see
Notes on the Introd. to Ps. cxiii.), is
occupied in celebrating the praises of
God for what he had done in the delivering of his people from Egyptian bondage,
and in conducting them to the promised
land. It is the language of exultation,
joy, and triumph, in view of the gracious
interpositions of God in their deliverance.
The psalmist sees the mountains and
hills seized as it were with consternation, leaping and skipping like sheep;
Jordan, as it were, frightened and fleeing back; the very earth trembling,—
at the presence of God. Everything is
personified. Everything is full of life;
everything recognizes the presence and
the power of the Most High. It would
be appropriate to use such a psalm on
the great festivals of the Jewish nation,
for nothing could be more proper than

PSALM CXIV.

WHEN *i* Israel went out of
Egypt, the house of Jacob
from a people of strange language,*k*
2 Judah *l* was his sanctuary,
and *m* Israel his dominion.

to keep these events in their history
before the minds of the people.
    The author of the psalm is unknown;
and the occasion on which it was composed cannot now be determined. It is
a most animated, elevated, cheering
psalm, and is proper to be used at all
times to make the mind rejoice in God,
and to impress us with the feeling that
it is easy for God to accomplish his purposes.

1. *When Israel went out of
Egypt.* Literally, "In the going out
of Israel from Egypt." This is not
to be confined to the exact act of the
exodus, but embraces all that properly entered into that migration,—
the whole train of events which resulted in their being brought into the
promised land. ¶ *The house of Jacob.*
The family of Jacob,—a name appropriately used here, since it was the
family of Jacob that had gone down
into Egypt, and that had increased to
these great numbers. ¶ *From a people of strange language.* Speaking a
foreign or a barbarian tongue. See
Notes on Ps. lxxxi. 5.
2. *Judah was his sanctuary.* His
home; his abode; his sacred dwelling-place. Judah was the principal
or leading tribe, recognized as the
tribe where power was to be concentrated, and from which the Messiah
was to proceed (Gen. xlix. 8-12);
and hence the name was early used
to denote the entire people, and ultimately, as modified in the word *Jews*,
became the common name of the
nation. ¶ And *Israel his dominion.*
The nation that he ruled; the nation
that had his law; the nation that he
governed by his presence,—or, of
which he was the recognized king.
There can be no doubt that the reference here is to God, but it is remark-

3 The sea saw *n* *it*, and fled :
Jordan *o* was driven back.

4 The mountains *p* skipped like
rams, *and* the little hills like
lambs.

5 What *ailed* thee, O thou sea,
that thou fleddest ? thou Jordan,

n Ex. xiv. 21.　　*o* Jos. iii. 13, 16.

that thou wast driven back ?

6 Ye mountains, *that* ye skipped like rams; *and* ye little hills,
like lambs ?

7 Tremble, *q* thou earth, at the
presence of the Lord, at the
presence of the God of Jacob;

p Hab. iii. 6, 8.　　*q* Micah vi. 1, 2.

able that the name " God " is not used.
Perhaps the reason may be that this
psalm was designed to be employed in
connexion with the preceding one, and
as that consists entirely of the praises
of God, it was not necessary to repeat
the name when his praise was to be
continued under another form, and in
connexion with another line of thought.

3. *The sea saw it.* The word *it* is
supplied, not very properly, by our
translators. It would be more expressive to say, " The sea saw :" that
is, The sea—(the Red Sea)—saw the
mighty movement—the marshalled
hosts—the moving masses—the cattle
—the pursuing enemies—the commotion—the agitation—on its usually
quiet shores. We are to conceive of
the usual calmness of the desert—the
waste and lonely solitudes on the
banks of the Red Sea,—and then all
this suddenly broken in upon by vast
hosts of men, women, children, and
cattle, fleeing in consternation, followed by the embattled strength of
Egypt,—all rolling on tumultuously
to the shore. No wonder that the
sea is represented as astonished at
this unusual spectacle, and as fleeing
in dismay. ¶ *And fled.* As if affrighted at the approach of such an
host, coming so suddenly upon its
shores. ¶ *Jordan was driven back.*
Referring to the dividing of the waters
of the Jordan when the children of
Israel passed over to the promised
land. Josh. iii. 13–17. They also
seemed astonished at the approach of
the Hebrews, and retired to make a
way for them to pass over.

4. *The mountains skipped like rams.*
As flocks in their gambols. They
seemed to move from place to place ;
everything seemed to be unsettled,

and acknowledged the presence of
the Omnipotent One. The word rendered *skipped* means to leap for joy ;
to dance. See Notes on Ps. xxix. 6.
The reference here is to the agitations
and commotions of the peaks of Sinai,
when God came down to deliver the
law. Ex. xix. 16–18. ¶ And *the
little hills like lambs.* Heb., Like
the sons of the flock. The reference
here is to the less prominent emi-
nences of Sinai. The lofty hills, and
the smaller hills surrounding, seemed
to be all in a state of commotion.

5, 6. *What* ailed *thee, O thou sea,
that thou fleddest ?* etc. Literally,
" What to thee, O sea," etc. That is,
What influenced thee,—what alarmed
thee,—what put thee into such fear,
and caused such consternation ?　Instead of *stating* the cause or reason
why they were thus thrown into dismay, the psalmist uses the language
of surprise, as if these inanimate objects had been smitten with sudden
terror, and as if it were proper to ask
an explanation from themselves in
regard to conduct that seemed so
strange.

7. *Tremble, thou earth, at the presence of the Lord,* etc. This is at the
same time an explanation of the facts
referred to in the previous verses, and
the statement of an important truth
in regard to the power of God. The
true explanation—as here implied—of
what occurred to the sea, to the Jordan, to the mountains, and to the
hills, was the fact *that God was there ;*
the inference from that, or the truth
which followed from that, was, that
before that God in whose presence
the very mountains shook, and from
whom the waters of the sea fled in
alarm, the whole earth should tremble.

8 Which [r] turned the rock *into* a standing water, the flint into a fountain of waters.

r Ex. xvii. 6; Num. xx. 11.

8. *Which turned the rock into a standing water.* That is, Before him who could do this, the earth should tremble ; the inhabited world should stand in awe of such amazing power. The words rendered *a standing water,* mean properly *a pool of water.* They indicate nothing in regard to the *permanency* of that pool ; they do not imply that it remained *as* a standing pool during the sojourn of the Israelites in the wilderness,—whatever may have been the fact in regard to that. The simple idea is, that, at the time referred to, the rock was converted into a pool ; that is, the waters flowed from the rock, constituting such a pool. ¶ *The flint.* Another name for the rock,—used here to describe the greatness of the miracle. ¶ *Into a fountain of waters.* That is, The waters flowed from the rock as from a fountain. The Bible is a book of miracles, and there is nothing more improbable in this miracle than in any other.

In the Septuagint, the Latin Vulgate, the Syriac, the Arabic, and in many manuscripts, there is no division of the psalm here, but the following psalm is united with this, as if they were a single poem. *Why,* in those versions, the division of the Hebrew was not followed, cannot now be ascertained. The division in the Hebrew is a natural division, and was evidently made in the original composition.

PSALM CXV.

It is not possible now to ascertain on what occasion this psalm was composed, or who was its author. It has been generally believed that it was written in the later periods of the Jewish history, and after the captivity in Babylon. There is no improbability in the supposition, though there is nothing so marked in the psalm as to make this supposition necessary. It is evident from vers. 2, 3,

PSALM CXV.

NOT [s] unto us, O LORD, not unto us, but unto thy name

s Isa. xlviii. 11 ; Ez. xxxvi. 32.

that it was composed in a time of national calamity, and especially of such national disaster as might lead the surrounding nations to say of them that they were forsaken by the God whom they worshipped. This charge is replied to by saying that what had occurred had taken place under the Divine permission, and was no proof that Jehovah was not the true God. This thought leads the author of the psalm to prove the utter powerlessness of idols as compared with Jehovah, and, in view of this, to exhort the people of Israel still to trust in their own God as the Being in whom alone they could hope for protection and safety.

The psalm, therefore, comprises the following parts :—

I. A statement that all which they had was to be traced to God, ver. 1.

II. The existing troubles of the nation as being so great that the heathen were led to infer that Jehovah could not help them, and to ask, with some show of plausibility, where now was the God in whom they trusted ? ver. 2.

III. The general statement of the psalmist that what had occurred was to be traced to God ; that it was not evidence that he had *forsaken* them, but was proof that he was a *sovereign,* ver. 3.

IV. A statement of the utter weakness, helplessness, and inefficiency of idols ; of their entire powerlessness as being without life ; and of the stupidity and folly of worshipping such lifeless objects, vers. 4-8.

V. An exhortation to trust in the Lord, on the ground of what he had done, and of the blessings which were to be expected of him, vers. 9-16.

VI. An exhortation to do this at once, since death would soon occur, and praise could not be rendered to him in the grave, vers. 17, 18.

1. *Not unto us, O LORD, not unto us, but unto thy name give glory.* This apparently abrupt commencement of the psalm was undoubtedly in reference to some circumstances which would be well understood at the time when the psalm was composed, but which cannot be definitely ascertained

give glory, for thy mercy, *and* for thy truth's sake.

2 Wherefore *t* should the heathen say, Where *is* now their God?

t Joel ii. 17.　　*u* Dan. iv. 35.

3 But *u* our God *is* in the heavens; he hath done whatsoever he hath pleased.

4 Their idols *v* *are* silver and gold, the work of men's hands.

v Ps. cxxxv. 15—18; Isa. xl. 19; Jer. x. 3—7.

now. It seems to have been in view of some existing troubles, and the language at the same time expresses a hope of the Divine interposition, and a feeling that the praise of such interposition would belong wholly to God. The phrase "give glory" means, give all the honour and praise. See Notes on Ps. xxix. 1, 2. ¶ *For thy mercy.* The mercy or the favour which we seek and look for,—thy gracious help in the time of trouble. ¶ And *for thy truth's sake.* Thy faithfulness to thy promises; thy faithfulness to thy people. The psalmist anticipated this manifestation of faithfulness with confidence; he felt that all the praise for such an anticipated interposition would belong to God.

2. *Wherefore should the heathen say.* The nations; they who worshipped idols, and who claimed that those idols were true gods. Why should we, thy people, be so left, so forsaken, so afflicted, as to lead these idolaters to suppose that *we* worship a false God, or that the God whom we adore is destitute of power or faithfulness;—either that he does not exist, or that he cannot be relied on. It is evident that they were now in circumstances which would give some plausibility to the question here asked. ¶ *Where* is *now their God?* They seem to be forsaken. God, the God whom they worship, does not come forth for their defence. If he exists at all, he is destitute of power, or he is not true to the people who worship him, and he cannot be trusted. Comp. Notes on Ps. xlii. 3, 10; lxxix. 10.

3. *But our God* is *in the heavens.* The Septuagint adds, "and in the earth." This is not, however, in the Hebrew. The idea is, Our God really exists. He is the true God. He reigns in heaven. His plans are such as are and should be formed in heaven: —lofty, vast, incomprehensible. But he is still *our* God; our Ruler; our Protector. He is not a god of earth—whose origin is earth,—who dwells on earth alone,—like the idols of the heathen; but the whole vast universe is under his control. ¶ *He hath done whatsoever he hath pleased.* And, therefore, what has been done is right, and we should be submissive to it. He is a sovereign God; and mysterious as are his doings, and much as there *seems* to be occasion to ask the question "Where is now your God?" yet we are to feel that what has occurred has been in accordance with his eternal plans, and is to be submitted to as a part of his arrangements. It is, in fact, always a sufficient answer to the objections which are made to the government of God, *as if* he had forsaken his people in bringing affliction on them, and leaving them, apparently without interposition, to poverty, to persecution, and to tears, that he is "in the heavens;" that he rules there and everywhere; that he has his own eternal purposes; and that all things are ordered in accordance with his will. There *must*, therefore, be some good reason why events occur as they actually do.

4. *Their idols.* Their gods—the gods which *they* worship, as contrasted with the God whom we adore. The design of this description (vers. 4-8) is to show the utter vanity of trusting in such gods, and to lead the people of Israel to put *their* trust in the true God—in Jehovah. ¶ *Are silver and gold.* Made of silver and gold, and they must have, therefore, the properties of silver and gold. They can be of value only *as* silver and gold. They cannot do the work of mind; they cannot do the work of

5 They have mouths, but they speak not; eyes have they, but they see not;

6 They have ears, but they hear not; noses have they, but they smell not;

7 They have hands, but they

handle not; feet have they, but they walk not; neither speak they through their throat.

8 They that make them are like unto them; *so is* every one that trusteth in them.

9 O Israel, trust thou in the

God. The psalmist was not disposed to depreciate the *real* value of these idols, or to throw contempt on them which they did *not* deserve. He was disposed to treat them fairly. They *were* silver and gold; they had an intrinsic value as such; they showed in the value of the material how much the heathen were disposed to honour their objects of worship; and they were not held up to contempt as shapeless blocks of wood or stone. The psalmist *might* have said that most of them *were* made of wood or stone, and were mere shapeless blocks; but it is always best to do justice to an adversary, and not to attempt to underrate what he values. The argument of an infidel on the subject of religion *may* be utterly worthless *as* an argument for infidelity, but it may evince ability, learning, subtilty, clearness of reasoning, and even *candour;*—and it is best to admit this, if it is so, and to give to it all the credit which it deserves *as* a specimen of reasoning, or *as* stating a real difficulty which ought to be solved by somebody,—to call it "silver and gold" if it is so, and not to characterize it as worthless, weak, stupid—the result of ignorance and folly. He has great advantage in an argument who owns the *real* force of what an opponent says; he gains nothing who charges it as the offspring of stupidity, ignorance, and folly—unless he can show that it *is* so.

¶ *The work of men's hands.* Shaped and fashioned by men's hands. They *cannot,* therefore, be superior to those who made them; they cannot answer the purpose of a God.

5–7. *They have mouths,* etc. They are shaped like men, but have none of the attributes of intelligent beings.

8. *They that make them are like unto them.* Stupid; senseless; irrational. See Notes on Isa. xliv. 9–20. ¶ So is *every one that trusteth in them.* Men who do this show that they are destitute of all the proper attributes of reason, since such gods *cannot* help them. It is most strange, as it appears to us, that the worshippers of idols did not themselves see this; but this is in reality no more strange than that sinners do not see the folly of their course of sin; that men do not see the folly of worshipping no God. In fact, there is less of folly among the heathen than there is in this class of men. The worship of an idol shows at least that there is some religious tendency in the mind; some conviction that God ought to be worshipped; some aspiration after a proper object of worship; some appreciation of the true dignity and rank of man as made for worship; but what shall be said of the man who evinces no such tendency,—who has no such aspiration or desire,—who endeavours to extinguish in his nature all that was designed to express the idea of worship, or to lead him to God,—who never starts the inquiry whether there *is* a God,—who never prays for light, for guidance, for pardon, for a preparation for death and eternity,—who never even testifies so much interest in religion as to set up an image of gold, or wood, or stone, as indicative of the fact that he is made above the brutes? There are multitudes of the heathen *less* stupid and foolish than men in Christian lands.

9. *O Israel, trust thou in the* LORD. This exhortation is founded in a great measure on what had been just said in regard to idols. They

LORD: he *is* *w* their help and their shield.*x*

10 O house of Aaron, trust in the LORD: he *is* their help and their shield.

11 Ye that fear the LORD, trust in the LORD: he *is* their help and their shield.

12 The LORD hath been mind-

w Ps. xxxiii. 20.
x Ps. lxxxiv. 11 ; Prov. xxx. 5.

ful *y* of us: he will bless *us* : he will bless the house of Israel; he will bless the house of Aaron.

13 He *z* will bless them that fear the LORD, *both* small *1* and great.

14 The LORD shall increase you more and more, you and your children.

y Isa. xliv. 21.   *z* Ps. xxix. 11.
1 with.

had no power. There was no reason why they should be confided in. They could not help in the day of trouble; and as men need a god, and as the idols cannot be to them as gods, the exhortation is addressed to his people to trust him. He would be to them all that was implied in the name *God;* all that was wanted in a *God.* ¶ *He* is *their help.* The help of those who trust in him. He is able to help them in the time of trouble; he is willing to help them; he *will* help them. They who put their trust in him will find him a sure and certain help. This is the experience of all who confide in him. ¶ *And their shield.* Their protector. See Notes on Ps. v. 12; xviii. 2; xxxiii. 20. Comp. Gen. xv. 1 ; Deut. xxxiii. 29; Prov. xxx. 5.

10. *O house of Aaron,* etc. Ministers of religion; descendants of Aaron. His family was consecrated to the various services of the sanctuary.

11. *Ye that fear the* LORD, etc. All the people that reverence God; all his true worshippers.

12. *The* LORD *hath been mindful of us.* This would be peculiarly appropriate if the psalm was written, as is commonly supposed, after the return from the captivity of Babylon. In such circumstances it would be every way proper to bring before the mind of the people the fact that God had remembered them and had delivered them. ¶ *He will bless* us. Our past experience furnishes the fullest evidence that he will continue to bless us. He who has delivered

us from so great calamities, and who has restored us to our native land after so long and so painful a captivity, will not forsake us now. There can be now no circumstances in which he *cannot* bestow on us all the blessings which we need; there will be none when we may not hope that he will bless us. If he could save us from such troubles, he can save us from all; if he did thus interpose, we may argue that he will always grant us his help when we need it. ¶ *He will bless the house of Israel; he will bless the house of Aaron.* Comp. vers. 9, 10.

13. *He will bless them that fear the* LORD. Comp. ver. 11. ¶ *Both small and great.* Marg., as in Heb., *with.* The little *with* the great; children and grown persons; the poor and the rich ; the ignorant and the learned; those of humble rank, and those of most exalted birth and condition.

14. *The* LORD *shall increase you more and more.* He will increase your numbers and your power. We may suppose that the people were greatly diminished by the captivity, and that on their return to their country their number was comparatively small. This promise of a great increase was in accordance with the cherished wishes of the Hebrew people, and with the repeated promises which God had made to their fathers. Comp. Gen. xv. 5; xxii. 17; xxxii. 12. ¶ *You and your children.* The blessing shall be not only on you, but it shall go down to future generations.

15 Ye *a are* blessed of the
LORD, which made heaven and
earth.

16 The heaven, *even* the heavens, *are* the LORD's: but the
earth hath he given to the children of men.

a Ps. iii. 8; Eph. i. 3, 4.

17 The dead *b* praise not the
LORD, neither any that go down
into silence.

18 But we *c* will bless the LORD
from this time forth and for
evermore. Praise the LORD.

b Ps. lxxxviii. 10—12; Isa. xxxviii. 18, 19.
c Dan. ii. 20.

---

15. *Ye* are *blessed of the* LORD.
Blessed in your present comforts and
mercies; blessed in his promises in
regard to the time to come; blessed
in the prospects which are before
you. ¶ *Which made heaven and
earth.* The true God; the great
Creator of all things. It was not the
blessing of a creature—man or angel
—it was the blessing of the living
God.
16. *The heaven.* Heb., *The heavens.* ¶ Even *the heavens* are *the*
LORD's. A more literal and correct
rendering of this would be, "The
heavens are heavens for Jehovah."
That is, he has reserved the heavens
as a home for himself, or as his peculiar possession and abode. Comp.
Isa. lxvi. 1; Matt. v. 34; Acts vii.
49. ¶ *But the earth,* etc. He prepared earth for the abode of man; he
has placed man upon it to cultivate
it; he has given its fruits and productions to man, to be held and enjoyed by man; he has made all on
earth subject to man,—the dwellers
in the air, the land, and the waters.
All this he has given to *man;* not to
the angels. Earth is the home of
man, the birth-place of man; the
place where he lives, where he shows
the result of his toil, his skill, and
his ingenuity; the place where he
builds houses, bridges, monuments,
works of art; the place where he
prepares for another state of existence; the place where he dies, and is
buried. It is, as formed by the
Creator, a beautiful abode fitted up
for man; how much more beautiful
would it be, if man never defiled or
desolated it by sin! how happy an
abode would it have been if sin had
never entered it!

17. *The dead praise not the* LORD.
The meaning of this is, that *as* those
who are dead cannot praise God, or
cannot worship him, this should be
done while we are in the land of the
living. This opportunity, like all
other opportunities, will be cut off
in the grave, and hence we should
be faithful in this duty, and should
avail ourselves of this privilege, while
life lasts. In regard to the sentiment here expressed, and the grounds
on which that sentiment was entertained, see Notes on Isa. xxxviii. 18,
19; Ps. vi. 5. ¶ *Neither any that
go down into silence.* Into the grave
—the land of silence. Ps. xciv. 17.
Nothing is more impressive in regard
to the grave than its utter *silence.*
Not a voice, not a sound, is heard
there,—of birds or men—of song or
conversation—of the roaring of the
sea, the sighing of the breeze, the
fury of the storm, the tumult of
battle. Perfect stillness reigns there;
and the first sound that shall be
heard there will be the archangel's
trump.
18. *But we will bless the* LORD,
etc. While life lasts; now and ever
onward. Our lives are spared; and
while those lives shall be continued
they shall be spent in praise. We
will transmit the praise to future
times; and when we are dead, the
voice of praise shall be prolonged by
those who come after us. It may be
added here that we have now higher
and clearer views of the grave and
of the future world than the psalmist had, and that though it is certain that our voices of praise must
be stilled by death, yet in another world we shall continue the
work of praise in strains more lofty

PSALM CXVI.

I LOVE ^d the LORD, because he hath heard my voice *and* my supplications.

2 Because he hath inclined his ear unto me, therefore will I call upon *him* [1] as long as I live.

d Ps. xviii. 1—6.　　[1] *in my days.*

than here, and in a continuance of service that shall never end. The grave is, indeed, before us all; but so is also heaven, if we belong to those who truly fear the Lord, and who sincerely worship him through Christ Jesus.

PSALM CXVI.

The author and date of this psalm are unknown. It seems to be rather of a private than a public character, and there are expressions in it which must have been drawn from the personal experience of its writer. It is adapted to public use only because in all public assemblages there are those who would find their own experience represented by the language of the psalm. It *may* have been composed after the return from Babylon, but there is nothing in the psalm to limit it to that time, and the language is such that it *may* have been composed at any period after Jerusalem became the place of public worship, ver. 19.

The Septuagint and the Latin Vulgate, which combined the two previous psalms into one, divide this into two, at the end of ver. 9. The reason why this was done is unknown.

The psalm appears to have been composed in reference to a dangerous sickness, or some deep affliction which threatened life, vers. 3, 8, 9, 15; and it expresses a purpose to praise and serve God in view of the fact that the author had been delivered from impending death, and that his days had been lengthened out upon the earth.

The psalm embraces the following points:—

I. An expression of love and gratitude in view of the mercies of God, and of a purpose to serve him as long as life should last, vers. 1, 2.

II. A description of his sufferings, as if the pains of hell had seized him, vers. 3, 4.

III. A description of the mercy and goodness of God as interposing in answer to his prayer, and delivering him, vers. 5-11.

IV. A solemn declaration of his pur-

pose to praise God for all his mercies; to take the cup of salvation and call on his name; to pay his vows in the presence of the people of God; to offer the sacrifice of thanksgiving; to worship in the courts of the Lord's house, in the midst of Jerusalem, vers. 12-19.

1. *I love the* LORD. The Hebrew rather means, "I love, because the Lord hath heard," etc. That is, the psalmist was conscious of *love;* he felt it glowing in his soul; his heart was full of that peculiar joy, tenderness, kindness, peace, which love produces; and the source or reason of this, he says, was that the Lord had heard him in his prayers. ¶ *Because he hath heard,* etc. That is, This fact was a *reason* for loving him. The psalmist does not say that this was the *only* reason, or the *main* reason for loving him, but that it was *the* reason for that peculiar joy of love which he then felt in his soul. The main reason for loving God is his own excellency of nature; but still there are other reasons for doing it, and among them are the benefits which he has conferred on us, and which awaken the love of gratitude. Comp. Notes on 1 John iv. 19.

2. *Because he hath inclined his ear unto me.* See Notes on Ps. v. 1. Because he has been gracious to me, and has heard my prayers. This is a *good* reason for serving God, or for devoting ourselves to him, but it is not the *only* reason. We *ought* to worship and serve God whether he hears our prayers or not; whether he sends joy or sorrow; whether we are favoured with prosperity, or are sunk in deep affliction. Men *have* worshipped God even when they have had no evidence that he heard their prayers; and some of the most pure acts of devotion on earth are those which come from the very depths of darkness and sorrow. ¶ *Therefore will I call upon* him *as*

3 The sorrows of death compassed me, and *e* the pains of hell [1] gat hold upon me: I found trouble and sorrow.

e Jonah ii. 2, etc.   [1] *found me.*

4 Then *f* called I upon the name of the LORD: O LORD, I beseech thee, deliver my soul.

5 Gracious *g is* the LORD, and

f Ps. xxxiv. 6.   *g* Ps. ciii. 8.

long as I live. Marg., as in Heb., *in my days.* Encouraged by the past, I will continue to call upon him in the future. I will retain a firm faith in the doctrine that he hears prayer, and I will express my practical belief in the truth of that doctrine by regular and constant habits of worship. When a man once has evidence that God has heard his prayer, it is a reason why he should always call on him in similar circumstances, for God does not change.

3. *The sorrows of death.* What an expression! We know of no intenser sorrows pertaining to this world than those which we associate with the dying struggle—whether our views in regard to the *reality* of such sorrows be correct or not. We may be—we probably are—mistaken in regard to the intensity of suffering as ordinarily experienced in death; but still we dread those sorrows more than we do anything else, and all that we dread *may be* experienced then. Those sorrows, therefore, become the representation of the intensest forms of suffering; and such, the psalmist says, he experienced on the occasion to which he refers. There would seem in his case to have been two things combined, as they often are:—(1) actual suffering from some bodily malady which threatened his life, vers. 3, 6, 8–10; (2) mental sorrow as produced by the remembrance of his sins, and the apprehension of the future, ver. 4. See Notes on Ps. xviii. 5. ¶ *And the pains of hell.* The pains of *Sheol*—Hades; the grave. See Notes on Ps. xvi. 10; Job x. 21, 22; Isa. xiv. 9. The pain or suffering connected with going down to the grave, or the descent to the nether world; the pains of death. There is no evidence that the psalmist here refers to the pains of *hell,* as we understand the word, as

a place of punishment, or that he means to say that he experienced the sorrows of the damned. The sufferings which he referred to were those of death—the descent to the tomb. ¶ *Gat hold upon me.* Marg., as in Heb., *found me.* They discovered me —as if they had been searching for me, and had at last found my hiding-place. Those sorrows and pangs, ever in pursuit of us, will soon find us all. We cannot long escape the pursuit. Death tracks us, and is upon our heels. ¶ *I found trouble and sorrow.* Death found *me,* and *I* found trouble and sorrow. I did not seek it, but in what I *was* seeking I found *this.* Whatever we fail to "find" in the pursuits of life, we shall *not* fail to find the troubles and sorrows connected with death. They are in our path wherever we turn, and we cannot avoid them.

4. *Then called I upon the name of the* LORD. Upon the Lord. I had no other refuge. I felt that I must perish unless he should interpose, and I pleaded with him for deliverance and life. Comp. Notes on Ps. xviii. 6. ¶ *O* LORD, *I beseech thee, deliver my soul.* My life. Save me from death. This was not a cry for salvation, but for life. It is an example for us, however, to call on God when we feel that the soul *is* in danger of perishing, for then, as in the case of the psalmist, we have no other refuge but God.

5. *Gracious* is *the* LORD. This fact was his encouragement when he called on God. He believed that God was a gracious Being, and he found him to be so. Comp. Notes on Heb. xi. 6. ¶ *And righteous,* etc. Just, true, faithful. This, too, is a proper foundation of appeal to God:—not that we are righteous, and have a claim to his favour, but that he is a Being who will do what is *right;* that is, what

righteous ; *h* yea, our God *is* merciful.

6 The LORD preserveth the simple: I was brought low, and he helped me.

7 Return unto thy rest,*i* O my

h Ezra ix. 15; Neh. ix. 8; Dan. ix. 7.

soul; for the LORD hath dealt bountifully with thee.

8 For thou hast delivered my soul from death, mine eyes from tears, *and* my feet from falling.*k*

i Jer. vi. 16; Matt. xi. 29; Heb. iv. 3.
k Jude 24.

is best to be done in the case. If he were an unjust Being; if he were one on whose stability of character, and whose regard for right, no reliance could be placed, we could never approach him with confidence or hope. In this sense we may rely on his *justice*—his *justness* of character—as a ground of hope. Comp. Notes on 1 John i. 9: "If we confess our sins, he is faithful and *just* to forgive us our sins."

6. *The* LORD *preserveth the simple.* The LXX. render this *babes* — νήπια. The Hebrew word has reference to simplicity or folly, as in Prov. i. 22. It then refers to those who are the opposite of cautious or cunning; to those who are open to persuasion; to those who are easily enticed or seduced. The *verb* from which the word is derived—פָּתָה, *pathah*—means *to open, to expand;* then, *to be* open, frank, ingenuous, easily persuaded or enticed. Thus it may express either the idea of being *simple* in the sense of being foolish, easily seduced and led astray; or, *simple* in the sense of being open, frank, ingenuous, trustful, sincere. The latter is evidently its meaning here. It refers to one of the characteristics of true piety,—that of unsuspecting trust in God. It would describe one who yields readily to truth and duty; one who has singleness of aim in the desire to honour God; one who is without guile, trick, or cunning. Such a man was Nathanael (John i. 47): "Behold an Israelite indeed, in whom is no guile." The Hebrew word used here is rendered *simple*, Ps. xix. 7; cxix. 130; Prov. i. 4, 22, 32; vii. 7; viii. 5; ix. 4; xiv. 15, 18; xix. 25; xxi. 11; xxii. 3; xxvii. 12; Ezek. xlv. 20; and *foolish*, Prov. ix. 6. It does not elsewhere

occur. The meaning here is, that the Lord preserves or keeps those who have simple and unwavering trust in him; those who are sincere in their professions; those who rely on his word. ¶ *I was brought low.* By affliction and trial. The Hebrew literally means to hang down, to be pendulous, to swing, to wave—as a bucket in a well, or as the slender branches of the palm, the willow, etc. Then it means to be slack, feeble, weak, as in sickness, etc. See Notes on Ps. lxxix. 8. Here it probably refers to the prostration of strength by disease. ¶ *And he helped me.* He gave me strength; he restored me.

7. *Return unto thy rest, O my soul.* Luther, "Be thou again joyful, O my soul." The meaning seems to be, "Return to thy former tranquillity and calmness; thy former freedom from fear and anxiety." He had passed through a season of great danger. His soul had been agitated and terrified. That danger was now over, and he calls upon his soul to *resume* its former tranquillity, calmness, peace, and freedom from alarm. The word does not refer to *God* considered as the "rest" of the soul, but to what the mind of the psalmist *had* been, and *might* now be again. ¶ *For the* LORD *hath dealt bountifully with thee.* See Notes on Ps. xiii. 6.

8. *For thou hast delivered my soul from death.* My life. Thou hast saved me from death. This is such language as would be used by one who had been dangerously ill, and who had been restored again to health. ¶ *Mine eyes from tears.* Tears which he had shed in his sickness, and in the apprehension of dying. It *may* refer to tears shed on other occasions, but it is most natural to refer it to this.

9 I will walk before the LORD
in the land of the living.
10 I [l] believed, therefore have

[l] 2 Cor. iv. 13.

I spoken : I was greatly afflicted.
11 I said in my haste, All men
are liars.

Comp. Notes on Ps. vi. 6. ¶ And *my
feet from falling.* From stumbling.
That is, he had not, as it were, fallen
by the way, and been rendered unable
to pursue the journey of life. All this
seems to refer to one occasion—to a
time of dangerous illness.

9. *I will walk before the* LORD, etc.
Comp. Notes on Ps. xxvii. 13; Isa.
xxxviii. 20. This expresses a full belief that he would live, and a purpose
to live " before the Lord *;*" that is, as
in his presence, in his service, and enjoying communion with him.

10. *I believed, therefore have I spoken.*
This, in the Septuagint and Latin Vulgate, begins a new psalm, but without
any good reason. This language is
borrowed by the Apostle Paul to express his confidence in the truth of
the gospel, and the effect which that
confidence had on him in causing him
to declare the truth. 2 Cor. iv. 13.
The meaning here is, that in the time
of his affliction the psalmist had true
faith in God; and, as a result of that,
he was able now to speak as he did.
At that time he trusted in God; he
called on him; he sought his mercy,
and God heard his prayer; and now,
as the consequence of that, he was
enabled to give utterance to these
thoughts. Faith was at the foundation of his recovery, and he was now
reaping the fruits of faith. ¶ *I was
greatly afflicted.* In danger of death.
The psalmist reviewed this now, and
he saw that all that he had felt and
dreaded was real. He *was* in imminent danger. There *was* occasion for
the tears which he shed. There *was*
reason for the earnestness of his cry
to God.

11. *I said in my haste.* The Hebrew
word here used means to flee in haste;
to be in alarm and trepidation; and
the idea seems to be, that the assertion
referred to was made under the influence of excitement,—or that it was

not the result of sober reflection, but
of an agitated state of mind. It does
not necessarily imply that that which
was said was false, for many true statements may be made when the mind is
agitated and excited; but the meaning is, that he was then in such a state
of mind as *to suggest* the belief, and to
cause the assertion that all men are
liars. Whether calm reflection would,
or would not, confirm this impression
of the moment would be a fair question after the excitement was over.
¶ *All men* are *liars.* Are false; no one
is to be relied on. This was said in
the time of his affliction, and this
added much *to* his affliction. The
meaning is that, in those circumstances of distress, no one came to his
aid; no one sympathized with him;
there was no one to whom he could
unbosom himself; no one seemed to
feel any interest in him. There were
relatives on whom he might have supposed that he could rely; there may
have been those to whom he had
shown kindness in similar circumstances; there may have been old
friends whose sympathy he might
have had reason to expect; but all
failed. No one came to help him. No
one shed a tear over his sorrows. No
one showed himself true to friendship,
to sympathy, to gratitude. All men
seemed to be false; and he was shut
up to God alone. A similar thing is
referred to in Ps. xli. 5–9; lxxxviii.
18; comp. also Job xix. 13–17. This
is not an unnatural feeling in affliction.
The mind is then sensitive. We need
friends then. We expect our friends
to show their friendship then. If
they do not do this, it seems to us
that the entire world is false. It is
evident from the whole course of remark here that the psalmist on reflection felt that he had said this *without*
due thought, under the influence of
excitement,—and that he was dis-

12 What shall I render unto the LORD *for* all his benefits toward me?

13 I will take the cup of salvation, and call upon the name of the LORD.

14 I [m] will pay my vows unto the LORD now in the presence of all his people.

m Jonah ii. 9.

posed, when his mind was restored to calmness, to think better of mankind than he did in the day of affliction and trouble. This also is not uncommon. The world *is* much better than we think it is when our own minds are morbid and our nerves are unstrung; and bad as the world is, our opinion of it is not unfrequently the result rather of our own wrong feeling than of just reflection on the real character of mankind.

12. *What shall I render unto the* LORD for *all his benefits toward me?* All his "recompences,"—the same word which in ver. 7 is rendered "hath dealt bountifully." The question here has reference to that. What return can be equal to his bounties; what will be a proper acknowledgment of them; with what can I repay him for them all? The question is a natural and a proper question. It is one which we naturally ask when we have received a favour from our fellow-mortals; how much more proper is it in view of the favours which we receive from God,—especially in view of the mercy of God in the gift of a Saviour; the love manifested in the redemption of the soul! What CAN be an adequate return for love like that,—for mercies so great, so undeserved?

13. *I will take the cup of salvation.* Comp. Notes on Ps. xi. 6. The "cup of salvation" means the cup by which his sense of the greatness of the salvation might be expressed—the cup of thanksgiving. Comp. Notes on 1 Cor. x. 16. The reference seems to be to a custom in festivals of drinking a cup of wine as a special expression of thanks or of obligation. The act would be more solemn, and the truth more deeply impressed on the mind, when accompanied by some religious rite—some ceremonial, as in the Lord's

Supper, expressly designed to call the mercy of God to remembrance. ¶ *And call upon the name of the* LORD. Engage in a solemn act of devotion; make it a matter of special ceremony or observance to call the mercy of God to remembrance. This was *one* way of rendering to the Lord a return for the benefits received at his hands;—as it is now. Christians do this at the table of the Lord—in the observance of the Lord's Supper.

14. *I will pay my vows,* etc. I will perform or execute. The word *vows* here refers probably to the solemn promise which he had made in his sickness—the promise to devote himself to God, should he be restored to health. Comp. Notes on Isa. xxxviii. 15, 20. Such promises are commonly made in sickness, and, alas! almost as commonly disregarded and forgotten on a restoration to health. Yet such vows *should* be sacredly observed, for (*a*) They are right and proper; (*b*) they are made in most solemn circumstances; (*c*) they are usually sincere; (*d*) they are of the nature of a covenant with God; (*e*) they are made when we are in the best position to take just views of life—of this life, and of the life to come; (*f*) the subsequent life would be happier and better if they were faithfully carried out. Comp. Notes on Ps. xxii. 25; lxvi. 13, 14. ¶ *In the presence of all his people.* Publicly. The vows were made in private; on the sick bed; when alone; in the silence of the night-watches; when no eye was upon him who made them but the eye of God. There is a propriety, however, that the expression of thanksgiving should be public. Comp. Isa. xxxviii. 20. Indeed, nothing is more proper than public thanks for a restoration from sickness; and as in our public assemblies prayer is often specially

15 Precious *n* in the sight of the LORD *is* the death of his saints.

16 O LORD, truly I *am* thy servant; I *am* thy servant, *and*

offered for the sick at their own request, so it would be equally proper that, at their request, public thanks should be rendered for their recovery.

15. *Precious in the sight of the* LORD is *the death of his saints.* Of his people ; his friends. Luther renders this, " The death of his saints is held to be of value "—(*ist werth gehalten*)—" before the Lord." The word rendered *precious—*קָר, *yakar* —means *costly,* as precious stones, 1 Kings x. 2, 10, 11 ; *dear, beloved,* as relatives and friends, Ps. xlv. 9 ; *honoured, respected,* Ecc. x. 1 ; *splendid, beautiful,* Job xxxi. 26 ; *rare,* 1 Sam. iii. 1. The idea here is, that the death of saints is an object of *value;* that God regards it as of importance ; that it is connected with his great plans, and that there are great purposes to be accomplished by it. The idea *here* seems to be that the death of a good man is in itself of so much importance, and so connected with the glory of God and the accomplishment of his purposes, that he will not cause it to take place except in circumstances, at times, and in a manner, which will best secure those ends. The *particular* thought in the mind of the psalmist seems to have been that as *he* had been preserved when he was apparently so near to death, it must have been because God saw that the death of one of his friends was a matter of so much importance that it should occur *only* when the most good could be effected by it, and when the ends of life had been accomplished ; that God would not decide on this hastily, or without the best reasons ; and that, therefore, he had interposed to lengthen out *his* life still longer. Still, there *is* a general truth implied here, to wit, that the act of removing a good man from the world is, so to speak, an act of deep deliberation on the part of God ; that good, and sometimes great, ends are

to be accomplished by it ; and that, therefore, God regards it with special interest. It *is* of value or importance in such respects as the following :— (1) As it is the removal of another of the redeemed to glory—the addition of one more to the happy hosts above ; (2) as it is a new triumph of the work of redemption,—showing the power and the value of that work ; (3) as it often furnishes a more direct proof of the reality of religion than any abstract argument could do. How much has the cause of religion been promoted by the patient deaths of Ignatius, and Polycarp, and Latimer, and Ridley, and Huss, and Jerome of Prague, and the hosts of the martyrs ! What does not the world owe, and the cause of religion owe, to such scenes as occurred on the death-beds of Baxter, and Thomas Scott, and Halyburton, and Payson ! What an argument for the truth of religion,—what an illustration of its sustaining power,—what a source of comfort to us who are soon to die,—to reflect that religion does not leave the believer when he most needs its support and consolations ; that it can sustain us in the severest trial of our condition here ; that it can illuminate what seems to us of all places *most* dark, cheerless, dismal, repulsive—" the valley of the shadow of death !"

16. *O* LORD, *truly I* am *thy servant.* In view of thy mercy in delivering me from death, I feel the obligation to give myself to thee. I see in the fact that thou *hast* thus delivered me, evidence that I *am* thy servant—that I am so regarded by thee ; and I recognize the obligation to live as becomes one who has had this proof of favour and mercy. ¶ *The son of thine handmaid.* Of a pious mother. I see now the result of my training. I call to my recollection the piety of a mother. I remember how *she* served thee ; how

the son of thine handmaid: thou hast loosed my bonds.
17 I will offer to thee the sacrifice [o] of thanksgiving, and will call upon the name of the LORD.
18 I [p] will pay my vows unto the LORD now in the presence of all his people,
19 In the courts [q] of the LORD'S house, in the midst of thee, O Jerusalem. Praise ye the LORD.

PSALM CXVII.

O PRAISE [r] the LORD, all ye

o Lev. vii. 12. p Ec. v. 5. q Ps. xcvi. 8; c. 4. r Rom. xv. 11.

she trained me up for thee; I see now the evidence that her prayers were heard, and that her efforts were blessed in endeavouring to train me up for thee. The psalmist saw now that, under God, he owed all this to the pious efforts of a mother, and that God had been pleased to bless those efforts in making *him* his child, and in so guiding him that it was not improper for him to speak of himself as possessing and carrying out the principles of a sainted mother. It is not uncommon—and in such cases it is proper—that all the evidence which we may have that we are pious,—that we are living as we ought to live,—that we are receiving special favours from God,—recalls to our minds the instructions of early years, the counsels and prayers of a holy father or mother. ¶ *Thou hast loosed my bonds.* The bonds of disease; the fetters which seemed to have made me a prisoner to Death. I am now free again. I walk at large. I am no longer the captive—the prisoner—of disease and pain.

17. *I will offer to thee the sacrifice of thanksgiving.* I will publicly thank and praise thee. See Notes on Ps. cvii. 22. ¶ *And will call upon the name of the* LORD. Will worship and praise the Lord.

18. *I will pay my vows,* etc. See ver. 14.

19. *In the courts of the* LORD'S *house.* See Notes on Ps. lxv. 4. Comp. Ps. lxxxiv. 2; xcii. 13; xcvi. 8; c. 4; cxxxv. 2. ¶ *In the midst of thee, O Jerusalem.* Where the tabernacle, and afterwards the temple, was reared. ¶ *Praise ye the* LORD. Hallelujah. A call on others to join in the praise of God. The psalmist felt his own heart drawn to the service of praise by all the mercies of God; he desired, as an expression of his own feelings, that others should unite with him in that sacred exercise. When our own hearts are filled with gratitude, we wish that all others may partake of the same feeling.

PSALM CXVII.

The occasion and the author of this psalm are alike unknown. De Wette regards it as a *Temple-psalm*, and agrees with Rosenmüller in the supposition that it was sung either at the beginning or the end of the service in the temple. Knapp supposes that it was used as an intermediate service, sung during the progress of the general service to vary the devotion, and to awaken a new interest in the service, either sung by a choir or by the whole people.

In many manuscripts of Kennicott and De Rossi, and in several editions of the Scriptures, this psalm is united with the following. The psalm has no independent character or meaning of its own, and seems to have been designed, like the "Doxologies" in our Books of Psalms and Hymns, to be attached to other psalms as occasion might require. There is no psalm designed for public worship to which it might not thus properly be attached.

1. *O praise the* LORD, *all ye nations.* The idea is that God has a claim to universal worship, and that all the nations of the earth are under obligations to adore him as the true God. He is not the God of the Hebrew people only, but of all people; his praise should be celebrated not merely by one nation, but by all. This is one of the passages in the Old Testament, anticipating what is more fully disclosed in the New Testament,

nations: praise him, all ye people,

2 For his merciful kindness is great toward us: and the truth

⁸ of the LORD *endureth* for ever. Praise ye the LORD.

s Isa. xxv. 1; John xiv. 6; 1 John v. 6.

in which the sacred writer extends his vision beyond the narrow boundaries of Judea, and looks to the world, the whole world, as the theatre on which the true religion was to be displayed, and for which it was designed. It is language such as *would* be indited by the Spirit of inspiration on the supposition that the time would come when the barrier between Jews and Gentiles would be broken down, and when all the nations of the earth would be in the possession of the true religion, and would unite in the worship of the same God. This doctrine, however, was not fully made known until the coming of the Redeemer. The announcement of this was made by the Redeemer himself (comp. Matt. viii. 11; xii. 21; xxviii. 19); it was the occasion of no small part of the trouble which the Apostle Paul had with his countrymen (comp. Acts xiii. 46; xviii. 6; xxi. 21; xxii. 21; xxvi. 20, 23); it was one of the doctrines which Paul especially endeavoured to establish, as a great truth of Christianity, that all the barriers between the nations were to be broken down, and the Gospel proclaimed to all men alike, Rom. iii. 29; ix. 24, 30; xi. 11; xv. 9–11, 16, 18; Gal. ii. 2; Eph. ii. 11–18; iii. 1–9. It is under the gospel that this language becomes peculiarly appropriate. ¶ *Praise him, all ye people.* People of all lands. The word here rendered *praise* — שָׁבַח, *shabahh* — means properly to soothe, to still, to restrain,— as, for example, billows (Ps. lxxxix. 9); and then, to praise, *as if* to soothe with praises, — *mulcere laudibus,* Pacuv. The idea of *soothing* or *mitigating,* however, is not necessarily in the word, but it may be understood in the general sense of *praise.* We may in fact often soothe or appease men—angry, jealous, suspicious men —by skilful flattery or praise—for

there are few, even when under the influence of anger or hatred, who may not thus be approached, or who do not value praise and commendation more than they do the indulgence of passion; but we cannot hope thus to appease the anger of God. We approach him to utter our deep sense of his goodness, and our veneration for his character; we do not expect to turn him from anger to love—to make him forget his justice or our sins—by soothing flattery.

2. *For his merciful kindness is great toward us.* His kindness; his compassion; his love. All nations— all people—may say this, and therefore the psalm is adapted to universal praise. Especially may this be said in view of the love of God to mankind in the gift of a Saviour—a Saviour not for any one people peculiarly or exclusively, but for the world, John iii. 16. ¶ *And the truth of the* LORD *endureth for ever.* All that God has said:—his declarations; his promises; his assurances of mercy. They are the same in all lands where they are made known, and they are the same in all ages of the world. *Truth* is a representation of things as they are; and truth, therefore, must be ever the same. What was true in the first ages of the world in regard to the relation of the sum of the squares on the two sides of a right-angled triangle to the square of the hypothenuse is true now, and will always be true; and so, what God has affirmed at any one time will always remain the same in all ages and in all lands. What was truth to Abraham is truth to us; what was truth to Paul is truth to us; what was truth to the martyrs is truth to us; what is truth to us will be truth to all generations of the world in all lands, and will be truth for ever. *This* fact, too, is a just foundation

for universal praise, and therefore the psalm is so adapted to be used in all lands and among all people. How often in our own language has this psalm been the medium of the utterances of praise in Christian sanctuaries :—

> " From all that dwell below the skies,
> Let the Creator's praise arise ;
> Let the Redeemer's name be sung,
> Through every land, by every tongue.
> Eternal are thy mercies, Lord ;
> Eternal truth attends thy word ;
> Thy praise shall sound from shore to shore,
> Till suns shall rise and set no more."

PSALM CXVIII.

Of the authorship of this psalm, and the occasion on which it was composed, nothing can now be ascertained with certainty. The common opinion has been that it is a psalm of David, and that it was composed when his troubles with Saul ceased, and when he was recognized as king. Some, however, have referred it to Hezekiah on the occasion of his restoration from sickness ; others to the time of the return from the Babylonish exile ; and others to the time of the Maccabees. It would be useless to examine these opinions, as they are all of them mere conjecture, and as no certainty can now be arrived at.

What is apparent on the face of the psalm is, that it was a psalm of thanksgiving, to be employed in the temple when an *offering* or *sacrifice* was led up to the altar (ver. 27) to be presented as an acknowledgment of mercy from God, on some occasion of deliverance from danger, by some one whose claim to rule had been rejected, but who was now victorious over his enemies, and recognized as the rightful leader and ruler of the people. The psalm is in a measure *dramatic.* The author is the speaker in the first twenty-one verses ; in the remainder of the psalm the priests and the people speak, and at the close, the psalmist again utters praise.

The psalm consists of the following parts :—

I. The author of the psalm speaks, vers. 1-21.

(1) He calls on all to praise the Lord, and to unite with him in the expression of thanks, because what had occurred was a matter of interest to all the people ;—to Israel, to the house of Aaron, to the priesthood, to all that feared God, vers. 1-4.

(2) A description of his peril and deliverance, vers. 5-18. He had been in distress ; he had called on the Lord ; he had seen the benefit of trusting in the Lord rather than in man. All nations had compassed him about as bees ; they had thrust sore at him ; they had sought his life ; but he had not been dismayed ; he had felt, even in the midst of his dangers, that he would live to declare the works of the Lord, vers. 17, 18.

(3) The speaker approaches the temple. He asks that the doors may be opened that he may enter and praise the Lord. He addresses those who have charge of the temple — the ministers of religion—and desires leave to come and present his offering, vers. 19-21.

II. The priests and people speak, vers. 22-27.

(1) They recognize him now *as* the Ruler—the corner-stone—the foundation of the nation's prosperity, and its hope. He had been rejected by those who were professedly laying the foundation of empire, but he had now established his claims to being regarded as the very corner-stone on which the whole edifice must rest, ver. 22.

(2) They recognize this as a marvellous work of God, and as fitted to excite the deepest admiration, ver. 23.

(3) They recognize this as a joyful day, *as if* God had *created a day* for the very purpose of celebrating an event so joyous, ver. 24.

(4) They pronounce him blessed who thus came in the name of the Lord ; they bless him out of the house of the Lord, vers. 25, 26.

(5) They direct him to bring his offering, and to bind it to the horns of the altar preparatory to sacrifice. He is permitted freely to come. His offering is recognized as proper, so that he can approach with an assurance of acceptance, ver. 27.

III. The author of the psalm again speaks, vers. 28, 29. He acknowledges

PSALM CXVIII.

O GIVE ^{t} thanks unto the LORD; for *he is* good; because his mercy ^{u} *endureth* for ever.

2 Let ^{v} Israel now say, that his mercy *endureth* for ever.

t 1 Chron. xvi. 8, 34.

3 Let the house of Aaron now say, that his mercy *endureth* for ever.

4 Let them now that fear the LORD say, that his mercy *endureth* for ever.

u Ps. ciii. 17.   *v* Ps. cxv. 9, etc.

God as his God, and calls on all to praise him.

Portions of the psalm are, in the New Testament, applied to Christ; and it has been made a question whether it had, or had not, an original reference to him. Thus in Matt. xxi. 42; Mark xii. 11; Luke xx. 17, it is quoted by the Saviour as illustrating a truth in regard to himself. In Acts iv. 11, the twenty-second verse of the psalm is applied by Peter to the Saviour, as having been fulfilled in him,—or, as meaning that the *language* of the psalm would properly describe the fact which had occurred in the treatment of Jesus of Nazareth. Many of the Jewish rabbins regarded the psalm as referring to the Messiah, and not a few Christian interpreters have supposed that it had such an original reference.

It seems clear, however, from the psalm itself that it could not have been composed primarily with reference to him. There are portions of it which cannot, without a very forced use of language, be applied to him, as for example, the allusion to the attack made by "all nations" on the person referred to in the psalm (ver. 10), and in the allusion to the danger of death (vers. 17, 18). The person referred to in the psalm was in danger of death, but he was not given over to death. He had the assurance in the very midst of the danger that he would *not* die, but would continue to live (ver. 17). The Redeemer, however, did die. His enemies accomplished their purpose in this respect. They put him to death, though he rose again from the dead.

It is clear, therefore, I think, that the psalm had not an original reference to the Messiah. Still, there is much in it which is applicable to him, and which might be used as expressive of what occurred to him. It contains *principles* also which may be as applicable to him as they were to the psalmist; and, therefore, it is used by the Saviour to enforce the moral of his own parable in reference to himself, as having had a coun-

terpart in their own history, *in a case* which must have been familiar to them all. As such, it is right to use it now, as *illustrating* what occurred in the treatment of the Redeemer.

1. *O give thanks unto the* LORD, etc. Let others unite with me in giving thanks to the Lord; let them see, from what has occurred in my case, what occasion there is for praise. Every instance of a particular favour shown to any one is to others an occasion for praise, inasmuch as it is an illustration of the general character of God. On this verse comp. Notes on Ps. cvi. 1. The language is nearly the same.

2. *Let Israel now say*, etc. The Hebrew people; the people of God. They have now, in my case, a new illustration of the mercy of God which ought to animate them, and to encourage their hearts. Comp. Ps. cxv. 9.

3. *Let the house of Aaron now say*, etc. Comp. Ps. cxv. 10. The ministers of religion. They are appointed to serve God; to lead in his worship; to defend his truth; to keep up faith in the truth of religion. They are, therefore, interested in my case, and may derive from it a new proof of the merciful character of God which they may employ, not only for their own encouragement in personal piety, but in the duties of their office. My case furnishes a new argument, of which they can make use in defending the truth, and in illustrating the power of religion.

4. *Let them now that fear the* LORD *say*, etc. Comp. Ps. cxv. 11. All that worship God are interested in what God has done for me. It is a manifestation of the Divine character which should cheer them. They are called, therefore, to unite with

5 I ^w called upon the LORD ¹ in distress : the LORD answered me, *and set me* in a large place.

6 The ^x LORD *is* ² on my side ; I will not fear : what can man do unto me ?

w Ps. cxx. 1.   ¹ *out of distress.*
x Ps. xxvii. 1; Heb. xiii. 6.

7 The LORD taketh my part with them that help me : therefore shall I see *my desire* upon them that hate me.

8 *It* ^y *is* better to trust in the LORD, than to put confidence in man :

² *for me.*   *y* Jer. xvii. 5, 7.

the author of the psalm in praise and thanksgiving, not merely from sympathy with him, but because great truths of religion had been illustrated, in his case, which were of as much importance to them as to him.

5. *I called upon the* LORD *in distress.* Marg., as in Heb., *out of distress.* In the very midst of trouble he called upon the Lord; his voice was heard, as it were, coming from the depth of his sorrows. See Notes on Ps. xviii. 6. ¶ *The* LORD *answered me.* That is, he heard my prayers, and delivered me. See Notes on Ps. xviii. 6. ¶ And set me *in a large place.* I was before pressed on every side; sorrows compassed me around; I could not move; I had no liberty. Now he gave me space and freedom on every side, so that I could move without obstruction or pain. This is literally, "The LORD"—(not *Jehovah* here, but *Jah*)—"answered me in a large place." See Notes on Ps. iv. 1; xviii. 19.

6. *The* LORD is *on my side.* Marg., as in Heb., *for me.* The Lord is with me. He is my helper. He defends my cause. ¶ *I will not fear.* I have nothing to be afraid of. God is more mighty than any or all of my foes, and he can deliver me from them all. Comp. Ps. lvi. 4, 9, 11. ¶ *What can man do unto me ?* Any man; all men. They can do no more than God permits. They cannot destroy me when he means to save me ; they cannot defeat his gracious designs towards me. I am safe if God is my Friend. Comp. Notes on Rom. viii. 31.

7. *The* LORD *taketh my part with them that help me.* The psalmist had friends. There were those who stood

by him. He relied, indeed, on their aid, but not on their aid without God. He felt that even *their* help was valuable to him only as God was with them. There was direct dependence on God in reference to himself; and there was the same sense of dependence in respect to all who were engaged in his defence. This might be rendered, however, simply "for my help," and is so rendered by De Wette. The Septuagint and Latin Vulgate render it, "The Lord is my helper." ¶ *Therefore shall I see* my desire *upon them that hate me.* Literally, " I shall see upon those that hate me ;" that is, I shall look upon them according to my wish; I shall see them overthrown and subdued. See Notes on Ps. liv. 7. Comp. Ps. xcii. 11; cxii. 8.

8. It is *better to trust in the* LORD *than to put confidence in man.* This is stated apparently as the result of his own experience. He had found men weak and faithless ; he had not so found God. Comp. Ps. xl. 4; lxii. 8, 9. Literally, "Good is it to trust in Jehovah more than to confide in man." This is the Hebrew form of comparison, and is equivalent to what is stated in our version, " It is *better,*" etc. It is better, (1) because man is weak,—but God is Almighty; (2) because man is selfish,—but God is benevolent; (3) because man is often faithless and deceitful,—God never; (4) because there are emergencies, as death, in which man cannot aid us, however faithful, kind, and friendly he may be,—but there are no circumstances in this life, and none in death, where God cannot assist us : and (5) because the ability of man to help us pertains at best only to this present

9 *It is* better to trust in the
LORD, than to put confidence in
^z princes.

10 All nations compassed me
about: but in the name of the
LORD will I ¹ destroy them.

11 They compassed me about;

z Ps. cxlvi. 3.   ¹ *cut them off*
          a Deut. i. 14.

yea, they compassed me about:
but in the name of the LORD I
will destroy them.

12 They compassed me about
like bees; ^a they are quenched as
the fire of thorns: ^b for in the
name of the LORD I will ² destroy
them.

b 2 Sam xxiii. 6; Nahum i. 10.   ² *cut down.*

---

life,—the power of God will be commensurate with eternity.

9. It is *better . . . than to put confidence in princes.* Even in the most
mighty of the human race; in those
who of all men may be supposed to
have the most ability to aid us; in
those whose favour is often sought
more than the favour of God. Princes
are but men; often as faithless and
deceitful as other men; often less reliable in their character than those
in more humble life: and in the great
matters where we most need aid—in
sickness, in danger, in death, in the
eternal world—as absolutely powerless as men in the lowest condition of
poverty, or in the most humble rank.

10. *All nations compassed me about.*
They surrounded me; they hemmed
me in on every side, so that I seemed
to have no chance to escape. It would
seem from this that the psalm was
composed by some one who was at
the head of the government, and
whose government had been attacked
by surrounding nations. This would
accord well with many things that occurred in the life of David; but there
were also other times in the Jewish
history to which it would be applicable, and there is nothing that necessarily confines it to the time of David.
¶ *But in the name of the* LORD *will
I destroy them.* Marg., as in Heb.,
cut them off. This is the language
which he used at that time; the purpose which he then formed; an expression of the confidence which he
then cherished. He meant to subdue
them; he had no doubt that he would
be able to do it.

11. *They compassed me about; yea,
they compassed me about,* etc. The

sentiment and the language of the
previous verse are here repeated, as
if to give force to what he had said,
or to deepen the impression. His
own mind dwelt upon it, and the
events to which he referred came so
vividly to his recollection, and were
so important, that he dwells upon
them. The subject was worth more
than a passing remark. The mind
was full, and the language comes
from an overflowing heart.

12. *They compassed me about like
bees.* (*a*) As thick or numerous as
bees; (*b*) armed as bees,—or, their
weapons might be compared to the
stings of bees. ¶ *They are quenched
as the fire of thorns.* The Septuagint and the Vulgate render this,
"They *burn* as the fire of thorns."
The connexion would seem to demand
this, but the Hebrew will not bear it.
The figure is changed in the Hebrew,
as is not uncommon. The mind of
the psalmist at first recalls the *number* and the *malignity* of his foes;
it then instantly adverts to the rapid
manner in which they were destroyed.
The illustration from the "fire of
thorns" is derived from the fact that
they quickly kindle into a blaze, and
then the flame soon dies away. In
Eastern countries it was common to
burn over their fields in the dry time
of the year, and thus to clear them
of thorns and briars and weeds. Of
course, at such a time they would
kindle quickly, and burn rapidly, and
would soon be consumed. So the
psalmist says it was with his enemies.
He came upon them, numerous as
they were, as the fire runs over a
field in a dry time, burning everything before it. Comp. Notes on Isa.

13 Thou hast thrust sore at me, that I might fall : but *c* the LORD helped me.

14 The LORD *d is* my strength and song, and is become my salvation.

15 The voice of rejoicing and salvation *is* in the tabernacles of

c Mic. vii. 8.   *d* Ex. xv. 2, 6; Isa. xii. 2.

the righteous : the right hand of the LORD doeth valiantly.

16 The right hand of the LORD is exalted ; the right hand of the LORD doeth valiantly.

17 I *e* shall not die, but live, and declare the *f* works of the LORD.

e Hab. i. 12.   *f* Ps. lxxiii. 28.

---

xxxiii. 12. ¶ *For in the name of the* LORD *I will destroy them.* That is, such was his purpose *then ;* such was the reason why they so soon and suddenly disappeared.

13. *Thou hast thrust sore at me that I might fall.* Literally, "Thrusting thou hast thrust at me." This is the Hebrew mode of expressing intensity, repetition, or emphasis. The meaning is, that they had made a deadly thrust at him ; that they had repeated the blows ; that they had come with a fierce determination to crush and destroy him. The psalmist, as it were, sees the enemy again before him, and addresses him as if he were present. Everything is vivid to the mind ; the whole scene appears again to pass before him.

14. *The* LORD is *my strength and song.* He is the source of strength to me ; and he is the subject of my praise. There is no ground of praise in myself for anything that I have done, but all is due to him. ¶ *And is become my salvation.* He has saved me. I live because *he* preserved me. So we shall be saved in heaven solely because *he* saves us, and there, more than can be possible here, we shall say, "God is our strength and our song, and is become our salvation."

15, 16. *The voice of rejoicing and salvation.* Rejoicing *for* salvation ; — song, praise, thanksgiving. Luther renders this beautifully ; "They sing with joy for victory in the houses of the righteous." ¶ Is *in the tabernacles of the righteous.* The *tents* of the righteous ; their dwellings. That is, (*a*) it is a *fact* that the voice of joy and rejoicing is

there ; (*b*) it is *appropriate* that it should be so, or that a righteous family *should* be happy,—the dwelling-place of praise ; (*c*) God will *add* to the happiness of the righteous, or will make their habitation happy, peaceful, blessed. There is nothing that diffuses so much happiness through a family as religion ; there is no joy like that when a member of a family is converted ; there is no place on earth more happy than that where a family bows before God with the feeling that all are children of God and heirs of salvation. ¶ *The right hand of the* LORD *doeth valiantly.* Heb. *Doeth strength.* That is, God does great things, laying the foundation for joy and praise.

17. *I shall not die, but live.* Evidently the psalmist had apprehended that he would die ; or, he had felt that he was in imminent danger of dying. In this language he seems, as in ver. 13, to go back again to the scenes referred to in the psalm. He lives them over again. He describes the feelings which he had then. He saw that he was in danger. His enemies were thick round about him, and sought his life. But he had *then* the assurance that they would not be victorious ; that they would not accomplish their object ; that he would be protected ; that he would live to declare what God had done for him. He does not say *how* he had this assurance, but there is no impropriety in supposing that he had it, as Hezekiah had in similar circumstances (see Isa. xxxviii. 5-8, 21), by a direct Divine intimation. Things *like* this are not uncommon now, when, in danger or in sickness, the

18 The LORD hath chastened *g* me sore: but he hath not given me over unto death.

19 Open *h* to me the gates of righteousness: I will go into them, *and* I will praise the LORD;

g 2 Cor. vi. 9.
h Isa. xxvi. 2; Rev. xxii. 14.

20 This gate of the LORD, into which the righteous shall enter.

21 I will praise thee; for thou hast heard me, and art become my salvation.

22 The *i* stone *which* the build-

i Matt. xxi. 42; Acts iv. 11; Eph. ii. 20;
1 Pet. ii. 4, 7.

mind is strongly impressed with the belief that there will be a restoration to health and safety, and when the mind is made calm and peaceful *by* that belief—the very calmness of the mind under such a belief contributing not a little to that result. Why should we hesitate to believe that such a faith and hope *may* come from the Lord? Comp. Acts xxvii. 22–25. ¶ *And declare the works of the* LORD. Declare what he has done.

18. *The* LORD *hath chastened me sore.* Heb., "The Lord has chastened —has chastened me." See Notes on ver. 13. The psalmist had been greatly afflicted, and he now looked upon his affliction in the light of a fatherly chastisement or correction. It had been a severe trial, and he was not insensible to its severity, though he regarded it as designed for his own good. ¶ *But he hath not given me over unto death.* He interposed when I was in danger; he rescued me when I was on the verge of the grave. This is the close of the psalmist's statement in regard to the Divine dealings with him. He had passed through great danger; he had been sorely afflicted; but he had been rescued and spared, and he came now to express his thanks to God for his recovery. In the following verse he addresses those who had the care of the sanctuary, and asks that he might be permitted to enter and offer his thanks to God.

19. *Open to me the gates of righteousness,* etc. The gates of the house devoted to a righteous God; the gates of a house where the principles of righteousness are strengthened, and where the just emotions of the heart may be expressed in the

language of praise. Comp. Notes on Isa. xxvi. 2. The language here may be regarded as addressed to those who had charge of the house of the Lord—the priests — requesting that they would open the doors and permit him to enter to praise God for his mercy. Comp. Isa. xxxviii. 20.

20. *This gate of the* LORD. This gate dedicated to the service of the Lord; that belongs to the house of the Lord. ¶ *Into which the righteous shall enter.* Through which the righteous pass. That is, It is *for* such persons, and all who come with a purpose to serve and worship God should be permitted to pass through them; I claim the privilege, therefore, of so passing through these gates into the house of God, for I come to praise him. All who are truly righteous, all who desire to worship God, all who wish and purpose to be holy, have a *right* thus to enter the house of God—to be recognized as his friends—to be permitted to join in all the devotions of his people; all such will have a right to enter the temple above. None have a right to exclude them here; none in heaven will be disposed to exclude them there.

21. *I will praise thee.* Within thy courts. ¶ *For thou hast heard me, and art become my salvation.* See ver. 14.

22. *The stone* which *the builders refused.* See Notes on Matt. xxi. 42, 43. Comp. Mark xii. 10, 11; Acts iv. 11; 1 Pet. ii. 7. This is an allusion to a building, as if a stone should be cast away by workmen as unfit to be worked into the edifice. The figure would then be applicable to any one who, for any purpose, was

ers refused is become the head *stone* of the corner.

23 This is 1 the LORD's doing;

it *is* marvellous in our eyes.

24 This *is* the day *which* the

1 *from the LORD.*

---

rejected. Thus it might have been applied many a time to David; so, doubtless, to others who urged claims to authority and power; and so, eminently, to the Lord Jesus Christ. We are not to suppose that this had original reference to the Messiah, but the *language* was applicable to him; and it is used in the passages above referred to, in addresses to the Jews, merely to show them how the *principle* was found in their own writings, that one who was rejected, like a stone regarded as unfit to be worked into any part of a building, *might* be in reality so important that it would be laid yet at the very corner, and become the most valuable stone in the edifice,—that on which the whole superstructure would rest. ¶ *Is become the head* stone *of the corner.* The principal stone placed at the corner of the edifice. This is usually one of the largest, the most solid, and the most carefully wrought of any in the edifice. Of course one would be needed at each corner of the building to constitute a firm support, but usually there is one placed at one corner of an edifice larger and more carefully wrought than the others, often laid with imposing ceremonies, and prepared to contain whatever it may be thought necessary to deposit in the foundation of the building to be transmitted to future times as preserving the names of the builders, or expressing the design of the edifice. Such a position he who had been rejected was to occupy in the civil polity of his country; such a position eminently the Lord Jesus occupies in relation to the church. Eph. ii. 20.

23. *This is the* LORD's *doing.* Marg., as in Heb., *This is from the Lord.* That is, It is to be traced to the Lord alone. It is not the result of human wisdom or power. The deliverance from danger,—the raising

up from the low condition,—the change by which he who was rejected was restored to his rightful place,—all this was to be traced to God alone. So it was in the case of the psalmist; so it was in the case of the Redeemer. None but God could have made him who was rejected, despised, crucified, and laid in the grave, the Saviour of a world. The place which the once-rejected Redeemer now bears in the church,—the honours bestowed on him as the head of the church,—the triumph of his gospel in the world, —all prove that it is the work of God. ¶ *It is marvellous in our eyes.* It is fitted to excite wonder. It is not one of those things which are to be ranked with the common and well-known events that are easily explained, and that excite no wonder; it is one of those things which cannot be explained by any known law; which belong to the "supernatural;" which bear the marks of a direct Divine interposition; which are fitted to excite the admiration of mankind. Thus it was in the case of the psalmist; thus, pre-eminently, it was in the case of the Redeemer. No operation of natural laws will constitute a sufficient explanation of the latter. It is a matter for wonder, for rejoicing, and for praise, that one, despised, rejected, crucified, has been raised from the grave; that his religion has spread so far over the world; that it influences mankind as it does; and that he himself is exalted to a rank "far above all principality, and power, and might, and dominion, and every name that is named, not only in this world, but also in that which is to come." Eph. i. 21.

24. *This* is *the day* which *the* LORD *hath made.* As if it were a new day, made for this very occasion; a day which the writer of the psalm did not expect to see, and which *seemed* therefore to have been *created* out of the

LORD hath made; we will rejoice and be glad in it.

25 Save now, I beseech thee, O LORD : O LORD, I beseech thee, send now prosperity.

---

ordinary course, and *added* to the other days. He was in danger of death; his days were likely to be cut off and ended, so that he should see no more. But God had spared him, and added *this* joyous day to his life; and it was meet that for this he should be praised. It was so full of joy, so unexpected, so bright, so cheerful, that it appeared to be a new day coming fresh from the hand of the Almighty, unlike the other days of the year. So the Sabbath—the day that commemorates the resurrection of the Redeemer—is God's day. He claims it. He seems to have *made* it anew for man. Amidst the other days of the week,—in a world where the ordinary days are filled up with so much of earth, so much toil, trouble, care, vexation, vanity, wickedness, — it *seems* like one of the days that God made when he first made the world; before sin and sorrow entered; when all was calm, serene, happy. The Sabbath is so calm, so bright, so cheerful, so benign in its influence; it is so full of pleasant and holy associations and reminiscences, that it *seems* to be a day fresh from the hand of God, unlike the other days of the week, and *made especially,* as if by a new act of creation, for the good of mankind. So when a man is raised up from sickness—from the borders of the grave — it seems to be a *new* life given to him. Each day, week, month, year that he may live, is so much *added* to his life, as if it were created anew for this very purpose. He should, therefore, regard it not as his own, but *as* so much given to him by the special mercy and providence of God,—as if *added on* to his life. Comp. Isa. xxxviii. 5. ¶ *We will rejoice and be glad in it.* The psalmist, and all who united with him in his thanksgivings. So the Christian Sabbath. It is a day of joy—all joy, and no sorrow. It is a

day to be happy in;—a day of rest; a day, when the cares and toils of life are suspended; a day, when we are no longer harassed with those things which vex us in the worldliness of the week; a day, when we think of God, of redemption, of hope, of heaven. The Sabbath *should* be a day of joy, and not of gloom; it *would* be the happiest of all days to weary and jaded men everywhere, if they observed it aright. In a world of toil and sorrow, it is among the richest of God's blessings to men; it strengthens, refreshes, and cheers the heart of burdened and sorrowful man here; it lifts the soul to joyous contemplation of that eternal Sabbath where wearisome toil and sorrow shall be no more.

25. *Save now, I beseech thee, O* LORD, etc. The word *save* here seems to be used in the general sense of imploring the Divine interposition and mercy. It is a part of the word which in the New Testament is rendered " Hosanna"—*save now* (Matt. xxi. 9),—and is the language which the multitudes employed when they followed the Saviour as he went from the Mount of Olives to Jerusalem. The language which they used on that occasion was borrowed from this psalm, and was eminently appropriate to the occasion—" Hosanna,—blessed be he that cometh in the name of the Lord ;"—but the fact that it was thus employed does not prove that the psalm had original reference to the Messiah. The language was not improbably used on high festivals, and would be *naturally* employed when the Messiah came. ¶ *Send now prosperity.* Give success; be favourable. God *had* interposed, and now the prayer is, that there might be continued and uninterrupted prosperity; that as the tide had begun to turn in the psalmist's favour, it might recede no more; that the calamities and woes

26 Blessed *k be* he that cometh in the name of the LORD: we have blessed you out of the house of the LORD.

k Matt. xxi. 9; xxiii. 39.

27 God *is* the LORD, which hath shewed us light; *l* bind the sacrifice with cords, *even* unto the horns of the altar.

l Esther viii. 16; 1 Pet. ii. 9.

---

which he had experienced might not be repeated. This was omitted in the acclamations of the multitude that attended the Saviour (Matt. xxi. 9); but it is eminently an appropriate prayer to be used in connexion with his coming,—since his coming, whether to the world, to an individual, to a church, or to a community, brings the highest kind of "prosperity" in its train.

26. *Blessed* be *he that cometh in the name of the* LORD. See Notes on Matt. xxi. 9. This is the language of those who had charge of the sanctuary, addressing him who came in the name of the Lord to present his thank-offering. It is the language of welcome; the assurance that his offering would be acceptable to God. It was *applicable* to the Messiah, as coming in the name of the Lord, and was so used by the multitudes (Matt. xxi. 9), and by the Saviour himself (Matt. xxiii. 39); but this use of the language does not prove that it had original reference to him. The Old Testament abounds in language which may thus be employed to express ideas under the Christian dispensation; but this does not prove that all such language was originally designed to refer to that dispensation. ¶ *We have blessed you out of the house of the* LORD. We, the priests, the ministers of religion, have pronounced and do pronounce you blessed. We welcome your approach. You may come freely with your thank-offering. It will be accepted of the Lord. You come under our benediction, and the benediction of God.

27. *God* is *the* LORD. Still the language of the priests in their official capacity. The meaning here seems to be "God is Jehovah;" or, Jehovah is the true God. It is an utterance of the priesthood in regard to the great truth which they were appointed specifically to maintain,—that Jehovah is the true God, and that he only is to be worshipped. This truth it was appropriate to enunciate on all occasions; and it was peculiarly appropriate to be enunciated when a prince, who had been rescued from danger and death, came, as the restored leader of the people of God, to acknowledge his gracious intervention. On such an occasion,—in view of the rank and character of him who came,—and in view of what God had done for him, —it was proper for the ministers of religion to announce in the most solemn manner, that Jehovah was the only true and living God. ¶ *Which hath showed us light.* Who has given us light in the days of our darkness and adversity; who has restored us to prosperity, and bestowed on us the blessings of safety and of peace. ¶ *Bind the sacrifice with cords.* Come freely with the sacrificial victim; with the offering which is to be presented to God in sacrifice. The word —חג, *hhag*—commonly means a festival or feast, Ex. x. .9; xii. 14; and then it means a festival-sacrifice, a victim, Ex. xxiii. 18; Mal. ii. 3. The Septuagint and Vulgate render it, "Prepare a solemn feast." Our translation probably expresses the true sense. The word rendered *cords,* means properly anything interwoven or interlaced. Then it means a cord, a braid, a wreath; and then a branch with thick foliage. Different interpretations have been given of the passage here, but probably the word is correctly rendered *cords.* ¶ *Unto the horns of the altar.* Altars were often made with projections or "horns" on the four corners. Ex. xxvii. 2; xxx. 2; xxxvii. 25; 1 Kings ii. 28. Whether the animal was actually bound to the altar when it was

28 Thou *m art* my God, and I will praise thee; *thou art* my God, I will exalt thee.

m Isa. xxv. 1.

29 O *n* give thanks unto the LORD; for *he is* good; for his mercy *endureth* for ever.

n ver. 1.

---

slain, is not certain; but there would seem to be an allusion to such a custom here. Lead up the victim; make it ready; bind it even to the altar, preparatory to the sacrifice. The language is that of welcome addressed to him who led up the victim,—meaning that his sacrifice would be acceptable.

28. *Thou* art *my God, and I will praise thee.* This is the language of the author of the psalm,—his solemn profession before the sanctuary and the altar; his response to the priesthood. In ver. 27, they had declared that "Jehovah alone was God;" to this he now replies, that he acknowledges it; he recognizes him as the true God, and as his God; he comes to praise him; and he professes his purpose always to exalt him as his God. ¶ Thou art *my God, I will exalt thee.* Repeating the solemn declaration that Jehovah alone was the God whom he worshipped, and that it was his purpose always to magnify his name.

29. *O give thanks unto the* LORD, etc. The psalm closes, as it began, with an exhortation to praise God. In the beginning of the psalm, it was a general exhortation; here it is an exhortation founded on the course of thought in the psalm, or as a proper conclusion from what had been referred to in the psalm. Evidence had been given that the Lord was good; on the ground of that, all men are exhorted to give him thanks.

PSALM CXIX.

This is an Alphabetical Psalm,—the longest, and most perfect in its kind, in the collection of Psalms. The peculiarity of the composition consists in this, —that the first *eight* verses of the psalm begin with the first letter of the Hebrew alphabet—א, *Aleph;* the next eight verses with the second letter—ב, *Beth;* and so on, through the twenty-two letters of the alphabet. These parts are designated in our common version by the names of the Hebrew letters respectively indicating the parts,—Aleph, Beth, Gimel, Daleth, etc.

The general subject of the psalm is THE LAW OF GOD considered as a rule of life; as sanctifying the soul; as a support in trial; as imparting happiness to the mind,—in its contemplation, and in obedience to it. The psalm appears to have been intended to set forth the excellency of that law, and the happy effects of obeying it, in every variety of form, and with every variety of expression. In its great length, extending to one hundred and seventy-six verses, there was ample opportunity to illustrate this; and the purpose of the author of the psalm seems to have been to see how much could be said on this, and to say all that could be said on it. It is remarkable that a single subject *could* be pursued so far with so much variety, and with so little that can be regarded as repetition; for there are perhaps no two verses in the psalm so exactly similar that there cannot be seen, either in themselves, or in their connexion, some new phase given to the subject, or some new shade of thought not expressed elsewhere. So marked is this design of the psalm, so constant is the reference to the law of God—the testimonies of God—the statutes of God—that, according to the Masora, there is "only one verse in the psalm which does not contain some title or description of the word of God."

The psalm seems to be a record of the personal experience of the author, or the result of his meditations on the subject. It is not the Jewish people speaking, or the church, as many have supposed, but it is evidently an individual—not improbably a man of years —giving the result of his experience in regard to the influence of the law or the word of God in the various circumstances of life:—in regard to what he had *found* that to be to himself personally. At the same time, the language is such as will express the experience of others, and is such as might be employed in public worship.

It is not probable, however, that a psalm so long was commonly used in public worship, as many of the shorter psalms were. It is a great storehouse of truths, most precious and valuable, on one of the most important subjects of religion—the word of God; and it *may* have been intended, as would seem not improbable from the alphabetical arrangement, to be committed to memory by the young, that their minds might be early stored with valuable precepts to be their guide in the journey of life. A young man could not have a better treasure laid up in his mind than he would possess by committing this psalm to memory.

Whether the psalm was the work of David or of some later writer cannot be ascertained. Many have ascribed it to David; and it has been supposed that he wrote it either when he was an exile among the Philistines (1 Sam. xxvii.), or when he was young, and had not yet obtained the authority of the government. This last opinion is derived—Rosenmüller thinks correctly—from vers. 9, 23, 46, 141, 161. Gurlitt supposed that its author was some youth who was made captive by the Assyrians, and who composed the psalm in his captivity, as expressive of his attachment to his religion:—a youth who could not, though away from his country and home, and surrounded by temptations, be turned away from the religion of his fathers by threats or bribes;—who rejected all the allurements and blandishments which could be presented to him to induce him to abandon that religion, and to conform to the customs of idolatry,—or who resisted all temptations to sensual gratifications. This idea is derived from vers. 22, 23, 25, 28, 29, 36, 39, 42, 43, 46, 50, 51, 53, 56, 67, 72, 74, 78, 83, 84, 95, 109. Thus understood, it would be applicable to the condition of such a young Hebrew as Joseph or Daniel, and would express the feelings which *such* young men would have in the temptations by which they were surrounded, and the firmness of their attachment to the principles of the religion in which they had been trained. The idea is a beautiful one, and may properly be used for an *illustration*, but there is no certain evidence that the psalm was composed under those circumstances. Others have

supposed that the psalm was written by Jaddo (Neh. xii. 22), the high-priest in the time of Alexander the Great—amidst the troubles which then existed in Judea, and amidst the opposition of the Samaritans,—and that the design was to show his own firmness in the Jewish religion, and to excite the Hebrews to the same firmness by setting forth the authority and excellence of the word of God, and the authority of the law. Rüdinger supposes that it was composed in the time of the persecutions under Antiochus,—the times of the Maccabees,—with the same design. All these are mere conjectures, and it is now impossible to ascertain the occasion on which the psalm was composed, or to determine who was its author. Nor is it necessary. The psalm is so applicable to the people of God at all times, so fitted to strengthen the mind in trial, so adapted to guide, comfort, and support the soul, and so true in regard to the influence and value of the law of God, that it is not needful to know when it was composed, or who its author was. It is sufficient to know that it was composed under the guidance of the Holy Spirit, and is a repository of truths which will be of inestimable value in all ages of the world.

There is no *grouping* or *arrangement* of the subjects in the psalm, and little or no connexion between the sentiments in the verses of it. Much in it has a proverbial cast, or is presented in the form of aphorisms; and the order of thought *seems* to have been suggested by the necessity of choosing a particular letter with which to commence each verse, and the succession of eight verses under each letter. It might be possible to make an arrangement of the psalm under particular heads, — such as the following, under the general title of THE WORD OF GOD, or THE LAW OF GOD;—

I. In youth.	V. At night.
II. In trial.	VI. In public.
III. In duty.	VII. In private.
IV. In meditation.	VIII. In prosperity.
IX. In adversity, etc., etc. ;—	

but, in an *exposition* of the psalm, such an arrangement or classification, changing the structure of the psalm, might be of doubtful propriety, and it will be right to adhere to the order which the Spirit of Inspiration has seen fit to observe.

PSALM CXIX.

ALEPH.

BLESSED *are* the [1] undefiled in the way, who *o* walk in the law of the LORD.

[1] Or, *perfect,* or, *sincere.* *o* Ps. cxxviii. 1.

2 Blessed *are* they that keep his testimonies, *and that* seek him with the whole heart.*p*

3 They *q* also do no iniquity: they walk in his ways.

p Prov. xxiii. 26 ; 1 John iii. 20.
q 1 John iii. 9 ; v. 18.

1. *Blessed* are *the undefiled in the way.* In the way or journey of life ; in the path of religion ; in the road which leads to heaven. As life—the religious life—is represented under the image of a *journey*, the expression here is equivalent to saying, " Blessed are those who in the journey of life— in their religious course—are pure, sincere, uncontaminated." On the word *way*, see Notes on Ps. i. 6. The margin here on the word *undefiled*, is *perfect,* or *sincere.* So the Hebrew. The word is the same as in Job i. 1, where it is rendered *perfect.* See Notes on that passage. The Greek translation is *undefiled—ἄμωμοι.* So the Latin, *immaculati.* Luther renders it, " Who live without blemish" or stain. The idea is, " Blessed are they who are upright, sincere, perfect, in their course." The whole psalm is designed to illustrate this thought, by showing what the influence of a sincere and conscientious attachment to the principles of the law or word of God in the various circumstances of life must be. ¶ *Who walk in the law of the* LORD. Who habitually obey his law. This *constitutes* sincerity, uprightness, perfection in a man's life ; for the law of the Lord is the only just rule of human conduct.

2. *Blessed* are *they that keep his testimonies.* His commandments or laws, considered as what *he bears witness to* concerning that which is just, wise, good. Every law of a parent is to his children a *testimony* on his part of what is wise and right and good ; and so every law of God is *his* solemn testimony as to what is right and good for man. See Notes on Ps. xix. 7 ; xxv. 10. ¶ And that *seek him with the whole heart.* With a sincere

desire to know his will and to do it ; without hypocrisy or guile ; with no selfish or sinister aims. As God *knows* the heart, all other modes of "seeking" him must be in vain. It is impossible for man to impose on him by appearances.

3. *They also do no iniquity.* See Notes on 1 John iii. 9. The meaning is, that they are righteous ; their character is that they *do* that which is right. It cannot mean that all persons who are religious are actually and absolutely perfect,—for no man would hold this opinion ; no one does hold it. It is general language such as is commonly used to describe an upright or righteous man. The declaration is true of all who are the friends of God,—or, who are truly religious,—in the following senses : (1) That they are habitually and characteristically righteous ; (2) That they intend to do right,—for a man who deliberately purposes to do wrong —to lead a life of sin and disobedience, *cannot* be a pious man. (3) That when they do err, it is not the result of intention, or the design of their life, but because they are tempted ; are overcome with passion ; are led by the power of their native corruption of heart to act *contrary* to their better judgment and their true character. See Rom. vii. 14–17. On the other hand, it is true that a man who is not characteristically *righteous;* who is not an upright man in his dealings ; who is not true, and honest, and temperate, and just, and benevolent, *cannot* be a child of God and heir of heaven. No exactness of orthodoxy, and no fervour of emotion, and no zeal in the cause of religion, can constitute true piety without this. ¶ *They walk in his*

4 Thou *r* hast commanded *us* to keep thy precepts diligently.

5 O that my ways were directed to keep thy statutes!

6 Then shall I not be ashamed,*s*

r Deut. vi. 17; xi. 13, 22.
s 1 John ii. 28.   *t* ver. 171.

when I have respect unto all thy commandments.

7 I *t* will praise thee with uprightness of heart, when I shall have learned [1] thy righteous judgments.

[1] *judgments of thy righteousness.*

---

ways. Habitually; constantly; characteristically. They are not *merely* honest, upright, and just in their dealings with men, but they walk in the ways of God; they are *religious.*

4. *Thou hast commanded.* All this is here traced to the *command* of God; to the fact that he has required it. It is not mere human prudence; it is not mere morality; it is not because it will be for our interest; it is because God requires it. This is the foundation of all true virtue; and until a man acts from this motive it cannot be said that he is in the proper sense a righteous man. ¶ *To keep thy precepts diligently.* Heb., *very much;* that is, to do it constantly; faithfully. Each one of his laws is to be observed, and to be observed always, and in all circumstances.

5. *O that my ways were directed,* etc. Indicating the desire of the pious heart. That desire—a prevailing, constant, uniform desire—is to keep the law of God. It is the aim of the life; it is the supreme purpose of the soul; it is the ruling wish of the man, thus to keep the law of God. He in whose bosom this is *not* the constant wish cannot be a pious man. The Hebrew particle used here, and rendered "O that," is a particle denoting a wish, or an earnest desire. The word "ways" denotes the course of life. The whole is expressive of an earnest *desire* to live in accordance with the law of God. It implies also a sense of dependence on God.

6. *Then shall I not be ashamed.* On the word *ashamed*, see Notes on Job vi. 20; Ps. xxv. 2, 3. The meaning here is, that he would not have occasion to be ashamed; he would not be disappointed; all his hopes

would be realized. He would have full evidence of piety; he would enjoy the comforts which he sought in religion; he would feel assured of ultimately obtaining eternal life. ¶ *When I have respect unto all thy commandments.* Literally, "In my looking at all thy commandments." That is, in his regarding them; in his feeling that all were equally binding on him; and in his having the consciousness that he had not intentionally neglected, violated, or disregarded any of them. There can be no true piety except where a man *intends* to keep ALL the commands of God. If he makes a selection among them, keeping this one or that one, as may be most convenient for him, or as may be most for his interest, or as may be most popular, it is full proof that he knows nothing of the nature of true religion. A child has no proper respect for a parent if he obeys him only as shall suit his whim or his convenience; and no man *can* be a pious man who does not purpose, in all honesty, to keep ALL the commandments of God; to submit to his will *in everything.*

7. *I will praise thee with uprightness of heart.* With an upright and sincere heart. ¶ *When I shall have learned.* Heb., "In my learning." In the practice or act of learning them. His own experience of their nature, influence, and value would lead him to sincere praise. He had no doubt of finding that they were worthy of his praises, and of seeing in them more and more occasion to glorify and honour God. The more we know of God, the more shall we see in him to praise. The larger our acquaintance and experience, the more our hearts will be disposed to

8 I will keep thy statutes : O forsake me not utterly.

BETH.

9 Wherewithal shall a young "

man cleanse his way ? By taking heed *thereto* according to thy word.

u Prov. i. 4.

magnify his name. This remark must extend to all that there is in God *to be learned ;* and as that is infinite, so there will be occasion for renewed and more elevated praise to all eternity. ¶ *Thy righteous judgments.* Marg., as in Heb., *Judgments of thy righteousness.* The laws or statutes which God, as a righteous or just God, appoints to be the rule of conduct to his creatures.

8. *I will keep thy statutes.* Thy commands ; thy laws. This expresses the firm purpose of the psalmist. He *meant* to keep the law of God ; he could confidently say that he *would* do it,—yet coupled with the prayer which follows, that God would not forsake him. ¶ *O forsake me not utterly.* Heb., " To very much ;" so as to leave me to myself. His confidence that he would keep the commandments of God was based on the prayer that God would not leave him. There is no other ground of persuasion that we shall be able to keep the commandments of God than that which rests on the belief and the hope that He *will* not leave us.

9. *Wherewithal.* This begins the second portion of the psalm, extending to ver. 16, in which all the verses begin with the *second* letter of the Hebrew alphabet, indicated in our translation by the word *Beth.* These names of the letters, inserted for convenience, are no part of the psalm, as it is not so marked in the original. This mode of indicating the divisions of the psalm is peculiar to our version. It is not in the Septuagint, the Latin Vulgate, or the German versions. The word *wherewithal* means " *by what* " (Heb.) ; that is, What means shall a young man adopt by which he may " cleanse his way ?" It indicates a state of inquiry. The case supposed is that of a young man pondering the question how he

may be saved from the corruptions of his own heart, and escape the temptations to which he is exposed in early years, and lead a pure and upright life. There can be no more important inquiry for one just entering on the journey of life ; there can be found nowhere a more just and comprehensive answer than is contained in this single verse. All the precepts of ancient and modern wisdom, all the teachings of heathen morality and religion, and all the results of the experience of mankind, could furnish nothing in addition to what is here suggested. The world has no higher wisdom than this by which to guide a young man, so that he may lead a holy life. ¶ *Shall a young man.* The remark here *might* be applied also to those who are in middle life, or even to those who are in more advanced years, but it is applied here especially to the young, because it may be supposed that in the other cases the matter may be regarded as settled by experience ; because to the young, as they commence life, the inquiry is so momentous ; and because it is a question which it may be supposed *will* come up before the mind of every young man who has any right aspirations, and any proper conception of the dangers which encompass his path. ¶ *Cleanse his way ?* Make his course of life pure and upright. The *language* does not necessarily imply that there had been any previous impurity or vice, but it has particular reference to the future : —not how he might cleanse himself from past offences, but how he might make the future pure. The inquiry is, how he might conduct himself,—what principles he could adopt, — under what influence he could bring himself,—so that his future course would be honest, honourable, upright. ¶ *By taking heed* thereto, etc. . The word

10 With *v* my whole heart have I sought thee: O let me not wander from thy commandments.

11 Thy *w* word have I hid in

v 2 Chron. xv. 15.

mine heart, that I might not sin against thee.

12 Blessed *art* thou, O LORD: teach *x* me thy statutes.

w Ps. i. 2.   *x* ver. 26, etc.   Ps. xxv. 4.

"thereto" is not in the original. The Hebrew is, "To keep according to thy word;" or, "in keeping according to thy word." Prof. Alexander supposes that this means "to keep it [his way] according to thy word;" and that the whole is a question,—"How may a young man so cleanse his way as to keep it according to thy word?"—and that the answer to the question is to be found in the general strain of the psalm, or in the general principles laid down in the psalm. But it is clear that the answer to the question must be found *in* the verse, or not found at all; and the most natural construction is that in our translation. So De Wette renders it: "How can a young man walk guiltless? If [or, when] he holds [or, keeps] himself according to thy word." The meaning clearly is, If he governs himself according to the law of God,—if he makes that law the rule of his life and conduct, he would be enabled to do it. All other things might fail; this rule would never fail, in making and keeping a man pure. The more principles of common honesty, the principles of honour, the considerations of self-interest, the desire of reputation,—valuable as they may be,—would not constitute a security in regard to his conduct; the law of God would, for that is wholly pure.

10. *With my whole heart have I sought thee.* See Notes on ver. 2. The psalmist in ver. 2 speaks of the "blessedness of those who seek the Lord with the whole heart;" in this verse he says that this blessedness was his. He could affirm that he had thus sought God. He had such a consciousness that this was the aim and purpose of his life that he could say so without hesitation. Every man who claims to be a

religious man *ought* to be able to say this. Alas, how few can do it! ¶ *O let me not wander*, etc. Keep me in this steady purpose; this fixed design. This is the language of a heart where there is a consciousness of its weakness, and its liability to err, strong as may be its purpose to do right. Such an apprehension is one of the best means of security, for such an apprehension will lead a man to *pray*, and while a man prays he is safe.

11. *Thy word have I hid in mine heart.* Comp. Notes on Ps. xxxvii. 31. The word rendered *hid* means properly to conceal, so that a thing may be secret, private, inaccessible; then, to lay up in private, to treasure up, to hoard—as money or jewels—commonly *hidden* from public view. Job xx. 26; Ps. xvii. 14. Then it means to lay up in one's heart, as a secret, inaccessible place; to hide one's thoughts, purposes, designs; or to lay up knowledge or wisdom in the heart as a treasure, Job x. 13; Prov. ii. 1; vii. 1. The meaning here is, that he had *treasured* up the word of God, as the most valuable thing, in his heart; it was *there*, though unseen; it constituted the secret power by which he was governed; it was permanently deposited there, as the most valuable of his treasures. ¶ *That I might not sin against thee.* That it might protect me from sinning against thee. That I might be continually guided by its precepts; that I might be admonished of duty; that I might be deterred from going astray.

12. *Blessed* art *thou*, O LORD. Blessed art thou as the author of such a law. This language of benediction or doxology is an outbreak of feeling or adoration in view of such a law,—so good, so holy, so fitted to

13 With my lips have I declared all the judgments of thy mouth.

14 I have rejoiced in the way of thy testimonies as *much as* in all riches.

15 I will meditate *y* in thy precepts, and have respect unto

y Ps. i. 2.

thy ways.

16 I will delight myself in thy statutes : I will not forget thy word.

GIMEL.

17 Deal *z* bountifully with thy servant, *that* I may live, and keep thy word.

z Ps. cxvi. 7.

---

direct and guide man. The mind is full of the subject; and the lips give vent to the feeling of gratitude and joy that such a law had been revealed to men. ¶ *Teach me thy statutes.* Make me more and more acquainted with a law so pure, so rich, so valuable.

13. *With my lips have I declared.* That is, I have openly and publicly made thy words known to others; I have defended and vindicated them. ¶ *All the judgments.* The word *judgments* here means the same as statutes or laws: and the idea is, that he had been on the side of those laws, and had endeavoured by argument and persuasion to bring others under their influence. *How* he had done it we are not informed; but we have no reason to suppose that the author of the psalm was a minister of religion, and if not, then we have here an example of what a man who does not claim to be a public teacher may do, and should do, in making known and defending Divine truth. Every man is as much bound to do this in his sphere as the minister of religion is in his; and private members of the church have often an opportunity of doing this to more advantage than the ministers of the gospel possess. ¶ *Of thy mouth.* With my mouth I speak those things which have proceeded from thine. I speak in thy name; I declare thy truth. It is not my own; it is thine.

14. *I have rejoiced,* etc. I do rejoice; I exult in this; I find my happiness there. The word expresses a high degree of joy. ¶ *As* much as *in all riches.* Heb., "as upon all wealth."

As men rejoice who have great wealth. I find *my* happiness in religion, as if in the possession of real wealth. Prov. x. 22.

15. *I will meditate in thy precepts.* I will think of them; I will find my happiness in them. See Notes on Ps. i. 2. ¶ *And have respect unto thy ways.* And look to thy ways—thy commands. I continually regard them, or refer to them in my mind as the guide of my life. See Notes on ver. 6.

16. *I will delight myself in thy statutes.* I will find my happiness in thy laws. See Notes on Ps. i. 2; cxii. 1. ¶ *I will not forget thy word.* I will not allow the world to crowd it out of my mind.

17. *Deal bountifully,* etc. This commences the next portion of the psalm, indicated by the letter *Gimel,* the *third* letter of the Hebrew alphabet, answering to our letter *g.* Each verse of this portion (vers. 17–24) begins with this letter. There is a resemblance between the first *word* of this verse—גְּמֹל, *gemol* — and the letter —*Gimel*—which commences the eight verses of this portion of the psalm. The noun (derived from the verb)—גָּמָל, *gamal*—means a camel, and the letter *gimel* has been supposed to have derived its name from its having originally a resemblance to the camel's neck. In some of the Phenician inscriptions, and in the Ethiopic alphabet, it has this form (Gesenius, *Lex*). The *verb* used here means to do, or show, or cause good or evil to any one; and then to reward, or to recompense, either good or evil. Here it seems to be used in

18 ¹ Open thou mine eyes, that I may behold wondrous things out of thy law.

¹ *Reveal.*

19 I *am* a stranger *a* in the earth; hide not thy commandments from me.

a Ps. xxxix. 12; Heb. xi. 13; 1 Pet. ii. 11.

a general sense of doing good, or showing favour, as in Ps. xiii. 6; cxvi. 7; cxlii. 7. Comp. Prov. xi. 17. It does not necessarily imply that the author of the psalm had any claim, or demanded this on the ground of merit. He begged the favour, the friendship, the interposition of God in his behalf. ¶ That *I may live.* The continuance of life was dependent on the favour of God. ¶ *And keep thy word.* For grace to do this he was equally dependent on God; and he asked that life might be continued, in order that he might honour the word of God by obeying it.

18. *Open thou mine eyes.* Marg., *Reveal.* So the Septuagint and the Latin Vulgate. The Hebrew word means to be naked; then to make naked, to uncover, to disclose, to reveal. Here it is the same as *uncover;* that is, take away from the eyes what is before them to prevent clear vision. Comp. Num. xxii. 31; xxiv. 4, 16. ¶ *That I may behold wondrous things.* Things which are fitted to excite wonder and amazement :—that is, things which are secret or hidden from the common view; the deep, spiritual meaning of the word of God. By natural vision he might see the surface—the letter; to see the deep, hidden, real, meaning, he needed the special influence of God. Comp. 1 Cor. ii. 12, 14, 15. He believed that there *were* such things in the law of God; he desired to ˙see them. ¶ *Out of thy law.* Out of the written word; out of the Scriptures. The word *law* here is used to denote *all* that God had revealed to mankind; all that is contained in the volume of inspiration. The truths taught here are (1) That there are deep, hidden, secret things in the word of God, which are not perceived by the natural man; (2)

That those things, when understood, are fitted to excite wonder, or to fill the mind with admiring views of God; (3) That a special illumination of God is necessary that man may perceive these things; and (4) That the proper understanding of these things is connected with prayer, and can be hoped for only in answer to prayer. No one has a proper appreciation of Divine truth—of the beauty, the spiritual meaning, the grandeur, the sublimity of the Bible —until he is a renewed—a praying—man. Comp. Notes on 1 Cor. ii. 6-15.

19. *I am a stranger in the earth.* A wayfaring man; a pilgrim; a sojourner; a man whose permanent home is not in this world. The word is applicable to one who belongs to another country, and who is now merely passing through a foreign land, or sojourning there for a time. Comp. Notes on Heb. xi. 13. The home of the child of God is heaven. Here he is in a strange—a foreign— land. He is to abide here but for a little time, and then to pass on to his eternal habitation. ¶ *Hide not thy commandments from me.* Make me to know them; keep them continually before me. In this strange land, away from my home, let me have the comfort of feeling that thy commands are ever with me to guide me; thy promises to comfort me. The feeling is that of one in a strange land who would desire, if possible, to keep up constant communications with his *home*—his family, his friends, his kindred there. On earth, the place of our sojourning —of our pilgrimage—the friend of God desires to have constant intercourse with heaven, his final home; not to be left ·to the desolate feeling that he is cut off from all intercourse with that world where he is for ever to dwell.

20 My *b* soul breaketh for the longing *that it hath* unto thy judgments at all times.

21 Thou hast rebuked the proud

b Ps. lxiii. 1.   *c* 1 Pet. v. 5.

---

c that are cursed, which do err from thy commandments.

22 Remove from me reproach and contempt; for I have kept thy testimonies.

---

20. *My soul breaketh.* This word means to break; to crush; to break in pieces by scraping, rubbing, or grating. The *idea* would seem to be, not that he was crushed as by a single blow, but that his soul—his strength—was worn away by little and little. The desire to know more of the commands of God acted continually on him, exhausting his strength, and overcoming him. He *so* longed for God that, in our language, "it wore upon him"—as any ungratified desire does. It was not the *possession* of the knowledge of God that exhausted him; it was the intenseness of his *desire* that he might know more of God. ¶ *For the longing.* For the earnest desire. ¶ That it hath *unto thy judgments at all times.* Thy law; thy commands. This was a constant feeling. It was not fitful or spasmodic. It was the steady, habitual state of the soul on the subject. He had never seen enough of the beauty and glory of the law of God to feel that all the wants of his nature were satisfied, or that he could see and know no more; he had seen and felt enough to excite in him an ardent desire to be made fully acquainted with *all* that there is in the law of God. Comp. Notes on Ps. xvii. 15.

21. *Thou hast rebuked the proud.* Comp. Ps. ix. 5. The meaning is, that God had done this not by word but by deed. The proud were everywhere rebuked by God, alike in his law, and in his providence. The *connexion* seems to be this:—the psalmist is meditating on the benefit or advantage of keeping the law of God; of a humble, pious life. His mind naturally adverts to what would be the opposite of this,—or to this in contrast with an opposite course of life; and he says, therefore, that

God had in every way, and at all times, manifested his displeasure against that class of men. *Such* a course, therefore, must be attended with misery; but the course which *he* proposed to pursue must be attended with happiness. ¶ *That are cursed.* The accursed; those who are regarded and treated by God *as* accursed, or as objects of his disapprobation. ¶ *Which do err from thy commandments.* Who depart from thy law. The sense is, "*I* propose and intend to keep thy law. As a motive to this, I look at the consequences which must follow from disobeying it. I see it everywhere in the Divine treatment of those who *do* disregard that law. They are subject to the displeasure—the solemn rebuke—of God. So all must be who disregard his law; and it is my purpose not to be found among their number."

22. *Remove from me reproach and contempt.* Show me thy favour, and let me not suffer in the estimation of mankind on account of my religion. Let me not be exposed to malicious charges; to accusations of hypocrisy, insincerity, and unfaithfulness on account of my religion. This "reproach and contempt" might arise from two sources; (1) On account of religion itself, or *because* he was a true friend of God; or (2) he may have been charged with hypocrisy and insincerity; with doing things inconsistent with the profession of religion. These accusations he prays may be removed from him (*a*) In order that the true religion might not be in itself a matter of reproach, but that God might honour his own religion, and make it esteemed among men; (*b*) Because he was conscious that so far as he was concerned, the charges were

23 Princes also did sit *and* speak against me: *but* thy servant did meditate in thy statutes.

24 Thy testimonies also *are*

d vers. 77, 92.   1 *men of counsel.*

my *d* delight, *and* 1 my *e* counsellors.

DALETH.

25 My soul cleaveth unto the

e Prov. vii. 1—4.

unfounded. He did not deserve the "reproach and contempt" that properly belong to a life of hypocrisy and insincerity. ¶ *For I have kept thy testimonies.* My conscience assures me of this. I can appeal to thee, my God, in proof that I do not deserve the charge of insincerity and hypocrisy. Every professedly pious man *ought* to be able thus to appeal to conscience and to God, and to say, in the most solemn manner, that he does not *deserve* the reproach of hypocrisy and insincerity.

23. *Princes also did sit* and *speak against me.* This would have been applicable to David many times in his life, but it was also applicable to many others, and there is nothing in the language which would limit it to David. It is evident that the author of the psalm had been subject to reproach from those who were of exalted rank; it is clear also that he felt this keenly. It is natural, whether proper or not, that we should feel the reproach and contempt of those in elevated life—the rich, the honoured, the learned—more than of those in humbler life. Their good opinion can be of value only as they may be better qualified than others to judge of what constitutes true excellence, or as they may have it in their power to do us more harm, or to do more to aid us in doing good, than others have; but truth and principle are never to be sacrificed that we may secure their favour; and if, in the faithful discharge of our duty, and the zealous adherence to the principles of our religion, we incur their frowns, we are to bear it, —as the great Lord and Saviour of his people did. Heb. xiii. 13. ¶ But *thy servant did meditate in thy statutes.* I was engaged in this; I continued to do it; I was not de-

terred from it by their opposition; I found comfort in it, when they sat and talked against me. This would *seem* to have reference to some occasion when they were together—in public business, or in the social circle. They, the princes and nobles engaged in the ordinary topics of conversation, or in conversation connected with revelry, frivolity, or sin. Unwilling to participate in this,—having different tastes,—feeling that it was improper to be one of their companions in such a mode of spending time, or in such subjects of conversation, *he* withdrew, he turned his thoughts on the law of God, he sought comfort in meditation on that law and on God. He became, therefore, the subject of remark—perhaps of their jests—*because* he thus refused to mingle with them, or because he put on what seemed to be hypocritical seriousness, and was (what they deemed) stern, sour, unsocial, as if he thus publicly, though tacitly, meant to rebuke them. Nothing will be more *likely* to subject one to taunting remarks, to rebuke, to contempt, than to manifest a religious spirit, and to introduce religion in any way in the circles of the worldly and the gay.

24. *Thy testimonies also* are *my delight.* See Notes on ver. 16. He found his main happiness in the word of God. ¶ And *my counsellors.* Marg., as in Heb., *men of my counsel.* He sought direction and advice from them as from a friend who would give him counsel. He looked to the revealed law of God to ascertain what was right; to know how he should act in the emergencies of life.

25. *My soul cleaveth unto the dust.* This commences a new division of the psalm, in which each verse begins with the *fourth* letter of the Hebrew

dust: quicken thou me according to thy word.

26 I have declared my ways, and thou heardest me: teach me thy statutes.

27 Make me to understand the way of thy precepts: so shall I talk of thy wondrous works.

28 My soul [1] melteth for heavi-

[1] *droppeth.*

---

alphabet,—*Daleth*, equivalent to the English *d*. There is nothing in the sense to separate it from the other parts of the psalm. The word rendered *cleaveth* means to be glued to; to stick fast. It has the sense of adhering firmly to anything, so that it cannot easily be separated from it. Comp. Notes on Ps. lxiii. 8. The word *dust* here may mean either the earth, and earthly things, considered as low, base, unworthy, worldly; or it may mean the grave, as if he were near to that, and in danger of dying. De Wette understands it in the latter sense. Comp. Ps. xliv. 25; xxii. 29. Yet the word *cleave* would hardly suggest this idea; and the force of that word would be better represented by the idea that his soul, as it were, *adhered* to the things of earth; that it seemed to be so fastened to them—so *glued* to them— that it could not be detached from them; that his affections were low, earthly, grovelling, so as to give him deep distress, and to lead him to cry to God for life and strength that he might break away from them. This expresses what is often felt by good men, and thus presents one of the forms of religious experience. Comp. Rom. vii. 14, 15. ¶ *Quicken thou me.* Cause me to live; give me vigour and strength to break away from this which binds me fast, and to rise above these low propensities. ¶ *According to thy word.* That is, either according to thy *promises* made to thy people to aid them when they are in distress; or, according to the principles of thy word, that I may live as thy word requires. Who has not found his soul so cleaving to dust —to earth—to worldly things—as to feel himself degraded by it, and to lead him to cry out with earnestness that God would give him strength,

life, vigour, that his soul might rise to better things?

26. *I have declared my ways.* That is, I have declared or recounted them to thee. I have made mention of my cares, troubles, anxieties, purposes. I have laid them all before thee, reserving or keeping back nothing. ¶ *And thou heardest me.* Thou didst answer me. It is only when we declare all our ways before God, that we can hope he *will* hear us. It is right and proper that we should go before God with *all* our cares and troubles. There is nothing that gives us anxiety, of which we may not speak to him, however trivial it may seem to be,— even as a child speaks to a mother of the smallest matter that troubles him. *When* this is done, we may be assured that God will not turn away from us, or disregard our cry.

" I told him all my secret grief;
    My secret groaning reached his ears;
  He gave my inward pains relief,
    And calmed the tumult of my fears."

¶ *Teach me thy statutes.* Make known to me thy will. Acquaint me with what thou wouldst have me to do. See ver. 12.

27. *Make me to understand*, etc. See Notes on ver. 18. ¶ *So shall I talk of thy wondrous works.* The things in thy works—thy providential dealings — that are wondrous. That is, with a heart full of the subject, he could not but speak of those things,—for " out of the abundance of the heart the mouth speaketh." See Notes on Ps. xxxix. 2–4.

28. *My soul melteth.* Marg., *droppeth.* The Hebrew word here employed—דָּלַף, *dalaph*—means to drop, to drip, to distil, spoken of a house, as when the rain drops through the roof, Eccl. x. 18; then, to shed tears, to weep, Job xvi. 20,—and this seems to be the meaning here. The idea of

ness: strengthen thou me according unto thy word.

29 Remove *f* from me the way of lying; and grant me thy law graciously.

30 I have chosen the way of

truth : thy judgments have I laid *before me.*

31 I have stuck unto thy testimonies : O LORD, put me not to *g* shame.

f Prov. xxx. 8.   *g* Isa. xlix. 23.

melting is not properly in the word, and the term *weep* would better express the meaning. His soul seemed to drop tears. It overflowed with tears. Yet there is an idea of *abundant* or *constant* weeping. It is not a gush of emotion, as when we say of one that he is "*bathed* in tears;" it is the idea of a steady flow or dropping of tears—slow, silent, but constant—as if the soul were dripping away or dissolving. Thus the idea is more striking and beautiful than that of *melting.* It is quiet but continuous grief that slowly wears away the soul. There are two kinds of sorrow :—(*a*) the one represented by *floods* of tears, like fierce torrents that sweep all away, and are soon passed ; (*b*) the other is the gentle dropping—the constant wearing—the slow attrition caused by inward grief, that secretly but certainly wears away the soul. The latter is more common, and more difficult to be borne than the other. The Septuagint and the Latin Vulgate render this, "My soul slumbereth." ¶ *For heaviness.* This word means grief, sorrow, vexation. Prov. xiv. 13; xvii. 21. It is here silent grief; hidden sorrow. How many thus pine in secret, till life slowly wears away, and they sink to the grave. ¶ *Strengthen thou me.* Give me strength to meet this constant wearing away—this slow work of sorrow. We need strength to bear great and sudden sorrow ; we need it *not less* to bear that which constantly wears upon us; which makes our sleep uneasy; which preys upon our nerves, and slowly eats away our life. ¶ *According unto thy word.* See vers. 9, 25.

29. *Remove from me.* Take it from me ; cause it to depart ; let me not be under its influence or power. ¶ *The*

way of lying. Every false, deceitful, hypocritical way. We are not to suppose that the psalmist was addicted to lying, but that he felt he was, like all men, in danger of acting from false views, from wrong motives, or under the influence of delusion and deceit. It is a prayer that he might always be sincere and truthful. No man who knows his own heart can doubt the propriety of this prayer. On nothing does a man need more to examine himself; in nothing does he more need the grace of God, than that he may be *sincere.* ¶ *And grant me thy law graciously.* The knowledge of thy law ; grace to obey thy law. The single word rendered " grant graciously " is a word which implies the idea of *mercy* or *favour.* It was not a thing which he claimed as a right; it was that for which he was dependent on the mercy of God.

30. *I have chosen the way of truth.* Among all the paths of life I have selected this. I prefer this. I desire to walk in this. Religion is, wherever it exists, a matter of *preference* or *choice;* and the friend of God *prefers* his service to the service of the world. ¶ *Thy judgments.* Thy statutes; thy laws. ¶ *Have I laid* before me. I have set them before my mind as the guide of my conduct; I have made their observance the end and aim of my life.

31. *I have stuck unto thy testimonies.* The word here rendered *stuck* is the same which in ver. 25 is rendered *cleave :*—" My soul cleaveth unto the dust." It means here that he had adhered to the testimonies of God as if he had been *glued* to them, or as if he and they were firmly united together. He had so adhered to them that he could not be detached from them. ¶ *O* LORD, *put me not to*

32 I will run the way of thy commandments, when thou shalt enlarge *h* my heart.

HE.

33 Teach me, O LORD, the way of thy statutes, and I shall keep *i* it *unto* the end.

34 Give *k* me understanding, and

h Isa. lx. 5; 2 Cor. vi. 11.
i Rev. ii. 26.   *k* Prov. ii. 6.

l I shall keep thy law; yea, I shall observe it with *my* whole heart.

35 Make me to go in the path of thy commandments; for therein do I delight.

36 Incline my heart *m* unto thy testimonies, and not to *n* covetousness.

l Deut. iv. 6.   *m* Jer. xxiv. 7.
n Luke xii. 15; 1 Tim. vi. 10; Heb. xiii. 5.

shame. Let me not be disappointed or confounded; let all my anticipations of the good effects of obeying thy law be realized; let me find all that I have hoped for; let me partake of thy friendship and favour as I desire. See Notes on ver. 6.

32. *I will run the way of thy commandments.* That is, I will not merely keep them—which might be expressed by "I will *walk* in them,"—but I will *hasten* to keep them; I will do it with alacrity, as when one runs to accomplish an object. I will devote to them all the energies of my life. ¶ *When thou shalt enlarge my heart.* Or, more literally, "For thou wilt enlarge my heart;" expressing confidence that God *would* do this, so that he would be thus inclined and enabled to keep his commandments. It is an acknowledgment of dependence, and at the same time the expression of a confident belief that God *would* grant him the grace needful for him. The phrase "to enlarge the heart" means to make it free; to deliver it from all hindrances to what is right; to fill it with noble and holy purposes; to stimulate and animate it. The heart is contracted or made narrow by selfishness, pride, vanity, ambition, covetousness; it is made large by charity, love, hope, benevolence. Sin narrows the soul; religion enlarges it.

33. *Teach me, O LORD, the way of thy statutes.* This begins a new division of the psalm, indicated by the letter *He* (or *h*). The word rendered *teach* means properly to throw, to cast, to hurl; and then, to teach,—as if truth were thrown and scattered

abroad. The sentiment is the same as in ver. 12. ¶ *And I shall keep it unto the end.* Always. To the end of life. His keeping it depended on grace given to him continually to dispose and enable him to do it.

34. *Give me understanding, and I shall keep thy law.* Give me right views of it, of its nature and obligation. It is not a prayer that God would give him the *faculty* of understanding or intelligence; but that he would enable him to take just views of the law. The word is the same as in ver. 27, rendered there, "Make me to understand." ¶ *Yea, I shall observe it with* my *whole heart.* See ver. 2. I will keep it with undivided affections; I will make it the sole guide of my life.

35. *Make me to go in the path,* etc. That is, Incline me to it; so direct me that I shall thus walk. It is an acknowledgment of his dependence on God, that he might be able to carry out the cherished purposes of his soul. ¶ *For therein do I delight.* See ver. 16. I am conscious of having pleasure in thy commandments; of having a strong desire to keep them, and I pray for grace that I may be able to do it. Real *delight* in the law of God is one of the best means of securing its observance; one of the best evidences that it will be kept.

36. *Incline my heart unto thy testimonies.* Cause my heart to be inclined to them, or to be disposed to keep them. This, too, is a recognition of dependence, and a prayer for guidance. ¶ *And not to covetousness.* To gain; to the love of money. This

37 ¹ Turn away mine eyes from beholding ⁰ vanity; *and* quicken thou me in thy way.

¹ *Make to pass.*   o Isa. xxxiii. 15.

38 Stablish ᵖ thy word unto thy servant, who *is devoted* to thy fear.
39 Turn away my reproach

p 2 Sam. vii. 25; 2 Cor. i. 20.

seems to be referred to here as the principal thing which would turn away the heart from religion, or as that from which the most danger was to be feared. There are undoubtedly many other things which will do this, —for all sin will do it; but this was the chief danger which the psalmist apprehended in his own case, and perhaps he meant to refer to this as the principal danger on this subject which besets the path of man. There are many more persons turned away from the service of God, and kept away from it, by covetousness than there are by any other one sin. When the psalmist prays that God would not " *incline* " his heart to covetousness, the language is similar to that in the Lord's prayer—" And lead us not into temptation." That is, Restrain us from it; let us not be put in circumstances where we shall be in danger of it. We are not to suppose that God exerts any *positive* influence either to make a man covetous, or to tempt him. See James i. 13, 14.

37. *Turn away mine eyes from beholding vanity.* Vain things; wicked things; things which would be likely to lead me astray from what is real and true. Comp. Isa. xxxiii. 15; Job xxxi. 1. Marg. here, as in Heb., *make to pass.* Make my eyes to pass rapidly from such objects, that I may not look at them, may not contemplate them, may not dwell upon them. There is danger in looking on sin steadily; in surveying its features; in returning to contemplate it. An ugly object loses much of its deformity when we look often upon it;—and this is a benevolent law, lest we should be miserable when we are under a necessity of looking on it. Sin follows this general law, and is to be avoided altogether, even in its contemplation, if we would be safe. A man should be thankful in this world that he has

eyelids; and as he *can* close his eyes, so he should often do it. ¶ And *quicken thou me in thy way.* Endow me with life, energy, vigour, that I may walk in thy way.

38. *Stablish thy word unto thy servant.* Confirm it; make it *seem* firm and true; let not my mind be vacillating or sceptical in regard to thy truth. This seems to be a prayer against the influence of doubt and scepticism; a prayer that doubts might not be suffered to spring up in his mind, and that the objections and difficulties of scepticism might have no place there. There is a class of men whose minds are naturally sceptical and unbelieving, and for such men such a prayer is peculiarly appropriate. For none can it be improper to pray that the word of God may always seem to them to be true; that their minds may never be left to the influence of doubt and unbelief. ¶ *Who* is devoted *to thy fear.* Literally, " Who," or which, " to thy fear." This may refer either to the author of the psalm, or to the word of God. It may mean that *he* was among those who feared,—that is, worshipped God; or, that the word of God had reference to the "fear,"—that is, to the worship of God, or was designed to secure that. The construction seems to demand the latter interpretation; and then the prayer is, that God would confirm his faith in that "word "—in that revealed truth—which was designed to secure the worship of God.

39. *Turn away my reproach.* The reproach which is likely to come upon me from being a professed worshipper of God. In all ages good men have been exposed to this reproach. ¶ *Which I fear.* Which I have reason to apprehend will come upon me. This may not mean that he was personally afraid of it, but merely that he had reason to apprehend that he was exposed to

which I fear : for thy judgments *are* good.

40 Behold, I have longed after thy precepts : quicken *q* me in thy righteousness.

VAU.

41 Let thy mercies come also unto me, O LORD ; *even* thy sal-

q John x. 10.

vation, according to thy word.

42 So shall I [1] have wherewith to answer him that reproacheth me : for I trust in thy word.

43 And take not *r* the word of truth utterly out of my mouth ; for I have hoped in thy judgments.

[1] Or, *answer him that reproacheth me in a thing.*
r Isa. lix. 21.

it. The prayer is proper, for there is nothing which our nature makes us shrink back from more than *reproach.* Comp. ver. 22 ; Ps. lxix. 9, 20 ; Rom. xv. 3 ; 2 Cor. xii. 10. The word *reproach* in the original is the same which denotes shame or dishonour. ¶ *For thy judgments* are *good.* Thy statutes ; thy laws. I *know* they are good. I feel that I desire to obey them. I pray, therefore, that obedience on my part to that which is good may not subject me to shame ; that men may see that thy laws are good, and that it is *not* a matter of reproach to obey them.

40. *Behold, I have longed after thy precepts.* I have earnestly desired them. See Notes on ver. 20. ¶ *Quicken me in thy righteousness.* Make me to live ; to live in obedience to thy righteous laws. See Notes on vers. 25, 37.

41. *Let thy mercies come also unto me, O* LORD. This commences a new portion of the psalm, in which each verse begins with the letter *Vau,* or *v.* There are almost no words in Hebrew that begin with this letter, which is properly a conjunction, and hence in each of the verses in this section of the psalm (vers. 41–48) the beginning of the verse is in the original a conjunction,—*vau.* This does not here indicate a *connexion,* as with us the conjunction " *and* " would naturally do ; but is a mere artificial arrangement in order that the verse *may* begin with that letter, and it in no manner affects the sense. The phrase " Let thy mercies come " is literally, " and thy mercies shall come," or " and let thy mercies come." That

is, Let thy mercy be manifested to me ; let me experience thy mercy and thy favour. ¶ Even *thy salvation.* Mercy connected with salvation, or that leads to salvation. ¶ *According to thy word.* According to the promises of thy word ; according to the arrangements which thou hast made, and hast revealed. The only hope of mercy is that which is held out in the word of God.

42. *So shall I have wherewith to answer him that reproacheth me.* I shall have something by which I may reply to those who calumniate me. So the Saviour replied to the suggestions of the tempter almost wholly by passages of Scripture (Matt. iv. 4, 7, 10) ; and so, in many cases, the best answer that can be given to reproaches on the subject of religion will be found in the very words of Scripture. A man of little learning, except that which he has derived from the Bible, may often thus silence the cavils and reproaches of the learned sceptic ; a man of simple-hearted, pure piety, with no weapon but the word of God, may often thus be better armed than if he had all the arguments of the schools at his command. Comp. Eph. vi. 17. ¶ *For I trust in thy word.* I believe it ; I rely on it ; I confide in that, as my only comfort and protection.

43. *And take not the word of truth utterly out of my mouth.* Do not take it entirely or altogether from me. Let me not be utterly hopeless ; let me be at no time without *some* evidence that thy word dwells in me with sustaining and sanctifying power. The prayer seems to have been offered

44 So shall I keep thy law continually for ever and ever.

45 And I will walk at [1] liberty: *s* for I seek thy precepts.

46 I will speak of thy testimonies also before kings, *t* and will not be ashamed.

47 And I will delight myself in

[1] *large.*   *s* John viii. 32, 36; Gal. v. 1, 13.

thy commandments, which I have loved.

48 My hands also will I lift up unto thy commandments, which I have loved; and I will meditate in thy statutes.

ZAIN.

49 Remember the word unto

t Matt. x. 18, 19; Acts xxvi. 1, etc.

---

when the mind was troubled and in doubt, and when it *seemed* as if all hope and all trust in the truth of God would vanish. The words rendered "utterly" mean "to very much;" that is, *altogether* or *entirely.* Let it not be done until the *extreme* shall be reached. ¶ *For I have hoped in thy judgments.* I *do* trust in thy word, and it is my *only* trust. If that is gone, all is gone. As long as I can hold on to that, even in the slightest degree, I am safe. When all else fails, if *that* has not utterly failed me, I shall be secure.

44. *So shall I keep thy law continually for ever and ever.* At all times and in all places; in this world and the world to come. This indicates a purpose to do it, and an assurance that he would do it, if God should enable him to retain *even the slightest hold* on the truth.

45. *And I will walk at liberty.* Marg., *at large.* Luther renders it, *"freely."* The Septuagint, *"in a broad place."* The Hebrew word means *wide, broad, large, spacious.* The reference is to that which is free and open; that in which there are no limits, checks, restraints;—where a man does what he pleases. The meaning here is, that he would feel he was free. He would not be restrained by evil passions and corrupt desires. He would be delivered from those things which seemed to fetter his goings. This does not here refer so much to external troubles or hindrances, to being oppressed and straitened by external foes, as to internal enemies —to the servitude of sin—to the slavery of appetite and passion. Comp. Notes on Rom. vii. 9–14. See

also Job xxxvi. 16; Ps. cxviii. 5. The margin well expresses the sense of the passage. ¶ *For I seek thy precepts.* I seek or endeavour to obey them. I seek them as the guide of my life. I ask nothing else to direct me.

46. *I will speak of thy testimonies also before kings,* etc. In the presence of men of most elevated rank. I will not be ashamed to avow my belief in thy word before those in power—whether friendly or unfriendly to thee and to thy cause. I will not disguise my belief in thy truth with any desire to secure their favour; I will not be intimidated from expressing my faith by any dread of their frowns. Comp. Matt. x. 18, 19; Acts iv. 19; v. 29; xxvi. 2.

47. *And I will delight myself,* etc. See Notes on ver. 16.

48. *My hands also will I lift up unto thy commandments,* etc. As an expression of delight or rejoicing, as men lift up their hands with their voice when they give expression to joy. It denotes a high state of joy, such as leads to an outward expression; not merely that which exists in calm contemplation, but where the heart is full, and when it finds outward expression. ¶ *And I will meditate in thy statutes.* See Notes on Ps. i. 2. I will indicate my joy—my happiness—in thy commandments in every way possible;—by outward expressions, and by deep and calm contemplation when I am alone;—in my daily employments, in solitude, in the night-watches. This is indicative always of true religion.

49. *Remember the word unto thy servant.* This commences a new division of the psalm, in which each

thy servant, upon which thou hast caused me to *u* hope.

50 This *is* my comfort in my affliction: for thy word hath quickened me.

51 The proud have had me

u 1 Pet. i. 13, 21.

greatly in derision; *yet* *v* have I not declined from thy law.

52 I remembered thy judgments of old, O LORD: and have comforted myself.

v Job xxiii. 11; Isa. xxxviii. 3.

---

verse begins with the Hebrew letter *Zain*—answering to our *z*. There is nothing peculiar in this portion of the psalm as indicated by the letter. The language here is a prayer that God would not forget what he had promised; that all that he had said might be fulfilled; that the expectations and hopes which he had raised in the mind might be realised. It is language which *may* be used with reverence, and without any implication that God *would* forget,—as a child might with propriety and love ask a parent to *remember* a promise which he had made. ¶ *Upon which thou hast caused me to hope.* That is, All the hope which I have has been excited by thy word; thy promises. I have no other source of hope; I cherish no other hope. I pray now, since that hope has been thus excited in me, that I may realise all I have been led to desire and to expect. The word of God is the only foundation of hope for men; and when our hopes are fairly built on that, we have a right to appeal to God that he will make it good.

50. *This is my comfort in my affliction.* Comp. Rom. xv. 4. The word here rendered *comfort* occurs only here and in Job vi. 10. The obvious meaning is, that his only consolation in his affliction was derived from the word of God; the word which had caused him to hope, and the word by which he had been quickened or made alive. The particular design of this is to show the value of the word of God as a source of comfort in trouble. ¶ *For thy word hath quickened me.* Has made me alive; or, caused me to live. That is, the word, the truth of God, had been the instrument of calling him

from the death of sin, and of imparting to him new life, or had been the means of his regeneration. Comp. James i. 18; 1 Cor. iv. 15; Heb. iv. 12; 1 Pet. i. 23. As it was by this "word" that he had been made alive, so his only comfort was in that word, and it was to him a just ground of consolation that God *had* brought him from the death of sin, and had imparted to him spiritual life.

51. *The proud have had me greatly in derision.* Those of rank; those in high life:—perhaps, as we should say, the gay and fashionable world. They have ridiculed me; they have held me up to contempt for my scruples, my seriousness, my conscientiousness, my unwillingness to mingle with them in the pursuits, the pastimes, the frivolities of life. It is now no new thing to be held in contempt by the "proud" and the gay, on account of serious piety; to be thus held in contempt has been rather the rule than the exception in the treatment which the friends of religion have received from the world. ¶ Yet *have I not declined from thy law.* I have not been deterred from the avowal of my religious belief; I have not turned away from the duties of piety on account of the ridicule and scorn to which I have been exposed. Comp. Ps. xliv. 17–19.

52. *I remembered.* In my troubles. ¶ *Thy judgments of old.* The word *judgments* here seems to refer to the Divine dealings, whether expressed in the law of God, or in the actual administration of his government over the world. The words "of old" do not seem here to refer to the *eternity past*, as the phrase sometimes does now, but to the constancy and uniformity of the principles of the Divine administra-

53 Horror [w] hath taken hold upon me because of the wicked that forsake thy law.

w Ezra ix 3.

54 Thy statutes have been my songs in the house of my pilgrimage.

tion. The psalmist remembered that the principles of that administration had been always the same; that the law of God was always the same; and that, therefore, he might *confide* in God. What God had done formerly he would do now; the favour which he had shown in times past he would continue to show now. In the trials of life, in the changes which occur, in the apparent wreck of things, in the fearful prospect of disaster and ruin at any time, it is well for us to *think* of the unchanging principles which mark the Divine dealings. Under such an administration, all who put their trust in God *must* be safe. ¶ *And have comforted myself.* I have found consolation in this. When all else seemed to fail, it was a comfort to reflect that an unchangeable God presided over the affairs of men. We could not put confidence in a God given to change.

53. *Horror hath taken hold upon me.* Has seized me; has overpowered and overwhelmed me. I shudder; I tremble; I am afraid; I am filled with distress. Luther, " I am burnt up." The Hebrew word—זַלְעָפָה, *zalaphah*—is from a verb meaning to be hot; to glow; and the idea in the word is that of violent heat; then, a glow or burning, as of a wind—the *simoom* of the desert. See Ps. xi. 6, where the word is translated *horrible tempest,*—in the margin, *burning.* The word occurs only in that passage, in the one before us, and in Lam. v. 10, where it is rendered *terrible* [*famine*],—in the margin, *terrors,* or *storms.* The state referred to here is that of one who sees the storm of burning wind and sand approaching; who expects every moment to be overcome and buried; whose soul trembles with consternation. ¶ *Because of the wicked*, etc. Their conduct alarms me. Their

danger appals me. Their condition overwhelms me. I see them rebelling against God. I see them exposed to his wrath. I see the grave just before them, and the awful scenes of judgment near. I see them about to be cast off, and to sink to endless woe, and my soul is transfixed with horror. The contemplation overwhelms me with uncontrollable anguish. Can such things be? Can men be thus in danger? And can they be calm and composed, when so near such awful horrors? No man can look on the world of despair without horror; no one can truly realize that his fellow-men are exposed to the horrors of that abode without having his soul filled with anguish. Strange that all men do not feel thus,—that impenitent men can walk along on the verge of the grave and of hell *without* horror,— that pious men, good men, praying men, can look upon their friends in that condition without having their souls filled with unutterable anguish. Comp. Ps. cxix. 136; Rom. ix. 1–4; Luke xix. 41.

54. *Thy statutes.* Thy law; thy commandments. ¶ *Have been my songs.* Have been to me a source of joy; have been my happiness, my consolation, my delight. I have found pleasure in meditating on them; I have had peace and joy in them in the day of loneliness and trouble. The psalmist rejoiced, doubtless, as the good now do, (*a*) In law itself; law, as a rule of order; law, as a guide of conduct; law, as a security for safety; (*b*) in *such* a law as that of God—so pure, so holy, so fitted to promote the happiness of man; (*c*) in the stability of that law, as constituting his own personal security, the ground of his hope; (*d*) in law in its influence on the universe, preserving order, and securing harmony.

55 I have remembered thy name, O LORD, in the night, [x] and have kept thy law.

56 This I had, because I kept thy precepts.

CHETH.

57 *Thou art* my portion, [y] O

x Ps. lxiii. 6; lxxvii. 6.

LORD : I have said that I would keep thy words.

58 I entreated thy [1] favour with *my* whole [z] heart : be merciful unto me according to thy word.

59 I thought [a] on my ways,

y Jer. x. 16; Lam. iii. 24.   [1] *face.*
z Heb. x. 22.   a Lam. iii. 40, 41; Lu. xv. 17, 18.

¶ *In the house of my pilgrimage.* In my life considered as a journey to another world; in my pilgrimage through the desert of this world; amidst rocks, and sands, and desolation; among tribes of savage men, wanderers, robbers, freebooters; with no home, no place of shelter; exposed to cold, and rain, and sleet, and ice, and snow, as pilgrims are,—for to all these is the "pilgrim"—the wayfarer—exposed, and all these represent the condition of one passing through this world to a better (comp. Heb. xi. 13). Here, says the psalmist, I sang. I found joy in these scenes by thinking on the pure law—the pure and holy truth of God. I comforted myself with the feeling that there *is* law; that there is just government; that there is a God; that I am under the protection of law; that I am not alone, but that there is one who guides me by his truth. Comp. Notes on Job xxxv. 10. See Acts xvi. 25; Ps. xxxiv. 1.

55. *I have remembered thy name, O Lord, in the night*, etc. I have thought on thee in the night, when on my bed; I have done it in the night of calamity and sorrow. See Notes on Ps. lxiii. 6.

56. *This I had, because I kept thy precepts.* Literally, "This was to me;" that is, This has happened to me; this has occurred. This joyful remembrance of thy law in the night of affliction (ver. 50); this stability and firmness on my part in keeping thy law when proud men have derided me (ver. 51); this comfort which I have derived from meditating on thy statutes (ver. 52); this solicitude for the welfare of others

(ver. 53); this peace which I have enjoyed in thy law in the house of my pilgrimage (ver. 54); and this consolation which I have had in thee in the night-season (ver. 55);—all this has been granted to me because I have kept thy statutes; because I have sought to be obedient—to serve thee—to find my happiness in thee. These are the proper fruits and effects of keeping the law of God. Such peace does it impart; so much does it do to sustain and comfort the soul.

57. Thou art *my portion*, O LORD. This begins a new division of the psalm, indicated by the Hebrew letter *Cheth*, which may be represented in English by *hh.* On the meaning of the language here, see Notes on Ps. xvi. 5. God was to him what other men seek in wealth, honour, pleasure, fame. To him, God was all and in all. He asked nothing else. ¶ *I have said.* I have formed the purpose, and have expressed it. It is the deliberate and settled design of my life. ¶ *That I would keep thy words.* That I would obey thee at all times; that I would keep all thy commandments.

58. *I entreated thy favour.* Marg., as in Heb., *face.* That is, he prayed that God would lift upon him the light of his countenance; that he would not avert his face from him in anger. ¶ *With* my *whole heart.* With sincere, undivided affections. See vers. 2, 10, 34; Ps. ix. 1. ¶ *Be merciful unto me according to thy word.* See Notes on ver. 41.

59. *I thought on my ways.* This language most naturally refers to the time of conversion, and may be employed without impropriety to de-

and turned my feet unto thy testimonies.

60 I made haste, and delayed not, to keep thy commandments.

61 The [1] bands of the wicked have robbed me : *but* I have not forgotten thy law.

[1] Or, *companies.*

---

scribe the process of a sinner's turning to God. It would seem to be descriptive of the experience of the author of the psalm when he became personally interested in the subject of religion. The first step in such a work is reflection on the course of life which has been led ; on the guilt of such a course ; and on the consequences. It is a *pause* in the career of sin and folly—a pause for reflection and thought. Comp. Luke xv. 17, 18. No one is converted without such reflection ; and as soon as a sinner can be made to pause and reflect on his course, there is hope that he will be converted. Assuredly it is proper for all, whatever may be their circumstances in life, to pause from time to time ; to reflect ; to ask what will be the consequences of the course of life which is pursued. ¶ *And turned my feet.* Changed my course of life. He himself did this in fact ; and he does not hesitate to say that it was he who thus turned. His own agency was employed. He does not say that he "*waited*" for God to turn him ; or that he found he could not turn of himself, but that *he* turned ; *he* paused ; *he* reflected ; *he* changed his course of life. This is true in conversion always. There is an actual *turning from sin ;* an actual *turning to God.* The sinner turns. He leaves an old path, and treads a new one. He does this as the conscious result of reflection on the course which he was pursuing ; and there is nothing in his actual turning, or in his whole future course, which is not the proper result of reflection, or which a proper reflection on the course of life would not lead to and justify. Man himself is always *active* in conversion. That is, he does something ; he changes ; he repents ; he believes ; he turns to God ; it is not *God* that changes, that repents, that believes, that turns ;—it is the

man himself. It is, indeed, by the grace and help of God ;—but the effect of that grace is not to make him idly wait ; it is to rouse him to effort ; to lead him to *act.* ¶ *Unto thy testimonies.* Thy law, considered as the Divine testimony in regard to what is right.

60. *I made haste.* This language further describes the process of conversion. There was no delay ; there was no excuse offered. He acted at once under his conviction of what was right. He did not ask permission to defer it to a future time ; he did not attempt to avoid the duty ; he did not plead inability ; he did not give himself merely to the "use of means ;" he did not rely on prayer, and reading, and reflection ; but *he did the thing, and he did it at once.* This is conversion ; and if all convicted sinners would follow this example, and do at once that which they are commanded to do, and which they know they ought to do, there would be in no case any difficulty about conversion, for the main difficulty in conversion lies in the fact that the sinner is not willing to obey God at once ; that he will not break away from his sins ; that he endeavours to excuse himself ; that he pleads for delay ; that he waits for *God* to do what *he himself* ought to do. ¶ *And delayed not to keep thy commandments.* I did not continue to go on in a course of sin, but I forsook my sin and obeyed.

61. *The bands of the wicked.* Marg., *companies.* The Hebrew word properly means a cord, a rope ; then a snare, gin, net ; then, a band or a company of men. The reference is to some time in the life of the psalmist when he was surrounded by wicked men. ¶ *Have robbed me.* Rather, have surrounded me ; have environed me—for so the Hebrew word means. ¶ But *I have not forgotten thy law.*

62 At midnight I will rise to give thanks unto thee, because of thy righteous judgments.

63 I *am* a companion *b* of all *them* that fear thee, and of them that keep thy precepts.

64 The earth, O LORD, is full of thy mercy: teach me thy statutes.

TETH.

65 Thou hast dealt well with

b Prov. xiii. 20.

I have not been deterred from keeping it by the dangers to which I have been exposed.

62. *At midnight I will rise to give thanks unto thee.* In the usual times of repose; when men are commonly lying in unconscious slumber. My heart is so interested in thy law—my soul is so full—that I am kept wakeful by meditating upon it, and I arise from my bed and offer thee praise. The Hebrew here means, literally, *the half,* or *halving* of the night, the night considered as divided into two equal portions. The idea is, that his mind was so full of the subject that he would take this unusual time to give vent to his feelings. The mind *may* be so full of love to the law—the word—of God, that nothing will satisfy it but such unusual acts of devotion. The Saviour rose up a great while before day, and went out into a solitary place and there prayed (Mark i. 35); and on one occasion at least he continued all night in prayer to God (Luke vi. 12). ¶ *Because of thy righteous judgments.* I do this on account of the interest which I have in those judgments or laws of righteousness. I love them *as* laws; I love them as *righteous* laws.

63. *I* am *a companion of all* them *that fear thee.* I find my associates and friends among those who worship thee; not with the profane and the wicked. "A man is known by the company that he keeps;" and it is an evidence of piety when we seek our companions and friends among the pious. It shows where the heart is; what the preferences are; what are the tastes; what is the real condition of the soul. We seek our friends in accordance with our tastes and preferences; our love to God is indicated by our love to his friends.

Comp. Ps. cxxxix. 21, 22. ¶ *And of them that keep thy precepts.* That obey thy law. On the sentiment here, comp. Notes on Ps. i. 1. A man may determine much in regard to his own character by asking himself what is the character of his chosen friends and companions. A member of a church should regard it as a dark sign against himself in regard to his piety, if his chosen friends are taken from the world, and not from the professed friends of God; if he finds more pleasure in their society, and in the scenes where they meet, than he does in the society of Christians however humble, or in places where they assemble for prayer and praise.

64. *The earth, O* LORD, *is full of thy mercy.* Full of the proofs of thy goodness and compassion. See Notes on Ps. xxxiii. 5. This is the expression of a heart full of love to God and to his word. In such a state of mind as the psalmist was in, the goodness of God is seen everywhere. The best preparation for seeing evidence that God is good is a heart full of love. Then the proofs of that love spring up on every side—as when we truly love a friend we find constant proofs of his excellency of character. ¶ *Teach me thy statutes.* I desire to see more and more of thy law. Thou art so gracious and merciful, the evidence of thy goodness is so wide-spread round about me, that it leads me to desire to see more and more of thyself and thy law.

65. *Thou hast dealt well with thy servant.* This begins a new division of the psalm, indicated by the Hebrew letter *Teth,* corresponding to our *t.* The use of this letter, however, does nothing to mark the sense. The literal meaning of the phrase here is,

thy servant, O LORD, according unto thy word.

66 Teach *c* me good judgment and knowledge: for I have be-

c Jer. iii. 15.

lieved thy commandments.

67 Before I was afflicted *d* I went astray; but now have I kept thy word.

d Jer. xxxi. 18, 19; Heb. xii. 11.

"Good hast thou done with thy servant;" and the idea is, that God had been good, and had done good to him. In the review of his own life he sees good, and good alone. Even in afflictions and trials this is all that he sees. ¶ *According unto thy word.* According to thy promises; or, according to the principles of thy word. That is, the whole effect of the revealed truth of God upon him had been good. It was designed for his good; it had produced good only. Truth and law do nothing but good, and the welfare of individuals, and of a community, is promoted just in proportion as truth and law prevail.

66. *Teach me good judgment.* The word here rendered *judgment* means, properly, *taste*,—that power by which we determine the quality of things as sweet, bitter, sour, etc. Then it is applied to the mind or understanding, as that by which we determine the moral quality of things, or decide what is right or wrong; wise or foolish; good or evil. Here it means that he desired to have in full exercise the faculty of appreciating what is right, and of distinguishing it from what is wrong. ¶ *And knowledge.* Knowledge of the truth; knowledge of thy will; knowledge of duty. ¶ *For I have believed thy commandments.* I have confided in thy commandments. He believed that such a keeping of the law of God would be connected with a correct view of things. The keeping of the commands of God is one of the best means of growing in true knowledge, and of cultivating the understanding;—of promoting a just taste or perception of what is true, and of developing the powers of the soul in the best proportions. Comp. John vii. 17.

67. *Before I was afflicted.* The Septuagint and the Latin Vulgate,

"Before I was humbled." The Hebrew word has the general sense of being afflicted, and may refer to any kind of trial. ¶ *I went astray.* The Hebrew word means to wander; to err; to do wrong; to transgress. Num. xv. 28; Job xii. 16. It here means that he forgot his duty; that he fell into sin; that he departed from what was right; that he embraced erroneous views; that he lived in the neglect of his soul, the neglect of duty, and the neglect of God. Prosperity had not led him to fulfil duty; to seek salvation; to trust in God. This was, in his case, as it is in thousands of others, the experience of his life. Hence affliction often becomes so necessary to check us when we are going astray, and so useful in recalling us to the ways of duty and of truth. ¶ *But now have I kept thy word.* Since I was afflicted. The effect has been to recall me from my wanderings, and to turn me to paths of duty and holiness. This is an effect often—very often—experienced; this is language which can be used by many a child of God. Of those who are the children of God it may be said that they are *always* benefited *sooner* or *later* by afflictions. It may not be at the time of the affliction (comp. Heb. xii. 11), but the *ultimate* effect is in all cases to benefit them. Some error is corrected; some evil habit changed; some mode of life not consistent with religion is forsaken;—pride is humbled; the heart is quickened in duty; habits of prayer are resumed or formed; the affections are fixed on a better world; the soul is made more gentle, calm, humble, spiritual, pure. Afflictions are among the most precious means of grace. They are entirely under the direction of God. They may be endlessly varied, and adapted

68 Thou *e art* good, and doest good: teach me thy statutes.

69 The proud have forged a lie

e Ps. xxv. 8; Matt. xix. 17.

against me: *but* I will keep thy precepts with *my* whole heart.

70 Their heart is as fat as grease: *but* I delight in thy law.

to the case of every individual. God knows every heart, and the best way to reach any heart. By sickness; by disappointment; by loss of property; by bereavement; by blighted hopes; by the ingratitude of others; by the unkindness of professed friends, and the malice of enemies; by domestic troubles; by the misconduct of children—perhaps the sorest of all human ills, and the hardest to bear;—in ten thousand ways God can reach the heart, and break and crush it, and make it ready for the entrance of truth,—as the farmer breaks and pulverizes the soil by the plough and the harrow, so that it shall be prepared to receive the seed. Comp. Notes on Isa. xxviii. 24–29. Among those things for which good men have most occasion for thankfulness are afflictions; and when we lie down on the bed of death, and look over life and the Divine dealings with us through life, as the glories of heaven are about to open upon us, we shall feel that among the chiefest mercies of God are those dealings of his holy hand, trying at the time, which kept us from going astray, or which recalled us when we had wandered from him, —and *that in our life, now closing, there has not been one trial too much.*

68. *Thou* art *good.* See Notes on Ps. c. 5; cvii. 1. ¶ *And doest good.* As the expression or manifestation of goodness. The goodness of God is not a mere sentiment; not mere feeling; not an inactive principle; not a mere wish:—it finds expression in acts which tend to promote the happiness of his creatures everywhere. ¶ *Teach me thy statutes.* See Notes on vers. 12, 26. As one of the acts of the Divine goodness, the psalmist prays that God will make him more and more acquainted with his law.

69. *The proud.* The psalmist had before referred to the *proud* as those

from whom he had suffered injury, or as having been exposed to their derision. See Notes on ver. 51. He here reverts to another form in which he had suffered from them. ¶ *Have forged a lie against me.* Comp. Job xiii. 4. The word rendered *forged,* means to patch together; and then it is applied to charges or accusations against any one, perhaps from their being *made up* (as they often are) of shreds and patches, — hints, small matters, things having no necessary connexion in themselves, but brought together as if they pertained to the same transaction, — words dropped here and there in conversation, which, being artfully woven together, seem to make out a plausible case against a man. Most slanders are formed and sustained in this way; for it is rare that an absolutely forged slander is uttered against a man, or that a charge is brought which cannot be made to have plausibility from such circumstances as those referred to above. Even the most pure and circumspect cannot always avoid this; for there is something in every man's life of which a malignant and cunning enemy may take advantage, and which he may weave into a story which some will believe, and which it may not be easy to confute. A malicious man may thus start a slander which may require years to correct, and which may even operate injuriously against a man all his life. ¶ But *I will keep thy precepts with* my *whole heart.* Notwithstanding their accusations, and their attempts to turn me away from thee, or to represent me as false and hypocritical. Whatever they may do; whatever reports they may start to my disadvantage, it is my fixed purpose to obey entirely and always thy law. See Notes on ver. 51.

70. *Their heart is as fat as grease.*

71 It *f is* good for me that I
have been afflicted; that I might
learn thy statutes.

72 The *g* law of thy mouth *is*
better unto me than thousands of
gold and silver.

f ver. 67.   *g* Ps. xix. 10; Prov. viii. 11, 19.

JOD.

73 Thy hands have made me,
and fashioned me: give me understanding, *h* that I may learn
thy commandments.

h vers. 34, 144; Ps. cxi. 10.

They are prospered. They have
health, property, influence, comforts
of all kinds. Heaven appears to smile
upon them, and it *seems* as if it were
one effect of a wicked course of life
to *make* men prosperous. See Notes
on Ps. xvii. 10; lxxiii. 7. ¶ But *I
delight in thy law.* Though its observance should not be attended by
any such results as seem to follow
wickedness, though I am poor, emaci-
ated, pale,—disappointed, slandered,
persecuted,—though my lot in life is
among the lowly and the despised,—
yet I will adhere to my purpose to keep
thy law. It is, and it shall be, my
delight, whatever may be the effects
of so observing it. See ver. 35.

71. It is *good for me that I
have been afflicted.* See Notes on
ver. 67. Whatever may have been
the form of the affliction, it was good
for me. The design was benevolent;
the result has been my own benefit.
This will be the experience sooner or
later resulting from all the afflictions
of the righteous. ¶ *That I might
learn thy statutes.* That I might be
brought more fully to understand
what they require; and that I might
be led to conform to them. It is implied here (*a*) that this is the *tendency*
of affliction; and (*b*) that this is an
advantage—a *good.* Anything that
will lead a man to obey God is a
blessing and a favour. Whatever
leads a sinner to secure the salvation
of his soul is a gain to him. No
matter what it may cost; no matter
what he may be required to give up;
no matter to what persecutions and
troubles it may expose him; no matter
what he may suffer, or how long he
may suffer; no matter though poverty,
contempt, toil—even the rack or the
stake—may be the consequence of his

religion,—yet it is a *gain* to him; and
he will be thankful for it in the end,—
for nothing that can be endured in this
life can be compared with the sufferings of the world of despair; nothing
on earth can be " compared with the
glory which shall be revealed in us in
heaven." See Notes on Rom. viii. 18.

72. *The law of thy mouth.* The law
which proceeds out of thy mouth, or
which thou hast spoken. ¶ Is *better
unto me.* The Hebrew is, " Good to
me is the law of thy mouth above
thousands of gold and silver." ¶ *Than
thousands of gold and silver.* Than
any amount of wealth. It is to me
the most valuable possession; that
which I prize above all other things.
Comp. Notes on Ps. xix. 10.

73. *Thy hands have made me.* This
commences a new division of the
psalm, in which each verse begins
with the Hebrew letter *Jod*—or *i*—
the smallest letter in the Hebrew
alphabet, called in Matt. v. 18, *jot;*
" one *jot* or tittle shall in no wise
pass from the law." The words " thy
hands" have made me" are expressive of the idea that he had been
formed or moulded by God,—as the
hands are the instruments by which
we do anything. See Notes on Job
x. 8; comp. Ps. c. 3. ¶ *And fashioned me.* Fitted me; shaped me;
formed me as I am. He had received
alike his existence and the particular
form of his existence from God—as a
man makes a statue or image. Comp.
Ps. cxxxix. 13–16. ¶ *Give me understanding,* etc. As I have derived
my being from thee, so I am wholly
dependent on thee to carry out the
purpose for which I have been made.
My Maker alone can give me understanding. I have no resources in
myself. See ver. 34.

74 They *i* that fear thee will be glad when they see me ; because I have hoped in thy word.

75 I know, O Lord, that thy judgments *are* [1] right, and *that* thou in faithfulness *k* hast afflicted me.

i Ps. xxxiv. 2.   [1] *righteousness.*

76 Let, I pray thee, thy merciful kindness be 2 for my comfort, according to thy word unto thy servant.

77 Let thy tender mercies come unto me, that I may live : for thy law *is* my delight.

k Rev. iii. 19.   2 *to comfort me.*

---

74. *They that fear thee.* Those who worship thee; thy friends; the pious and the good. ¶ *Will be glad when they see me.* They will welcome me to their society ; they will regard and treat me as a friend and brother. It is implied here that he considered this to be an honour—a thing to be desired. He valued the friendship and affection of those who feared and served God, and he made it an object so to live as to be worthy of their affection. Wicked men—men of the world—do *not* value that. They are satisfied with the friendship of those who, like themselves, have no fear of God. To a truly pious mind, the friendship of those who love God is of more value than that of any others ; though in the one case they are poor and despised, and though in the other they are rich and of exalted rank. See Notes on ver. 63. *Because I have hoped in thy word.* See Notes on ver. 49.

75. *I know, O* Lord. I feel assured ; I entertain no doubt on the subject. This was the conviction of the mind of the psalmist in affliction. Mysterious as the trial may have been, hard as it may have been to bear, long as it may have been continued, and varied as may have been the forms of the trial, yet he had no doubt that it was all right; that it was for the best purposes; and that it was in strict accordance with what was best. ¶ *That thy judgments.* This does not here refer to the *laws* of God, but to the Divine dealings; to those afflictions which came in the way of *judgments,* or which might be regarded as expressive of the Divine view of his conduct and life. ¶ *Are right.* Marg., as in Heb., *righteous-*

ness. They were in accordance with what was right; they were so strictly just, that they might be called *righteousness itself.* This implied the utmost confidence in God, the most absolute submission to his will. ¶ *And that thou in faithfulness hast afflicted me.* In faithfulness to my soul; in faithfulness to my own best interest. It was not arbitrary ; it was not from malice ; it was not that the affliction had come by chance; it was because God loved his soul, and sought his welfare. It was because *God* saw that there was some good reason why it should be done; that there was some evil to be checked; some improper conduct to be corrected ; some lesson which he would be the better for learning; some happy influence on his life here, and on his happiness in heaven, which would be more than a compensation for all that he would suffer.

76. *Let, I pray thee, thy merciful kindness be for my comfort.* Marg., as in Heb., *to comfort me.* The word rendered *merciful kindness* means mercy, favour, grace, kindness; and the idea is, that all his consolation—all that he expected or desired—must be derived from mere favour; from the goodness of God. He had no source of comfort in himself, and he had no claim on God for comfort. It was through mercy alone that he could have happiness of any kind. ¶ *According to thy word,* etc. See Notes on ver. 25.

77. *Let thy tender mercies come unto me.* See Notes on ver. 41. ¶ *That I may live.* It is evident that this was uttered in view of some great calamity by which his life was threatened. He was dependent for

78 Let the proud be ashamed;
for they dealt perversely with me
without [l] a cause: *but* I will meditate in thy precepts.
79 Let those that fear thee

[l] 1 Pet. ii. 20.

turn unto me, and those that
have known thy testimonies.
80 Let my heart be sound [m] in
thy statutes, that I be not [n]
ashamed.

[m] Deut. xxvi. 16; Ez. xi. 19.   [n] ver. 6.

life,—for recovery from sickness, or
for deliverance from danger,—wholly
on the compassion of God. ¶ *For
thy law* is *my delight*. See Notes on
ver. 16; comp. vers. 24, 47. This is
urged here as a reason for the Divine
interposition. The meaning is, that
he was a friend of God; that he had
pleasure in his service and in his
commandments; and that he might,
therefore, with propriety, appeal to
God to interpose in his behalf. This
is a proper ground of appeal to God
in our prayers, not on the ground of
merit or claim, but because we may
reasonably suppose that God will be
disposed to protect his friends, and
to deliver them in the day of trouble.

78. *Let the proud be ashamed*. Referring here to his enemies, who appear to have been in the higher ranks
of life, or to have been those who
prided themselves on their wealth,
their station, or their influence. See
Notes on ver. 51. The psalmist asks
here that they might be confounded
or put to shame; that is, that they
might fail of accomplishing their purposes in regard to him. See Notes on
Ps. xxv. 2, 3; Job vi. 20. ¶ *For they
dealt perversely with me*. They were
not honest; they deceived me; they
took advantage of me; they were not
true to their professions of friendship. Comp. Notes on Isa. lix. 3;
Job viii. 3; xxxiv. 12. ¶ *Without a
cause*. Heb., *by a lie*. That is, They
have been guilty of falsehood in their
charges or accusations against me. I
have given them no occasion for such
treatment, and their conduct is based
on an entire misrepresentation. See
Notes on John xv. 25. ¶ But *I will
meditate in thy precepts*. See Notes
on Ps. i. 2. I will not be diverted
from thee, from thy law, from thy
service, by all that man can do to

me; by all the false charges which
the enemies of religion may bring
against me; by all the contempt or
persecution that I may suffer for my
attachment to thee. See Notes on
vers. 23, 69.

79. *Let those that fear thee turn
unto me*. Let thy friends be my friends.
Let them show me favour, and count
me among their companions. If the
great and the powerful turn away
from me; if they persecute me, and
do me wrong; if they cast out my
name as evil, and are unwilling to
associate with me, yet let thy friends,
however poor and humble, regard me
with kindness, and reckon me among
their number, and I shall be satisfied.
¶ *And those that have known thy
testimonies*. Thy law. Those who can
see and appreciate the beauty of thy
commandments. This is the ground
of true friendship in religion,—the
common love of God, of his law, and
of his service. This is a permanent
ground of affection. All friendship
founded on earthly distinctions; all
derived from titled birth,—from rank,
—from affluence,—from civil, military, or naval renown,—from beauty,
strength, or nobleness of form,—must
be temporary; but that which is
founded on attachment to God, to
his law, and to the Saviour, will
abide for ever.

80. *Let my heart be sound*, etc. Heb.,
Be perfect. See Notes on Job i. 1.
The Septuagint here is *immaculate*,
ἄμωμος. So the Latin Vulgate. It
is the expression of a desire that the
heart might be pure; that there
might be no improper attachment
for other objects; that there might
be no defect of love to God. ¶ *That
I be not ashamed*. See Notes on ver. 6.
A man has no occasion to be ashamed
of a pure heart; and that which can

CAPH.

81 My soul fainteth *o* for thy salvation; *but* I hope in thy word.

82 Mine eyes fail for thy word, saying, When wilt thou comfort me?

83 For I am become like a bottle in the smoke; *yet* do I not forget thy statutes.

84 How many *are* the days of thy servant? when *p* wilt thou execute judgment on them that persecute me?

o Ps. lxxxiv. 2.   *p* 2 Thess. i. 6; Rev. vi. 10.

alone keep us from being ultimately ashamed is sincerity, uprightness, and purity in the service of God.

81. *My soul fainteth for thy salvation.* The new division of the psalm, which begins here, is indicated by the Hebrew letter *Caph*, equivalent to *k* or *c* (hard). The word here rendered *fainteth* is the same that in Ps. lxxiii. 26 is translated *faileth:* "My flesh and my heart *faileth.*" The idea is, that his strength gave way; he had such an intense *desire* for salvation that he became weak and powerless. Any strong emotion *may* thus prostrate us; and the love of God—the desire of his favour—the longing for heaven—may be so intense as to produce this result. ¶ *I hope in thy word.* I trust in thy promises, and am sustained. My powers, which would otherwise wholly fail, are upheld *by* thy word, and on that I rely. See ver. 74.

82. *Mine eyes fail for thy word.* The same word in Hebrew as in the previous verse and in Ps. lxxiii. 26. The idea here is that of looking out for a thing—of "*straining* the eyes"—so that their power becomes exhausted. The language expresses a longing desire — a waiting — an intense wish—for a thing, as when we look for a ship long expected, or for a friend long absent, or for help when in danger. Such a desire the psalmist had for the word of God; for Divine truth. ¶ *Saying, When wilt thou comfort me?* How long shall I be compelled to wait for comfort? How often in the Psalms do the expressions occur, "*When,*" and "*How long!*" How often in the life of the believer now are similar expressions appropriate! God often seems greatly to try the faith and patience of his people by mere *delay;* and the strength of faith and the power of religion are shown in such circumstances by persevering faith in the Divine promises, even when there seems to be no evidence that he will interpose.

83. *For I am become like a bottle in the smoke.* Bottles in the East were commonly made of skins. See Notes on Matt. ix. 17. Such "bottles," hanging in tents where the smoke had little opportunity to escape, would, of course, become dark and dingy, and would thus be emblems of distress, discomfort, and sorrow. The meaning here is, that, by affliction and sorrow, the psalmist had been reduced to a state which would be well represented by such a bottle. A somewhat similar idea occurs in Ps. xxii. 15: "My strength is dried up like a potsherd." See Notes on that place. ¶ Yet *do I not forget thy statutes.* Comp. Notes on ver. 51. Though thus deeply afflicted, though without comfort or peace, yet I do, I will, maintain allegiance to thee and thy law. The doctrine is that distress, poverty, sorrow, penury, and rags—the most abject circumstances of life—will not turn away a true child of God from obeying and serving him. True religion will abide all these tests. Lazarus from the deepest poverty—from beggary—from undressed sores—went up to Abraham's bosom.

84. *How many* are *the days of thy servant?* I cannot hope to live long. I am sinking under my burdens. If I am, therefore, to see the accomplishment of my desires—my deliverance from my enemies and my troubles—it must be soon. This is not a desire to be told how long he was to live, as if it were an object of desire to know

85 The proud have digged *q* pits for me, which *are* not after thy law.

86 All *r* thy commandments *are* [1] faithful : they persecute me wrongfully ; help thou me.

87 They had almost consumed me upon earth : but I forsook not

q Ps. xxxv. 7.   *r* ver. 138.

thy precepts.

88 Quicken me after thy loving-kindness ; so shall I keep the testimony of thy mouth.

LAMED.

89 For *s* ever, O LORD, thy word is settled in heaven.

[1] *faithfulness.*   *s* Matt. xxiv. 34, 35.

---

this, but it is a method of saying that he could not live long under these circumstances, and therefore he offered this earnest prayer that God would interpose and save him *soon.* ¶ *When wilt thou execute judgment on them that persecute me?* How long shall this be delayed? I look for this ; I expect it ; I rely on thy promise that it shall be done ; but if done so that *I* shall see it, it must soon be done, for I shall soon sink into the grave. It is a prayer that God would come and do quickly what he felt assured he would do, in delivering him from his foes.

85. *The proud.* Those in high life, or of exalted rank. See Notes on ver. 51. ¶ *Have digged pits for me.* See Notes on Ps. vii. 15. Comp. Ps. xxxv. 7 ; lvii. 6 ; xciv. 13. ¶ *Which* are *not after thy law.* The word *which* here refers not to the *pits,* but to the *proud.* They who have done this are men who do not regard thy commands ; men who are open and public offenders. It is that class of men with whom I have to contend—men who set at defiance all the laws of God ; men high in rank, who wield great power, and who have no regard to the law of God in their conduct. Even they have sought my destruction in the meanest way possible—by covert arts, by underhanded means, by digging pits, as they would for wild beasts.

86. *All thy commandments* are *faithful.* Marg., *faithfulness.* The idea in the Hebrew is that they are worthy to be relied on. They are founded in truth, and they should secure our confidence. ¶ *They persecute me wrongfully,* etc. Heb., a *lie,*

or *falsehood.* That is, There is a *lie* or *falsehood* at the foundation of their persecutions. Those persecutions are not based on any just views of what I am, or of the treatment which I ought to receive at the hand of my fellow-men. They charge on me things which are not true, and they act accordingly. See Notes on ver. 78.

87. *They had almost consumed me upon earth.* The word which is here translated *consumed* is the same which is used in ver. 81, and there rendered *fainteth.* See Notes on that verse. The idea is, that their persecutions had been so severe, and so long continued, that his strength was almost exhausted ; he was ready to faint and to die. ¶ *But I forsook not thy precepts.* I still adhered to thee, even in the extremity of my suffering. The effect of persecution was not to drive me from thee, or to lead me to abandon thee. See Notes on vers. 61, 69.

88. *Quicken me.* Cause me to live ; revive me. See Notes on Ps. lxxi. 20 ; Eph. ii. 1. Comp. Ps. lxxx. 18 ; Rom. viii. 11 ; 1 Pet. iii. 18 ; John vi. 63. ¶ *After thy loving-kindness.* Thy mercy ; thy grace ; thy compassion. That is, Let the measure of the grace given to me be thine own benevolent nature, and not my deserts. That is all I ask ; that is all I could desire. ¶ *So shall I keep the testimony of thy mouth.* Which proceeds out of thy mouth. His hope of being able to keep it was founded on the grace and mercy which he besought God to bestow upon him.

89. *For ever, O LORD, thy word is settled in heaven.* This commences a

90 Thy faithfulness *is* [1] unto
all generations; thou hast established the earth, and it [2] abideth.

91 They continue this day according to thine ordinances: *t*
for all *are* thy servants.

[1] *to generation and generation, Ps. lxxxix. 1.*

92 Unless thy law *had been* my
delights, I should then have
perished in mine affliction.

93 I will never forget thy precepts: for with them thou hast
quickened me.

[2] *standeth.*   *t* Jer. xxxiii. 25.

---

new division of the psalm, indicated
by the Hebrew letter *Lamed*, or *l.*
On the meaning of the passage, see
Notes on Ps. lxxxix. 2. The word
rendered *settled* means properly *to
set, to put, to place;* and then, to
stand, to cause to stand, to set up, as
a column, Gen. xxxv. 20; an altar,
Gen. xxxiii. 20; a monument, 1 Sam.
xv. 12. The meaning here is, that
the word—the law—the promise—
of God was made firm, established,
stable, in heaven; and would be so
for ever and ever. What God had
ordained as law would always remain
law; what he had affirmed would
always remain true; what he had
promised would be sure for ever.

90. *Thy faithfulness.* The accomplishment of thy promises. ¶ *Is
unto all generations.* Marg., to *generation and generation.* From one
generation to another. The generations of men change and pass away,
but thy promises do not change.
They are as applicable to one generation as to another; they meet every
generation alike. The people of no
one age can lay any exclusive claim
to them, or feel that they were made
only for them. They are as universal—as much adapted to the new
generations that come upon the earth
—as the light of the sun, ever-
enduring, is; or as the fountains and
streams, which flow from age to age.
¶ *Thou hast established the earth,
and it abideth.* Marg., *Standeth.* It
is firm. The earth thus established
or made firm, is an illustration of thy
faithfulness, and of the stability and
permanence of thy promises. It is
the same from generation to generation, with its rivers, streams, and
fountains; with its fruits and flowers;
with its balmy air and its sweet

prospects; with its riches of gold
and silver; with its pearls and dia-
monds; with its treasures of land
and ocean. So is the word of God
—so are the gracious promises which
he has addressed to men—the same
in every age.

91. *They continue this day according to thine ordinances.* According
to thy *judgments* (Heb.); that is, thy
commands. They *stand* (Heb.) as
thou hast appointed; they are what
thou didst design them to be. The
original purpose in their creation is
carried out, and they thus furnish an
illustration of the stability of thy
government and the permanency of
thy law. ¶ *For all* are *thy servants.*
All worlds obey thy commands; all
are under thy control. They *show*
that they are thy servants by the
conformity of their movements to
the laws which thou hast impressed
on them.

92. *Unless thy law* had been *my
delights.* See Notes on vers. 16, 24.
Unless I had had pleasure in thy
law, thy word, thy truth; unless I
had derived support and consolation
in that. ¶ *I should then have perished
in mine affliction.* I should have
sunk under my burden. I should
not have been able to hold up under
the weight of sorrow and trial. How
often the people of God can say this!
How often may each one in the
course of his life say this! "I should
have sunk a thousand times," said a
most excellent, but much afflicted,
man to me, "if it had not been for
one declaration in the word of God,
—'The Eternal God is thy refuge,
and underneath are the everlasting
arms.'"

93. *I will never forget thy precepts.* Thy laws; thy truth. I will

94 I *am* thine, save " me : for I have sought thy precepts.

95 The wicked have waited for me, to destroy me : *but* I will

u Zeph. iii. 17.

consider thy testimonies.

96 I have seen an end of all perfection : *but* thy commandment *is* exceeding broad.

bear them in mind for ever. To all eternity they shall be the object of my meditation. ¶ *For with them thou hast quickened me.* By them thou hast given me life, spiritual life. Comp. Notes on James i. 18. This is stated as a reason why he would never suffer the truth of God to pass out of his mind. By that truth he had been made really to live. He had been brought from spiritual death to spiritual life. He saw before him now, as the result of that, an endless career of blessedness. How *could* he ever forget that which had wrought such a change in his character and condition; which had inspired such hopes; which had opened before him such an immortal career of glory !

94. *I* am *thine.* All that he had, and was, belonged to God. This is an expression of a *fact*, and of a *purpose*:—a *fact* about which he had no doubt; a *purpose* ever to be the Lord's. This is indicative of the real state of feeling in the heart of a pious man. He feels that he *is* the Lord's; he has no other desire than to *be* his for ever. ¶ *Save me.* Deliver me from my enemies; from sin; from hell. As he *belonged* to God, he prayed that God would save and preserve his own. ¶ *For I have sought thy precepts.* I feel assured or confident that this has been the aim and purpose of my life. On this ground I plead that thou wilt keep and preserve me. A man who feels assured that he is a friend of God has a *right* to appeal to him for protection, and he will not appeal to him in vain.

95. *The wicked have waited for me to destroy me.* That is, they have lain in wait ; or, they have laid a plan. They are watching the opportunity to do it. ¶ But *I will*

consider thy testimonies. I will think of them; I will adhere to them; I will find my support in them; I will not be driven from my adhesion to them by an apprehension of what man can do to me.

96. *I have seen an end of all perfection.* The word which is here rendered *perfection*—תִּכְלָה, *tichlah* —occurs only in this place ; but a similar word from the same root— תַּכְלִית, *tachlith*—occurs in the following places : — in Neh. iii. 21, and Job xxvi. 10, rendered *end ;* in Job xi. 7, xxviii. 3, rendered *perfection ;* and in Ps. cxxxix. 22, rendered *perfect.* It means properly *completion, perfection ;* or, as others suppose, *hope, confidence.* It is rendered, in the Septuagint and Latin Vulgate, *consummation.* Luther renders it, "of all things." It is proper here to apply it to character ; to perfect virtue, or to claims to perfect virtue, — either in one's-self or in others. The word rendered *end* here refers not to the fact of its existence, or to its duration, but to a limit or boundary as to its extent. To all claims to perfection made by man, he had seen an end or limit. He had examined all which claimed to be perfect ; he had found it defective ; he had so surveyed and examined the matter, as to be able to say that there could be no claim to perfection which would prove good. All claim to perfection on the part of man must be abandoned for ever. ¶ But *thy commandment* is *exceeding broad.* The word *but* is not in the original, and enfeebles the sense. The idea is, that the law of God, as he now saw it, was of such a nature—was so "*broad* "—as to demonstrate that there *could* be no just claim to perfection among men. All claims to perfection had arisen from the fact

MEM.

97 O how love I thy law! it *is*
v my meditation all the day.
98 Thou, through thy com-
mandments, hast made me wiser

v Ps. i. 2.   [1] *it* is.

than mine enemies: for [1] they
are ever with me.
99 I *w* have more understanding than all my teachers : for thy
testimonies *are* my meditation.

w Deut. iv. 6, 8; 2 Tim. iii. 15.

that the law was *not* properly understood, that its true nature was
not seen. Men thought that they
were perfect, but it was because
they had no just view of the extent and the spirituality of the law
of God. They set up an imperfect
standard; and when they became
conformed to that standard, as they
might do, they imagined themselves
to be perfect; but when their conduct was compared with a higher
and more just standard—the law of
God—it could not but be seen that
they were imperfect men. That law
had claims which they had not met,
and never would meet, in this life.
It is very easy to flatter ourselves
that we are perfect, if we make our
own *standard* of character; it is not
possible for man to set up a claim to
perfection, if he measures himself by
the standard of God's word; and all
the claims of men to perfection are
made simply because they do not
properly understand what the law of
God requires. Comp. Notes on Job
ix. 20.
97. *O how love I thy law!* This
commences a new division of the
Psalm, indicated by the Hebrew
letter *Mem—m.* The expression here,
"O how love I thy law," implies *intense* love,—as if a man were astonished at the fervour of his own emotion. His love was so ardent that it
was amazing and wonderful to himself;—perhaps wonderful that he, a
sinner, should love the law of God at
all; wonderful that he should ever
have been brought *so* to love a law
which condemned himself. Any man
who reflects on what his feelings are
by nature in regard to religion, will
be filled with wonder that he loves it
at all; all who are truly religious
ought to be so filled with love to it,

that it will be difficult for them to
find words to express the intensity of
their affection. ¶ *It* is *my meditation
all the day.* See Notes on Ps. i. 2.
98. *Thou, through thy commandments.* By the teaching and power
of thy law. ¶ *Hast made me wiser
than mine enemies.* I have a better
understanding of thee, of thy law, of
the duties of this life, and in regard to
the life to come, than my enemies
have,—not because I am naturally
better, or because I have higher endowments by nature, but because *thou*
hast made me wiser than they are.
The rendering of this first clause of
the verse now most approved by interpreters is, "Thy commandments
make me more wise than my enemies
are," though this requires a singular
verb to be construed with a plural
noun (Professor Alexander). So De
Wette renders it. ¶ *For they* are
ever with me. Marg., as in Heb., *it
is ever with me.* The reference is to
the law or commandments of God.
The meaning is, that that law was
never out of his mind; that he was
constantly thinking about it; and
that it unfolded such wisdom to him
as to make him superior to all his
foes;—to give him a better understanding of life, its design, its duties,
and its obligations, than his enemies
had. The best instructor in true
wisdom is the revealed word of God,
—the Bible.
99. *I have more understanding than
all my teachers.* Referring perhaps
to those who had given him instruction in early life. By constant meditation on the law of God, he had, in
the progress of years, advanced to a
point beyond that to which they had
arrived. He had improved upon their
suggestions and instructions, until he
had surpassed them in knowledge.

100 I understand more than the ancients; *x* because I keep thy precepts.

101 I have refrained *y* my feet

x Job xxxii. 7—9.   *y* Prov. i. 15.

from every evil way, that I might keep thy word.

102 I have not departed from thy judgments : for thou hast taught me.

His *design* in saying this was to set forth the excellency and the fulness of the law of God, and to show how the study of it was fitted to enlarge the understanding. In early life the wisdom of teachers seems to be far beyond anything that we can hope to reach ; yet a few years of study and meditation may place us far beyond them. What those teachers *seemed* to be to us, however, when we were young, may serve ever onward as a means of comparison when we wish to speak of the greatness of human attainments. So the psalmist says that he had now reached a point which seemed to him in early life to be wonderful, and to be beyond what he had then hoped ever to attain. He had now reached that point ; he had gone beyond it. ¶ *For thy testimonies* are *my meditation.* Comp. Ps. i. 2 ; 2 Tim. iii. 15. All this knowledge he had obtained by meditation on the law of God ; by the study of Divine truth. The effect of that constant study was seen in the knowledge which he now possessed, and which seemed to surprise even himself as compared with the brightest anticipations of his early years.

100. *I understand more than the ancients.* Heb., The old men. It does not refer, as the word *ancients* does with us, to the men of former times, but to aged men. They have treasured up wisdom. They have had the advantage of experience, of study, and of observation. They, therefore, like teachers, become a standard by which we measure our own attainments, as the boy hardly hopes to gain that amount of knowledge which he observes in men who are venerable in years, and who are remarkable for their acquirements. Comp. Job xii. 12 : " With the ancient is wisdom, and in length of days under-

standing." Job xxxii. 7 : " I said, Days should speak, and multitude of years should teach wisdom." Comp. 1 Kings iv. 30, 31. Yet the psalmist says that he *had* reached this point, and had even gone *beyond* what he had once thought he could never attain. ¶ *Because I keep thy precepts.* It is all the result of an honest endeavour to do right ; to observe law; to keep the commands of God. Obedience to the law of God will do more than any mere human teaching to make a man truly wise.

101. *I have refrained my feet from every evil way.* I have walked in the path which thy law marks out. I have avoided the way of wickedness, and have not yielded to the seductions of a sinful life. ¶ *That I might keep thy word.* I have avoided all those allurements which would turn me from obedience, and which would prevent a right observance of thy commands. This indicates a *purpose* and a *desire* to keep the law of God, and shows the method which he adopted in order to do this. That method was to guard against everything which would turn him from obedience ; it was, to make obedience to the law of God the great aim of the life.

102. *I have not departed from thy judgments.* Thy law ; thy commands. This cannot mean that he had *never* done this, but that as a great rule of life he had not done it. The character and aim of his life had been obedience, not disobedience. A man may honestly say this, though he may be conscious of much imperfection, and may feel that he has not *perfectly* carried out such an aim and purpose. No one can be a truly pious man, or have evidence of personal religion, who cannot say in sincerity that he has " not departed " in this sense, " from

103 How sweet *z* are thy words
unto my ¹ taste ! *yea, sweeter* than
honey to my mouth !
104 Through thy precepts I
get understanding : therefore I
hate *a* every false way.

z Job xxiii. 12 ; Ps. xix. 10.			¹ *palate.*

NUN.

105 Thy word *is* a ² lamp *b* unto
my feet, and a light unto my
path.
106 I have sworn, *c* and I will

a Prov. viii. 13.			² Or, *candle.*
b Prov. vi. 23.			*c* Neh. x. 29.

the judgments " (the commands) of
God ; who cannot look back on his
life and say that his course—his aim
—his *character*—since he became a
professor of religion—*has* been one of
obedience to God. Comp. 1 John iii.
7-9. ¶ *For thou hast taught me.*
Not to himself was this to be traced,
but to God ; not to any wisdom of
his own, but to that which was given
him from on high.
103. *How sweet are thy words unto
my taste,* etc. Marg., as in Heb.,
palate. The reference is to the
taste, perhaps because the sense of
taste was supposed to reside in the
palate. The Hebrew word *may* include also the whole of the inside of
the mouth. The word rendered *sweet*
does not occur elsewhere. It properly means *to be smooth,* and hence
is applied to kind or agreeable words.
On the sentiment here, see Notes on
Ps. xix. 10.
104. *Through thy precepts I get
understanding.* A true understanding ; a correct view of things ; a
knowledge of thee, of myself, of the
human character, of the destiny of
man, of the way of salvation—the
best, and the only essential knowledge for man. This knowledge the
psalmist obtained from the " precepts " of God ; that is, *all* that God
had communicated by revelation. This
passage expresses in few words what
had been said more at length in vers.
98-100. ¶ *Therefore I hate every
false way.* I see that which is right
and true, and I pursue it. In proportion as I have a just knowledge of
truth and duty, I hate that which is
false and evil.
105. *Thy word* is *a lamp unto my
feet.* This begins a new portion of
the psalm, indicated by the Hebrew

letter *Nun,* equivalent to our *n.* The
margin here is *candle.* The Hebrew
word means a light, lamp, candle.
The idea is, that the word of God is
like a torch or lamp to a man in a
dark night. It shows him the way ;
it prevents his stumbling over obstacles, or falling down precipices, or
wandering off into paths which would
lead into danger, or would turn him
away altogether from the path to life.
Comp. Notes on 2 Pet. i. 19. ¶ *And
a light unto my path.* The same idea
substantially is presented here. It is
a light which shines on the road that
a man treads, so that he may *see* the
path, and that he may see any danger
which may be *in* his path. The expression is very beautiful, and is full of
instruction. He who makes the word
of God his guide, and marks its teachings, is *in* the right way. He will
clearly see the path. He will be able
to mark the road in which he ought
to go, and to avoid all those by-paths
which would lead him astray. He
will see *where* those by-roads turn off
from the main path,—often at a very
small angle, and so that there seems
to be no divergence. He will see any
obstruction which may lie in his path ;
any declivity or precipice which may
be near, and down which, in a dark
night, one might fall. Man *needs*
such a guide, and the Bible *is* such a
guide. Comp. Notes on ver. 9.
106. *I have sworn.* I have solemnly
purposed ; I have given to this purpose the solemnity and sanction of an
oath. That is, I have called God to
witness ; I have formed the purpose
in his presence, and with the consciousness that his eye is upon me.
So all who make a profession of religion solemnly vow or swear. They
do it in the house of God ; they do it

perform *it,* that I will keep thy righteous judgments.

107 I am afflicted very much : quicken me, O LORD, according unto thy word.

108 Accept, I beseech thee,

d Heb. xiii. 15.

the *d* freewill offerings of my mouth, O LORD, and teach me thy judgments.

109 My soul *is* continually in *e* my hand : yet do I not forget thy law.

e Job xiii. 14.

in the presence of the Discerner of hearts ; they do it at the communion table ; they do it at the family altar ; they do it in the closet, when alone with God. ¶ *And I will perform* it. Heb., I will establish it, or make it to stand. It shall not be a mere purpose. It shall be accomplished. This also is the resolution of all who make a true profession of religion. It is their intention—their solemn determination —to carry out that vow to its full accomplishment, always, and in every place, while life lasts, and for ever. A man who makes a profession of religion, intending *not* to carry out what is fairly implied in such a profession, is a hypocrite. Unless there is a solemn purpose to keep the law of God, and always to keep it,—to do what is fairly implied in a profession of religion, and always to do it,—to defend the truth according to his best means of knowing it, and always to defend it,—he cannot possibly be a sincere friend of God ; he cannot be truly a religious man. He cannot be loyal to his country who *designs* to violate any one of its just laws ; he cannot be an obedient child who *intends* to disobey the laws of a parent. ¶ *That I will keep thy righteous judgments.* Not implying that there are any of the judgments of God which are *not* righteous, but meaning to characterize all his judgments or laws *as* righteous.

107. *I am afflicted very much.* The form of the affliction is not mentioned. There are frequent allusions in the psalm to the fact that the author was and had been afflicted—as, in fact, must be the case in the life of every good man. Comp. vers. 71, 75. If David was the author of the psalm, we know that there were numerous

VOL. III.

occasions in his life when this language would be appropriate. As designed for the people of God at all times, it was important that there should be these allusions to affliction. ¶ *Quicken me,* etc. Make me live ; give me life and vigour, that I may bear up under my trials. See Notes on ver. 25.

108. *Accept, I beseech thee, the free-will offerings of my mouth.* On the meaning of the word here rendered *free-will,* see Notes on Ps. cx. 3. It conveys the idea that there is no constraint or compulsion ; that the offering is a prompting of the heart. The offering might be that of flour, or grain, or fruits, or property of any kind, as devoted to God ; or it might be, as here, an offering of the lips, expressed in prayer and praise. Either of them might be acceptable to God ; —their being accepted in either case would depend on the good pleasure of God, and hence the psalmist prays that his offering *might* be thus acceptable. Comp. Heb. xiii. 15. ¶ *And teach me thy judgments.* Thy commands ; thy laws. See Notes on ver. 12.

109. *My soul* is *continually in my hand.* The Septuagint renders this, " My soul is always in *thy* hands," but the Hebrew will not admit of this construction. The idea in the original is that his soul—his life— was always in jeopardy. The expression seems to be proverbial. Anything taken in the hand is liable to be rudely snatched away. Thus a casket of jewels, or a purse of gold in the hand, may at any moment be seized by robbers. See Notes on Job xiii. 14. Comp. 1 Sam. xix. 5 ; Judges xii. 3. The meaning here is, that his life was constantly in danger. ¶ *Yet*

P

110 The wicked have laid a snare *f* for me: yet I erred not from thy precepts.

111 Thy testimonies have I taken as an heritage for ever: for they *are* the rejoicing *g* of my heart.

f Prov. i. 11, 12.   *g* Jer. xv. 16.

112 I have inclined *h* mine heart to ¹ perform thy statutes alway, *even unto* the end.

SAMECH.

113 I hate *vain* *k* thoughts: but thy law do I love.

h 2 Chron. xix. 3.   ¹ *do.*
i Rev. ii. 10.   *k* Jer. iv. 14.

do I not forget thy law. Notwithstanding the danger to which I am exposed, and the care necessary to defend my life, I do not allow my mind to be turned from meditating on thy law, nor do I suffer any danger to deter me from obeying it. Comp. Notes on ver. 61.

110. *The wicked have laid a snare for me.* As men do to take wild beasts or birds. See Notes on ver. 85. Comp. Notes on Job xviii. 8, 10; Ps. ix. 15; lxix. 22. See also vers. 61, 69. ¶ *Yet I erred not from thy precepts.* Notwithstanding the danger to which I was exposed, I maintained a steadfast adherence to thy commandments. I was not deterred from obeying them by any peril which beset me.

111. *Thy testimonies.* Thy law; thy revealed will;—the revelation which thou hast given considered as thy solemn *testimony* as to what is true and right. ¶ *Have I taken as an heritage for ever.* As my inheritance; as my property; as that which I consider to be of real and permanent value. The Hebrew word here used —לַחֵנ, *nahhal*—means to receive as a possession; to acquire; to possess as wealth; and then, to inherit. It is usually applied to the possession of the promised land as an inheritance. Here it means that the law of God was to him *as* such a possession. He regarded it as one does a rich inheritance. He chose it as his portion above all things else. ¶ *For they* are *the rejoicing of my heart.* My happiness is in them. I find constant comfort in them. See vers. 77, 92. Comp. Notes on Ps. i. 2.

112. *I have inclined mine heart.* The Hebrew word means properly to stretch out; to extend—as the hand.

Ex. viii. 6, 17. Then it means to incline, to bow, to depress. Here the idea is, that he had *given* that *direction* to the inclinations of his heart; he had resolved or purposed. He refers to an act of choice on his part, meaning that he had preferred this course, or that he had made this a solemn intention. Though every right inclination of the human heart is to be traced to the Divine agency, yet it is also true that man is active in religion,—or that his own mind resolves, chooses, and prefers,—and that true religion *is* the actual *choice* or *preference* of all who serve God aright. See Notes on ver. 59. ¶ *To perform thy statutes alway.* Marg., as in Heb., *to do.* He meant to do the will of God. He intended to do this constantly; even for ever. No man can be a truly pious man who has any disposition, or any purpose, *ever* to turn away from the service of God. ¶ *Even unto the end.* See ver. 33. To the end of life; to the end of all things.

113. *I hate* vain *thoughts.* This commences a new portion of the psalm, distinguished by the Hebrew letter *Samech*, answering to our *s.* The word rendered "vain thoughts" occurs only in this place. It is rendered by the Septuagint, παρανόμους —transgressors. So the Latin Vulgate. Luther renders it *die Flatter-geister*, the frivolous-minded. The word means *divided;* a man of a *divided mind;* a man who has no sure faith in regard to Divine things, but is driven hither and thither; a sceptic; a doubter. Comp. James i. 8. Thus it refers not to his own thoughts primarily, as being "vain" or worthless, but to a state of mind or heart

114 Thou *l art* my hiding place and my shield: I hope in thy word.

115 Depart *m* from me, ye evildoers: for I will keep the commandments of my God.

116 Uphold me according unto

l Ps. xxxii. 7.. *m* Ps. cxxxix. 19; 1 Cor. xv. 33.

thy word, that I may live: and let me not be ashamed *n* of my hope.

117 Hold thou me up, and I shall be safe: and I will have respect unto thy statutes continually.

n Rom. v. 5.

in general, where there is no firmness, no stability, no settled view:—a state of mind wavering, doubtful, sceptical, in regard to religion. What is implied here in reference to what he *loved*,— by stating (in the way of contrast) what he "hated,"—would be a mind which was settled in its convictions of truth, and firm in its adherence to truth; a mind which was steadfast in religion, and not vacillating, sceptical, or uncertain on the subject. This denotes that the psalmist sought such a state of mind for himself, and that he valued it in others. ¶ *But thy law do I love.* I have no "divided" or unsettled feelings in regard to that. I am conscious of a firm attachment to it. This thought he has repeatedly expressed in the psalm.

114. *Thou* art *my hiding place.* See Notes on Ps. xxxii. 7, where the same expression occurs. ¶ *And my shield.* See Notes on Ps. v. 12; lxxxiv. 11. ¶ *I hope in thy word.* See vers. 74, 81.

115. *Depart from me, ye evil-doers.* Workers of iniquity; bad men. See Notes on Ps. vi. 8. This indicates a determined purpose that nothing should deter or allure him from the service of God. A man who wishes to serve God, and lead a religious life, *must* separate himself from the society, as such, of unprincipled men. ¶ *For I will keep the commandments of my God.* This is my fixed resolution. It may be remarked here (1) that bad men *will* turn away from the society of one who has formed such a resolution, and who carries it out; (2) the resolution is a necessary one to be formed and executed, if a man will serve God; (3) the formation and execution of

such a purpose, is the best way to get rid of the society of bad men.

116. *Uphold me.* Sustain me in the trials and the temptations of life. Help me to bear afflictions without sinking under them; to meet temptations without yielding to them; to encounter opposition from the enemies of religion without being overcome. ¶ *According unto thy word.* (1) According to the requirements of thy word,—that I may be conformed to them; (2) according to the promises of thy word,—that they may be verified in me. ¶ *That I may live.* That my life may not be cut off by my foes, and that I may not sink under my burdens. ¶ *And let me not be ashamed of my hope.* The meaning of this is, Let not my hope prove to be delusive and vain; let it not be seen at last that it is worthless, or that religion has no power to accomplish what it promises. See Notes on Ps. vi. 10; xxv. 2, 3; xxxi. 1. The phrase does not mean, as it would seem to signify, Let me not blush, or be unwilling to acknowledge my hope, or to profess that I am a friend of God. That *would be*, indeed, a proper prayer, but it is not the prayer here.

117. *Hold thou me up.* Keep me from falling in the trials and temptations of life. The Hebrew word means to prop, uphold, support. The Septuagint is, "Aid me." ¶ *And I shall be safe.* And I shall be *saved;* or, that I may be *saved.* It is an acknowledgment of entire dependence on God for salvation—temporal and eternal. ¶ *And I will have respect,* etc. I will *look* to thy statutes; I will have them always in my eye. Comp. Notes on ver. 6.

118 Thou hast trodden *o* down all them that err from thy statutes: for their deceit *is* *p* falsehood.

119 Thou [1] puttest away all the wicked of the earth *like* dross : *q*

o Mal. iv. 3.   *p* 1 John ii. 21.
          [1] *causest to cease.*

therefore I love thy testimonies.

120 My flesh trembleth *r* for fear of thee; and I am afraid of thy judgments.

AIN.

121 I have done judgment and

q Ez. xxii: 18.   *r* Hab. iii. 16.

---

118. *Thou hast trodden down all them that err from thy statutes.* Comp. Notes on ver. 21. Rather, "Thou hast made light of," or "thou despisest." The Hebrew word means properly to suspend in a balance; to weigh. Then it means to lift up lightly or easily; and then, to make light of; to contemn; to regard anything as *light.* The Septuagint and Latin Vulgate render it, *Thou dost despise.* That is, God regards them as of no account; as a light substance of no value; as chaff which the wind carries away. Comp. Job xxi. 18; Ps. i. 4; xxxv. 5; Isa. xvii. 13. ¶ *For their deceit* is *falsehood.* This *seems* to be a truism—for deceit must imply falsehood. In the original this is an emphatic way of declaring the whole thing to be false, as the Hebrew language often expresses emphasis by mere repetition,—thus *"pits, pits,"* meaning *many pits.* The psalmist *first* characterizes their conduct as *deceitful*—as that which cannot be relied on—as that which must fail in the end; he then speaks of this *system* on which they acted as altogether a *"lie"*—as that which is utterly "false;"—thus giving, as it were, *a double emphasis* to the statement, and showing how *utterly* delusive and vain it must be.

119. *Thou puttest away all the wicked of the earth.* Marg., *causest to cease.* Literally : "Dross—thou makest all the wicked of the earth to cease." They are seen by the psalmist as dross, and then he says that God had treated them as such. ¶ Like *dross.* The *scoriæ* of metals, or of a furnace. This dross is cast out as of no value. So the wicked are regarded by God. ¶ *Therefore I love*

thy testimonies. I love a law which condemns sin. I love a government which ferrets out and punishes the guilty. This is a leading object with all just governments; and this we approve in all governments. As the Divine government makes this an object, and as it will accomplish this more perfectly than any other administration, so it is more worthy of confidence than any other. As it is the only government that does this perfectly, so it is the only one that is worthy of unlimited confidence.

120. *My flesh trembleth for fear of thee.* I stand in awe of thee. I shudder at the consciousness of thy presence. See Hab. iii. 16; Heb. xii. 21; Joel ii. 10; Nah. i. 5. There is nothing unaccountable in this. Any man would tremble, should God manifest himself to him as he might do; and it is possible that the *mind* may have such an overpowering sense of the presence and majesty of God, that the *body* shall be agitated, lose its strength, and with the deepest alarm fall to the earth. Comp. Dan. x. 8; Rev. i. 17. No man could meet one of the departed dead, or a good angel, without this fear; how much less could he meet God! ¶ *And I am afraid of thy judgments.* Of thy laws or commands. My mind is filled with awe at the strictness, the spirituality, the severity of thy law. Reverence—awe—is one of the essential elements of all true religion.

121. *I have done judgment and justice.* This commences a new division of the psalm, indicated by the Hebrew letter *Ain*—a letter which cannot well be represented in the English alphabet, as there is, in fact, no letter in our language exactly cor-

justice: leave ˢ me not to mine oppressors.

122 Be surety ᵗ for thy servant for good: let not the proud oppress me.

123 Mine eyes fail for thy salvation, and for the word of thy

ˢ Ps. xxxvii. 32, 33.   ᵗ Heb. vii. 22.

righteousness.

124 Deal ᵘ with thy servant according unto thy mercy, and teach me thy statutes.

125 I ᵛ am thy servant; give me understanding, that I may know thy testimonies.

ᵘ Ps. ciii. 10.   ᵛ Ps. cxvi. 16.

responding with it. It would be best represented probably by what are called "*breathings*" in Greek. The meaning of the first part of this verse is, "I have led a righteous and upright life." It is equivalent to saying that he had kept the law of God, or had made that the rule of his conduct. ¶ *Leave me not to mine oppressors.* To the men who would do me wrong; who seek my hurt. He urged this on the ground that he had been obedient to the Divine law, and might, therefore, with propriety, make this request, or might claim the Divine protection. Man has no merit of his own, and no claim on God; but when he is his true friend, it is not improper to expect that he will interpose in his behalf; nor is it improper to present this in the form of a prayer. Our loving God, and serving him, though it *is* done imperfectly, is, in fact, a reason why he should and will interpose in our behalf.

122. *Be surety for thy servant for good.* On the meaning of the word here rendered "be surety," see Notes on Job xvii. 3, and Isa. xxxviii. 14, in both which places the same Hebrew word occurs. In Isaiah it is rendered "*undertake* for me." The word means, properly, *to mix, to mingle;* hence, to braid, to interweave; then, to exchange, to barter. Then it means to mix or intermingle *interests;* to unite ourselves with others so that their interests come to be our own; and hence, to take one under our protection, to become answerable for, to be a surety for:—as, when one endorses a note for another, he *mingles* his own interest, reputation, and means with his. So Christ becomes

the security or surety—ἔγγυος—of his people, Heb. vii. 22. The prayer here is, that God would, so to speak, mix or mingle his cause and that of the psalmist together, and that he would then protect the common cause as his own; or, that he would become a *pledge* or *surety* for the safety of the psalmist. This now, through the Mediator, we have a right to ask at the hand of God; and when God makes our cause his own, we must be safe. ¶ *Let not the proud oppress me.* See Notes on ver. 51. Let them not triumph over me, and crush me.

123. *Mine eyes fail for thy salvation.* See Notes on vers. 81, 82. ¶ *And for the word of thy righteousness.* Thy righteous word,—that it may be made known to me, and that I may see its beauty and enjoy it.

124. *Deal with thy servant according unto thy mercy.* Not according to justice—for, sinners as we are, we can never urge that as a plea before God. No man who knows himself *could* ask of God to deal with him according to the strict and stern principles of justice. But we may ask him to deal with us according to mercy—for mercy is our only plea, and the mercy of God—vast and boundless—constitutes such a ground of appeal as we need. No man can have any other; no man need desire any other. ¶ *And teach me thy statutes.* See Notes on ver. 12. Show thy mercy to me in teaching me thy law.

125. *I am thy servant.* See Notes on Ps. cxvi. 16. ¶ *Give me understanding, that I may know thy testimonies.* Since I am thy servant, instruct me in the knowledge of thy

126 *It is* time for *thee*, LORD, to work; *for* they have made void thy law.

127 Therefore I love thy com-

w Ps. xix. 10; Prov. viii. 11.

mandments above *w* gold, yea, above fine gold.

128 Therefore I esteem all *thy* precepts *concerning* all *things to be* right; *and* I hate every false way.

---

will. As I desire to obey thee, show me what will be acceptable obedience, or what thou dost require in order to acceptable service. This is a prayer of piety. A man who sincerely desires to obey God will make it a first point to ascertain what is his will, or what will constitute true obedience.

126. It is *time for* thee, LORD, *to work.* Literally, " Time to do for Jehovah;" and the construction might be either that it is time to do [something] for Jehovah; or, that it is time for Jehovah himself to do [something]. The direct address to the Lord in the latter part of the sentence would seem, however, to show that the latter is the true interpretation:—to wit, that since men make void the law of God, it is time for *him* to work, that is, to interpose by his power and restrain them; to bring them to repentance; to assert his own authority; to vindicate his cause. Thus understood, it is an appropriate prayer to be used when iniquity abounds, and when some peculiar form of sin has an ascendancy among a people. The other interpretation, however, " It is time [for us] to do [something], since men make void thy law," suggests a truth of great importance. Then is the time when the people of God should arouse themselves to efforts to stay the tide of wickedness, and to secure the ascendancy of religion, of virtue, and of law. ¶ For *they have made void thy law.* They have broken it. They have set it at defiance. They regard and treat it as if it had no claim to obedience; as if it were a thing of nought. This the psalmist urges as a reason for the putting forth of power to arrest the evil; to bring men to repentance; to secure the salvation of souls. By all the evil done when the law of God is set at nought,

by all the desirableness that the law should be obeyed, by all the danger to the souls of men from its violation, this prayer may now and at all times be offered, and that with earnestness. Comp. ver. 136.

127. *Therefore I love thy commandments*, etc. The more men break them (ver. 126), the more I see their value; the more precious they are to me. The fact that they make thy law void, and that evil consequences result from their conduct, only impresses my mind the more with a sense of the value of the law, and makes my heart cling to it the more. There is almost nothing that will so impress upon our minds the importance of *law* as the sight of the effects which follow when it is disregarded. ¶ *Above gold*, etc. See Notes on ver. 72. Comp. Ps. xix. 10.

128. *Therefore I esteem all* thy *precepts* concerning *all* things to be *right.* Literally, " Therefore all the commandments of all I regard as right." The idea seems to be, that he regarded as right and just all the commandments of God pertaining to *every* thing and *every* person; all, considered in every way; all, wherever the law extended, and whomsoever it embraced; all the law pertaining to duty towards God and towards man. He saw in the *violation* of the laws of God (ver. 126) a reason for approving *all* law; all that would restrain men from sin, and that would bind them to duty and to virtue. The effect had been to lead him to reflect on the worth of law *as* law, and he had come to the conclusion that *all* the laws of God were to be approved and loved, inasmuch as they would, in their observance, prevent the wrongs and sorrows which he saw to be consequent on their violation. ¶ And *I hate every false way.* Every course

PE.

129 Thy testimonies *are* ^x wonderful: therefore doth my soul keep them.

130 The entrance of thy words giveth light; *y* it ^z giveth understanding unto the simple.

x ver. 18; Isa. xxv. 1.   *y* 2 Cor. iv. 4, 6.

131 I opened my mouth, and panted: for I longed for thy commandments.

132 Look thou upon me, and be merciful unto me, ¹ as thou usest to do unto those that love thy name.

z Prov. i. 4; ix. 4—6.

¹ *according to the custom toward.*

of life not based on truth, or on a right view of things. All just law is based on a perception of what is *true ;* on the reality of things; on what is required in the nature of the case; on what will tend to promote the best interests of society. Comp. Notes on ver. 104.

129. *Thy testimonies* are *wonderful.* This commences a new division of the psalm, indicated by the Hebrew letter *Pe,* corresponding to our *p.* The meaning of the expression here is, that the laws of God—the revelations of his will—are adapted to fill the mind with wonder. The mind is awed by their wisdom; their comprehensiveness; their extent; their spirituality; their benevolence:—by the fact that laws are framed, so perfectly adapted to the end; so well fitted to secure order, and to promote happiness. ¶ *Therefore doth my soul keep them.* Because they are so surpassingly wise and benevolent; because they are so manifestly the work of wisdom and goodness.

130. *The entrance of thy words giveth light.* The Septuagint translates this, "the manifestation (or declaration)—ἡ δήλωσις—of thy words enlightens." So the Vulgate. Luther renders it, "When thy word is revealed, so it delivers us, and makes the simple wise." De Wette, "The opening [revelation] of thy word," etc. The Hebrew word—פֵּתַח, *paith-ahh*—means an *opening* or *entrance* —as of a gate, Josh. xx. 4; Judges ix. 35; and then *a door,* as of a tent or the temple, Gen. xviii. 1; 1 Kings vi. 8; or the gate of a city, Isa. iii. 26; and then it means opening, insight, instruction. The word as here used seems to denote the opening or

unfolding of the word of God; the revelation of that word to the mind. A door is open so that we enter into a house; a gate, so that we enter into a city; and thus the meaning of the word of God is *opened* to us, so that we may, as it were, enter in and see its beauty. The language does not, therefore, denote the entrance of that word *into* the mind, but, its being made open *to us* so that we may perceive its beauty, or may ourselves " enter " into its meaning, its mysteries, and its beauties. ¶ *It giveth understanding unto the simple.* The word rendered *simple* literally means *those who are open to persuasion,* or who are easily enticed or seduced. Then it refers to the credulous, Prov. xiv. 15, and then to the *inexperienced.* See Notes on Ps. xix. 7; cxvi. 6.

131. *I opened my mouth and panted.* All this is the language of deep emotion. We breathe hard under the influence of such emotion; we open the mouth wide, and pant, as the ordinary passage for the air through the nostrils is not sufficient to meet the wants of the lungs in their increased action. The idea is, that his heart was full; that he had such an intense desire as to produce deep and rapid breathing; that he was like one who was exhausted, and who " panted " for breath. Comp. Notes on Ps. xlii. 1. ¶ *For I longed for thy commandments.* The word here rendered *longed* occurs nowhere else. It means to desire earnestly. See Notes on ver. 20.

132. *Look thou upon me.* Turn not away from me. Regard me with thy favour. ¶ *And be merciful unto me, as thou usest to do unto those that*

133 Order *a* my steps in thy word : and *b* let not any iniquity have dominion over me.

134 Deliver me from the oppression of man ; so will I keep thy precepts.

a Ps. xvii. 5.
b Ps. xix. 13; Rom. vi. 12, 14.

135 Make *c* thy face to shine upon thy servant; and teach me thy statutes.

136 Rivers *d* of waters run down mine eyes, because they keep not thy law.

c Num. vi. 25, 26.
d Jer. xiii. 17; xiv. 17; Ez. ix. 4.

love thy name. Marg., *According to the custom toward those*, etc. The Hebrew word is *judgment* :—" according to the *judgment* to the lovers of thy name." The word seems here to be used in the sense of *right ;* of what is *due ;* or, of what is usually *determined :* that is, as God usually determines, judges, acts towards those who love him. The idea is, Treat me according to the rules which regulate the treatment of thy people. Let me be regarded as one of them, and be dealt with accordingly. On the sentiment in this passage, see Notes on Ps. cvi. 4.

133. *Order my steps in thy word.* My goings, or, my conduct and life,— by thy word; according to thy requirements. Let me be wholly obedient to thy will. ¶ *And let not any iniquity have dominion over me.* See Notes on Ps. xix. 13. The prayer is, that *no* form of sin, that no wicked passion or propensity, might be allowed to rule over him. He who is willing that any one sin should rule in his heart, though he should be free from *all* other forms of sin, cannot be a pious man. See Notes on James ii. 10.

134. *Deliver me from the oppression of man.* From constraint on the part of man, so that I may be free to act as I please. Give me true religious liberty, and let me not be under any compulsion or constraint. The word rendered *" deliver"* is that which is usually rendered *redeem.* It is used here in the large sense of deliverance; and the prayer is an expression of what the true friends of religion have always sought, desired, and demanded — *freedom* of opinion—the richest blessing which man can enjoy. ¶ *So will I keep thy precepts.* My heart inclines to

that ; I desire it ; and, if suffered to act without constraint, I will do it. As it is the purpose and the wish of my soul, I pray that all hindrances to the free exercise of my religion may be removed. How often has this prayer been offered in times of persecution ! By how many millions of the dwellers on the earth might it even now be offered ! What a blessing it is to those who *are* free from oppressive laws, that they *are* permitted to carry out the wishes of their hearts, and to worship God according to the dictates of their conscience, with none to molest them or make them afraid.

135. *Make thy face to shine upon thy servant.* Heb., " Let thy face give light to thy servant." See Notes on Ps. iv. 6. ¶ *And teach me thy statutes.* See Notes on ver. 12.

136. *Rivers of waters run down mine eyes.* My heart is sad, and my eyes pour forth floods of tears. It is not a gentle weeping, but my eyes are like a fountain which pours out full-flowing streams. See Jer. ix. 1. " Oh that my head were waters, and mine eyes a fountain of tears," etc. Comp. Jer. xiv. 17; Lam. i. 16; ii. 18. ¶ *Because they keep not thy law.* On account of the sins, the follies, the stupidity, and the transgressions of men. So the Saviour wept over Jerusalem (Luke xix. 41); and so the apostle said that he had " great heaviness and continual sorrow " in his heart, on account of his " brethren," his " kinsmen according to the flesh." Rom. ix. 2, 3. Such a feeling is right. There is nothing for which we should be excited to deeper emotion in respect to our fellow-men than for the fact that they are violators of the law of God,

TZADDI.

137 Righteous *e art* thou, O
LORD, and upright *are* thy judgments.

138 Thy testimonies *that* thou
hast commanded *are* [1] righteous

e Dan. ix. 7.   [1] *righteousness.*

and very [2] faithful.

139 My zeal *f* hath [3] consumed
me, because mine enemies have
forgotten thy words.

140 Thy word *is* very [4] pure :
therefore thy servant loveth it.

[2] *faithfulness.*   *f* Ps. lxix. 9.
[3] *cut me off.*   [4] *tried,* or, *refined.*

and exposed to its fearful penalty.
There is nothing which more certainly indicates true piety in the soul
than such deep compassion for men
as sinners, or *because* they are sinners. There is nothing which is
more certainly connected with a work
of grace in a community, or revival
of true religion, than when such a
feeling pervades a church. Then
Christians will pray ; then they will
labour to save sinners ; then they
will feel their dependence on God ;
and then the Spirit of God will descend and bless the efforts put forth
for the salvation of men. It may be
added, nothing is more remarkable
than that pious men ordinarily feel
so little on account of the danger of
their friends and fellow-sinners, —
that the occasions are so rare on
which they imitate the example of
the psalmist and of the Saviour in
weeping over the condition of a
perishing world !

137. *Righteous* art *thou, O* LORD,
etc. This commences a new division
of the psalm, indicated by the Hebrew letter *Tzaddi*—corresponding
with *tz.* The thought in this verse
is, that God is right, or righteous, in
his judgments, that is, in his law ;
or, in other words, that his law is
founded on principles of equity.

138. *Thy testimonies* that *thou hast
commanded.* Thy law, considered as
a *testimony* as to what is right and
best. ¶ Are *righteous and very faithful.* Marg., as in Heb., *righteousness*
and *faithfulness.* They are *so* righteous, and so deserving of confidence,
—so certain to be accomplished, and
so worthy to be trusted in,—that they
may be spoken of as *righteousness*
and *fidelity* of the most perfect kind ;
the very essence of that which is right.

139. *My zeal hath consumed me.*
Marg., *cut me off.* The word which
is here translated *consumed* is rendered *cut off* in Lam. iii. 53 ; Job
xxiii. 17 ; Ps. liv. 5 ; lxxxviii. 16 ;
xciv. 23 ; ci. 5 ; cxliii. 12 ; *vanish,*
Job vi. 17 ; *destroyed,* Ps. lxxiii. 27 ;
2 Sam. xxii. 41 ; Ps. xviii. 40 ; ci. 8 ;
lxix. 4. It means here, that he
pined away ; that his strength was
exhausted ; that he was sinking under
the efforts which he had put forth as
expressive of his deep interest in the
cause of God and of truth. On the
sentiment here expressed, see Notes
on Ps. lxix. 9. ¶ *Because mine
enemies have forgotten thy words.*
Thy law ; thy commands. It was
not because they were *his* foes,—not
because he was endeavouring to destroy them, or to take vengeance on
them,—but because they were unmindful of God, and of the claims of
his law. It is a great triumph which
religion gains over a man's soul,
when, in looking on the conduct of
persecutors, calumniators, and slanderers—of those who are constantly
doing us wrong,—we are more grieved
because they violate the law of God
than because they injure us ; when
our solicitude is turned from ourselves, and terminates on our regard
for the honour of God and his law.
Yet *that* is the nature of true religion ; and *that* we should be able to
find in ourselves in such circumstances. A man should doubt the
evidence of his personal religion, if
all his feelings terminate on the
wrong done to himself by the wicked
conduct of. others ; if he has no
feeling of solicitude because the law
of God has been violated, and God
has been dishonoured. Comp. Notes
on ver. 136.

141 I *am* small and despised;
yet do not I forget thy precepts.
142 Thy righteousness *is* an
everlasting righteousness, and *g*

g John xvii. 17.

thy law *is* the truth.
143 Trouble and anguish have
¹ taken hold on me; *yet* thy commandments *are* my delights.

¹ *found me.*

140. *Thy word* is *very pure.* Marg.,
tried or *refined.* See the word explained in the Notes on Ps. xviii. 30.
¶ *Therefore thy servant loveth it.*
Therefore *I* love it. I love it *because*
it is pure, holy, true; not merely because it will save *me.* Apart from all
reference to myself. I *love* thy truth
as truth; I love purity *as* purity;
I love law *as* law; I love holiness *as*
holiness. This is true religion.

141. *I* am *small and despised.*
The word here rendered *small* may
mean "small" in respect to number,—
that is, *few,* Micah v. 2; Isa. lx. 22;
or in respect to age,—*young,* Gen.
xix. 31; or in respect to dignity,—
low; least in rank or esteem. The
language here may be applied to the
church as comparatively few; to one
who is young; or to one in humble
life. Either of these may be a reason
why one is regarded as of little consequence, or may be subject to reproach and ridicule. It is not possible to determine in which of these
senses the word is used here, or in
which sense it was applicable to the
psalmist. The word *despised* means
treated as unworthy of notice; passed
by; looked upon with contempt. This
might be on account of age, or poverty, or ignorance, or humble rank:
—or it might be simply on account
of his religion, for the friends of God
have been, and often are, despised
simply *because* they are religious.
The Saviour was *despised* by men;
the apostles were; the most excellent
of the earth in all ages have been.
Comp. Heb. xi. 36–38; 1 Cor. iv. 13.
¶ Yet *do not I forget thy precepts.*
I am not ashamed of them. I am
not deterred from keeping them, and
from avowing my purpose to obey
them, because I am despised for it.
This is often one of the severest tests
of religion, and to be faithful in
such circumstances is one of the

clearest proofs of true attachment to
God. There are few things which
we are less able to bear than *contempt,* and one of the best evidences
of attachment to *principle* is when
we adhere to what we regard as right
and true, though we are despised for it
by the gay, the worldly, the rich—
by those who claim to be "*wise.*"
He who can bear *contempt* on account of his opinions, can usually
bear anything.

142. *Thy righteousness* is *an everlasting righteousness.* It never changes.
The principles of thy law, of thy
government, and of thy method of
saving men, are the same under all
dispensations, in every land, in all
worlds; and they will remain the
same for ever. Human governments
change. Old dynasties pass away.
New laws are enacted under new administrations. Customs change. Opinions change. Men change. The
world changes. But as God himself
never changes, so it is with his law.
That law is founded on eternal truth,
and can *never* change. ¶ *And thy law*
is *the truth.* It is founded on "truth;"
on the reality of things. It is so
essentially founded on truth, it springs
so certainly out of truth, or out of the
reality of things, that it may be said
to be the truth itself. He who understands the law of God understands
what truth is, for it is the expression
and the exponent of that which is true.

143 *Trouble and anguish.* The
word rendered *trouble* means affliction of any kind; the word rendered
anguish would probably express that
which results from being *pressed,
compressed, straitened.* It properly
refers to a situation where there is
no room to move, and where we are
pent up in a narrow place. The two
words denote *deep affliction.* ¶ *Have
taken hold on me.* Marg., as in Heb.,
found me. That is, they were in pur-

144 The righteousness of thy testimonies *is* everlasting : give me understanding, and I shall [h] live.

KOPH.

145 I cried with *my* whole

heart ; hear me, O LORD : I will keep thy statutes.

146 I cried unto thee; save me, [1] and I shall keep thy testimonies.

147 I [i] prevented the dawning

h Prov. x. 21.   [1] Or, *that I may.*
i Ps. cxxx. 6.

suit of me, and have at last apprehended me. Trouble, anguish, death, are *in pursuit* of us all our lives, and are never very far in the rear of us. Often, when we least expect them, they come suddenly up to us, and make us their victims. ¶ Yet *thy commandments* are *my delights.* Notwithstanding this trouble, and *in* this trouble—no matter what comes—I have the same unfailing source of comfort, the truth of God ; and notwithstanding what *may* occur, I still make God and his law the source of my happiness. See Notes on ver. 24.

144. *The righteousness of thy testimonies.* The principles of righteousness on which they are founded. Those testimonies—those laws—are not arbitrary, or the mere expressions of *will.* They are founded on right and justice as seen by God, and his laws are his *testimony* as to what truth and justice are. ¶ Is *everlasting.* See Notes on ver. 142. ¶ *Give me understanding, and I shall live.* Give me a right view of thy law, and thy truth, and I shall have real *life.* See Notes on ver. 34.

145. *I cried with* my *whole heart,* etc. This commences a new division of the psalm, indicated by the Hebrew letter *Koph,* answering to our letter *k.* The expression " I cried with my whole heart " means that he did it earnestly, fervently. He had no divided wishes when he prayed. Not always is this so, even with good people. They sometimes offer a form of prayer, that they may be spiritually-minded, when their hearts are intensely worldly, and they would be unwilling to be otherwise ; or that religion may be revived, when their hearts have no lively interest in it, and no wish for it ; or that they may live wholly to God, when they are making all their

arrangements to live for the world, and when they would be greatly disappointed if God should take means to *make* them live entirely to him ; or that they may be humble, childlike, sincere, when they have no wish to be any otherwise than they are now, and when they would regard it as an affront if it should be assumed by any that they are *not* so now, and if they were exhorted to change their course of life. Often it would be a great surprise—perhaps *grief*—even to professedly religious persons, if God should answer their prayers, and should *make* them what they professedly desire to be, and what they pray that they may be. See Notes on Ps. ix. 1 ; comp. Ps. cxi. 1 ; cxxxviii. 1 ; cxix. 2, 10, 34, 58, 69 ; Jer. xxiv. 7. ¶ *I will keep thy statutes.* It is my purpose and desire to keep thy law perfectly.

146. *I cried unto thee.* I called upon thee in trouble. ¶ *Save me, and I shall keep thy testimonies.* Marg., *That I may keep.* The correct rendering is, " I will keep." The idea is, that if God would interpose and save him, he *would* henceforward faithfully keep the law of God. It is one of the designs of affliction to lead men to make such vows as this. They *are* commonly made on beds of sickness, alike by the religious and the irreligious ; the saint and the sinner. How often, alas, are they forgotten even by the friends of God ! How seldom are they remembered at all by the sinner when he is raised up from the verge of the grave, and restored again to health !

147. *I prevented the dawning of the morning, and cried.* I *anticipated* it ; I rose up to pray *before* the morning dawned. On the word *prevent,* see Notes on 1 Thess. iv. 15 ; Ps. xxi. 3 ; lix. 10 ; lxxix. 8. The meaning here

of the morning, and cried; I hoped in thy word.

148 Mine eyes prevent the *night* watches, that I might meditate in thy word.

149 Hear my voice, according unto thy loving-kindness : O LORD, quicken me according to thy judgment.

150 They draw nigh that follow after mischief : they are far from thy law.

151 Thou *k art* near, O LORD; and all thy commandments *are* truth.

k Ps. cxxxix. 2, etc.

---

is, that he rose up before the dawn, to pray. Thus the Saviour did, Mark i. 35. (*a*) It is *proper* thus to pray; for our earliest thoughts should be those of devotion ; our earliest acts should be in acknowledgment of God. (*b*) Such a time is eminently favourable to devotion. Calm, still, quiet; —before the thoughts are engaged in the world, and before the cares of life press upon us,—when the thoughts are clear, and the mind tranquil,—the soul is in the best state for devotion. (*c*) All men, if they will, can secure this time, before the " dawning of the morning," to pray. Comp. Notes on Ps. v. 3; lxxxviii. 13 ; see also Ps. cxxx. 6. The word rendered " dawning of the morning," is from a verb which means to blow ; to blow gently ; and is usually applied to the evening, when the breezes blow gently. It may be applied, however, as it clearly is here, also to the morning. ¶ *I hoped in thy word.* I prayed *because* I had hope in thy word ; I exercised hope in thy word *then.* Alone with thee in the morning, I found consolation by trusting in thy gracious promises.

148. *Mine eyes prevent the* night *watches.* Luther renders this, " I wake up early." The Hebrew word means *a watch*—a part of the night, so called from military watches, or a dividing of the night to " keep guard." See Notes on Ps. xc. 4. The idea of the psalmist here is, that he *anticipated* these regular divisions of the night in order that he might engage in devotion. Instead of waiting for their return, he arose for prayer *before* they recurred—so much did his heart delight in the service of God. The language would seem to be that of one

who was accustomed to pray in these successive " watches " of the night— the early, the middle, and the dawn. This may illustrate what occurs in the life of all who love God. They will have regular seasons of devotion, but they will often *anticipate* those seasons. They will be in a state of mind which prompts them to pray ; when nothing will meet their state of mind *but* prayer ; and when they cannot wait for the regular and ordinary season of devotion,—like a hungry man who cannot wait for the usual and regular hour of his meals. The meaning of the phrase, " *mine eyes* prevent," is that he awoke before the usual time for devotion. ¶ *That I might meditate in thy word.* See Notes on Ps. i. 2.

149. *Hear my voice, according unto thy loving-kindness.* According to thy mercy; thy goodness. Let *that* be the rule in answering me ; not *my* deserts, or even the fervour of my prayers. We can desire no better rule in answer to our prayers. ¶ *O LORD, quicken me.* Give me life; cause me truly to live. See Notes on ver. 40. ¶ *According to thy judgment.* Thy law as a rule of judgment; thy revealed truth, with all its gracious promises.

150. *They draw nigh.* They follow me; they press hard upon me. ¶ *That follow after mischief.* That seek to do me wrong. ¶ *They are far from thy law.* They yield no obedience to it ; they are not influenced by it in their conduct towards me.

151. *Thou* art *near, O LORD.* God was present with him ; he was ready to hear his cry ; he was at hand to save him. Comp. Ps. cxlv. 18. The psalmist had the assurance, springing from deep feeling, and the conscious

152 Concerning thy testimonies, I have known of old that thou hast founded them for *l* ever.

RESH.

153 Consider *m* mine affliction, and deliver me; for I do not forget thy law.

l Luke xxi. 33.   *m* Lam. v. 1.

154 Plead *n* my cause, and deliver me: quicken me according to thy word.

155 Salvation *is* far *o* from the wicked: for they seek not thy statutes.

n Mic. vii. 9; 1 John ii. 1.   *o* Luke xvi. 23, 24.

presence of God, which the people of God often have, that God is very *near* to them; that he is ready to hear them; that their prayers are answered; that they are in the presence of a Heavenly Friend. Such are among the precious experiences of the life of a religious man. ¶ *And all thy commandments* are *truth.* All that thou hast ordained; all that thou hast promised. The psalmist *felt* this. He was experiencing the truth of what God had assured him of. Not a doubt came into his mind, —for God was *near* him. This conviction that God is "*near*" us—this manifestation of God to the soul as a present God,—is one of the most certain assurances to our own minds of the truth of religion, and of our acceptance with him.

152. *Concerning thy testimonies.* In regard to all that thou hast *testified* to as true and best. Every command of God is in fact a *testimony* of his as to what is right; every promise is a testimony of his own purpose in regard to mankind. ¶ *I have known of old.* The word here used is a noun, and means properly, *the front,* what is *before;* then, the East; then, what pertains to olden time or ancient days—*before* the present. The meaning here is, that he had known this *before* what had now occurred; it was not a new thing—a new experience. It was deeply impressed on his mind as the result of all his reflection and observation. ¶ *That thou hast founded them for ever. From* eternity, and *for* eternity. They were laid in the eternity past; they will continue in the eternity to come. They are based on eternal principles of right; they will never

be changed. Such a conviction will do much to keep the soul steady and firm in the trials and uncertainties of life. Whatever may change, God's law does not change; whatever is new, that is not new; whatever will vanish away, that will remain.

153. *Consider mine affliction,* etc. This commences a new division of the psalm, indicated by the Hebrew letter *Resh,* corresponding to our *r.* The prayer here is, that God would look upon his trial; that he would regard it as it really was; that he would not turn away from it, or pass it by, as if it were a trifle—a thing not worthy to claim his attention. See Notes on Ps. ix. 13. ¶ *For I do not forget thy law.* I endeavour to be obedient, submissive, patient. *As* a suffering child of thine, I come to thee, and beseech thee to interpose and save me.

154. *Plead my cause,* etc. Undertake my cause, as an advocate does. See Notes on Ps. xxxv. 1. ¶ *Quicken me,* etc. Give me life. See Notes on ver. 25.

155. *Salvation* is *far from the wicked.* That is, (*a*) in their present course :—they are very far from being *safe,* or from having a prospect of salvation. (*b*) They are constantly going farther and farther off,—making their salvation less probable,—not going *toward* heaven, but *from* it. (*c*) Destruction is very near to them, and they are constantly *making* it nearer and nearer. (*d*) In their present course it may be said that salvation is *far*— is *infinitely* remote—from them, so that they can never come to it. (*e*) If they would be saved, they must change their course altogether, and go *towards* salvation and not *from* it. ¶ *For they seek not thy statutes.* They do not

156 ¹ Great *are* thy tender mercies, O LORD; quicken me according to thy judgments.

157 Many *are* my persecutors and mine enemies; *yet* do I not decline from thy testimonies.

158 I beheld the transgressors, and was grieved; because they

¹ Or, *Many.*

kept not thy word.

159 Consider how I love thy precepts : quicken me, O LORD, according to thy loving-kindness.

160 ² Thy word *is* true *from* the beginning : and every one of thy righteous judgments *endureth* for ever.

² *The beginning of thy word* is true.

regard thy law; they do not make it a principle to obey thy commandments.

156. *Great* are *thy tender mercies,* O LORD. They are many, or multiplied. The word rendered " tender mercies " is the same which occurs in Ps. xl. 11; li. 1; lxix. 16; lxxix. 8; ciii. 4. See Notes on Ps. xxv. 6. ¶ *Quicken me,* etc. See ver. 149.

157. *Many* are *my persecutors and mine enemies.* The thought here turns on the *number* of his enemies, and on the effect which *numbers* might have in turning one from the way of truth. We might meet *one* such enemy, and overcome him; we might resist the influence of *one* in endeavouring to turn us away from the truth, but the danger of falling is much increased when *numbers* are combined in persecuting us, or in seeking to turn us away from our religion,—when it becomes *unpopular* to be a professed friend of God. ¶ Yet *do I not decline from thy testimonies.* I still adhere to thee; I still maintain my integrity, notwithstanding all this. See Notes on ver. 51.

158. *I beheld the transgressors.* Those who wronged me; those who violated the law of God. ¶ *And was grieved.* Or, *sickened.* The word here used means commonly to loathe, to nauseate, to sicken. Ezek. xvi. 47; Ps. xcv. 10. I was made sad, sorry, sick at heart. I did not look on them with anger; I did not desire to take revenge upon them; I did not return evil for evil. My heart was sad that men *would* do wrong; that they *would* expose themselves to such danger. See Notes on ver. 136. ¶ *Because they kept not thy word.* Be-

cause they violated thy law; because they were sinners.

159. *Consider how I love thy precepts.* Search me. Behold the evidence of my attachment to thy law. This is the confident appeal of one who was conscious that he was truly attached to God; that he really loved his law. It is similar to the appeal of Peter to the Saviour (John xxi. 17), " Lord, thou knowest all things; thou knowest that I love thee." A man who truly loves God *may* make this appeal without impropriety. He may be so confident—so certain—that he has true love for the character of God, that he may make a solemn appeal to him on the subject—as he might appeal to a friend, to his wife, to his son, to his daughter, with the utmost confidence that he loved them. A man *ought* to have such love for *them,* that he could affirm this without hesitation or doubt; a man *ought* to have such love for *God,* that he could affirm this with equal confidence and propriety. ¶ *Quicken me,* etc. See Notes on ver. 25.

160. *Thy word* is *true* from *the beginning.* Literally, " The head of thy word is truth." Probably the meaning is, that the *principles* of God's word were truth, or were based on truth. The main thing—that on which all relied—was truth, absolute truth. It was not *made* truth by the mere will of God, but it was *founded on* essential truth. Comp. Notes on vers. 142, 144. Marg., *The beginning of thy word is true.* Its origin is truth; its foundation is truth; its essential nature is truth. See Ps. xix. 9. ¶ *And every one of thy righteous judgments* endureth *for*

SCHIN.

161 Princes *p* have persecuted me without a cause: but my heart standeth in awe of thy word.

162 I rejoice *q* at thy word, as

p 1 Sam. xxiv. 11, 17; xxvi. 21, 23.

one that findeth great spoil.

163 I hate and abhor lying; *but* thy law do I love.

164 Seven times a day do I praise thee because of thy righteous judgments.

q ver. 111.

ever. Since any one of thy laws is as certainly founded in truth as any other, it must be that all alike are eternal and unchanging. It must be so with all the essential principles of morality. Mere regulations in regard to rites and ceremonies may be altered, as local and municipal laws among men may be; but essential principles of justice cannot be. A civil corporation—the government of a city or borough—may change its regulations about streets, and culverts, and taxes; but they can never enact laws authorizing murder or theft; nor can they alter the essential nature of honesty and dishonesty; of truth and falsehood.

161. *Princes have persecuted me without a cause.* This commences a new division of the psalm, indicated by the Hebrew letter *Schin*—corresponding to our *s*, or *sh*. On the meaning of the expression here, see Notes on vers. 23, 78. ¶ *But my heart standeth in awe of thy word.* I still reverence thy word. I am not deterred from keeping thy law by any threats or intimidations. This is in accordance with the uniform statements in the psalm, that *nothing* deterred him from manifesting his adherence to the law of God.

162. *I rejoice at thy word, as one that findeth great spoil.* Plunder in a camp; prey; booty:—as the hunter or the warrior, when he lights on great and unexpected success.

163. *I hate and abhor lying.* The mention of *lying* here particularly seems to have been suggested by the necessity, from the structure of the psalm, of finding some word at the beginning of the verse which commenced with the letter *Schin.* At the same time, it is an illustration of

the nature of piety, and doubtless there had been numerous occasions in the life of the psalmist when he had seen and experienced the effects of falsehood. *This* sin, therefore, might occur to him as readily as any other. It is unnecessary to say that religion *forbids* this sin in all its forms. ¶ But *thy law do I love.* Particularly here the law which forbids lying. The psalmist was conscious, as every good man must be, that he truly *loved* that pure law which forbids falsehood in all its forms.

164. *Seven times a day.* The word *seven* may be used here, as it is often in the Scriptures, indefinitely to denote *many*, or *often.* There is, however, nothing which makes it necessary to understand it in this sense. The number of times in which it is proper and profitable to engage in secret or public devotion is nowhere specified in the Scriptures, but it is left, under a general direction, to be determined by each one as he shall find it desirable and convenient; as his feelings or his circumstances shall suggest. On another occasion (Ps. lv. 17) David mentions that he prayed " evening, and morning, and at noon ;" at other times, perhaps, he might have found it in accordance with his feelings, or with his circumstances, to engage in devotion *seven* times in a day. There are circumstances in the lives of all good men when they are prompted to do this:—times of trouble, of sickness, of bereavement, of danger, or of religious interest. There are states of mind which prompt to this, and when secret devotion becomes frequent, and almost constant; —when nothing will satisfy the mind *but* prayer. No one would be injured

165 Great peace ^r have they which love thy law: and ¹ nothing shall offend them.

166 LORD, I have hoped for thy salvation, and done thy commandments.

r Prov. iii. 2; Isa. xxxii. 17; John xiv. 27; Phil. iv. 7.

167 My soul hath kept thy testimonies; and I love them exceedingly.

168 I have kept thy precepts and thy testimonies: for ^s all my ways *are* before thee.

1 *They shall have no stumbling-block,*
1 Pet. ii. 8; 1 John ii. 10.
s Ps. cxxxix. 3; Prov. v. 21.

by making it a rule, unless unavoidably prevented, to engage seven times each day in secret prayer, though, at the same time, no one could maintain that this is required *as* a rule by the Scriptures. The times, the circumstances, the manner, the place of secret devotion are wisely and properly left to each individual to be determined by himself. Religion is essentially voluntary, and the times of secret devotion must be voluntary, and *therefore* a man can easily determine, by his own secret devotions, whether he *has* any peculiar interest at any particular time in religion, or whether he has any religion at all. ¶ *Do I praise thee.* Do I engage in devotion. ¶ *Because of thy righteous judgments.* Thy law, considered *as* righteous. I love that law, as such, and I praise thee for it.

165. *Great peace have they.* See Notes on Isa. xxvi. 3; comp. Notes on Phil. iv. 6, 7. They have great calmness of mind. They are not troubled and anxious. They believe and feel that all things are well-ordered by thee, and will be conducted to the best result. They, therefore, calmly leave all with thee. As a matter of fact, the friends of God *have* peace and calmness in their minds, even amidst the troubles, the disappointments, and the reverses of life. The love of God is the best—the only—way to secure permanent peace in the soul. ¶ *Which love thy law.* It is the love of *law*, and the belief that the law of God is in accordance with justice, that gives peace to their minds. God's government is a government of law, and therefore it is loved. ¶ *And nothing shall offend them.* Marg., *They shall have no*

stumbling-block. "Heb., "And to them no stumbling," or stumbling-block. See Notes on Matt. v. 29, 30; xviii. 6; xvi. 23; 1 Pet. ii. 8; James ii. 10. The meaning here is, that they would not fall into sin; they would be kept safe; they would be preserved from the power of temptation. The meaning is not, as it would seem to be in our version, that nothing would pain, grieve, or irritate them; but, as above, that as long as they were obedient to the law, and disposed to obey it, they would be safe from the power of temptation.

166. LORD, *I have hoped for thy salvation.* As a prevailing habit or principle in my life. I have looked to thee for deliverance in the time of danger; I have looked to thee for salvation in the world to come. ¶ *And done thy commandments.* That is, habitually. This is not, necessarily, a claim to absolute perfection.

167. *My soul hath kept thy testimonies, and I love them exceedingly.* I am conscious of loving them; I feel an inward assurance that I do love them.

168. *I have kept thy precepts and thy testimonies.* This is an appeal which is several times made in the psalm; not with boasting, but as indicating the tenor and purpose of his life. Every man *ought* to be able to make such an appeal. ¶ *For all my ways* are *before thee.* Thou hast seen my manner of life, and I may appeal to thee in proof that I have thus kept thy law. No one can lay claim to entire perfection, but there is many a man who, while conscious of much imperfection, and many shortcomings, can appeal to God for the truth of the statement that his great aim of

TAU.

169 Let my cry come near before thee, O LORD : give *t* me understanding according to thy word.

170 Let my supplication come before thee : deliver me according to thy word.

t Prov. ii. 6, 7 ; James i. 5.

171 My lips shall utter praise, when thou hast taught me thy statutes.

172 My tongue shall speak of thy word : for all thy commandments *are* righteousness.

173 Let thine hand help me : for I " have chosen thy precepts.

174 I have longed for thy sal-

u Jos. xxiv. 22 ; Luke x. 42.

---

life has been to keep his commandments.

169. *Let my cry come near before thee, O* LORD. This commences a new division of the psalm, indicated by the last letter of the Hebrew alphabet, the letter *Tau*, corresponding to our *t*, or *th*. The petition here is, that his prayer might be heard ; that it might come into the very presence of God ; that there might be no obstructions to its reaching where God was. Let nothing from my unworthiness, from my past sins, from my ignorance, prevent its coming before thee. Something often *apparently* hinders our prayers so that they do not reach the ear of God. The psalmist prays here that there may be no such hindrance in the prayer which he now offers. ¶ *Give me understanding according to thy word.* According to the promises of thy word ; or, give me the same views of truth which are set forth in thy word. This prayer had been several times offered before, and it shows how earnest was his desire to know the truth. See vers. 34, 73, 144.

170. *Let my supplication come before thee.* The word here rendered *supplication* properly means *favour, mercy, pity,* Josh. xi. 20 ; Ezra ix. 8 ; then, that by which favour or mercy is sought,—prayer or petition, Ps. vi. 9 ; lv. 1. ¶ *Deliver me according to thy word.* From my enemies, my sins, my dangers. According to thy promises ; according to the arrangements *in* thy word.

171. *My lips shall utter praise, when thou hast taught me thy statutes.* The sentiment here is the

same as in ver. 7. The language is varied, but the meaning here, as in that verse, is, I will praise thee in proportion as I learn thy precepts or thy law. The more I learn of thy will, the more I will praise thee. I shall see more for which to offer praise and adoration, and I shall be more and more inclined to praise and adore thee. Each new degree of knowledge will excite a corresponding desire to praise thee. This *will* be true of all who love God, while this life lasts, and for ever. The ever-increasing knowledge of God will excite ever-increasing praise ; and as God is infinite and eternal, it follows that the increase of knowledge and of happiness, in those who are saved, will be eternal. These things will go hand in hand for ever and ever.

172. *My tongue shall speak of thy word.* It shall speak of it in the language of praise ; it shall speak of it in making it known to others. ¶ *For all thy commandments* are *righteousness.* I see this ; I feel it ; and, therefore, I will speak of it. My impression that thy commandments are all *righteous* is so deep, that I cannot but speak of them. I must vindicate them ; I must praise thee for them.

173. *Let thine hand help me.* Do *thou* help me,—the hand being that by which we accomplish anything. ¶ *For I have chosen thy precepts.* I have chosen them as my comforters and my guide. I have resolved to obey them, and I pray that thou wilt help me to accomplish the purpose of my heart.

174. *I have longed for thy salva-*

vation, O Lord; and thy law *is* my *v* delight.

175 Let my soul live, and it shall praise thee; and let thy judgments help me.

v Ps. i. 2.

176 I *w* have gone astray like a lost sheep : seek thy servant; for I do not forget thy commandments.

w Isa. liii. 6 ; Luke xv. 4, etc. ; 1 Pet. ii. 25.

---

tion, O Lord. See Notes on ver. 166. The word rendered *I have longed* denotes an earnest desire or wish. Comp. Notes on Ps. xlii. 1, and on ver. 20 of this psalm. ¶ *And thy law* is *my delight.* It is so much the object of my delight that I earnestly long or desire to see more and more of its richness and fulness.

175. *Let my soul live, and it shall praise thee.* I desire life that I *may* praise thee ; if I do live, I *will* praise thee. My life is consecrated to thy service ; if lengthened out, and as far as it shall be lengthened out, it shall be devoted to thee. ¶ *And let thy judgments help me.* The dealings of thy hand ; the interpositions of thy providence. Let them all be such as will be favourable to the great purpose of my soul—the service of my God.

176. *I have gone astray like a lost sheep.* A sheep that has wandered away from its fold, and is without a protector. Comp. Isa. liii. 6 ; Matt. x. 6 ; xv. 24 ; xviii. 12 ; Luke xv. 6 ; 1 Pet. ii. 25. I am a wanderer. I have lost the path to true happiness. I have strayed away from my God. I see this ; I confess it ; I desire to return. It is remarkable that this is almost the only confession of sin in the psalm. This psalm, more than any other, abounds in confident statements respecting the life of the author, his attachment to the law of God, the obedience which he rendered to that law, and his love for it,—as well as with appeals to God, founded on the fact that he *did* love that law, and that his life was one of obedience. This is not, indeed, spoken in a spirit of self-righteousness, or as constituting a claim on the ground of merit ; but it is remarkable that there is so frequent reference to it, and so

little intermingling of a confession of sin, of error, of imperfection. The psalm would not have been complete as a record of religious experience, or as illustrating the real state of the human heart, without a distinct acknowledgment of sin, and hence, in its close, and in view of his whole life, upright as in the main it had been, the psalmist confesses that he had wandered ; that he was a sinner ; that his life had been far from perfection, and that he needed the gracious interposition of God to seek him out, and to bring him back. ¶ *Seek thy servant.* As the shepherd does the sheep that is lost, Luke xv. 4–6. So the Saviour came to seek and to save that which was lost, Luke xix. 10. So God seeks the wanderer by his word, by his providence, by his Spirit, to induce him to return and be saved. ¶ *For I do not forget thy commandments.* In all my wandering ; with my consciousness of error ; with my sense of guilt, I still *do* feel that I love thy law—thy service— thy commandments. They are the joy of my heart, and I desire to be recalled from all my wanderings, that I may find perfect happiness in thee and in thy service evermore. Such is the earnest wish of every regenerated heart. Far as such an one may have wandered from God, yet he is conscious of true attachment to him and his service ; he desires and earnestly prays that he may be " sought out," brought back, and kept from wandering any more.

PSALM CXX.

This is the first of fifteen psalms (cxx.–cxxxiv.) to each of which is prefixed the title "A Song of Degrees." Four of these psalms are ascribed to David, one of them to Solomon, and the rest are by unknown authors.

There has been a great diversity of opinion as to the meaning of the title, and the reason why it was prefixed to these psalms. Some have supposed that the title, "Song of Degrees," or "*Ascents*," was applied to them as being psalms which were sung during the periodical journeys or pilgrimages to Jerusalem at the times of the great yearly festivals—the *going up* to Jerusalem. Others have supposed that they were psalms which were composed or sung during the return from the exile—the *going up* again to Jerusalem after their long captivity in Babylon. Some of the Jewish rabbins supposed that they were psalms which were sung as the people ascended the fifteen steps—going up to the temple represented by Ezekiel, seven on one side and eight on the other, Ezek. xl. 22, 37. Others have supposed that the title refers to some peculiarity of structure in the psalms—a gradation or elevation of thought—approaching to a climax. Michaelis (Notes on Lowth's Lectures on Hebrew Poetry, xxv., p. 512) supposes that the title is a musical term, and that the reference is to something peculiar in the rhythm, or what is called by us, "feet" of the psalm, but which in the East would be called *steps* or *ascents*. See De Wette, Einleitung, p. 35.

In this variety of conjecture—for it can be regarded as little more than conjecture—it is impossible now to determine with any degree of certainty what is the true meaning of the title, or why it was given to these psalms. It is evident that, from some cause, there was such a *unity* in them, either from the nature of the composition, or from the occasion on which they were used, that they could properly have a general title given to them, as indicating what would be well understood among the Hebrews in regard to their design. But I apprehend that the *reason* for that title cannot now be positively ascertained. Something *negative*, however, may be determined in regard to this. (1) It is quite clear that the opinion of the rabbins that they were fifteen in number, and named Songs of *Degrees*, because they were sung on ascending the steps to the temple, is purely fanciful. In the *real* temple there was no such ascent; and it is only in the visions of Ezekiel that there is any such allusion. (2) It seems equally clear that they were not so called because they were composed and used

for the *going up* from the captivity in Babylon, or to be sung during the march through the desert. Several of them—those of David and Solomon—were composed long before that event, and could have had no allusion to it. Besides, there are but two of them (cxxii., cxxvi.) that have any reference to the return from Babylon, or that would have any applicability to that journey. Moreover, it is extremely improbable that any such selection of psalms should have been used on such a journey, or that any arrangement should have been made for such a purpose. (3) It seems to me equally improbable that they were called "Songs of Degrees or Ascents," because they were used by the people when *going up* to Jerusalem to attend on the great festivals. As in the previous specification, it may be remarked that the psalms here referred to had no special applicability to such a use; that there is no evidence that any such practice prevailed; that it is wholly improbable that there would be any such set and fixed arrangement, or that the people in going up to Jerusalem on those occasions *would* move along to measured music.

The word rendered *degrees* in the title, —מַעֲלָה, *maalah*, in the singular,—and מַעֲלוֹת, *maaloth*, in the plural, the form used here—means properly an *ascent*, a *going up*, as from a lower to a higher region, Ezra vii. 9 (marg.); or of the thoughts that ascend in the mind, Ezek. xi. 5. Then it means a *step*, by which one ascends, 1 Kings x. 19; Ezek. xl. 26, 31, 34. Then it means a degree of a dial, or a dial as divided into degrees, where there is an *ascent* on the dial, 2 Kings xx. 9-11. See Notes on Isa. xxxviii. 8. After what has been said above, there seem to be but *two* suppositions which have probability in regard to its meaning here :—(*a*) The one is the opinion of Gesenius, that these psalms are called Songs of Degrees, or Ascents, because of a certain *ascent* in the mode of composition, as when the first or last words of a preceding line are repeated at the beginning of a succeeding line, and then some new *increase* in the sense or idea,—or some *ascent* in the meaning,—follows by such an addition. The following instances may be referred to as illustrating this view. Ps. cxxi. 1, 2 : "I will lift up mine eyes unto the hills, from whence cometh *my help :— My help* cometh from the Lord," etc.

PSALM CXX.

A Song of degrees.

1 N *x* my distress I cried unto the

LORD, and he heard me.

x Jonah ii. 2.

Vers. 3, 4 : "He that *keepeth* thee will not slumber :—Behold, he that *keepeth* Israel shall neither slumber nor sleep." Vers. 7, 8 : "The Lord shall *preserve* thee from all evil ; he shall *preserve* thy soul : — The Lord shall *preserve* thy going out, and thy coming in," etc. So also Ps. cxxiv. 1, 2 : "If it had not been the Lord who was *on our side*, now may Israel say : If it had not been the Lord who was *on our side ;* when men rose up against us,—*then* (ver. 3) they had swallowed us up quick ; *then* (ver. 4) the waters had overwhelmed us ; *then* (ver. 5) the proud waters had gone over our soul." See also Ps. cxxii. 2, 3, 4 ; cxxiii. 3, 4 ; cxxvi. 2, 3 ; and cxxix. 1, 2. There is doubtless some foundation for this supposition, but, after all, it seems far-fetched, and though the remark may be true of some of these fifteen psalms, yet it can by no means be made applicable to all of them, nor could it be shown to be so *peculiar* to them that no others could have been for the same reason included in the number. (*b*) The remaining supposition seems to have much more plausibility than any one here suggested. It is that the term is a *musical* expression ; that there was something peculiar in the "*scale*" of the music to which these psalms were sung, though that is now lost to us. This is akin to the opinion of J. D. Michaelis, as alluded to above. This is, also, referred to by Asseman (Biblioth. Orient., t. i., p. 62), and by Castell (Lex. Syr.) It is impossible, however, now to ascertain *what* there is that would make this appellation peculiarly appropriate to these psalms. All that can be *known* is, that there was some reason why these psalms were, so to speak, bound up together, and designated by a common title. This does not prevent a *special* title being prefixed to some of them in regard to their author and design.

The psalm now before us has no other title, and nothing to designate its author. It pertains to a sufferer who calls earnestly upon the Lord for deliverance. The particular form of trial is that caused by the *tongue*,—slander. The author was suffering from some unjust aspersions cast upon him ; from some

effort to destroy his reputation ; from some charge in regard to his character, which made him miserable, as if he sojourned in Mesech, and dwelt in the tents of Kedar, ver. 5. He says that it was in vain for him to attempt to live in peace with the men who calumniated him. He was himself disposed to peace. He earnestly desired it. But they were for war, and they kept up the war, vers. 6, 7. Among the forms of suffering to which the people of God are exposed, this is not uncommon ; and it was proper that it should be referred to in a book designed, as the Book of Psalms was, to be useful in all ages, and in all lands, as a record of religious experience.

1. *In my distress.* In my suffering, as arising from *slander*, vers. 2, 3. There are few forms of suffering more keen than those caused by slander—

"Whose edge is sharper than the sword ; whose tongue
Outvenoms all the worms of Nile ; whose breath
Rides on the posting winds, and doth belie
All corners of the world : kings, queens, and states,
Maids, matrons, nay, the secrets of the grave
This viperous slander enters."
                    Cymbeline, iii. 4.

It is one of those things which a man cannot guard against ; which he cannot repel by force ; whose origin he cannot always trace ; which will go where a vindication will not follow ; whose effects will live long after the slander is refuted ; which will adhere to a man, or leave a trait of suspicion, even after the most successful vindication, for the effect will be to make a *second* slander more easily credited than the first was. ¶ *I cried unto the* LORD, *and he heard me.* I had no other resource. I could not meet the slander. I could not refute it. I could not prevent its effects on my reputation, and all that I could do was to commit the case to the Lord. See Notes on Ps. xxxvii. 5, 6.

6 My soul hath long dwelt with him that hateth peace.

7 I *am* [1] *for* peace : but when I speak, they *are* for war.

[1] Or, *a* man of *peace*.

and Meshech they were thy merchants." Ezek. xxxix. 1: "I am against . . . the chief prince of Meshech and Tubal." Herodotus (iii. 94; vii. 78) connects them with the Tibarenes. The idea here is, that they were a barbarous, savage, uncivilized people. They dwelt outside of Palestine, beyond what were regarded as the borders of civilization ; and the word seems to have had a signification similar to the names Goths, Vandals, Turks, Tartars, Cossacks, in later times. It is not known that they were particularly remarkable for slander or calumny ; but the meaning is that they were barbarous and savage,—and to dwell among slanderers and revilers seemed to the psalmist to be *like* dwelling among a people who were strangers to all the rules and principles of civilized society. ¶ That *I dwell in the tents of Kedar*. The word *Kedar* means properly *dark skin*, a *dark-skinned man*. Kedar was a son of Ishmael (Gen. xxv. 13), and hence the name was given to an Arabian tribe descended from him, Isa. xlii. 11 ; lx. 7 ; Jer. xlix. 28. The idea here also is, that to dwell among slanderers was like dwelling among barbarians and savages.

6. *My soul hath long dwelt with him that hateth peace*. This trouble is no new thing. It has been long continued, and has become intolerable. Who this was that thus gave him trouble is, of course, now unknown. It is only necessary to remark that there can scarcely be any source of trouble more bitter than that of sustaining such relations to others either in business, or in office, or by family-ties—whether by marriage or by blood —in school, in college, or in corporate bodies—as to expose us always to a quarrel :—to be compelled to have constant intercourse with men of sour, perverse, crooked tempers, who

are satisfied with nothing ; who are suspicious or envious; who pervert our motives and our conduct; who misrepresent our words; who demand more than is due to them ; who refuse to perform what may reasonably be expected of them ; and who make use of every opportunity to involve us in difficulties with others. There are many trials in human life, but there are few which are more galling, or more hard to bear than this. The literal rendering of the passage would be, " Long for her has my soul dwelt," etc. That is, long (or too long) for her good,— for the welfare of my soul. It has been an injury to me; to my piety, to my comfort, to my salvation. It has vexed me, tried me, hindered me in my progress in the Divine life. Nothing would have a greater tendency of this kind than to be compelled to live in the manner indicated above.

7. *I* am for *peace*. Marg., *A man of peace*. Literally, " I [am] peace." It is my nature. I desire to live in peace. I strive to do so. I do nothing to provoke a quarrel. I would do anything which would be right to pacify others. I would make any sacrifices, yield to any demands, consent to any arrangements which would promise peace. ¶ *But when I speak*. When I say anything on the subject, when I propose any new arrangements, when I suggest any changes, when I give utterance to my painful feelings, and express a desire to live differently—they will listen to nothing ; they will be satisfied with nothing. ¶ *They* are *for war*. For discord, variance, strife. All my efforts to live in peace are vain. They are determined to quarrel, and I cannot prevent it. (*a*) A man in such a case should separate from such a person, if possible, as the only way of peace. (*b*) If his posi-

PSALM CXXI.
A Song of degrees.

I ¹ will lift up mine eyes unto the hills, from whence cometh my help.

tion and relations are such that *that* cannot be done, then he should be careful that he does nothing himself to irritate and to keep up the strife. (*c*) If all that he does or can do for peace is vain, and if his relations and position are such that he cannot separate, then he should bear it patiently—as coming from God, and as the discipline of *his* life. God has many ways of testing the patience and faith of his people, and there are few things which will do so more effectually than this; few situations where piety will shine more beautifully than in *such* a trial; (*d*) He who is thus tried should look with the more earnestness of desire to another world. There *is* a world of peace; and the peace of heaven will be all the more grateful and blessed when we go up to it from such a scene of conflict and war.

PSALM CXXI.

This psalm is entitled simply, "A Song of Degrees." See Notes on the title to Psalm cxx. Nothing is known, or can be known, of the author or of the occasion on which it was composed. De Wette and Rosenmüller suppose that it was composed in the exile; Rosenmüller regarding it as a psalm to be sung on the return to Palestine after the captivity,—De Wette, as the psalm of a pensive exile looking toward the hills of Palestine, his native land, as the source from whence all his help must come,—and expressing confidence in God that he would bring him out of his exile and his trouble. There is no *proof*, however, that either of these suppositions is correct. The language is such, indeed, as *might* then be employed, but it is also such as might be used on many other occasions. It might be the language of the leader of an army, endangered, and looking to the "hills" where he expected reinforcements; it might be that of a pious man encompassed with dangers, and using this expression as illustrative of his looking up to God; or it might be the language of one looking directly to heaven, represented as the heights, or the exalted place where God dwells; or it might be the language of one looking to the hills of Jerusalem—the seat of the worship of God—the place of His abode—as his refuge, and as the place from whence only help could come. This last seems to me to be the most probable supposition; and thus the psalm represents the confidence and hope of a pious man (in respect to duty, danger, or trial) as derived from the God whom he worships,—and the place where God has fixed his abode,—the church where he manifests himself to men.

1. *I will lift up mine eyes.* Marg., *Shall I lift up mine eyes to the hills? Whence should my help come?* The expression would properly denote a condition where there was danger; when no help or aid was visible; and when the eyes were turned to the quarter from which help might be expected to come. What the danger was cannot now be ascertained. ¶ *Unto the hills.* Heb., *the mountains.* To the quarter from whence I look for assistance. This (as has been shown in the Introduction) may refer (1) to the mountains whence one in danger expected help; or (2) to heaven, considered as high, and as the abode of God; or (3) to the hills on which Jerusalem was built, as the place where God dwelt, and from whence aid was expected. The third of these is the most probable. The first would be applicable to a state of war only, and the second is forced and unnatural. Adopting the *third* interpretation, the language is natural, and makes it proper to be used at all times, since it indicates a proper looking to God as he manifests himself to men, particularly in the church. ¶ *From whence cometh my help.* A more literal rendering would be, "Whence cometh my help?" This accords best with the usage of the

2 My *a* help *cometh* from the LORD, which made heaven and earth.

3 He *b* will not suffer thy foot to be moved: he *c* that keepeth thee will not slumber.

4 Behold, he that keepeth Israel shall neither slumber nor sleep.

5 The LORD *is* thy keeper; the LORD *is* thy shade *d* upon thy right hand.

6 The *e* sun shall not smite

Hebrew word, and agrees well with the connexion. It indicates a troubled and anxious state of mind—a mind that asks, *Where* shall I look for help? The answer is found in the following verse.

2. *My help* cometh *from the* LORD. From Jehovah. This is the answer to the anxious inquiry in ver. 1. It indicates (*a*) a consciousness that help *could* come only from God; (*b*) a belief that it *would* come from him; and a confident yet humble reliance on him. ¶ *Which made heaven and earth.* The great Creator of the universe. He must, therefore, be able to protect me. The Creator of all can defend all.

3. *He will not suffer thy foot to be moved.* He will enable you to stand firm. You are safe in his protection. Comp. Notes on Ps. xxxviii. 16. This, with the remainder of the psalm, seems to be of the nature of an answer to the anxious question in ver. 1,—an answer which the author of the psalm, in danger and trouble, makes to his own soul, imparting confidence to himself. ¶ *He that keepeth thee will not slumber.* He will be ever watchful and wakeful. Comp. Isa. xxvii. 3. All *creatures*, as far as we know, sleep; God never sleeps. Comp. Ps. cxxxix. 11, 12. His eyes are upon us by day, and in the darkness of the night—the night literally; and also the night of calamity, woe, and sorrow.

4. *Behold, he that keepeth Israel.* The Keeper—the Guardian—of his people. The psalmist here passes from his own particular case to a *general* truth—a truth to him full of consolation. It is, that the people of God must always be safe; that their

great Guardian never slumbers; and that he, as one of his people, might, therefore, confidently look for his protecting care. ¶ *Shall neither slumber nor sleep.* Never slumbers, never ceases to be watchful. Man sleeps; a sentinel *may* slumber on his post, by inattention, by long-continued wakefulness, or by weariness; a pilot *may* slumber at the helm; even a mother *may* fall asleep by the side of the sick child; but God is never exhausted, is never weary, is never inattentive. He never closes his eyes on the condition of his people, on the wants of the world.

5. *The* LORD *is thy keeper.* Thy Preserver; thy Defender. He will keep thee from danger; he will keep thee from sin; he will keep thee unto salvation. ¶ *The* LORD *is thy shade.* The Lord is as a shadow:—as the shadow of a rock, a house, or a tree, in the intense rays of the burning sun. See Notes on Isa. xxv. 4. ¶ *Upon thy right hand.* See Ps. xvi. 8; cix. 31. Perhaps the particular allusion to *the right hand* here may be that that was the place of a protector. He would thus be at hand, or would be ready to interpose in defence of him whom he was to guard. It is *possible*, however, that the idea here may be derived from the fact that in Scripture the geographer is represented as looking to the east, and not towards the north, as with us. Hence the south is always spoken of as the *right*, or at the right hand (comp. Notes on Ps. lxxxix. 12); and as the intense rays of the sun are from the south, the idea may be, that God would be as a shade in the direction from which those burning rays came.

6. *The sun shall not smite thee by*

thee by day, nor the moon by night.

7 The [f] LORD shall preserve thee from all evil : he shall preserve thy soul.

8 The LORD shall preserve thy [g] going out, and thy coming in, from this time forth, and even for evermore.

[f] 2 Tim. iv. 18.   [g] Deut. xxviii. 6 ; Prov. ii. 8.

day. The Septuagint renders this, "shall not *burn* thee"—συγκαύσει. So the Latin Vulgate. The Hebrew word means to smite, to strike, as with a rod or staff, or with the plague or pestilence ; and then, to kill, to slay. The allusion here is to what is now called a "sun-stroke"—the effect of the burning sun on the brain. Such effects of the sun are often fatal now, as doubtless they were in the time of the psalmist. ¶ *Nor the moon by night.* The psalmist here refers to some prevalent opinion about the influence of the moon, as endangering life or health. Some have supposed that he refers to the sudden cold which follows the intense heat of the day in Oriental countries, and which, because the moon rules the night, as the sun does the day, is either poetically or literally attributed to the moon. Lackmann and Michaelis suppose that there is some allusion to the influence of the moon in producing various kinds of disease, and especially *lunacy*—an idea which gave origin to that name. Comp. Notes on Matt. iv. 24. See Matt. xvii. 15 ; Mark ix. 17 ; Luke ix. 39. Knapp supposes the idea is, that from the moon's not giving a clear and full light like the sun, travellers trusting to its guidance may be led into rivers or quagmires. Macrobius refers to a custom among the Orientals of covering the faces of children when asleep, from some imagined effect of the moon on the health of the child. Andersen (Orient. Reise-Beschreib. i. 8) refers to an effect, which he says is common, and which he had often seen, of sleeping in the moon-beams, of making the neck stiff, so that it could not be turned from side to side as before. See Rosenmüller, *Morgenland, in loc.* Others have supposed that the allusion is to the effect of the moon, and

of sleeping under the open air, in producing ophthalmia—a disease very common in the East, — an effect guarded against by covering the face. The influence of the moon, in producing madness or disease,— the general influence of it on health, —is often referred to. Thus Shakspeare says :—

"The moon, the governess of floods,
 Pale in her anger, washes all the air,
 That rheumatic diseases do abound."
                Midsummer Night's Dream, ii. 2.

"It is the very error of the moon ;
 She comes more near the earth than she
        was wont,
 And makes men mad."
                            Othello, v. 2.

Some of these things are evidently purely imaginary. The true idea seems to be that there were effects to be dreaded from the sudden changes from the heat of day to the cold of night, and that these effects were attributed to the moon. See Gen. xxxi. 40. The meaning is, that God would be a Protector alike in the dangers of the day and of the night.

7. *The* LORD *shall preserve thee from all evil.* This is an advance of the thought. The psalmist had in the previous verses specified some particular evils from which he says God would keep those who put their trust in him. He now makes the remark general, and says that God would not only preserve from these particular evils, but would keep those who trusted in him from *all* evil :— he would be their Protector in *all* the perils of life. ¶ *He shall preserve thy soul.* Thy life. See Ps. xli. 2 ; xcvii. 10.

8. *The* LORD *shall preserve thy going out and thy coming in.* Preserve thee in going out and coming in ; in going from thy dwelling, and returning to it ; in going from home and coming back ; that is, every-

PSALM CXXII.

A Song of degrees of David.

I WAS glad when they said

unto me, Let *h* us go into the house of the LORD.

h Isa. ii. 2, 3 ; Jer. l. 5 ; Zec. viii. 21.

---

where, and at all times. Comp. Deut. xxviii. 6. See Notes also on Job v. 24. ¶ *From this time forth, and even for evermore.* Through this life and for ever. This is the gracious assurance which is made to all who put their trust in God. At home and abroad; in the house, in the field, and by the way; on the land and on the ocean; in their native country and in climes remote; on earth, in the grave, and in the eternal world, they are always safe. No evil that will endanger their salvation can befal them ; nothing can happen to them here but what God shall see to be conducive to their ultimate good ; and in the heavenly world they shall be safe for ever from every kind of evil, for in that world there will be no sin, and consequently no need of *discipline* to prepare them for the future.

" In foreign realms, and lands remote,
  Supported by thy care,
Through burning climes they pass unhurt,
  And breathe in tainted air.
When by the dreadful tempest borne,
  High on the broken wave,
They know thou art not slow to hear,
  Nor impotent to save.
The storm is laid—the winds retire,
  Obedient to thy will ;
The sea that roars at thy command,
  At thy command is still.
In midst of dangers, fears, and death,
  Thy goodness we'll adore ;
We'll praise thee for thy mercies past,
  And humbly hope for more.
Our life, while thou preserv'st that life,
  Thy sacrifice shall be;
And death, when death shall be our lot,
  Shall join our souls to thee."
  Addison's Spec.

PSALM CXXII.

This psalm is expressly ascribed to David, though it is not known why it should be classed among the "Songs of Degrees." On the supposition that these were used by the pilgrims in "going up" to Jerusalem to worship, and that they were sung by the way, this psalm would be particularly appropriate, and is one of the very few, in the entire collection of fifteen, that would

be appropriate. This psalm evidently *was* used on some such occasion, and is beautifully suited to such a design. There is no reason to doubt that it is a composition of David, but it is not now possible to ascertain at what period of his life, or on what particular occasion, it was composed. De Wette has endeavoured to show that the psalm must have been composed at a later period in the Jewish history than the time of David. His arguments are— (1) That these "Psalms of Degrees" mostly pertain to a later period, and yet that they are closely connected together in sense; (2) that the language indicates a later period than the time of David; (3) that the pilgrimage to Jerusalem was not instituted until a later age than that of David; (4) that the mention of the "thrones of the house of David" (ver. 5) indicates a later age; and (5) that Jerusalem is represented (ver. 3) as a city already built,—probably, as De Wette thinks, referring to Jerusalem as *rebuilt* after the captivity. It will be found, however, in the exposition of the psalm, that there is no part of it which is not applicable to David and his times.

1. *I was glad.* It was a subject of joy to me. The return of the happy season when we were to go up to worship filled me with joy. The language is expressive of the happiness which is felt by those who love God and his sanctuary, when the stated season of worship returns. The heart is drawn to the house of prayer ; the soul is filled with peace at the prospect of being again permitted to worship God. *Who* the speaker here is, is not known. It *may* have been David himself; more probably, however, it was designed by him to be used by those who should go up to worship, as expressive of their individual joy. ¶ *When they said unto me.* When it was said unto me. When the time arrived. When I was invited by others to go. The announcement was joyful; the in-

2 Our feet shall stand within thy gates, O Jerusalem.

3 Jerusalem is builded as a city that is compact together:

4 Whither the tribes go up, the tribes of the LORD, unto the testimony of Israel, to give thanks unto the name of the LORD.

---

vitation was welcome. It met the desires of my heart, and I embraced the invitation cheerfully and joyfully. ¶ *Let us go into the house of the* LORD. Up to the place where God dwells; the house which he has made his abode. If the psalm was composed in the time of David, this would refer to the tabernacle as fixed by him on Mount Zion; if at a later period, to the temple. The *language* will admit of either interpretation. Comp. Notes on Isa. ii. 3.

2. *Our feet shall stand within thy gates, O Jerusalem.* We shall enter the sacred city. It appears now in full view before us,—its walls, its palaces, its sacred places. We shall not stand and gaze upon it at a distance; we shall not merely be charmed with its beauty as we approach it; we shall accomplish the object of our desire, and enter within its walls and gates. So the believer approaches heaven—the New Jerusalem above. He will not merely admire its exterior, and look upon it at a distance; but he will enter in. He draws nearer and nearer to it, and as he approaches it when he is dying, its beauty becomes the more charming to his view, and the joy of his heart increases as he now feels the assurance that he will "stand within its gates:"—that he will enter there, and dwell there for ever. So said Dr. Payson, when approaching the end of life:— "The celestial city is full in my view. Its glories beam upon me, its breezes fan me, its odours are wafted to me, its sounds strike upon my ears, and its spirit is breathed into my heart. Nothing separates me from it but the river of death, which now appears but as an insignificant rill, that may be crossed at a single step, whenever God shall give permission. The Sun of Righteousness has been gradually drawing nearer and nearer, appearing

larger and brighter as he approached, and now he fills the whole hemisphere, —pouring forth a flood of glory, in which I seem to float like an insect in the beams of the sun; exulting, yet almost trembling, while I gaze on this excessive brightness, and wondering with unutterable wonder why God should deign thus to shine upon a sinful worm." Works, i. 407. See also the exquisite description of the glories of heaven, familiar to all, as described by Bunyan, as the Christian pilgrims were about to cross the river of death.

3. *Jerusalem is builded as a city that is compact together.* Literally, "joined to itself together;" that is, when one part is, as it were, bound closely to another part; not scattered or separate. The walls are all joined together; and the houses are all united to one another so as to make a compact place. The ground occupied by Jerusalem never could be large, as it was surrounded with valleys, except on the north, and hemmed in with hills, so that, from the necessity of the case, when it became the capital of the nation, it was densely crowded. This, moreover, was usual in ancient cities, when they were made compact for the sake of defence and protection.

4. *Whither the tribes.* The twelve tribes of the children of Israel. ¶ *Go up.* To the great feasts and festivals of the nation. See Ex. xxiii. 17. This language of *going up* is such as would be used anywhere respecting the capital of a nation,— as it is now of London; but it was literally true of Jerusalem, since it was elevated far above most parts of the land. ¶ *The tribes of the* LORD, *unto the testimony of Israel.* The " *ark* of testimony ;" the ark within which were the tables of stone, containing the law considered as God's

5 For ⁱ there ¹ are set thrones of judgment, the thrones of the house of David.

i Deut. xvii. 8, 9 ; 2 Chron. xix. 8.

6 Pray for the peace of Jerusalem : they shall prosper that love thee.

¹ do sit.

---

testimony or *witnessing* as to justice, right, equity, duty, truth. See Ex. xvi. 34 ; xxv. 16, 21 ; xl. 3, 20 ; xxx. 6, 36 ; xxxi. 18. ¶ *To give thanks unto the name of the* LORD. To worship Jehovah,—the *name* often being put for the Being himself. A main part of Hebrew worship was *praise*, and hence this is often put for the whole of worship.

5. *For there are set.* Marg., *Do sit.* The Hebrew is, "For there sit thrones for judgment." They are established there ; or, That is the appointed place for administering justice. ¶ *Thrones of judgment.* Seats for dispensing justice. The word *throne* is now commonly appropriated to the seat or chair of a king, but this is not necessarily the meaning here. The word may denote a seat or bench occupied by a judge. The meaning here is, that Jerusalem was the supreme seat of justice; the place where justice was dispensed for the nation. It was at once the religious and the civil capital of the nation. ¶ *The thrones of the house of David.* Of the family of David, who performed the office of magistrates, or who administered justice. The family of David would naturally be employed in such a service as this. This office Absalom—who had not been appointed to it—earnestly desired, in order that he might secure popularity in his contemplated rebellion. "Oh that I were made a judge in the land, that every man which hath any suit or cause might come unto me, and I would do him justice!" 2 Sam. xv. 4.

6. *Pray for the peace of Jerusalem.* The prosperity, the welfare of Jerusalem,—for peace is everywhere the image of prosperity and happiness. Comp. Ps. li. 18. This is the language which those who were going up to the city—to the house of the Lord—addressed to each other, expressing the joyful feelings of their hearts at their own near approach to the city. It breathes the desire that all would pray for the peace and prosperity of a city so dear to their own souls ; where the worship of God was celebrated ; where God himself dwelt ; where justice was administered :—a city of so much importance and so much influence in the land. To us now it inculcates the duty of praying for the church : —its peace ; its unity ; its prosperity ; its increase ; its influence on our country and on the world at large. It is a prayer that the church may not be divided by schism or heresy ; that its members may cherish for each other right feelings ; that there may be no jealousies, no envyings, and no jars; that the different branches of the church may regard and treat each other with kindness, with respect, and with mutual recognition ; that prosperity may attend them all. ¶ *They shall prosper that love thee.* Or rather, They shall have peace that love thee; or, May they have peace that love thee. The word *prosper* conveys an idea which is not in the original. The Hebrew word means *to be secure, tranquil, at rest*, spoken especially of one who enjoys quiet prosperity, Job iii. 26 ; xii. 6. The essential idea is that of quietness or rest; and the meaning here is, that those who love Zion *will* have peace ; or, that the tendency of that love is to produce peace. See Rom. v. 1. The prayer was for "peace ;" the thought in connexion with that was naturally that those who loved Zion *would* have peace. It is indeed true, in general, that they who love Zion, or who serve God, *will* "prosper" (comp. Notes on 1 Tim. iv. 8), but that is not the truth taught here. The idea is that

7 Peace be within thy walls, *and* prosperity within thy palaces.

8 For my brethren and companions' sakes, I will now say,

Peace *be* within thee.

9 Because of the house of the LORD our God I will seek *k* thy good.

k Neh. ii. 10.

---

they will have *peace:*—peace with God; peace in their own consciences; peace in the prospect of death and of the future world ; peace amidst the storms and tempests of life ; peace in death, in the grave, and for ever.

7. *Peace be within thy walls.* The word here rendered *walls,* means properly an host, an army; then a fortification, an entrenchment, especially the ditch or trench with the low wall or *breastwork* which surrounds it. *Gesenius,* Lex.   It refers here to the fortifications or defences around Jerusalem.   ¶ And *prosperity.* Peace ; —the same word which is used in the previous verse, and expressing the same idea—that of tranquillity. ¶ *Within thy palaces.* This word properly means a *fortress, castle;* then, a palace, a residence of a king or a prince, 1 Kings xvi. 18 ; 2 Kings xv. 25 ; Isa. xxv. 2.   The idea is, that such places abounded in Jerusalem ; and the prayer is, that in those abodes of power, where the rulers of the land resided, there might be peace.   The particular reason for this prayer is suggested in the following verse.

8. *For my brethren and companions' sakes.* Because they dwell there ; or, because they go up there to worship ; or, because they love thee, and find their happiness in thee ; or, because they are unconverted, and all my hope of their salvation is to be derived from thee,— from the church, from the influence of religion.   ¶ *I will now say, Peace be within thee.* I will pray for thy peace, for thy prosperity, for the blessing of God upon thee,—because their good, their comfort, their hope of salvation, depends on thee, — on the influence which shall go out from thee.   So the Christian prays that the church may prosper,—that the

Divine blessing may rest upon it,— that there may be in it harmony, peace, love, and zeal,—that a blessing may attend the preaching of the gospel,—not only because *he* loves it, and seeks his own comfort and edification in it, but that his friends and kindred—his wife, his parents, his children, his neighbours—those whom he loves, and whose salvation he desires, may be saved. This expresses the true feelings of piety all over the world ; this is one of the grounds of the strong love which the friends of God have for the church,—because they hope and desire that through the church those most dear to their hearts will find salvation.

9. *Because of the house of the* LORD *our God I will seek thy good.* Because of the sanctuary within thee ; because that is the place where God is worshipped. The principal attraction in thee is the fact that in thee is the place where the worship of God is celebrated. It is this which gives its main importance in my view to the place ; it is for this, and because I desire its influence to be perpetuated and extended, that I seek thy prosperity. This expresses a deep feeling in the mind of a pious man. To him the church of God is the most important of all objects, gives the principal interest to a place, and is everywhere to him the chief attraction. The church does more to adorn a place than anything else ; it is that which exerts the best influence on a place, and sends the best influence abroad ; it is that which to him is the source of chief comfort and delight. His heart is there ; his main delight is there ; his arrangements will be made so as best to enjoy the privileges of the sanctuary ; and his plans of life will all contemplate the welfare, the extension, and

PSALM CXXIII.

A Song of degrees.

UNTO thee *l* lift I up mine eyes, O thou that dwellest in the heavens.

2 Behold, as the eyes of servants *look* unto the hand of their masters, *and* as the eyes of a maiden unto the hand of her

l Ps. cxxi. 1.

---

the influence of the church of God. It is *religion* which in his view is the chief ornament of a place; religion which in any community is the principal fountain of its happiness and prosperity; religion which is the central and controlling influence on the private dwellings, and the public institutions, of a nation.

PSALM CXXIII.

This psalm is entitled simply "A Song of Degrees." See Notes on the title of Psalm cxx. Nothing is intimated in regard to the authorship of the psalm, or to the occasion on which it was composed. The only circumstance which throws any light on its origin is the statement in ver. 4, that the author and his friends—the people of God referred to in the psalm—were exposed to derision and contempt for their attachment to religion, especially the contempt and reproach of those who were in circumstances of ease and affluence, or who were in the more elevated ranks of life. This might accord well with the condition of the exiles returning from Babylon, or with the condition of the returned captives when rebuilding the walls of the city, and when they met with scorn and contempt from the Samaritans and the Ammonites; from Sanballat and Tobiah; from the Arabians and the Ashdodites (Neh. iv. 1-8); but there is no certain evidence that the psalm was composed on that occasion. The pious Hebrews of antiquity—David and others —and the people of God at all times have been too much exposed to this kind of treatment to make the mere applicability of the psalm to that particular time a reason for concluding that it *must* have been composed then; and it is now impossible to determine by whom, or on what occasion it was composed. It refers to what may occur in any age of the world; and it expresses the proper feelings of piety at all times when we are, on account of our religion, exposed to "the scorning of those that are at ease, and to the contempt of the proud."

1. *Unto thee.* To God. ¶ *Lift I up mine eyes.* In supplication and prayer. Nature prompts us to *look up* when we address God, as if he dwelt *above* us. It is the natural prompting of the heart that he must be the most exalted of all beings, dwelling above all. See Ps. cxxi. 1. ¶ *O thou that dwellest in the heavens.* Whose home—whose peculiar abode —is in heaven—above the sky. This is in accordance with the common feelings of men, and the common description of God in the Bible, though it is true also that God is everywhere. Comp. Ps. ii. 4; xi. 4.

2. *Behold, as the eyes of servants* look *unto the hand of their masters,* etc. Or, *are* to the hands of their masters; or, regard the hands of their masters. That is, we look to God with the same spirit of deference, dependence, and readiness to mark the will of God, which is evinced by servants in regard to their masters, and by maidens in regard to the will of a mistress. There has been some difference of view in regard to the meaning of this comparison. Some have supposed that the allusion is to the fact that servants, when in danger, look to their masters for protection; others, that they look to them for the supply of their wants; others, that when they have been guilty of an offence they look to them alone for pardon. See Rosenmüller, *in loc.* The true idea, however, seems to be, that they look to them with deference and respect; that they attentively mark every expression of their will; that they are ready to obey their commands on the slightest intimation of their wishes—standing in a waiting posture, with no will of their own,— their own wills absorbed in the will of the master or the mistress. The following extracts from Oriental tra-

mistress; so our eyes *wait* upon the LORD our God, until that he have mercy upon us.

3 Have mercy upon us, O LORD, have mercy upon us: for

vellers may illustrate the idea here: —Maundrell (Reise von Aleppo nach Jerusalem, s. 13), speaking of an interview with the Pasha at Tripoli, says, "The servants all stood in great numbers with the utmost respect, and in profoundest silence, and served the guests with the utmost attention and respect." Pococke remarks that in Egypt the slaves stand in the profoundest silence at the end of the table, their hands laid cross-wise over one another, and that they mark with the deepest attention the slightest movement of their master, who conveys his wishes to them through signs and winks. Savary, in his Letters from Egypt (p. 135), says, "The slaves stand with their hands laid cross-wise over their breasts, silent, at the end of the hall. *Their eyes are directed to the master,* and they are attentive to the slightest indication of his will." See other illustrations in Rosenmüller, Morgenland, ii. 109, 110. It is to such a custom as this that the psalmist refers; and the idea is, that his eyes were directed to God, in his troubles, in profound silence, and with deep attention, resembling that of servants waiting in stillness on their master, and catching the slightest intimation of his will—a movement of the head or hand—or anything which would indicate his pleasure. ¶ *Until that he have mercy upon us.* We have nothing to do but wait. We have no other resource. We can do nothing if we turn away from him. Our only hope and expectation is there, and if we ever find relief, it must be there. The surest—the only—hope of relief is to wait on God; and it is the purpose of our souls to do this until we find help and deliverance. This is the attitude in which the earnest prayer in the next verse is offered.

we are exceedingly filled with contempt.

4 Our soul is exceedingly filled with the scorning of those that are at ease, *and* with the contempt of the proud.

3. *Have mercy upon us, O* LORD, *have mercy upon us.* The language of earnest pleading, repeating with emphasis the object of the prayer. The supplicants are represented as standing and urging this petition, feeling that help could come only from God; looking only to him; and watching his countenance, as servants do their master's. ¶ *For we are exceedingly filled.* The Hebrew word here used means *to be saturated;* to have the appetite fully satisfied—as applied to one who is hungry or thirsty. Then it comes to mean to be entirely full, and the idea here is, that as much contempt had been thrown upon them as could be;—they could experience no more. ¶ *With contempt.* Contempt has been shown us in every possible way. We are thoroughly despised.

4. *Our soul is exceedingly filled.* Thoroughly sated. This verse states the *nature* and the *source* of the contempt which they were called to bear. ¶ *With the scorning of those that are at ease.* According to one view of these "Psalms of Degrees" (see Introd. to Ps. cxx.) this would be an instance of an "*ascent*" in the sense, or of the *going up* of the thought, where in ver. 3 there was mention made in general of "*contempt*," and in this verse the thought is carried onward and upward, or there is an additional idea which gives intensity to it. It is the scorn proceeding from those who are at ease; that is, the gay, the affluent, the proud. The word *scorning* means derision, mockery. The idea in the Hebrew is derived from stammering, which the word properly means; and then, mockery, as repeating over the words of another, or imitating the voice of one in derision. Comp. Ps. ii. 4; Job xxii. 19. The

PSALM CXXIV.
A Song of degrees of David.

IF *m* *it* *had* *not* *been* the LORD

who was on our side, now may Israel say;

m Ex. xv. 1, etc.

phrase "those that are at ease" properly refers to those who are tranquil or quiet, Job xii. 5; Isa. xxxii. 18; xxxiii. 20; and then it is used of those who are living at ease; those who are living in self-indulgence and luxury, Amos vi. 1; Isa. xxxii. 9, 11. Here it would seem to refer to those who, in our language, are "in easy circumstances;" the affluent; those who are not compelled to toil :—then, the gay, the fashionable, those in the upper walks of life. The contempt was aggravated by the fact that it came from that quarter; not from the low, the ignorant, the vulgar, but from those who claimed to be refined, and who were distinguished in the world of gaiety, of rank, and of fashion. This, even for good people (such is human nature), is much more hard to bear than contempt is when it comes from those who are in the lower walks of life. In the latter case, perhaps, we feel that we can meet contempt with contempt; in the former we cannot. We disregard the opinions of those who are beneath us; there are few who are not affected by the opinions entertained of them by those who are above them. ¶ And *with the contempt of the proud.* Those who are lifted up; either in rank, in condition, or in feeling. The essential idea is, that it was the contempt of those to whom mankind *look up.* Religious people have always had much of this to encounter, and often it is in fact a more severe test of the reality and power of religion than the loss of goods, or than bodily pains and penalties. We can bear much if we have the respect—the praise—of those above us; it is a very certain test of the reality and the power of our religion when we can bear the scorn of the great, the noble, the scientific, the gay, and the fashionable. Piety is more frequently checked and obscured by this than it is by per-

secution. It is more rare that piety shines brightly when the gay and the fashionable frown upon it than when princes attempt to crush it by power. The church has performed its duty better in the furnace of persecution than it has in the gay scenes of the world.

PSALM CXXIV.

This psalm, one of the *Songs of Degrees*, is, like Ps. cxxii., ascribed to David. See the Introductory Notes to that psalm. There is nothing in the one before us to render it improbable that it was composed by him, but it is now impossible to ascertain on what occasion it was written. It would be appropriate to be sung on the return from Babylon, and there is no improbability in the supposition that it may have been *used* on that occasion. But there is nothing in it to prove that it was composed then, or to make it applicable to that occasion alone. Very many were the occasions in the Jewish history when such a psalm was applicable; very many have been the occasions in the history of the Christian church; very many, also, in the lives of individual believers.

The *idea* in the psalm is, that deliverance from trouble and danger is to be ascribed wholly to God; that the people of God are often in such circumstances that there is no human help for them, and that the praise of their deliverance is due to God alone.

1. *If* it had not been *the* LORD *who was on our side.* Unless it was Jehovah who was with us. The idea is, that some one had been with them, and had delivered them, and that such was the nature of the interposition that it could be ascribed to no one but Jehovah. It bore unmistakeable evidence that it was his work. The deliverance was of such a kind that it could have been accomplished by him only. Such things often occur in life, when the intervention in our behalf is so remarkable that we *can* ascribe it to no one else but God.

2 If *it had not been* the LORD who was on our side, when men rose up against us ;

3 Then they had swallowed us up quick, when their wrath was kindled against us :

4 Then the waters had overwhelmed us, the stream had gone

over our soul :

5 Then the proud waters had gone over our soul.

6 Blessed *be* the LORD, who hath not given us *as* a prey to their teeth.

7 Our soul is escaped as a bird out of the snare of the fowlers :

¶ *Now may Israel say.* May well and truly say. The danger was so great, their helplessness was so manifest, and the deliverance was so clearly the work of God, that it was proper to say that *if* this had not occurred, ruin would have been inevitable and entire.

2. *If* it had not been *the* LORD *who was on our side.* Repeating the idea, since the mind was full of it, and carrying the thought forward. This is one of the instances of an *ascent* of thought in these psalms, from which it has been supposed that the title "Songs of *Degrees*" was given to this collection. See, however, Introd. to Ps. cxx. ¶ *When men rose up against us.* When we were assailed by our enemies. On what occasion this occurred, it is now impossible to determine.

3. *Then they had swallowed us up quick.* There was no other help, and ruin—utter ruin—would have soon come upon us. The word *quick* here means *alive;* and the idea is derived from persons swallowed up in an earthquake, or by the opening of the earth, as in the case of Korah, Dathan, and Abiram. Num. xvi. 32, 33. Comp. Ps. cvi. 17. The meaning here is, that they would have been destroyed *as if* they were swallowed up by the opening of the earth ; that is, there would have been *complete* destruction. ¶ *When their wrath was kindled against us.* Heb., In the kindling of their wrath against us. Wrath is often represented in the Scriptures as *burning* or *heated*—as that which consumes all before it.

4. *Then the waters had overwhelmed us.* Our destruction would have been *as if* the waves of the ocean had

overwhelmed us. ¶ *The stream had gone over our soul.* The torrent would have swept us away. Comp. Ps. xviii. 4, 16.

5. *Then the proud waters had gone over our soul.* Over us. The word *proud* here is applied to the waters as if raging, swelling, rolling, tumultuous; as if they were self-confident, arrogant, haughty. Such raging billows, as they break and dash upon the shore, are a striking emblem of human passions, whether in an individual, or in a gathering of men—as an army, or a mob. Comp. Ps. lxv. 7. This is again an amplification, or an *ascent* of thought. See Notes on ver. 2. It is, however, nothing more than a poetical embellishment, adding intensity to the expression.

6. *Blessed be the* LORD. The Lord be praised ; or, We have reason to praise the Lord because we have been delivered from these calamities. ¶ *Who hath not given us* as *a prey to their teeth.* The figure is here changed, though the same idea is retained. The image is now that of destruction by wild beasts—a form of destruction not less fearful than that which comes from overflowing waters. Such changes of imagery constantly occur in the Book of Psalms, and in impassioned poetry everywhere. The mind is full of a subject ; numerous illustrations occur in the rapidity of thought ; and the mind seizes upon one and then upon another as best fitted to express the emotions of the soul. The next verse furnishes another instance of this sudden transition.

7. *Our soul is escaped.* We have escaped ; our life has been preserved. ¶ *As a bird out of the snare of the*

the snare is broken, and we are escaped.

8 Our help *is* in the name of the LORD, who made heaven and earth.

PSALM CXXV.
A Song of degrees.

THEY that trust in the LORD *shall be* as mount Zion, *which* cannot be removed, *but* abideth for ever.

fowlers. By the breaking of the snare, or the gin. The bird is entangled, but the net breaks, and the bird escapes. See Notes on Ps. xci. 3. ¶ *The snare is broken,* etc. It was not strong enough to retain the struggling bird, and the captive broke away. So we seemed to be caught. The enemy appeared to have us entirely in his power, but escape came to us as it does to the bird when it finds the net suddenly break, and itself again at large.

8. *Our help* is *in the name of the* LORD. In the Lord; in the great Jehovah. See Ps. cxxi. 2. ¶ *Who made heaven and earth.* The great Creator; the true God. Our deliverances have led us up to him. They are such as can be ascribed to him alone. They could not have come from ourselves; from our fellow-men; from angels; from any or all created beings. Often in life, when delivered from danger, we may feel this; we always may feel this, and should feel this, when we think of the redemption of our souls. That is a work which we of ourselves could never have performed; which could not have been wrought for us by our fellow-men; which no angel could have accomplished; which all creation combined could not have wrought out; which could have been effected by no one but by him who "made heaven and earth;" by him who created all things. See Col. i. 13–17.

PSALM CXXV.

This psalm is entitled merely "A Song of Degrees." Its author, and the occasion on which it was composed, are unknown. The contents of the psalm accord well with the supposition that it may have been written after the return from the Babylonish captivity, and may

have been designed to strengthen and comfort those who were engaged in rebuilding the city, and restoring the ancient worship, either against the Samaritans and those who opposed them (Neh. vi. 12, 13), or against the lukewarmness of a part of the people themselves. There is nothing, however, so exclusively applicable to that time as to make it *necessary* to suppose that it was composed on that occasion. There is, indeed, evidence in the psalm (ver. 5), that there were some among the people who were disposed to turn away from the service of Jehovah, or who were perverse and rebellious; but such a state of things was not peculiar to the time of the return from the captivity, nor was it peculiar to the Jews, for it has occurred often; it exists still. The psalm is designed to encourage those who were disposed to trust in the Lord, by the assurance that they would be safe; that the blessing of God would be upon them; and that the church was firm and secure.

1. *They that trust in the* LORD. His people; his friends. It is, and has been always, a characteristic of the people of God that they *trust* or *confide* in him. ¶ Shall be *as mount Zion.* The mountain which David fortified, and on which the city was at first built, 2 Sam. v. 6–9. The name *Zion* became also the name by which the entire city was known. ¶ Which *cannot be removed,* but *abideth for ever.* A mountain is an emblem of firmness and stability; and it is natural to speak of it as that which could not be removed. There is something more than this, however, intended here, as there is some ground of comparison *peculiarly* in regard to Mount Zion. This must have been either the idea that Zion was particularly strong by position, or that it was under the Divine protection, and was therefore safe. Most

2 *As* the mountains *are* round about Jerusalem, so the LORD *is* round about his people from henceforth even for ever.

3 For the rod of [1] the wicked shall not rest upon the lot of the righteous; lest *n* the righteous put forth their hands unto iniquity.

[1] *wickedness.*   *n* 1 Cor. x. 13.

---

probably it refers to Zion as a place secure by nature, and rendered more so by art.

2. As *the mountains* are *round about Jerusalem.* Heb., " Jerusalem — the mountains are round about her." Jerusalem, except on the north, is encompassed with hills or mountains, so that although the city was built on hills — Zion, Moriah, Bezethah, Acra,—it was itself surrounded by hills higher than any of these, and was, in a certain sense, in a valley. See Notes on Matt. ii. 1. Comp. Notes on Ps. xlviii. ¶ *So the* LORD is *round about his people,* etc. As Jerusalem is thus protected by the hills around, so the people of God are protected by Jehovah. He surrounds the church; he is exalted far above the church; he guards the approaches to the church; he can defend it from all its foes. Under his protection it is safe. Jerusalem, as surrounded by hills and mountains, has thus become an *emblem* of the church at all times; its security was an emblem of the security of all who trust in the Lord.

3. *For the rod of the wicked.* Marg., as in Heb., *wickedness.* The word " rod,"—the staff, the sceptre, the instrument of inflicting punishment,—here means dominion, power, that condition in which the wicked are commonly found, as one of prosperity or power. God will not deal with the righteous as the wicked are often dealt with:—that is, God will not give his people prosperity as he does them. The righteous will be afflicted, and will be placed in circumstances to keep them from putting forth their hands to iniquity; that is, from indulging in iniquity. They will be afflicted; they will be kept in the ways of virtue and religion by trial; they will not be left

to act out the depravity of the heart as the wicked are. ¶ *Shall not rest upon.* Permanently abide; or, be the constant condition of the righteous. They *may* be prospered, but they must expect that there will be changes, and that God will so deal with them as to keep them from putting forth their hands to iniquity. ¶ *The lot of the righteous.* The righteous, considered as the " lot " or portion of the Lord. The *language* is derived from dividing a land by *lot* (comp. Ps. cv. 11; lxxiv. 2); and the idea is, that the " lot " pertaining to the Lord, or his " portion " among men, is the righteous. ¶ *Lest the righteous put forth their hands unto iniquity.* Lest the effect of prosperity should be to lead them away from God,—like the wicked. Hence they are dealt with in a different manner. They are afflicted; they are thus kept under proper discipline, and their hearts and lives are made what they should be. The statement in this verse, therefore, accords with the uniform statements in the Scriptures, that prosperity is dangerous to the spiritual interests of men, and that, therefore, men are often afflicted in order that they may be led to seek higher interests than those which pertain to this life. The *connexion* here seems to be, that God will defend his people, even as Jerusalem was defended by hills and mountains; but that the *real* welfare and prosperity of his people was not what the wicked seek—wealth and honour, — but the favour of the Lord. Another meaning may, however, be suggested in regard to this verse, which to some may appear more probable than the one above. It is this:—that the " rod "—the dominion of the wicked — of bad rulers — of a harsh and oppressive

4 Do good, O Lord, unto
those that be good, and to *them
that are* upright in their hearts.

5 As for such as turn aside

unto their crooked ways, the
Lord shall lead them forth with
the workers of iniquity : *but* peace
º shall be upon Israel.

o Gal. vi. 16.

---

government—will not *always* be upon
the people of God, lest, being crushed,
they should be led to acts of iniquity ;
or lest, being kept from the free
service of God, they should abandon
themselves to sin.

4. *Do good, O* Lord, *unto* those
that be *good,* etc. To the good ; to
the pious. Let them be under the
Divine protection. Possibly this is
not merely a prayer, but is expressive
of the belief of the psalmist as to
what *would* occur under the Divine
administration — that the favour of
God *would* rest upon his people.

5. *As for such as turn aside unto
their crooked ways.* The wicked.
Those who leave the right or straight
path, and wander in forbidden ways.
The word here rendered *crooked ways*
occurs nowhere else except in Judges
v. 6, where it is rendered *by-ways,*—
meaning unfrequented paths or roads ;
narrow and crooked paths, remote
from the highways, or the ways commonly traversed. Hence the word
means also paths of sin — as devia-
tions from the straight road which
man should travel. ¶ *The* Lord
*shall lead them forth with the work-
ers of iniquity.* They shall be dealt
with *as* sinners. They shall be
punished. The allusion is to back-
sliders ; to those who forsake the
worship of God ; who cease to do
"good ;" who, though among the
professed people of God, wander
from him in by-paths and forbidden
ways. The idea is, that their profession of religion will not save them ;
that they will not obtain the Divine
blessing merely because they are
avowedly the people of God, or are
numbered among them, but that
they will be treated as all other sinners are : — they will be led forth
with all the wicked, and will be
treated like them. Comp. Ezek.

xxxiii. 12, 13 ; Matt. vii. 22, 23 ; xxv.
11, 12. ¶ But *peace* shall be *upon
Israel.* Upon the real Israel ; upon
the true people of God. Gal. vi. 16 ;
Isa. liv. 13 ; lv. 12 ; lvii. 2 ; lxvi. 12 ;
John xiv. 27 ; xvi. 33 ; Eph. ii. 17 ;
Phil. iv. 7.

PSALM CXXVI.

This psalm is entitled simply "A
Song of Degrees." See the Introd. to
Psalm cxx. There can be no reasonable
doubt as to the occasion on which it was
composed, for it bears internal evidence
of having been composed with reference
to the return from Babylon. It may
have been designed to be sung as the
returning captives went up to Jerusalem, but was more probably composed
subsequently to that event, as designed
to keep it in remembrance. It was evidently, however, written not long after
the return, and by some one who had
been personally interested in it, for the
author manifestly, in describing the feelings of the people (vers. 1, 2), speaks of
himself as one of them, or as participating in those feelings which they had
when the exile was closed, and when
they returned to their own land. Who
the author was, it is in vain now to conjecture.

It is evident from the psalm (ver. 5),
that, when it was composed, there was
still some trouble, — something that
might be called a "captivity,"—from
which the psalmist prays that they
might be delivered ; and the object of
the psalm would seem to be in part, in
that trial to find encouragement from
the former interposition of God in their
case. As he *had* "turned the captivity
of Zion," as he *had* filled their "mouth
with laughter," so the psalmist prays
that he would again interpose in similar
circumstances, and renew his goodness.
It is, of course, now impossible to determine precisely to what this refers. It
may be, as Rosenmüller supposes, to a
portion of the people who remained in
exile ; or it may be to some other captivity or danger to which they were exposed after their return. The psalmist,

PSALM CXXVI.

A Song of degrees.

WHEN the LORD [1] turned [p] again the captivity of Zion, we were like them that dream.

2 Then was our mouth filled with laughter, and our tongue

[1] *returned the returning.*

with singing: then said they among the heathen, The LORD hath [2] done great things for them.

3 The LORD hath done great things for us; *whereof* we are glad.

p Ps. liii. 6 ; lxxxv. 1.
[2] *magnified to do with them.*

---

however, expresses entire confidence that there would be such interposition, and that, though then in trouble, they would have joy, such as the farmer has who goes forth sowing his seed with weeping, and who comes with joy in the harvest, bearing his sheaves with him, vers. 5, 6.

1. *When the LORD turned again the captivity of Zion.* Marg., as in Heb., *returned the returning of Zion.* The Hebrew word which is rendered in the text *captivity* means properly *return;* and then, those returning. The ancient versions render it *captivity.* The reference clearly is to those who were returning to Zion, and the psalmist fixes his eye on them *as* returning, and immediately says that it was *the Lord* who had thus restored them. The whole was to be traced to God. ¶ *We were like them that dream.* The Latin Vulgate and the LXX. render this, "we were comforted." The meaning is, "It seemed like a dream; we could hardly realize that it was so; it was so marvellous, so good, so full of joy, that we could scarcely believe it was real." This state of mind is not uncommon, when, in sudden and overpowering joy, we ask whether it can be real; whether it is not all a dream. We *fear* that it is; we apprehend that it will all vanish away like a dream.

2. *Then was our mouth filled with laughter.* Then were we happy; completely happy. See Job viii. 21. ¶ *And our tongue with singing.* We expressed our joy in songs—the natural expression of joy. Young converts—those "*turned*" from sin to God—sing. Their feelings find expression in the songs of Zion. This is natural; this is proper; this *will* occur when sinners are converted.

An assemblage of young converts is always a happy assemblage; a place where there is a "revival" of religion is always a happy place,—full of songs and singing. ¶ *Then said they among the heathen.* The nations; the people among whom they dwelt. ¶ *The* LORD *hath done great things for them.* In causing their return to their own land; in ordering the arrangements for it; in bringing their captivity to an end; in securing such interposition from the civil rulers as to facilitate their return. This would indicate that the surrounding people had not an unfriendly feeling towards them, but that they pitied them in exile, and were disposed to acknowledge the hand of God in what was done. Their deliverance, in the circumstances, was such as evidently to have been the work of God. This will agree well with the account of the return of the exiles from Babylon, and with all that had been done for them by Cyrus. Comp. Ezra i. 1–4.

3. *The* LORD *hath done great things for us.* All that the people around us say is true. We see it; we feel it; we acknowledge it. Those to whom this appertained would see it more clearly than those who had merely observed it. A surrounding world may see in the conversion of a man, in his being turned from sin, in the influence of religion upon him, in his comfort, calmness, and peace, that "the Lord has done great things" for him; but he himself, while he responds most fully to what they say, will see this more clearly than they do. There is more in his redemption, his conversion, his peace and joy, than they do or can perceive, and with emphasis he himself will say, "The

4 Turn again our captivity, O LORD, as the streams in the south.

5 They *q* that sow in tears shall reap in ¹ joy.

6 He that goeth forth and

Lord HAS done great things for me." ¶ Whereof *we are glad.* It fills our souls with joy. If this is understood of the returning Hebrews—coming back from the captivity in Babylon— all must see how appropriate is the language; if it be applied to a sinner returning to God, it is no less suitable, for there is nothing that so fills the mind with joy as a true conversion to God.

4. *Turn again our captivity, O LORD.* Literally, "Turn our captivity." The word *"again"* is inserted by the translators, and conveys an idea which is not necessarily in the original. It is simply a prayer that God would "turn" their captivity; *i. e.*, looking upon the captivity as not wholly ended, or as, in some sense, still continuing, that it might please him *wholly* to turn it, or to end it. The *language* would be applicable, if there was a new "captivity" similar to the one from which they had been delivered, or if the one mainly referred to was not complete; that is, if a part of the people still remained in bondage. The latter is probably the idea, that while a considerable part of the nation had been restored, and while an order had been issued for the restoration of all the captives to their native land, it was still true that a portion of them remained in exile; and the prayer is, that God would interfere in their behalf, and complete the work. A portion of the exiles, in fact, returned under Cyrus; a part under Darius; a part under Xerxes and his successors. The return was by no means accomplished at once, but occupied a succession of years. ¶ *As the streams in the south.* In the southern parts of Palestine, or in the regions bordering it on the south, —Idumea and Arabia. That is, As those streams when dried up by the summer heat are swelled by autumnal

and winter rains, so let the streams of the returning people, which seem now to be diminished, be swelled by augmenting numbers coming again to their own land. Let the companies of returning emigrants be kept full, like swollen streams, until all shall have been brought back.

5. *They that sow in tears shall reap in joy.* Though the sowing of seed is a work of labour and sorrow, —often a work so burdening the farmer that he weeps,—yet the return—the harvest—is accompanied with rejoicing. The truth is expressed in a general form, as illustrating the idea that enterprises which are begun under many difficulties, and which require much labour, will be crowned with success, and that the joy is more than an equivalent for all the weariness and sorrow. Thus it is in respect to the toil of the husbandman; the cares and anxieties of the student; the work of conversion and repentance; the labours of the Christian pastor; the efforts of the Sabbathschool teacher; the faithfulness of the Christian parent; the endeavours of a church for a revival of religion; the zeal and sacrifice of the Christian missionary. The particular allusion here is to the exiles, in their long and weary march to their native land. It was a work of toil and tears, but there would be joy, like that of the harvest, when, their long journey over they should again come to their native land. Comp. Isa. ix. 3.

6. *He that goeth forth and weepeth.* He that goes forth weeping—still an allusion to the farmer. He is seen moving slowly and sadly over the ploughed ground, burdened with his task, and in tears. ¶ *Bearing precious seed.* Marg., *seed-basket.* Literally, "bearing *the drawing out of seed ;*" perhaps the seed as drawn out of his bag; or, as scattered or sown

weepeth, bearing [1] precious seed, shall doubtless come again with

[1] Or, *seed-basket.*

rejoicing, *r* bringing his sheaves *with him.*

r Ps. xxx. 5.

---

regularly in furrows, so that it seems to be *drawn out* in regular lines over the fields. ¶ *Shall doubtless come again.* Shall come to this sown field again in the time of harvest. He will visit it with other feelings than those which he now has. ¶ *With rejoicing,* etc. Then his tears will be turned to joy. Then the rich harvest will wave before him. Then he will thrust in his sickle and reap. Then he will gather the golden grain, and the wain will groan under the burden, and the sheaves will be carried forth with songs of joy. He will be abundantly rewarded for all his toil; he will see the fruit of his labours; he will be filled with joy. The design of this illustration was, undoubtedly, to cheer the hearts of the exiles in their long and dangerous journey to their native land; it has, however, a wider and more universal application, as being fitted to encourage all in their endeavours to secure their own salvation, and to do good in the world,— for the effort is often attended with sacrifice, toil, and tears. The joy of heaven will be more than a compensation for all this. The following remarks by Dr. Thomson (Land and the Book, vol. i., pp. 118, 119) will furnish an illustration of the meaning of this passage :—" I never saw people sowing in tears exactly, but have often known them to do it in fear and distress sufficient to draw them from any eye. In seasons of great scarcity, the poor peasants part in sorrow with every measure of precious seed cast into the ground. It is like taking bread out of the mouths of their children ; and in such times many bitter tears are actually shed over it. The distress is frequently so great that government is obliged to furnish seed, or none would be sown. Ibrahim Pasha did this more than once within my remembrance, copying the example, perhaps, of his great prede-

cessor in Egypt when the seven years' famine was ended. The thoughts of this psalm may likewise have been suggested by the extreme danger which frequently attends the farmer in his ploughing and sowing. The calamity which fell upon the husbandmen of Job when the oxen were ploughing, and the asses feeding beside them, and the Sabeans fell upon them and took them away, and slew the servants with the edge of the sword (Job i. 14, 15), is often repeated in our day. To understand this, you must remember what I just told you about the situation of the arable lands in the open country ; and here again we meet that verbal accuracy : the sower *goes forth*—that is, from the village. The people of Ibel and Khiem, in Merj 'Aiyûn, for example, have their best grain-growing fields down in the 'Ard Hûleh, six or eight miles from their homes, and just that much nearer the lawless border of the desert. When the country is disturbed, or the government weak, they cannot sow these lands except at the risk of their lives. Indeed, they always *go forth* in large companies, and completely armed, ready to drop the plough and seize the musket at a moment's warning ; and yet, with all this care, many sad and fatal calamities overtake the men who must thus sow in tears. And still another origin may be found for the thoughts of the psalm in the extreme difficulty of the work itself in many places. The soil is rocky, impracticable, overgrown with sharp thorns; and it costs much painful toil to break up and gather out the rocks, cut and burn the briers, and to subdue the stubborn soil, especially with their feeble oxen and insignificant ploughs. Join all these together, and the sentiment is very forcibly brought out, that he who labours hard, in cold and in rain, in

PSALM CXXVII.

A Song of degrees [1] for Solomon.

EXCEPT [s] the LORD build the house, they labour in vain 2 that build it; except the LORD

keep the city, the watchman waketh *but* in vain.

[1] Or, *of;* Ps. lxxii., *title.*
[s] 1 Cor. iii. 6, 7.
[2] that are *builders of it in it.*

---

fear and danger, in poverty and in want, casting his precious seed in the ground, will surely come again, at harvest-time, with rejoicing, and bearing his sheaves with him."

PSALM CXXVII.

This psalm is entitled "A Song of Degrees for Solomon;" in the margin, "Of Solomon." In the Syriac Version the title is, "From the Psalms of the Ascent; spoken by David concerning Solomon; it was spoken also of Haggai and Zechariah, who urged the rebuilding of the Temple." The meaning of the title may be either "*for* Solomon," or "*of* Solomon;" that is, it may have been either composed by him, or with reference to him. Many have supposed that it was written by David near the close of his life, and was designed to be a guide to Solomon, his successor, in regard to the principles which should govern him in his reign. There is nothing, however, in the title in the Hebrew which would indicate that it was composed by David; and there is nothing in the psalm which would seem to be *peculiarly* appropriate to address to a young monarch just entering on his reign, unless it was the mere fact of dependence on God. The allusion to children (vers. 3–5), beautiful and proper as it is, would seem to have no particular pertinency to an entrance on the administration of a government, and would not be the topic which would most naturally be suggested in such circumstances. The probability, therefore, is, that the psalm was composed *by* Solomon. On what occasion, however, it was written, it is now impossible to determine. The sentiments and style are such as agree well with the idea that Solomon was the author, and the whole psalm *might* have been introduced into the Book of Proverbs without any manifest discrepancy with the general character and style of that book. From the psalm itself it would seem that it was composed mainly with reference to one who was entering on domestic life, and

that it was intended to set before such a one the views which ought to guide him, or the thoughts which ought to occur to him. Nothing could be more appropriate in such circumstances than the sentiments of the psalm :—I. The entire dependence on God for success, ver. 1. II. The vanity of all efforts—rising early, and sitting up late—without the Divine blessing, ver. 2. III. The fact that children belong to God, and are to be regarded as his, ver. 3. IV. The aid which children might be expected to render to a father in supporting or defending him, ver. 4. V. The comfort which he might expect to derive from them, and the honour which, being properly trained, they would reflect on him and on the family, ver. 5.

1. *Except the* LORD *build the house.* Or rather, "*a* house." The word *house* may refer either to an ordinary dwelling; to the temple, as a place of worship; or to a family, with reference to its success and prosperity, as the word *house* is often used now. The statement is universal, and is designed to indicate a universal dependence on God in human undertakings, though it is not improbable that there may have been an allusion, when the psalm was composed, to some building which was contemplated or commenced. If the psalm was a composition of David or Solomon, the allusion *may* have been to the temple about to be erected. The language, however, is so general as to be applicable to *any* enterprise of that kind. ¶ *They labour in vain that build it.* Literally, "In vain toil its builders in it." The idea is, that they are entirely dependent on God. No matter what their skill, their strength, their industry may be—all will be in vain unless God shall assist them. They are dependent on Him for life, for health, for strength, for practical wisdom, for a disposition to continue

2 *It is* vain for you to rise up
early, to sit up late, to eat *¹* the
t Gen. iii. 17, 19.

bread of sorrows : *for* so he giveth
his beloved sleep.

their work, and for success in it.
Their work might be destroyed by
fire, by a tempest, by an earthquake,
or by an irruption of enemies; and
for the result, therefore, they are entirely dependent on God. ¶ *Except
the* LORD *keep the city.* The same
idea of dependence is here repeated
in another form. The preservation
of a city depends wholly on God,
whatever care or precaution may be
used. ¶ *The watchman waketh* but
in vain. Literally, "In vain waketh
the keeper." The word rendered
waketh means to be sleepless; and
then, to watch. The allusion is to
the watch or guard appointed to keep
a city, and the idea is, that, whatever
may be the diligence, the care, the
fidelity of one thus appointed to guard
a city, its safe keeping must depend
on God alone. Fires may break out
in spite of the watchmen; a tempest
may sweep over it; bands of armed
men may assail it; or the pestilence
may suddenly come into it, and
spread desolation through its dwellings. There *may* have been an allusion in this to some immediate arrangement for guarding Jerusalem
when the psalm was composed; but
the remark is so general that it is
not necessary to confine it to that.
It is universally true that, after all
the care for their own preservation
which men can employ, their safety
depends wholly on God.
2. It is *vain for you to rise up
early.* The psalmist does not here
say that it is improper to rise early;
or that there could be *no* advantage
in it; or that men would be more
likely to be successful in their undertakings if they did *not* rise early;
but that, although this was done,
they would be still altogether dependent on God. *Mere* early rising,
without his blessing, would not secure
what they hoped to accomplish, for
everything is still in the hand of God.

Health, strength, clearness of mind,
and success, are all under his control;
and though early rising *may* tend to
produce all these—as it *does* in fact
—yet still men are not the less dependent on God for success. ¶ *To
sit up late.* That you may labour or
study. As in the former case the
psalmist does not express any opinion
about the propriety or impropriety of
early rising, so it is in respect to this.
He merely says that if it *is* done, this,
of itself, will not accomplish the object; men are still dependent on God
for success *though* they do it. As a
matter of fact, however, sitting up
late has *less* tendency to promote
success in life than early rising; but
in either case there is the same dependence on God. ¶ *To eat the bread
of sorrows.* Bread of care, anxiety,
or trouble; that is, bread earned or
procured by the severity of toil.
There may be an allusion here to the
original sentence pronounced on man,
Gen. iii. 17. The meaning is, that it
is in vain that you labour hard, that
you exhaust your strength, in order
to get bread to eat, unless God shall
bless you. After all your toil the result is with him. ¶ For *so he giveth
his beloved sleep.* The word *"for"*
is not in the original. The sentence
is very obscure in the connexion in
which it stands. The Septuagint and
Latin Vulgate render it, "Ye who eat
the bread of care—rise when you have
rested—when he hath given his beloved sleep." Some have supposed it
to mean that God gives his people rest
without toil,—or that, while others
labour, his "beloved"—his friends—
sleep; but this interpretation is not
necessarily demanded by the Hebrew,
and is inconsistent with the general
doctrine of the Bible. Others have
supposed the idea to be, that God
gives his beloved rest *after* labour;
but though this is true, it is not true
of them peculiarly or exclusively.

3 Lo, children " *are* an heritage of the Lord : *and* the fruit of the womb *is his* reward.

u Gen. xxxiii. 5 ; 1 Sam. ii. 5.

4 As arrows *are* in the hand of a mighty man ; so *are* children of the youth.

5 Happy *is* the man that hath

Some suppose, with as little probability, that the meaning is, that what others hope (but hope in vain) to get by labour, the Lord bestows upon his people in sleep, they know not how. The meaning evidently is, that God bestows "sleep" upon his people in some sense in which it is *not* bestowed on others, or that there is, in regard to their case, something in which they differ from those who are so anxious and troubled,—who rise so early for the sake of gain,—who toil so late,—who eat the bread of care. The idea seems to be that there would be calmness, repose, freedom from anxiety or solicitude. God makes the mind of his people—his beloved—calm and tranquil, while the world around is filled with anxiety and restlessness—busy, bustling, *worried.* As a consequence of this calmness of mind, and of their confidence in him, they enjoy undisturbed repose at night. They are not kept wakeful and anxious about their worldly affairs as other men are, for they leave all with God, and *thus* he "giveth his beloved sleep." The particle " *so* "—יֵ, *kēn* — or "thus," I apprehend, refers to the general sense of what had been said, rather than to what *immediately* precedes it ;—to the fact that all success depends on God (ver. 1), and that it is always by his interposition, and not as the result of human skill, toil, or fatigue, that men find calmness, success, repose. It is only by the favour of God, and by their recognizing their dependence on him, that they find repose, success, and freedom from care.

3. *Lo, children* are *an heritage of the* Lord. They are an inheritance derived from the Lord. They are bestowed by him as really as success is in building a house, or in guarding a city. The idea is, that everything which we value, or which we desire,

is a gift from God, and is to be received as from him, and to be acknowledged as his gift. The general idea here, as in the previous verses, is that of entire dependence on God. ¶ And *the fruit of the womb* is his *reward.* Or rather, " *a* reward ;" that is, they are of the nature of a reward for a life of devotion to God ; they are among the blessings which God promises, and are evidences of his favour. Our translation by inserting the words " *is his* " obscures the sense, as if the meaning were that they belong to God as his " reward " for what he does for us. The reverse of this is the true idea,—that they are a blessing with which he rewards or favours his people. Of course, this is not universally true, but the promise is a general one, in accordance with the usual promises in the Bible in regard to the result of piety. Children are to be reckoned among the Divine favours bestowed on us, and for their lives, their health, their virtues, and the happiness derived from them, we are, as in other things, dependent on him,—as in building a house, in guarding a city, or in the rest and comfort derived from toil.

4. *As arrows* are *in the hand of a mighty man.* They are what a parent may rely on for defence in danger, or for help in securing provision for himself and family,—as the warrior or the hunter relies on his arrows. ¶ *So* are *children of the youth.* Sons in their youth ; in their prime and vigour. The comparison of sons with arrows or spears is common in Arabic poetry. See Rosenmüller, Com. *in loc.* Also Morgenland, *in loc.*

5. *Happy* is *the man.* Heb., The happiness of the man. See Notes on Ps. i. 1. ¶ *That hath his quiver full of them.* The *quiver* is a case in which arrows are carried ; and as a man—a hunter or warrior—feels se-

¹ his quiver full of them: they shall not be ashamed, but they shall ² speak with the enemies in the *v* gate.

¹ *filled his quiver with.*
² Or, *subdue,* Ps. xviii. 47, or, *destroy.*
v Job v. 4.

cure when he has his quiver full of arrows, so a man is blessed in proportion to the number of his sons. This is in accordance with the idea often presented in the Bible, and the promise often made there of a numerous posterity as a proof of the Divine favour. ¶ *They shall not be ashamed.* They shall not turn back discomfited, hanging their heads with shame and confusion. See Notes on Job vi. 20. ¶ *But they shall speak with the enemies in the gate.* Marg., *shall subdue,* or *destroy.* The Hebrew word, however, means *to speak ;* and the meaning is, that they would *speak* to their foes in the place of conflict,—for a battle occurred often in the gate of a city, as the possession of a *gate,* or an entrance to a city was of so much importance to those who attacked, and those who defended it. The idea is, that they would speak *with effect ;* they would distinguish themselves; they would let their presence be known. The connexion does not allow us to understand this of forensic controversy, or of transactions in business, though these were usually performed at the gates of cities. The meaning is, that they would do honour to the family, and gratify the heart of the parent, by their valour in defending their city and home, or in attacking the cities of the enemies of their country. The psalm is designed to inculcate the lesson of dependence on God for success in everything.

PSALM CXXVIII.

The author of this psalm is unknown, as is also the occasion on which it was composed. It is not known, either, why *this* psalm was placed among those which are called "Songs of Degrees." The scope and

PSALM CXXVIII.

A Song of degrees.

BLESSED *w is* every one that feareth the LORD : that walketh in his ways.

2 For *x* thou shalt eat the

w Ps. cxii. 1.　　*x* Isa. iii. 10.

design of it, however, cannot be misunderstood. It is intended to show the advantage of religion on the affairs of this life, and especially *on the domestic relations ;*—in a numerous family, in the character of children, and in being permitted to see numerous descendants. In connexion with this, the possessor of true religion would be permitted to see the prosperity of Zion—the good of Jerusalem, and peace upon Israel. Of course this is to be regarded as a *general* statement, or as indicating what will *commonly* be true as the result of religion. See Notes on Ps. xxxvii. 9, 33; cxii. 2, 3. Thus industry, temperance, prudence, tend to promote health and long life, so that health and a long life are the *general* result ; but it would be unfair to regard one who should assert this as meaning to say that it is *universally* true, or that men who are industrious, temperate, and prudent, are *never* sick, and *never* die.

The psalm states, in general (ver. 1), the blessedness of those who fear the Lord. This blessedness is seen (1) in their success in life, ver. 2; (2) in a numerous and happy family, ver. 3; (3) in being permitted to see children's children, ver. 6; (4) in being permitted to see the prosperity of religion—the "good of Jerusalem," and "peace upon Israel," vers. 5, 6.

1. *Blessed* is *every one that feareth the* LORD. That honours God ; that is truly pious. See Notes on Ps. i. 1 ; cxii. 1. What that blessedness is, is indicated in the following verses. ¶ *That walketh in his ways.* The ways which God commands or directs. On the word *walketh,* see Notes on Ps. i. 1.

2. *For thou shalt eat the labour of thine hands.* Thou shalt enjoy the avails of thy labour ; thou shalt be secure in thy rights. See Notes on Isa. iii. 10. This is a general promise respecting the prosperity which re-

the good of Jerusalem all the days of thy life.

6 Yea, thou shalt see thy children's *b* children, *and* *c* peace upon Israel.

b Gen. l. 23 ; Job xlii. 16.
c Ps. cxxv. 5.

---

to would be permitted to enjoy a view of the continual prosperity of religion in the world. ¶ *All the days of thy life.* To the very close of life. No h gher blessing could be promised to a pious man than that he should see religion always prospering ; that the last view which he would have of the world should be the rapid advances of religion ; that he should die in a revival of religion.

6. *Yea, thou shalt see thy children's children.* This is a continuation of the idea of blessedness as connected with a numerous posterity—an object of so much interest to the Hebrews (see Notes on ver. 3), and having its foundation in our nature. ¶ And *peace upon Israel.* See Ps. cxxv. 5. As the crowning blessing ; a blessing above that of success in worldly affairs ; above that of seeing a numerous and happy posterity. The love of God is the supreme affection in the mind of a pious man ; the desire that his cause may prosper and triumph is to him a supreme desire. Man is truly and completely blessed only in religion.

PSALM CXXIX.

This psalm is entitled merely " A Song of Degrees." Its author is unknown ; and the occasion on which it was written cannot now be ascertained. It is a psalm which would be applicable to many periods of the Jewish history, and it is not of such a nature that it can with certainty be referred to any one of them. There is nothing in it which would forbid us to suppose that it was composed on the return from the Babylonish exile, but there is nothing to fix it definitely to that event. Why it was made one of the " Songs of Degrees" is equally unknown. It merely refers to the fact that Israel had often been roughly and severely treated ; and

PSALM CXXIX.

A Song of degrees.

MANY [1] a time have they afflicted me from *d* my youth, may Israel now say :

2 Many a time have they afflicted

[1] Or, *Much.*   *d* Ex. i. 13, 14 ; Lam. i. 3.

---

it contains a prayer that those who were the enemies of Zion might be punished in a proper manner. It would seem probable that it was composed during a time of trouble, of war, or of persecution, and that the main purpose of the writer was to refer to the fact that the same thing had often occurred before, and to find consolation and support *in* that fact. The principle on which it is founded is, that there is nothing to be dreaded as the result of trial, if we have passed through the same form of trial before, and if we have not sunk but have been sustained under it. This furnishes an assurance that the same thing may occur again.

1. *Many a time.* Marg., as in Heb., *much.* Probably, however, the idea is, as expressed in our translation, *many a time ; often.* So it is in the Latin Vulgate and the Septuagint ; and this accords better with the connexion. ¶ *Have they afflicted me from my youth.* Have I been afflicted ; have others dealt unjustly by me. The *youth* here is the beginning of the history of that people :—since we began to be a people ; since the nation was founded. ¶ *May Israel now say.* May the nation now say. It is clear from this that the psalm was not written at an early period of their history.

2. *Many a time,* etc. This repetition is designed to fix the thoughts on the fact, and to impress it on the mind. The mind dwells on the fact as important in its bearing on the present occasion or emergency. The idea is, that it is no new thing to be thus afflicted. It has often occurred. It is a matter of long and almost constant experience. Our enemies have often attempted to destroy us, but in vain. What we experience now we have often experienced, and when

me from my youth; yet *e* they have not prevailed against me.

3 The plowers plowed upon my back; they made long their furrows.

e John xvi. 33.   *f* 1 Cor. xvi. 22.

thus tried we have been as often delivered, and have nothing now therefore to fear. We are not to regard it as a strange thing that we are now afflicted; and we are not to be discouraged or disheartened as if our enemies could overcome us, for they have often tried it in vain. He who has protected us heretofore can protect us still. He who defended us before can defend us now, and the past furnishes an assurance that he will defend us if it is best that we should be protected. It does much to support us in affliction if we can recall to mind the consolations which we had in former trials, and can avail ourselves of the result of past experience in supporting us now. ¶ *Yet they have not prevailed against me.* They have never been able to overcome us. We were safe then in the Divine hands; we shall be safe in the same hands now.

3. *The ploughers ploughed upon my back.* The comparison here is undoubtedly taken from the *ploughing* of land, and the idea is that the sufferings which they had endured were such as would be well represented by a plough passing over a field, tearing up the sod; piercing deep; and producing long rows or furrows. The direct allusion would seem to be to stripes inflicted *on* the back, *as if* a plough had been made to pass over it; and the meaning is, that they had been subjected to sufferings as slaves or criminals were when the lash cut deep into the flesh. Probably the immediate thing in the mind of the psalmist was the hard bondage of the children of Israel in Egypt, when they were subjected to all the evils of servitude. ¶ *They made long their furrows.* On my back. The word here used, and

4 The LORD *is* righteous: he hath cut asunder the cords of the wicked.

5 Let *f* them all be confounded and turned back that hate Zion.

6 Let them be as the grass

rendered *made long*—אָרַךְ, *arach*, means to make long, to prolong, to extend in a right line, and it may be used either in the sense of making long as to extent or space, or making long in regard to time, prolonging. The latter would seem to be the meaning here, as it is difficult to see in what sense it could be said that stripes inflicted on the back could be made long. They might, however, be continued and repeated; the sufferings might be *prolonged* sufferings as well as *deep.* It was a work of long-continued oppression and wrong.

4. *The LORD is righteous.* Righteous in permitting this; righteous in what he has done, and will do, in the treatment of those who inflict such wrongs. We may now safely commit our cause to him in view of what he has done in the past. He was not indifferent then to our sufferings, or deaf to the cries of his people; he interposed and punished the oppressors of his people, and we may trust him still. ¶ *He hath cut asunder the cords of the wicked.* By which they bound us. He did this in our "youth;" when we were oppressed and beaten in Egypt. Then he interposed, and set us free.

5. *Let them all be confounded and turned back,* etc. This might be rendered in the indicative, "they *are* ashamed," but the connexion seems to require the rendering in our version. It is a prayer that God would now interpose as he had done in former times, and that he would cause *all* the haters of Zion to be put to shame as formerly.

6. *Let them be as the grass* upon *the housetops.* The housetops, or roofs of houses, covered with sand or earth, in which seeds of grass may germinate and begin to grow, but

upon the house-tops, *g* which withereth afore it groweth up;

7 Wherewith the mower filleth not his hand, nor he that bindeth sheaves his bosom.

8 Neither do they which go by say, The blessing *h* of the LORD *be* upon you : we bless you in the name of the LORD.

g 2 Kings xix. 26.　　*h* Ruth ii. 4.

---

where, as there is no depth of earth, and as the heat of the sun there would be intense, it would soon wither away. See Notes on Isa. xxxvii. 27. ¶ *Which withereth afore it groweth up.* This, even if it has any meaning, is not the meaning of the original. The idea in the Hebrew is,—and it is so rendered in the Septuagint, the Latin Vulgate, and by Luther,—"which before [one] pulls it, withers." Grass would wither or dry up, of course, if it were pulled up or cut down, but the grass here spoken of withers even *before* this is done. It has no depth of earth to sustain it; having sprouted, and begun to grow, it soon dies—a perfect image of feebleness and desolation; of hopes begun only to be disappointed. " This morning " (says Dr. Thomson, " Land and the Book," vol. ii., p. 574) " I saw a striking illustration of this most expressive figure. To obtain a good view of the Tyropean, my guide took me to the top of a house on the brow of Zion, and the grass which had grown over the roof during the rainy season was now entirely withered and perfectly dry."

7. *Wherewith the mower filleth not his hand.* It cannot be gathered and laid up for the use of cattle, as grass can that grows in the field. It is valueless for any such purpose; or, is utterly worthless. The phrase " filleth not his hand " seems to be derived from the idea of reaping, where the reaper with one hand takes hold of the grain which he reaps, and cuts it off with the sickle in the other. ¶ *Nor he that bindeth sheaves.* The man who gathers in the harvest. This was commonly performed by a different person from the reaper. ¶ *His bosom.* This word would commonly refer to the bosom of the garment, in which things were carried; or that part above the girdle. It may

be used here, however, in a larger sense,—since it is incongruous to suppose that sheaves of grain would be carried thus,— as meaning simply that one who gathered the sheaves would usually convey them in his arms, folding them to his bosom.

8. *Neither do they which go by say, The blessing of the* LORD, *etc.* As in a harvest-field, where persons passing by express their joy and gratitude that their neighbours are reaping an abundant harvest. The phrase " The blessing of the Lord be upon you," was expressive of good wishes; of pious congratulation; of a hope of success and prosperity ; as when we say, " God be with you ;" or, " God bless you." The meaning here is, that such language would never be used in reference to the grass or grain growing on the house-top, since it would never justify a wish of that kind :—it would be ridiculous and absurd to apply such language to any one who should be found gathering up that dry and withered, and worthless grass. So the psalmist prays that it may be in regard to all who hate Zion (ver. 5), that they may have no such prosperity as would be represented by a growth of luxuriant and abundant grain ; no such prosperity as would be denoted by the reaper and the binder of sheaves gathering in such a harvest; no such prosperity as would be indicated by the cheerful greeting and congratulation of neighbours who express their gratification and their joy at the rich and abundant harvest which has crowned the labours of their friend, by the prayer that God would bless him. ¶ *We bless you in the name of the* LORD. Still the language of pious joy and gratification addressed by his neighbours to him who was reaping his harvest. All this is simply language drawn from com-

PSALM CXXX.

A Song of degrees.

OUT of the depths *i* have I cried unto thee, O LORD.

2 Lord, hear my voice; *k* let thine ears be attentive to the voice of my supplications.

i Lam. iii. 55; Jonah ii. 2.   *k* 2 Chron. vi. 40.

mon life, uttering a prayer that the enemies of Zion might be "confounded and turned back" (ver. 5); a prayer that they might not be successful in their endeavours to destroy the Church. Such a prayer cannot but be regarded as proper and right.

PSALM CXXX.

This psalm also is entitled "A Song of Degrees." See Notes on Introd. to Ps. cxx. The author and the occasion on which it was composed are unknown, as is also the reason why it was included in this group of psalms.

The language of the psalm seems to be that of an individual; but most interpreters suppose that it is an individual speaking in the name of the nation, and representing its calamities and its penitence. Some have imagined that the person represented as speaking in vers. 7, 8, is a different individual from the one speaking in the other part of the psalm, but there seems to be no ground for this opinion. It is commonly supposed that the psalm had reference to the state of the Jews in the Babylonish captivity, but there is no necessity for limiting it to that period, if indeed it has any reference to the people of Israel. There were many occasions in their history when the language of the psalm would not be less appropriate than at that time. But there is no *necessity* at all for supposing that it refers to the nation as such. It may be the language of an individual, mourning over his sins, and pleading for mercy, expressing deep conviction of sin, and humble trust in God as the only hope for a convinced, condemned, and penitent sinner. As such, it would represent what has occurred in thousands of cases when sinners have been brought to conviction of sin, and have cried for mercy. Understood in this manner, it is one of the most instructive and touching of the psalms. I know of no reason why it may not be so regarded.

1. *Out of the depths.* The word rendered *depths* is from a verb—עָמַק, *amak*—which means to be deep; then,

to be unsearchable; then, to make deep; and it would apply to anything low, deep, or profound, as the ocean, a pit, or a valley. The word here used occurs elsewhere only in the following places:—Ps. lxix. 2, 14, where it is rendered *deep*, applied to waters; and Isa. li. 10; Ezek. xxvii. 34, where it is rendered *depths*. The word, as used here, would be applicable to deep affliction, dejection, or distress. It would be applicable (*a*) to affliction —the depths of sorrow from loss of friends, property, or bodily suffering; (*b*) sin—the depths into which the soul is plunged under the consciousness of guilt; (*c*) mental trouble— low spirits—melancholy—darkness of mind—loss of comfort in religion— powerful temptation — disappointment—the anguish caused by ingratitude—or sadness of heart in view of the crimes and the sorrows of men—or grief at the coldness, the hardness, the insensibility of our friends to their spiritual condition. From all these depths of sorrow it is our privilege to call upon the Lord; *in* those depths of sorrow it is proper thus to implore his help. Often he brings us into these "depths" that we *may* be led to call upon him; always when we are brought there, we should call upon him. ¶ *Have I cried unto thee, O* LORD. Or rather, "do I now invoke thee," or call earnestly upon thee. The language does not refer so much to the past as the present. I *now* cry for mercy; I *now* implore thy blessing. The condition is that of one who in deep sorrow, or under deep conviction for sin, pleads earnestly that God would have compassion on him.

2. *Lord, hear my voice.* This is the prayer; this is *what* he cried. It is the language of earnest pleading. ¶ *Let thine ears be attentive to the voice of my supplications.* Do not

3 If *l* thou, LORD, shouldest mark iniquities, O Lord, who shall stand?

4 But *m* there *is* forgiveness

l Ps. cxliii. 2; Rom. iii. 20—24.
m Ex. xxxiv. 7; Dan. ix. 9; Rom. viii. 1.

with thee, that *n* thou mayest be feared.

5 I wait for the LORD, my soul doth wait, and in his word do I hope.

n Jer. xxxiii. 8, 9; 2 Tim. ii. 19.

---

turn away from me; do not disregard my cry. See Notes on Ps. v. 1.

3. *If thou, LORD, shouldest mark iniquities.* If thou shouldst observe, note, attend to, regard all the evil that I have done. The Hebrew word means properly to keep, to watch, to guard. The word, as used here, refers to that kind of vigilance or watchfulness which one is expected to manifest who is on guard; who keeps watch in a city or camp by night. The idea is, If God should thus look with a scrutinizing eye; if he should try to see all that he could see; if he should suffer nothing to escape his observation; if he should deal with us exactly as we are; if he should overlook nothing, forgive nothing, we could have no hope. ¶ *Who shall stand?* Who shall stand upright? Who could stand before thee? Who could hope to be acquitted? This implies (1) that the petitioner was conscious of guilt, or knew that he was a sinner; (2) that he felt there was a depth of depravity in his heart which *God* could see, but which *he* did not,—as every man must be certain that there is in his own soul; (3) that God had the power of bringing that to light if he chose to do it, so that the guilty man would be entirely overwhelmed; (4) that he who urged the prayer rested his only hope on the fact that God would *not* mark iniquity; would *not* develope what was in him; would *not* judge him by what he saw in his heart; but would deal with him otherwise, and show him mercy and compassion. Every man must feel that if God should "mark iniquity" as it is,—if he should judge us as we are,—we could have no hope. It is only on the ground that we may be forgiven, that we can hope to come before him.

4. *But* there is *forgiveness with thee.* The Septuagint renders this ἱλασμός, propitiation, reconciliation; the Latin Vulgate *propitiatio*, propitiation. The Hebrew word means *pardon.* The idea is, that sin may be forgiven; or, that God is a Being who does pardon sin, and that this is the only ground of hope. When we come before God, the ground of our hope is not that we can justify ourselves; not that we can prove we have not sinned; not that we can explain our sins away; not that we can offer an apology for them; it is only in a frank and full confession, and in a hope that God will forgive them. He who does not come in this manner can have no hope of acceptance with God. ¶ *That thou mayest be feared.* That thou mayest be reverenced; or, that men may be brought to serve and worship thee— may be brought to a proper reverence for thy name. The idea is, not that pardon produces *fear* or *terror,*—for the very reverse is true,—but that God, by forgiving the sinner, brings him to reverence him, to worship him, to serve him:—that is, the sinner is truly reconciled to God, and becomes a sincere worshipper. The offender is *so* pardoned that he is disposed to worship and honour God; for God has revealed himself as one who forgives sin, *in order* that the sinner may be encouraged to come to him, and be his true worshipper.

5. *I wait for the* LORD. That is, in this state of distress and trouble— from these "depths" of woe, and sorrow, and conviction of sin. This implies two things: (1) that he had no other dependence; (2) that his soul was actually in a waiting posture, or that he actually looked to the Lord for his interposition. ¶ *My*

6 My soul *waiteth* for the Lord more than they that watch for the morning; ¹ *I say, more than*
¹ Or *which watch unto the morning.*

they that watch for the morning.
7 Let Israel hope *o* in the LORD : for with the LORD *there*
o Ps. lxxi. 5; Rom. viii. 24; Heb. x. 35.

soul doth wait. I wait, with all my soul and heart. ¶ *And in his word do I hope.* In his promise. I believe that he will fulfil that promise, and that I shall find a gracious answer to my prayers. Under conviction for sin, under deep sorrow and distress of any kind, this is the only hope of man. If God does *not* interpose, there is no deliverer; that he *will* interpose we may feel assured, if we come to him with a humble, a believing, and a penitent heart.

6. *My soul* waiteth *for the Lord more than they that watch for the morning.* More intently; more anxiously. The Septuagint and Latin Vulgate render this, "My soul hopeth in the Lord from the morning watch till night." The idea is that of watchers — night guards — who look anxiously for the break of day that they may be relieved. It is not that of persons who simply look for the return of day, but of those who are on guard—or it may be who watch beside the sick or the dying—and who look out on the east to mark the first indications of returning light. To them the night seems long; they are weary, and want repose; all around is cheerless, gloomy, and still; and they long for the first signs that light will again visit the world. Thus in affliction—the long, dark, dreary, gloomy night of sorrow—the sufferer looks for the first indication, the first faint ray of comfort to the soul. Thus under deep conviction for sin, and deep apprehension of the wrath of God—that night, dark, dreary, gloomy, often long—the soul looks for some ray of comfort, some intimation that God will be merciful, and will speak peace and pardon. ¶ I say, more than *they that watch for the morning.* Marg., *which watch unto the morning.* The translation in the text best expresses the sense.

There is something exceedingly beautiful and touching in this language of repetition, though it is much enfeebled by the words which our translators have inserted, "I say, more than." The Hebrew is, "more than they that watch for the morning,— watch for the morning," as if the mind dwelt upon the words as better expressing its own anxious state than any other words could do. Every one who has been afflicted will feel the force of this; every one who has been under conviction of sin, and who has felt himself in danger of suffering the wrath of God, will remember how anxiously he longed for mercy, for light, for peace, for *some* indication, even the most faint, like the first ray which breaks in the east, that his soul *would* find mercy and peace.

7. *Let Israel hope in the* LORD. In such circumstances of affliction and distress, let not the people of God despair. In the darkest night, in calamities deep and prolonged, let not those who love God despair. The morning will dawn; the light will break in the east; deliverance and joy will come. The Hebrew here is, "Trust, O Israel, in the Lord." The *design* of the psalmist seems to be, from his own experience, to persuade others—the afflicted people of God—to put their trust in Him in whom he had himself hoped. From the very depths of affliction, guilt, and almost despair, he had looked to the Lord:—encouraged and persuaded by his example, he would now entreat the people of God everywhere and always, in like manner, to trust him. ¶ *For with the* LORD *there is mercy.* He is merciful, and in his mercy we may trust. ¶ *And with him* is *plenteous redemption.* It is ample; it is full; it abounds. It is not limited; it is not exhausted; it cannot be exhausted. So we may always feel when

is mercy, and with him *is* plenteous [p] redemption.

p Ps. ciii. 8.

8 And [q] he shall redeem Israel from all his iniquities.

q Matt. i. 21.

we come before God, that his mercy is ample for all the wants of all the sinful and the suffering; that the provisions of his grace are unexhausted and inexhaustible. Applying this, as we may, to the work of the Saviour, we may feel that the redemption which is in him is adequate to the wants of a world, and that although numberless millions have been saved by it, yet that it is still as rich, as full, and as free as it was in the beginning;—as the ocean, though from the beginning of the world it has supplied the materials for rain and dew to water the hills, the vales, the continents, and the islands, is still full; as the light of the sun, though for thousands of ages it has poured its light on the planets, and on all the vast space between itself and those orbs, and has sent out its light into the vast regions beyond, still shines with undiminished splendour, and pours its floods of day and of glory on all those worlds.

8. *And he shall redeem Israel from all his iniquities.* His people. He will completely deliver them from the power and the pollution of sin. This will ultimately be accomplished in reference to his whole church, and to every true member of that church. This was the highest object before the mind of the psalmist—that with which the psalm appropriately closes. And this is the highest object before the mind of every true child of God—that he may be completely and for ever delivered from the power and the dominion of sin. This will be perfectly accomplished in heaven only; but there and then the bliss will be complete. The psalm begins with an earnest cry from the "depths;" it closes with the triumphant hope of complete and eternal deliverance. There is one world where there is no occasion to cry to God from the "depths" of sorrow and of sin.

PSALM CXXXI.

This brief psalm is entitled "A Song of Degrees of David." There is nothing in it to forbid the idea that it was composed by him, for it is wholly in his spirit and manner. It is not known, however, on what occasion it was written, nor why it has a place among the "Songs of Degrees." It would *seem* to have been prepared on some occasion when the author had been charged with being of a lofty and proud spirit; with meddling in matters that were above him, or above his condition in life; or with making such suggestions about public affairs as were considered to indicate a self-confident, or an aspiring mind. Without being able to determine this by any certain facts, the supposition which would seem most to accord with the contents of the psalm would be that it was written when he was a young man; when he had expressed, in the presence of others, some sentiments on public affairs which were interpreted by them as denoting a forward and self-confident spirit. If so, then this psalm was probably a private meditation on what he had done, and was of the nature of a personal examination of his spirit and motives. Knowing, as we do, what David was afterwards—his great talents as a warrior and a king, and his ability to manage public affairs—it would not, in itself, be strange or improbable that, in early life, and even when a shepherd-boy, he might have advanced opinions which would be regarded as beyond his age, as unbecoming his condition, and as manifesting a disposition to meddle with matters above him; and that he might have been rebuked for this. If it were so, we may suppose that a pious and a modest youth would give himself to self-examination, to determine whether that *was* the spirit which actuated him, and this psalm may have been the result of such an examination:—a deep self-consciousness that such was *not* the spirit which influenced him; that these were *not* the motives which prompted him to do what he had done. The psalm, therefore, may, perhaps, without impropriety, be regarded as furnishing evidence of the early manifestation of a disposition on the part of David to

PSALM CXXXI.

A Song of degrees of David.

LORD, my heart is not haughty,
nor mine eyes lofty: neither
do I [1] exercise myself in great
matters, or in things too [2] high
for me.

2 Surely I have behaved and
quieted [3] myself, as a child [r] that

[1] walk.   [2] wonderful, Job xlii. 3.
[3] my soul.   [r] Matt. xviii. 3.

study public affairs, and of an early
manifestation of a knowledge on that
subject which was regarded as above his
years and his station; and, at the same
time, of his readiness to profit by rebuke,
and to examine his real motives; and of
his consciousness that he was *not* actuated by self-confident and aspiring views.
The psalm manifests a humble spirit,
and a spirit of confident trust in God.
If the interpretation thus suggested
could be confirmed,—or if it may be
allowed,—the psalm would be one of
the most valuable records of the early
life and character of David. It would
add to the interest of this conjecture, if
we might suppose that this psalm was
left among the effusions of his early
years—among, as we should say, his
"private papers,"—and was discovered
after he was dead, and was then arranged
and published among these "Songs of
Degrees."

1. LORD, *my heart is not haughty.*
Though this is charged upon me;
though I may have said things which
seem to imply it; though this might
appear a just inference from my conduct,—yet I am conscious that this is
not my real character. What I have
said was not the result of ambition.
¶ *Nor mine eyes lofty.* I am conscious that I am not ambitious and
aspiring—as I am accused of being.
What I have said is not the result of
such a feeling, nor should such a
charge be brought against me. ¶ *Neither do I exercise myself.* Marg., as
in Heb., *walk.* I do not walk about
among such things; I do not pry into
them; I do not meddle with them.
What I have said or done is not, as
has been said concerning me, the result of a meddlesome and interfering
spirit. It may *seem* to be so; my
own consciousness tells me it is *not*
so. The interpretation put upon my
conduct may be natural; but I am
conscious to myself that it is not the
right interpretation. ¶ *In great
matters, or in things too high for me.*
Marg., as in Heb., *wonderful.* The
word *wonderful* would apply to matters fitted to excite astonishment by
their vastness, or their unusual nature
—as prodigies or miracles; and then,
great and lofty truths. It would
apply also to things which might be
regarded as far above the capacity of
a child, or of one in obscure life, and
with slight advantages of education;
and, as above suggested, it may have
been the accusation brought against
him, that, in respect to public matters,
matters of state,— or to the more elevated doctrines of religion,—he had
manifested a spirit unbecoming one in
early years, and of humble rank, and
that this indicated a desire to meddle
with matters which he could not understand, and which could not pertain
to him. He was conscious, he says,
that he was *not* actuated by that
spirit.

2. *Surely I have behaved and quieted
myself.* Marg., as in Heb., *my soul.*
The Hebrew is, "If I have not soothed
and quieted my soul." This is a strong
mode of affirming that he *had* done it.
The negative form is often thus used
to denote a strong affirmation. The
full form would be, " God knows if I
have not done this;" or, "If I have
not done this, then let me bear the
consequences; let me be punished."
The idea is that he was *conscious* he
had done this. Instead of being arrogant, proud, and ambitious,—instead
of meddling with matters above him,
and which did not belong to him, he
had known his proper place. He had
been gentle, calm, retiring. The word
rendered *behaved* means properly to be
even or level; then, in the form here
used, to make even, smooth, or level;
and it is here used in the sense of

is weaned of his mother: my soul *is* even as a weaned child.

3 Let Israel hope in the LORD, [1] from henceforth and for ever.

[1] *from now.*

calming the mind; smoothing down its roughnesses; keeping it tranquil. Comp. Notes on Isa. xxxviii. 13, in our version, " I *reckoned* " (the same word as here) " till morning,"—but where the correct translation would be, " I *composed* or calmed myself until morning." So the meaning here is, that he had kept his mind calm, and even, and gentle. ¶ *As a child that is weaned of his mother.* See Isa. xxviii. 9. There have been very various interpretations of this passage. See Rosenmüller *in loc.* Perhaps the true idea is that of a child, when weaned, as leaning upon its mother, or as reclining upon her breast. As a weaned child leans upon its mother. That is, as a child, accustomed to the breast, and now deprived of it, lays its head gently where it had been accustomed to derive its nutriment, feeling its dependence, hoping to obtain nourishment again: not angry, but gently grieved and sad. A little child thus clinging to its mother— laying its head gently down on the bosom — languishing — looking for nourishment—would be a most tender image of meekness and gentleness. ¶ *My soul* is *even as a weaned child.* Literally, " As a weaned child upon me my soul ;" that is probably, My soul leans upon me as a weaned child. My powers, my nature, my desires, my passions, thus lean upon me, are gentle, unambitious, confiding. The Septuagint renders this in a different manner, and giving a different idea, " Had I not been humble, but exalted myself as a weaned child doth against its mother, how wouldst thou have retributed against my soul !" The Hebrew, however, requires that it should be otherwise interpreted. The *idea* is, that he *had* been gentle ; that he had calmed down his feelings ; that whatever aspirations he might have had, he had kept them under; that though he might have made in-

quiries, or offered suggestions that *seemed* to savour of pride or ambition, he had been conscious that this was not so, but that he had known his proper place, and had kept it. The sentiment here is, that religion produces a child-like spirit ; that it disposes all to know and keep their right place ; that to whatever inquiries or suggestions it may lead among the young, it will tend to keep them modest and humble ; and that whatever suggestions one in early life may be disposed to make, they will be connected with a spirit that is humble, gentle, and retiring. Religion produces self-control, and is inconsistent with a proud, an arrogant, and an ambitious spirit.

3. *Let Israel hope in the* LORD, etc. The connexion would seem to require us to understand this as the assertion of him who had been accused of thoughts which seemed to be too lofty. As the *result* of all his reflections (of those reflections for which he was rebuked and charged with pride, but which were really conceived in a modest spirit),—as expressing what he *saw* that seemed to be in advance of what others saw, or to indicate a habit of thought beyond his years,— he says that there were reasons *why* Israel should hope in the Lord ; that there was a foundation for confident trust ; that there was that in the Divine character which was a just ground of reliance ; that there was that in the course of events—in the tendencies of things—which made it proper for the people of God, for the church, to hope, to confide, to feel assured of its ultimate and permanent safety. This would indicate the nature of the suggestions which he had expressed, and which had exposed him to the charge of arrogance ; and it *would* also indicate a ripe and mature habit of thinking, beyond what might be expected from one in very early

PSALM CXXXII.

A Song of degrees.

LORD, remember David, *and* all his afflictions ;

2 How he sware unto the LORD, *and* vowed *ˢ* unto the mighty God of Jacob ;

ˢ 2 Sam. vii. 1, etc.

---

life. All this was, probably, applicable to David in his early years, as to the reflections which might have foreshadowed what he *would* be in future ; this was eminently applicable to David's Descendant,—greater than he,—who, at twelve years of age, astonished the Hebrew doctors in the temple with "his understanding and answers" (Luke ii. 47) ; this gives a beautiful view of modesty joined with uncommon gifts in early life ; this shows what is always the nature of true religion—as producing modesty, and as prompting to hope.

PSALM CXXXII.

This psalm is simply entitled "A Song of Degrees." The author of it is not known, nor can the occasion on which it was written be certainly ascertained. It would seem to have been composed in a time of public distress and disaster ; when the affairs of the nation were in jeopardy, and especially when the line of the monarchy seemed about to fail, and the promises made to David seemed about to come to nought. It would have been a suitable occasion for such a psalm at the time immediately preceding the captivity in Babylon, or on the return from Babylon, when the throne was tottering or had fallen, and when God seemed to be about to forsake his house, the temple,—or had forsaken it, and suffered it to fall to ruin. At such a time of national disaster, when it appeared as if the house of God was to be permanently destroyed, and the government to be overturned for ever, it was natural and proper thus to make mention of the zeal, the toil, and the sacrifice of him who had sought a "habitation" for God ;—who had planned and laboured that there might be a permanent dwelling-place for the Most High, and who had received gracious promises from God himself in regard to the permanent establishment of his family on the throne. It would be appropriate, also, to recall this as a foundation for the prayer that God would

again visit Zion, and would fulfil the promises which he had given to David.

The psalm therefore consists properly of two parts : I. A statement of the zeal of David for the ark, in securing a permanent abode for it, vers. 1-8 ; and II. A reference to the promises made to David and his posterity, and a prayer that these promises might be carried out and accomplished, vers. 9-18.

1. LORD, *remember David.* Call to remembrance his zeal, his labour, his trials in order that there might be a permanent place for thy worship. Call this to remembrance in order that his purpose in thy cause may not be frustrated ; in order that the promises made to him may be accomplished. ¶ And *all his afflictions.* The *particular* trial here referred to was his care and toil, that there might be a settled home for the ark. The word used would not refer merely to what is specified in the following verses (his bringing up the ark to Mount Zion), but to his purpose to build a house for God, and —since he was not permitted himself to build it because he was a man of war, and had been engaged in scenes of blood, (1 Kings v. 3 ; 1 Chron. xxii. 8) — to his care and toil in collecting materials for the temple to be erected by his son and successor. It is not, therefore, his *general* afflictions which are here meant, but his anxiety, and his efforts to secure a lasting place for the worship of God.

2. *How he sware unto the* LORD. The solemn oath which he took that he would make this the first object ; that he would give himself no rest till this was done ; that he would sacrifice his personal ease and comfort in order that he might thus honour God. This oath or purpose is not recorded in the history. The fair interpretation of this would be either (1) That these words properly ex-

3 Surely I will not come into the tabernacle of my house, nor go up into my bed;

4 I will not give sleep to mine eyes, *or* slumber to mine eyelids,

5 Until I find out a place for the LORD, [1] an habitation for the mighty *God* of Jacob.

6 Lo, we heard of it at Ephra-

[1] *habitations.*

pressed what was in the mind of David at the time,—that is, his acts implied that this purpose was in his heart; or (2) that this vow was actually *made* by David, though not elsewhere recorded. Such a vow might have been made, and the remembrance of it kept up by tradition, or it might have been suggested to the author of the psalm by direct inspiration. ¶ And *vowed unto the mighty* God *of Jacob.* See Gen. xlix. 24. The God whom Jacob worshipped, and who had manifested himself so signally to him as a God of might or power.

3. *Surely I will not come into the tabernacle of my house.* The tent of my dwelling; the place where I abide. ¶ *Nor go up into my bed.* The couch of my bed, or where I sleep. I will make it my first business to find a dwelling-place for the Lord; a place where the ark may repose.

4. *I will not give sleep to mine eyes,* etc. There is no difference here between the words *sleep* and *slumber.* The meaning is, that the house of the Lord should be his first care.

5. *Until I find out a place for the* LORD. A place for the ark of God; a place where it may constantly and safely remain. The symbol of the Divine presence rested on the mercy-seat, the cover of the ark, and hence this was represented as the seat or the house of God. ¶ *An habitation for the mighty* God *of Jacob.* Heb., "For the mighty One of Jacob." The reference is to a *permanent* dwelling-place for the ark. It had been moved from place to place. There was no house appropriated to it, or reared expressly for it, and David resolved to provide such a house,—at first, a tent or tabernacle on Mount Zion,—and then, a more spacious and magnificent structure,

the temple. The latter he was not permitted to build, though the purpose was in his heart.

6. *Lo, we heard of it at Ephratah.* Most probably this is the language of the contemporaries of David; or this is what they might be supposed to say; or this is what tradition reports that they *did* say. David's purpose, as referred to in the previous verses, is not recorded in the history, and the memory of the whole transaction may have been handed down by tradition. Or, this *may* be merely poetic language, expressing the feelings of those who, when sent out by David, or accompanying him, found the ark. Much difficulty has been felt in regard to this verse. There is no mention in the history of the fact that the ark was "heard of" at Ephrata, or that it was ever there. The name *Ephrata*—אֶפְרָתָה—is applied (1) to a region of country to which was subsequently given the name Bethlehem, Gen. xxxv. 16–19; Ruth iv. 11. (2) Properly to Bethlehem, a city of Judah, the full name of which was Bethlehem-Ephratah, Gen. xlviii. 7; Micah v. 2. (3) It is a proper name, 1 Chron. ii. 19, 50; iv. 4. (4) It *may* perhaps be the same as *Ephraim.* Comp. Judges xii. 5; 1 Sam. i. 1; 1 Kings xi. 26. Some have supposed the meaning to be, that they found it within the limits of the tribe of *Ephraim,* and that the word *Ephratah* is used here with reference to that; but this is a forced construction. It may have been indeed true that the ark was found within the limits of that tribe, but the word Ephratah would not *naturally* denote this; and, besides, the tribe of Ephraim was so large, and covered such an extent of territory, that this would convey no distinct information; and it cannot

tah ; we found it in the fields of
the wood.

7 We *t* will go into his tabernacles ; we will worship *u* at his

t Ps. cxxii. 1.   *u* Ps. xcix. 5.

footstool.

8 Arise, O LORD, into thy
rest ; thou, and the ark of *r* thy
strength.

r Ps. lxxviii. 61.

---

be supposed that the writer meant
to say merely that they found it
within the limits of a *tribe*. Nor can
it mean that they actually found the
ark *at* Ephrata, or Bethlehem, for
this would not be true. A simple
and natural interpretation of the passage has been suggested, which seems
to make it plain :—that, in their
search for the ark, it was at Ephratah
or Bethlehem that they first *heard* of
it, but that they actually *found* it in
the fields of the wood. It may seem
strange that there should have been
so much uncertainty about the ark
as is here implied ; that David did
not know where it was ; and that
none of the priests knew. But, while
it must be admitted that it *seems*
to be strange, and that the fact is
not of easy explanation, it is to be
remembered that the ark was at one
time in the possession of the Philistines ; that when it was re-taken it
seems to have had no very permanent
resting-place ; that it may have been
removed from one spot to another as
circumstances required ; that it may
have been committed now to one, and
now to another, for safe keeping ; and
thus it *might* have occurred, in the
unsettled and agitated state of affairs,
that its exact situation might be unknown, and that a somewhat diligent
search was necessary in order to find
it. We know too little of the times
to enable us to pronounce upon the
subject with much confidence. ¶ *We
found it in the fields of the wood.*
Continuing our search, we found it
there. Perhaps Kirjath-jearim, 1 Sam.
vii. 1 ; 1 Chron. xiii. 5. It was to
Kirjath-jearim that the ark was carried after it had been taken by the
Philistines (1 Sam. vi. 21). The
literal meaning of the passage here
is, "The fields of the wood "—or of
Jear, where the word in Hebrew is

the same as in Kirjath-*jearim*. The
name Kirjath-jearim means Forest
Town, or, city of the woods ; and the
allusion here is the same as in 1 Sam.
vii. 1. The interpretation, then,
seems to be that they heard of the
ark, or learned where it was, when
they were at Ephrata or Bethlehem ;
but that they actually found it in
the vicinity of Kirjath-jearim. The
ignorance in the case may have been
merely in regard to the exact place
or house where it was at that time
kept. Bethlehem was the home or
city of David, and the *idea* is, that,
when there, and when it was contemplated to remove the ark to
Mount Zion, information or intelligence was brought there of its exact
locality, and they went forth to bring
it to its new abode or its permanent
resting-place.

7. *We will go into his tabernacles.*
His tents, or the fixed resting-place
prepared for the ark. This is evidently language supposed to have
been used on bringing up the ark
into its place in Jerusalem :—language such as they may be supposed
to have *sung* or *recited* on that occasion. ¶ *We will worship at his
footstool.* See Notes on Ps. xcix. 5.
The meaning is, the footstool of God :
—let us bow humbly at his feet.
The language denotes profound adoration. It expresses the feelings of
those who bare the ark to its assigned
place.

8. *Arise, O LORD, into thy rest.*
Into that which is appointed for its
permanent place of repose, that it
may no longer be removed from spot
to spot. This is spoken of the ark,
considered as the place where God,
by an appropriate symbol, abode.
That symbol—the Shechinah—rested
on the cover of the ark. The same
language was used by Solomon at

9 Let thy priests be clothed with righteousness; and let thy saints shout ^w for joy.

10 For thy servant David's sake turn not away the face of

w Isa. lxv. 14.   x 1 Kings viii. 25.

thine anointed.

11 The LORD hath sworn <i>in</i> truth unto David, he will not turn from it, Of ^x the fruit of thy ¹ body will I set upon thy throne;

¹ belly.

the dedication of the temple: "Now, therefore, arise, O Lord God, into thy resting-place, thou and the ark of thy strength," 2 Chron. vi. 41. ¶ <i>Thou, and the ark of thy strength.</i> The ark, the symbol of the Divine power, <i>as if</i> the power of God resided there, or as if the Almighty had his abode there. Perhaps the language was derived from the fact that the ark, in the wars of the Hebrews against their foes, was a symbol of the Divine presence and protection, —that by which the Divine power was put forth.

9. <i>Let thy priests be clothed with righteousness.</i> This is also substantially the same language that was used by Solomon at the dedication of the temple. See again 2 Chron. vi. 41. The idea is, that in the service of such a God, the priests, the ministers of religion, should be holy. The honour of religion demanded it. It was the first qualification of those who "served the altar;" a qualification without which all other endowments would be valueless. On the word <i>clothed,</i> see Notes on Ps. xxxv. 26; comp. Ps. lxv. 13; xciii. 1; civ. 1; Isa. lxi. 10 ; 1 Pet. v. 5. ¶ <i>And let thy saints shout for joy.</i> Thy holy ones; all who truly worship and honour thee. Let them be happy <i>in</i> such a God; in thy presence; in thy service. The fact that there <i>is</i> a God, and such a God, and that this God is <i>ours</i> —that we <i>may</i> serve him, glorify him, enjoy him—is fitted to fill the mind with joy.

10. <i>For thy servant David's sake.</i> Because of the promise made to him; because of the zeal which he has shown in securing a place for the ark. Let it not be in vain that he has shown such a regard to the honour of God; let not the promises made to him fail. Such a prayer is proper now. There

is nothing wrong in our beseeching God to carry out and accomplish the purposes cherished by his church for promoting the honour of his name; or for a child to pray that the purposes of a pious parent in regard to himself may not fail. It is an expression of nature—a desire that the labour and sacrifices of those who have gone before us should not be lost. This is the language of the author of the psalm, and of those for whom the psalm was composed. See ver. 1. In view of all that David has done, do thou now show favour and mercy. ¶ <i>Turn not away the face of thine anointed.</i> As if in displeasure, or in forgetfulness. The word <i>anointed</i> would refer to one who was set apart as a king, a priest, or a prophet. See Notes on Matt. i. 1. The word would be applicable to David himself, as the anointed king; in a higher sense it is applicable to the Messiah, the Christ. The reference here is probably to David himself, <i>as if</i> a failure to carry out his purposes in regard to the sanctuary, or to fulfil the promises made to him, would be a turning away the face from him; would be a mark of the Divine displeasure against him. The prayer is, that God would carry out those purposes <i>as if</i> his face was continually turned with benignity and favour towards David.

11. <i>The LORD hath sworn in truth unto David.</i> He has made a gracious promise, confirmed by an oath, which we may plead in our present necessities. That promise was made "in truth,"—that is, sincerely,—so that it will certainly be carried out,—so that we may appeal to God, on the ground of his faithfulness, to keep his word. ¶ <i>He will not turn from it.</i> We may be certain that he will carry it out. We may appeal to him on the

12 If thy children will keep my covenant, and my testimony that I shall teach them, their children shall also sit upon thy throne for evermore.

13 For the LORD hath chosen Zion: he hath desired *it* for his habitation.

14 This *y is* my rest for ever: here will I dwell; for I have

y Ps. lxviii. 16.   ¹ Or, *surely.*   *z* Luke i. 53.

desired it.

15 I will ¹ abundantly bless her provision: I will satisfy her poor with *z* bread.

16 I *a* will also clothe her priests with salvation; and her saints shall shout aloud for joy.

17 There will I make the horn of David to bud: I have ordained a ² lamp *b* for mine anointed.

a ver. 9.   ² Or, *candle.*   *b* 2 Chron. xxi. 7.

basis of that promise with the utmost confidence. ¶ *Of the fruit of thy body will I set upon thy throne.* Marg., as in Heb., *of thy belly.* The throne would descend to his posterity, 2 Sam. vii. 12; see Notes on Ps. lxxxix. 3, 4.

12. *If thy children will keep my covenant,* etc. This was the condition implied in the promise,—that they were to keep the law of God, and to serve and obey him. If they did not, they could not, of course, plead the promise. This principle is universal. We cannot plead any promise of God in our behalf, or in behalf of our children, unless we obey his commands, and are ourselves faithful to him. See the sentiment in this verse illustrated in the Notes on Ps. lxxxix. 30–37.

13. *For the* LORD *hath chosen Zion.* He has selected it as the place where he will abide; the seat of his religion. This is a new plea or argument, and shows that the psalm had reference to Zion or Jerusalem, as then in danger, or as having been in danger. See Notes on Ps. xlviii. 1, 2. ¶ *He hath desired* it *for his habitation.* A place where to abide. He had selected this as the permanent place of his worship.

14. *This* is *my rest for ever.* My home; my permanent abode. I will no more remove from place to place— as when the ark was carried in the wilderness, and as it has been since; but Zion shall now be the fixed seat of religion. See Notes on Ps. lxviii. 16. ¶ *Here will I dwell,* etc. Permanently; constantly.

15. *I will abundantly bless her provision.* Marg., *surely.* Hebrew, " Blessing I will bless,"—a strong

affirmation, meaning that he would certainly do it; that he would do it in every way; that every needed blessing would be imparted. The word rendered *provision* is a cognate form of the word in Ps. lxxviii. 25, translated *meat :* " He sent them *meat* to the full." It properly refers to food for a journey, but it is applicable to any kind of food. The original idea is that of food obtained by hunting—as game, venison: Gen. xxv. 28; Job xxxviii. 41. The meaning here is, that God would provide abundantly for their support. ¶ *I will satisfy her poor with bread.* I will give them what they need. See Notes on Ps. xxxvii. 25.

16. *I will also clothe her priests with salvation.* See Notes on ver. 9, where—instead of the word which in 2 Chron. vi. 41, as here, is *" salvation,"*—we find the word *" righteousness."* The promise here corresponds to the prayer in ver. 9. It is a reason why God should interpose. What they prayed for (ver. 9), had been expressly *promised,* and that promise is now urged as a plea why the prayer should be granted. ¶ *And her saints shall shout aloud for joy.* See ver. 9. In 2 Chron. vi. 41 the prayer is, " And let thy saints rejoice in goodness." The sense is not materially varied. The Hebrew is, " And let thy saints rejoicing rejoice;" that is, *let them shout, shout ;* let them be full of joy.

17. *There will I make the horn of David to bud.* The horn was an emblem of power; and then, of success or prosperity. See Notes on Luke i. 69. The word rendered " to bud"

18 His enemies will I clothe with shame; but upon himself shall his crown flourish.

means to grow, or to shoot forth as a plant, or as grass grows; and then it may be applied to anything which shoots forth or grows. The allusion here would seem to be to a horn as it shoots forth on the head of an animal. So David would be endowed with growing strength; would have the means of defending himself against his enemies, and of securing victory. The language had no original reference to the Messiah, but it is not improperly applied to him (as springing from David) in Luke i. 69. On the word *horn*, see Notes on Ps. lxxv. 4. Comp. Ps. lxxxix. 17, 24; xcii. 10; cxii. 9; Dan. vii. 8; viii. 5. ¶ *I have ordained a lamp for mine anointed.* Marg., *a candle.* I have appointed; that is, I have given him that which will always be as a lamp or guide to him; that by which he will see to walk. I have given him true and precious promises, which will be to him as a lamp, a candle, a lantern is to one walking in the night. See Notes on Ps. xviii. 28; cxix. 105.

18. *His enemies will I clothe with shame.* They shall be so confounded that shame shall seem to cover them as a garment. See Notes on Ps. cix. 29. That is, David would be triumphant. ¶ *But upon himself shall his crown flourish.* His crown shall be as a fresh, blooming garland. The Hebrew word used here may mean either to *glitter*, or to *flower*, to *flourish* or *bloom*. As applied to a crown, it may mean either that it would. sparkle or glitter, as set with precious stones,—or (under the idea of a garland) it may mean that it would appear to bloom or blossom. In either case it denotes success, joy, triumph,—and is a promise of prosperity to David as a king. This was a part of the promise referred to by the psalmist, and a ground of the plea in the psalm. God had made these precious promises to David and

PSALM CXXXIII.
A Song of degrees of David.

BEHOLD, how good and how

his posterity; and now, in a time of sorrow and disaster, when the glory of the crown seemed about to pass away, the psalmist, in the name of the people, and in language to be used by the people, prays that those ancient promises might be remembered and fulfilled. So, in a time of general religious declension, we may plead the promises, so rich and so abundant, which God has made to his church, as a reason for his gracious interposition; for his coming to revive his work.

PSALM CXXXIII.

This psalm is entitled "A Song of Degrees of David." It is one of the four in this collection ascribed to him, and there is no reason to doubt the correctness of the inscription. As to the occasion on which the psalm was composed, however, we have no information. Perhaps there was nothing special in the occasion which called it forth, since it may have been written at any time to set forth the beauty and the power of brotherly love. It may have been composed either for the service of the people when gathered in their annual festivals, or in view of the harmony—the beauty and order—evinced when they *were* thus gathered together.

The psalm is an illustration, in most beautiful language, of brotherly love, particularly in regard to its calm, and gentle, and sweet influence—like the ointment which flowed down from the head of the anointed priest, or like the gentle dew on Hermon or Zion. It is a psalm applicable alike to a church; to a family; to a gathering of friends.

1. *Behold.* As if he looked upon such a gathering, and saw there the expressions of mutual love. This may have been uttered in the actual contemplation of such an assemblage; or it may have been a picture of the imagination. ¶ *How good.* How good in itself; how proper; how fitted to promote happiness, and to diffuse good influences abroad. ¶ *And*

pleasant *it is* for brethren to dwell [1] together in unity!

[1] *even together.*

2 *It is* like the precious ointment *c* upon the head, that ran

c Ex. xxx. 25, 30.

---

how pleasant. The word here used means lovely, charming, attractive; that which fills the mind with delight, spoken of one beloved, Cant. vii. 6; of a friend, 2 Sam. i. 26; of a place, Gen. xlix. 15; of words, Prov. xv. 26; of beauty or glory, as of Jehovah, Ps. xxvii. 4. It is descriptive of the pleasure which we derive from a picture, from a landscape, from sweet sounds and gentle voices, or from love. ¶ *For brethren to dwell together in unity.* Marg., *even together.* Heb., "The dwelling of brethren also together." Perhaps the idea in the word "*also*" may be, that while the unity of brethren when separate, or as they were seen when scattered in their habitations, was beautiful, it was *also* pleasant to see them when actually assembled, or when they actually came together to worship God. As applicable to the church, it may be remarked (1) that all the people of God—all the followers of the Redeemer—*are brethren*, members of the same family, fellow-heirs of the same inheritance, Matt. xxiii. 8. (2) There is a peculiar fitness that they *should* be united, or dwell in unity. (3) There is much that is beautiful and lovely *in* their unity and harmony. They are redeemed by the same Saviour; they serve the same Master; they cherish the same hope; they are looking forward to the same heaven; they are subject to the same trials, temptations, and sorrows; they have the same precious consolations. There is, therefore, the beauty, the "goodness," the "pleasantness" of obvious fitness and propriety in their dwelling together in unity. (4) Their unity is adapted to produce an important influence on the world, John xvii. 21. No small part of the obstructions to the progress of religion in the world has been caused by the strifes and contentions of the professed friends of God. A

new impulse would be given at once to the cause of religion if all the followers of the Lord Jesus acted in harmony :—if every Christian would properly recognize every other Christian as his brother; if every true church *would* recognize every other church *as* a church; if all ministers of the Gospel would recognize all other ministers as such; and if all who *are* Christians, and who walk worthy of the Christian name, were admitted freely to partake with all others in the solemn ordinance which commemorates the Saviour's dying love. Until this is done, all that is said about Christian *union* in the church is a subject of just derision to the world,—for how *can* there be union when one class of ministers refuse to recognize the Christian standing, and the validity of the acts, of other ministers of the Lord Jesus,—when one part of the Christian church solemnly refuses to admit another portion to the privileges of the Lord's table,—when by their actions large portions of the professed followers of the Redeemer regard and treat others as having no claims to a recognition as belonging to the church of God, and as left for salvation to his "uncovenanted mercies."

2. It is *like the precious ointment upon the head.* That is, which was poured upon the head of the high priest, when consecrated to the holy office. The Hebrew is, "the *good* ointment." For a description of the ointment which was used in the consecration of the high priest, and the holy things of the sanctuary, see Ex. xxx. 22–30. Comp. Notes on Isa. lxi. 3, on the phrase "oil of joy." Anointing with oil was common on festivals and joyous occasions (see Notes on Ps. xxiii. 5), and hence it became an emblem of anything joyous, happy, beautiful; and the idea seemed to be carried to the highest degree when it

down upon the beard, *even* Aaron's beard; that went down to the skirts of his garments;

3 As the dew of Hermon, *d and*

d Deut. iv. 48.

was connected with the anointing of a high priest to the sacred duties of his office. There is no other resemblance between the idea of anointing with oil and that of harmony among brethren than this which is derived from the gladness—the joyousness—connected with such an anointing. The psalmist wished to give the highest idea of the pleasantness of such harmony; and he, therefore, compared it with that which was most beautiful to a pious mind—the idea of a solemn consecration to the highest office of religion. The comparison is one which would not unnaturally occur to a Jew. ¶ *That ran down upon the beard.* Descending from the head upon the long, flowing beard. The idea here is that of *copiousness*, or *abundance*—as if so *much* ointment was poured forth as to descend on the whole person, consecrating the entire man. ¶ *Even Aaron's beard.* The word "even" here, introduced by our translators, weakens the force and beauty of the comparison. The psalmist had the simple image of Aaron before his mind, without intending to compare him with any other. ¶ *That went down to the skirts of his garments.* Literally, "to the *mouth* of his garment." The idea is that the anointing oil was abundant enough to flow down so as to fall on his entire robe, diffusing a sweet fragrance all around. It is *possible*, though it may seem like a conceit, that the psalmist may have had an idea of *unity* in this, as if in the anointing of the high priest the whole *man* was consecrated, or was "*united*" in the consecration. It was not merely the head, but the beard, the raiment, the entire person, that partook of the fragrance of the anointing oil. Thus love in a Christian community is so abundant—so

as the dew that descended upon the mountains of Zion: for there the LORD commanded the blessing, *even* life for evermore.

overflowing—that it spreads over all the spiritual body, the church; the same sweet and holy influence, represented by the oil of anointing, pervades all, and combines all in one.

3. *As the dew of Hermon,* etc. On the situation of Mount Hermon, see Notes on Ps. lxxxix. 12. The literal rendering of this passage would be, "Like the dew of Hermon which descends on the mountains of Zion." According to our version *two* things are referred to: the dew of Hermon, *and* the dew on the mountains of Zion. But this is not in the original. There no *dew* is referred to but that which belongs to Hermon. It has, of course, been made a question how the dew of Hermon, a remote mountain, could be said to descend on the mountains of Zion, and our translators have sought to solve the difficulty by inserting the words "and as the dew." Some have supposed that the proper interpretation is to refer the *comparison* in the passage to the dew of Hermon, and that all which follows is an application of the thought:— "Like the dew of Hermon is the influence which comes down upon the mountains of Zion," etc. The most probable and plausible interpretation, however, it seems to me, is, that the mind of the poet was turned to the dew of Hermon—to the gentleness, and the copiousness, and the vivifying nature of that dew,—diffusing beauty and abundance all around,—and that he thought of *that* dew, or dew *like* that, as descending on the mountains of Zion. Not that the dew *of* Hermon actually descended there; but when changing the comparison, in illustration of brotherly love, from oil to dew, he most naturally thought (perhaps from some former observation) of the dew of Hermon, and immediately thought of Zion *as if* that dew de-

PSALM CXXXIV.
A Song of degrees.

BEHOLD, bless ye the LORD, all

ye servants of the LORD, which by night stand in the house of the LORD.

---

scended there :—that is, love, unity, and concord there would be as if the dew of Hermon should descend on the barren hills of Zion or Jerusalem, there diffusing beauty, abundance, fertility. The comparison of the influence of brotherly love, or unity, with *dew* is not a forced or unnatural one. So calm, so gentle, so refreshing on the tender grain, on the young plants, on the flowers, is *dew*, that it is a striking image of the influences which produce brotherly love and harmony. ¶ *For there the* LORD *commanded the blessing.* He appointed that as the place of worship; as the seat of his residence; the source of all holy influences. See Notes on Ps. lxxviii. 67–69; lxxxvii. 2. ¶ Even *life for evermore.* Literally, "Life to eternity." That is, such influences go from that place as to lead to eternal life, or as to secure eternal life. It is in Zion, in his church, that he has made known the way to eternal life, and the means by which it may be obtained. To the end of the world this beautiful psalm will be sung in the church alike as *expressing* the charm which there is in unity among brethren and in the church; and as *tending to promote* that unity whose beauty it is designed to commend. Happy will be that day when the church shall be so united that it may be sung everywhere, as expressing what *is*, and not merely what *should be.*

PSALM CXXXIV.

This is the last psalm of the collection or group called "Songs of Degrees," and it is of the nature of a *doxology* as now sung in our places of worship. Its author is unknown. From anything that appears in the psalm itself, it may have been composed originally to occupy the very place which it does occupy here. The psalm is a summons to praise, and it would seem not improbable that it was designed to be sung by

alternate choirs, — the first (vers. 1, 2) representing the people approaching the sanctuary, calling on those who habitually serve God there—the ministers of religion—to lift up their hands in the sanctuary and to praise the Lord ;—the second (ver. 3), the response of the priests or the ministers of religion, pronouncing a blessing on the people—a blessing as proceeding out of Zion.

1. *Behold.* As if calling attention to the fact that they were there, or had come. ¶ *Bless ye the* LORD. Praise Jehovah. Making known their desire that God should be praised, and calling on those who presided over the public worship of the sanctuary to engage now in that service as expressive of *their* feelings. ¶ *All* ye *servants of the* LORD. The priests or ministers of religion, appointed especially to this service. ¶ *Which by night stand in the house of the* LORD. There was a class of singers in the temple who devoted the night, or a part of the night, to praise; and it is possible that this service may have been, as it was subsequently in some of the monasteries, continued by succeeding choirs, during the entire night. Thus in 1 Chron. ix. 33, it is said, "And these are the singers, chief of the fathers of the Levites, who remaining in the chambers were free; for they were employed in that work day and night." This class is particularly addressed in this psalm, as if they were especially favoured, or as if they had peculiarly the ear of God in the silence of the night, and when the world slumbered around them. There *is* something favourable to devotion in the silence of the night; when the world sleeps; when we are alone with God; when it *seems* as if God would more particularly attend to our cry since the rest of the world is still, and does not (as it were) need his care. All this may be fancy; but the effect may be to

2 Lift *e* up your hands *in* [1] the sanctuary, and bless the LORD.

3 The LORD, that made heaven and earth, bless thee out of Zion.

PSALM CXXXV.

PRAISE ye the LORD. Praise *f* ye the name of the LORD;

praise *him,* O ye servants of the LORD.

2 Ye *g* that stand in the house of the LORD, in the courts of the house of our God,

e 1 Tim. ii. 8.   *Or, holiness.*
f Ps. cxlv. 1; Neh. ix. 5.
g Ps. xcii. 13.

make the mind more solemn, and better fitted for devotion.

2. *Lift up your hands* in *the sanctuary.* Marg., *In holiness.* The Hebrew word properly means *holiness,* but it may be applied to *a holy place.* See Ps. xx. 2. The lifting up of the hands is properly expressive of prayer, but the phrase *may* be used to denote praise or worship in general. ¶ *And bless the* LORD. In the night-watches,—while all around is still,—let there be one place where the voice of praise shall ascend on high.

3. *The* LORD *that made heaven and earth.* The great Creator of all things. This is probably the language of those who were thus employed in the service of the Lord at night; their response to the address in the first two verses. ¶ *Bless thee out of Zion.* That is, bless those who thus approached the sanctuary, and called on those within to praise the Lord. This is the answer. Let the blessing of God rest on *you.* It is language showing that they appreciated the kind and encouraging salutation, and that they reciprocated the feelings and the good wishes of those who came to worship. In the name of the Lord whom they served, therefore, and appealing to him, they pronounced a blessing on those who thus approached the sanctuary. Men do not come near the house of God— the place of public worship — with kind and sympathising feelings without a blessing from the sanctuary, without a response that welcomes them, and that meets all their aspirations. There is always in Zion— in the church—a voice, by day and night, which pronounces a blessing

on those who wish it well, who seek its good, and who desire to partake of the favour of God. ¶ *Out of Zion.* That is, may God speak to you out of Zion; may he confer on you such blessings as properly go out of Zion; or such as Zion (or his church) can furnish. Go not away unblessed; go not without a token of Divine favour,—for God *will* bless you.

PSALM CXXXV.

This psalm has no title in Hebrew; and the author, and the occasion on which it was written, are alike unknown. It is general in its character, though its imagery is taken mostly from Hebrew history.

The sole design of the psalm is to excite to the praise of God; or to show reasons for that praise. As grounds or reasons for this, the psalmist refers to the fact that God is good, ver. 3; to the fact that he had chosen Jacob for himself, ver. 4; to the greatness of God as seen in the works of nature, vers. 5-7; to the history of the Hebrew people, vers. 8-12; to the inability of idols to aid, vers. 13-18; and, in view of all this, he calls on all classes of the people to praise the Lord, vers. 19-21.

1. *Praise ye the* LORD. Heb., *Hallelu-jah.* Literally, "Praise *Jah,*" —an abridged name for Jehovah. See Notes on Ps. lxviii. 4. ¶ *Praise ye the name of the* LORD. The same as praising God himself. ¶ *Praise* him, *O ye servants of the* LORD. You who are especially designated or appointed to this service, Ps. cxxxiv. 1.

2. *Ye that stand in the house of the* LORD. See Notes on Ps. cxxxiv. 1. That is, those who were appointed to conduct the services of religion, the priests and Levites. ¶ *In the courts of the house of our God.* The

T

3 Praise the LORD; for the LORD *is* good: sing praises unto his name; for *h it is* pleasant.

4 For *i* the LORD hath chosen Jacob unto himself, *and* Israel for his peculiar treasure.

5 For I know that the LORD *is* great, and *that* our Lord *is* above all gods.

h Ps. cxlvii. 1.
i Ex. xix. 5; Deut. vii. 6, 7; 1 Pet. ii. 9.

6 Whatsoever *k* the LORD pleased, *that* did he in heaven, and in earth, in the seas, and all deep places.

7 He *l* causeth the vapours to ascend from the ends of the earth: he *m* maketh lightnings for the rain: he bringeth the wind out of his treasuries.

k Ps. xxxiii. 9, 11; Dan. iv. 35.
l Jer. xiv. 22; Zech. x. 1.　*m* Jer. x. 13.

areas, or parts assigned for different classes of worshippers around the tabernacle and the temple. See Notes on Matt. xxi. 12; Ps. xcii. 13.

3. *Praise the* LORD; *for the* LORD *is good.* See Ps. cvii. 1. ¶ *Sing praises unto his name; for it is pleasant.* See Ps. xxxiii. 1; xcii. 1. The idea here is, that it is a source of happiness, and that it is proper in itself.

4. *For the* LORD *hath chosen Jacob unto himself.* The descendants of Jacob. He has selected them from among all the inhabitants of the earth to be his peculiar people. ¶ And *Israel for his peculiar treasure.* The word here rendered *treasure,* means that which is acquired; property; wealth. They were what God possessed, owned, or claimed among all the people of the earth as peculiarly his own. He had chosen them; he had redeemed them; he had made them his own, and he regarded them with the interest with which any one looks on his own property, the fruit of his own toil. See Ex. xix. 5; Deut. vii. 6; xxxii. 9; 1 Kings viii. 53.

5. *For I know.* I, as the representative of Israel, and speaking in the name of the people. This is said as the foundation or the reason for praise. It was the thorough conviction of the psalmist that God was great above all who were claimed to be gods, and that he only was worthy of worship. ¶ *That the* LORD *is great.* See Notes on Ps. xcv. 3. ¶ *And* that *our Lord is above all gods.* All that are worshipped as gods.

6. *Whatsoever the* LORD *pleased.* God is an absolute sovereign. He has formed a plan, and has carried it out. He has made the world as he chose, and he has ordered all its arrangements according to his own pleasure. As a universal sovereign, he has a right to universal adoration. See Notes on Ps. cxv. 3. ¶ *In heaven, and in earth,* etc. These are put for the universe; these *are* the universe. In these places—in all worlds—on the land and in the ocean—even in the profound depths of the sea, there is nothing which has not been placed there by his will, and which he has not arranged according to his eternal plan.

7. *He causeth the vapours to ascend from the ends of the earth.* The word rendered *vapours* means literally *risings;* things *raised up;* and it may be applied, therefore, to vapours or clouds. The Septuagint, the Latin Vulgate, and Luther render it *clouds.* It is among the proofs of the Divine wisdom and power that he causes them to *ascend* contrary to the common law which drags all things down towards the earth. The arrangement by which this is done is among the most wise and wonderful of all the works of God. See Notes on Job xxvi. 8; xxxviii. 25–28. ¶ *He maketh lightnings for the rain.* To accompany the rain. See Notes on Job xxviii. 26. ¶ *He bringeth the wind out of his treasuries.* Where he has, as it were, treasured it up, to be used when there should be occasion for it. See Notes on Job xxxviii. 22.

8 Who smote *n* the first-born of Egypt, ¹ both of man and beast.

9 *Who* sent tokens *o* and wonders into the midst of thee, O Egypt, upon Pharaoh, and upon all his servants.

10 Who *p* smote great nations, and slew mighty kings:

11 Sihon king of the Amorites, and Og king of Bashan, and all the kingdoms of Canaan:

n Ex. xii. 29. ¹ *from man unto.*
o Ex. vii., etc.
p Num. xxi. 24—35 ; Ps. cxxxvi. 17, etc.

12 And gave *q* their land *for* an heritage, an heritage unto Israel his people.

13 Thy *r* name, O LORD, endureth for ever; *and* thy memorial, O LORD, throughout ² all generations.

14 For *s* the LORD will judge his people, and he will repent himself concerning his servants.

q Jos. xii. 1—7 ; Ps. xliv. 1—3 ; lxxviii. 55.
r Ex. iii. 15.
² *to generation and generation.*
s Deut. xxxii. 36.

8. *Who smote the firstborn of Egypt.* As the last and the greatest of the plagues brought upon the Egyptians; the chief and crowning judgment under which they were made willing that the children of Israel should go, and which was in fact *the* judgment which secured their freedom. This is selected here evidently for this reason, instead of recounting *all* the plagues which were brought upon the Egyptians. ¶ *Both of man and beast.* Ex. xi. 5. Marg., as in Heb., *From man unto beast.* That is, including both ; smiting both.

9. Who *sent tokens and wonders.* Tokens :—that is, signs or evidences of the Divine power. Wonders :— things fitted to impress the mind with awe ; things outside of the ordinary course of events ; things not produced by natural laws, but by the direct power of God. The allusion here is, of course, to the plagues of Egypt, as recorded in Exodus. See Notes on Ps. cv. 27—36.

10. *Who smote great nations,* etc. To wit, those specified in the following verse.

11. *Sihon king of the Amorites,* etc. These are *specimens* of what was done, or *instances* of the mighty kings who were subdued. It is not pretended that all were enumerated. The subjugation of these nations and kings showed the power of God, and laid the foundation for praise.

12. *And gave their land* for *an heritage,* etc. See Notes on Ps. cxi. 6.

13. *Thy name, O LORD, endureth for ever.* Thou art the ever-living, the unchanging God. The generations of men pass away ; the kingdoms of the earth change ; the idols perish, but thou art the same. The object here seems to be to bring the image or the idea of God before the mind as he was *when* he performed these great works, as a God interposing in behalf of his people, and as worthy of praise. The idea is that he is the same now that he was then ; and as he then impressed the world with a sense of his majesty and power, and as he then interposed in behalf of his people by mighty signs and wonders, we should feel that, being an unchangeable God, he can do it now, and is now equally worthy of confidence, adoration, and praise. ¶ And *thy memorial.* Thy remembrance ; the memory of thyself. That is, What thou hast done to secure a remembrance among men is of such a nature as to make the same impression to all coming time. The events were such that the memory of them should never pass away from mankind. ¶ *Throughout all generations.* Marg., as in Heb., *To generation and generation.* There never will be a generation on the earth, in the latest periods, to which the memory of these things should not be transmitted.

14. *For the LORD will judge his people.* He will interpose in their behalf by his judgments, or by di-

15 The ⁱ idols of the heathen
are silver and gold, the work of
men's hands.

16 They have mouths, but they
speak not; eyes have they, but
they see not;

17 They have ears, but they
hear not; neither is there *any*
breath in their mouths.

18 They that make them are

ⁱ Ps. cxv. 4, etc.; Isa. xliv. 12, etc.

like unto them: *so is* every one
that trusteth in them.

19 Bless the LORD, O house of
Israel: bless the LORD, O house
of Aaron:

20 Bless the LORD, O house of
Levi: ye that fear the LORD,
bless the LORD.

21 Blessed be the LORD out of
Zion, which dwelleth at Jerusalem. Praise ye the LORD.

recting the course of events in their
favour. This language is copied literally from Deut. xxxii. 36: "For the
Lord shall judge his people, and repent himself for his servants." It is
there a part of the song of Moses
after the journey through the wilderness, after smiting the kings of the
Amorites and of Bashan; and when,
delivered from their enemies, the
Israelites had come to the borders of
the promised land, Deut. xxxi. The
language was, therefore, peculiarly
appropriate to the design of this
psalm. ¶ *And he will repent himself
concerning his servants.* In behalf
of his people. That is, he will do
as if he repented, or had changed his
mind. He will stay his judgments.
He will not suffer his people to be
destroyed. He will not permit the
judgments which seemed to threaten
their entire ruin to be carried out to
the full. They shall be arrested mid-
way *as if* God had then changed his
mind. Of course, all this is language
accommodated to human weakness,
and to the manner of speaking among
men.

15–18. *The idols of the heathen* are
silver and gold, etc. To show more
fully the propriety of praising God,
and him alone as God, the psalmist
instituted a comparison between him
and idols, showing that the gods
worshipped by the heathen lacked
every ground of claim to Divine
worship and homage. They were,
after all that could be done to fashion,
to decorate, and to adorn them, nothing *but* silver and gold, and could

have no better claim to worship than
silver and gold as such. They had,
indeed, mouths, eyes, ears, but they
could neither speak, see, hear, nor
breathe. The passage here is substantially the same as in Ps. cxv.
4–8; and the one was evidently copied
from the other, though in the latter
the description is in some respects
amplified; but which was the original
it is impossible to determine. See
Notes on that passage.

19–21. *Bless the* LORD, *O house of
Israel,* etc. This passage, also, is
evidently an imitation of the passage
in Ps. cxv. 9–13. The *form* in Ps.
cxv., however, is rather an exhortation to *trust* in the Lord, and an assurance that God *would* bless the
classes spoken of, than a call on them
to bless the Lord. Still the same
classes of persons are referred to;—
the house of Israel; the house of
Aaron; and those who feared the
Lord. The passage needs no further
illustration than what is found in the
Notes on Ps. cxv. 9–13. It is an
earnest call on all classes of the people to bless and praise the Lord. It
is language expressive of overflowing
joy; the utterance of a heart full of
exalted conceptions of the majesty,
the glory, and the mercy of God; of
a heart which feels to the utmost the
fitness of praise, and desires that all
classes of men—priests and people,
—that all created things should unite
in the praise of Jehovah. Who, in
reading the psalm, can fail to catch
the feelings of the psalmist, and to
say AMEN AND AMEN!

PSALM CXXXVI.

O GIVE thanks unto the LORD; for *he is* ^u good: for *v* his mercy *endureth* for ever.

2 O give thanks unto ^w the God of gods: for his mercy *en-dureth* for ever.

u Ps. cxix. 68.

3 O give thanks to the Lord of lords: for his mercy *endureth* for ever.

4 To him who alone ^x doeth great wonders: for his mercy *endureth* for ever.

v 1 Chron. xvi. 34; 2 Chron. xx. 21.
w Deut. x. 17; Dan. ii. 47. *x* Ps. lxxii. 18.

PSALM CXXXVI.

This psalm also has no title to indicate the author, or to explain the occasion on which it was composed. It is a psalm of very peculiar construction, and stands alone in the form of its poetry. The peculiarity consists in repeating at the close of each verse the language "for his mercy endureth for ever." This is a kind of *refrain*, and may have been designed, in public worship, to be a response by a choir, or by the people. That it *may* have been intended to be so used cannot be disproved, nor can any one show that such a response in public worship is, itself, improper or wrong. It is not certain, however, that it was meant to be so used; and it should not, therefore, be appealed to as *proving* that such responses are proper in public worship, whatever may be true on that point. It may have been merely a specimen of the poetic art among the Hebrews,—one of the forms in which Hebrew poetry expressed itself. The subjects referred to as laying the foundation for the response in each verse,— "for his mercy endureth for ever,"--are such as have been often introduced in the previous psalms, and will require but little additional illustration. The general idea is, that *all* these acts of the Divine interposition,—all that God has done, even though it seemed to be a display of power or of justice, of severity or of wrath,—was, in fact, an illustration of the "*mercy*" of God, and laid a foundation for praise. That is, All this was connected with the good of his people, with favours to mankind, with the accomplishment of great and benevolent purposes, and, *therefore*, was expressive of *mercy*,—a proof that the "mercy of God endures for ever."

1. *O give thanks unto the* LORD; *for* he is *good*. This whole verse is the same as Ps. cvi. 1, except that that is introduced by a *Hallelujah*.

See Notes on that verse. ¶ *For his mercy* endureth *for ever*. See also Notes on Ps. cvi. 1; cvii. 1. Literally, "For unto eternity his mercy." That is, It is ever the same; it never changes; it is never exhausted; it is found in all his dealings—in all his acts towards his creatures, and ever will be.

2. *O give thanks unto the God of gods*. See Deut. x. 17. The supreme God; the God superior to all that is called God, or that is adored by the nations of the earth; above all to whom the name God is ever applied. ¶ *For his mercy*, etc. The ground of praise here is, that it is a characteristic of the supreme God that he is a merciful Being; that there is blended in his character eternal mercy with infinite power. Mere *power* might fill us with dread; power mingled with mercy, and able to carry out the purposes of mercy, must lay the foundation for praise.

3. *O give thanks to the Lord of lords*. The Lord or Ruler of all in authority,—all kings, princes, rulers. He is supreme over all. This is an attribute of Divinity; yet this is ascribed to the Lord Jesus, thus proving that he is Divine. See Notes on Rev. xix. 16. ¶ *For his mercy*, etc. The ground of praise here, as in the previous verse, is, that this God,— the Supreme Ruler over all the potentates and magistrates of earth,—is a merciful Being. He is kind and benignant *towards* those rulers, and *through* them to mankind.

4. *To him who alone doeth great wonders*. Miracles; marvellous things; things which spring from his direct and absolute power; things lying beyond the range of natural laws.

5 To him that *v* by wisdom made the heavens : for his mercy *endureth* for ever.

6 To him that stretched *z* out the earth above the waters : for his mercy *endureth* for ever.

7 To him that made great

y Prov. iii. 19.　*z* Gen. i. 9, etc. ; Jer. x. 12.

lights : for his mercy *endureth* for ever ;

8 The sun [1] to rule by day : for his mercy *endureth* for ever :

9 The moon and stars to rule by night : for his mercy *endureth* for ever.

[1] *for the ruling.*

See Notes on Ps. lxxii. 18. ¶ *For his mercy*, etc. For all these mighty wonders are performed in carrying out purposes of mercy. So the wonders which were done in Egypt were for the deliverance of an oppressed people ; so the miracles performed by the Saviour and his apostles were to remove disease and pain, and to establish a religion of mercy ; so the Divine interpositions among the nations are to assert the principles of righteousness, to secure the reign of order and love, and to promote the welfare of mankind.

5. *To him that by wisdom made the heavens.* Made them in so wise a manner ; where so much wisdom was manifested. See Prov. iii. 19 ; viii. 24–31. ¶ *For his mercy*, etc. The making of the heavens was a manifestation of mercy and goodness as furnishing an abode for unfallen and holy beings ; as a dwelling-place for redeemed sinners when they shall be removed there from the earth ; and as, by their order, their beauty, their harmony, and their happy influences, tending to promote the happiness of man on earth.

6. *To him that stretched out the earth above the waters.* Gen. i. 1, 9 ; see Notes on Ps. xxiv. 2. ¶ *For his mercy*, etc. As an illustration of his benignity and kindness in preparing an abode for man, and for other creatures in the world. Whatever there is of life or happiness, on the continents and islands, has resulted from that act of God when " he made the dry land appear."

7. *To him that made great lights.* Gen. i. 14. The sun and the moon are here particularly referred to. ¶ *For his mercy*, etc. As manifested

in all that has followed from the creation and diffusion of *light*,—(all the beauty in the universe as *seen;* all the life, beauty, and vigour in the vegetable and animal world ; all that there *is* of life and happiness in the universe—for there could be neither if darkness reigned everywhere) ; *light*, the emblem of happiness ; the source of joy ; the producer, in a great measure, of the beauties of the universe, and the revealer of those beauties everywhere. How *can* a man think of *light* and not praise its Author ?

8. *The sun to rule by day.* Gen. i. 16. Marg., as in Heb., *for the ruling of the day.* That is, to control, as it were, the day ; to determine its length—its beginning—its ending—to make it what it *is*. ¶ *For his mercy*, etc. By all the blessings of day as distinguished from night and darkness,—by all that the sun in his daily course does to diffuse life, joy, peace, comfort, happiness on the earth,—by all that are warmed by its beams, cheered by its light, guided in labour, guarded from dangers,—do we derive an argument for the mercy of God ; by all this there is laid a foundation for his praise.

9. *The moon and stars to rule by night.* Gen. i. 16. ¶ *For his mercy*, etc. As a proof also of his benignity and mercy. By all the beauty of the moon and stars in their course through the heavens,—by all that there is in the harmony and order of their movements,—by all that there is to make night less hideous and fearful,—by all that there is to reveal a countless number of worlds whose existence could not have been discovered but for the night,—by all that there is to

10 To *a* him that smote Egypt in their first-born : for his mercy *endureth* for ever :

11 And brought out Israel from among them : for his mercy *endureth* for ever :

12 With a strong hand, and with a stretched-out arm : for his mercy *endureth* for ever :

a Ps. cxxxv. 8, etc.; Ex. xii. 29.

13 To him which divided *b* the Red sea into parts : for his mercy *endureth* for ever.

14 And made Israel to pass through the midst of it : for his mercy *endureth* for ever.

15 But [1] overthrew Pharaoh and his host in the Red sea : for his mercy *endureth* for ever.

b Ps. lxxviii. 13. [1] *shaked off.*

guide the mariner on the ocean, enabling him to determine his position and to mark his course when on the deep,—and therefore by all the blessings of navigation and commerce, binding the different parts of the world together,—by all that there is in the " North-star," fixed and true in guiding those who flee from bondage, —by all these and kindred things without number, do we see the benignity, the goodness, the mercy of God, in forming the moon and stars " to rule by night."

10. *To him that smote Egypt in their first-born.* Ex. xii. 29. That is, he struck them down, or destroyed them, by his own direct power. ¶ *For his mercy,* etc. It was in mercy to his people. It was the means of their deliverance from bondage, for the Egyptians would not otherwise have suffered them to depart. By all the results of their deliverance both to themselves and to mankind, the act was seen to be an act of mercy to the world. It was better for mankind that the Hebrews should be delivered even at this sacrifice than it would have been that they should *not* be brought into the promised land.

11. *And brought Israel out from among them.* From the land of Egypt. By all the wonders manifested in their deliverance, and in conducting them out of the land so that they should escape from their pursuers. ¶ *For his mercy,* etc. His mercy in this respect was to be measured by all that there was of power in conducting them forth in safety, and by the results of it.

12. *With a strong hand.* A powerful hand ; as by a hand that could grasp and subdue all that opposed. ¶ *And with a stretched-out arm.* As if the arm were stretched out to strike with the utmost force, or to exert its utmost power. See Ex. vi. 6; Deut. iv. 34; v. 15; vii. 19; xxvi. 8; Jer. xxxii. 21. ¶ *For his mercy,* etc. The exertion of his power in delivering his people was the expression of a mercy, the consequences of which are to endure for ever, for the results of that deliverance will never cease in the history of the world; will never cease in heaven.

13. *To him which divided the Red sea into parts.* More literally, "Parted it into parts;" made parts of that which before was unbroken and a whole. It was actually divided into *two* parts, so that the Hebrews passed between them : Ex. xiv. 21, 22. ¶ *For his mercy,* etc. This, too, was an exercise of mercy, or a manifestation of benevolence toward them and toward the world, to be measured by all the good which would result from it in itself, and by all the power which was put forth to effect it.

14. *And made Israel to pass through the midst of it.* Ex. xiv. 29. ¶ *For his mercy,* etc. The mercy manifested in keeping the waves from returning on them and overwhelming them.

15. *But overthrew Pharaoh and his host in the Red sea.* Marg., as in Heb., *shaked off.* The word is applicable to a tree shaking off its foliage. Isa. xxxiii. 9. The same word is used in Ex. xiv. 27 : " And the Lord overthrew (Marg., *shook off*) the Egyptians in the midst of the sea."

16 To him which led *c* his people through the wilderness: for his mercy *endureth* for ever.

17 To him which smote great kings: for his mercy *endureth* for ever:

18 And *d* slew famous kings; for his mercy *endureth* for ever:

19 Sihon *e* king of the Amorites: for his mercy *endureth* for ever:

20 And Og the king of Bashan: for his mercy *endureth* for ever:

21 And gave *f* their land for an heritage: for his mercy *endureth* for ever:

22 *Even* an heritage unto Israel his servant: for his mercy *endureth* for ever.

23 Who remembered *g* us in our low estate: for his mercy *endureth* for ever:

c Ex. xiii. 18; Deut. viii. 15.
d Deut. xxix. 7.   *e* Num. xxi. 21, 23.

f Jos. xii. 1, etc.
g Deut. xxxii. 36; Luke i. 48.

He shook them off as if he would no longer protect them. He left them to perish. ¶ *For his mercy,* etc. Their destruction was wrought in mercy to his people and to the world; for it was the means of deliverance to Israel. The death of a wicked man is a benefit to the world, and the act of removing him may be really an act of the highest benevolence to mankind. No wrong is done to such men, for they deserve to die; and the only service which can be rendered to the world through them is by their removal from the earth.

16. *To him which led his people through the wilderness.* For all the manifestations of his care during a period of forty years. ¶ *For his mercy,* etc. That is, his mercy was to be measured by all the protection extended over them; by all the provision made for their wants; by all that God did to defend them; by all his interposition when attacked by their enemies; by safely bringing them to the land to which he had promised to conduct them.

17–22. *To him which smote great kings.* On this passage see Notes on Ps. cxxxv. 10–12. There is little difference in the two places, except that here the statement is divided by the *refrain,* "For his mercy endureth for ever." The idea in the whole passage, in view of the Divine interposition in slaying the mighty kings, and in giving their land for a possession to the Hebrew people, is, that it was a proof of mercy and benevolence. It is

benevolence to mankind and to the church of God,—it is in the interests of humanity, of domestic peace, and of the charities of life, to remove wicked men from the world. This mercy may be manifested further, not merely in removing the wicked, but in transferring their possessions to those who will make a better use of them. Thus the possessions of these mighty kings, Sihon and Og, were transferred to the people of God, and lands which had been devoted to the service of blood, ambition, crime, pollution, and idolatry, became devoted to the service of religion and righteousness. In like manner, through the removal of a wicked man from the world by death, God may cause his wealth, accumulated by avarice and dishonesty, to be transferred to the hands of children who wil. make a good use of it—children converted as if in anticipation of this, and with a view to this. Among the highest expressions of mercy to the world may be, therefore, the removal of wicked princes in war,—or the removal of wicked men, in other ranks of life, by death in any form.

23. *Who remembered us in our low estate.* When we were few in number; when we were a feeble people; when we were a people unable to contend with such mighty foes. ¶ *For his mercy,* etc. By all that he did for us *when* thus feeble; by all his power put forth to defend us from our enemies, he has showed his mercy and kindness to us and to the world.

24 And hath redeemed us from our enemies : for his mercy *endureth* for ever.

25 Who *h* giveth food to all

h Ps. cxlv. 15, 16.

flesh : for his mercy *endureth* for ever.

26 O give thanks unto the God of heaven : for his mercy *endureth* for ever.

24. *And hath redeemed us from our enemies.* Has rescued or delivered us from all our foes; has given to us freedom and peace. ¶ *For his mercy,* etc. By all that he has done in order to redeem us; and by all the prosperity, happiness, and peace which have followed as the result of that, he has showed his mercy. So it is in the greater work of the redemption of the soul. By all the love manifested in the gift of a Saviour,—by all the sufferings and toils of his life, —by his "agony and bloody sweat" in the garden of Gethsemane,—by his "cross and passion,"—by all the blessings of salvation here, all our peace, all our purity, all our consolations, all our hopes, and by all the glories of heaven hereafter,—the mercy of God in our redemption is to be estimated and measured. Who can take the full account of it ?

25. *Who giveth food to all flesh.* To all living things :—all in the air, on the earth, in the waters. See Notes on Ps. civ. 27, 28; comp. Ps. cxv. 16. ¶ *For his mercy,* etc. All this is a proof of his benignity and kindness. To see this, it would be necessary to have a view of what is *done* every day in the providence of God to meet the wants of the countless multitudes thus dependent on him. Let it be remembered, also, that the wants of *each* insect, fowl, animal, fish, is to be provided for *as an individual,*—and who can take in a full view of the care, the wisdom, the benevolence of what is done every day by the Father of all in providing for their wants ? Let it be remembered, also, that this has been continued without ceasing from the foundation of the world, and will be demanded until its close, and then let us try to imagine what is necessary to be done to provide for the

wants of all the dwellers in distant worlds,—and who, in this view, can form any proper estimate of the wisdom and the goodness of God ?

26. *O give thanks unto the God of heaven.* The God who reigns in heaven; whose home is heaven. ¶ *For his mercy,* etc. In view of all this— of all that he does in heaven and on earth—let praise be ascribed to him. To know the measure of the praise due to him ; to see how great is his "mercy," it would be necessary to know *all* that he does in heaven and on earth. That will not be known here. It will constitute the theme of contemplation and praise for ever and ever. Enough, however, *is* known here to show the propriety of repeating again, again, and again, as in this psalm, the language, "For his mercy endureth for ever ;" "For his mercy endureth for ever ;" "For his mercy endureth for ever."

PSALM CXXXVII.

Though there is no title prefixed to this beautiful psalm, and no direct intimation as to the occasion on which it was composed, yet there can be no doubt as to the circumstances in which it was written. There is, indeed, no mention of the name of the author, and no possibility of recovering that name now, but there can be no doubt that it was composed by one of the exiles in Babylon, —one who had witnessed and shared the sufferings of the exiles there, and who had also a lively recollection of the wrongs done to Jerusalem when it was attacked and destroyed by its foes. The writer was a *Jew* to the heart's core ; an "Hebrew of the Hebrews ;" embodying and expressing in this short psalm all that there was which was peculiar in Hebrew feeling, patriotism, devotion. Nowhere else in a short compass is so much *Judaism*—so much Jewish piety —to be found concentrated as in this psalm. There is grief at their lonely

PSALM CXXXVII.

B Y the rivers of Babylon, there
we sat down; yea, we wept,

when we remembered Zion.

2 We hanged our harps upon
the willows in the midst thereof.

and desolate condition in Babylon; profound and submissive silence in the midst of their troubles; indignation that they should be taunted and derided by their captors; a strong—earnest—supreme love for their native land; deep resentment at the remembrance of the many wrongs done to Jerusalem when it was destroyed; and an earnest invocation to God that he would remember those wrongs alike in relation to Edom and Babylon, and treat those wrongdoers as they deserved. It would seem most probable that the psalm was composed soon after the return from Babylon, and before the temple was finished, —while the ruins of the city caused by the Edomites and Babylonians were visible everywhere. The combined remembrance of the insults in Babylon, and of the wrong done to the city at its capture, animates the poet, and fills his mind with this deep and burning indignation.

1. *By the rivers of Babylon.* The streams, the water-courses, the rivulets. There was properly only one river flowing through Babylon,—the Euphrates; but the city was watered, as Damascus now is, by means of canals or water-courses cut from the main river, and conveying the water to different parts of the city. For a description of Babylon, see the introductory Notes to Isaiah, ch. xiii. If the reference here is to *Babylon proper*, or the city, the allusion would be to the Euphrates flowing through it; if to Babylonia, the allusion would be to the Euphrates, and the other rivers which watered the country, as the Tigris, the Chaboras, and the Ulai. As it is most probable that the captive Hebrews were not scattered through the empire, but were concentrated in one or a few places, it is, perhaps, not improper to understand this of Babylon itself. ¶ *There we sat down.* There we were sitting. Perhaps a little company of friends; perhaps those assembled for worship; perhaps those who happened to come

together on some special occasion; or, perhaps, a poetic representation of the general condition of the Hebrew captives, as sitting and meditating on the desolations of their native land. ¶ *Yea, we wept.* We sat there; we meditated; we wept. Our emotions overpowered us, and we poured forth tears. So now, there is a place in Jerusalem, at the south-west corner of the area on which the temple was built, where the Jews resort on set occasions to weep over the ruins of their city and nation. ¶ *When we remembered Zion.* When we thought on our native land; its former glory; the wrongs done to it; the desolations there; when we thought of the temple in ruins, and our homes as devastated; when we thought of the happy days which we had spent there, and when we contrasted them with our condition now.

2. *We hanged our harps upon the willows.* The harps once used to accompany the songs of praise and the service of God in the temple; the harps with which they had sought to beguile their weary hours, and to console their sad spirits in their captivity. The word rendered *willows* —עֲרָבִים, *arabim*—used only in the plural, denotes the willow or *osier*, so called from its white, silvery leaves. Gesenius, *Lex.* Comp. Isa. xv. 7. It is probable that the weeping willow —the willow with long pendulous branches—is here referred to. Trees in desert lands spring up along the courses of the streams, and appear, in the wide desolation, as long and waving lines of green wherever the rivers wind along. The course of a stream can thus be marked by the prolonged line of meandering green in the desert as far as the eye can reach. It has been objected to the statement here that the *willow* is not now found in the neighbourhood of ancient Babylon, but that the palm

3 For there they that carried us away captive required of us [1] a song : and they that [2] wasted *i* us

[1] *the words of a song.* [2] *laid us on heaps*
i Ps. lxxix. 1.

required of us mirth, *saying*, Sing us *one* of the songs of Zion.
4 How shall we sing the LORD's song in a [3] strange land?

[3] *land of a stranger.*

is the only tree which grows there. I saw, however, in 1852, in St. James's Park in London, a willow-tree with a label on it, stating that it was taken from the site of ancient Babylon; and there seems no reason to doubt the correctness of the account. The willow may be less abundant there now than it was in former times, as is true of the palm-tree in Palestine, but there is no reason to doubt that it grew there. All that the psalm, however, would necessarily demand in a fair interpretation would be that there should have been even a single clump of these trees planted there, under which a little band of exiles may have seated themselves when they gave utterance to the plaintive language of this psalm. ¶ *In the midst thereof.* In the midst of Babylon; showing that this referred to the city proper. They could not sing, such was their grief, though they had their harps with them; and they hung them up, therefore, on the branches of the trees around them;—or, poetically, they were as dumb *as if* they had hung up their harps there.
3. *For there they that carried us away captive.* The Babylonians. ¶ *Required of us a song.* Asked of us a song. The word does not express the idea of compulsion or force. Marg., as in Heb., *words of a song.* Perhaps the idea is that they did not merely ask *music,* but they wished to hear the *words*—the songs themselves —in which they were accustomed to praise God. This *may* have been a taunt, and the request may have been in derision; or it may have been seriously, and with no desire to reproach them, or to add to their sorrows. We are not to impute bad motives to others where there is no evidence that there are any, and

where the supposition of good motives will answer just as well; and the expression here may have been a kind and natural wish to hear the songs of these foreigners,—songs of which they might have heard much by report; perhaps songs which they had *over-heard* them singing when they were in a less desponding state of mind, and when they sought to comfort themselves by these ancient national melodies. As the only reason assigned for *not* complying with this request was that they *could* not "sing the Lord's song in a strange land" (ver. 3), we are rather led to infer that there was no bad motive—no disposition to taunt and ridicule them by the request that was made. ¶ *And they that wasted us.* Marg., *laid us on heaps.* The Hebrew word means a tormentor; properly, one who extorts lamentation from others, or who causes them to howl,—to wit, under oppression or wrong. The Septuagint and Latin Vulgate render it, "They who led us away." The general idea is, those under whom they were then suffering; or, who had caused these trials to come upon them. ¶ *Required of us mirth.* Literally, "Our tormentors, joy." The Hebrew word means *joy;* and the sense is, that they asked them to give the usual indications of joy and happiness—to wit, a song. The language means, "Cheer up; be happy; give us one of the beautiful songs which you were accustomed to sing in your own land." It *may*, indeed, have been in derision; but there is no proof that it was. ¶ Saying, *Sing us* one *of the songs of Zion.* The songs—the sacred hymns—which you were accustomed to sing in worship in your own land.
4. *How shall we sing the* LORD's *song.* The song designed to cele-

5 If *k* I forget thee, O Jerusalem, let my right hand forget *her
cunning.*

6 If I do not remember thee,

k Dan. vi. 10.   *l* Ps. lxxxiv. 10.

let my tongue cleave to the roof
of my mouth : if I prefer *l* not
Jerusalem above ¹ my chief joy.

¹ *the head of my joy.*

---

brate his praise; that is, appropriate
to the worship of Jehovah. ¶ *In a
strange land.* Far from our home;
far from the temple; exiles; captives:—how *can* we find spirit in
such circumstances to sing? How
can we do that which would be indicative of what we do not feel, and
cannot feel,—joy and happiness! The
idea is not that those psalms or songs
would be profaned by being sung
there, or that there would be anything improper in itself in singing
them, but that it would be misplaced
and incongruous to sing them in their
circumstances. It would be doing
violence to their own feelings; their
feelings would not allow them to do
it. There are states of mind when
the language of joy is appropriate
and natural; there are states where
the heart is so sad that it cannot
sing.

5. *If I forget thee, O Jerusalem.*
The meaning here is, that to sing in
such circumstances would *seem* to
imply that they had forgotten Jerusalem; that they were unmindful of
its sorrows, and cared not that it was
desolate. The remembrance of its
calamities pressed hard upon them,
and they could not do anything which
would seem to imply that they had
become unmindful of the sufferings
that had come upon their nation.
One will not make merry when a
wife or child lies dying,—or on the
day of the funeral,—or over the grave
of a mother. A gay and brilliant
party, accompanied with music, feast-
ing, dancing, when a friend has been
just laid in the grave, when the
calamities of war are abroad, when
the pestilence is raging in a city, we
feel to be untimely, unseemly, and
incongruous. So these captives said
it would be if they should make
merry while their temple was in

ruins; while their city was desolate;
while their people were captives in a
foreign land. ¶ *Let my right hand
forget her cunning.* Let my right
hand forget its skill in music—all its
skill. If I should now play on the
harp—as indicative of joy—let the
hand which would be employed in
sweeping over its strings become
paralyzed and powerless. Let the
punishment come where it would
seem to be deserved—on the hand
which *could* play at such a time. So
Cranmer held the hand which had
been employed in signing a recanta-
tion of his faith in the fire, until it
was burned off, and dropped in the
flames.

6. *If I do not remember thee.*
Equivalent to, "If I forget thee."
If I ever fail to remember thee; if I
shall ever act as if I had forgotten
thee. Singing in a strange land,
among those who had perpetrated
such wrongs in thee,—appearing to
be happy, cheerful, joyous, gay, merry
there,—would be understood to imply
that I had ceased to remember thee,
and cared nothing for thee. ¶ *Let
my tongue cleave to the roof of my
mouth.* Comp. Ezek. iii. 26. Let me
be unable to speak; let my tongue
be as it were attached to the upper
part of the mouth, so that it could
not be used. If I employ it in an unworthy purpose,—in any way whereby
it can be inferred that I have ceased
to remember my native land, and the
city of our solemnities, let my tongue
be ever after useless. This language
is often employed by Virgil: Vox
faucibus hæsit. ¶ *If I prefer not
Jerusalem.* Literally, "If I do not
cause to ascend." That is, If I do
not exalt Jerusalem in my estimation
above everything that gives me pleasure; if I do not find my supreme
happiness in that. ¶ *Above my chief*

7 Remember, O LORD, the children of Edom in the day of Jerusalem; who said, [1] Rase *it*, rase *it, even* to the foundation thereof.

[1] *make bare.*

joy. Marg., as in Heb., *the head of my joy.* The chief thing which gives me joy; as the head is the chief, or is supreme over the body. This is expressive of a great truth in regard to religion. Anything else—everything else—is to be sooner sacrificed than that. The happiness which is found in religion is superior to that found in every other source of enjoyment, and is preferred to every other. If either is to be sacrificed—the joy of religion, or the pleasure derived from society, from the gay world, from literature, from music, from dancing, from works of art—it will be the latter and not the former. There are other sources of joy which are not in any way inconsistent with religion:—the joy of friendship; of domestic life; of honourable pursuits; of the esteem of men. So of music, the arts, gardens, literature, science. But when one interferes with the other, or is inconsistent with the other, the joy of the world is to be sacrificed to the joy of religion. When the joy of religion is sacrificed *for* the joy of the world, it proves that there is no true piety in the soul. Religion, if it exists at all, will always be supreme.

7. *Remember, O* LORD, *the children of Edom.* The Edomites; the people of Idumea. On the situation of Edom or Idumea, see introductory Notes to Isa. xxxiv. ¶ *In the day of Jerusalem.* In the day when Jerusalem shall be restored; in the day when punishment shall be inflicted on the nations that destroyed it;—then, do not forget the Edomites, who took so large and so active a part in its overthrow. This is to be understood as a continued " *remembrance* " of Zion; as a purpose not to "forget" Jerusalem. The psalmist, representing the feelings of the captives in Babylon, says, that so far from doing anything which would imply a forgetfulness of their native land,—as singing cheerful

songs there might be understood to be,—they would do *everything* to call Jerusalem to remembrance. They would remember her former splendour; they would remember her desolations; *they would go further*—they would not forget those who had brought these calamities upon her; those who had done most for her overthrow. As among the most prominent, they would remember particularly the ancient enemies of their nation—the Edomites—who had been among the most active in its destruction, and who had united with the Babylonians in the work of ruin. They would remember all this; and they prayed God that *he* also would remember the desolation itself, and all the *actors* in that work of desolation. ¶ *Who said.* Implying that they had been associated with the Babylonians in the destruction of the city. On the hostility of that people to the Hebrews, and the grounds of their hostility,—and on their agency as united with the Babylonians in destroying Jerusalem, and the Divine vengeance threatened them on that account,—see, as above, the introd. to Isa. xxxiv. ¶ *Rase* it. *rase* it. Marg., as in Heb., *make bare.* That is, Strip it of everything,—temple, houses, ornaments, fountains,—and leave it *a bare and naked rock.* Let nothing remain but the rocks—the foundations—on which it is built. In the history of the Edomites, as stated in the introd. to Isa. xxxiv., there were abundant facts to show that they were particularly zealous and active in seeking the destruction of the hated city. This verse and the one following constitute a portion of the " imprecatory" Psalms; of those which seem to cry for vengeance, and to manifest a revengeful and unforgiving spirit; the portion of the Psalms which has been regarded as so difficult to be reconciled with the forgiving spirit enjoined

8 O daughter of Babylon, who
m art to be ¹ destroyed; happy
shall he be that ² rewardeth thee
as thou hast served us

m Isa. xiii. 1, etc.; Rev. xviii. 6.   ¹ *wasted.*

9 Happy *shall he be* that taketh
and dasheth thy little ones against
the ³ stones.

² *recompenseth unto thee thy deed which thou*
didst to us.   ³ *rock.*

---

in the gospel. On this subject, see
General Introd., § 6.

8. *O daughter of Babylon.* That
is, Babylon itself; the city of Babylon.
On the word *"daughter"* as thus
used, see Notes on Isa. i. 8. ¶ *Who
art to be destroyed.* Certainly to be
destroyed; of whose destruction there
are fixed and absolute prophecies. See
Notes on Isa. xiii. 19–22. ¶ *Happy
shall he be that rewardeth thee as thou
hast served us.* Marg., *that recompenseth unto thee thy deed which thou
didst to us.* Literally, "Happy
shall he be who shall repay to thee
the recompence which thou hast re-
compensed unto us." The idea is,
Who shall repay thee for thy treatment of us; or, as we should say in
common language, "Who shall pay
thee back?" That is, he will be
esteemed a fortunate man who is
made the instrument of inflicting deserved punishment on a city so guilty
and so cruel. He will acquire fame
and honour by doing it; his name
will be made known abroad and perpetuated among men. In fact, the
name of Cyrus, who conquered Babylon, *is* among the names of the most
celebrated of conquerors; and the
manner in which he took Babylon
and overthrew the government and
kingdom, has given him a most eminent place among successful princes
and conquerors.

9. *Happy* shall he be *that taketh*,
etc. Marg., as in Heb., *rock.* This
refers to what was not uncommon in
ancient warfare, as it is now among
savage tribes, — the indiscriminate
slaughter of those of all ages, and of
both sexes, in war. It was expressly
foretold of Babylon that this would
occur (see Isa. xiii. 16, and the Notes
on that place), and there may be a
reference here to that prediction, and
the psalmist may mean to say that

the man would be accounted happy,
or would be happy, who wreaked
vengeance on Babylon in carrying
out that prophecy. The idea is, "This
will certainly occur, for it is foretold,
and happy or fortunate will he be
who is the instrument in fulfilling
it." Comp. 2 Kings viii. 12; Nahum
iii. 10; Hos. xiii. 16. See also Homer,
Il. xxii. 63, 373, *seq.* It is impossible to reconcile such barbarous
customs with the idea of "honourable war," or with the principles of
war as carried on among "civilized"
nations now. It should be added,
however, that there is much—very
much—that *is* practised in war by
"civilized" nations still, which it is
equally *impossible* to reconcile with
any just notions of morality or humanity, and which in coming ages,
and when men shall come to view
things aright, will seem to the people
of those times to be not less monstrous,
strange, and barbarous. In regard
to this passage, we are not *necessarily*
to suppose that the author of the
psalm approved of this, or desired it,
or prayed for it. He looked forward
to the fulfilment of a prediction; he
saw that a just and terrible judgment
would certainly come upon Babylon;
he expressed that in the common
language of the times, and states the
manner in which it would occur; he
described the feelings—the gratification—of those who would execute the
Divine purpose in the overthrow of
Babylon; he referred to the estimate
in which the conqueror would be held
by men, and the glory of the achievement as giving him fame among men.
It must be admitted that the feelings
of the author of the psalm appear to
accord with this; that he considers
it proper that the city should be destroyed; and that he regards its overthrow as a righteous judgment, and

PSALM CXXXVIII.
A Psalm of David.

I WILL praise thee with my whole heart; before the gods

will I sing praise unto thee.

2 I will worship toward thy holy temple, and praise thy name for thy loving-kindness and for

as a thing to be desired in the Divine administration. It is true that he *might* approve of such an overthrow, and see it to be right,—he *might* describe the feelings of those by whom it would be wrought, *their* joy, *their* exultation, and even their barbarity, without himself approving of their barbarity, or sympathising with their feelings, or partaking of their spirit; but still it cannot in fairness be denied that there is an apparent approval of the act here referred to, which savours more of imprecation than forgiveness, and which is apparently prompted more by the spirit of revenge than by a desire of just punishment. On this subject, however, see General Introd., § 6 (4); and Notes on Ps. cix. 10. A correct *record* may be made, whether of facts or of feelings, without any design of expressing either approbation or disapprobation on the part of the historian, the prophet, or the poet.

PSALM CXXXVIII.

This is the first of a series of *eight* psalms (Ps. cxxxviii.-cxlv.), placed together in this part of the book, and ascribed to David. They appear to be of the nature of a *supplement* to the Book of Psalms, composed of psalms unknown to the original collector and arranger of the book, and subsequently discovered and ascertained to be the works of David. It is not to be regarded as strange that there should be psalms of this nature composed by David at different periods of his life, which might have been preserved in different branches of his family, and which might not have been generally known to exist. It is rare that the works of an author, especially a poet, are collected and published, and that things of this kind—fugitive and occasional pieces—are not subsequently found; nor is it very unusual that such pieces may, after all, be among the most tender, touching, and beautiful of

his compositions. Burns's "Highland Mary," so much admired, and his "When wild War's deadly blast was blown,"—a poem which no one can read without tears,—with not a few others of his, are of this description. They are said, in his Biography, to have been "extracted from the *correspondence* of Burns." (Works of Robert Burns, Philad., 1834, pp. 76, 85, 89.)

The occasion on which this psalm was composed cannot now be determined. It was evidently written in view of trouble (vers. 3, 7), and it expresses confidence that God would interpose in the future in behalf of the author, as he had done in the past; and it is, therefore, adapted to inspire confidence and hope in all who are called to pass through scenes of trial. The psalm does not admit of any particular analysis.

1. *I will praise thee with my whole heart.* Reserving nothing in my heart to give to idols or to other gods. All that constitutes praise to God as God, he would address to him alone. He would use no language, and cherish no feeling, which implied a belief that there was any other God; he would indulge in no attachment which would be inconsistent with supreme attachment to God, or which would tend to draw away his affections from him. See Notes on Ps. ix. 1. ¶ *Before the gods will I sing praise unto thee.* The idols; all idols;—in preference to them all. This does not mean that he would do this *in the presence* of other gods; but that Jehovah should be acknowledged to be God *in preference* to any or all of them.

2. *I will worship.* I will bow down and adore. ¶ *Toward thy holy temple.* See Notes on Ps. v. 7. The word *temple* here undoubtedly refers to the tabernacle. ¶ *And praise thy name for thy loving-kindness.* Praise thee for thy benignity; thy mercy; thy benevolence. ¶ *And for thy truth.*

thy truth: for ^{n} thou hast magnified thy word above all thy name.

3 In the day when I cried thou answeredst me, *and* strengthenedst me *with* strength in my soul.

n Isa. xlii. 21.

4 All the kings of the earth shall praise thee, O LORD, when they hear the words of thy mouth.

5 Yea, they shall sing in the ways of the LORD: for great *is* the glory of the LORD.

Thy truthfulness; thy faithfulness to thy promises. ¶ *For thou hast magnified thy word.* Thou hast made it great. Comp. Isa. xlii. 21. The reference here is to the promises of God, and especially to the promise which God had made to David that the Messiah would descend from him. Comp. 2 Sam. vii. ¶ *Above all thy name.* Above all else that thou hast done; above all the other manifestations of thyself to me or to the world. The word *name* here would refer properly to all that God had done to make himself known,—since it is by the *name* that we designate or distinguish any one; and, thus understood, the meaning would be, that the word of God—the revelation which he has made of himself and of his gracious purposes to mankind—is superior in clearness, and in importance, to all the other manifestations which he has made of himself; all that can be known of him in his works. Beyond all question there are higher and clearer manifestations of himself, of his being, of his perfection, of his purposes, in the volume of revelation, than any which his works have disclosed or can disclose. Comp. Ps. xix. There are very many points in relation to God, of the highest interest to mankind, on which the disclosures of science shed no light; there are many things which it is desirable for man to know, which cannot be learned in the schools of philosophy; there are consolations which man needs in a world of trouble which cannot be found in nature; there is especially a knowledge of the method by which sin may be pardoned, and the soul saved, which can never be disclosed by the blow-pipe, the telescope, or the microscope. These things, if learned at all, must

be learned from revelation, and these are of more importance to man as a traveller to another world than all the learning which can be acquired in the schools of philosophy—valuable as that learning is.

3. *In the day when I cried.* Referring to some former period of his life when he was in trouble. ¶ *Thou answeredst me.* In the very day when I called, thou gavest me the answer:—that is, immediately. ¶ And *strengthenedst me* with *strength in my soul.* Literally, " Thou didst embolden,—or, didst make me courageous with strength." Thou didst enable me to meet danger, and to overcome fear. It would seem probable that this was on some occasion when he was in danger from his enemies.

4. *All the kings of the earth shall praise thee,* etc. That is, kings, princes, and rulers shall learn the words of promise; shall be made acquainted with the words which thou hast graciously spoken, and with their fulfilment, and shall be led to praise thee. This refers to a time, of which frequent prophetic mention is made in the Scriptures, when kings and rulers shall be converted to the true religion, and when they shall act an important part, by their example and influence, in maintaining and diffusing it. Comp. Ps. lxviii. 31, 32; Isa. xlix. 23.

5. *Yea, they shall sing in the ways of the* LORD. In the ways which God has appointed. They shall join with all that love him—with the humblest of the people—in acknowledging God. Kings and people shall thus bow before God in common acts of praise, and as being on the same level before him. As men, as sinners, as redeemed, as travelling to the grave, they are

6 Though *o* the LORD *be* high, yet hath he respect unto the lowly: but the proud he knoweth afar off.

7 Though *p* I walk in the midst of trouble, thou wilt revive me; thou shalt stretch forth thine

o Isa. lvii. 15 ; lxvi. 1, 2 ; 1 Pet. v. 5.
p Micah vii. 8, 9.

hand against the wrath of mine enemies, and thy right hand shall save me.

8 The LORD will perfect *q that which* concerneth me: thy mercy, O LORD, *endureth* for ever: forsake not the works of thine own hands.

q Phil. i. 6 ; 1 Thess. v. 24.

all alike before God. ¶ *For great* is *the glory of the* LORD. Great is his character; great his dignity; great his honour; and all this will be seen to be so when those of most exalted rank thus worship and adore him. The most lofty on earth shall acknowledge that there is one who is more exalted than they are, and their own dignity and splendour shall thus contribute to deepen the impression of the honour and glory of God.

6. *Though the* LORD *be high.* This might be rendered "For lofty is Jehovah—and the humble he sees—and the proud he knows from afar." The idea is, that God—so high and exalted—sees and knows all of every rank among men. The mind of the psalmist had been impressed with a sense of the greatness and majesty of God, but (as if it might be said that one so great could not regard man, so humble and insignificant) he adds, that the fact of God's exaltation does not prevent his noticing the affairs of men: that the lowly in life need not fear lest they should be overlooked; the proud need not hope that they will escape the notice of his eye. ¶ *Yet hath he respect unto the lowly.* Those in humble life; the obscure; the unknown. It does not mean here that he has any special favour towards them, but merely that he *sees* them. Their low and obscure condition does not prevent his observing them, and they need have no fear that he will overlook them, or that they will be forgotten. Comp. Notes on James iv. 6; 1 Pet. v. 5. ¶ *But the proud.* Those of lofty rank, and of lofty feelings;—the haughty. ¶ *He knoweth afar off.* From afar. Though he is exalted,—though he is in heaven,—yet he is not so far removed but that he sees them, and knows them altogether. Distance from him is no protection for them; nor can the wicked hope to escape notice from the fact that God reigns over distant worlds.

7. *Though I walk in the midst of trouble.* Though *I* am in the low vale of sorrow, I shall not be overlooked or forgotten. This implies that the writer was *then* in trouble, and it expresses the conviction that *whenever* he should be in trouble God would remember him, and give him life and strength. ¶ *Thou wilt revive me.* Thou wilt cause me *to live;* thou wilt give me life. Ps. xxx. 3. Comp. Notes on Ps. lxxi. 20. The meaning is, Thou wilt give me life—vigour—strength—to bear the trouble. ¶ *Thou shalt stretch forth thine hand.* As one does when he is about to inflict a blow. ¶ *Against the wrath of mine enemies,* etc. In reference to all their attempts to destroy me. Thou wilt meet their wrath by thy power, and I shall be safe.

8. *The* LORD *will perfect* that which *concerneth* me. He will complete what he has begun. He will not begin to interpose in my behalf, and then abandon me. He will not promise to save me, and then fail to fulfil his promise. He will not encourage me, and then cast me off. So of us. He will complete what he begins. He will not convert a soul, and then leave it to perish. "Grace will complete what grace begins." See Notes on Phil i. 6. ¶ *Thy mercy, O* LORD, endureth *for ever.* See Notes on Ps. cxxxvi. 1. ¶ *Forsake not the works of thine own hands.* What thou hast

VOL. III.   U

PSALM CXXXIX.
To the chief Musician. A Psalm of David.

O LORD, thou hast searched

^r me, and known *me*.

r Jer. xvii. 10; Rev. ii. 23.

made; what thou hast begun to do.
Do not leave *me* to perish. Prayer is
one of the means—and an *essential*
means—by which the saints are to be
kept unto salvation. The doctrine
of the " perseverance of the saints"
is not inconsistent with prayer, but
rather prompts to it; and he who
professes to rely on that doctrine, and
feels so safe that he does not need to
pray, and does *not* pray, gives certain
evidence that he has never been converted, and has no true religion.

PSALM CXXXIX.

This psalm purports to be a psalm of
David, and there is no reason to doubt
that it is properly attributed to him.
See introd. to Ps. cxxxviii. At what
time it was composed is, however, unknown. It contains reflections which
might have occurred at any period of
his life; yet it would seem most probable that it was not written in his early
years, but that it is a record of his most
mature thoughts on a great and very
important subject.

The psalm relates to the omnipresence
of God, and contains such reflections as
would occur to one meditating on that
attribute of the Deity. It is the most
distinct and full statement of that doctrine which is to be found in the Hebrew Scriptures, and the doctrine is
presented in language which has never
been surpassed for sublimity and beauty.
The leading idea in the psalm seems to
be that of *comfort* from the fact that
God is everywhere; that he knows all
that pertains to us; that we can never
be hidden from his view; that he has
known us from the beginning; that as
he fashioned and formed us—making us
what we are—he knows all our necessities, and can supply them.

The psalm consists of three parts :--
I. A celebration of the Omniscience
and Omnipresence of God, as a ground
of confidence and hope, vers. 1–18.
   (*a*) The fact that he knows all that
      there is in the heart, vers. 1-6.
   (*b*) The fact that he is everywhere
      present, vers. 7-12.
   (*c*) The fact that all in our past life

has been known to God; that
he has created us, and that his
eye has been upon us from the
beginning of our existence,
vers. 13–16.
   (*d*) The fact that his thoughts to-
      wards us are precious, and
      numberless as the sand, vers.
      17, 18.
II. The feelings of the psalmist in
relation to the acts of the wicked as a
proof that he loved God, vers. 19–22.
These reflections seem to have sprung
from his contemplation of the Divine
character and perfections, as leading
him to hate all that was opposed to a
Being so pure, so benevolent, so holy.
On looking into his own heart, in view
of what God was, he was conscious that
he had no sympathy with the enemies
of God as such; that such was his love
for the character of God, and such his
confidence in him, that he could have
nothing in common with them in their
feelings towards God, but wished to be
dissociated from them for ever.
III. The expression of a desire that,
as God saw all the recesses of the human
soul, he would search *his* heart, and
would detect *any* evil he might see
there, and deliver him from the evil,
and lead him in the way which conducted to life eternal, vers. 23, 24. Any
one may feel, and must feel, that after
all which he knows of himself,—after
all the effort which he makes to ascertain what is within his heart,—there
are depths there which his eye cannot
penetrate, and that there may be sins
of thought and feeling there which
he has not detected; but it is only from
the consciousness of sincerity, and a
true desire to honour God, that one can
pray that *God* would search him, and
that he would detect and bring out every
form of sin which *he* may see concealed
and lurking in the soul. He who can
sincerely offer this prayer is a pious man.

1. *O* LORD, *thou hast searched me.*
The word rendered *searched*, has a
primary reference to searching the
earth by boring or digging, as for
water or metals. See Job xxviii. 3.
Then it means to search accurately

2 Thou *s* knowest my down-sitting and mine up-rising; thou *t* understandest my thought afar off.

3 Thou ¹ compassest my path and my lying down, and art acquainted *with* all my ways.

s 2 Kings vi. 12; xix. 27.

4 For *there is* not a word in my tongue, *but*, lo, O LORD, thou *u* knowest it altogether.

5 Thou hast beset me behind and before, and laid thine hand upon me.

t Ps. xciv. 11; Ezek. xi. 5.
¹ Or, *winnowest.* *u* Mal. iii. 13, 16.

or closely. ¶ *And known* me. As the result of that search, or that close investigation. Thou seest all that is in my heart.. Nothing is, or can be, concealed from thee. It is with this deep consciousness that the psalm begins; and all that follows is but an expansion and application of this idea. It is of much advantage in suggesting right reflections on our own character, to have this full consciousness that God knows us altogether; that he sees all that there is in our heart; that he has been fully acquainted with our past life.

2. *Thou knowest my downsitting,* etc. In the various circumstances of life, thou knowest me. Thou knowest me in one place as well as in another. I cannot so change my position that thou will not see me, and that thou wilt not be perfectly acquainted with all that I say, and all that I do. In every posture, in every movement, in every occupation, thou hast a full knowledge of me. I cannot go out of thy sight; I cannot put myself into such a position that thou wilt not see me. ¶ *Thou understandest my thought.* Heb., As to my thought. That is, Thou seest what my plans are; what I design to do; *what I am thinking about.* A most solemn reflection! How unwilling would bad men be—would even good men be—to have those round about them know always *what they are thinking about.* ¶ *Afar off.* Not when the *thought* is far off; but *thou,* being far off, seest us as clearly as if thou wert near. I cannot go to such a distance from thee that thou wilt not see perfectly all that I am thinking about.

3. *Thou compassest my path,* etc. Marg., *winnowest.* The Hebrew

word—זָרָה, *zarah*—means properly *to scatter,* to cast loosely about—as the wind does dust; and then, to winnow,—to wit, by throwing grain, when it is thrashed, up to the wind: Isa. xxx. 24; Jer. iv. 11; Ruth iii. 2. Then it means *to winnow out;* that is, to winnow out all the chaff, and to leave all the grain—to save all that is valuable. So here it means that God, as it were, *sifted* him. Comp. Isa. xxx. 28; Amos ix. 9; Luke xxii. 31. He scattered all that was chaff, or all that was valueless, and saw what there was that was real and substantial. When it is said that he did this in his "path and his lying down," it is meant that he did it in every way; altogether; entirely. ¶ *And art acquainted* with *all my ways.* All the paths that I tread; the whole course of my life. All that I do, in all places and at all times, is fully known to thee.

4. *For* there is *not a word in my tongue.* All that I say; all that I have power to say; all that I am disposed at any time to say. ¶ But *lo, O LORD, thou knowest it altogether.* All that pertains to it. What is *said,* and what is *meant.* Merely to *hear* what is spoken does not imply necessarily a full knowledge of what is said,—for it may be false, insincere, hypocritical. God knows exactly what is *said* and what is *meant.*

5. *Thou hast beset me behind and before.* The word rendered *beset—* צוּר, *tzur*—means properly to press; to press upon; to compress. It has reference commonly to the siege of a city, or to the pressing on of troops in war; and then it comes to mean to besiege, hem in, closely surround,

6 *Such* knowledge *is* too wonderful for me; it is high, I cannot *attain* unto it.

7 Whither *v* shall I go from thy spirit? or whither shall I flee from thy presence?

v Jer. xxiii. 24 ; Jonah i. 3.
w Amos ix. 2—4.

8 If I *w* ascend up into heaven, thou *art* there : if I make my bed in hell, *x* behold, thou *art there.*

9 *If* I take the wings of the morning, *and* dwell in the uttermost parts of the sea :

x Job xxvi. 6 ; Prov. xv. 11.

so that there is no way of escape. This is the idea here,—that God was on every side of him ; that he could not escape in any direction. He was like a garrison besieged in a city so that there was no means of escape. There is a transition here (not an unnatural one), from the idea of the *Omniscience* of God to that of his *Omnipresence,* and the remarks which follow have a main reference to the latter. ¶ *And laid thine hand upon me.* That is, If I try to escape in any direction I find thine hand laid upon me there. Escape is impossible.

6. Such *knowledge* is *too wonderful for me.* Literally, " Wonderful knowledge away from me," or, more than I can comprehend. It is beyond my reach ; it surpasses all my powers to comprehend it. ¶ *It is high, I cannot* attain *unto it.* It is so exalted that I cannot grasp it ; I cannot understand how it can be.

7. *Whither shall I go from thy spirit ?* Where shall I go where thy spirit is not ; that is, where thou art not ; where there is no God. The word *spirit* here does not refer particularly to the Holy Spirit, but to God *as* a spirit. " Whither shall I go from the all-pervading Spirit— from God, considered as a spirit ?" This is a clear statement that God is a " Spirit " (comp. John iv. 24) ; and that, as a spirit, he is Omnipresent. ¶ *Or whither shall I flee from thy presence ?* Heb., From his face ; that is, where he will not be, and will not see me. I cannot find a place—a spot in the universe, where there is not a God, and the same God. Fearful thought to those that hate him— that, much as they may wish or desire it, they can never find a place

where there is not a holy God ! Comforting to those that love him—that they will never be where they may not find a God,—their God ; that nowhere, at home or abroad, on land or on the ocean, on earth or above the stars, they will ever reach a world where they will not be in the presence of that God — that gracious Father — who can defend, comfort, guide, and sustain them.

8. *If I ascend up into heaven.* The word *heaven* here, in the original is in the plural number—*heavens,*— and includes all that there is above the earth—the highest worlds. ¶ *If I make my bed.* Properly, " If I strew or spread my couch." If I should seek that as the place where to lie down. ¶ *In hell.* Heb., *Sheol.* See Notes on Isa. xiv. 9, where the word is fully explained. The word here refers to the under-world—the abodes of the dead ; and, in the apprehension of the psalmist, corresponds in depth with the word " heaven " in height. The two represent all worlds, above and below ; and the idea is, that in neither direction, above or below, could he go where God would not be. ¶ *Thou* art there. Or, more emphatically and impressively in the original, " *Thou !*" That is, the psalmist imagines himself in the highest heaven, or in the deepest abodes of the dead,—and lo ! God is there also ! he has not gone from *him !* he is still in the presence of the same God !

9. If *I take the wings of the morning.* Literally, " I will take the wings of the morning." That is, I will take this as a supposable case ; I will imagine what would occur, should I be able to take to myself the wings

10 Even there shall thy hand lead me, and thy right hand shall hold me.

11 If I say, Surely the darkness shall cover me; even the

night shall be light about me.

12 Yea, the darkness ¹ hideth not from thee; *y* but the night

¹ *darkeneth.*   *y* Dan. ii. 22.

of the morning, and endeavour to escape *by flight* from the presence of God, or go where he could not pursue me, or where he would not be. The "wings of the morning" evidently mean that by which the light of the morning *seems to fly* — the most rapid object known to us. It is not to be supposed that the psalmist had an idea of the exact velocity of light, but to him that was the most rapid object known; and his language is not the *less* striking because the laws of its flight have become accurately known. The word rendered *morning* refers to the dawn —the daybreak—the Aurora—the *first* beams of the morning light. The beams of light are in fact no swifter then than at any other time of the day, but they *seem* to be swifter, as they so quickly penetrate the darkness. ¶ And *dwell in the uttermost parts of the sea.* The end of the sea; that is, the *west,* as the sea referred to undoubtedly is the Mediterranean, which was *west* of Palestine, and which became another name for the west. The idea is, that if he could fly with the rapidity of light, and could be in an instant over the sea, even beyond its remotest border, still God would be there before him. He could not escape from the Divine presence.

10. *Even there shall thy hand lead me.* I shall find thee there; thy hand would be upon me; I should not have gone from thy presence. ¶ *And thy right hand shall hold me.* Still hold me; still be laid upon me. I should find myself there, as certainly as here, in thy hand;—and in the same sense,—either to seize upon me if I went astray, or to protect me, if obedient, supported by thee in all the perils of the flight. God, still the same—the same in all re-

spects—would be with me there as he is here.

11. *If I say, Surely the darkness shall cover me.* If I seek to find refuge in the darkness of the night so that God would not see me. The word rendered *cover*—שׁוּף, *shuph*—means properly to snap, to gape after; then, to lie in wait for; and then, to attack, or fall upon any one, unexpectedly. It is rendered *bruise* (twice) in Gen. iii. 15, "He shall *bruise* thy head, and thou shalt *bruise* his heel;" *breaketh* in Job ix. 17, "He *breaketh* me with a tempest;" and in this place *cover.* It does not occur elsewhere. Here it means to fall upon; to overpower; to cover. The idea is, If it should come suddenly upon me; if I should be involved in sudden darkness—*as if* the darkness should come and attempt to *snatch* me away from God. All this would be in vain, for it would be, so far as God is concerned, bright day around me. ¶ *Even the night shall be light about me.* In respect to me. It shall be as if I stood in the full blaze of light. God can see me still; he can mark my goings; he can perceive all that I do as plainly then as at mid-day. This *is* so:—and what a thought this is for a wicked man who seeks to escape detection in his crimes by perpetrating them in the night! What a thought for a good man, that in the darkest night of sorrow, when there seems to be nothing but deep midnight, when there appears to be not a ray of light in his dwelling, or on his path, that all to the eye of God is as clear as noon-day! For in that night of sorrow God sees him as plainly as in the brightest days of prosperity and joy.

12. *Yea, the darkness hideth not from thee.* Marg., as in Heb., *darken-*

shineth as the day : ¹ the darkness and the light *are* both alike *to thee.*

13 For thou hast possessed my

¹ *as is the darkness, so is the light.*

reins : thou hast covered me in my mother's womb.

14 I will praise thee : for I am fearfully *and* wonderfully made : marvellous *are* thy works, and

eth not. Darkness does not make darkness to thee. It makes things dark to us; not to him. So it is in natural darkness; so in moral darkness. It seems dark to us; it is not so to him. Things appear dark to us, — disappointment, bereavement, trouble, care, losses; but all is light to God. The existence of sin and suffering on the earth seems dark to us;—not to him, for he sees the reasons and the end of all. ¶ *But the night shineth as the day.* One is as bright and clear to him as the other. ¶ *The darkness and the light* are *both alike* to thee. Marg., as in Heb., *As is the darkness so is the light.* To thee there is no difference. All is light.

13. *For thou hast possessed my reins.* The word here rendered *possessed* means properly to *set upright,* to *erect,* and hence the derivative of the verb is applied to a cane or reed, as being erect. Then the word means to found, to create, Gen. xiv. 19, 22, —as the heavens and the earth ; and then, to get, to gain, to purchase, etc. Here the word seems to be used in its original sense, to make, create, etc. The idea is, not as in our translation, that God *possessed* or *owned* them but that he had *made* them, and that, *therefore,* he knew all about them. The word *reins* means literally the *kidneys ;* and then, it comes to denote the inward part, the mind, the soul, the seat of the desires, affections, and passions. Jer. xi. 20. See Notes on Ps. vii. 9; Job xix. 27. The meaning here is, that God had made him ; that the innermost recesses of his being had been constituted as they are by God ; and that, *therefore,* he must be able to see all that there is in the very depths of the soul, however it may be hidden from the eye of man. ¶ *Thou hast*

covered me in my mother's womb. The word here rendered *cover* means properly to interweave ; to weave ; to knit together, and the literal translation would be, " Thou hast *woven* me in my mother's womb, meaning that God had put his parts together, as one who weaves cloth, or who makes a basket. So it is rendered by De Wette and by Gesenius (*Lex.*). The original word has, however, also the idea of protecting, as in a booth or hut, woven or knit together, — to wit, of boughs and branches. The former signification best suits the connexion ; and then the sense would be, that as God had made him,—as he had formed his members, and united them in a bodily frame and form before he was born,— he must be able to understand all his thoughts and feelings. As he was not concealed from God before he saw the light, so he could not be anywhere.

14. *I will praise thee.* I will not merely admire what is so great and marvellous, but I will acknowledge thee in a public manner as wise, and holy, and good : — as entitled to honour, love, and gratitude. ¶ *For I am fearfully* and *wonderfully made.* The word rendered " fearfully " means properly *fearful things ;* things fitted to produce fear or reverence. The word rendered " wonderfully made " means properly to distinguish; to separate. The literal translation of this—as near as can be given—would be, " I am distinguished by fearful things;" that is, by things in my creation which are fitted to inspire awe. I am distinguished among thy works by things which tend to exalt my ideas of God, and to fill my soul with reverent and devout feelings. The idea is, that he was *distinguished*

that my soul knoweth [1] right well.

15 My [2] substance was not hid from thee, when [z] I was made in

[1] *greatly.* [2] Or, *strength,* or, *body.*

secret, *and* curiously wrought in the lowest parts of the earth.

16 Thine eyes did see my substance, yet being unperfect; and

[z] Job x. 8, 9.

among the works of creation, or so "separated" from other things in his endowments as to work in the mind a sense of awe. He was made different from inanimate objects, and from the brute creation; he was *so* made, in the entire structure of his frame, as to fill the mind with wonder. The more any one contemplates his own bodily formation, and becomes acquainted with the anatomy of the human frame, and the more he understands of his mental organization, the more he will see the force and propriety of the language used by the psalmist. ¶ *Marvellous* are *thy works.* Fitted are they to excite wonder and admiration. The particular reference here is to his own formation; but the same remark may be made of the works of God in general. ¶ *And* that *my soul knoweth right well.* Marg., as in Heb., *greatly.* I am fully convinced of it. I am deeply impressed by it. We can see clearly that the works of God are "wonderful," even if we can understand nothing else about them.

15. *My substance was not hid from thee.* Thou didst see it; thou didst understand it altogether, when it was hidden from the eyes of man. The word *substance* is rendered in the margin, *strength* or *body.* The Septuagint, the Latin Vulgate, the Syriac, the Arabic, and Luther render it, "my bone," or "my bones." The word properly means strength, and then anything strong. Another form of the word, with different pointing in the Hebrew, means a bone, so called from its strength. The allusion here is to the bodily frame, considered as strong, or as that which has strength. Whatever there was that entered into and constituted the vigour of his frame, the psalmist says, was seen and known by God,

even in its commencement, and when most feeble. Its capability to become strong,—feeble as it then was,—could not even at that time be concealed. or hidden from the view of God. ¶ *When I was made in secret.* In the womb; or, hidden from the eye of man. Even then thine eye saw me, and saw the wondrous process by which my members were formed. ¶ And *curiously wrought.* Literally, *embroidered.* The Hebrew word— רקם, *rakam*—means to deck with colour, to variegate. Hence it means to variegate a garment; to weave with threads of various colours. With us the idea of *embroidering* is that of working various colours *on* a cloth by a needle. The Hebrew word, however, properly refers to the act of *weaving in* various threads — as now in weaving carpets. The reference here is to the various and complicated tissues of the human frame — the tendons, nerves, veins, arteries, muscles, *as if* they had been woven, or as they appear to be curiously interweaved. No work of tapestry can be compared with this; no art of man could *weave* together such a variety of most tender and delicate fibres and tissues as those which go to make up the human frame, even if they were made ready to his hand :—and who but God could *make* them? The comparison is a most beautiful one; and it will be admired the more, the more man understands the structure of his own frame. ¶ *In the lowest parts of the earth.* Wrought in a place as dark, as obscure, and as much beyond the power of human observation as though it had been done low down beneath the ground where no eye of man can penetrate. Comp. Notes on Job xxviii. 7, 8.

16. *Thine eyes did see my substance,*

in thy book ¹ all *my members* were written, ² *which* in continuance were fashioned, when *as yet there was* none of them.

¹ *all of them.*

17 How precious also are thy thoughts unto me, O God! how great ª is the sum of them!

² Or, what *days they should be fashioned.*
ª Ps. xl. 5.

---

yet being unperfect. This whole verse is very obscure, but the *idea* in this expression clearly is, " Before I had shape or form thou didst see what I was to be." The single word in the original translated " my substance, yet being unperfect," is גֹּלֶם, *golem.* It occurs only in this place, though the verb—גָּלַם, *galam*—is found in 2 Kings ii. 8, where it is used in reference to the mantle of Elijah: "And Elijah took his mantle, and *wrapped it together,* etc. That is, he rolled it up, or he folded it. The noun, then, means that which *is* rolled or wrapped together; that which is folded up, and, hence is applicable to anything folded up or undeveloped; and would thus most aptly denote the embryo, or the fœtus, where all the members of the body are as yet folded up, or undeveloped; that is, before they have assumed their distinct form and proportions. This is undoubtedly the idea here. Before the embryo had any such form that its future size, shape, or proportions could be marked by the eye of man, it was clearly and distinctly known by God. ¶ *And in thy book.* Where thou recordest all things. Perhaps the allusion here would be to the book of an architect or draftsman, who, before his work is begun, draws his plan, or sketches it for the direction of the workmen. ¶ *All* my members *were written.* The words *my members* are not in the original. The Hebrew is, as in the margin, *all of them.* The reference may be, not to the members of his body, but to his *days* (see the margin on the succeeding phrase),—and then the sense would be, " all my *days,* or all the periods of my life, were delineated in thy book. That is, When my substance—my form—was not yet developed, when yet an embryo,

and when nothing could be determined from that by the eye of man as to what I was to be, all the future was known to God, and was written down,—just what should be my form and vigour; how long I should live; what I should be; what would be the events of my life. ¶ Which *in continuance were fashioned.* Marg., *What days they should be fashioned.* Literally, " Days should be formed." De Wette renders this, " The days were determined before any one of them was." There is nothing in the Hebrew to correspond with the phrase " in continuance." The simple idea is, The days of my life were determined on, the whole matter was fixed and settled, not by anything seen *in* the embryo, but *before* there was any form—before there were any means of judging from what I then was to what I would be—all was seen and arranged in the Divine mind. ¶ *When* as yet there was *none of them.* Literally, " And not one among them." Before there was one of them in actual existence. Not one development had yet occurred from which it could be inferred what the rest would be. The entire knowledge on the subject must have been based on Omniscience.

17. *How precious also are thy thoughts unto me, O God!* On the word *thoughts,* see Notes on ver. 2. Comp. ver. 23. The remark is made here doubtless in view of the numberless *thoughts* involved in planning and forming a frame so wondrous, and in the care necessary to bring it to perfection; to develop it; to provide for it; to guard and defend it. How many *thoughts* of a parent are employed in behalf of his children, in providing for them; teaching them; counselling them; anticipating their wants. How many more

18 *If* I should count them, they are more in number than the sand: when I awake, I am still with thee.

19 Surely thou wilt slay the wicked, O God: depart from me, therefore, ye bloody men.

20 For they speak against thee

---

thoughts are needful on the part of God in reference to each one of us: — for there are numberless things necessary for us which cannot occupy the mind of a parent, since he cannot accomplish these things for us ; they do not lie within his province, or in his power. ¶ *How great is the sum of them.* Literally, "How strong are the heads of them." That is, The heading of them, or the summing of them up, would be a task beyond the power of man. And who *could* estimate the number of the *thoughts* necessarily bestowed on himself by his Maker in all the care exercised over him ; all the arrangements for his development and growth ; all that is done to defend him from danger ; all that is indispensable in providing for his wants ; all that was necessary to secure the salvation of his soul ! See Notes on Ps. xl. 5.

18. If *I should count them.* If I could count them. ¶ *They are more in number than the sand.* Numberless as the sand on the sea-shore. ¶ *When I awake, I am still with thee.* When I am lost in deep and profound meditation on this subject, and am aroused again to consciousness, I find the same thing still true. The fact of *my* being forgetful, or lost in profound meditation, has made no difference with thee. Thou art still the same ; and the same unceasing care, the same thoughtfulness, still exists in regard to me. Or, the meaning may be, sleeping or waking with me, it is still the same in regard to thee. Thine eyes never close. When mine are closed in sleep, thou art round about me; when I awake from that unconscious state, I find the same thing existing still. I have been lost in forgetfulness of thee in my slumbers ; but thou hast not forgotten me. There has been

no change — no slumbering — with thee.

19. *Surely thou wilt slay the wicked, O God.* Comp. Notes on Isa. xi. 4. The literal translation of this would be, "If thou wilt slay the wicked." It is not easy to account for the sudden and remarkable transition or diversion of the train of thought from the main subject of the psalm, in these verses (19–22), in which the psalmist gives vent to his feelings towards the wicked, and prays that they may depart from him. Perhaps the explanation of it may be, that as the psalmist was reflecting on the fact that God is everywhere present, that he searches the hearts of men, that he must know all their conduct, he was suddenly struck with the idea of the condition of wicked men in the presence, and under the eye, of such a Being. As God knows all things, he must know them ; and this instantaneously suggested the idea of their guilt and danger. Men of such characters could not deceive such a God. They could not but be known to him, and could not but be objects of his aversion. They could not, therefore, but be in danger. ¶ *Depart from me, therefore, ye bloody men.* See Ps. cxix. 115. The Hebrew is, "Men of bloods ;" that is, men who shed blood. The language is used to denote wicked men in general. The idea here is not that the psalmist was in danger from them at that time, but that he desired to be separate from that class of men ; he did not wish to be ranked with them, to partake of their conduct, or to share in their fate. He had no sympathy with them, and he desired to be separate from them altogether.

20. *For they speak against thee wickedly.* This is one form or manifestation of their character as wicked men, that they speak maliciously

wickedly, *and* thine enemies take *thy name* in vain.

21 Do [b] not I hate them, O LORD, that hate thee? and am not I grieved with those that rise

b 2 Chron. xix. 2.

up against thee?

22 I hate them with perfect hatred; I count them mine enemies.

23 Search me, O God, and

---

against God. The psalmist, therefore, desired to have nothing to do with them. It is always a sufficient reason for avoiding the society, the friendship, and the fellowship of others, when they profane, blaspheme, or calumniate the name of God. From such men we should at once withdraw. Piety shrinks from the society of such men, whatever may be their rank, or their social qualities, and turns away in pain, in sorrow, in abhorrence. See Notes on Ps. xxvi. 9. ¶ And *thine enemies take* thy name *in vain.* It is proof that they are thine enemies that they take thy name in vain, or that they are profane men; it is a sufficient reason for desiring to be separated from them.

21. *Do not I hate them, O* LORD, *that hate thee?* This is in the consciousness of the psalmist a proof of his own real piety, as derived from his feelings towards those who were the enemies of God. The word *hate* here, as applied to them, must be understood in the sense that he disapproved of their conduct; that he did not desire to be associated with them; that he wished to avoid their society, and to find his friends among men of a different character. See Notes on Ps. i. 1. Comp. Ps. v. 5. ¶ *And am not I grieved with those that rise up against thee?* The expression here—" grieved "—explains the meaning of the word "hate" in the former member of the verse. It is not that hatred which is followed by malignity or ill-will; it is that which is accompanied with grief —pain of heart—pity—sorrow. So the Saviour looked on men : Mark iii. 5 : "And when he had looked round about on them with *anger,* being *grieved* for the hardness of

their hearts." The Hebrew word used here, however, contains *also* the idea of being disgusted with; of loathing; of nauseating. See Notes on Ps. cxix. 158. The feeling referred to is anger, — conscious disgust—at such conduct; and grief, pain, sorrow, that men should evince such feelings towards their Maker.

22. *I hate them with perfect hatred.* With no approval whatever of their conduct; with no sympathy for the evil they do; with no words of apology for their sinful acts; with entire disapprobation. ¶ *I count them mine enemies.* As they are the enemies of God, so I regard them as *my* enemies. I do not wish to be associated with them, or to be regarded as one of them.

23. *Search me, O God.* The word *search* here is the same as in ver. 1. See Notes on that verse. The psalmist had stated the fact that it is a characteristic of God that he *does* search the heart; and he here prays that God *would* exercise that power in relation to himself; that as God could know all that there is within the heart, he would examine him with the closest scrutiny, so that he might be under no delusion or self-deception; that he might not indulge in any false hopes; that he might not cherish any improper feelings or desires. The prayer denotes great *sincerity* on the part of the psalmist. It indicates also self-distrust. It is an expression of what all must feel who have any just views of themselves,—that the heart is very corrupt; that we are liable to deceive ourselves; and that the most thorough search *should* be made that we be *not* deceived and lost. ¶ *And know my heart.* Know or see all that is within it. ¶ *Try me.* As metal is

know my heart; try me, and know my thoughts;

24 And see if *there be any* [1] wicked way in me, and lead me in the way everlasting.

[1] *way of pain,* or, *grief.*

---

tried or proved that is put to a *test* to learn what it is. The trial here is that which would result from the Divine inspection of his heart. ¶ *And know my thoughts.* See what they are. The word rendered *thoughts* occurs only in one other place, Ps. xciv. 19. The idea is, Search me thoroughly; examine not merely my outward conduct, but what I think about; what are my purposes; what passes through my mind; what occupies my imagination and my memory; what secures my affections and controls my will. He must be a very sincere man who prays that God will search his thoughts, for there are few who would be willing that their fellow-men, even their best friends, should know all that they are thinking about.

24. *And see if* there be any *wicked way in me.* Marg., *way of pain,* or *grief.* The Hebrew word properly means an image, an idol (Isa. xlviii. 5), but it also means pain, 1 Chron. iv. 9; Isa. xiv. 3. The word in the form used here does not occur elsewhere. Gesenius (*Lex.*) renders it here idol-worship. De Wette, "way of idols." Prof. Alexander, "way of pain." The Septuagint and Vulgate, "way of iniquity." So Luther. The Syriac, "way of falsehood." Rosenmüller, "way of an idol." According to this, the prayer is that God would search him and see if there was anything in him that partook of the nature of idolatry, or of defection from the true religion; any tendency to go back from God, to worship other gods, to leave the worship of the true God. As idolatry comprehends the sum of all that is evil, as being alienation from the true God, the prayer is that there might be nothing found in his heart which

PSALM CXL.

To the chief Musician. A Psalm of David.

DELIVER me, O LORD, from the evil man: preserve me from the [2] violent man;

[2] *man of violences.*

---

tended to alienate him from God, —would indicate unfaithfulness or want of attachment to him. ¶ *And lead me in the way everlasting.* The way which leads to eternal life; the path which I may tread for ever. In any other way than in the service of God his steps must be arrested. He must encounter his Maker in judgment, and be cut off, and consigned to woe. The path to heaven is one which man may steadily pursue; one, in reference to which death itself is really no interruption,—for the journey commenced here will be continued through the dark valley, and continued for evermore. Death does not interrupt the journey of the righteous for a moment. It is the same journey continued, — as when we cross a narrow stream, and are on the same path still.

PSALM CXL.

This, also, is a psalm of David. The occasion on which it was composed is not indicated in the title, but the contents of the psalm leave no room to doubt that it was written at an early period of his life, in the time when he was subjected to persecution—most probably in the time of Saul. The psalm bears every mark of David's style and spirit; and there can be no doubt that he was the author of it. For the reasons why it may have had a place *here* in the Book of Psalms, see Introd. to Ps. cxxxviii. On the phrase, "To the chief Musician," see Introd. to Ps. iv.

1. *Deliver me, O LORD, from the evil man.* That is, evidently from some particular man who was endeavouring to injure him; some personal enemy. All the circumstances mentioned agree well with the supposition that Saul is intended. ¶ *Preserve me from the violent man.* Marg.,

2 Which imagine mischiefs in *their* heart: continually are they gathered together *for* war.

3 They have sharpened their tongues like a serpent: adders' *c* poison *is* under their lips. Selah.

4 Keep me, O LORD, from the

c Rom. iii. 13.

hands of the wicked; preserve me from the violent man; who have purposed to overthrow my goings.

5 The proud have hid a snare *d* for me, and cords; they have spread a net by the wayside: they have set gins for me. Selah.

d Jer. xviii. 22.

---

as in Heb., *man of violences*. That is, one who has committed violence so often, who has so frequently done wrong, that this may be considered a characteristic of the man. This would apply well to the repeated acts of Saul in persecuting David, and endeavouring to do him injury.

2. *Which imagine mischiefs in* their *heart*. Here the language is changed to the plural number in the Hebrew, implying that while there was one man who was eminent in his wickedness and his wrong-doing, there were many others associated with him, acting under his direction. The word *mischiefs* in the Hebrew means *evils; wickednesses*. It was not a single purpose; the plan embraced many forms of evil,—doing him wrong in every way possible. ¶ *Continually are they gathered together* for *war*. They are organized for this purpose; they are constantly prepared for it. The word rendered *gathered together* properly means to sojourn, to dwell for a time; and it has been proposed by some to render this, "All the day they dwell with wars;" that is, they are constantly involved in them. But the word may mean also *to gather together*, as in Ps. lvi. 6.

3. *They have sharpened their tongues like a serpent*. Comp. Notes on Ps. lxiv. 3. The idea here is, that since the tongue of the serpent *seems* to be sharp, pointed, adapted to penetrate (and probably the original reference in the image was derived from that idea), the wound inflicted is by the serpent's tongue—*as if* with a hard, penetrating point. It is now known, however, that it is by a tooth —a single tooth, made flexible for the

purpose, — at the root of which a small bag containing the poison is located, which is injected through an orifice in the tooth into the wound. The meaning here is, that the words spoken by such persons — by their tongues — were like the poison produced by the bite of a serpent. ¶ *Adders' poison* is *under their lips*. The asp or adder is among the most poisonous of serpents. Thus Cleopatra of Egypt is said to have destroyed her own life by an asp, which she had concealed for that purpose. This passage is quoted in Rom. iii. 13, as a proof of human depravity. See Notes on that verse.

4. *Keep me, O* LORD, *from the hands of the wicked*, etc. See Notes on Ps. lxxi. 4. This is a repetition of the prayer in ver. 1. ¶ *Who have purposed to overthrow my goings*. To thrust me down as I go; to defeat my plans; to destroy me. They endeavour to prevent my accomplishing what I had designed to do.

5. *The proud have hid a snare for me*. Haughty; arrogant; oppressive men. See Notes on Ps. xxxv. 7; lvii. 6. ¶ *And cords*. Strings; twine; —as those do who lay a net to catch birds, and who design to spring it upon them unawares. ¶ *They have spread a net by the wayside*. Where I may be expected to walk, and where it may be suddenly sprung upon me. ¶ *They have set gins for me*. Snares, toils—such as are set for wild beasts. The meaning is, that they had not only made open war upon him, but they had sought to bring him into an ambush—to rush upon him suddenly when he was not on his guard, and did not know that danger was near.

6 I said unto the LORD, Thou *art* my God: hear the voice of my supplications, O LORD.

7 O GOD the Lord, the strength of my salvation, thou hast covered my head in the day of battle.

8 Grant not, O LORD, the de-

sires of the wicked: further not his wicked device, [1] *lest* they exalt themselves. Selah.

9 *As for* the head of those that compass me about, let the mischief of their own lips cover them.

[1] Or, *let them* not *be exalted.*

---

6. *I said unto the* LORD, *Thou* art *my God*, etc. In all these dangers from open war, in all these perils from a crafty enemy lying in ambush, my only refuge was God; my hope was in him alone. From all these dangers, seen and unseen, I knew that he could defend me, and I confidently believed that he would.

7. *O* GOD *the Lord*, etc. Literally, "Jehovah, Lord, the strength of my salvation." The word rendered "God," in the original, is *Jehovah.* The address is to Jehovah as the Lord; that is, as the supreme Ruler, —who presides over all things. Him the psalmist acknowledged as *his* Lord and Ruler. The phrase "the strength of my salvation" means the strength or power on which my safety depends. I have no other hope of deliverance but in thee. ¶ *Thou hast covered my head in the day of battle.* Thou hast been a shield unto me. Literally, "In the day of arms," or of armour, 1 Kings x. 25; Ezek. xxxix. 9, 10.

8. *Grant not, O* LORD, *the desires of the wicked.* That is, in the matter under consideration. Let them not accomplish their desire in my destruction. Let them not succeed in their designs against me. The prayer, however, *may* be used more generally. It is proper to pray that the desires of the wicked, as wicked men, may not be granted to them; that they may *not* be successful in their purposes. Success in such desires would be only an injury to themselves and to the world. It is proper to pray that the purposes of the wicked may be defeated, and that they may be led to abandon their designs and to seek better ends. For this, in fact, we

always pray when we pray for their conversion. ¶ *Further not his wicked device.* His purpose against me. ¶ Lest *they exalt themselves.* Lest they attribute it to their own skill, wisdom, or valour, and lest they pride themselves on their success. To succeed in a righteous cause makes a man humble and grateful; in a bad cause, proud, and forgetful of God. The margin here is, "*Let them not be exalted.*" The meaning is, that success would at the same time elate them in their own estimation, and increase their bad influence in the world. It is, on every account, a benevolent prayer that wicked men may *not* be successful in their plans of iniquity.

9. As for *the head of those that compass me about.* Luther renders this, "The calamity which my enemies design against me must fall upon their own heads." The passage stands in contrast with ver. 7: "Thou hast covered my head," etc. As for his own head, it had been protected in the day of battle. In reference now to the heads of his enemies,—of those that compassed him about,—he prays that what they had designed for *his* head might come by a just retribution on their own. The phrase "compass me about" refers to his enemies as being numerous, and as surrounding him on every side. See Ps. xl. 12; lxxxviii. 17; cix. 3; cxviii. 10-12. ¶ *Let the mischief of their own lips cover them.* Come upon them. The mischief which they have designed against me; that which they have conspired to bring on me. The reference is to a combination against him, or to some agreement which they had made to destroy him.

10 Let *e* burning coals fall
upon them : let them be cast into
the fire; into deep pits, that they
rise not up again.

11 Let not [1] an evil speaker be
established in the earth : evil
shall hunt the violent man to

e Ps. xi. 6.

[1] *a man of tongue, or, an evil speaker, a wicked
man of violence, be established in the earth:
let him be hunted to* his *overthrow.*

overthrow *him.*

12 I *f* know that the LORD
will maintain the cause of the
afflicted, *and* the right of the
poor.

13 Surely the righteous shall
give thanks unto thy name: the
upright shall dwell in thy presence.

f 1 Sam. ii. 8.

10. *Let burning coals fall upon
them.* Let them be punished, *as if*
burning coals were poured upon them.
See Notes on Ps. xi. 6; xviii. 12, 13;
cxx. 4. ¶ *Let them be cast into the
fire.* Punished as if they were cast
into the fire and consumed. ¶ *Into
deep pits, that they rise not up again.*
That they may utterly perish. This
was one mode of punishing, by casting a man into a deep pit from
which he could not escape, and leaving him to die, Gen. xxxvii. 20, 24;
Ps. ix. 15; xxxv. 7; Jer. xli. 7.

11. *Let not an evil speaker.* Literally, " A man of tongue." That is,
a man whom the tongue rules; a man
of an unbridled tongue; a man who
does not control his tongue. See
Notes on James iii. 2–12. ¶ *Be established in the earth.* Be successful
or prosperous; let him not carry out
his designs. It is not desirable that
a man *should* prosper in such purposes; and therefore, this is not a
prayer of malignity, but of benevolence. ¶ *Evil shall hunt the violent
man,* etc. More literally, " A man of
violence — a bad man — they shall
hunt him down speedily;" or, " let
him be hunted down speedily. Let
him who forms a project of violence
and wrong—a bad man—be hunted
as the beasts of prey are, and let his
destruction come quickly." Marg.,
Let him be hunted to his overthrow.
But the explanation now given suits
the connexion, and is a literal expression of the sense of the original.

12. *I know that the* LORD *will
maintain the cause of the afflicted.*
See Notes on Ps. ix. 4. The psalmist here doubtless refers primarily to

himself, as having a confident belief
that the Lord would maintain *his*
cause, or would defend *him.* At the
same time he makes the statement
general, implying that what would
be done to him would be done to all
in similar circumstances. The idea
is that God, in all his attributes, in
all his providential arrangements, in
all his interpositions on earth, would
be found to be on the side of the
oppressed, the afflicted, and the
wronged. He has no attribute that
can take part with an oppressor or a
wrong doer. The wicked cannot
come to him with the belief that
he will be on their side :—the righteous—the oppressed—the afflicted—
can. ¶ And *the right of the poor.*
He will defend the right of the poor.
Literally, *The judgment of the poor.*
That which will be just and right in
their case.

13. *Surely the righteous shall give
thanks unto thy name.* Unto thee.
(1) They will have occasion to do it;
(2) they will be disposed to do it.
They will not be unmindful of the
favours conferred upon them; it will
be a characteristic of them that they
will be thankful. ¶ *The upright
shall dwell in thy presence.* They
shall be under thy protection; they
shall be admitted to thy favour; they
shall dwell in thy dwelling-place.
(1) On earth they shall enjoy his
favour,—*as if* they abode with God.
(2) In heaven they will be permitted
to dwell with him for ever. The
general idea of the psalm is, that the
poor, the persecuted, the afflicted, if
righteous, shall enjoy the favour and
protection of God. God is on their

side, and not on the side of the wicked who oppress them. But then, men *should be righteous* in order that they may find the favour of God and dwell with him. There is no reason why a *poor* wicked man should enjoy the favour of God any more than why a *rich* wicked man should. It is not poverty or riches that commend us to God; it is faith, and holiness, and love, and obedience, in the condition of life in which we are placed, be it in a cottage or a palace.

PSALM CXLI.

This, also, is a psalm of David, and apparently composed under circumstances similar to the former. It is impossible, however, to determine the precise time at which it was written, or the exact circumstances of the psalmist at the time.

The circumstances, as far as they can be gathered from the psalm, are these :—

(1) He was in a situation of peril ;— so much so as to have almost no hope for himself or his followers. Snares and gins were laid for him (ver. 9), and his followers and friends were scattered and dispirited, as if their bones were scattered at the grave's mouth, ver. 7. Everything looked dark and discouraging.

(2) In these circumstances it occurred to his mind, or was suggested to him, to say or do something which, not honourable or right in itself, might have brought relief, or which might have rescued him from his peril, and secured the favour of his enemies ;— some trick—some artful scheme—some concession of principle—which would have delivered him from his danger, and which would have secured for him a position of safety, plenty, and honour, vers. 3, 4. Many considerations, derived from his danger, might have been suggested for this, even by those who were not bad men, but who might have been timid men, and who might have felt that their cause was hopeless, and that it would be proper to avail themselves of this opportunity to escape from their peril in any way.

(3) David knew that to resist this,— to abstain from following this apparently wise and prudent counsel,—to refuse to do what the circumstances

might seem to others to justify,—would expose him to the rebukes of sincere and honest men who thought that this would be right. Yet knowing all this, he resolved to bear their reproach rather than to follow such advice by doing a wrong thing. He says (ver. 5), that though they should smite him, it would (he knew) be in kindness, with the best intention ; though they should reprove him, it would be like a "gentle oil"—it would not break his head or crush him. He would cherish no resentment ; he would still pray for them as usual in the time of their calamities, ver. 5. Even when the "judges," the rulers,—his enemies—should be overthrown, as they might be, he would take no advantage of that circumstance ; he would not seek for revenge ; his words should be "sweet" kind words still, ver. 6.

(4) David prays, therefore, in view of this temptation, and of the counsel suggested to him, that he might be able to set a watchful guard over his own lips, and to keep his heart, that he might not be betrayed into anything which would be dishonourable or wicked ; that he might not be allured to that which was wrong by any prospect of temporal advantage which might follow. vers. 1-4.

(5) As the result of all, he put his trust in God, that he might be enabled to pursue an upright course ; and that, in such a course, he might be preserved from the snares which had been laid for him, vers. 8-10.

Perhaps what is here said in illustration of the design of the psalm will best agree with the supposition that it refers to the time mentioned in 1 Sam. xxiv. 1-7. Saul was then in his power. He could easily have put him to death. His friends advised it. The *suggestion* was a natural one ; it would seem to many to be a justifiable measure. But he resisted the temptation, trusting in the Lord to deliver him, without his resorting to a measure which could not but have been regretted ever afterwards.

The practical truth which would be illustrated by this view of the psalm would be, *that we are not to say or do anything that is wrong, though good men, our friends, advise it* ; *though it should subject us to their reproaches if we do it not* ; *though to do it would be followed by great personal advantages* ; *and though not to do it would leave us still in danger—a danger from which the course advised would have delivered*

PSALM CXLI.

A Psalm of David.

LORD, I cry unto thee : make haste unto me; give ear unto my voice, when I cry unto thee.

2 Let my prayer be [1] set forth before thee *as* incense, *g and* the

[1] *directed.*

lifting up of my hands *as* the evening sacrifice.

3 Set a watch, O LORD, before my mouth : keep the door of my lips.

4 Incline not my heart to *any* evil thing, to practise wicked

g Rev. v. 8.

---

us. It is better to act nobly, honourably, and in a high-minded manner, and to leave the result with God, still trusting in him.

1. LORD, *I cry unto thee.* In view of my perils ; in view of the suggestions of my friends ; in view of my temptation to do a wrong thing at their advice, and with the prospect of the advantage which it might seem to be to me. ¶ *Make haste unto me.* To save me from all this danger :— the danger from my enemies ; the danger from the counsels of my friends. See Notes on Ps. xxii. 19 ; comp. Ps. xl. 13 ; lxx. 1, 5 ; lxxi. 12. The meaning is, that there is need of *immediate* interposition. There is danger that I shall be overcome ; that I may be tempted to do a wrong thing ; that I may be ruined if there is any delay. ¶ *Give ear unto my voice,* etc. See Notes on Ps. v. 1.

2. *Let my prayer be set forth before thee.* Marg., *directed.* The Hebrew word means to fit ; to establish ; to make firm. The psalmist desires that his prayer should not be like that which is feeble, languishing, easily dissipated, but that it should be like that which is firm and secure. ¶ *As incense.* See the Notes and illustrations on Luke i. 9, 10. Let my prayer come before thee in such a manner as incense does when it is offered in worship ; in a manner of which the ascending of incense is a suitable emblem. See Notes on Rev. v. 8 ; viii. 3. ¶ And *the lifting up of my hands.* In prayer ;—a natural posture in that act of worship. ¶ As *the evening sacrifice.* The sacrifice offered on the altar at evening. Let my prayer be as acceptable as that is when it is offered in a proper manner.

3. *Set a watch, O* LORD, *before my mouth.* That I may not say anything rashly, unadvisedly, improperly. Comp. Ps. xxxix. 1. The prayer here is, that God would guard him from the temptation to say something wrong. To this he seems to have been prompted by the circumstances of the case, and by the advice of those who were with him. See introduction to the psalm. Comp. Notes on Ps. xi. 1. ¶ *Keep the door of my lips.* That my lips or mouth may not open except when it is proper and right ; when something good and true is to be said. Nothing can be more proper than *this* prayer ; nothing more desirable than that God should keep us from saying what we ought not to say.

4. *Incline not my heart to* any *evil thing.* Heb., to a word that is evil ;" that is, wrong. The connexion seems to demand that the term should be thus explained. The expression "Incline not" is not designed to mean that God exerts any *positive* influence in leading the heart to that which is wrong ; but it may mean "Do not place me in circumstances where I may be tempted ; do not leave me to myself ; do not allow any improper influence to come over me by which I shall be led astray." The expression is similar to that in the Lord's Prayer : "Lead us not into temptation." The psalmist's allusion here has been explained in the introduction to the psalm. ¶ *To practise wicked works with men that work iniquity.* To be united or associated with men who do wrong ; to do the things which wicked and unprincipled men do. Let me not be permitted to do anything that will be regarded as identifying me with

works with men that work iniquity: and *h* let me not eat of
their dainties.

h Prov. xxiii. 6.

5 Let the righteous smite me:
¹ *it shall be* a kindness: and let

¹ Or, *kindly, and reprove me; let not* their
precious oil break my head.

---

them. Let me not, in the circumstances in which I am placed, be left
to act so that the fair interpretation
of my conduct shall be that I am one of
their number, or act on the same principles on which they act. Literally,
" To practise practices in wickedness
with men." ¶*And let me not eat of
their dainties.* Let me not be tempted
by any prospect of participating in
their mode of living—in the luxuries
and comforts which they enjoy—to do
a wicked or wrong thing. Let not a
prospect or desire of this overcome my
better judgment, or the dictates of my
conscience, or my settled principles of
what is right. Men often *do* this.
Good men are often tempted to do it.
The prospect or the hope of being
enabled to enjoy what the rich enjoy,
to live in luxury and ease, to be
" clothed in fine linen and fare sump-
tuously every day," to move in circles
of splendour and fashion, often leads
them to a course of action which their
consciences condemn; to practices inconsistent with a life of godliness; to
sinful indulgences which utterly ruin
their character. Satan has few temptations for man more attractive and
powerful than the " dainties " which
wealth can give; and there are few of
his devices more effectual in ruining
men than those which are derived
from these allurements. The word
here rendered *dainties* properly refers
to things which are pleasant, lovely,
attractive; which give delight or
pleasure. It may embrace *all* that
the world has to offer as fitted to give
pleasure or enjoyment. It refers here
to what those in more elevated life
have to offer; what they themselves
live for.

5. *Let the righteous smite me.* This
verse is exceedingly difficult and obscure (comp. the margin); and there
have been almost as many different
opinions in regard to its meaning as

there have been commentators on the
psalm. A large number of these
opinions may be seen in Rosenmüller
in loc. De Wette explains it, " I
gladly suffer anything that is unpleasant from my friends, that may be for
my good; but the wickedness of my
enemies I cannot endure." The Septuagint and Latin Vulgate render it,
" Let a righteous man correct me with
mercy, and he will work convictions
in me; but let not the oil of a sinner
(for this shall still be my prayer)
anoint my head at their pleasure."
Thompson's translation. According
to this, the sense would be, " If the
righteous smite me with severity of
words I shall take it as an act of kindness and benevolence; on the other
hand, the bland words of a sinner,
smooth as oil, which wound more
than sharp arrows, may God avert
from me." Or, in other words, " I
had rather be slain by the severe
words of the righteous than anointed
by the oily and impious words of the
wicked." The sense proposed by
Hengstenberg (Com. *in loc.*) is, "Even
as I through the cloud of wrath can
see the sunshine of Divine goodness, I
will not give myself over to doubt and
despair, according to the course of the
world, when the hand of the Almighty
rests upon me; but I will, and can,
and should, in the midst of trouble,
be joyful, and that is the high privilege of which I will never be deprived."
According to this, the idea is, that the
sufferings endured by good men, even
at the hand of the wicked, are chas-
tisements inflicted by a gracious God
in justice and mercy, and as such may
be likened to a festive ointment,
which the head of the sufferer should
not refuse, as he will still have occasion for consolation to invoke God in
the midst of trials yet to be experienced. The word *righteous* is evidently
employed in the usual sense of the

him reprove me; *it shall be* an
excellent oil, *which* shall not

break my head : for yet my prayer
also *shall be* in their calamities.

---

term. It refers to those who love and
serve God. The word translated
smite — חָלַם *halam* — is rendered
broken in Judges v. 22; Isa. xvi. 8;
xxviii. 1 (*margin*, but rendered by our
translators *overcome*, sc. with wine);
smote, Judges v. 26; Isa. xli. 7;
beaten, Prov. xxiii. 35; *beating down*,
1 Sam. xiv. 16; *break down*, Ps.
lxxiv. 6. It does not elsewhere occur,
except in the verse before us. It would
apply to any beating or smiting, with
the fist, with a hammer, with a weapon
of war, and then with *words*—words
of reproof, or expressions of disapprobation. According to the view above
taken (Introd.), it is used here with
reference to an apprehended rebuke
on the part of good men, for not following their advice. ¶ It shall be *a
Kindness*. Literally, " A kindness ;"
that is, an act of kindness. The idea
is, that it would be so intended on
their part ; it should be so received
by him. Whatever might be the
wisdom of the advice, or the propriety
of yielding to it, or whatever they
might say if it were not followed, yet
he could regard it as on their part
only well-intended. If a certain
course which they had advised should
be rejected, and if by refusing or declining to follow it one should incur
their displeasure, yet that ought to be
interpreted only as an act well-intended and meant in kindness. ¶ *And
let him reprove me*. As I may anticipate that he will, if his advice is not
taken. I must expect to meet this
consequence. ¶ It shall be *an excellent oil*. Literally, " *Oil of the
head*." That is,—like oil which is
poured on the head on festive occasions, or when one is crowned, as a
priest, or a prophet, or a king. See
Notes on Mark vi. 13 ; Luke iv. 18,
19. *Oil* thus used for the head, the
face, etc., was an indispensable article
for the toilet among Orientals. The
idea is here that the reproof of the
righteous should be received as readily

as that which contributed most to
comely adorning and comfort ;—or
that which diffused brightness, cheerfulness, joy. ¶ Which *shall not break
my head*. Or rather, Which my head
shall not (or, should not) refuse;
which it should welcome. The word
rendered *break* should not have been
so translated. The Hebrew word—
יָנִי *yani* — is from נוּא, *noo* — in
Hiphil, to negative; to make naught ;
then to refuse, to decline, to deny.
It is rendered *discourage* in Num.
xxxii. 7, 9 (Marg., *break*); *disallow*,
Num. xxx. 5 (*twice*), 8, 11 ; *make of
none effect*, Ps. xxxiii. 10 ; *break*, in
the passage before us. It does not
elsewhere occur. The idea is, " If
such reproof comes on me for the
faithful doing of what I regard as
wise and best, I ought no more to reject it than the head would refuse the
oil poured on it, to make the person
healthful and comely." ¶ *For yet
my prayer also* shall be *in their calamities*. I will not be sullen, displeased,
angry, revengeful. I will not refuse
to pray for them when trials come
upon them, because they have not
approved of my course, because they
have reproved me for not following
their counsel, because they have used
words that were like heavy blows. I
will cherish no malice ; I will not be
angry ; I will not seek to be revenged.
I will not turn away from them when
trouble comes on them. I will love
them, cherish with gratitude the
memory of the kindness they meant,
and pray for them in the time when
they specially need prayer. Should
they now rebuke me rather than pray
for me, yet I will not in turn rebuke
them in similar trials, but *will pray
for them*, as though nothing of this
had happened. Noble spirit,—indicative of what should always be the
spirit of a good man. Our friends—
even our pious friends—may not
be always *wise* in their advice, and
they may be severe in their reproofs

6 When their judges are overthrown in stony places, they shall hear my words; for they are *i* sweet.

i 2 Sam. xxiii. 1.

if we do not follow their counsel; yet let us receive all as well-intended, and let us not in anger, in sullenness, or in revenge, refuse to aid them, and to pray for them in trouble, though they were *not* wise, and though they used words of severity towards us.

6. *When,* etc., etc. This passage is no less difficult than the preceding, and it seems almost impossible to determine its exact meaning. What is meant by *judges?* What judges are referred to by the word *their?* What is meant by their being *overthrown?* What is the sense of the words *in stony places?* Does the passage refer to some certain prospect that they *would be* overthrown, or is it a mere supposition which relates to something that *might* occur? Who are meant by *they,* in the phrase "they shall hear my words?" It seems to me that the most plausible interpretation of the passage is founded on that which has been assumed thus far in the explanation of the psalm, as referring to the state of things recorded in 1 Sam. xxiv. 1–7. David was in the wilderness of En-gedi, in the midst of a rocky region. Saul, apprised of his being there, came with three thousand chosen men to apprehend him, and went into a cave to lie down to rest. Unknown, probably, to him, David and his men were in the "sides of the cave." They now saw that Saul was completely in their power, and that it would be an easy thing to enter the cave, and kill him when off his guard. The men urgently advised David to do this. David entered the cave, and cut off the skirt of Saul's robe, showing how completely Saul was in his power, but he proceeded no farther; he did not follow the suggestions of his friends; he did not take the life of Saul, as he might have done; and he even regretted what he *had* done, as implying a want of due respect for the anointed

of the Lord, 1 Sam. xxiv. 11. Yet he had the fullest confidence that the king and his forces *would* be overthrown, and that it would be done in a way consistent with open and manly war, and not in an underhanded and stealthful way, as it would have been if he had cut him off in the cave. With this in view, it seems to me that the difficult passage before us may be explained with, at least, some degree of plausibility. ¶ *Their judges.* By the judges, are to be understood the rulers of the people; the magistrates; those in office and power,—referring to Saul and the officers of his government. "*Their* judges;" to wit, the judges or rulers of the hosts in opposition to me,—of those against whom I war; Saul and the leaders of his forces. ¶ *Are overthrown.* Are discomfited, vanquished, subdued; as I am confident they will be, in the regular prosecution of the war, and not by treachery and stealth. ¶ *In stony places.* Literally, " in the hands of the rock;" or, as the word *hands* may sometimes be used, "in the *sides* of the rock." It might mean *by the power of the rock,* as thrown upon them; or, *against its sides.* The essential idea is, that the *rocks,* the rocky places, would be among the means by which they would be overthrown; and the sense is, that now that Saul was in the cave—or was in that rocky region, better known to David than to him—Saul was so completely in his power, that David felt that the victory, in a regular course of warfare, would be his. ¶ *They shall hear my words.* The followers of Saul; the people of the land; the nation. Saul being removed—subdued—slain—the people will become obedient to me who have been anointed by a prophet as their king, and designated as the successor of Saul. David did not doubt that he would himself reign when Saul was overcome, or

7 Our bones are scattered at the grave's mouth, as when one cutteth and cleaveth *wood* upon the earth.

8 But mine eyes *are* unto thee, O GOD the Lord: in thee is my trust, ¹ leave not my soul ² destitute.

¹ *make.*   ² *bare.*

9 Keep me from the snares *ᵏ which* they have laid for me, and the gins of the workers of iniquity.

10 Let the wicked fall into their own nets, whilst that I withal ³ escape.

ᵏ Prov. xiii. 14.   ³ *pass over.*

---

that the people would hear his words, and submit to him as king. ¶ *For they are sweet.* They shall be pleasant; mild; gentle; equitable; just. After the harsh and severe enactments of Saul, after enduring his acts of tyranny, the people will be glad to welcome me, and to live under the laws of a just and equal administration. The passage, therefore, expresses confidence that Saul and his hosts would be overthrown, and that the people of the land would gladly hail the accession to the throne of one who had been anointed to reign over them.

7. *Our bones are scattered at the grave's mouth.* We are, indeed, now like bones scattered in the places of graves; we seem to be weak, feeble, disorganized. We are in a condition which of itself seems to be hopeless: as hopeless as it would be for dry bones scattered when they were buried to rise up and attack an enemy. The reference is to the condition of David and his followers as pursued by a mighty foe. His hope was not in his own forces, but in the power and interposition of God (ver. 8). ¶ *As when one cutteth and cleaveth wood upon the earth.* Like chips, blocks, splinters, that have no strength; as when these lie scattered around—a fit emblem of our feeble and scattered forces.

8. *But mine eyes are unto thee, O GOD the Lord.* My hope is in thee. I do not rely on my own power. I do not trust in my armed forces. I know that they are weak, dispirited, scattered,—like strewed bones,—like the chips and splinters lying around the place where wood is chopped. I look, therefore, solely to God. I believe

that he *will* interpose; and now that my enemy has placed himself in this position, I do not need to resort to stealthful arts—to dishonourable acts —to assassination—as my friends advise, but the object will be accomplished, and I shall be placed on the throne by the act of God, and in a manner that will not subject my name and memory to reproach by a base and treacherous deed. ¶ *In thee is my trust.* I rely on thee alone. ¶ *Leave not my soul destitute.* My life; my all. Do not now leave me without thy gracious interposition; do not suffer this juncture to pass by without such an interposition as will end the war, and restore peace to me and to a distracted land.

9. *Keep me from the snares,* etc. See Notes on Ps. xi. 6. Comp. Ps. xxxviii. 12; lxix. 22; xci. 3. The secret plans which they have laid against me. ¶ *And the gins of the workers of iniquity.* Wicked men; men who seek my destruction. On the word *gins,* see Notes on Isa. viii. 14. The gin is a trap or snare to catch birds or wild animals. The word here used is the same which occurs in Ps. xviii. 5, and which is there rendered *snare.* See Notes on that passage. Comp. also Ps. lxiv. 5; lxix. 22; cvi. 36; cxl. 5, where the same word occurs.

10. *Let the wicked fall into their own nets.* See Notes on Ps. xxxv. 8. Comp. Ps. vii. 15, 16. ¶ *Whilst that I withal escape.* Marg., as in Heb., *pass over.* While I safely pass over the net or snare which has been secretly laid for me. The word *withal* means, in the Heb., *together, at the same time;* that is, At the same time that they fall into the net, let me pass over it in safety. See Notes on Job v. 13.

PSALM CXLII.

[1] Maschil of David; a Prayer when he was in the *l* cave.

I CRIED unto the LORD with my voice : with my voice unto the LORD did I make my supplication.

[1] Or, A Psalm *of David giving instruction.*
l 1 Sam. xxii. 1.   *m* Ps. lxii. 8; cii., *title.*

2 I poured out *m* my complaint before him : I showed before him my trouble.

3 When *n* my spirit was overwhelmed within me. then thou knewest my path : in *o* the way wherein I walked have they privily laid a snare for me.

n Ps. cxliii. 4.   *o* Ps. cxl. 5.

PSALM CXLII.

This also is a psalm of David. It is entitled, like not a few others of the Psalms, *Maschil;* marg., *giving instruction :*—a didactic hymn. See the word explained in the Introd. to Ps. xxxii. It is said, in the title, to be "A prayer when he was in the cave;" that is, either a prayer which he composed while there, or which he composed afterwards, putting into a poetic form the substance of the prayer which he breathed forth there, or expressive of the feelings which he had when there. The reference may be either to the cave of Adullam (1 Sam. xxii. 1), or to that in Engedi (1 Sam. xxiv. 3). In both cases the circumstances were substantially the same, for David had fled to the cave to escape from Saul. The prayer is such as would be appropriate to a condition of danger such as was that in which David then was. It is a cry of distress when there was no refuge—no hope—but in God; when there seemed to be no way of escape from his enemies; and when, forsaken by his friends, and pursued by an enemy who sought his life, he seemed now to be in the power of his foe. It may also be *used* to express the feelings of one now in danger,—as of a sinner under condemnation, seeing no way of escape, exposed to ruin, and shut up entirely to the mercy of God. Such a one feels, as David did on this occasion, that there can be no escape but through the interposition of God.

1. *I cried unto the* LORD *with my voice.* See Notes on Ps. iii. 4, where the language is the same. He uttered a loud and audible prayer, though he was alone. It was not a mental ejaculation, but he gave expression to his desires. ¶ *With my voice unto the* LORD *did I make my supplication.* See Ps. xxx. 8. The Hebrew word rendered "did make my supplica-

tion," means to implore favour or mercy. It denotes the language of petition and entreaty, not the language of claim.

2. *I poured out my complaint before him.* Literally, my meditation; that is, What so much occupied my thoughts at the time I expressed aloud. The word *complaint* does not express the idea. The meaning is, not that he *complained* of God or of man; but that his mind *meditated* on his condition. He was full of care and of anxiety; and he went and poured this out freely before God. The Septuagint and the Latin Vulgate render this, *my prayer.* See Ps. lv. 2, where the same Hebrew word is used. ¶ *I showed before him my trouble.* I made mention of it. I spoke of it.

3. *When my spirit was overwhelmed within me.* Luther renders this, "When my spirit was in distress." The Hebrew word rendered *overwhelmed* means, in Kal, to cover as with a garment; then, to be covered as with darkness, trouble, sorrow; and then, to languish, to faint, to be feeble : Ps. lxxvii. 3; cvii. 5. The idea here is, that, in his troubles, he had no vigour, no life, no spirit. He did not see how he could escape from his troubles, and he had no heart to make an effort. ¶ *Then thou knewest my path.* Thou didst see all. Thou didst see the way that I was treading, and all its darkness and dangers, implying here that God had made it an object to mark his course; to see what egress there might be—what way to escape from the danger. It was in no sense concealed from God, and no danger of the way was hidden from him. It is much for us to feel when

4 I ¹ looked *p* on *my* right hand, and beheld, but *there was* no man that would know me: refuge ² failed me; no man ³ cared for my soul.

5 I cried unto thee, O LORD: I said, Thou *art* my *q* refuge, *and*

¹ Or, *look on the right hand and see.*
p Ps. lxix. 20.   ² *perished from me.*

my portion *r* in the land of the living.

6 Attend unto my cry; for I am brought very low: deliver me from my persecutors; for they are stronger *s* than I.

³ *sought after.*   *q* Ps. xlvi. 1.
r Ps. lxxiii. 26; Lam. iii. 24.
s Rom. viii. 31, 37.

---

we are in danger or difficulty that God knows it all, and that nothing can be hidden from him. ¶ *In the way wherein I walked.* In my path; the path that I was treading. ¶ *Have they privily laid a snare for me.* They treated me as a man would treat his neighbour, who should spread a snare, or set a trap, for him in the path which he knew he must take. The word rendered "have privily laid" means to hide, to conceal. It was so concealed that I could not perceive it. They did it unknown to me. I neither knew that it was laid, nor where it was laid. They meant to spring it upon me at a moment when I was not aware, and when I should be taken by surprise. It was not open and manly warfare; it was stealth, cunning, trick, art.

4. *I looked on* my *right hand, and beheld.* Marg., *Look on the right hand and see.* The words translated *looked* and *beheld* are in the imperative mood in the Hebrew. They are not, however, improperly rendered as to the sense. They refer to David's state of mind at the time, and give vividness to the description. The psalmist seems to be in the presence of others. He calls upon them to look around; to see how he was encompassed with danger. Look, says he, in every direction; see who there is on whom I may rely; what there is to which I may trust as a refuge. I can find none; I see none; there is none. The "right hand" is referred to here as the direction where he might look for a protector: Ps. cix. 6, 31. ¶ *But* there was *no man that would know me.* No man to be seen who would recognize me as his friend;

who would stand up for me; on whom I could rely. ¶ *Refuge failed me.* Marg., as in Heb., *perished from me.* If there had been any hope of refuge, it has failed altogether. There is none now. ¶ *No man cared for my soul.* Marg., *No man sought after my soul.* Heb., after my *life.* That is, No one sought to save my life; no one regarded it as of sufficient importance to attempt to preserve me.

5. *I cried unto thee, O LORD.* When there was no help; when I saw myself encompassed with dangers; when I looked on every hand and there was no *man* that would undertake for me. ¶ *I said, Thou art my refuge.* (*a*) My *only* refuge. I can go nowhere else. (*b*) Thou *art in fact* my refuge. I can and do put my trust in thee. See Notes on Ps. xlvi. 1. ¶ And *my portion.* See Notes on Ps. xvi. 5. ¶ *In the land of the living.* Among all those that live—all living beings. There is no one else among the living to whom I can come but to thee, the living God. My hope is not in men, for they are against me; not in angels, for they have not the power to rescue me. It is God only, the living God, whom I make my confidence and the ground of my hope.

6. *Attend unto my cry.* Give ear to me when I cry to thee. Do not turn away and refuse to hear me. ¶ *For I am brought very low.* I am reduced greatly; I am made very poor. The language would be applicable to one who had been in better circumstances, and who had been brought down to a condition of danger, of poverty, of want. It is language which is commonly applied

7 Bring my soul out of prison, [t] that I may praise thy name; the righteous shall compass me about, for thou shalt deal bountifully [u] with me.

t Ps. cxlvi. 7 ; Isa. lxi. 1.
u Ps. xiii. 6 ; cxix. 17.

PSALM CXLIII.
A Psalm of David.

HEAR my prayer, O LORD; give ear to my supplications : in thy faithfulness answer me, *and* in thy righteousness.

---

to poverty. ¶ *Deliver me from my persecutors.* Saul and his followers. ¶ *For they are stronger than I.* More in number; better armed; better fitted for battle.

7. *Bring my soul out of prison.* Bring me out of my present condition which is like a prison. I am as it were shut up ; I am encompassed with foes; I do not know how to escape. Comp. Ps. xxv. 17. ¶ *That I may praise thy name.* Not merely for my own sake, but that I may have occasion more abundantly to praise thee; that thus *thou* mayest be honoured ; — an object at all times much more important than our own welfare — even than our salvation. ¶ *The righteous shall compass me about.* They shall come to me with congratulations and with expressions of rejoicing. They will desire my society, my friendship, my influence, and will regard it as a privilege and an honour to be associated with me. David looked to this as an object to be desired. He wished to be associated with the righteous ; to enjoy their friendship; to have their good opinion; to be reckoned as one of them here and for ever. Comp. Notes on Ps. xxvi. 9. It *is* an honour—a felicity to be desired—to be associated with good men, to possess their esteem ; to have their sympathy, their prayers, and their affections ; to share their joys here, and their triumphs in the world to come. ¶ *For thou shalt deal bountifully with me.* Or, when thou shalt deal bountifully with me. When thou dost show me this favour, then the righteous will come around me in this manner. They will see that I am a friend of God, and they will desire to be associated with me as his friend.

PSALM CXLIII.

This psalm also is entitled " A Psalm of David." There is, however, no intimation in the title as to the time or the occasion on which it was composed. In the Septuagint version, and the Latin Vulgate, it is said to have been written " when Absalom his son persecuted him." There is nothing in the psalm inconsistent with this supposition, nor is there anything which necessarily restricts the application to that period of David's life. It would seem most natural that it should refer to the same trials as the previous psalm; and the sentiments in it are as applicable to the persecutions under Saul as to the rebellion of Absalom. There can be no doubt that it was composed when he was in danger and in trouble on account of malignant and powerful enemies ; and it is of the same general character as many in the collection that were composed on those occasions. It is a psalm written in trouble ; and, in a world like this, there will be always many hearts that can fully sympathize with the sentiments which are expressed in it.

1. *Hear my prayer, O LORD, give ear,* etc. See Notes on Ps. iv. 1 ; v. 1. ¶ *In thy faithfulness answer me.* That is, Show thy faithfulness to thy promises. God had made gracious promises to David (comp. Ps. lxxxix. 19–37), and he now pleads that he would remember those promises, and accomplish in his behalf what he had said he would. God has also made gracious promises to his people, and they may always plead those promises as a reason why they should be heard, and why their prayers should be answered. ¶ And *in thy righteousness.* Comp. Ps. xxxi. 1. In thy disposition to do right; to vindicate a righteous cause; to interpose when wrong is done. We, though sinners before God, may feel that our cause is a just one as towards our fellow-

2 And enter not *v* into judgment with thy servant: for *w* in thy sight shall no man living be justified.

3 For the enemy hath persecuted my soul; he hath smitten my life down to the ground: he

v Job xiv. 3.

hath made me to dwell in darkness, as those that have been long dead.

4 Therefore is my spirit overwhelmed within me: my heart within me is desolate.

w Ps. cxxx. 3; Ex. xxxiv. 7; Job ix. 2, 3; Eccles. vii. 20; Rom. iii. 20; Gal. ii. 16.

---

men, and, when wronged, we may ask God to interpose, as a righteous God, in our behalf. We cannot, however, ask him to save us on the ground of our righteousness towards him, for we have no such righteousness. See ver. 2.

2. *And enter not into judgment with thy servant.* Do not deal with me on the ground of justice as towards *thee;* do not mark my own offences against thee, when I plead that justice may be done as between me and my fellow-men. While I plead that thou wouldst judge righteously between me and them, I am conscious that I could not claim thy needed interposition on the ground of any righteousness towards thee. There I must confess that I am a sinner; there I can rely only on mercy; there I could not hope to be justified. ¶ *For in thy sight.* As before thee; in thy presence; by thee. ¶ *Shall no man living.* No one of the race, no matter what his rank, his outward conduct, his gentleness, his amiableness, his kindness;—no matter how just and upright he may be towards his fellow-men. ¶ *Be justified.* Be regarded as righteous; be acquitted from blame; be held to be innocent. The meaning is, "I do not come before thee and plead for thy favour on the ground of any claim on thee, for I am conscious that I am a sinner, and that my only hope is in thy mercy." See Notes on Rom. iii. 20. Comp. Job iv. 17; ix. 2, 20; xv. 14–16; xxv. 4–6. This is a great and momentous truth in regard to man; it is the foundation of the necessity for a plan of salvation through an atonement—for some way in which man *may* properly be regarded and

treated as righteous. Assuredly every man, conscious of what he is in himself, may and should fervently pray that God *would* not enter into judgment with him; that he would not mark his offences; that he would not judge him as strict justice would demand. Our hope is in the *mercy,* not in the *justice* of God.

3. *For the enemy hath persecuted my soul.* Has persecuted me; has sought my life. ¶ *He hath smitten my life down to the ground.* He has, as it were, trampled me down to the earth. The word rendered *smitten* means to break in pieces, to beat small, to crush. See Ps. lxxii. 4; lxxxix. 10; Job vi. 9. His very life seemed to be crushed out as one that is trodden down to the ground. ¶ *He hath made me to dwell in darkness.* He has made my life like that of one who dwells in darkness; he has made it a life of sorrow, so that I have no comfort—no light. ¶ *As those that have been long dead.* A similar expression occurs in Lam. iii. 6: "He hath set me in dark places, as they that be dead of old." The same Hebrew words are used. The word rendered "*long*" means, age, duration, eternity: Ps. cxxxix. 24. The idea here is, that his condition was like that of those who had been long in their graves; who had long since ceased to see any light; whose abode was utter and absolute gloom.

4. *Therefore is my spirit overwhelmed within me.* See Notes on Ps. lxxvii. 3. Comp. Ps. xlii. 5–7. His spirit was broken and crushed. He was in a state of despair as to any human help. ¶ *My heart within me is desolate.* I have no comfort; no cheerfulness; no hope. My soul

5 I remember the days of old; *x* I meditate on all thy works; I muse on the work of thy hands.

6 I stretch forth my hands unto thee: my soul *thirsteth* *y* after thee, as a thirsty land. Selah.

7 Hear me speedily, O LORD; my spirit faileth: hide not thy

x Ps. lxxvii. 5, 11.   *y* Ps. lxiii. 1.
[1] Or, *for I am become*, Ps. lxxxviii. 4.

face from me, [1] lest I be like unto them that go down into the pit.

8 Cause me to hear thy loving-kindness in the morning; *z* for in thee do I trust: cause me to know the way *a* wherein I should walk; for I lift up my soul unto thee.

9 Deliver me, O LORD, from

z Ps. xxx. 5.   *a* Ps. lxxiii. 24.

is like the waste desert where there is no water; where nothing grows; where there are only rocks and sands.

5. *I remember the days of old.* Former times. (1) As contrasted with my present condition. (2) As times when I called upon thee, and thou didst interpose. (3) As encouraging me now to come to thee, and spread out my case before thee. See Notes on Ps. lxxvii. 5–11; xlii. 4. ¶ *I meditate on all thy works*, etc. On what thou hast done; on thy gracious interpositions in the time of trial; on the manifestations of thy power in my behalf, and in behalf of thy people. I call all this to mind, remembering that thou art an unchangeable God; that thou hast the same power still; that thou canst interpose now as thou didst then; and that, as an unchangeable God, thou wilt do it in the same circumstances. I, therefore, come to thee, and pray that thou wilt interpose in my behalf.

6. *I stretch forth my hands unto thee.* In prayer. I have nowhere else to go. See Ps. lxxxviii. 9. ¶ *My soul* thirsteth *after thee, as a thirsty land.* As land in a time of drought *seems* to thirst for rain. See Notes on Ps. lxiii. 1. Comp. Ps. xlii. 1. The word rendered *thirsty* here means properly *weary*. The idea is that of a land which seems to be weary; which has no vigour of growth; and where everything seems to be exhausted. The same word occurs in Isa. xxxii. 2: "As the shadow of a great rock in a *weary* land."

7. *Hear me speedily, O LORD.* Hasten to hear me; do not delay. Literally, "Hasten; answer me." I

am in imminent danger. Do not delay to come to my relief. ¶ *My spirit faileth.* My strength is declining. I can hold out no longer. I am ready to give up and die. ¶ *Hide not thy face from me.* Do not refuse or delay to look favourably upon me; to lift up the light of thy countenance upon me. ¶ *Lest I be like unto them that go down into the pit.* Marg., *For I am become like.* The idea is, Unless thou shalt lift up the light of thy countenance,—unless thou shalt interpose and help me, I shall die. The *pit* here refers to the grave. See Notes on Ps. xxviii. 1.

8. *Cause me to hear thy loving-kindness.* The voice of thy loving-kindness, or thy mercy and favour. Permit me to hear thee addressing me in the language of kindness, and with the assurances of mercy. ¶ *In the morning.* Early; speedily; with the first rays of the morning. Let it be, as it were, the first thing in the day; the first thing that is done. The idea is not that he would wait for another day, but that he would interpose as the very first act,—as when one enters on a day. See Notes on Ps. xlvi. 5, where the margin is, *when the morning appeareth;* Hebrew, *In the faces of the morning.* ¶ *For in thee do I trust.* I have no other confidence or ground of reliance; but I have confidence in thee. ¶ *Cause me to know the way wherein I should walk*, etc. The safe way; the way in which I may find safety. See Notes on Ps. v. 8.

9. *Deliver me, O LORD, from mine enemies.* See Notes on Ps. lxix. 14. ¶ *I flee unto thee to hide me.* Marg.,

mine enemies: I [1] flee unto thee
to hide me.

10 Teach [b] me to do thy will;
for thou art my God; thy spirit
is good; [c] lead me into the land
of uprightness.[d]

11 Quicken [e] me, O LORD, for

[1] hide me with thee.
[b] Micah iv. 2; 1 John ii. 27.

thy name's sake: for thy righteousness' sake bring my soul out
of trouble.

12 And of thy mercy cut off
mine enemies, and destroy all
them that afflict my soul: for I
am thy servant.

[c] Neh. ix. 20.　　[d] Isa. xxvi. 10.
[e] Hab. iii. 2; Eph. ii. 1.

Hide me with thee. The Hebrew is,
I hide myself with thee; that is, I
take refuge with thee; I put myself
under thy protection; I make myself
thus secure, as thou art secure. See
Notes on Ps. xvii. 8. Comp. Ps.
xxvii. 5; xxxi. 20.

10. *Teach me to do thy will*, etc.
To do that which will be agreeable or
pleasing to thee; which will meet
with thy approbation. That is, Teach
me in the present emergency to do
that which thou wilt approve; which
will be wise; which will be best
adapted to secure my deliverance and
my safety. ¶ *Thy spirit is good.*
The spirit which guides those who
trust in thee; the spirit with which
thou dost guide men. That spirit is
wise, prudent, judicious, reliable. It
will not lead astray. Grant me *that*
spirit, and I shall be certain that I
am going in the right path. There
is no certain evidence that the psalmist
here refers distinctively to the Holy
Ghost, considered as the Third Person of the Trinity; but the prayer
is one for guidance from on high in
the day of darkness and trouble. It
is an acknowledgment of dependence
on God for direction, and the expression of confidence that under the
Divine guidance he would not go
astray. ¶ *Lead me into the land of
uprightness.* Or rather here, "land
of evenness;" level ground; ground
where I may walk without the
dangers to which I am exposed where
I am now, in a place of ambuscades,
caverns, rocks, where I may be assailed at any moment without the
power of seeing my enemy, or of defending myself. See this use of the
word in the following places where it

is rendered *plain*,—meaning a level
country, Deut. iii. 10; iv. 43; Josh.
xiii. 9, 16, 17, 21; 1 Kings xx. 23,
25; Ps. xxvii. 11; Jer. xxi. 13;
xlviii. 8, 21; Zech. iv. 7. He desired to be led, as it were, into a *level*
country where he might be safe. It
is not a prayer, as would seem from
our translation, to be so guided that
he might lead an upright life. Such
a prayer is proper, but it is not the
prayer offered here.

11. *Quicken me, O LORD.* Give
me life. Comp. Notes on Eph. ii. 1.
Make me equal to my circumstances,
for I am ready to sink and to yield.
¶ *For thy name's sake.* For thine
honour. Comp. Notes on Dan. ix. 17,
18. It is in thy cause. Thou wilt
thus show thy power, thy faithfulness, thy goodness. Thou wilt thus
get honour to thyself. This is the
highest motive which can influence
us,—that God may be glorified. ¶ *For
thy righteousness' sake.* Thy justice;
thy truth; thy faithfulness in per-
forming thy promises and pledges.
¶ *Bring my soul out of trouble.* Out
of this trouble and distress. See Notes
on Ps. xxv. 17.

12. *And of thy mercy*, etc. Thy mercy
to me; thy mercy to the world. The
destruction of the wicked is a favour
to the universe; just as the arrest and
punishment of a robber or a pirate is
a mercy to society, to mankind; just
as every prison is a display of *mercy*
as well as of *justice:*—mercy to society
at large; justice to the offenders.
¶ *And destroy all them that afflict my
soul.* Cut them off; render them
powerless to do mischief. ¶ *For I*
am *thy servant.* Not as a matter of
private feeling,—not for personal re-

PSALM CXLIV.

A Psalm of David.

BLESSED *be* the LORD my
¹ strength, *f* which teacheth
my hands to ² war, *and* my fingers to fight.

¹ *rock*, Ps. xviii. 2, 31.   *f* Isa. xlv. 24.

2 My ³ goodness and my fortress; my high tower, and my
deliverer; my shield, and *he* in
whom I trust; who subdueth my
people under me.

² *the war.*   ³ Or, *mercy.*

venge,—but because I am in thy service, and it is only by being delivered
from these dangers that I can honour
thee as I would. It is thine own
cause, and I ask that they may be cut
off *in order* that the service which I
might render thee may be unembar-
rassed.

PSALM CXLIV.

This psalm is also ascribed to David.
It is almost entirely a compilation of
passages from other psalms,—particularly
Ps. xviii.,—newly arranged. Comp. Ps.
xviii. 34, with ver. 1; xviii. 2, 46, with
ver. 2; xviii. 9, with ver. 5; xviii. 14,
with ver. 6; xviii. 16, with ver. 7.
Comp. also Ps. viii. 4, with ver. 3; civ.
32, with ver. 5; xxxiii. 2, 3, with ver.
9; xxxiii. 12, with ver. 15; cxxviii. 3,
with ver. 12. In itself considered there
is nothing improbable in the supposition
that David himself should have made
such a selection, or should have employed language which he had used
before, adapting it now to a new purpose, and making such additions as
would fit it for the new occasion for
which it was intended. It would not
be possible now, however, to ascertain
the occasion on which this arrangement
was made, or its specific design. There
is, evidently, a remembrance of former
mercies; there was impending danger;
there is an earnest prayer that God
would interpose as he had done in
former times; there is a promise of new
songs of praise if God would interpose;
there is a looking forward to the prosperity—the joy—which would result if
God did thus interpose and save the
nation. In regard to the occasion on
which the psalm was written, perhaps
the conjecture of Kimchi is the most
probable, that it is a prayer against the
attempts of foreign nations to overthrow
the Hebrew people, in some of the
numerous wars in which David was engaged after he had come to the possession
of the crown. The different parts of the

psalm can be better explained on this
supposition than perhaps on any other.
This would make proper all the expressions in regard to the past (vers. 1, 2);
the uncertainty and instability of
earthly things and the weakness of man
(vers. 3, 4); the necessity of the Divine
interposition as in former times (vers.
5-8); the reference to foreigners (vers.
7, 8, 11); the purpose to praise God
(vers. 9, 10); the allusion to the happiness of a people whose God is the Lord,
and to the prosperity which would follow his interposition (vers. 12-15).

1. *Blessed* be *the* LORD *my strength.*
Marg., as in Heb., *my rock.* See
Notes on Ps. xviii. 46, where the same
expression occurs in the Hebrew.
¶ *Which teacheth my hands to war.*
Heb., *To the war.* See Notes on Ps.
xviii. 34. The Hebrew is not precisely alike, but the sense is the same.
¶ And *my fingers to fight.* Heb., my
fingers to the fight. That is, he
teaches my fingers so that I can skilfully use them in battle. Probably
the immediate reference here is to the
use of the bow,—placing the arrow,
and drawing the string.

2. *My goodness.* Marg., *my mercy.*
That is, He shows me mercy or favour.
All the favours that I receive come
from him. ¶ *And my fortress; my
high tower, and my deliverer.* See Notes
on Ps. xviii. 2, where the same words
occur. ¶ *My shield.* The same word
which in Ps. xviii. 2 is rendered
buckler. See Notes on that passage.
¶ *And* he *in whom I trust.* The same
idea as in Ps. xviii. 2. The tense of
the verb only is varied. ¶ *Who subdueth my people under me.* See Notes
on Ps. xviii. 47. The language is
slightly different, but the idea is the
same. It is to be remarked that
David *here* refers to his people,—

3 LORD, *g* what *is* man, that thou takest knowledge of him; *or* the son of man, that thou makest account of him!

4 Man *h* is like to vanity: his days *are* as a shadow that passeth away.

5 Bow *i* thy heavens, O LORD, and come down: touch the mountains, and they shall smoke.

6 Cast forth lightnings, and scatter them: shoot out thine arrows, and destroy them.

g Ps. viii. 4.　*h* Ps. xxxix. 5.　*i* Isa. lxiv. 1.

" who subdueth *my* people,"—meaning that those over whom God had placed him had been made submissive by the Divine power.

3. LORD, *what* is *man, that thou takest knowledge of him?* The sentiment here is the same as in Ps. viii. 4, though the language is not precisely the same. See Notes on that passage. The word rendered " that thou takest knowledge of him," means here to take notice of; to regard. The idea is, It is amazing that a being so insignificant as man should be an object of interest to God, or that One so great should pay any attention to him and to his affairs. In Ps. viii. 4, the language is " that thou art mindful of him,"—that is, that thou dost remember him,—that thou dost not altogether pass him over. In Ps. viii. the remark is made in view of the heavens as being so exalted in comparison with man, and the wonder is, that in view of worlds so vast occupying the Divine attention, and needing the Divine care, *man*, so insignificant, does not pass out of his view altogether. Here the remark seems to be made in illustration of the idea that there is no strength in man; that he has no power to accomplish anything of himself; that he is entirely dependent on God. ¶ *Or the son of man.* Man—any of the race. See Notes on Ps. viii. 4. ¶ *That thou makest account of him!* Ps. viii. 4, " that thou visitest him." See Notes on that passage. The word here means " that thou shouldest *think* of him,"—that he should ever come into thy thought at all.

4. *Man is like to vanity.* See Notes on Ps. xxxix. 5, 6; lxii. 9. The idea here is, that man can be compared only with that which is utterly vain—which is emptiness—which is nothing. ¶ *His days* are *as a shadow that passeth away.* See Notes on Ps. cii. 11: " My days are like a shadow that declineth." The idea is essentially the same. It is, that as a shadow has no substance, and that as it moves along constantly as the sun declines, until it vanishes altogether, so man has nothing substantial or permanent, and so he is constantly moving off and will soon wholly disappear:

5. *Bow thy heavens, O* LORD, etc. Come to my aid *as if* the heavens were bent down; come down with all thy majesty and glory. See Notes on Ps. xviii. 9: " He bowed down the heavens also, and came down." What it is there declared that the Lord *had* done, he is here implored to do again. ¶ *Touch the mountains, and they shall smoke.* See Notes on Ps. civ. 32: " He toucheth the hills, and they smoke." It is there affirmed as a characteristic of God that he *does* this; here the psalmist prays that, as this belonged to God, or was in his power, he *would* do it in his behalf. The prayer is, that God would come to his relief *as if* in smoke and tempest—in the fury of the storm.

6. *Cast forth lightnings, and scatter them.* See Notes on Ps. xviii. 14: " He sent out his arrows, and scattered them." The allusion there is to lightning. The psalmist prays that God would do now again what he had then done. The Hebrew here is, " Lighten lightning;" that is, Send forth lightning. The word is used as a verb nowhere else. ¶ *Shoot out thine arrows,* etc. So in Ps. xviii. 14: " He shot out lightnings." The words are the same here as in that psalm, only that they are arranged differently. See Notes on that place.

7 Send thine [1] hand from above: rid me, and deliver me out of great waters, from the hand of strange children;

8 Whose mouth speaketh vanity, and their right hand *is* a right hand of falsehood.

9 I will sing a new song unto

[1] *hands.*

thee, O God: upon a psaltery, *and* an instrument of ten strings, will I sing praises unto thee.

10 *It is he* that giveth [2] salvation unto kings: who delivereth David his servant from the hurtful sword.

11 Rid me, and deliver me

[2] Or, *victory.*

---

7. *Send thine hand from above.* Marg., as in Heb., *hands.* See Notes on Ps. xviii. 16: "He sent from above." ¶ *Rid me, and deliver me out of great waters.* Thus Ps. xviii. 16: "He took me, he drew me out of many waters." As God had done it once, there was ground for the prayer that he would do it yet again. ¶ *From the hand of strange children.* Strangers:—strangers to thee; strangers to thy people; foreigners. See Ps. liv. 3: "For strangers are risen up against me." The language would properly imply that at the time referred to in the psalm he was engaged in a warfare with foreign enemies. Who they were, we have no means now of ascertaining.

8. *Whose mouth speaketh vanity.* Vain things; things not real and true; falsehood; lies. See Notes on Ps. xxiv. 4. The idea is, that what they said had no foundation in truth—no reality. Truth is solid and reliable; falsehood is unreliable and vain. ¶ *And their right hand is a right hand of falsehood.* The meaning here seems to be that even under the solemnities of an oath, when they lifted up their hands to swear, when they solemnly appealed to God, there was no reliance to be placed on what they affirmed or promised. Oaths were taken by lifting up the right hand as towards God. See Gen. xiv. 22; Ex. vi. 8 (Marg., and Heb.); Deut. xxxii. 40.

9. *I will sing a new song unto thee, O God.* There will be occasion *in* such a deliverance, or manifestation of mercy, for a new expression of praise. On the phrase, "a new song," see Notes on Ps. xxxiii. 3.

¶ *Upon a psaltery,* and *an instrument of ten strings.* The word "and" should not have been inserted here. The idea is, "Upon a lyre or harp [Nebel] of ten strings, will I sing praise." See Notes on Isa. v. 12; and Ps. xxxiii. 2.

10. It is he *that giveth salvation unto kings.* Marg., *Victory.* The Hebrew word means *salvation,* but it is here used in the sense of deliverance or rescue. Even *kings,* with all their armies, have no hope but in God. They seem to be the most powerful of men, but they are, like all other men, wholly dependent on him for deliverance from danger. David thus recognizes his own entire dependence. Though a king in the Divine purpose and in fact, yet he had no power but as derived from God; he had no hope of deliverance but in him. It is implied further that God might as readily be supposed to be willing to interpose in behalf of kings as of other men when their cause was right, and when they looked to him for aid. See Notes on Ps. xxxiii. 16: "there is no king saved by the multitude of an host." Comp. Ps. xliv. 5, 6. ¶ *Who delivereth David his servant from the hurtful sword.* Who has done it; who can do it again; on whom alone David is dependent as all other men are. David speaks of himself by name elsewhere. See Ps. xviii. 50; 2 Sam. vii. 26. He refers to himself also under the name of "the king," Ps. lxi. 6; lxiii. 11. Cæsar, in his writings, often speaks of himself in the same way.

11. *Rid me, and deliver me,* etc. See Notes on vers. 7, 8. The language is here repeated. The prayer had been

from the hand of strange children, whose mouth speaketh vanity, and their right hand *is* a right hand of falsehood.

12 That our sons *may be* as plants *k* grown up in their youth; *that* our daughters *may be* as

k Ps. cxxviii. 3.

corner-stones, [1] polished *after* the similitude of a palace:

13 *That* our garners *may be* full, affording [2] all manner of store; *that* our sheep may bring forth thousands and ten thousands in our streets:

[1] cut.   [2] from kind to kind.

---

interrupted by the thought that the answer to it would lay the foundation for praise, and by an acknowledgment of entire dependence on God. The psalmist now, after repeating the prayer, suggests what would result from the answer to it, and dwells on the happy consequences which must follow; the bright scenes in his own reign, in the prosperity of the people, in the happiness of the nation, in domestic comforts, and in the abundance which the land would produce when these dangers should pass away, when men now engaged in the conflict of arms might return to the peaceful pursuits of life, when families would be safe in their dwellings, and when the earth cultivated in time of peace would again produce abundance, vers. 12–14.

12. *That our sons* may be *as plants grown up in their youth.* That our sons—not called forth to the hardships of the tent and the field, the perils and the exposures of war—may grow up under the culture of home, of the family, in quiet scenes, as plants carefully cultivated and flourishing. Comp. Ps. cxxviii. 3. The Hebrew here is, "grown large in their youth;" not *grown up,* which has a paradoxical appearance. The meaning is, that they may be stout, strong, vigorous, well-formed, even in early life; that they may not be stunted in their growth, but be of full and manly proportions. ¶ That *our daughters* may be *as corner-stones.* The word here used — זָוִיֹת, *zaviyoth*—occurs only in the plural form, and means properly corners,—from a verb meaning to hide away, to conceal. The word is used respecting the corners of an altar, Zech. ix. 15; and seems

here to refer to the corner columns of a palace or temple:—perhaps, as Gesenius (*Lex.*) supposes, in allusion to the columns representing female figures so common in Egyptian architecture. ¶ *Polished.* Marg., *cut.* The idea is not that of *polishing* or *smoothing,* but of cutting or sculpturing. It is the stone carefully cut as an ornament. ¶ After *the similitude of a palace.* A more literal translation would be, "The likeness or model of a temple;" or, for the building of a temple. That is, that they may be such as may be properly compared with the ornamental columns of a temple or palace. The comparison is a very beautiful one, having the idea of grace, symmetry, fair proportions:— that on which the skill of the sculptor is most abundantly lavished.

13. That *our garners* may be *full.* That our fields may yield abundance, so that our granaries may be always filled. ¶ *Affording all manner of store.* Marg., *From kind to kind.* Heb., *From sort to sort;* that is, every sort or kind of produce or grain; all, in variety, that is needful for the supply of man and beast. ¶ That *our sheep may bring forth thousands and ten thousands in our streets.* A great part of the wealth of Palestine always consisted in flocks of sheep; and, from the earliest periods, not a few of the inhabitants were shepherds. This language, therefore, is used to denote national prosperity. ¶ *In our streets.* The Hebrew word here used means properly whatever is *outside;* what is out of doors or abroad, as opposed to what is within, as the inside of a house; and then, what is outside of a town, as opposed to what is within. It may, therefore, mean a

14 *That* our oxen *may be* ¹ strong to labour: *that there be* no breaking in, nor going out; that *there be* no complaining in

¹ *able to bear burdens,* or, *loaden* with flesh.

---

street (Jer. xxxvii. 21 ; Job xviii. 17 ; Isa. v. 25) ; and then the country, the fields, pastures, etc. : Job v. 10 ; Prov. viii. 26. Here it refers to the pastures ; the fields ; the commons.

14. That *our oxen* may be *strong to labour.* Marg., *able to bear burdens ;* or, *laden with flesh.* The Hebrew is simply loaded or laden :—that is, with a burden ; or, with flesh ; or, as Gesenius renders it, with young. The latter idea would best suit the connexion, — that of cattle producing abundantly or multiplying. ¶ That there be *no breaking in, nor going out.* No breaking in of other cattle into enclosed grounds, and no escape of those which are shut up for pasture. That property may be safe everywhere. The image is that of security, peace, order, prosperity. ¶ *That* there be *no complaining in our streets.* Literally, *outcry ; clamour.* That the land may be at peace ; that order and law may be observed ; that the rights of all may be respected ; that among neighbours there may be no strifes and contentions.

15. *Happy* is that *people that is in such a case.* In such a condition ; or, where these things prevail. ¶ Yea, *happy* is that *people, whose God is the* LORD. Whose God is JEHOVAH ; who worship and serve HIM as their God. The worship of Jehovah—the religion of Jehovah—is *adapted* to make a people happy ; peaceful ; quiet ; blessed. Prosperity and peace, such as are referred to in the previous verses, are, and must be, the result of pure religion. Peace, order, abundance, attend it everywhere, and the best security for a nation's prosperity is the worship of God ; that which is most certain to make a nation happy and blessed, is to acknowledge God and to keep his laws.

---

our streets.

15 Happy *ᶦ is that* people that is in such a case : yea, *ᵐ* happy *is that* people, whose God *is* the LORD.

l Deut. xxxiii. 29.   *m* Ps. lxxxix. 15.

PSALM CXLV.

This is also a Psalm of David, and the last of the series in this part of the collection. It is entitled simply, " Of Praise," or, in the Hebrew, " Praise by David," or " Praise *of* David ;"—that is, one of David's songs of praise. It is an *alphabetical* psalm ; that is, each verse begins with a letter of the Hebrew alphabet. The arrangement in this respect is complete, except that the letter נ, *Nun—n—*is omitted, for which no reason can be assigned, unless it was from a desire that the psalm might consist of three equal parts of seven verses each. In the Septuagint, Syriac, Arabic, Latin Vulgate, and Æthiopic Versions, this omission is attempted to be supplied by inserting between vers. 13 and 14 a verse which in Hebrew would begin with a נ, *Nun,—*נאמן, etc. :—" Faithful is the Lord in all his words, and holy in all his works." This is taken from ver. 17 of the psalm by the change of a word in the beginning—*faithful* for *righteous,—*נאמן for צדיק. There is no authority for this, however, in the MSS., and it is evidently an attempt to supply what seemed to be an omission or defect in the composition of the psalm. The verse is not in the Chaldee Paraphrase, or in the version of Aquila and Theodotion ; and it is certain that as early as the time of Origen and Jerome it was not in the Hebrew text. The Masorites and the Jewish commentators reject it. The sense is in no way affected by the insertion or omission of this, since the verses of the psalm have no necessary connexion in meaning— the composition, as in most of the alphabetical psalms, being made up of independent sentiments suggested in part at least by the necessity of commencing each verse with a particular letter.

The psalm does not admit of any particular analysis, and it is impossible now to ascertain the occasion on which it was written.

PSALM CXLV.

David's *Psalm* of praise.

I WILL extol thee, my God, O King; and I will bless thy name for ever and ever.

2 Every day will I bless thee, and I will praise thy name for ever and ever.

3 Great *is* the LORD, and greatly to be praised; and [1] his

---

[1] *of his greatness* there is *no search.*

---

greatness *is* ᴨ unsearchable.

4 One generation shall praise thy works to another, and shall declare thy mighty acts.

5 I will speak of the glorious honour of thy majesty, and of thy wondrous [2] works.

6 And *men* shall speak of the might of thy terrible acts : and I will declare [3] thy greatness.

ᴨ Rom. xi. 33.   [2] *things*, or, *words.*   [3] *it.*

---

1. *I will extol thee,* etc. I will lift thee up ; I will lift up thy name and praise, so that it may be heard afar. ¶ *And I will bless thy name for ever and ever.* I will bless or praise thee. I will do it now ; I will do it in all the future. I will do it in time; I will do it in eternity. See Notes on Ps. xxx. 1.

2. *Every day will I bless thee,* etc. Comp. Ps. xcii. 2 ; lv. 17. As we receive blessings from God every day (comp. Lam. iii. 23), it is proper that we should render to him daily thanks ; as God is the same always—" yesterday, to-day, and for ever "—it is proper that he should receive from day to day the tribute of praise ; as we are daily dependent on him—one day as much as another—our recognition of that dependence should be daily ; and as he will always be unchangeably the same, it will be proper that he should be praised for ever and ever. Two things are apparent from this verse : —(1) That a truly religious man *will* worship God every day ; (2) that it is the fixed purpose of a truly religious man to continue this for ever.

3. *Great* is *the* LORD, *and greatly to be praised.* See Notes on Ps. xcvi. 4; xviii. 3. ¶ *And his greatness* is *unsearchable.* See Notes on Job v. 9 ; ix. 10; xi. 7, 8.

4. *One generation shall praise thy works,* etc. Shall praise thee on account of thy works or thy doings. That is, Thy praise shall be always kept up on the earth. See Notes on Isa. xxxviii. 19; Ps. xix. 2. One generation shall transmit the know-

ledge of thy works to another by praise—by hymns and psalms recording and celebrating thy praise. Successive generations of men shall take up the language of praise, and it shall thus be transmitted to the end of time. ¶ *And shall declare thy mighty acts.* Thy works of strength or power. God's greatness—his infinity—is in itself a just ground of praise, for we should rejoice that there is One Infinite Eternal Being ; and as all that greatness is employed in the cause of truth, of law, of good order, of justice, of kindness, of mercy, it should call forth continued praise in all parts of his dominions.

5. *I will speak.* That is, in my acts of praise. I will not be ashamed to be known as his worshipper ; I will publicly declare my belief in his existence, his greatness, his goodness. ¶ *Of the glorious honour of thy majesty.* The glory of the honour of thy majesty. This accumulation of epithets shows that the heart of the psalmist was full of the subject, and that he laboured to find language to express his emotions. It is beauty ; it is glory ; it is majesty :—it is all that is great, sublime, wonderful— all combined— all concentrated—in one Being. ¶ *And of thy wondrous works.* Marg., *things,* or *words.* The reference is to wondrous deeds or acts considered as the subject of discourse or praise.

6. *And* men *shall speak of the might of thy terrible acts.* The force, the power of those things done by thee which are fitted to inspire fear

7 They shall abundantly utter the memory of thy great goodness, and shall sing of thy righteousness.

8 The LORD *o* *is* gracious, and full of compassion; slow to anger, and ¹ of great mercy.

9 The LORD *is* good *p* to all;

o Num. xiv. 18.　　¹ *great in.*

and his tender mercies *are* over all his works.

10 All thy works shall praise thee, O LORD; and thy saints shall bless thee.

11 They shall speak of the glory of thy kingdom, and talk of thy power;

p Nahum i. 7.

---

or reverence. The great *power* displayed in those acts shall be a ground or reason for celebrating thy praise. The manifestations of that power will so deeply impress the minds of men, that they will be led to speak of them. ¶ *And I will declare thy greatness.* Heb., "And thy greatness, I will declare it." In respect to that, I will recount it, or I will make it known to others.

7. *They shall abundantly utter the memory of thy great goodness.* Heb., The memory of the greatness of thy goodness they will pour forth. The word rendered "abundantly utter" means to bud forth, to gush out, to flow, as a fountain. Prov. xviii. 4; i. 23; xv. 2, 28. It is applied to words as poured forth in praise. The meaning is, that the heart is full, as a fountain is full of water, and that it naturally overflows, or seeks to discharge itself. The thought of the goodness of God fills the heart, and makes it overflow with gratitude. ¶ *And shall sing of thy righteousness.* They shall shout for joy at the displays of thy justice; at the manifestations of thy righteous character.

8. *The* LORD is *gracious.* See Notes on Ps. lxxxvi. 5, 15. ¶ *And full of compassion.* Kind; compassionate; ready to do good. See Notes on Ps. ciii. 8. ¶ *Slow to anger.* See Ps. ciii. 8, where the same expression occurs. ¶ *And of great mercy.* Marg., *great in mercy.* His greatness is shown in his mercy; and the manifestation of that mercy is great:—great, as on a large scale; great, as manifested towards great sinners; great, in the sacrifice made that it may be displayed; great, in the completeness

with which sin is pardoned—pardoned so as to be remembered no more.

9. *The* LORD is *good to all.* To all his creatures. That is, he is kind and compassionate towards them; he is disposed and ready to do them good. There is not one of them whom he is not ready and willing to bless; not one whose happiness would not be agreeable to him, or whose welfare he is not ready to promote. Comp. Ps. c. 5. ¶ *And his tender mercies* are *over all his works.* In all that he has made there is evidence that he is a kind and benevolent God. He has a heart to love, to bless, what he has made; everywhere arrangements are made for happiness; he is not disposed to cast off the feeble, the erring, and the suffering; he is willing to receive back again those who have wandered from him, to pardon the offending, to wipe away the tears of the sorrowful.

10. *All thy works shall praise thee.* Or, do praise thee; that is, all thy works show what thou art, and combine in setting forth thy perfections. See Notes on Ps. xix. 1. ¶ *And thy saints shall bless thee.* Or, do bless thee. All those who are holy in heaven and on earth, the angels around thy throne, and thy people below, all combine to proclaim thy praise.

11. *They shall speak of the glory of thy kingdom.* Of thy reign; of the great principles of thy government and laws. They see in that reign evidence that thou art worthy of universal praise. Seeing this, it becomes to them a subject on which they talk or converse (comp. Mal. iii. 16)—a subject of interest to their

12 To make known to the sons of men his mighty acts, and the glorious majesty of his kingdom.

13 Thy kingdom *is* [1] an everlasting [q] kingdom, and thy dominion *endureth* throughout all generations.

[1] *a kingdom of all ages.*

14 The LORD upholdeth all that fall, and raiseth up all *those that be* bowed down.

15 The eyes of all [2] wait upon thee; and thou givest them their meat in due season.

[q] Dan. ii. 44.　　[2] *look unto.*

---

hearts, and "out of the abundance of the heart the mouth speaks." Men talk about that which interests them; those things in which they have pleasure; those which they desire to understand; those in which they see difficulties that they would wish to have solved. It is one of the characteristics of the "saints"—of the people of God — that they *do* talk about God and his kingdom; that the subject is to them a pleasant theme of meditation and conversation; that *they* have the kind of pleasure in talking about God which other men have in conversing about their farms or their merchandise, their children and friends, the news of the day, politics, literature, or science. ¶ *And talk of thy power.* As put forth in the works of creation; as manifested in the dispensations of thy providence; as evinced in the conversion of sinners; as displayed in carrying thy truth around the world; as exhibited in sustaining the sufferer, and in giving peace and support to the dying.

12. *To make known to the sons of men his mighty acts.* To bring other men to understand and to appreciate the evidences of the power of God. A man who sees this himself will wish that others may see it also. This is the foundation of the desire which warms and animates the heart of the Christian missionary—the desire to make the great truths of redemption known as far as possible, even to the ends of the earth. ¶ *And the glorious majesty of his kingdom.* And the glory of the majesty of his reign. They wish to communicate the knowledge of this to those ignorant of it. They themselves see this

to be glorious, and they wish that all others may see it also.

13. *Thy kingdom* is *an everlasting kingdom,* etc. See Notes on Ps. x. 16; Dan. iv. 34. The meaning is, that the reign of God will continue for ever and ever. It will never pass away as other dominions do; it will not change as dynasties do among men; it will not be overthrown as they are; its great principles will stand firm for ever and ever. Comp. Notes on Ps. lxxii. 17.

14. *The* LORD *upholdeth all that fall.* The word here used is a participle, literally, "The Lord sustaining;" that is, the Lord *is* a Sustainer or Upholder of all that fall. The allusion is to those who have no power to go of themselves; who would sink under the burdens of life if they were not supported. The idea is, that it is a characteristic of the Lord, that he *does* sustain such; that all such may confidently look to him to uphold them. ¶ *And raiseth up all* those that be *bowed down.* The word here also is a participle: "he is lifting up;" that is, he is a lifter up. The reference is to those who are bent and bowed under the duties, the cares, the trials of life; who go bowed down under those burdens. God is able to strengthen them so that they can bear those burdens without being crushed under them.

15. *The eyes of all wait upon thee.* Marg., *Look unto thee.* All creatures, on the land, in the air, in the waters; all in heaven; all throughout the universe. That is, It is *as if* all directed their eyes to thee imploringly for the supply of their wants. To no one else can they look for those things which are needful for

16 Thou *r* openest thine hand, and satisfiest the desire of every living thing.

17 The LORD *is* righteous in all his ways, and ¹ holy in all his

works.

18 The LORD *is* nigh unto all them that call upon him, to all that call upon him in truth.

r Ps. civ. 28.

¹ Or, *merciful, or, bountiful.*

---

them. A universe thus looks every day, every hour, every moment, to its God! How sublime the scene! ¶ *And thou givest them their meat in due season.* See Notes on Ps. civ. 27, where the same words occur.

16. *Thou openest thine hand.* By the mere opening of the hand all needful gifts are bestowed on the creatures dependent on thee. The same words are found in Ps. civ. 28; see Notes on that passage. ¶ *And satisfiest the desire of every living thing.* All kinds of creatures:—men, fowls, beasts, fishes, insects—the innumerable multitudes that swarm on the earth, in the air, in the waters. In Ps. civ. 28, it is, "They are filled with good." The meaning is essentially the same. Of course this is to be taken in a general sense. It cannot mean that absolutely no one ever wants, or ever perishes from want, but the idea is that of the amazing beneficence and fulness of God in being able and willing to satisfy such multitudes; to keep them from perishing by cold, or hunger, or nakedness. And, in fact, how few birds perish by hunger; how few of the infinite number of the inhabitants of the sea; how few animals that roam over deserts, or in vast plains; how few men; how few even of the insect tribes—how few in the world revealed by the microscope—the world beneath us—the innumerable multitudes of living things too small even to be *seen* by the naked eye of man !

17. *The* LORD *is* righteous in all *his ways.* In his own character; in his laws; in his providential dealings; in his arrangements for the redemption and salvation of man. In his own character he is what it is desirable that a God should be; in all his laws he ordains that only which it

is desirable should be enacted; in all his dealings with men he does that which it is desirable should be done. He violates no right; he wrongs no one; he demands of no one a service which would be unjust; he makes no arrangements for pardon and salvation which it is not best should be made. It is much for a man to be able to say in all that occurs to him under the Divine administration, "It is *right;*" it is much for a man to have such confidence in God as to be able to feel that all he does in respect to nations is the best thing that could be done. Comp. Notes on Ps. lxxxix. 14; xcvii. 2. ¶ *And holy in all his works.* Marg., *merciful,* or *bountiful.* The Hebrew word is *merciful.* The idea seems to be that righteousness and mercy are equally consulted in his arrangements; that they meet together, and act harmoniously in the Divine plans. Comp. Notes on Ps. lxxxv. 10.

18. *The* LORD *is nigh unto all them that call upon him.* There is a sense in which he is "nigh" to all, for he is everywhere present; but there is a special sense in which he *seems* to be nigh to us; in which he *manifests* himself to us; in which he gives us *evidence* of his presence. It is in prayer, in praise, in his ordinances,—in his gracious interpositions in our behalf,—in the peace and joy which we have in communion with him. Comp. Notes on Ps. xxxiv. 18: "The Lord is nigh unto them that are of a broken heart." ¶ *To all that call upon him in truth.* In sincerity; not hypocritically; worshipping him as the true God, and with a sincere desire to obtain his favour. Comp. Notes on John iv. 24. We can have no hope that God will hear us unless we are sincere in our worship. He sees

19 He will fulfil the desire of them that fear him; he also will hear their cry, and will save them.

20 The LORD preserveth all

s Ex. xx. 6.   t Rev. v. 13.

them that love *s* him; but all the wicked will he destroy.

21 My mouth shall speak the praise of the LORD; *t* and let all flesh bless his holy name for ever and ever.

the heart, and he will act towards us as we *are,* and not as we *profess* to be.

19. *He will fulfil the desire of them that fear him.* Of those who worship him with reverence,—those who are his true friends. See Notes on Matt. vii. 7, 8; John xiv. 14; 1 John v. 14; Ps. xxxiv. 15. ¶ *He also will hear their cry, and will save them.* He will regard their *expressed* desire —their earnest prayer.

20. *The LORD preserveth all them that love him.* He keeps them; watches over them; defends them; makes them the object of his care. See Notes on Ps. xxxi. 20, 23; xcvii. 10. ¶ *But all the wicked will he destroy.* All that are found ultimately to be wicked; all that on the final trial deserve to be classed with the wicked. See Notes on Ps. ix. 17; xi. 6; Matt. xxv. 46.

21. *My mouth shall speak the praise of the* LORD. That is, I will utter his praise. In view of all these things, in view of his character and doings, I will praise him. I will be found among those who honour him; who acknowledge him as the true God; who render homage for what he is, and thanks for what he has done. ¶ *And let all flesh bless his holy name for ever and ever.* All men; all that dwell upon the earth. Let his praise be universal and eternal. This is the language of true piety; all in whose bosom there is any true religion will heartily say *Amen.* No desire of a pious heart is more constant and strong than that God should be praised, adored, honoured by all intelligent creatures; that he should be known and acknowledged in all the earth as the true God; that his praise should ascend from all parts of the universe for ever. See Notes on Ps. c.

PSALM CXLVI.

This psalm is without a title, and it is impossible to ascertain by whom, or on what occasion, it was composed. In the Septuagint and the Latin Vulgate, the title is, "Hallelujah. Of Haggai and Zechariah." But this is without authority, and it is not known how it came to be prefixed. The same title occurs in the Arabic Version. The Syriac Version has the title still more in full: "Spoken by Haggai and Zechariah the prophets, who ascended from the captivity at Babylon, concerning the morning ministration of the priests;" that is, to be used in their morning services. The tradition, therefore, would seem to be that this is a composition of those prophets. That it *may* have belonged to the times of Haggai and Zechariah is certainly possible, nor is there anything *in* the psalm inconsistent with that supposition, though there is no positive evidence that it is so. In this portion of the Psalms (cxlvi.--cl.) all begin and end in the same manner, with a Hallelujah; they all belong to one group, and seem to pertain to the same occasion; and it is not improbable that they constitute a series of psalms intended to commemorate the completion of the walls of Jerusalem, and the finishing of the temple. They would be eminently appropriate to such an event.

This psalm is a general psalm of praise which might be used at any time, containing thoughts such as are appropriately suggested by a contemplation of the character of God, and his dealings with men. The idea is that of the blessedness of trusting in God; the security of those who do it; the superiority of this confidence and peace over any which is reposed in princes; and the evidence that it will be safe to trust in him, furnished by his merciful interpositions in behalf of the oppressed, the hungry, the prisoner, the blind, the bowed down, the righteous, the stranger, the fatherless, and the widow.

The psalm, then, has these parts:—

I. An expression of a purpose to praise

PSALM CXLVI.

PRAISE ye the LORD. Praise u the LORD, O my soul.

2 While v I live will I praise the LORD: I will sing praises unto my God while I have any being.

3 Put w not your trust in princes, nor in the son of man, in whom there is no 2 help.

4 His breath goeth forth, he

1 Hallelujah. u Ps. ciii. 1.
v Ps. civ. 33. w Isa. ii. 22; Jer. xvii. 5, 7.
2 Or, salvation.

God; or, God as an object of praise, vers. 1, 2.
II. Reliance is not to be put in man, even in princes, since all are mortal, vers. 3, 4.
III. God is the only Being on whom we can rely, 5–9.
(1) The happiness of that reliance, ver. 5.
(2) Reasons for such reliance, vers. 6–9. He is the Creator of all things; he keeps truth; he executes judgment for the oppressed; he shows his kindness towards the hungry, the prisoner, the blind, the bowed down, the righteous, the stranger, the fatherless, and the widow.
IV. God will reign for ever, and he is the God of Zion. His people, therefore, should praise him, ver. 10.

1. Praise ye the LORD. "Ye;"— all people. Marg., Hallelujah. See Ps. civ. 35; cvi. 1. ¶ Praise the LORD, O my soul. See Notes on Ps. ciii. 1; civ. 1.
2. While I live will I praise the LORD, etc. See Notes on Ps. civ. 33, where the same language occurs substantially as in this verse: "I will sing unto the Lord as long as I live; I will sing praise to my God while I have my being." The idea is, not merely that he would praise him during this life—short and fleeting as it is—but that as long as he had an existence— in the future world — for ever he would praise him.

"Through every period of my life
Thy goodness I'll pursue;
And after death, in distant worlds,
The glorious theme renew.
Through all eternity to Thee
A joyful song I'll raise;
But, oh! eternity's too short
To utter all thy praise."—Addison.

3. Put not your trust in princes.

Rely on God rather than on man, however exalted he may be. There is a work of protection and salvation which no man, however exalted he may be, can perform for you; a work which God alone, who is the Maker of all things, and who never dies, can accomplish. See Notes on Ps. cxviii. 8, 9. Comp. also Notes on Isa. ii. 22: "Cease ye from man, whose breath is in his nostrils; for wherein is he to be accounted of?" ¶ Nor in the son of man. Any son of man; any human being, no matter what his rank or power. The phrase is often used to denote man. See Notes on Ps. viii. 4. The appellation "Son of man" was often applied by the Saviour to himself to express emphatically the idea that he was a man— that he had a human nature; that he was identified with the race; that he was a brother, a fellow-sufferer, a friend of man:—that he was not a cold and abstract being so exalted that he could not feel or weep over the sins and woes of a fallen and suffering world. The language here, however, does not refer to him. It is right to put our trust in him; we have no other trust. ¶ In whom there is no help. Marg., salvation. So the Hebrew. The idea is, that man cannot save us. He cannot save himself; he cannot save others.

4. His breath goeth forth. He dies like other men, no matter how exalted he is. See Notes on Isa. ii. 22. ¶ He returneth to his earth. See Notes on Ps. xc. 3. The earth— the dust—is "his:"—(a) It is his, as that from which he was made:—he turns back to what he was. Gen. iii. 19: "Dust thou art, and unto dust shalt thou return." (b) The earth—

x returneth to his earth; in that very day his thoughts perish.

5 Happy *is he* that *hath* the God of Jacob for his help, whose hope *is* in the LORD his God.

6 Which *y* made heaven, and

x Eccles. xii. 7.   *y* Rev. xiv 7.
z Luke i. 53.

the dust—the grave is *his*, as it is his home—the place where he will abide. (*c*) It is *his*, as it is the only property which he has in reversion. All that a man—a prince, a nobleman, a monarch, a millionaire—will soon have will be his grave,—his few feet of earth. *That* will be his by right of possession; by the fact that, for the time being, he will occupy it, and not another man. But that, too, may soon become another man's grave, so that even there he is a tenant only for a time; he has no permanent possession *even of a grave*. How poor is the richest man! ¶ *In that very day*. The very day—the moment—that he dies. ¶ *His thoughts perish.* His purposes; his schemes; his plans; his purposes of conquest and ambition; his schemes for becoming rich or great; his plans of building a house, and laying out his grounds, and enjoying life; his design of making a book, or taking a journey, or giving himself to ease and pleasure. Luke xii. 19, 20: "And I will say to my soul, Soul, thou hast much goods laid up for many years; take thine ease, eat, drink, and be merry; but God said unto him, Thou fool! this night thy soul shall be required of thee." Such are all the purposes of men!

5. *Happy is he that hath the God of Jacob for his help.* Who may rely for protection on the God who defended Jacob in his travels and dangers. Or, perhaps the word *Jacob* is here used collectively to denote *Israel* —the Jewish people :—the God whom they adore and worship, rather than the gods of the heathen. Comp. Notes on **Ps.** cxliv. 15; liv. 4. ¶ *Whose hope* is *in the* LORD *his God.* In Jehovah, worshipped as his God. That is, who

earth, the sea, and all that therein *is*; which keepeth truth for ever;

7 Which executeth judgment for the oppressed : which giveth food to the *z* hungry. The LORD looseth *a* the prisoners :

a Ps. lxviii. 6; cvii. 14.

truly worships Jehovah, or makes Jehovah his God.

6. *Which made heaven and earth,* etc. Who is the true God, the Creator of all things. Happy is he who can address the God who called all this wondrous universe into being, and who sustains all by his power, as *his* God. ¶ *Which keepeth truth for ever.* Who is always true to his promises. In this verse there are *two* reasons given why the lot of the people of God would be a happy one : (1) That Jehovah is the true God, the Creator of all things, and, therefore, able to protect and provide for them. (2) That he is faithful, and may always be relied on. Idol-gods have no power, and every reliance placed on them is a vain reliance; men are often false and cannot be trusted, but Jehovah has infinite power, and every promise that he makes will be fulfilled; all that he says is eternally and unchangeably true. The reasons for trusting in him, or the reasons why they who trust in him are " happy," are further stated in the following verses.

7. *Which executeth judgment for the oppressed.* This is the *third* reason why the lot of those is a happy one who trust in God. It is because he has power to pronounce and execute a right judgment or sentence in regard to the oppressed and the wronged, and because it is characteristic of his nature that he does thus execute judgment. See Notes on Ps. ciii. 6: "The Lord executeth righteousness and judgment for all that are oppressed." ¶ *Which giveth food to the hungry.* See Notes on Ps. cvii. 9: "For he satisfieth the longing soul, and filleth the hungry soul with

8 The Lord ^{b} openeth *the eyes of* the blind: the Lord raiseth them ^{c} that are bowed down: the Lord loveth the righteous:

b Matt. ix. 30; John ix. 6, etc.; 1 Pet. ii. 9.
c Ps. cxlvii. 6; Luke xiii. 13.

9 The Lord preserveth the strangers; he ^{d} relieveth the fatherless and widow: but the way of the wicked he ^{e} turneth upside down.

d Prov. xv. 25. *e* Job xii. 13, 14; Prov. iv. 19.

goodness." This is the *fourth* reason why they who confide in God are happy. Comp. Luke i. 53: "He hath filled the hungry with good things." ¶ *The* Lord *looseth the prisoners.* This is the *fifth* reason why they who trust in the Lord are "happy." Comp. Notes on Ps. lxviii. 6: "He bringeth out those which are bound with chains." See also Notes on Ps. cvii. 10: "Being bound in affliction and iron." Comp. Job xxxvi. 8, 9.

8. *The* Lord *openeth* the eyes of *the blind.* . This is the *sixth* reason for what is stated as to the blessedness of those who put their trust in the Lord. The language here would be applicable to bodily or to mental blindness. Comp. Notes on Ps. cxix. 18: "Open thou mine eyes, that I may behold wondrous things out of thy law." See also Notes on Isa. xxxv. 5: "Then the eyes of the blind shall be opened." ¶ *The* Lord *raiseth them that are bowed down.* This is the *seventh* reason why they are happy who trust in the Lord. It is that those who are crushed and bowed down under the weight of care, trouble, and calamity, are raised up by him, or are sustained and comforted. See Notes on Ps. cxlv. 14: "The Lord upholdeth all that fall, and raiseth up all those that be bowed down." ¶ *The* Lord *loveth the righteous.* This is the *eighth* reason why those who trust in the Lord are happy. It is a characteristic of God, and a foundation for praise, that he loves those who obey law; who do that which is right.

9. *The* Lord *preserveth the strangers.* He regards them with interest; he defends and guides them. This is the *ninth* reason why those who trust in the Lord are happy. The stranger—

away from home and friends; with no one to feel an interest in him, or sympathy for him; with the feeling that he is forsaken; with no one on whom he can call for sympathy in distress—may find in God one who will regard his condition; who will sympathize with him; who is able to protect and befriend him. Comp. Ex. xii. 49; xxii. 21; xxiii. 9; Lev. xix. 33; Deut. i. 16; x. 18, 19; Isa. lvi. 3, 6. ¶ *He relieveth the fatherless and widow.* He is their friend. This is the *tenth* reason why those who put their trust in the Lord are happy. It is that God is the Friend of those who have no earthly protector. See Notes on Ps. lxviii. 5: "A father of the fatherless, and a judge of the widows, is God in his holy habitation." ¶ *But the way of the wicked he turneth upside down.* He overturns their plans; defeats their schemes; makes their purposes accomplish what they did not intend they should accomplish. The Hebrew word here means to bend, to curve, to make crooked, to distort; then, to overturn, to turn upside down. The same word is applied to the conduct of the wicked, in Ps. cxix. 78: "They dealt perversely with me." The idea here is, that their path is not a straight path; that God makes it a crooked way; that they are diverted from their design; that through them he accomplishes purposes which they did not intend; that he prevents their accomplishing their own designs; and that he will make their plans subservient to a higher and better purpose than their own. This is the *eleventh* reason why those who put their trust in God are happy. It is that God is worthy of confidence and love, because he has all the plans of wicked men entirely under his control.

10 The LORD shall reign for ever, *even* thy God, O Zion, unto all generations. Praise ye the LORD.

PSALM CXLVII.

PRAISE ye the LORD: for *it is f* good to sing praises unto

our God: for *it is* pleasant; *and* praise is comely.

2 The LORD doth build up Jerusalem; he gathereth together the outcasts *g* of Israel.

3 He *h* healeth the broken in

f Ps. xcii. 1.   *g* Deut. xxx. 3, 4.
            h Isa. lxi. 1.

---

10. *The* LORD *shall reign for ever.* See Notes on Ps. x. 16: "The Lord is King for ever and ever." Comp. Ex. xv. 18. ¶ *Even thy God, O Zion, unto all generations.* As long as the world shall endure. There shall be no change of dynasty as there is in human governments; but the same King shall reign from age to age. ¶ *Praise ye the* LORD. Hallelu-jah. The psalm closes as it commences. It is a call on all persons to unite in the praise of Jehovah.

PSALM CXLVII.

The author of this psalm is unknown; nor can the occasion on which it was composed be ascertained with any degree of certainty. In the Septuagint, the Arabic, and the Syriac Versions, it is ascribed, like the previous psalm, to the prophets Haggai and Zechariah. The Syriac has this title:—"A Psalm of Haggai and Zechariah, when they urged the completion of the temple of Jerusalem." It is quite manifest, from vers. 2, 13, 14, that the psalm was written after the return from the Babylonish captivity, and that probably on the completion of the temple after that return, with a view to be employed at its dedication. See Introd. to Ps. cxlvi.

This psalm comprises two themes:— praise to God for his goodness to his creatures generally; and special praise for his goodness to his people. These topics are intermingled in the psalm, but the former is more prominent in the first part of the psalm; the latter in the close. Both were proper themes at the rebuilding of the temple and the walls of the city, after the return from the exile. Both are proper now, and will be so always.

1. *Praise ye the* LORD. Hallelu-jah. See Ps. cxlvi. 1. ¶ *For* it is *good to sing praises unto our God.* See Notes

on Ps. xcii. 1: "It is a good thing to give thanks unto the Lord." ¶ *For* it is *pleasant.* See Notes on Ps. cxxxv. 3: "Sing praises unto his name; for it is pleasant." The Hebrew word is the same. ¶ And *praise is comely.* Becoming; proper. See Notes on Ps. xxxiii. 1: "praise is comely for the upright." The Hebrew word is the same. If these psalms were composed for the re-dedication of the temple, it would not be unnatural that much of the language employed should be borrowed from earlier psalms with which the people were familiar.

2. *The* LORD *doth build up Jerusalem.* He builds up the walls; he restores the city; he has caused the temple to be reconstructed. This language would be applicable to a return from the captivity. There *may* be an allusion here to the language in Ps. cii. 16: "When the Lord shall build up Zion, he shall appear in his glory." See Notes on that passage. What is there spoken of as what would be in the future is here spoken of as accomplished, and as a ground of praise. ¶ *He gathereth together the outcasts of Israel.* Those who have been exiled from their native land, and who have been scattered as outcasts in a foreign country. This is appropriate language to use on the supposition that the psalm was composed after the return from the exile, for it is in such language that that return was predicted by the prophets. Isa. xi. 12: "And he shall assemble the outcasts of Israel, and gather together the dispersed of Judah," etc. Isa. lvi. 8: "The Lord God which gathereth the outcasts of Israel," etc.

3. *He healeth the broken in heart.* Referring primarily to the fact that

heart, and bindeth up their [1] wounds.

4 He telleth the number of the stars; he calleth them all by *their* names.

5 Great *is* our Lord, and of great power: [2] his understanding

[1] *griefs.*

[2] *of his understanding* there *is no number.*

[i] *is* infinite.

6 The LORD lifteth up the [k] meek: he casteth the wicked down to the ground.

7 Sing unto the LORD with thanksgiving; sing praise upon the harp unto our God;

[i] Isa. xl. 28.   [k] Ps. xxv. 9; Matt. v. 5; 1 Pet. iii. 4.

---

he had healed those who were crushed and broken in their long captivity, and that he had given them comfort by returning them to their native land. At the same time, however, the language is made general, as describing a characteristic of God that he *does* this; that it is his character to do this. See Notes on Ps. xxxiv. 18. See also Ps. li. 17. Comp. Isa. lxi. 1; Luke iv. 18. ¶ *And bindeth up their wounds.* See Notes on Isa. i. 6. Marg., *griefs.* The word refers to those who are afflicted with griefs and troubles. The reference is to mental sorrows; to a troubled spirit; to a heart made sad in any way. God has provided healing for such; on such he bestows peace.

4. *He telleth the number of the stars.* He counts them all. God only can do this. The stars are so numerous that no astronomer can count them; they lie so far in the depths of space, and are so remote from each other, that no man can be so presumptuous as to suppose that he has even *seen* any considerable part of them, even by the aid of the most powerful telescopes. ¶ *He calleth them all by* their *names.* As if each one had a name, and God could call them forth one by one by their names, like the muster-roll of an army. This language seems to be taken from Isa. xl. 26: " Lift up your eyes on high, and behold who hath created these things, that bringeth out their host by numbers; he calleth them all by names, by the greatness of his might, for that he is strong in power; not one faileth." See Notes on that passage.

5. *Great is our Lord.* See Notes on Ps. xlviii. 1. ¶ *And of great*

power. This seems to be added, as in Isa. xl. 28, in view of the power required in making the heavens, and in guiding and numbering the stars: " Hast thou not known? Hast thou not heard, that the everlasting God, the Lord, the Creator of the ends of the earth, fainteth not, neither is weary?" ¶ *His understanding* is *infinite.* Marg., *Of his understanding there is no number.* That is, This corresponds with his power to number the stars. There is no limit to it. It is not bounded; there is no point reached where it can be said that *there is no more;* that it is exhausted. See Notes on Isa. xl. 28: " There is no searching of his understanding."

6. *The* LORD *lifteth up the meek.* The humble; the poor; the bowed down; the oppressed. See Notes on Ps. cxlvi. 8: " The Lord raiseth them that are bowed down." ¶ *He casteth the wicked down to the ground.* See Notes on Ps. cxlvi. 9: " The way of the wicked he turneth upside down."

7. *Sing unto the* LORD *with thanksgiving.* Accompany the praise of God —the expression of worship—with a grateful remembrance of the past. The one will aid the other, and the two will constitute acceptable and proper worship. The first word here means properly to answer, or respond; and the idea would seem to be, that we are to make a suitable *response* or *answer* to the manifold favours which we have received at the hand of God. ¶ *Sing praise upon the harp unto our God.* On the word *harp*, see Notes on Isa. v. 12. The harp was an instrument commonly employed in Divine worship. See Notes on Ps. xxxiii. 2:

8 Who covereth the heaven
with clouds, who prepareth rain
for the earth, who maketh grass
to grow upon the mountains.

9 He giveth to the beast his
food, *and* to the young ravens
l which cry.

10 He delighteth not in the

l Job xxxviii. 41; Matt. vi. 26.

strength of the horse; he taketh
not pleasure in the legs of a
man.

11 The *m* LORD taketh pleasure
in them that fear him, in those
that hope in his mercy.

12 Praise the LORD, O Jerusalem; praise thy God, O Zion.

m Isa. lxii. 4; Mal. iii. 16, 17.

"Praise the Lord with harp." Comp.
Ps. xliii. 4; xlix. 4; lvii. 8; lxxi. 22.

8. *Who covereth the heaven with
clouds.* Clouds that are designed to
convey refreshing rain to the earth.
The reasons for praise here stated
(vers. 8, 9) are derived from the goodness of God as exhibited in his providential arrangements for the good of
man. ¶ *Who prepareth rain for the
earth.* By causing it to be taken
from the sea, carried by the clouds,
and conveyed through the air to the
places where it is needed, and then
gently sprinkled on the earth. Comp.
Notes on Ps. civ. 13: "He watereth
the hills from his chambers." See
also Notes on Job v. 10; xxviii. 26;
xxxvi. 27, 28; xxxviii. 28, 37. ¶ *Who
maketh grass to grow upon the mountains.* Which would be barren but
for the rain. Who conveys the water
thus to the very tops of the mountains, and causes it to descend on
their sides, so that even the mountains are clothed with verdure and
beauty. Comp. Notes on Ps. civ. 14:
"He causeth the grass to grow for
the cattle."

9. *He giveth to the beast his food.*
To the wild beast; to the animals that
cannot toil for it themselves, as man
does. Comp. Notes on Ps. civ. 21,
27, 28. ¶ *To the young ravens which
cry.* Comp. Notes on Job xxxviii. 41.
See also Ps. cxlv. 15.

10. *He delighteth not in the strength
of the horse.* The horse is among the
noblest works of God—perhaps the
noblest of all the animals that he has
made. See Notes on Job xxxix. 19–
25. Yet God regards with more interest and pleasure humble piety than
he does any mere power, however

great and wonderful it may be.
¶ *He taketh not pleasure in the legs
of a man.* Not the same pleasure as
in piety; he prefers the humble heart
to this. The reference is to man as
capable of rapid marches, of quick
movements in assaulting an enemy;
the allusion being, perhaps, to an
army prepared for war,—cavalry and
infantry,—the horse moving on with
resistless force,—the foot-soldiers with
rapid motion.

11. *The LORD taketh pleasure in
them that fear him.* In those who
truly worship him, however humble,
poor, and unknown to men they may
be; however unostentatious, retired,
unnoticed may be their worship. Not
in the "pride, pomp, and circumstance
of war" is his pleasure; not in the
march of armies; not in the valour
of the battle-field; not in scenes where
"the garments of the warrior are
rolled in blood,"—but in the closet,
when the devout child of God prays;
in the family, when the group bend
before him in solemn devotion; in the
assembly—quiet, serious, calm—when
his friends are gathered together for
prayer and praise; in the heart that
truly loves, reverences, adores him.
¶ *In those that hope in his mercy.*
It is a pleasure to him to have the
guilty, the feeble, the undeserving *hope*
in him—trust in him—seek him.

12. *Praise the LORD, O Jerusalem,*
etc. In addition to this general
praise in which all may unite, there
are special reasons why Jerusalem
and its inhabitants should praise
God:—just as now, in addition to
the general reasons pertaining to all
men why they should praise God,
there are special reasons why Chris-

13 For he hath strengthened the bars of thy gates; he hath blessed thy children [n] within thee.

14 [1] He maketh peace *in* thy borders, *and* filleth thee with the [2] finest of the wheat.

15 He [o] sendeth forth his commandment *upon* earth : his word runneth very swiftly.

[n] Ps. cxv. 14.
[1] *Who maketh thy border peace.*

16 He giveth snow like wool : he scattereth the hoarfrost like ashes.

17 He casteth forth his ice like morsels : who can stand before his cold ?

18 He sendeth out his word, and melteth them : he causeth his wind to blow, *and* the waters flow.

[2] *fat of wheat,* Ps. lxxxi. 16; Deut. xxxii. 14.
[o] Ps. cvii. 20.

---

tians—why his redeemed people—should do it. What those reasons, as pertaining to the inhabitants of Jerusalem, were, is specified in the following verses.

13. *For he hath strengthened the bars of thy gates.* He has made thee safe and secure—as if he had given additional strength to the fastenings of the gates of the city. Cities were surrounded by walls. They were entered through gates. Those gates were fastened by bars passed across them, to which the gates were secured. The *language* here might be applicable to any period, but it is probable that there is particular reference to Jerusalem as made strong in rebuilding it after the return from Babylon. ¶ *He hath blessed thy children within thee.* The inhabitants, by giving them safety and peace.

14. *He maketh peace* in *thy borders.* Marg., *he maketh thy border peace.* The word *border* here refers to a boundary, and stands for all the domain or territory included within the boundaries of a country. The idea is, that peace prevailed throughout the land. ¶ And *filleth thee with the finest of the wheat.* Marg., as in Heb., *fat of wheat.* Literally, "He satisfies thee with the fat of wheat." There is no want of wheat, and that of the best kind. Comp. Notes on Ps. cxxxii. 15: "I will satisfy her poor with bread."

15. *He sendeth forth his commandment* upon *earth.* That is, with reference to the productions of the

earth ; to the changes which occur ; to the seasons; to snow, frost, ice, cold, heat, wind; and he is universally and immediately obeyed. Nature everywhere yields a ready acquiescence to his will. ¶ *His word runneth very swiftly.* As if it hastened to obey him. There is no delay. Comp. Notes on Ps. xxxiii. 9 : " He spake, and it was done; he commanded, and it stood fast." Snow, and frost, and ice, and cold, and heat, and wind, are entirely obedient to him. There is no reluctance in obeying him ; there is no delay.

16. *He giveth snow like wool.* He covers the earth with snow, so that it *seems* to have a clothing of wool. Comp. Notes on Job xxxvii. 6 : " For he saith to the snow, Be thou on the earth." ¶ *He scattereth the hoarfrost like ashes.* As if ashes were strewed over the earth ; or, as easily as one strews ashes.

17. *He casteth forth his ice like morsels.* The word rendered *morsels* means properly a bit, a crumb, as of bread, Gen. xviii. 5 ; Judges xix. 5. The allusion here would seem to be to hail, which God sends upon the earth as easily as one scatters crumbs of bread from the hand. ¶ *Who can stand before his cold ?* Or, hail. The word is the same, except in pointing, as the preceding word rendered *ice.* The idea is that no one can stand before the peltings of the hail, when God sends it forth, or scatters it upon the earth.

18. *He sendeth out his word.* He commands : or, he speaks. ¶ *And*

19 He *p* sheweth his ¹ word unto Jacob, his statutes *q* and his judgments unto Israel.

20 He *r* hath not dealt so with

p Deut. xxxiii. 3, 4; Rom. iii. 2.

any nation; and *as for his* judgments, they have not known them. Praise ye the LORD.

¹ *words.*   *q* Mal. iv. 4.
      r Deut. iv. 32—34.

---

melteth them. Melts the snow and the ice. Comp. Notes on Job xxxvii. 10–12: " By the breath of God frost is given," etc. The idea is, that they are entirely under his control. They obey him when he speaks. ¶ *He causeth his wind to blow.* The warm south wind :—" *his* " wind, because he directs it, and causes it to perform his will. ¶ And *the waters flow.* The snow and the ice melt.

19. *He showeth his word unto Jacob.* Marg., *words.* His commands; his promises; his laws. The things which were before adverted to, pertain to the world in general. All men see his works ; all enjoy the benefits of his arrangements in the seasons,—in the changes which occur upon the earth ; but he has peculiarly favoured his own people by giving them his laws,—his revealed will. This distinguishes them above all other nations of the earth, and gives them peculiar occasion for gratitude. ¶ *His statutes and his judgments unto Israel.* His laws ; his written word. The word *judgments* here refers to the law of God as being that which he *judges* or *determines* to be right.

20. *He hath not dealt so with any nation.* He has favoured Israel more than any other people by giving them his revealed truth. This was so. There was no nation in the ancient world so favoured as the Hebrew people in this respect. There is no nation now so favoured as the nation that has the revealed will of God— the Bible. The possession of that book gives a nation a vast superiority in all respects over all others. In laws, customs, morals, intelligence, social life, purity, charity, prosperity, that book elevates a nation at once, and scatters blessings which can be derived from nothing else. The

highest benevolence that could be shown to any nation would be to put it in possession of the word of God in the language of the people. ¶ *And* as for his *judgments, they have not known them.* Other nations are ignorant of his laws, his statutes, his revealed will. They are consequently subjected to all the evils which arise from ignorance of those laws. The fact that the ancient people of God possessed them was a sufficient reason for the Hallelujah with which the psalm closes. The fact that *we* possess them is a sufficient reason why we should re-echo the shout of praise, and cry HALLELUJAH.

PSALM CXLVIII.

The author of this psalm is unknown. The occasion on which it was composed was probably the same as that on which the two previous psalms and the two following were written,—each commencing and closing with a *Hallelujah.* That occasion was, most probably, as before remarked, the rebuilding of Jerusalem after the captivity, and the dedication of the temple.

The psalm is, in general, a call on all parts of the universe to praise the Lord. It is properly divided into two portions. In the first (vers. 1–6), the call is addressed to the heavens—to all that is above the earth—to praise Jehovah; in the second (vers. 7–14), the call is addressed to all the dwellers on the earth to unite in that praise. The psalm is most animated and triumphant. The language accords with the sentiment. It is adapted to the most animating and spirit-stirring music; and these psalms —this and the two preceding and the two following—in style, in sentiment, in poetic beauty, in sublimity, in their adaptedness to fill the soul with lofty emotions—are eminently fitted to close the whole collection,—the entire Book of Psalms. Little can be needed, or can be added, in illustration of the sentiments of the psalm.

PSALM CXLVIII.

PRAISE [1] ye the LORD. Praise
ye the LORD from the hea-
vens : praise him in the heights.

2 Praise [s] ye him, all his angels:
praise ye him, all his hosts.

3 Praise ye him, sun and moon:
praise him, all ye stars of light.

4 Praise him, ye heavens [t] of

1 *Hallelujah.*		s Ps. ciii. 20.

heavens, and ye waters that *be*
above the heavens.

5 Let them praise the name of
the LORD : [u] for he commanded,
and they were created.

6 He hath also stablished
them for ever and ever : he hath
made a decree which shall not
pass.

t 1 Kings viii. 27 ; 2 Cor. xii. 2.
u Gen. i. 1, etc.

---

1. *Praise ye the* LORD. See Notes
on Ps. cxlvi. 1. ¶ *Praise ye the*
LORD *from the heavens.* On the
part of the heavens. Let those who
dwell in heaven begin the song.
¶ *Praise him in the heights.* All
that are *in* the heights ; to wit, in
the highest parts of the universe, or
the heavens.

2. *Praise ye him, all his angels.*
Dwelling in the heavens. Comp.
Notes on Ps. ciii. 20. ¶ *Praise ye
him, all his hosts.* See Notes on Ps.
ciii. 21, and on Isa. i. 9. All his
armies,—referring to the angels considered as marshalled into hosts, of
which God is the Head and Leader.

3. *Praise ye him, sun and moon.*
The most conspicuous and glorious
objects in the heavens, as apparent
to the eyes of men. ¶ *Praise him,
all ye stars of light.* A poetical expression to denote bright or shining
stars. The phrase embraces all the
stars as they strike the eyes of men.
Each one has something peculiar to
it for which to praise God ; and the
entire groups—the immense multitudes, as such—should join in one
chorus of praise.

4. *Praise him, ye heavens of heavens.* Referring to the idea that
there is one heaven rising above
another. See Notes on Ps. lxviii. 33.
See 1 Kings viii. 27 : " Behold, the
heaven and heaven of heavens cannot contain thee." Comp. 2 Chron.
ii. 6. ¶ *And ye waters that* be *above
the heavens.* Gen. i. 7 : "And God
made the firmament, and divided the
waters which were under the firmament from the waters which were

above the firmament." The allusion
here is to the waters which seem to
be above the *lower* heaven, *i.e.,* the
air, and which *seem* to come from
some higher region — some higher
heaven. See Notes on Ps. civ. 3 :
" Who layeth the beams of his chambers in the waters."

5. *Let them praise the name of the*
LORD. That is, Let them praise Jehovah himself,—the name being often
put for the person or thing referred
to. ¶ *For he commanded, and they
were created.* He showed his great
power by merely speaking, and they
came at once into being. Comp.
Notes on Ps. xxxiii. 6, 9.

6. *He hath also stablished them
for ever and ever.* He has made
them firm, stable, enduring. That
they *may* be eternal is possible ; that
they will *not* be, no one can prove.
Matter, when created, has no necessary tendency to decay or annihilation ; and the universe—the stars,
and suns, and systems—which *have*
endured so many millions of ages
may continue to exist any number of
millions of ages to come. Of course,
however, all this is dependent on the
will of God. On the meaning of this
passage, comp. Notes on Ps. cxix.
90 ; lxxii. 5 ; lxxxix. 2, 36, 37. See
also Notes on 2 Pet. iii. 7, 10, 13.
¶ *He hath made a decree which shall
not pass.* He has given a law or
statute which they cannot pass. The
word rendered *decree* here seems to
be used in the sense of *limit* or
bound ; and the idea is, that he has
bound them by a fixed *law ;* he has
established laws which they are com-

7 Praise the LORD from the earth, ye dragons, *v* and all deeps:
8 Fire, and hail; snow, and vapours; stormy wind fulfilling his word:

v Isa. xliii. 20.

9 Mountains, and all hills; fruitful trees, and all cedars:
10 Beasts, and all cattle; creeping things, and ¹ flying fowl:

¹ *birds of wing.*

---

pelled to observe. The fact is, in regard to them, that he has established great laws — as the law of gravitation—by which they are held from flying off; he has marked out orbits in which they move; he has so bound them that they perform their revolutions with unerring accuracy in the very path which he has prescribed. So accurate are their movements that they can be predicted with exact precision; and so uniform, that any succession of ages does not vary or affect them.

7. *Praise the* LORD *from the earth.* From among those who dwell on the earth. In respect to *terrestrial* objects, let these also unite in the praise of God. ¶ *Ye dragons.* On the meaning of this word, see Notes on Ps. xci. 13 ; Isa. xiii. 22. The word may mean a great fish, a whale, a sea-monster, or a serpent. It would seem to refer here to whales and sea-monsters. See Notes on Rev. xii. 3. ¶ *And all deeps.* All that are *in* the depths of the sea. Not merely the " dragons " or sea-monsters, but all that inhabit the oceans.

8. *Fire, and hail.* Fire, when accompanied by hail ; that is, the lightning. See Ps. xviii. 12. ¶ *Snow, and vapours.* Snow and clouds. It was not unnatural that these should be combined, or suggested together to the mind. ¶ *Stormy wind.* The storm; the tempest. ¶ *Fulfilling his word.* Obeying his command; accomplishing his purpose. Let the storm-wind, which seems to be so little under any control, speak his praise by showing how obedient it is to his will, and how exactly it carries out his designs. Its perfect submission to his laws,—the exactness with which, though apparently so fierce, raging, and lawless, it

carries out his plans, and pauses when he commands it,—is in fact an act of praise or homage, as it proclaims his majesty, his supremacy, and his power. On the sentiment here expressed, comp. Notes on Ps. cvii. 29 ; Ps. lxxxix. 9.

9. *Mountains, and all hills.* As being among the loftiest objects of earth, raising their heads highest towards the heavens. ¶ *Fruitful trees, and all cedars.* Fruitful trees, not as distinguished from those which are barren, but as distinguished from forest-trees, those whose nature is that they do not bear *fruit.* Of the latter, the cedar was the most prominent, and, therefore, is made the representative of the whole.

10. *Beasts, and all cattle.* Wild beasts and tame; those which roam the forest, and those which have been domesticated for the service of man. As fruitful trees and cedars might include *all* the trees, so the " beasts and cattle " here might include the whole of those that were wild and tamed. ¶ *Creeping things, and flying fowl.* Marg., as in Heb., *Birds of wing.* These are grouped together for a reason similar to that for which fruitful trees and cedars, and beasts and cattle, are grouped together, to embrace the whole. The expression embraces the loftiest and lowest; those which ascend farthest above the earth, and those which creep upon its surface. The word rendered *creeping things* would properly embrace the smaller animals which creep along upon the ground; both those which have four feet or more, as mice, lizards, crabs, etc., and those without feet, which glide or drag themselves upon the ground, as worms and serpents. (Gesenius, *Lex.*) These, in their lowly condition, and in their

11 Kings of the earth, and all people; princes, and all judges of the earth :

12 Both young men, and maidens ; old men, and children :

13 Let them praise the name of the LORD : for *w* his name

w Ps. viii. 1 ; Isa. xii. 4.

alone is [1] excellent; his glory *is* above the earth and heaven.

14 He also exalteth the horn of his people, the praise of all his saints, *even* of the children of Israel, a people near *x* unto him. Praise ye the LORD.

[1] *exalted.* *x* Eph. ii. 13, 17.

humble way, are called on to unite in the general chorus of praise. Accomplishing the purpose for which they are made, they will, with the most lofty of created beings, contribute to proclaim the wisdom, the power, and the goodness of God.

11. *Kings of the earth, and all people.* This would embrace all, as all are included in the idea of the rulers and the ruled. ¶ *Princes, and all judges of the earth.* Those of exalted rank ; those high in authority. This is proper in itself considered, as they are men like other men; and proper as an example to the rest. None of any rank are exempt from the obligation to praise God; none are cut off from the privilege.

12. *Both young men, and maidens.* Those in the morning of life,—just entering on their career ; just forming their character :—with ardour, elasticity, cheerfulness, hope ;—let them consecrate all this to God :—let all that there is in the buoyancy of their feelings, in the melody of their voices, in their ardour and vigour, be employed in the praise and the service of God. ¶ *Old men, and children.* Old men, with what remains of life, and children, with all that there is of joyousness—let all unite in praising God. Life, as it closes,—life, as it begins,—let it all be devoted to God.

13. *Let them praise the name of the* LORD. Let them praise Jehovah,— the *name* being often put for the *person.* ¶ *For his name alone is excellent.* Marg., as in Heb., *exalted.* He only is exalted as God. See Notes on Ps. viii. 1 : "O Lord, our Lord, how excellent is thy name in all the earth !" ¶ *His glory* is *above the earth and heaven.* Comp. Notes on

Ps. cxiii. 4 : "The Lord is high above all nations, and his glory above the heavens." See also Notes on Ps. viii. 1 : "Who hast set thy glory above the heavens."

14. *He also exalteth the horn of his people.* He gives them power and prosperity. See Notes on Ps. lxxxix. 17 : "And in thy favour our horn shall be exalted." Comp. Ps. xcii. 10 ; cxii. 9. ¶ *The praise of all his saints.* That is, "he has raised up praise for all his saints ;" or, has given them occasion for praise. He has so blessed them with special mercies as to make praise peculiarly appropriate for them. ¶ Even *of the children of Israel, a people near unto him.* Whom he admits to his presence as his friends; whom he regards as his own. See Notes on Eph. ii. 13 ; comp. Notes on Acts ii. 39. ¶ *Praise ye the* LORD. Hallelu-jah. Let all unite in his praise.

PSALM CXLIX.

This belongs to the group of psalms already referred to (cxlvi.-cl.), each beginning and ending with a *Hallelujah*, and probably composed after the return from the captivity, and the rebuilding of the walls of the city and the second temple. This psalm would be eminently appropriate to such an occasion, —first, as expressing the joy of the nation ; and secondly, as indicative of what the nation was to do in those circumstances in carrying out the purposes of God, and accomplishing his will. The people are considered as restored to their land ; as safe, peaceful, happy; their city is securely fortified, and they are armed to defend themselves, and are now in a position to carry their conquests over the heathen and hostile powers around them. The psalm, therefore, consists of two parts :—

I. The exhortation to praise, to joy,

PSALM CXLIX.

PRAISE [1] ye the LORD. Sing unto the LORD a new song, *and* his praise in the congregation of saints.

2 Let Israel rejoice in him that

[1] *Hallelujah.*   *y* Ps. c. 3.

y made him : let the children of Zion be joyful in their King.

3 Let them praise his name [2] in the dance : let them sing praises unto him with the timbrel and harp.

[2] Or, *with the pipe.*

to rejoicing—as appropriate to their deliverance; to their safe return; to their re-establishment in their own land, vers. 1–5.

II. The exhortation to carry out the purposes of God in regard to the people who had wronged them, and who were still hostile to them :—to inflict on them the punishment which was due to them, and which God designed to bring upon them,—regarding themselves as called of God to be his instruments in executing that punishment, in token of the Divine displeasure at the conduct of those who had oppressed and wronged them, vers. 6–9.

1. *Praise ye the* LORD. Marg., *Hallelujah.* See Notes on Ps. cxlvi. 1. ¶ *Sing unto the* LORD *a new song.* As if there was a new and a special occasion for praise. This would be so if the psalm was composed on the return from the exile; on the rebuilding of the city; and on the re-dedication of the temple. On the meaning of the language, see Notes on Ps. xxxiii. 3; Rev. v. 9; xiv. 3; see also Ps. xcvi. 1; Isa. xlii. 10. ¶ And *his praise in the congregation of saints.* In the assembly of the people of God. See Notes on Ps. cxlviii. 14; cxi. 1.

2. *Let Israel.* The people of Israel; the Hebrew people; the people of God. ¶ *Rejoice in him that made him.* Him, who has made the people what they are. All that they have and are is to be traced to him, as really as the universe of matter is to be traced to his power. Their condition is not one of *development,* or one which is the result of their own wisdom, grace, or power. See Notes on Ps. c. 3 : " It is he that hath made us, and not we ourselves." Comp. Isa. liv. 5. ¶ *Let the children of Zion.* Those who dwell in Zion or

Jerusalem. ¶ *Be joyful in their King.* In God *as* their king. (*a*) That they *have* a king, or that there *is* one to rule over them ; (*b*) That they have *such* a king ; one so wise, so powerful, so good; (*c*) That he administers his government with so much efficiency, impartiality, equity, wisdom, goodness. Comp. Ps. c. 3–5.

3. *Let them praise his name in the dance.* Marg., *with the pipe.* The Hebrew word here—מָחוֹל, *Mahhol* —is rendered *dancing* in Ps. xxx. 11; *dance,* as here, Ps. cl. 4 (where also the margin has *pipe*) ; Jer. xxxi. 13; Lam. v. 15; *dances,* Jer. xxxi. 4. It does not elsewhere occur. On the verb חוּל, *hhool,* see Notes on Ps. x. 5; li. 5. Here it cannot be improper to regard it as referring to that measured tread, or solemn movement which sometimes constituted a part of worship: 2 Sam. vi. 14. Such a movement cannot be *proved* to be wrong in worship; whether it is wise or expedient is a different matter. Customs in worship change as the customs of a people change; and that might be very proper in one stage of society, or in one period of the world, which, though not in itself wrong, might be very unadvisable in another. There was much in the Hebrew mode of worship which cannot be transferred to the forms of Christian worship without an obvious incongruity and disadvantage ; and because a thing has been done, and is not in itself wrong, we should not infer that it should always be done, or that it would be always best. If people like the Shakers dance in worship, they have an undoubted right to do so, and it *may* be the most edifying mode of worship for *them* with their

4 For [x] the LORD taketh pleasure in his people: he will beautify the meek with salvation.

5 Let the saints be joyful in
glory: let them sing aloud upon

their beds.

6 *Let* the high *praises* of God
be in their [1] mouth, and a two-
edged [y] sword in their hand;

x Ps. cxlvii. 11.   [1] *throat.*   *y* Heb. iv. 12.

low notions of religion; let not others
ridicule them; nor let others go to
see them as they would any other
outré performance from idle curiosity.
Such absurdities might soon die away
if they were not kept alive by the
notice which they attract, and by the
foolish curiosity of wiser people.
There are some things which are
more certain to come to an end by
neglect than they could by sober
argument; some things which live
merely because they *are* ridiculed,
and because they who practise them
are exalted into conspicuity by their
own folly, and by the idea that they
are martyrs. ¶ *Let them sing praises
unto him with the timbrel and harp.*
On these instruments, see Notes on
Isa. v. 12; Job xxi. 12; Ps. lxviii. 25;
lxxxi. 2.

4. *For the* LORD *taketh pleasure in
his people.* Let them rejoice on this
account. He loves them; he approves
their conduct; he bestows his favours
upon them. All this should add to
their joy, and fill their hearts with
gladness. Comp. Notes on Ps. xxxv.
27. The Hebrew word here rendered
"taketh pleasure" conveys the idea
of complacency, satisfaction, delight.
It is the opposite of being pained or
offended. God has complacency in
his people. He delights in their
welfare; he delights in doing them
good. ¶ *He will beautify the meek
with salvation.* The word here rendered *beautify* means to adorn, to
honour, as the sanctuary, Isa. lx. 7
(rendered *glorify*); and it here means
that the salvation which God would
bestow upon them would be of the
nature of an ornament, as if they
were clothed with costly or splendid
raiment. Comp. Ps. cxxxii. 16. The
word *meek* here means humble or
lowly, and may refer to those who
are humble in rank or condition, or

those who are humble in heart. Perhaps the two ideas are here combined.
They have not external adorning, but
God will give them an honour and
beauty in salvation which no outward
adorning could impart.

5. *Let the saints be joyful in glory.*
In the glory of their condition; in
the favour of God; in the honour
which he bestows upon them. Let
them rejoice in this; let them shout
and triumph over this. Other men
rejoice in honour; in wealth; in
houses, lands, parks, libraries, works
of art: let the saints rejoice in the
glory of being the friends of God;
in the hope of heaven. Comp. Ps.
lxxxiv. 11. ¶ *Let them sing aloud
upon their beds.* Comp. Notes on
Job xxxv. 10; Acts xvi. 25; Ps. xxxiv.
1. The idea is, that in the meditations of the night, when darkness is
around them, when alone with God,
they may find occasion for exultation
and praise. Their hearts may be full
of joy, and alone they may give expression to their joy in songs of
praise.

6. Let *the high* praises *of God* be
in their mouth. Marg., as in Heb.,
in their throat. Literally, "Praises
of God in their throat; and a sword
of two edges in their hand." That
is, In the very work of executing the
purposes of God on his enemies, there
should be the feeling and the language of praise. Their hearts should
be full of confidence in God; they
should feel that they are engaged in
his service; and while they defend
themselves, or inflict punishment on
the enemies of God, they should chant
his praise. The idea is, that even in
the work of war they might feel that
they were engaged in the service of
God, and that the passions usual in
war should be subdued and kept
under by the consciousness that they

7 To execute vengeance upon the heathen, *and* punishments upon the people;

8 To bind their kings with chains, and their nobles with fet-ters of iron;

9 To execute upon them the judgment written: this honour have all his saints. Praise ye the LORD.

are mere instruments in the hand of God to accomplish *his* purposes. Perhaps the Hebrew word rendered *high praises* — רוֹמְמוֹת, *romemoth* — may imply more than mere *praise*. It may embrace anything that is lofty and exalted, and *may* mean here that they would have the consciousness that they were engaged in high and lofty aims; that they were carrying out the great designs of God; that they were executing purposes more momentous than their own could be —even the eternal purposes of the Most High. This would give an importance, a dignity, an elevation to their conduct which could spring from no other source. ¶ *And a two-edged sword in their hand.* Literally, *a sword of edges;* that is, a sword with an edge on both sides of the blade. Roman swords were often made in this manner. They were made for piercing as well as for striking. See Notes on Heb. iv. 12.

7. *To execute vengeance upon the heathen.* To inflict punishment upon them as a recompence for their sins. The word *heathen* here means *nations.* The allusion is, doubtless, to those who had oppressed and injured the Hebrew people,—perhaps referring to those who had destroyed the city and the temple at the time of the Babylonish captivity. They were now to receive the punishment due for the wrongs which they had done to the nation; a just recompence at the hand of God, and by the instrumentality of those whom they had wronged. Comp. Notes on Ps. cxxxvii. 7–9. ¶ And *punishments upon the people.* The people of those lands. Those who had waged war with the Hebrew nation.

8. *To bind their kings with chains.* To make them prisoners and captives. This is but carrying out the idea in the previous verses, of inflicting punishment upon them for the wrongs which they had done to the people of God. There is no evidence that this refers to *a spiritual* conquest, or to a *spiritual* subjection of those nations to the true religion. The whole idea is in accordance with what is so often expressed in the Psalms—that of inflicting just punishment on the wicked. See General Introd., § 6. ¶ *And their nobles with fetters of iron.* To make them prisoners. That is, to subdue them. Captives in war, even those of elevated rank, were often led in chains to grace the triumph of conquerors.

9. *To execute upon them the judgment written.* Either, that which is written in the law in general as what is threatened to wicked men; or, that which was written for their particular case, or which they were specifically commanded to do. Comp. Deut. vii. 1, 2; xxxii. 41–43. Most probably the reference is to some particular command in this case. ¶ *This honour have all his saints.* (*a*) It *is* an honour to engage in executing or carrying out the purposes of God. As it is an honour to be a magistrate, a judge, a sheriff, a constable, a commander of an army, an admiral in a navy, to execute the purposes of a government, —an honour *sought* with great avidity among men as among the most valued distinctions of life,—why should it be *less* honourable to execute the purposes of God? Are the objects which he seeks in his administration *less* important than those which are sought among men? Are his laws of *less* importance? Are his aims *less* pure? Is there *less* of justice, and equity, and benevolence in his plans? (*b*) It is an honour which pertains to "*all* the saints"—to *all* who love and fear God—to be engaged in carrying out

PSALM CL.

PRAISE [1] ye the LORD. Praise
God in his sanctuary: praise
or executing his plans. In their own
way, and in their own sphere—it may,
indeed, be a very humble sphere—but
each and all *in* their own sphere, are
engaged in executing the purposes of
God. In the duties of a family; in
kindness to the poor; in the office of
a teacher or a magistrate; in clearing
a farm; in cultivating the land; in
building a schoolhouse; in founding
a church, a college, an asylum for the
blind, the dumb, the lame, the insane;
in contributing to send the gospel
abroad over our own land, or among
the heathen, or *in going to carry that
gospel to a benighted world,*—in some
of these ways all who are truly the
friends of God, or who are entitled to
be enrolled among the "saints of the
Lord" are, in fact, carrying out the
purposes of the Lord—the "judgments written" to guide mankind;
and man's highest honour here, as it
will be in heaven, is to carry out the
purposes of the Lord. ¶ *Praise ye
the* LORD. Hallelu-jah. It is a subject of praise and thanksgiving, it
should lead us to shout *Hallelujah,*
that we are permitted to be employed
in any way, however humble, in carrying out the Divine plans, or in accomplishing those great designs which he
contemplates toward our race.

PSALM CL.

This beautiful and animated psalm
closes the series of the Hallelujah Psalms
(cxlvi.-cl.), and appropriately also closes
the entire volume. Its author is unknown, but in respect to the object for
which it was composed there can be no
uncertainty. It was manifestly *designed,* whoever wrote it, to occupy the
very place which it does occupy,—to
complete the volume devoted to praise.
Praise is the suitable ending of the
book; praise is what the Spirit of inspiration meant to secure in the heart and
on the lips. In the review of the whole
there is occasion for praise. In view of
all that has been disclosed about God,

him in the firmament of his
power.

[1] *Hallelujah.*

about his religion, about the manifestations of his mercy and grace to his people, there is occasion for praise. After
all that has been experienced, observed,
and recorded in this book—all of trial,
sorrow, temptation, conflict, disappointment, sickness, bereavement, persecution, war, captivity, bondage, exile,
tears, pain, darkness, trouble—there is,
as the result of the whole, as there will
be at the end of our own troubled and
chequered lives, occasion for exultation,
praise, triumph,—songs, rejoicings, rap-
tures, hallelujahs. This psalm, then,
made up wholly of expressions of gratitude and praise, is an appropriate close
to the entire Book of Psalms. So may
our lives close, when its varied scenes
are over, with thanksgivings and praises,
as a proper expression in view of the
past, and as emblematic of the uninterrupted employment that awaits us in
the heavens.

1. *Praise ye the* LORD. See Notes
on Ps. cxlvi. 1. ¶ *Praise God in his
sanctuary.* His holy place; the place
where he dwells. The allusion here
is, probably, to the temple, the place
of his abode on earth. ¶ *Praise him
in the firmament of his power.* The
whole expression is equivalent to earth
and heaven;—Praise him on earth;
praise him in heaven. The word rendered *firmament* is the same which is
used in Gen. i. 6. It properly means
an expanse—a thing spread out. The
verb from which the word is derived
means to beat; then, to beat out,—
that is, to spread out by beating, as
gold is; and then, simply to *spread
out,* to expand. Comp. Ps. cxxxvi. 6;
Isa. xlii. 5; xliv. 24. In Syriac the
word means to make firm; but this
idea is not necessarily in the Hebrew
word. The idea of a *firmament* as
something *firm* is derived from the
Septuagint,—in Gen. i. 6, στερέωμα—
in this place, ἐν στερεώματι. The
Hebrew, however, merely means an
expanse—something spread out, as the
heavens *seem* to us to be "stretched
out;" and the call here is on all that

2 Praise him for his mighty acts: praise him according to his excellent greatness.

3 Praise him with the sound *z* of the [1] trumpet: praise him

z Dan. iii. 5, etc. [1] Or, *cornet*, Ps. xcviii. 6.

with the psaltery and harp.

4 Praise him with the timbrel and [2] dance: praise him with stringed instruments and organs.

[2] Or, *pipe*, Ps. cxlix. 3.

---

dwell *above* that expanse—in heaven —to unite with those on earth in his praise. It is called "the expanse *of his power*" because it is in the heavens —in the sun, the moon, the stars— that the *power* of God seems to be principally displayed.

2. *Praise him for his mighty acts.* See Notes on Ps. cxlv. 4: "One generation shall praise thy works to another, and shall declare thy *mighty acts.*" The Hebrew word is the same. The reference is to that which displays the *power* of God; the things which manifest his omnipotence. ¶ *Praise him according to his excellent greatness.* Heb., the *multitude* of his greatness. Let the praise in elevation *correspond* with this; let it be such as shall properly *express* this; let all be employed that will contribute to make this known, or that will be appropriate to this. Hence the psalmist proceeds to call on all to make use of everything, by instrument and voice, that would in any manner set forth the praise of God.

3. *Praise him with the sound of the trumpet.* Marg., *cornet.* In this verse and the verses following there is an allusion to the instruments of music which were commonly employed in Hebrew worship. The idea is, that *all* these—all that could properly express praise—*should* be used to celebrate the praises of God. Each one, with its own distinct note, and all combined in harmony, should be employed for this purpose. Most of these instruments, and many more, are now *combined* in the organ, where the instruments, instead of being played on by separate performers, are so united that they can be supplied with wind from one source—the bellows—and all played by one performer. Thus one mind directs the performance,

securing, if skilfully done, *perfect* unity and harmony. This instrument was unknown to the Hebrews. Among them, each instrument had its own performer. The *trumpet* was principally used to call the people together, but it was also an important instrument among those used by the bands of musicians that performed in the temple, as its tones are now important ones in the organ. ¶ *Praise him with the psaltery and harp.* Heb., the *nebel* and *kinnor.* See these instruments described in the Notes on Isa. v. 12. The word here rendered *psaltery* is there rendered *viol,*—"And the *harp* and the *viol,*" etc.

4. *Praise him with the timbrel.* Heb., *toph.* See this described in the Notes on Isa. v. 12. It is rendered *tabret* and *tabrets* in Gen. xxxi. 27; 1 Sam. x. 5; xviii. 6; Isa. v. 12; xxiv. 8; xxx. 32: Jer. xxxi. 4; Ezek. xxviii. 13; *timbrel* and *timbrels* in Ex. xv. 20; Judges xi. 34; 2 Sam. vi. 5; 1 Chron. xiii. 8; Job xxi. 12; Ps. lxxxi. 2; cxlix. 3; and in the margin in Jer. xxxi. 4. The word does not occur elsewhere. It was an instrument that was struck with the hands. ¶ *And dance.* See this word explained in the Notes on Ps. cxlix. 3. Dancing among the Hebrews seems to have accompanied the timbrel or tabret. See Ex. xv. 20. ¶ *Praise him with stringed instruments.* מִנִּים *minnim.* This word means *strings,* from a verb which means to divide; and the proper reference would be to *slender threads,* as if they were *divided,* or made small. It is nowhere else applied to instruments of music, but might be properly applied to a harp, a violin, a bass-viol, etc. The word *strings* is indeed applied elsewhere to instruments of music (Ps. xxxiii. 2; cxliv. 9; 1 Sam. xviii.

5 Praise him upon the loud ^a cymbals: praise him upon the high-sounding cymbals.

a 1 Chron. xv. 16, etc.

6 Let ^b every thing that hath breath praise the LORD. Praise ye the LORD.

b Rev. v. 13.

16; Isa. xxxviii. 20; Hab. iii. 19), but the Hebrew word is different. Such instruments were commonly used in the praise of God. See Notes on Ps. xxxiii. 2. ¶ *And organs.* Heb., *uggab.* See this word explained in the Notes on Job xxi. 12. It occurs elsewhere only in Gen. iv. 21; Job xxi. 12; xxx. 31;—in all of which places it is rendered *organ.* The word is derived from a verb meaning to breathe, to blow; and would be applicable to *any* wind-instrument. It here represents the whole class of wind-instruments. The word *organ* is a Greek word, and is found in the Septuagint in this place; and hence our word *organ* has been introduced into the translation. The Greek word properly denotes (*a*) something by which work is accomplished, as a machine; (*b*) a musical instrument; (*c*) the material from which anything is made; (*d*) the work itself. (*Passow. Lex.*). Our word organ, as used in music, suggests the idea of a *combination* of instruments or sounds. That idea is not found in the Hebrew word. It denotes merely a wind-instrument. Neither the Hebrews nor any of the ancient nations had an instrument that corresponded with the *organ* as we now use the term.

5. *Praise him upon the loud cymbals.* Literally, "the cymbals of sound" or hearing. That is, Let there be audibly expressed joy. The allusion here is to an instrument of music that was most distinctly *heard* in union with other instruments. The sound of the cymbal would be most clearly audible in its accompaniment of the other instruments referred to,—as the sound of cymbals, or as the "triangle" would be now. The Hebrew word rendered *cymbal* means *a tinkling, clanging, ringing,* as of metal, or of arms; then, a whirring, as of wings (comp. Notes on Isa. xviii. 1); then,

any tinkling or clanging instrument, as a fish-spear or harpoon; then, cymbals, instruments of music. The cymbal, as now used, is an instrument of brass, in a circular form, like a dish, producing, when two are struck together, a sharp, ringing sound.— *Webster.* An instrument of this kind is evidently referred to here. The word occurs in the Bible in the following places only:—Deut. xxviii. 42, rendered *locust;* 2 Sam. vi. 5, rendered, as here, *cymbal;* Job xli. 7, rendered *fish-spears;* and Isa. xviii. 1, rendered *shadowing with.* ¶ *Praise him upon the high-sounding cymbals.* The cymbals of joyful voice. On the word *teruah,* rendered *high,* see Notes on Ps. lxxxix. 16. A loud, lofty sound or shout, as on the reception of a conqueror, is the idea here; and the sense is, that the praise of God was to be celebrated with that which would in the highest sense express joy and triumph.

6. *Let everything that hath breath praise the* LORD. All living things in the air, the earth, the waters. Let there be one universal burst of praise. Let his praises be celebrated not only with instruments of music, but let all living beings unite in that praise; let a breathing universe combine in one solemn service of praise. ¶ *Praise ye the* LORD. Hallelu-jah. Thus, at the end of all the trials, the conflicts, the persecutions, the sorrows, the joys recorded in this book, the psalmist gives utterance to feelings of joy, triumph, transport, rejoicing; and thus at the end of all,—when the affairs of this world shall be closed,—when the church shall have passed through all its trials, shall have borne all its persecutions, shall have suffered all that it is appointed to suffer,—when the work of redemption shall be complete, and all the ransomed of the Lord shall have been recovered from sin, and

shall be saved, — that church, all heaven, the whole universe, shall break forth in one loud, long, triumphant Hallelujah. "The ransomed of the Lord shall return, and come to Zion with songs, and everlasting joy upon their heads: they shall obtain joy and gladness; and sorrow and sighing shall flee away," Isa. xxxv. 10.

Here I close my exposition of this Book, and with it all that I purpose or expect to prepare in attempting to furnish a commentary on the Holy Scriptures. The volumes which I have prepared have occupied me daily, almost without intermission, for nearly forty years of my life; and now, at sixty-eight years of age, and with the diminished power of vision with which it has pleased God to afflict me, I can hope to attempt no more. More than a generation has passed away while I have been engaged in these labours; and the finishing of this work, and the reason why I cannot hope to do more, admonish me that I am soon to follow that generation to the grave, and that all my work must soon be ended.

A man who has written so much may be pardoned, perhaps, for this personal reflection at the end of so long a journey, and in view of the thought that his labour of life, in this respect, is ended. It has been remarked that "the close of a literary undertaking is always contemplated as an event of great interest to the feelings of an author. It is the termination of his labours, and the commencement of his hopes and fears."[*] Mr. Gibbon has thought proper to record the precise day and hour in which he concluded his "Decline and Fall of the Roman Empire." "I have presumed," he says, "to mark the moment of conception:—I shall now commemorate the hour of my final deliverance. It was on the day, or rather night, of the 27th of June, 1787, between the hours of eleven and twelve, that I wrote the last lines of the last page, in a summer-house in my garden. After laying down my pen, I took several turns in a *berceau* or covered walk of acacias, which commands a prospect of the country, the lake, and the mountains. The air was temperate, the sky was serene, the silver orb of the moon was reflected from the waters, and all nature was silent. I will not dissemble the first emotions of joy on the recovery of my freedom, and, perhaps, the establishment of my fame. But my pride was soon humbled, and a sober melancholy was spread over my mind, by the idea that I had taken an everlasting leave of an old and agreeable companion, and that whatever might be the future date of my history, the life of the historian might be short and precarious."[†]

Nor is Pope's reflection less affecting. "The morning after my exit," he says, "the sun will rise as bright as ever, the flowers smell as sweet, the plants spring as green, the world will proceed in its old course, and people laugh and marry as they were used to do."

I may not compare myself with these men; but I am conscious of similar emotions, as I bring to a close this long series of works, designed to illustrate the Bible. God has blessed me in this work far above all that I had any reason to anticipate; and while I have cause to believe that he has made it useful in some measure to the world, and venture to hope that he *will* make it useful when the fingers which now move this pen shall be stiff in the grave, he has made it, during nearly forty years, a source of constant blessing to my own soul. In the review of this part of my life I can now conceive of no way possible in which I could have more profitably spent the early hours of each day

---

* *Life of Cowper*, vol. iii. London, 1835.

† *Miscellaneous Works*, vol. i., p. 170. Dublin, 1796.

than in the study of the Bible. That it has required some sacrifice to do it,—that it has demanded some resoluteness of purpose and steadiness of aim,—that it has required some discipline of mind to keep me firm to the purpose, is indeed true; but the very discipline—the necessity of carrying out a fixed purpose—has been useful to me, and apart from any other results would in itself have been worth all which it has cost me.

I cannot close this work without emotion. I cannot lay down my pen at the end of this long task without feeling that with me the work of life is nearly over. Yet I could close it at no better place than in finishing the exposition of *this* book; and the language with which the Book of Psalms itself closes seems to me to be eminently appropriate to all that I have experienced. All that is past,—all in the prospect of what is to come,—calls for a long, a joyful, a triumphant HALLELUJAH.

APPENDIX.

PSALM XC.

The Fourth Book of Psalms. The Fourth Book of the Psalter numbers, like the Third Book, seventeen psalms. It comprises, along with the psalm of Moses, those of the last hundred years of the Jewish monarchy, up to the date of the Babylonish captivity. At what time they were collected and arranged in their present order there is no certain evidence to show; perhaps not till the days of Nehemiah, when the Fifth Book of the Psalter was also arranged, and the canon of Old Testament Scripture closed. Of the psalms composing the Fourth Book, Ps. xc. is entitled "A Prayer of Moses the Man of God;" Ps. ci. ciii. bear the name of David; Ps. cii. is "A Prayer of the Afflicted," &c. In the superscriptions of the rest there is no indication of the authorship; they are probably the productions of the sons of Asaph, who formed during this period the only surviving temple-choir.

These psalms do not reflect, to the same extent as those of Book III., the political events and vicissitudes of their period. They were all written (excepting, of course, the prayer of Moses) after the irrevocable doom of destruction upon Jerusalem for the wickedness of Manasseh had been solemnly pronounced. In consequence of that doom, the expected full redemption of Israel and the glorification of the sovereignty of the house of David in the person of the promised Messiah were in the eyes of the people indefinitely deferred; and the continuity of progress to the future of glory being thus destroyed, the immediate political events of the times lost in great measure their prospective interest. Whatever impatient hopes the events of the reign of Hezekiah had served to nurture of a speedy fulfilment of God's promises to Israel, must have yielded with many to the recklessness of despair and indifference; but meanwhile the faith of the true servants of God was being disciplined, and their expectations spiritualized. Deeply prophetical as are many of the psalms on which we now enter, the result of the dissociation of the anticipations of the future from the contemplations of the present is that they depict the events of the future rather in their divine than in their human aspect; they speak not so much of the truth which should spring out of the earth as of the righteousness which should look down from heaven. These psalms have a freshness of their own; not the freshness of national youth, nor that of national rejuvenescence; but rather the freshness which will ever spring from solid depth of faith. They are the utterance of the traveller who, finding but little of interest in the long weary plain that extends around him, rejoices nevertheless in gazing on the glories of the distant hills; and, in the assurance that he will not fail to reach them in the end, contentedly plods on along his level road, aware that the journey, however dull, is necessary, and trusting that in the Lord even his present labours will not have been in vain.— *Thrupp.*

There is a very general concurrence in ascribing the ninetieth Psalm to Moses. The accuracy of the superscription is admitted by all the ancient versions, by Luther, Calvin, Fabricius, &c., by Tholuck, Delitzsch, Hengstenberg, Alexander, and Binnie, and by modern commentators generally. Even those who range themselves on the other side, such as Hupfeld and Ewald, seem to speak doubtfully, and admit that the internal evidence is of the strongest possible kind. We give one or two passages from distinguished writers on the side of the ascription to Moses:—

"There are important *internal* reasons

which may be urged in favour of the composition of the psalm by Moses, as announced in the title. The poem bears throughout the character of high antiquity; there is no other psalm which so decidedly conveys the impression of being the original expression of the feelings to which it gives utterance. There is, moreover, no other psalm which stands so much *by itself*, in regard to its fundamental tone and peculiarities, for which parallel passages furnish so little kindred matter in characteristic peculiarities. On the other hand, there occurs a series of striking allusions to the Pentateuch, especially to the poetical passages, and, above all others, to Deut. xxxii. (compare the exposition), allusions which are of another kind than those which occur in other passages in the Psalms, and which do not bear like them the character of *borrowing.* Luther, in the following quotation, intimates that even here the deep seriousness of the lawgiver may be seen: 'Just as Moses acts in teaching the law, so does he in this prayer. For he preaches death, sin, and condemnation, in order that he may alarm the proud who are secure in their sins, and that he may set before their eye their sin and evil, concealing, hiding nothing.' The strong prominence given to the doctrine of *death as the wages of sin* is especially characteristic, a doctrine which is not of frequent occurrence in Scripture, and especially not so in the Psalms, and which is proclaimed as distinctly and impressively as it is here only in the Pentateuch, Gen. ii. and iii., and in those ordinances of the ceremonial law which threaten death.

"The reasons which have been adduced *against* the composition of the psalm by Moses are of very little weight. The objection that ver. 10, where the length of human life is limited to seventy, or, at the most, eighty years, stands opposed to Deut. xxxiv. 7, according to which Moses reached the age of 120, is disposed of by the remark, that Moses, throughout the whole psalm, does not speak in *his own name*, but in that of *the people.* It is obvious from Deut. xiv. 22, 23, that among the Israelites at that time the exceptions to the general rule, as to the duration of human life, were much fewer than at ordinary times. Koester's assertion that ver. 15 supposes a long period of suffering, and scarcely applies to the Israelites in the

wilderness, who rather beheld the glorious deeds of Jehovah, is disposed of as soon as we direct our attention to 'that terrible oath which God had flashed down upon them in Num. xiv.' Eight-and-thirty years spent amidst the gradual destruction of men lying under the curse, were well fitted to call forth the prayer, 'Make us glad according to the days in which thou hast afflicted us, the years during which we have seen evil;' they are sufficient to explain 'the melancholy view of life' which here meets us, and the dread earnestness 'with which he instructs us of our melancholy necessities:' no glass was more suitable than this for giving a view of the common condition of human life. Finally, the assertion that the psalm could not have been composed by Moses, because it resembles the other psalms in language and general poetical structure, is an *a priori* assertion, which may be met with at least as much force by another, that Moses, 'the fountain out of which all the prophets have drunk divine wisdom,' gave at first the tone no less for prophecy, Deut. xxxii. and xxxiii., than for psalm poetry."—*Hengstenberg.*

"Viewed with reference to its author, this psalm is the utterance of the feelings of the great prophet and lawgiver of Israel during his pilgrimage through the wilderness. It was probably written towards the end of the forty years' wanderings (see ver. 15); but its solemnity makes it more likely that it was the result of the long and habitual contemplations of Moses during those wanderings, than that it was occasioned by any single incident. The leading thought of the psalm is that to which vent is given in the first verse; that God is the eternal abiding-place of his people. This thought is first expanded in ver. 2. 'There is indeed,'—so runs the current of the prophet's meditation, —'an earth, which some might deem their home, and which, with all its ancient hills, might verily be called permanent as compared with the short-lived beings that inhabit it; for across its fields have flitted the living bodies, and beneath its soil have rested the bones of successive generations of men, who, from the swiftness with which they passed away, knew nothing of each other, though the earth meanwhile remained the same, and experienced no sensible change. Yet even this earth is itself but the thing of a day in comparison of Him whose infinity of existence no language can express, and who from everlasting to everlasting is God: it is therefore in the Creator, rather than in the creature, that we recognize our true abiding-place.' In order further to illustrate the everlastingness and power of God, they are contrasted in ver. 3–6 with the transitoriness of man; as also, in ver. 7–11, with his misery, the result of the divine wrath upon his sin. Ver. 12, which stands in connection with the preceding, contains a short petition that by the contemplation of his own impotence man may acquire a heart of wisdom, so as to learn that God is his abiding-place indeed."—*Thrupp.*

"This psalm is one of the oldest of the inspired utterances. It is the prayer which is read over the mortal dust of some hundreds of the children of men every week in London alone. And so used, none of us finds it antiquated. The lapse of 3000 years has not made it necessary to discard this clause and that. Words that described the relation of the children of Israel to the eternal God, serve still to express the devotion of English hearts turning to God in their sorrow. As these grand words are uttered, the curtain that hangs round our life seems to draw back, and we see beyond depths that we dreamed not of. From time and the slow succession of events, from the minutes and the hours that seem so long and so many, we turn to God, whose eternal nature was as it now is even when the world was formed, and to whom a thousand years are no more than the middle watch of the night is to a sound sleeper. Nations that seem established for ever are carried off down the roaring cataract of time; men full of pride, and glory, and power, grow and perish like grass; and God alone remains unchangeable, the same yesterday, and to-day, and for ever."—Archbishop of York's sermons in *Perowne.*

"Three thousand years and more have passed away since the congregation of Israel made the solitudes of the wilderness vocal with the plaintive music of this ninetieth psalm. There is probably not another song now sung in any nation under heaven that possesses such a hoary antiquity. And yet there is about it the freshness of a perpetual youth. In what nation have God's people ceased to employ it? It forms part of the English Order for the Burial of the Dead, and in all Christian nations is in one form or another devoted to a similar use. Moreover, as each new year comes round, bringing its train of saddening memories and summoning us to count our days, who does not turn to the prayer of Moses for the most adequate expression of the thoughts and feelings awakened by the season? In the Protestant churches of Hungary it is sung every New Year's-Day, and the same custom is widely prevalent in other countries. It is a solemnizing and stimulating thought, that when we lift up our voices to the Eternal in this psalm, we put ourselves into communion with the church of all generations and of every nation, we yield our hearts to the guidance of a song given three-and-thirty centuries ago by the inspiration of the Holy Spirit, and which has been a fountain of pensive comfort to God's saints in all the hundred generations that have lived and died since its notes first awoke the echoes of the desert."—*Binnie.*

11. *Who knows the power of thine anger? even according to thy fear, so is thy wrath.* The English version is obscure. The common interpretation is that God's wrath is as terrible as any man apprehends it to be; that those fears of the Deity are not vain bugbears, but are most just, and are vindicated by the terrible effects of the Divine wrath upon mankind. Or, God's wrath is equal to the apprehensions which the most thoughtful and serious people have of it. So Pool and Henry. The real meaning of the words seems to us best brought out, and the connection with the general subject of the psalm best maintained, by the translation of Hengstenberg, Alexander, and others, which unites the two clauses of the text; and makes of both one interrogation implying the strongest possible negation—"Who knows the power of thine anger, and according to thy fear, thy wrath?" According to thy fear then has the sense "as true piety or reverence for God demands." No one has a just sense of the Divine wrath, or knows and feels it as it ought to be known and felt. We give the following from Hengstenberg, who quotes Luther largely:—

On ver. 11, Luther: "From this point he shows why and for whose sake he had given this narrative; for the sake, namely, of unfeeling sinners, in order that they may be brought to a sense of their misery. For this is the greatest misery that we men live in such great manifold innumerable distresses, have such a short life, and are in perpetual danger, yea, certain prospect of eternal death, and yet do not feel all this, nor know it sufficiently. Who can sufficiently express such stupidity!" The expression, "who knows the power of thy wrath," equivalent to "thy wrath as it is made known in the brevity of our existence, the power of death in all its strength," is in the first instance an expression of painful *lamentation* over the inconceivable blindness of men; it however contains within it the heartfelt wish that it may be otherwise, and the *prayer* that God would alter it, which in ver. 12 rises out of the lamentation. The הורע there refers manifestly to the ידע here. Luther: "This complaint also contains a prayer in it. For Moses wishes that such pestilential security may be torn out of his heart, and out of the hearts of all men, and that all hearts may be animated by faith, so that men may believe that such a thing is true, and may be alarmed at such great wrath of God." "As thy fear" is to be understood as equivalent to "in proportion as is demanded by that fear of thee, that piety which is becoming in thy people." Several explain after the example of Venema: according to thy dreadfulness, according to the infinite measure of which in God, are his wrath against sin, and his punishment of sin. But "the fear of God" is a phrase of constant occurrence in the sense of "fear *before* God" (compare Deut. ii. 25; Ps. v. 7), and, on the other hand, there is only one passage which can be referred to in the sense of dreadfulness—viz. Eze. i. 18, a writer who supplies so many anomalous expressions, and even in this one passage, the above sense depends upon a false exposition, compare Gesen. *Thes.*—For what object the psalmist, in ver. 12, wishes his days to be numbered, appears from the reference of the הורע to the ידע of the preceding verse, according to which, to number the days, and to know the wrath of God must be strictly connected together. May God, the sense is, lead us to lay rightly to heart the brevity of our life, thus cause us to know the greatness of his wrath, the depth of our corruption, and in this way lead us to repentance. Luther: "Such a thing would never have come into my mind as to pray for this, if I had not seen that Moses prayed here for it with all earnestness and valour. For I thought that the hearts of all men were as full of fear and terror as mine is. But if we carefully examine we shall find there are scarcely ten in ten thousand moved by these things as they ought to be; all the others live as if there were no God and no death. This is the greatest misery, and the one to be most deeply deplored, that men even in death dream of life. There are certainly to be found some men of experience who feel this misery very severely without any such prayer, but the greater part do not feel it; for these generally live in such a way that they value their moment of life as if it were an eternal existence." —*Hengstenberg.*

12. *So teach us to number our days,* &c. The serious consideration of our lives' frailty and shortness will confer to our right valuation (or esteem) of things, and consequently to our well-placing, and our duly moderating our cares, affections, and endeavours about them. . . . To begin with that which takes the chief place, which the world most dotes on, which seems most great and eminent among men; secular state and grandeur, might and prowess, honour and reputation, favour and applause of men, all the objects of human pride and ambition: of this kind St. Peter thus pronounces, *All the glory of men is as the flower of the grass; the grass is dried up, and the flower thereof doth fall off;* it is as the flower of the grass, how specious soever, yet the most fading and failing part thereof; the grass itself will soon wither, and the flower doth commonly fall off before that. We cannot hold this flower of worldly glory beyond our short time of life; and we may easily much sooner be deprived of it: many tempests of fortune may beat it down, many violent hands may crop it; it is apt of itself to fade upon the stalk; however the sun (the influence of age and time) will assuredly burn and dry it up, with our life that upholds it. . . . Perhaps, could it, without much care, trouble, and hazard, continue for ever, or for a long time, it might be thought somewhat considerable: but since its duration is uncertain and short; since *man in honour abideth not, but is like the beasts that perish;* that they who look so *like gods,* and are called so, and are worshipped as such, *yet must die like men,* like men, yea *like sheep shall be laid in the grave;* since,

as it is said of the king of Babylon in Isaiah, *their pomp must be brought down to the grave;* seeing that a moment of time shall extinguish all their lustre, and still all that tumult about them; that they must be disrobed of their purple, and be clothed with corruption; and that their so spacious and splendid palaces must soon be exchanged for close darksome coffins; that both their own breath and the breath of them who now applaud them, must be stopped; that they who now bow to them, may presently trample on them; and they who to-day trembled at their presence may the morrow scornfully insult their memory. *Is this the man* (will they say, as they did of that great king) *who made the earth to tremble, that did shake kingdoms; that made the world as a wilderness, and destroyed the kingdoms thereof?* Since this is the fate of the greatest and most glorious among men, what reason can there be to admire their condition, to prize such vain and short-lived pre-eminences? For who can account it a great happiness to be styled and respected as a prince, to enjoy all the powers and prerogatives of highest dignity for a day or two; then being obliged to descend into a sordid and despicable estate? Who values the fortune of him that is brought forth upon the stage to act the part of a prince; though he be attired there, and attended as such, hath all the garb and ceremony, the ensigns and appurtenances of majesty about him, speaks and behaves himself imperiously, is flattered and worshipped accordingly; yet who in his heart doth adore this idol, doth admire this mockery of greatness? Why not? Because, after an hour or two the play is over, and this man's reign is done. And what great difference is there between this and the greatest worldly state? Between Alexander in the history and Alexander on the stage? Are not (in the psalmist's account) *all our years spent as a tale that is told?*— Barrow, *Sermons.*

PSALMS XCI.—C.

General remarks on this decade of Psalms. The eve of the captivity was blessed with psalms which take rank amongst the brightest and the most joyous the church ever sang. As the coming on of night brings into view the far-off starry worlds, so God made choice of the age when the temporal glories of David's house were sinking into dark-

ness, for disclosing to the faith of the godly the higher glories he had in store for that house and for his people. . . . The decline of the temporal grandeur of the nation was fitted, as it was no doubt intended, to wean God's people from that transitory glory, and to prepare them for listening to predictions respecting a more excellent. It was at this epoch, accordingly, that the divine purposes regarding the church and the world, in the latter days, began to be fully opened up by the prophets, and especially by Isaiah. Assuming that the predicted captivity would certainly come to pass, they spoke of a happy return to Zion; and with their announcement of that return were mingled intimations regarding the advent of the Messiah, his sufferings and consequent glory, the mission of the Comforter, the calling of the Gentiles, the establishment of the kingdom of God in all the earth. Occasionally, as in Is. xii., the predictions of the prophets blossom into song. It would have been strange if, at such a time, the stock of psalmody in actual use had not been enriched with an increment of new psalms,— anthems in which the church might express her faith in the disclosures God had made, and the gladness with which they filled her heart.

Every devout reader will remember psalms of the character anticipated. The middle of the Psalter derives a peculiar brightness from a constellation of them; the decade, I mean, which closes with Ps. c. With perhaps one or two exceptions, all the ten, from Ps. xci.-c., belong to the prophetic order. They are Messianic in the sense of celebrating the kingdom of Christ, although not Messianic in the narrower sense of celebrating his person. They soar above the level of the Old Testament economy, several of them carrying the soul forward and upward to a state of things such as the apostolical church itself never saw. Dr. Delitzsch has, with much felicity, entitled them *apocalyptic psalms:* some of them I should prefer to call the *Songs of the Millennium.* Ps. c., for instance, how grandly does it anticipate the millennial time, and summon all the nations to unite in the high praises of the Lord! . . . The Ninety-third is another star in this constellation. The drift of it cannot be better expressed than in the two words with which it opens, JEHOVAH REIGNETH. It is a kind of proclamation in which God's people are invited to declare before men and angels that the Lord is King, He and He only. It is the response of the church to the preaching of the gospel, so rapturously hailed in Isaiah—the preaching of the message "that bringeth good tidings, that publisheth peace; that bringeth good tidings of good, that publisheth salvation; that saith unto Zion, Thy God reigneth."—*Binnie.*

PSALM XCI.

There are no marks of date in the psalm. The author and the occasion are alike unknown. Hengstenberg remarks as follows:—"Several expositors have incorrectly assumed the occasion to have been a destructive *disease.* How God affords protection at such an emergency is indeed brought prominently forward in ver. 6, and perhaps with the design that the church should use this psalm, among other occasions, also in a season of pestilence, as it has done at all times: among all the psalms, no one is more suitable for this purpose. But this reference, so far from being the exclusive, is not even once the preponderating one, which it would have been had the psalm been called forth by such an occasion. According to a correct exposition, it occurs only in the verse above referred to. And even here it is oppression arising from enemies that occupies the foreground, as is usually the case in the psalm, among the dangers against which the protection of God is sufficient.

"The alternation of *thou* and *I* in the psalm has led many expositors to divide it among alternating choruses. But that this is not the case is clear from the fact that in this way we are obliged to tear asunder what is manifestly connected together; thus, in the introduction, where the first portion in the first verse must belong to the first chorus, and the second in the second verse to the second chorus; next in ver. 9, where the change occurs in one and the same verse, and where the first portion allotted to a particular chorus is remarkably distinguished for its being far too short and bald. The fact, however, upon which this hypothesis leans may be far more easily explained by supposing that the psalmist speaks at one time from his own person to the soul of the righteous one who is in danger, and revives its courage, while at another time he expresses confidence from the soul of

the righteous man; and thus in that pleasant alternation which forms the characteristic peculiarity of the psalm, he employs at one time the *thou* in the character of *teacher*, and at another time the *I* in the character of *scholar.* If we take a right view of the *I* throughout the psalm, keeping our attention not so much upon the person of the psalmist, as upon those who were intended to appropriate the psalm to themselves, the difference between the *thou* and the *I* will be felt as less marked, and will occasion scarcely any difficulty. Under the *thou* an *I* is everywhere concealed; for the psalmist teaches what the person for whose use the psalm was designed ought to acknowledge: and, in like manner, under the *I* there is a *thou;* for the person using the psalm adopts language put into his mouth by the psalmist, who is only a *thou* in disguise. The call of instruction in Scripture (this is the meaning of the alternation) ought always to be responded to by the acknowledgment of the hearer."

5, 6. *Thou shalt not be afraid for the terror by night,* &c. "Here is, first," says Henry, "great danger supposed, the mention of it is enough to frighten us; night and day we lie exposed, and those that are apt to be timorous will, in neither period, think themselves safe. When we are retired into our chambers, our beds, and have made all as safe as we can about us, yet there is terror by night, from thieves and robbers, winds and storms, beside those things that are creatures of fancy and imagination, which are often most frightful of all; we read of *fear in the night,* Can. iii. 8. There is also a *pestilence that walketh in darkness,* as that was which slew the first-born of the Egyptians and the army of the Assyrians. No locks or bars can shut out diseases, while we carry about with us in our bodies the seeds of them. But surely in the daytime, when we can look about us, we are not so much in danger; yes, there is an *arrow that flieth by day* too, and yet flies unseen; there is a destruction that wasteth at high noon, when we are awake and have all our friends about us; even then we cannot secure ourselves, nor can they secure us. It was in the daytime that that pestilence wasted which was sent to chastise David for numbering the people, on occasion of which some think this psalm was penned. But, secondly, here is great security promised to believers in the midst of this danger, '*Thou shalt not be afraid*, God by his grace will keep thee from disquieting, distrustful fear (that fear which hath torment), in the midst of the greatest dangers. Wisdom shall keep thee from being causelessly afraid, and faith shall keep thee from being inordinately afraid. Thou shalt not be afraid of the arrow, as knowing that, though it may hit thee, it cannot hurt thee; if it take away the natural life, yet it shall be so far from doing any prejudice to the spiritual life, that it shall be its perfection.' A believer *needs not* fear, and therefore *should not* fear, any arrow, because the point is off, the poison is out; *O death, where is thy sting?* It is also under divine direction, and will hit where God appoints, and not otherwise. Every bullet has its commission. Whatever is done, our heavenly Father's will is done; and we have no reason to be afraid of that."

11. *He shall give his angels charge over thee.* This is added by the psalmist expressly with the view of obviating any fears which might arise from our infirmity; so that we cannot fail to be struck with the benignant condescension of God in thus not only forgiving our diffidence, but proposing the means by which it may be best removed. Does he exhibit himself to us as a fortress and shield, proffer the shadow of his protection, make himself known to us as a habitation in which we may abide, and stretch out his wings for our defence? Surely we are chargeable with the worst ingratitude if we are not satisfied with promises so abundantly full and satisfactory. If we tremble to think of his majesty, he presents himself to us under the lowly figure of the hen: if we are terrified at the power of our enemies, and the multitude of dangers by which we are beset, he reminds us of his own invincible power, which extinguishes every opposing force. When even all these attempts to encourage us have been tried, and he finds that we still linger and hesitate to approach him, or cast ourselves upon his sole and exclusive protection, he next makes mention of the angels and proffers them as guardians of our safety. As an additional illustration of his indulgent mercy and compassion for our weakness, he represents those whom he has ready for our defence as being a numerous host; he does not assign one solitary angel to each saint, but commissions the whole armies of heaven to keep watch over every individual believer. It is the individual believer whom the psalmist addresses, as we read also Ps. xxxiv. 7, that "angels encamp round about them that fear him." We may learn from this that there is no truth in the idea that each saint has his own peculiar guardian angel; and it is of no little consequence to consider that as our enemies are numerous, so also are the friends to whom our defence is intrusted. It were something no doubt to know that even one angel was set over us with this commission, but it adds weight to the promise when we are informed that the charge of our safety is committed to a numerous host, as Elisha was enabled, by a like consideration, to despise the great army of adversaries which was arrayed against him (2 Ki. vi. 16). Nor is this inconsistent with the passages of Scripture which seem to speak as if a distinct angel were assigned to each individual. It is evident that God employs his angels in different ways, setting one angel over several whole nations, and again several angels over one man. There is no necessity that we should be nice and scrupulous in inquiring into the exact manner in which they minister together for our safety; it is enough that, knowing from the authority of an apostle the fact of their being appointed ministers to us, we should rest satisfied of their being always intent upon their commission. We read elsewhere of their readiness to obey and execute the commands of God; and this must go to strengthen our faith, since their exertions are made use of by God for our defence.

The psalmist, in the passage now before us, speaks of the members of the church generally; and yet the devil did not wrest the words when, in his temptation in the wilderness, he applied them particularly to Christ. It is true that he is constantly seeking to pervert and corrupt the truth of God; but, so far as general principles are concerned, he can put a specious gloss upon things, and is a sufficiently acute theologian. It is to be considered that when our whole human family were banished from the divine favour, we ceased to have anything in common with the angels, and they to have any communication with us. It was Christ, and he only, who, by removing the ground of separation, reconciled the angels to us; this being his proper office, as the apostle observes (Eph. i. 10), to gather together in one what had been dispersed both in heaven and on earth. This was represented to the holy patriarch Jacob under the figure of a ladder (Gen. xxviii. 12); and, in allusion to our being united into one collective body with the angels, Christ said, "Afterwards ye shall see the heavens opened and the angels of God ascending and descending."—*Calvin.*

6. *A brutish man knoweth not, neither doth a fool understand this.* Comp. Ps. lxxiii. 22. Were God's thoughts less deep and glorious, did he repay the wicked at every particular transgression immediately with his punishment, and did he bestow salvation immediately upon the righteous according to the canon which Job's friends with their limited views lay down, the government of the world would become plain even to the dark eye of ungodliness. But its depth makes it a *secret*, the understanding of which very often in times of conflict is withheld even from the pious, as is manifest from the example of Job and the author of Ps. lxxiii., and in which there is always much that may be learned. He who has got a deep insight into this secret, and has seen that the conduct of God towards *his people* is always and only *grace*, even though often under the deepest covering; and that his conduct towards the wicked is always only *wrath*, even when they flourish and blossom, he alone can cry out, "O the depth of the riches," &c., and to him *these* works of God appear greater and more glorious still than the works of creation. On ver. 7 comp. Ps. xxxvii. 38. The *annihilation* of the wicked comes into notice here as the basis of the *deliverance of the righteous*, which is the proper theme of the psalm. Arnd: "Nothing, except it be of God, can stand, whether it be skill, or riches, or honour, or power. It rises and flourishes to appearance, but in the end it is only a thistle bush and a noxious weed, good for nothing but the fire."—*Hengstenberg.*

12. *He shall flourish like the palm-tree; he shall grow up like a cedar in Lebanon.* Of the wicked he had just said before, "When the wicked spring as the grass, and when all the workers of iniquity do flourish, it is that they shall be destroyed for ever." They flourish as the *grass*, which to-day is, and to-morrow is cast into the oven.

What a contrast with the worthlessness, the weakness, transitoriness, and destiny of grass—in a warm country too —are the palm-tree, and the cedar in Lebanon! They are evergreens. How beautifully, how firmly, how largely they grow! How strong and lofty is the cedar! How upright, and majestic, and tall the palm-tree—the palm also bears fruit, called dates, like bunches of grapes. It sometimes yields a hundredweight at once.—*Jay.*

Those that be planted in the house of the Lord, shall flourish in the courts of our God. The allusion is striking. It compares the house of God to a garden, or fine, well-watered soil, favourable to the life, and verdure, and fertility of the trees fixed there. The reason is, that in the sanctuary we have the communion of saints. *There* our fellowship is with the Father, and with his Son Jesus Christ. *There* are dispensed the ordinances of religion, and the Word of truth. *There* God commandeth the blessing, even life for evermore. "Blessed is the man that heareth me, watching daily at my gates, waiting at the posts of my doors." They that wait upon the Lord renew their strength. Hence, from their own experience, as well as from the word of promise, they are increasingly induced to say with David, "I will dwell in the house of the Lord for ever."—*Jay.*

They shall still bring forth fruit in old age. This is to show the permanency of their principles, and to distinguish them from natural productions—

"The plants of grace shall ever live;
Nature decays, but grace must thrive:
Time, that doth all things else impair,
Still makes them flourish strong and fair."

The believer does not escape all the effects of years. The eye may grow dim; the ear become dull of hearing. But as the outward man perisheth, the inward man is renewed day by day. The young Christian is lovely, like a tree in the blossoms of spring; the aged Christian is valuable, like a tree in autumn, bending with ripe fruit. We therefore look for something superior in old disciples. More deadness to the world, the vanity of which they have had more opportunities to see—more meekness of wisdom—more disposition to make sacrifices for the sake of peace —more maturity of judgment in divine things—more confidence in God—more richness of experience.—*Jay.*

PSALM XCIII.

3. *The floods have lifted up, O Lord,*
&c. Various meanings have been attached to this verse. Some think there
is an allusion to the violent assaults
made upon the church by her enemies,
and the goodness of God seen in re-
straining them. Others are of opinion
that the words should be taken literally, and not figuratively, in this sense:
Though the noise of many waters be
terrible, and the waves of the sea more
fearful still, God is more terrible than
all. I would not be inclined to insist
too nicely upon any comparison that
may have been intended. I have no
doubt the psalmist sets forth the power
of God by adducing one brief illustration out of many which might have
been given, intimating that we need
not go further for a striking instance
of divine power—one that may impress
us with an idea of his tremendous
majesty—than to the floods of waters,
and agitations of the ocean; as in Ps.
xxix. 4, the mighty voice of God is said
to be in the thunder. God manifests
his power in the sound of the floods,
and in the tempestuous waves of the
sea, in a way calculated to excite our
reverential awe.—*Calvin.*

To this the translator of Calvin has
added the following apposite note:—
"Dr. Morison, after stating the opinion
of Mudge, who thinks that this psalm
was composed on the occasion of some
violent inundation, which threatened a
general confusion to the world, adds,
'It is more probable, perhaps, that the
floods spoken of are entirely figurative;
and that they represent in eastern
phrase those powerful enemies by whom
the peace of David and the ancient
church was so often disturbed. But
though the floods were lifted high, and
threatened destruction to those who
were within their reach, yet Jehovah
was seen, as it were, riding on their
most tempestuous billows, and amidst
their mightiest tumult, his throne was
unshaken and his kingdom unmoved.' In
support of this view he refers to other
passages of Scripture, as Is. viii. 7, 8;
xvii. 12, 13; and Job xlvi. 7, 8, where the
confederated enemies of God's church
are compared to the tempestuous waves
of the mighty ocean, which roll one
after another with resistless fury upon
the storm-tossed bark."

5. *Holiness becometh thine house, O
Lord, for ever.* Hengstenberg quotes

Amyrald: "Thy house shall by thy
sacred august presence remain for ever
undefiled, nor shall it be violated or
polluted by the insolence of thine enemies." He adds, "The *holiness* which
becomes the house of such a God (comp.
Ps. xxxiii. 1) must be preserved for it
by himself. It is becoming in God that
he take care that it be not *desecrated*
by impious hand, comp. Ps. lxxiv.;
lxxix. 1. He can at times, in punishment of the sins of his people, give it
up to be laid waste by the ungodly
world, but he must always see to it
that it rise like a phœnix again from
the ashes, so that its holiness is again
restored to it. And he *has* seen to this.
In room of the *first* house destroyed by
the Chaldeans, there arose the *second*,
and the second was not destroyed till
it had become a mere shell without a
kernel, and a glorious new erection of
the house of God had come into life in
the Christian church. The *world* did
not destroy it; but God himself took
down the poor provisional building
when the proper one was completed:
and this last one shall preserve its
sanctity at all times in spite of all the
assaults of the destruction-loving world.
The fundamental passage is Ps. xxiii. 6,
'I dwell in the house of the Lord for
ever,' לְאֹרֶךְ יָמִים, properly 'for length of
days.' The import in both passages is
essentially the same. For the house on
behalf of whose preservation the psalmist
here expresses his confident hope is the
house where the Lord dwells with his
people and they with him; and it comes
into view only in connection with this
property. The preservation of the
house for its own sake is not what is
spoken of, but only in so far as it is
the seat of the church; it is therefore
the preservation of the *church* that lies
near the psalmist's heart. The common
translation is, the *maintenance of holiness* becomes thy house, it is becoming
that it should be held holy by us.
By this mistranslation the point of the
psalm is destroyed. There are to be
urged against it: that the thought in
the connection is wholly a strange one
—the design of the psalm is evidently
to impart confident reliance on the
protection of the Lord in oppressions
from the world—that in Ps. xciii. xcii.,
and even in xci., the subject spoken of
is what God does for his people, not
what they should do for him; besides
this, we have the analogous conclusion
in Ps. xcii., the parallelism, the funda-

mental passage Ps. xxiii. 6, and also 'for the length of days,' and finally, the קדש, which does not signify maintenance of holiness, but holiness."— *Hengstenberg.*

PSALM XCIV.

11. *The Lord knoweth the thoughts of man, that they are vanity.* Surely it is the design of God in all his dispensations, and by all the discoveries of his Word, to stain the pride of all flesh. The dust is the proper place for a creature, and that place we must occupy. What a humbling thought is here suggested to us! Let us examine it.—1. If vanity had been ascribed to the meaner parts of the creation—if all inanimate and irrational beings, whose days are as a shadow, and who know not whence they came nor whither they go, had been thus characterized—it had little more than accorded with our own ideas. But the humiliating truth belongs to man, the *lord* of the lower creation—to man, that distinguished link in the chain of being which unites in his person mortality and immortality, heaven and earth. The "Lord knoweth the thoughts of *man,* that they are vanity." 2. Had vanity been ascribed to the exercises of our sensual or mortal part, or of that which we possess in common with other animals, it had been less humiliating. But the charge is pointed at that which is the peculiar glory of man, the intellectual part, his *thoughts.* It is here, if anywhere, that we excel the creatures which are placed around us. We can contemplate our own existence, dive into the past and the future, and understand whence we came and whither we go. Yet in this tender part are we touched. Even the *thoughts* of man are vanity. 3. If vanity had been ascribed merely to those loose and trifling excursions of the imagination which fall not under the influence of choice, a kind of comers and goers, which are ever floating in the mind, like insects in the air on a summer's evening, it had been less affecting. The soul of man seems to be necessarily active. Everything we see, hear, taste, feel, or perceive, has some influence upon thought which is moved by it, as the leaves on the trees are moved by every breeze of wind. But "thoughts" here include those exercises of the mind in which it is voluntarily or intensely engaged, and in which we are in earnest; even all

our schemes, contrivances, and purposes. One would think, if there were anything in man to be accounted of, it should be those exercises in which his intellectual faculty is seriously and intensely employed. Yet the Lord knoweth that even these are vanity. 4, If, during our state of childhood and youth only, vanity had been ascribed to our thoughts, it would have been less surprising. This is a truth of which numberless parents have painful proof; yea, and of which children themselves, as they grow up to maturity, are generally conscious. Vanity at this period, however, admits of some apology. The obstinacy and folly of some young people, while they provoke disgust, often excite a tear of pity. But the charge is exhibited against *man.* "Man *at his best estate* is altogether vanity." 5. The decision proceeds from a quarter from which there can be no appeal: "The Lord knoweth" it. Opinions dishonourable to our species may sometimes arise from ignorance, sometimes from spleen and disappointment, and sometimes from a gloomy turn of mind which views mankind through a distorted medium. But the judgment given in this passage is the decision of him who cannot err; a decision therefore to which, if we had no other proof, it becomes us to accede.—*Fuller.*

19. *In the multitude of my thoughts within me, thy comforts delight my soul.* 1. Uneasy thoughts arise from the disordered state of the world. On this subject great consolation springs from the conviction that the Lord reigneth. There sit at the helm infinite power, wisdom, and goodness. These perfections are of such a nature that renders it impossible to lie dormant or inactive: they are in perpetual operation; and in the final result they will appear with ineffable splendour and beauty. "Clouds and darkness are round about him, righteousness and judgment are the habitation of his throne." Under the administration of such a being, all events will infallibly terminate well—well for the interests of his glory, and well for the interests of his people. With whatever uneasiness we may contemplate the prevalence of moral disorder, and its portentous effects in a future state, the page of revelation assures us that ultimately the world will be filled with holy and happy creatures; that religion and virtue will prove triumphant; and that all nations shall see the glory of

God and worship at his footstool. And with respect to the final state of the wicked, there is every reason to conclude that their numbers will bear no proportion to those of the blessed, and that thus no more misery will be inflicted than what will be rendered conducive to the order and happiness of the universe. 2. Under painful apprehensions respecting the state of the church, the comforts of God are neither few nor small. It behoves us, on such occasions, to reflect that it is incomparably more his care than ours; that as the Saviour bought it with his blood, he will not fail to guide and govern it in the best manner possible. He has promised, "The gates of hell shall not prevail against it." His interpositions in its favour afford a pledge of what he will still accomplish: "I gave Egypt for thy ransom, Ethiopia and Sheba for thee. Since thou wast precious in my sight thou hast been honourable, and I have loved thee; therefore will I give men for thee, and people for thy life." . . . Afflictions are designed to purify the church. 3. Under the distressing thoughts arising from the state of a Christian, as an individual, the divine comforts are proposed. In temporal affliction and privations how consoling is it to reflect that they are all ordered in infinite wisdom, and proceed from the purest benignity; that they will issue in our advantage, and that they will be but of short duration. This, may the afflicted Christian reflect, is not an eternal state; these afflictions are but for a moment. "Weeping may endure for a night, but joy cometh in the morning."—*Rev. Robert Hall.*

PSALM XCV.

The psalm is an invitation to the chosen people, the flock of God's pasture, to worship their divine Shepherd and to serve him with sincerity and willingness. The calling and training of a peculiar people were the means by which from an early period God had unfolded his design of bringing all mankind to a recognition of his sovereignty. Israel was thus the light that was to give light to the whole world; and in the dealings of God with Israel, and of Israel with God, were to be practically exemplified the mutual relation of the sheep and their Creator-shepherd. Hence the solemn summons to Israel to worship and bow down, and kneel before the Lord their Maker, who was their God, they being the people of his pasture and the sheep of his hand. But what if the light should itself become darkness? What if those who were to be the special witnesses for God's sovereignty should themselves become like the world who despised it? What if those whose history was designed specially to illustrate the blessings of obedience to God's shepherd-rule should themselves tempt and provoke the God who had called them? Alas! the fathers of the Israelites had already thus transgressed, and God had been forced to punish them by not suffering them to enter into his rest. And hence the solemn warning in the latter part of the psalm, to succeeding generations of the chosen flock not to harden their hearts in like manner.

The particular appropriateness of such a warning in the days of Josiah's reign, when this psalm was probably written, was long ago noticed by Theodoret. The discovery of the lost book of the law had then shown how fearfully the Israelites of that and the preceding generations had departed from the precepts that had been given for their observance. And the spirit of God's sentence upon the rebellious generation of the wilderness, that they should not enter into his rest, had been then again displayed in the doom uttered by the prophetess Huldah: "Thus saith the Lord, Behold I will bring evil upon this place, and upon the inhabitants thereof, even all the words of the book which the King of Judah hath read; because they have forsaken me, and have burned incense unto other gods, that they might provoke me to anger with all the works of their hands; therefore my wrath shall be kindled against this place, and shall not be quenched." The indirect evidence thus afforded of the date at which the psalm was written is corroborated by the protests which are introduced into the earlier portion of the psalm against the follies of idolatry, ver. 3-5: idolatry being the special sin for which the doom of God was in Josiah's reign hanging over the city of Jerusalem.

It would, however, have been mere mockery, after the doom of destruction on Jerusalem was pronounced, to bid the people be not hard-hearted like their fathers, had nothing more remained to which they might still look forward. But there were blessings in store. The series of psalms of which this forms a part, Ps. xciii.–c., is, as we have already explained, essentially prophetical. Behind the darkness of the approaching Chaldean catastrophe the prophets had already hailed the advancing light of the future manifestation of God's kingdom; and it was to this that the people's expectations were now being directed by the psalmist. In closing his psalm with an allusion to God's promised rest, he implied that for the people of God a rest still remained. His own generation might at least welcome from afar that promised glory of God which their children should behold; and in that prospect might, with Moses towards the close of the wanderings in the wilderness, seek to be taught to apply their hearts to wisdom.

With the above view of the import of this psalm agrees the practical exposition of its latter verses given in the epistle to the Hebrews; if at least we allow the fact that the New Testament writer, living under the Christian dispensation, necessarily looked forward not to the first but to the second advent. For it has been the property of each divine dispensation under which men have lived to show the incompleteness of past events with reference to the promises which God has made. The Israelites after entering Canaan found that God's rest should not be theirs till God's Messiah should appear : hence the "to-day if ye will hear his voice" of the psalmist. And in like manner, after the coming of the Messiah and the proclamation of the divine kingdom, Christian believers still found that God's rest could not be fully theirs till all earthly toil and sin should be ended by the second appearance of their King in glory : hence the "to-day if ye will hear his voice" of the apostle. The name David, Heb. iv. 7, is, it need scarcely be remarked, a general designation of the Psalter, and does not indicate the authorship of the particular psalm quoted : we in like manner still apply the name Samuel to two historical books narrating events long posterior to that prophet's death.— *Thrupp.*

PSALM XCVI.

We shall only arrive at a true appreciation of the contents of this psalm when we perceive that it is the companion-psalm to Ps. xcv. It is in some sort the jubilant outpouring of praise to which Ps. xcv. had invited. Being too purely lyrical, too much a mere utterance of the joyousness of thanksgiving to stand alone, it attaches itself to the preceding psalm, which was in part of a hortatory character. The subject which lies at the basis of each psalm is substantially the same; viz. Israel a witness to the world for the sovereignty of God. But this witness was twofold. There was the witness of the people and the witness of the sanctuary. Ps. xcv. dwells upon the former; Ps. xcvi. upon the latter. The Israelitish people witnessed for the sovereignty of God, or so should have witnessed by a holy and dutiful obedience to his commandments. The Israelitish sanctuary witnessed for the sovereignty of God by being the symbol of his divine presence in the midst of his people on earth, by the consequent reverence with which it was regarded, and by the purity and solemnity of its ritual. The "honour and majesty," the "strength and beauty" of the Lord God of Israel, the King of the whole earth, were symbolized in various ways within the wall of the sanctuary of Zion; *e.g.* in the figures of the cherubim overshadowing the mercy-seat. The reverence which was paid to the sanctuary by the Israelites, and which they claimed for it from all the world, was shown by the offerings which they brought into the temple-courts. The ritual of the sanctuary was pure; it repudiated the use of idols and likenesses, and bade the people bow down and worship the very Lord : it was also solemn; it ordered the use of holy apparel (E. V. *beauty of holiness*), and forbade such personal disfigurements as the heathen practised.

Such being the witness borne to the sovereignty of God by his dwelling-place, the Israelitish sanctuary, the people are in this psalm invited to sing a *new* song in anticipation of that future manifestation of God's sovereignty for which the establishment of his sanctuary in Israel was helping to prepare the way. They are bidden show forth day by day that salvation which they had been taught that he was working out. They are bidden proclaim in prophetical anticipation among the heathen that "the Lord reigneth;" in other words, that he has publicly assumed and displayed abroad his sovereignty. And at the tidings of his approaching advent to judge the world in righteousness all creation also is summoned to rejoice; which, had it but the needful consciousness, it might well do, seeing that the Lord's coming would be the signal for the removal of that curse which had been inflicted even on the ground for man's sake.

In illustration of the close alliance between the contents of this psalm and those of the latter part of the prophecy of Isaiah, Hengstenberg notes the literal agreement in particular expressions between ver. 1, 11 and Is. xlii. 10. "The verbal reference to Isaiah in ver. 1," he justly remarks, "is designedly placed at the beginning, for the purpose of pointing out the prophetical fountain from which the lyric stream has flowed." It may deserve notice that the same chapter of Isaiah furnishes towards the close—more especially in ver. 19—the best illustration of the subject treated in the preceding psalm, viz. the shortcomings of that Israel who had been expressly designed to be the messenger and witness for God in the world; but who would only fully realize that high calling in the person of the Servant-Son, in whom the Father should be well-pleased. The true Israel was Christ.

In reference to the present use by the Christian church of Ps. xcvi., it is sufficiently obvious that we, whose lot is cast upon these latter days, intervening between the two advents of Christ, occupy a place in the midst of the fulfilment of the events to which the worshippers in the days of the psalmist looked forward. Now already, we are told, is the day of salvation. Yet still we expect a salvation to come, and rejoice that it should be nearer than when we first believed. Long ago did the herald proclaim the time fulfilled, and the kingdom of heaven at hand; yet "thy kingdom come" is still our prayer. We have known of one who for judgment came into this world; yet to the great day of judgment we still look forward. And the result is that while we have already a new song to sing for what has been achieved, and find the psalms of Israel practically insufficient to express the manifold mercies of redemption which we have received of God through Christ, there must still be another new song for blessings yet to come; and thus the whole creation, which was to rejoice for the advent of the Lord to judgment, still groaneth and travaileth in pain together, even until now. Under these circumstances the church of Christ both in the several members of whom she consists and also in her collective capacity, must, like the Israelitish people and sanctuary of olden times, still witness for God's sovereignty to the world. "Say among the heathen that the Lord reigneth," must be the Christian's as it was the Israelite's motto.—*Thrupp.*

The exhortation, "Sing to the Lord a new song," could only be responded to by the heathen after the salvation which forms the subject of the poem had arisen. Behind the exhortation, however, addressed to the heathen to praise God, there lies concealed another address to the Israelites. The church of the Lord should be raised by this psalm to joyful hope, should be awakened to an active zeal to serve with uprightness the Lord who had formed such a mighty purpose with her. She beheld indeed the heathen preparing to destroy the kingdom of the Lord in the small corner which still remained to her. But at the same time she beheld at a greater distance with the eye of the Spirit of the Lord, the Lord himself coming, in the full glory of his being, to judge the whole earth, to judge the world in righteousness, and the nations in faithfulness.

As the promise which forms the basis of our psalm is as yet unfulfilled in its whole extent, the whole fulness of the heathen have not yet entered into the kingdom of God, the psalm is fraught with importance to us, not only in regard to its general thought, but even as to its very language. It is a *missionary hymn* for all ages of the church; and it becomes more and more appropriate to our times in proportion as the heathen begin to respond to the call, "Sing to the Lord a new song," and in proportion as we find in the melancholy condition of the church at home occasion to look with a hopeful eye towards the heathen world.—*Hengstenberg.*

8. *Give unto the Lord the glory . . . bring an offering, and come into his courts.* He calls upon the Gentile nations in so many words to render unto God the same worship which the Jews did; not that we must worship God now according to the outward ritual which was prescribed under the law, but he signifies that there would be one rule and form of religion in which all nations should accord. Now, unless the middle wall of partition had been broken down, the Gentiles could not

have entered along with God's children into the courts of the sanctuary. So that we have here a clear prediction of the calling of the Gentiles, who needed to have their uncleanness taken away before they could be brought into the holy assembly. The *mincha*, or oblation, was only one kind of sacrifice, but it is here taken to denote the whole worship of God, because it was a part of divine service more ordinarily practised. We see from this and other passages that the inspired penmen describe the inward worship of God under symbols common in the age when they lived. God would not have meat-offerings presented to him after Christ had come; but the words which the psalmist employs intimate that the doors of the temple, once shut, were now to be opened for the admission of the Gentiles. The apostle, in his epistle to the Hebrews (ch. xiii. 15), tells us what are those sacrifices with which God will now be worshipped. Hence the absurdity of the Papists, who would adduce such passages in support of the mass and their other fooleries. We may very properly learn from the words, however, that we ought not to come empty-handed into the presence of God, enjoined as we are to present ourselves and all that we have as a reasonable service unto him (Rom. xii. 1; 1 Pet. ii. 5).—*Calvin.*

PSALM XCVII.

The text here consists of the words of Isaiah, "The Lord reigneth," placed at the head of the psalm, and to which the psalmist looks, when on the eve of a time of great oppression, as to a clear light which shines at the end of a long dark cavern, and which he opposes to the cry of the world, which may be soon expected, "The king of Babylon reigns," or "Bel and Nebo reign." He brings forward, however, a new view of the reign of the Lord. The language here does not apply to the conversion of the worshippers of idols to the living God, but singly and alone to judgment on the idolatrous world, by which its pride shall be completely humbled, and with which Sion's salvation is connected. The figure of the indignant judge meets us in the whole of the first half. Nothing but shame is the portion of the worshippers of idols in ver. 7. Sion, according to ver. 8, only hears of it and is glad.

The beginning of the fulfilment of the hopes expressed here took place at the destruction of Babylon, and the deliverance of Israel connected with it; comp. Is. xlvi. These hopes, however, in their main import, are *Messianic.* The appearance of Christ was of the nature of a judgment even for those among the heathen who became obedient to the gospel; the nullity of their whole previous existence became thereby apparent, and, in place of their pride and high-minded contempt of Sion, there appeared deep shame. While, however, behind the judgment, which is alone brought prominently forward in our psalm, the *grace* was concealed, which comes clearly forward in other passages, and especially in the preceding psalm : the view which is here the only predominant one comes forward, in other passages, alone in its power, for those who, like Julian for example, will know nothing of "the Lord reigneth." Even in our day the hopes here expressed are in the act of fulfilment. The exclamation, "The Lord reigneth," always sounds forth anew; the church calls it out to the naked and to the clothed world, to the worshippers of wooden and of imaginary gods, till it shall have reached to full and absolute truth, and all the kingdoms of the earth have become the kingdom of the Lord and his Anointed. —*Hengstenberg.*

PSALM XCVIII.

This psalm, observes Theodoret, treats of the same subject as the preceding : it fore-announces both the advents of our Saviour. It is the only piece in the Psalter which, without any author's name attached, bears in the Hebrew the simple title *Mizmor—*"A Psalm." This marks it as emphatically a psalm among psalms, a genuine lyrical effusion : it forms, in fact, the lyrical complement to the more decidedly prophetical psalm by which it is preceded, standing to it in nearly the same relation as Ps. xcvi. to Ps. xcv., or as Ps. xxxiii. to Ps. xxxii. It is the "new song" of praise for the victory which the previous psalm represented the Lord as gaining, in behalf of his true worshippers, and for his own glory's sake, over the wicked, and over all that boasted themselves of idols. It contains, however, one new feature : the victory for which in Ps. xcvii. only Zion and the daughters of Judah were pictured as rejoicing, is in Ps. xcviii. treated as a source of gladness to all the earth. Thus almost instinctively, as it were, did the Jewish psalmists, especially at seasons when their hearts were most expanded in praise, recognize the world-wide importance of God's dealings with their own little nation, and virtually anticipate the day of the catholicity of Zion, when there should be neither Greek nor Jew, circumcision nor uncircumcision, barbarian, Scythian, bond, nor free; but Christ should be all and in all. That this levelling of all distinction between Jew and Gentile was never clearly present to their minds we may reasonably admit; but yet it was the legitimate development of their invitation to all the world to rejoice. In its formal structure the psalm falls into three parts. Announcing in the opening verses the victory that has been gained, and implying in the concluding words of ver. 6, "before the Lord, the King," that by that victory God has publicly vindicated his sovereignty abroad, the psalmist calls first on Israel (ver. 1–3), then on all mankind (ver. 4–6), lastly on all creation (ver. 7–9), to testify their joy.—*Thrupp.*

PSALM XCIX.

See under Psalm xci.

PSALM C.

See again under Ps. xci. for observations on the decade which closes with Ps. c.

There can be no doubt that Ps. xci.-c. belong to the same time and same author, that they form a connected series, that they are on the territory of the psalm poetry what the second part of Isaiah is on the territory of prophecy, and that we have before us in them a decalogue of psalms intimately connected together. The reference to the relation in which Israel stands to the might of the world is common to all these psalms. The objective view of suffering also is a common feature : the psalmist stands everywhere above it, no crying from the depths, no conflict with despair—the explanation being that the psalmist has to do with *future* suffering, and is preparing for it a shield of consolation. These psalms also are in common characterized by a confident expectation of a glorious revelation of the Lord, which the author, following up the prophetical writings, sees with the eye of faith as already present. It is common to them all to quote with marked intelligence from older passages, especially from the Davidic psalms, and from the second part of Isaiah, in connection with an originality of thought and expression which it is impossible to mistake. It is a common feature also that these quotations are in all cases taken from writings of a date prior to the captivity, in accordance with a series of other marks of a pre-Chaldaic era which are scattered everywhere throughout these psalms. It is common to them all that the tone never rises above a certain height, and never sinks beneath it, just as in the second part of Isaiah, in common with which our psalm bears the character of mild sublimity. There are common to them all a great many parallel passages (compare the exposition), the use of the anadiplosis, the predilection for the mention of musical instruments, proceeding from the *joyful* character of the psalm.

It is impossible also not to notice design in the arrangement. Two introductory psalms of a general character stand at the head : Ps. xci., an expression of joyful confidence in the help of God in all troubles and dangers ; Ps. xcii., the greatness of God, which brings on the destruction of the wicked, and the salvation of the just ; Ps. xciii. is then opened with the watchword, "the Lord reigneth," which henceforward is uttered on all sides, and applied for comfort and exhortation. The whole ends in the exhortation addressed to the whole earth to serve the Lord and to praise him, and to give him glory for the abundant salvation which he imparts—the full-toned chorus of all nations and tongues who know that the Lord is God.

We have already pointed to the intimate connection between this cycle of psalms and the second part of Isaiah. We have hence a very strong proof in behalf of the genuineness of this portion of Scripture.—*Hengstenberg.*

That the psalm depends upon the preceding one is clear, not only from the formal arrangement, but also from the entirely general character of what is here laid down as a basis for the exhortation "to serve the Lord," &c., by which many expositors, who did not observe the connection of both psalms, have been led to an entirely false view of the psalm, and a misapprehension of its Messianic character, which becomes clearly established as soon as it is observed that the address in the whole psalm is directed to the *heathen*, and that they are exhorted, not only to shout with joy to the Lord, but also to be subject to him. The psalm forms not merely a conclusion to Ps. xcix.: it is assuredly with design that it is put at the end of the whole series, the ecumenic character of which becomes very obvious in it at the close.—*Hengstenberg.*

This noble version, *Old Hundred*, is, I believe, the most ancient now in common use in our language, as it is certainly one of the very best; faithful to the original, and yet full of grace and strength. It was first printed in the psalm-book published for the English exiles at Geneva in 1561; and is believed to have been written by William Kethe, a native of Scotland, who joined the exiles at Geneva in 1556. See the Third of the learned and valuable "Dissertations" by the Rev. Neil Livingstone, prefixed to the sumptuous reprint of *The Scottish Metrical Psalter of* 1635 (Glasgow, 1864). From an allusion in Shakespeare, the psalm in this version and the well-known melody named after it, would appear to have been as great favourites in Queen Elizabeth's time as they are among ourselves.—*Binnie.*

Luther would have immortalized his name had he done no more than written the majestic air and harmony to which we are accustomed to sing this psalm, and which, when the mind is in a truly worshipping frame, seems to bring heaven down to earth, and to raise earth to heaven, giving us anticipations of the pure and sublime delight of that noble and general assembly in which saints and angels shall for ever celebrate the praises of God.—*Cobbin* (in *Plumer*).

The grandeur and simplicity of our metrical version will be best seen by placing alongside of it the version of one of our most gifted poets:—

"Be joyful in God, all ye lands of the earth!
O, serve him with gladness and fear!
Exult in his presence with music and mirth,
With love and devotion draw near.

"For Jehovah is God—and Jehovah alone,
Creator and ruler o'er all;
And we are his people, his sceptre we own;
His sheep, and we follow his call.

"O, enter his gates with thanksgiving and song,
Your vows in his temple proclaim;

His praise with melodious accordance prolong,
And bless his adorable name!

"For good is the Lord, inexpressibly good,
And we are the work of his hand;
His mercy and truth from eternity stood,
And shall to eternity stand.
—*Montgomery.*

PSALM CI.

It is not agreed whether David wrote this psalm in early life, before his accession to power; after he had been partly acknowledged as king; or after all the tribes had given in their adhesion. The psalm has in it a tone of authority, indicating that David was already invested with legal functions. It expresses his solemn purpose. Some old writers call this the *Householder's Psalm.* In the seventeenth century, and perhaps earlier, it was customary among pious people to have a sermon preached at the setting up of each new family, or at the occupation of a new domicile. Old books give us accounts of these discourses. Some of them are expositions of this psalm. Nor is this perverting Scripture. A good king in his dominions ought to be like a good father and head of a family in his house. We have here the principles on which David would rule the nation.—*Plumer.*

This is the psalm which the old expositors used to designate "The Mirror for Magistrates;" and an excellent mirror it is. It would mightily accelerate the coming of the time when every nation shall be Christ's possession, and every capital a "city of the Lord," if all magistrates could be persuaded to dress themselves by it every time they go forth to perform the functions of their godlike office. When Sir George Villiers became the favourite and prime minister of King James, Lord Bacon, in a beautiful letter of advice, counselled him to take this psalm for his rule in the promotion of courtiers. "In these the choice had need be of honest and faithful servants, as well as of comely outsides who can bow the knee and kiss the hand. King David (Ps. ci. 6, 7) propounded a rule to himself for the choice of his courtiers. He was a wise and a good king: and a wise and a good king shall do well to follow such a good example; and if he find any to be faulty, which perhaps cannot suddenly be discovered, let him take on him this resolution as King David did, *There shall no deceitful per-*

son dwell in my house." It would have been well, both for the philosopher and the favourite, if they had been careful to walk by this rule.—*Binnie.*

1. *I will sing of mercy and judgment.* Very different opinions obtain regarding the meaning of this clause. We leave the reader to choose between that given in the commentary and that of Hengstenberg and Alexander. We quote the words of the latter, having ourselves a decided preference for the view presented by them :—

"As such a declaration of a present purpose in the Psalms is always followed by its execution, the older interpreters suppose *mercy and judgment* to be those which David meant to practise, as he states more fully in the remainder of the psalm. But besides that he says nothing in what follows of his *mercy,* there is no usage of the Psalms more settled than that *mercy and justice* are combined to denote divine, not human attributes, and that to sing and make music to *Jehovah* never means to praise something else in an address to him, but always to sing praises to himself. See Ps. ix. 11; xiii. 5; xviii. 49; xxx. 4, 12; xxxiii. 2; lxviii. 4; lxxi. 22, 23, in all which cases the form of expression seems to be derived from Judg. v. 3. But the psalm before us contains no such celebration of God's mercy and justice beyond this first verse. The best solution of this fact appears to be the one proposed by Hengstenberg, according to which the execution of the purpose here avowed is contained in Ps. ciii., which then, together with the one before us, and of course the intervening one, compose a *trilogy* or series of three psalms, all by David, each complete in itself, and yet designed to be connected with the others and interpreted by them. Supposing this to be the case, we must regard them all as psalms of David, whose name is prefixed to the third and the one before us, in which he lays down a rule, as it were, for his own government and that of his successors in the regal office. The impression made by these inspired instructions on the first of these successors may account for the remarkable coincidences of expression between this psalm and the Book of Proverbs."

God's work toward his people is a checkered work; a mixture of mercy and judgment: and when he exercises us with both, it is our duty to sing of both, and to be suitably affected with

both; whether our circumstances be joyful or sorrowful, still we must give glory to God; and in everything give· thanks : neither the laughter of a prosperous condition nor the tears of an afflicted condition must put us out of tune for the sacred songs of praise. . . . We find the psalmist singing both of mercy and judgment; as Ps. xxx. 6-9; xlii. 7, 11. You have an elegant description of the lot of God's people while here, as consisting both of mercy and judgment, and so affording occasion to sing of both, 2 Cor. vi. 8-10; where you will see the blink and the shower, the mercies and judgments that are in their lot; how God hath set the one over against the other; by honour and dishonour, by evil report and good report, &c. Thus they have occasion to sing both of mercies and crosses, while they find the Lord supporting them under trials, and remembering mercy in the midst of wrath, and making all things work together for good to them; "I will sing of mercy and judgment; unto thee, O Lord, will I sing." The Chaldee paraphrase of this text is remarkable, and suitable to the doctrine I have raised from it, namely, it is as if the psalmist had said, "If thou bestowest mercies upon me; or if thou bringest any judgment upon me ; before thee, O Lord, will I sing my hymn for all !"—*Ralph Erskine.*

2. *O when wilt thou come unto me?* Hengstenberg retains the interrogative form as in our English version :—" The affecting and anxious question, '*When wilt thou come to me,*' *blessing and helping me in my trouble?* which follows immediately after the first words of the description of the pious resolutions, in order to render prominent the object of these resolutions, and to exhibit them as introductory to Ps. cii., depends upon Ex. xx. 21, 'In every place where I erect a memorial for my name, I shall come to thee, and bless thee,' and is equivalent to, When wilt thou, faithful to thy promises, come to me, and bless me, thou who hast erected in Sion 'the city of the Lord,' ver. 8, a memorial of thy name, and hast chosen it as the place of thy sanctuary. The reference is all the more suitable, as David speaks here in name of his *family,* and the family represents the people to whom, in the fundamental passage, the promise had been given. Other interpretations have arisen merely from failing to observe the reference to this fundamental

passage, from which the indefinite coming is defined to be a coming fraught with *blessing* and *help*, and also from failing to observe the reference to Ps. cii., which makes itself known as the expansion of the cry, 'When wilt thou come to me?' by the clauses at the very beginning, 'Lord, hear my prayer, and let my cry come before thee,' according to which the coming of the Lord here can only be such a coming as goes hand in hand with the coming of the cry of the miserable to him. A host of different interpretations, like Luther's entirely arbitrary one, 'with those who belong to me,' are set aside by the simple remark, that מָתַי is never anything else than an interrogative 'when;' it is so also in Prov. xxiii. 35; comp. Michaelis on the passage."

PSALM CII.

It must be confessed that the theory of Hengstenberg and Alexander which regards Ps. ci.–ciii. as a series of psalms, all by David, each complete in itself and yet connected (see on last psalm), is with difficulty maintained in the face of the obvious allusion to the times of the captivity in ver. 13–21. We give *Dr. Binnie's* note:—"Ps. cii. brings before us the captivity in its third phase. The Lord had, by Jeremiah, announced a return after seventy years. This was spoken in plain terms. We are not surprised therefore to find that, as the years wore away, the fearers of God among the exiles began to look out for the fulfilment of the prediction. Daniel had come to understand 'by books, the number of the years, whereof the word of the Lord came to Jeremiah the prophet, that he would accomplish seventy years in the desolations of Jerusalem.' He knew more. He knew that when God holds forth the promise of blessings, he desires to be inquired of by his Israel with respect to it. Accordingly, he 'set his face unto the Lord God, to seek by prayer and supplication, with fasting;' and the burden of his prayer was that the Lord would at length turn the captivity of his people. 'O our God, cause thy face to shine upon thy sanctuary that is desolate, for the Lord's sake.' I refer to these exercises of the man greatly beloved, because I am persuaded that the chapter which relates them, Dan. ix., furnishes the best and most apposite commentary on Ps. cii. There is no reason to attribute the psalm to Daniel,

but it gives expression to the very thoughts and feelings which filled his soul, as the time fixed for the return drew near."

This plaintive poem was written by some pious exile towards the expiration of the seventy years of captivity, during which the people of Israel were detained in Babylon. The holy land was now lying desolate and uncultivated; its towns and cities were demolished; Jerusalem was a heap of ruins; and the magnificent temple, which had so long been honoured with the presence of the Most High, was overthrown and consumed by the flames in which its enraged and victorious captors had involved it. How keenly this state of public and individual degradation was felt there are many expressive proofs in the Scriptures; and this psalm delineates the feeling by most affecting images and mournful exclamations. In the midst, however, of this intense and accumulated grief, the devout author seeks to draw for himself and his distressed compatriots some consolation from the unchangeable existence, the universal providence, and the faithful promises of God. He depicts with deep sensibility the ardent affection which still glowed in the bosoms of these outcasts from their native soil, and the fondness with which they cherished the hope that they should yet be restored to it; that the walls of their beloved and long-lost Zion should be rebuilt, and the praises of Jehovah yet again resound through the courts of his temple, and among the exulting multitudes of his worshippers.

But though these pious exiles did not altogether lose their hold upon the promises and covenant of God, the language of the psalm shows that their spirits were broken by the long years of their desolate condition, and their hearts depressed by the sorrows to which they were subjected in a strange land, dwelling amidst proud and insulting masters, and daily witnessing scenes of idolatry and impiety which pierced their bosoms with poignant grief. The author of the psalm had most probably been carried away captive in early youth; he had survived nearly to the end of the term, and now, worn with cares and anxieties, he was earnest with God that deliverance might speedily arrive, lest he should sink into the grave without revisiting the delightful scenes by which his imagination was enraptured, without witnessing the fulfilment of the hopes which the prophets of God, had excited by the predictions which they had delivered relative to the returning prosperity of his beloved country. He at length takes refuge in the eternity of God, and the everlasting continuance of his kingdom; and glancing at the bright display that was yet to come of the blessings of the reign of the Messiah, when the nations and kingdoms of the world should be numbered among his disciples and worshippers, he concludes by asserting the final triumph and ever-during glory of that brightest illustration of the wisdom, power, and benevolence of the Most High.—*Walford.*

6. *Like a pelican in the wilderness.* The pelican (*Pelicanus onocrotalus*) is spread over many parts of Asia, Africa, and Europe. Its plumage, when full grown, is nearly all white, with an expanse of wings that sometimes reaches to twelve feet. The most remarkable feature in the pelican is the pouch, a curious dilatation of the throat, for the bestowment of the food till the hour of retirement and eating has come round. We have often seen one of the species sitting on the ledge of a rock a foot or two above the surface of the water, in pensive silence during the whole day; the continuity of its proceeding being only interrupted at distant intervals by the near approach of some unlucky fish, upon which it darted with unerring certainty and then resumed its wonted stillness. At other times we have observed them urging their way, with rapid flight, thirty or forty miles into the country, after a day's fishing, to feast in the lonely wilderness upon the contents of their well-stored pouches: and were then reminded of the words, "I am like a pelican in the wilderness." These birds are very distinctly represented in the paintings of ancient Egypt, in which they are represented as congregated among the reeds in great numbers, the natives collecting basketfuls of their eggs. They still frequent the marshes of the Delta of the Nile, and the islands of the river high up the country; they are also seen on all the lakes of Palestine, except the Dead Sea. —*Kitto.*

7. *A sparrow alone on the house-top.* Some understand the screech-owl; others, *a solitary bird* simply. "The word," says Dr. Kitto on the verse, "we have explained elsewhere to be a general term for birds, or perhaps for small birds in particular, while at the same time it is the proper name of the sparrow. It is quite clear that the word should be understood here in its general, not in its restricted signification; for the intimations do not by any means agree with a pert, active, chattering bird, fond of society, like the sparrow, but seem rather to require some moping bird, that sits watching solitary upon the house-tops in the night season. The owl might well enough be understood; but it is safer to take the reference indefinitely, as indeed most translators do, having instead of '*sparrow alone,*'— '*solitary bird,*' or '*solitary little bird;*' and '*bird alone,*' or '*little bird alone.*'"

Waterston the naturalist fixes on the *Passer solitarius,* which is known in Egypt and Syria, and in the south of Italy. This bird is like a thrush in size, shape, habits, and has a sweet plaintive note: but never associates with others of its species, not even with its own mate, except in breeding time. It is seen sitting solitary on house-tops, warbling it may be its plaintive song.— *Bonar.*

Ver. 25–27. These verses are quoted in the epistle to the Hebrews (chap. i. 10-12) as addressed to Christ, and form a part of the writer's proof from the Old Testament that he, as the Son of God, is higher than the angels. The quotation stands between two others, one from Ps. xlv. the other from Ps. cx., bearing on the same argument. But these are both of them Messianic psalms, and the principle on which the quotation rests is sufficiently obvious. It is by no means so easy to understand why the words of this psalm should have been quoted, as it does not seem at first sight to be a Messianic psalm. It may be observed, however, (1) that it is in this sense Messianic, that it looks forward to Israel's redemption from captivity and the future glory of Zion; (2) that there are two great lines of Messianic hope running through the Psalms, the one human, the other divine; the one of which the reign of the Son of David, the other of which the advent of Jehovah, is the great end and object. Here the psalmist is occupied with the latter, the appearing of Jehovah in his glory. (3) This identification of the Jesus of the New Testament with the Jehovah of the Old, is what we find elsewhere: comp. John xii. 41 with Is. vi. (Isaiah sees the glory of Jehovah,

John tells us it was the glory of Christ), and John xix. 37, "They shall look on him whom they pierced ;" which in Zech. xii. 10, is language used directly of Jehovah. The difference between these quotations in John and the one in the epistle to the Hebrews is that the *argument* in the latter *requires* that the Messianic character of the psalm should be conceded. (4) Not only the revelation, the *appearing* of Jehovah in Zion, but also the creation of the world (ver. 25), would point to the great Mediator, the eternal Word, as the person here spoken of, and on this last ground especially the quotation in the epistle to the Hebrews seems to rest.—*Perowne.*

PSALM CIII.

Henry's first remark on this ode is: "This psalm calls more for devotion than exposition." He who with a warm heart and ordinary good sense enters into its spirit in any version of it extant, is more enriched by it, and has a better understanding of it, than he who with a cold heart can critically weigh every word in the original, and in each of the many translations given us by ripe scholars. The Hebrew and all the ancient versions give David as author. This is doubtless correct, although Clarke thinks it "refers to the times of the captivity, or rather to its *conclusion*." He dates it B.C. 536; Scott, B.C. 1030. Delaney, Patrick, Morison, and Scott think David wrote it on occasion of delivery from dangerous sickness. Yet I have never heard it repeated with more ardour, or more appropriateness, than by God's people enduring great bodily distress.—*Plumer.*

5. *Thy youth is renewed like the eagle's; i.e.* so that in strength and vigour thou art like the eagle. The rendering of the E. V. is grammatically justifiable, but very unnecessarily makes the psalmist responsible for the fable of the eagle's renewing its youth. This fable has received different embellishments. The version of Saadia, given by Kimchi, is as follows : The eagle mounts aloft into heaven till he comes near the seat of central fire in the sun, when, scorched by heat, he casts himself down into the sea. Thence he emerges again with new vigour and fresh plumage, till at last, in his hundredth year, he perishes in the waves. Augustine's story is more elaborate and far less poetical. According to him, when the eagle grows old, the upper curved portion of the beak be-

comes so enlarged that the bird is unable to open its mouth to seize its prey. It would die of hunger, therefore, did it not dash this part of its beak against a rock till the troublesome excrescence is got rid of. Then it can devour its food as before, vigour is restored to its body, splendour to its plumage, it can soar aloft ; a kind of resurrection has taken place. Thus it renews its youth. And then, wonderful to say, having told this story gravely, adding, "In Christ thy youth shall be renewed as the eagle's."—*Perowne.*

15-18. *His righteousness unto children's children.* The family is honoured in the Psalms, because it has a very honourable place assigned it in God's economy of salvation. Christian families are ordained to be nurseries for heaven. Not that the grace of God can be made an heirloom in any line of natural descent. It is not transmissible by man. Every child of Adam who is saved must have been the subject, in his own person, of a radical change, by the special grace of the Holy Spirit. But it is plain that we are not left altogether without information with regard to the quarters in which the ministration of the Spirit is ordinarily vouchsafed ; and both Scripture and experience bear witness that God is wont to pour out his quickening Spirit especially on the seed of true believers. "The promise is to them and to their children." Under the Old Testament, as under the New, the initial Sacrament, which was the "seal of the righteousness of faith," was appointed to be administered to believers and to their seed along with them ; and thus the Lord intimated that the children of those who are members of the covenant society are members along with them. That this is the principle underlying the domestic element which receives such honourable prominence in the Psalter, is plain from such passages as Ps. ciii. 15–18.

This promise respecting children and children's children, is intended, like every other, to be a stimulus to duty, not a pillow for sloth.—*Binnie.*

PSALM CIV.

The general argument of this divine ode of creation has been well expressed by Calvin. "This psalm," he says, "differs from the last, in that it neither treats of God's special mercies bestowed on his church, nor lifts us to the hope of a heavenly life ; but painting for us in the frame of the world, and the order of nature, the living image of God's wisdom, power, and goodness, exhorts us to praise him, because in this one frail mortal life he manifests himself to us as a Father." It is a bright and living picture of God's creative power, pouring life and gladness throughout the universe.

It is not surprising that this great hymn of creation should have called forth the warmest expressions of admiration from those who have studied it, and that they should have vied with one another in praising it as a master-piece which has rarely been exceeded. One writer (Amyraldus) "prefers it to all the lyric poetry of the Greeks and Romans." Another (Hupfeld) declares that "in Hebrew poetry there is little that can compare with it in precision of outline, and in the delicacy of its transitions, as well as in its warm sympathy with nature, and in the beauty of its images." A third (Sanchez) says, "The psalm is delightful, sweet, and instructive, as teaching us the soundest views of nature, and the best method of pursuing the study of it, viz. by admiring with one eye the works of God, and with the other God himself, their Creator and Preserver." The great naturalist, A. Von Humboldt, writes:—"It might almost be said that one single psalm represents the image of the whole cosmos. . . . We are astonished to find in a lyrical poem of such limited compass the whole universe—the heavens and earth—sketched with a few bold touches. The contrast of the labour of man with the animal life of nature, and the image of omnipresent, invisible power, renewing the earth at will, or sweeping it of inhabitants, is a grand and solemn poetical creation." "With what an eye of gladness," says Herder, "does the poet survey the earth! It is a green mountain of Jehovah, which he lifted above the waters; a paradise which he established for the dwelling-place of so many living creatures above the seas. The series of pictures which the poet here displays is in fact the natural history of the earth."—*Perowne.*

4. *Who maketh his angels spirits,* &c. According to the simplest and most obvious construction of this verse, it can only mean that God makes his angels or ministering spirits swift and ardent in his service. But such a statement would be wholly out of place in a psalm, the rest of which relates ex-

clusively to the material creation. The best interpreters are therefore of opinion that *angels* and *ministers* are predicates, not subjects, or in other words, that the idea meant to be conveyed is, that he makes the winds his messengers or angels, and the flaming fire his minister or servant. This agrees exactly with the previous declaration that he makes the cloud his chariot or conveyance, and moves upon the wings of the wind. It may seem, however, to be inconsistent with the use made of the passage in Heb. i. 7, as a proof that the angels are inferior to the Son of God. But how could this inferiority be proved by the fact that the angels are spirits, or even wind and fire? The latter cannot be literally true, and if metaphorical, can only mean that they are swift and ardent in God's service, which they might be and yet equal to the Son in nature, who, considered as a messenger or agent of the Father, exhibits precisely the same qualities. The truth is, that the passage, as thus understood, is perfectly irrelevant and useless to the argument, and therefore that this mode of explaining it is not entitled to the preference, whatever difficulties may attend the other. Let it be observed, too, that the LXX., which is quoted in Heb. i. 7, is an exact transcript of the Hebrew, both as to the sense and collocation of the words, so that if the original admits of a different construction, it may be extended to the version likewise. The most satisfactory conclusion is, that the words are not quoted as an argument or proof of the inferiority of angels, but merely as a striking yet familiar form of words in which to clothe the writer's own idea, which is this, that angels are mere messengers and ministers, and as such may be classed with the material agencies which God employs in execution of his purpose. The wind and the lightning are God's angels and his ministers, and are expressly so described in the Old Testament; but they are never called his sons, much less addressed directly as the sovereign, eternal, righteous, ever-blessed God. Nor are the ministering spirits who share with these material agencies the character of messengers and servants, ever so described or so addressed. By thus supplying the suppressed links of the chain of argument, the verse before us in the only sense of which the context really admits, will be found not only as appropriate as the other to the purpose for which it is quoted in the New Testament, but incomparably more so. —*Alexander.*

15. *Wine that maketh glad the heart of man,* &c. In these words we are taught, that God not only provides for men's necessity, and bestows upon them as much as is sufficient for the ordinary purposes of life, but that in his goodness he deals still more bountifully with them by cheering their hearts with wine and oil. Nature would certainly be satisfied with water to drink; and therefore the addition of wine is owing to God's superabundant liberality. . . . But as there is nothing to which we are more prone than to abuse God's benefits by giving way to excess, the more bountiful he is towards men, the more ought they to take care not to pollute, by their intemperance, the abundance which is presented before them. Paul had therefore good reason for giving that prohibition (Rom. xiii. 14), "Make not provision for the flesh, to fulfil the lusts thereof;" for if we give full scope to the desires of the flesh, there will be no bounds. As God bountifully provides for us, so he has appointed a law of temperance, that each may voluntarily restrain himself in his abundance. He sends out oxen and asses into pastures, and they content themselves with a sufficiency; but while furnishing us with more than we need, he enjoins upon us an observance of the rules of moderation, that we may not voraciously devour his benefits; and in lavishing upon us a more abundant supply of good things than our necessities require, he puts our moderation to the test. The proper rule with respect to the use of bodily sustenance, is to partake of it that it may sustain, but not oppress us. The mutual communication of the things needful for the support of the body, which God has enjoined upon us, is a very good check to intemperance; for the condition upon which the rich are favoured with their abundance is that they should relieve the wants of their brethren. As the prophet in this account of the divine goodness in providence makes no reference to the excesses of men, we gather from his words that it is lawful to use wine not only in cases of necessity, but also thereby to make us merry. This mirth must however be tempered with sobriety, first, that men may not forget themselves, drown their senses, and destroy their

strength, but rejoice before their God according to the injunction of Moses, Lev. xxiii. 40; and, secondly, that they may exhilarate their minds under a sense of gratitude, so as to be rendered more active in the service of God. He who rejoices in this way will also be always prepared to endure sadness whenever God is pleased to send it. That rule of Paul ought to be kept in mind (Phil. iv. 12), "I have learned to abound—I have learned to suffer want." If some token of the divine anger is manifest, even he who has an overflowing abundance of all kinds of dainty food will restrict himself in his diet, knowing that he is called to put on sackcloth and to sit among ashes. Much more ought he whom poverty compels to be temperate and sober, to abstain from such delicacies. In short, if one man is constrained to abstain from wine by sickness, if another has only vapid wine, and a third nothing but water, let each be content with his own lot, and willingly and submissively wean himself from those gratifications which God denies him.—*Calvin.*

35. *Let the sinners be consumed out of the earth.* Coming now to the great question brought up by these imprecatory psalms, are we in a condition to throw any light upon it? It is the undoubted law of Christ that we should love our enemies, bless them that curse us, do good to them that hate us, pray for them that despitefully use us and persecute us. Can we explain how the language of the psalmists can be reconciled with the sentiments and conduct enjoined in that command?

In some instances the reconciliation is easy. Take, for example, the prayer with which Ps. civ. concludes, "Let the sinners be consumed out of the earth, and let the wicked be no more." The psalm is a meditation on God's works in nature, and has excited the admiration of the historians of natural science as the fullest and brightest expression of that sympathy with nature, and appreciation of its unity, in which the sacred poets so remarkably excelled all the pagan writers. At first sight it seems unaccountable that such a sunny joyous ode should be wound up with a petition for the rooting out of wicked men; it seems a jarring note in the song with which the church expresses her participation in the joy of her Lord over this fair world, the product of his beneficent wisdom. But, in truth, the prayer is both in harmony with the song and necessary to its completeness. An anecdote will explain my meaning. It fell to my lot some years ago to undertake a walk of some miles, on a summer morning, along a sea-shore of surpassing beauty. It was the Lord's-day, and the language of Ps. civ. rose spontaneously in my mind as one scene after another unfolded itself before the eye. About half-way to my destination the road lay through a dirty hamlet, and my meditations were rudely interrupted by the brawling of some people, who looked as if they had been spending the night in a drunken debauch. Well, I thought, the psalmist must have had some such unpleasant experience. He must have fallen in with people, located in some scene of natural beauty, who, instead of being a holy priesthood to give voice to nature in praise of her Creator—instead of being, in the pure and holy tenor of their lives, the heavenliest note of the general song—filled it with a harsh discord. His prayer is the vehement expression of a desire that the earth may no longer be marred by the presence of wicked men—that they may be utterly consumed, and may give place to men animated with the fear of God, just and holy men, men that shall be a crown of beauty on the head of this fair creation. If this be the right explanation of the psalmist's prayer, it is not only justifiable, but there is something wrong in our meditations on nature, if we are not disposed to join in it.—*Binnie.*

PSALMS CV. CVI.

The Historical Psalms. I have not attempted to compute the relative space given to the historical element in the Psalter, but it must be very considerable. Several of the longest of the psalms are historical from beginning to end. Ps. lxviii., although it is brightened with an ultimate reference to Christ and the gospel times, is, in the first instance, a glowing recital of the march out of Egypt and the conquest of Canaan. Ps. lxxviii. cv. and cvi. all traverse the same field. In Ps. lxxviii. Asaph, taking up his parable, teaches the people to read the dangers and the duties of their own time in the light of the history of the nation between the exodus and the reign of Solomon. In Ps. cv., one of the later psalmists, taking the materials

furnished by the same history, builds them up into a lofty ode of thanksgiving, that so the Lord's name may be hallowed in the continual commemoration of his mighty acts. Ps. cvi., which is also from the later period of Old Testament psalmody, partakes of a quite different character: it is a sorrowful confession of the sins by which the nation had brought dishonour on the name of the Lord and provoked him to anger in every period of its long history. These are the most prominent of the historical psalms. Others of less note will occur to the reader's memory; and there are, besides, historical allusions in very many of the non-historical psalms.

This historical quality of the Psalter deserves more consideration than it has commonly received. It proceeds upon the great principle of the unity of the church in its successive generations. The events of the past are celebrated, not as matters foreign to the men of the present generation, but as matters in which they are vitally interested. They are summoned to humble themselves in the retrospect of sins long past, and to say with Daniel, "O Lord, to us belongeth confusion of face, to our kings, to our princes, and to our fathers, because we have sinned against thee." They are invited also to commemorate with thanksgiving the years of the right hand of the Most High—the times when the Lord revived his people and prospered the work of their hands. . . .

Running through these and many other passages there is a sentiment of national continuity, analogous to that of personal identity. I know I am the same person I was twenty years ago: and, believing as I do, that all the events of my life are governed by the provident wisdom of God, I feel it to be my duty carefully to keep in memory and often to meditate upon, the way he has led me and tended me from my youth. I know it would be both a dereliction of duty and a forfeiture of inestimable benefits, were I to forget the errors of my youth or the dispensations of God's providence in ordering my lot. How often in times of perplexity or sorrow has the believer found the strongest comfort in calling to remembrance instances in which God heard his prayer and sent him help in years gone by! Well, the psalmists recognize a similar identity—a corporate identity—as pertaining to the church, and linking together its successive generations. Accordingly, they represent the church of any given time as having very much the same interest in its prior history which any individual-has in his infancy or childhood: and, in their hands, the principle is wonderfully fruitful both of admonition and comfort. How admirably is it applied, for example, in Ps. lxxvii.! In a time of deep distress, a dark and cloudy day, the daughter of Zion is at the point of despair: "Will the Lord cast off for ever, and will he be favourable no more? Is his mercy clean gone for ever? doth his promise fail for evermore? Hath God forgotten to be gracious? Hath he in anger shut up his tender mercies?" How does her faith obtain the victory in this conflict? It is by reverting to her own history in better days, and calling to remembrance God's doings of old. "I said, this is my infirmity: but I will remember the years of the right hand of the Most High. I will remember the works of the Lord; surely I will remember thy wonders of old. I will meditate also of all thy work, and talk of thy doings." . . .

The facts of the history are viewed, not as mere *events*—things that fell out in those old times—but rather as divine dispensations, the judgments of the Most High, each of which, since it embodied a thought of God's heart, was full of instruction for the generations following. This is the view which the apostle teaches us to take of the history of God's ancient people; for the things which befell them, he writes, "happened unto them for ensamples: and they are written for our admonition, upon whom the ends of the world are come." As Christ during his personal ministry instructed the church with spoken parables, so during the long centuries of the Old Testament he instructed it with acted parables. It is impossible to estimate the profit, in the shape both of doctrine and reproof, and correction, and instruction in righteousness, which serious persons have derived from the events of the history of which so large a portion of the Psalter is the lyrical memorial.

Rationalists will, of course, sneer at this account of the historical psalms. They see in them nothing but national songs. If there be any lyrical faculty in a nation, it naturally applies itself to the celebration of the national heroes and the most memorable passages of the national history: and what more reasonable than to attribute to this source the historical poems of the Bible? The explanation can be dressed so as to captivate the unwary. But it will not stand. Not to dwell upon the fact that all the psalmists are careful to testify, either explicitly or by clear implication, that, in their judgment, the national history is a "parable," that it is everywhere replete with religious significance, and that their design in making it the burden of their song, is to spread abroad the lessons it was meant to teach—not to dwell, I say, on that fact, it is enough to remark, that there is no glorifying, either of the nation itself or of its great men. This is quite fatal to the notion that these psalms are national songs and nothing more. That the lyrical genius of the Hebrew bards was quite capable of celebrating great men and chivalrous deeds, is sufficiently proved by David's lament for Saul and Jonathan. Yet the Psalter does not contain one song of that order. There is not a single ode in praise of any national hero, Abraham or Joseph, Moses or Joshua or Samson. If David seems to be an exception, it is to be remembered that he occupies a singular place in the history, as the ancestor and type of Christ. When the Psalter extols him, it is not as a national hero, but as the Anointed of the God of Jacob; and the praise is intended for the royal office and the divine antitype. When David, in his individual person, comes before us, it is not as a hero at all, but in the totally different character of a sinner saved by grace. As for that glorifying of the nation, which is the habit of every other lyrical literature, there is no trace of it in the Scriptures. On the contrary, the ordinary drift of the historical psalms is to inculcate on the people the remembrance of their sins, and to make them feel that in no respect were they intrinsically better than their neighbours. Let any one who doubts this read Ps. cvi. The key-note is that sorrowful confession with which, as we have seen, it begins, "We have sinned with our fathers, we have committed iniquity, we have done wickedly," and that penitential tone is maintained to the close. The poets of the nations have never written in this humbling strain. The world does not contain another instance of a collection of national lyrics so totally devoid of everything that could inflame national vanity, so redolent of a sense of the unworthiness of the nation, and of the marvellous grace of the Most High.—*Binnie.*

PSALM CVII.

Here commences the Fifth and last Book of Psalms. (*See Introduction.*)

This Psalm may doubtless be regarded as based on the deliverance from the captivity. It is therefore a captivity hymn. It is not, however, to be regarded as historical in the strict sense, nor are the figures used to be explained as exclusively illustrating the condition of the Jews in Babylon and the joy of their deliverance. The psalm is a psalm of praise for the divine goodness illustrated by God's dealings with wilderness wanderers, with prisoners, with sick and dying men, and with sailors in a storm.

23, 32. *They that go down to the sea in ships,* &c. Fourth example : seafarers tossed and driven by the tempest, and brought at last safe into port. The description may be compared with the language of Jon. i. 11. It is the most highly finished, the most thoroughly poetical of each of the four pictures of human peril and deliverance. It is painted as a landsman would paint it, but yet only as one who had himself been in "perils of waters" could paint the storm—the waves running mountains high, on which the tiny craft seemed a plaything, the helplessness of human skill, the gladness of the calm, the safe refuge in the haven.

Addison remarks that he prefers this description of a ship in a storm before any others he had ever met with, and for the same reason for which "Longinus recommends one in Homer, because the poet has not amused himself with little fancies upon the occasion, as authors of an inferior genius, whom he mentions, had done, but because he has gathered together those circumstances which are the most apt to terrify the imagination, and which really happened in the raging of a tempest." "By the way," he adds, "how much more comfortable as well as rational is this system of the psalmist, than the pagan scheme in Virgil and other poets where one deity is represented as raising a storm and another as laying it! Were we only to consider the sublime in this piece of poetry, what can be nobler than the idea it gives us of the Supreme

Being thus raising a tumult among the elements, and recovering them out of their confusion ; thus troubling and becalming nature!"—*Spectator*, No. 489. *Perowne.*

Addison's beautiful rendering of this passage and application to Christian experience in the following hymn will be appreciated by the reader :—

"Think, O my soul! devoutly think,
How, with affrighted eyes,
Thou saw'st the wide-extended deep,
In all its horrors rise.

"Confusion dwelt on every face,
And fear in every heart ;
When waves on waves, and gulfs on gulfs,
O'ercame the pilot's art.

"Yet then, from all my griefs, O Lord!
Thy mercy set me free ;
Whilst in the confidence of prayer,
My soul took hold on thee.

"For though in dreadful whirls we hung
High in the broken wave,
I knew thou wert not slow to hear,
Nor impotent to save.

"The storm was laid, the winds retired,
Obedient to thy will ;
The sea that roared at thy command,
At thy command was still!"

PSALM CIX.

This is the last of the imprecatory psalms. An abler or more satisfactory exposition of the principles involved in these than that presented by our author in his Introduction, can scarcely be desired (xxv.-xl.) He expresses himself doubtful of the Messianic character of the psalm and the designed application of its maledictions (ver. 8) to Judas. For a full examination of these points the reader is referred to Ps. lxix., *Appendix.* The admission under ver. 10 of wrong feelings on the part of David seems unnecessary even on the author's own principles, and proceeds from misapprehension of the true character of the psalm. It is the utterance of a holy man and prophet in sympathy with the law and providence of God.

PSALM CX.

The Messianic interpretation is the only one that yields a tolerable sense. Several alternatives have been proposed. For example, Herder and Ewald affirm that *David himself* is the prince to whom the psalm refers ; that (like Ps. xxi.) it is a prayer for the king, in which the people speak of him as their Lord, whose throne was exalted at the right hand of the Lord's throne in Sion, and whom God had invested with such honour in connection with his house, that he might be said to be a priest like Melchizedek, the ancient king of Salem. The theory can be dressed so as to wear a plausible air. But it will not bear examination. For (1) the psalm is in the title attributed to David's pen, and there is not a tittle of evidence pointing to any other writer. Would he have written of himself as "My Lord?" (2) The king is invited to sit at the right hand of Jehovah: a manner of speech nowhere else in Scripture used with reference to an earthly king. The Jewish kings sat "on the throne of Jehovah," as his representatives or vicegerents: not "at his right hand," as his fellows. (3) The people are represented as following the king in sacred attire, the beauty of holiness; that is to say, in holy sacerdotal vestments as an army of priests: a thing of which we find no trace in the history of David or any of the kings. It is Christ alone of whom we ever read that his "armies followed him, clothed in fine linen, white and clean" when he went in righteousness to make war. (4) The king is, by the oath of God, constituted a priest, "a priest for ever after the order of Melchizedek." One would think this at least cannot apply to David. But the exigencies of the Rationalistic theory are great, and a bold attempt must be made. Ewald, girding up the loins of his ingenuity, sets himself to show that in David's reign there was a remarkable conjunction of the royal and sacerdotal functions. How he goes to work may be gathered from the picture of David's administration that has been recently sketched by the elegant pencil of the Dean of Westminster. Thus it is gravely related of the king, as if it were matter of ascertained fact, that "though not himself a priest, he yet assumed almost all the functions usually ascribed to the priestly office. He wore the priestly dress, offered the sacrifices, gave the priestly benedictions, walked round about the altar in sacred processions."

But all this is asserted without a shadow of warrant from the sacred narrative. No doubt David is related to have "offered burnt-offerings and peace-offerings" at the bringing up of the ark; but that he did so with his own hand is no more likely than that Solomon, on a yet more solemn occasion, offered with his own hand the twenty thousand oxen and the hundred and twenty thousand sheep which he is related to have offered at the dedication of the house. David doubtless sings in Ps. xxvi. of "compassing God's altar;" but that is no more to be taken literally than the prayer in Ps. xxvii., that he might "dwell in the house of the Lord all the days of his life." As for the allegation that he wore the priestly dress, it is enough to say that the ephod in which he arrayed himself at the bringing up of the ark was not the priestly robe so named; this was made of *byssus* (fine linen), whereas the king's was of ordinary linen—a festal robe, no doubt, but not peculiar to the priesthood. This is not all. Let it be supposed, for the moment, that all these fancies about David's intromissions with the functions of the priesthood had been matters of fact; let it be supposed that this man after God's own heart was accustomed to officiate often in rites which the law of Moses had so sacredly appropriated to the sons of Aaron, that Saul, for venturing to officiate in them on one solitary and pressing occasion, was rejected, he and his house, from reigning over Israel; let it be supposed that he performed habitually, with high commendation, sacred offices like that for which Uzziah, when he attempted to perform it but once, was sharply reproved and smitten on the spot with leprosy—would all this have sufficed to vindicate the application to David of the oracle in the psalm? Such conduct might, perhaps, have warranted the application of the priestly *title;* certainly it could not have warranted the lofty and emphatic declaration: "Jehovah hath sworn, and will not repent, Thou art a priest for ever after the order of Melchizedek." The allegations so boldly made, if they had been true, would have amounted merely to this, that David exercised such priestly functions as belonged to all princes and heads of families under the patriarchal dispensation, before the law restricted the priesthood to Aaron and his sons—that he was a priest in the sense in which Abraham and Jacob were priests. But how far is this from answering to the grandeur of the oracle! The king here addressed is constituted a priest after the order of Melchizedek, to whom Abraham, the patriarchal priest, paid tithe in token of homage, and from whom he was content to receive a benediction; and the priesthood is confirmed by the irrevocable oath of Jehovah, and declared to be a perpetual priesthood. It shows how hard men are pressed by the exigencies of their theory when they can plead for the application to David of a declaration so far-reaching and magnificent.

After all, it is no wonder the Rationalistic interpreters fight hard for the identification of David with the priest after the order of Melchizedek—the throned priest of Zion; for incredible as this is, it is less so than any other of the non-Messianic interpretations;— than that of Hupfeld, who suggests (not without a misgiving) that the psalm celebrates *the dynasty* of David rather than any individual king; and than that of some others who fancy they see in it a reference to the martial exploits of the priesthood in the age of the Maccabees. Besides these, I do not know that there is any other theory worth notice, unless it be the wild notion of De Wette, that the psalm comes from the pen of some prophet who chose in this way to express his approval of king Uzziah's presumptuous invasion of the priestly functions! It is to shifts like these that learned and able men are driven when they abandon the natural and obvious sense of this great Messianic psalm.—*Binnie*.

The reader will admire the following accurate and spirited paraphrase from *Perowne:*—"Thus saith Jehovah—it is his revelation that I hear, it is his word addres..ed to one who, though he be my son, is yet my lord—'I give thee honour and dignity equal to my own, I associate thee with myself in kingly rule and dominion, until I have subdued every enemy who shall dare to lift himself up against thee.'"

Then turning to the king who has thus been solemnly placed on the throne of Jehovah, and who rules as his vicegerent in Zion, the psalmist says, "From Zion, thy royal seat, shall Jehovah himself, on whose throne thou sittest, stretch out the sceptre of thy dominion. So close shall be the fellowship between him and thee. Thou shalt sit on his throne, he shall wield thy sceptre, his might shall be thy might, his kingdom shall be thy kingdom, and thou shalt not only subdue thine enemies, but before they are yet vanquished thou shalt rule in the midst of them. When thou goest forth to war, thine own people shall flock with glad and willing hearts to thy standard.

They shall come clad, not in armour, but in holy vestments as ministering priests, for thou hast consecrated them to be thy priestly soldiers. They shall come a youthful host, in numbers numberless as the dews, bright and fresh as the dew from the womb of the morning. "Yet another solemn word concerning thee have I heard. It is a word confirmed by an oath, the oath of the Most High which cannot be broken. By that oath he hath made thee Priest as well as King; King thou art, Priest thou shalt be henceforth. Priest not after the law of a carnal commandment, or by descent through the Levitical priesthood, but after the order of Melchizedek, Priest therefore not of the Jew only, but of the Gentile also,— Priest not for a time, but for ever."

Then, looking on the leader, the host, the conflict, the poet exclaims, "The Lord, the God of hosts who is with thee, O king, who is at thy right hand to succour and give thee the victory in the battle, hath already crushed the rival monarchs that dispute thy sway. Thou shalt be a judge and ruler among the nations whom he has given thee as thine inheritance. The vast battlefield is strewn with the corpses of thy foes. Far and wide hast thou extended thy conquests, vanquishing one leader after another; and thou shalt reap the fruit of thy victories like a warrior who, pressing hotly on the rear of his enemies as they flee before him, scarcely pauses for a moment to snatch a hasty draught from the wayside brook, and then with renewed ardour, with head erect and kindling eye, continues the pursuit. Thus shall victory be crowned and not a foe remain."

3. *From the womb of the morning thou hast the dew of thy youth.* Thy "youth-like soldiery are as dew for beauty" (*Hengstenberg*); some say also in perpetual succession; and we must add, for number too. But is there not this other idea—they come suddenly as the dew appears, seen all at once under the light of the new risen Sun of Righteousness? And may we not adopt yet another from Hengstenberg, "All begotten from above"—as Job xxxviii. 28 might lead us to remember. The metre version of Tate and Brady has thus expressed some of these views:—

"Shall all (redeemed from error's night)
    Appear as numberless and bright
As crystal drops of morning dew."
    —*Rev. A. A. Bonar.*

7. *He shall drink of the brook in the way; therefore shall he lift up the head.* Not a few interpreters expound this verse in a very harsh manner: that the carnage would be so great as to cause the blood of the slain to flow in torrents, out of which Christ, the Conqueror, might drink till he was satiated. Akin to this is the exposition of those who would have it to be a figurative representation of misery and grief, and thus descriptive of the many afflictions to which Christ was liable during this transitory life. The similitude seems rather to be drawn from the conduct of brave and powerful generals, who, when in hot pursuit of the enemy, do not suffer themselves to be diverted from their purpose by attending to luxuries; but without kneeling down are content to quench their thirst by drinking of the stream which they are passing. It was in this way that Gideon found out the brave and warlike soldiers; regarding such as kneeled down to drink as destitute of courage, he sent them back to their homes. It therefore appears to me that David figuratively attributes military prowess to Christ, declaring that he would not take time to refresh himself, but would hastily drink of the river which might come in his way. This is designed to strike his enemies with terror, intimating to them the rapid approach of impending destruction. Should any one be disposed to ask, Where, then, is that spirit of meekness and gentleness with which the Scripture elsewhere informs us he shall be endued? Is. xlii. 2, 3; lxi. 1, 2; I answer that as a shepherd is gentle towards his flock, but fierce and formidable towards wolves and thieves; in like manner Christ is kind and gentle towards those who commit themselves to his care, while they who wilfully and obstinately reject his yoke, shall feel with what awful and terrible power he is armed. In Ps. ii. 9 we saw that he had in his hand an iron sceptre, by which he will beat down all the obduracy of his enemies; and, accordingly, he is here said to assume the aspect of cruelty, with the view of taking vengeance upon them. Wherefore it becomes us carefully to refrain from provoking his wrath against us, by a stiff-necked and rebellious spirit, when he is tenderly and sweetly inviting us to come to him.—*Calvin.*

PSALM CXI. CXII.

Acrostic Psalms. See *Appendix* on Ps. xxv. The only feasible method (of exhibiting the structure of these psalms to an English reader) is to omit from our alphabet the four letters that are of least frequent use, and make the two and twenty that remain stand for the two and twenty letters of the Hebrew. Thus:—

PSALM CXI.

Hallelujah!

1. A dore will I Jehovah with all my heart:
   B oth in the meeting of the upright and in the congregation.
2. C onfessedly great are the deeds of Jehovah:
   D elighters in them search them out.
3. E xcellent for honour and majesty is his work:
   F or evermore doth his righteousness endure.
4. G racious and compassionate is Jehovah:
   H is wonderful works hath he made to be remembered.
5. J ehovah hath given food to them that fear him:
   K ept his covenant for ever.
6. L oudly hath he declared to his people the might of his deeds:
   M aking them to inherit the heathen.
7. N otable for truth and judgment are the deeds of his hand:
   O n all his commandments men may trust.
8. P lanted firmly are they for ever and ever:
   Q uestionless is their truth and uprightness.
9. R edemption hath he sent to his people:
   S tablished for ever his covenant:
   T errible and holy is his name.
10. U nderstanding pertaineth to all who obey the commandments:
    W isdom's beginning is the fear of Jehovah:
    Y ears without end shall his praise endure.
    —*Binnie.*

PSALM CXII.

6. *Surely he shall not be moved.* There is a strange power in piety to beget calmness, self-possession, and firmness of character, even in the midst of fierce assaults and of dire conflicts with every kind of adversity and adversary. *Luther:* "Unless there were in us divine strength communicated by Christ, it would be impossible that we could stand against such numerous and mighty assaults of temptation." The righteous will not be dismayed when all nature is dissolving. *Arnd:* "Look at examples —how Moses says at the Red Sea, Stand still and see the salvation of God. How does Jehoshaphat stand firm as a wall when a hundred thousand men invade

the land, and he slays them all with one song of praise! How firmly does David stand when hunted by Saul! How overwhelmed is Saul with despair when his land is invaded by the Philistines, and he seeks advice from a witch! What firmness is in Daniel when in the lions' den! What joy in Stephen! How did the holy Basilius say when Cæsar Valens threatened him so dreadfully: 'Such bugbears should be set before children!' Athenasius when Julian persecuted him: 'He is a mist, and will soon disappear!'" There is indeed a fascinating power in the world to make its devotees dream of happiness as long as their prosperity lasts. But it is only the child of God who can in triumph repeat Hab. iii. 17, 18.— *Plumer*.

PSALM CXIII.

With this psalm begins "the Hallel," which was sung at the three great feasts, at the feast of the dedication, and at the new moons. At the feast of the passover it was divided into two parts, the first of which, consisting of Ps. cxiii. cxiv., was sung before the meal, that is, before the second cup was passed round; and the second, consisting of Ps. cxv.–cxviii., after the meal, when the fourth cup had been filled. This last, probably, was "the hymn" which our Lord and his apostles are said to have sung (Mat. xxvi. 30; Mark xiv. 26) after his last passover.

Paulus Burgensis styles Ps. cxiii.–cxviii. *Alleluia Judaeorum Magnum*, and this has been a very usual designation. But according to the ancient Jewish tradition this series of psalms is called simply "the Hallel," or sometimes "the Egyptian Hallel," whereas the name "Great Hallel" is given to Ps. cxxxvi. (See Delitzsch, from whom the above is taken.) The psalm may be said to be a connecting link between the song of Hannah and the Magnificat of the Virgin.—*Perowne*.

9. *He maketh the barren woman to keep house*. Hannah's song in 1 Sam. ii. 5–8, seems kept in view, as well as God's own words to David, 2 Sam. vii. 8, 9, all to furnish suitable language to express redemption-acts. And the long-barren woman of ver. 9, while it reminds us of Sarah, Rebecca, Rachel, Manoah's wife, Elizabeth, who all in the end were "filled with joy," may point to one and the same period of the world's history from its full and final consummation, as does Is. liv. 1. Isaiah seems expressly to allude to this psalm as receiving its fulfilment to the full when the Messiah's work of suffering (Is. liii.) issues in illimitable blessing to Israel and the world.—*Rev. A. A. Bonar*.

PSALM CXIV.

2. *Judah was his sanctuary and Israel his dominion*. It is indeed remarkable that the name of God is not mentioned here, and is introduced only at the close of the psalm. It may be, as our author suggests, that the psalm was designed to be used in connection with Ps. cxiii., which consists entirely of the praises of God. But there is a reason for the omission of the name in the first instance, in the requirements of poetic structure and beauty. Addison was much struck with the fact in this view. "I perceived," says he, "a beauty in the psalm which was new to me. The poet utterly conceals the presence of God in the beginning of it, and rather lets a possessive pronoun go without a substantive than he will so much as mention anything of divinity there. . . . If God had appeared before, there could be no wonder why the mountains should leap and the sea retire; therefore, that this convulsion of nature may be brought in with due surprise, his name is not mentioned till afterwards, and then, with a very agreeable turn of thought, God is introduced at once with all his majesty." Hengstenberg has the same idea, and observes that the questions in ver. 5, 6 would have been anticipated, and their appropriateness destroyed, by an earlier introduction of the name of God.

PSALM CXV.

The general tenor of the psalm, and its particular contents, make it perfectly well suited to the state of things in which the series is supposed to have been written, namely, that succeeding the return from exile, but before the actual rebuilding of the temple.—*Alexander*.

PSALM CXVI.

Various opinions have been entertained regarding the date of this beautiful psalm. Some have assigned it to David, others to Hezekiah. The expression of feeling in the psalm, "the mingled joy and grief" (*Alexander*), answers well to the times immediately succeeding the return from the captivity; while the Chaldaic forms constantly occurring in the original seem to place the matter beyond a doubt. And to this date, and on these grounds, the psalm is assigned by Tholuck, Hengstenberg, Alexander, Thrupp, and Perowne.

13. *The cup of salvation*, &c. This is doubtless an allusion to the drink-offering of strong wine poured out before the Lord in the holy place (Num. xxviii. 7). But the Jews had also in their families a more private cup of thanksgiving, as well for the common benefits of life, as for the more marked instances of the Lord's mercies and deliverances. The use of this was daily, at each meal, and more solemn at a festival. On the daily occasions the master took the cup, and thus "called upon the name of the Lord:" "Blessed be our God, the Lord of the world, who hath created the fruit of the vine;" and having first drunk of it himself, it was presented in order to all who were present. This observance was more marked at the celebration of the passover, and was followed by Christ at the last passover which he kept with his disciples.—Kitto, *Pict. Bible.*

PSALM CXVII.

Of the psalms written after the return, a large proportion were primarily designed for use in the temple service. So strongly marked is this design, that, if they were collected into one book, it might be entitled, "The Songs of the Second Temple." Some of them are very short—Ps. cxxxiv. for example.

Ps. cxvii. belongs also to this time. It is the shortest of all the psalms; the shortest, but not the least weighty. It is cited in the epistle to the Romans as celebrating beforehand the calling of the Gentiles; for it invites them to unite with God's ancient people in worshipping him. Since the invitation is addressed to all the nations, we may look upon it as truly a millennial song. Overleaping the intervening centuries, it anticipates the happy time when the fulness of the Gentiles shall be brought in.—*Binnie.*

PSALM CXVIII.

These temple songs are not all short. Some of them are among the longest in the Psalter. Ps. cxviii. may be named as a beautiful example. It is evidently a temple song; and the critics, with great unanimity, ascribe it to the century after the return. The precise occasion on which it was written is a point on which opinions differ; some of the critics, like Ewald, holding that it was composed to be sung at the feast of tabernacles, when the remnant who returned commenced to offer again the daily sacrifice; others, with Hengstenberg, connecting it with the laying of the foundation of the house; while others again, with Delitzsch, connect it with the solemnity of the dedication. The truth seems to be that it is simply a festal psalm of the second temple, which may well have been sung on any or all of the occasions named by the critics, but is not to be restricted to any one in particular. It breathes a spirit of jubilant trust in the Lord, in the midst of infinite difficulties and perils. Its trumpet tones made it one of Luther's favourites. In the midsummer of 1530, when Melancthon was deputed to present the Confession of the Protestant churches of Germany to the diet at Augsburg, Luther was advised to abstain from any public appearance. Looking out from his retirement on the perils of the time, "the sea and the waves roaring, and men's hearts failing them from fear," he found in Ps. cxviii. a word in season, and set his pen to work on an exposition of it. In the dedication, which is dated "*ex Eremo*, the 1st of July, MDXXX.," he gives characteristic expression to his love for this portion of the divine Word. "Since I am obliged to sit here idle in the desert, and, moreover, must sometimes spare my head, and give it a rest and holiday from my great task of translating all the prophets, I have gone back to my mine of wealth, my treasure. I have taken in hand my precious psalm, the *Confitemini*, and put on paper my meditations upon it. For it is my psalm that I delight in. For although the whole Psalter and the Holy Scripture is dear to me, my proper comfort and life, I have taken so to this psalm in particular that I must call it my own. Many a service has it done me; out of many great perils has it helped me, when help I had none, either from emperor, or king, or saint, or wise and prudent. I would not give it in exchange for the honour, wealth, and power of all the world, pope, Turk, and emperor. In calling the psalm mine own, I rob no man of it. Christ is mine, nevertheless he is the same Christ to all the saints that he is to me. Would God that all the world would challenge the psalm for their own as I do; it would be such friendly contention as scarce any unity or love could compare with. Alas! that there should be so few, even among those who might well do it, who will once say to the Holy Scriptures, or to some particular psalm, Thou art my book: thou shalt be mine own psalm."—*Binnie.*

12. *They compassed me about like bees; they are quenched as the fire of thorns.* The reader has here in miniature two of the finest images in Homer; which, if his curiosity demands to be gratified, he will find illustrated and enlarged, *Iliad,* ii. ver. 86.

> The following host,
> Poured forth by thousands, darkens all the coast.
> As from some rocky cleft the shepherd sees,
> Clustering, in heaps on heaps, the driving bees,
> Rolling and blackening, swarms succeeding swarms,
> With deeper murmurs and more hoarse alarms;
> Dusky they spread, a close embodied crowd,
> And o'er the veil descends the living cloud;
> So from the tents and ships a lengthening train
> Spreads all the beach and wide o'ershades the plain,
> Along the region runs a deafening sound;
> Beneath their footsteps groans the trembling ground.
>
> —Pope's Translation.

The other image, *the fire consuming the thorns,* we find in the same book, ver. 455:

> As on some mountain, through the lofty grove,
> The crackling flames ascend and blaze above;
> The fires expanding, as the winds arise,
> Shoot their long beams, and kindle half the skies:
> So, from the polished arms and brazen shields,
> A gleaming splendour flashed along the fields.
>
> —Pope's Translation.

The arms resembling a gleaming *fire* is common both to the psalmist and Homer; but the idea of that fire being *quenched* when the army was *conquered* is peculiar to the psalmist.—*Adam Clarke.*

22. *The stone which the builders refused is become the head stone of the corner.* It is to be regretted that the author should have maintained that the psalm in general, and this verse in particular, had no original or designed reference to the Messiah, but simply contained principles and statements which might be accommodated to him, or "might be used as expressive of what occurred to him." There does not seem to be any serious difficulty in the way of Messianic reference either in ver. 10 or 17, to both of which the author has made his appeal. (See his introduction to the psalm.) For if we understand the compassing nations (ver. 10) of the Samaritans, Idumeans, and Ammonites, who sought to hinder the Jews in rebuilding the city and temple, it is not inconsistent with the usage of prophecy to carry the mind forward to the Redeemer and his church, against whom the nations rise in vain. Again, if we suppose the restored nation and church of Israel at this time to rejoice in the assurance that they should not be delivered over to death or extinction, have we not a foreshadowing of the grand assurance that Christ and his church shall endure for ever, and discover and proclaim the works of God?

But it is not necessary to the Messianic sense of particular passages in a psalm that we should be able to interpret the entire psalm in all its parts of him. Whatever, therefore, may be thought of the above remarks, we maintain that the express and frequent applications of ver. 22 in the New Testament to Christ by himself and his apostles must be held as setting the matter at rest for ever.

We subjoin *Perowne's* note, as it contains a just exposition of principles, and renders it unnecessary to remark on other prophetic parts of the psalm:—

"Under this figure, suggested, no doubt, by the building of the temple, and the poor aspect it presented as compared with the first temple, is denoted primarily the people of Israel. They had been despised by their heathen masters, but now, by the good hand of their God upon them, they had been lifted up into a place of honour. They, rejected of men, were chosen of God as the foundation-stone of that new spiritual building which Jehovah was about to erect; that temple of the world, the foundation of which was to be laid in Zion. In Mat. xxi. 42–44; Mark xii. 10, 11; Luke xx. 17, our Lord applies the words of this and the next verse to himself. The quotation was, it would seem, purposely taken from the same psalm from which the multitude had just before taken their words of salutation, as they went forth to meet him and conduct him in triumph into Jerusalem. But there is more than an application of the words. Israel is not only a figure of Christ, there is an organic unity between him and them. Whatever, therefore, is true of Israel in a lower sense, is true in its highest sense of Christ. Is Israel God's 'firstborn son?' The name in its fulfilment belongs to Christ (Mat. ii. 15); if Israel is 'the servant of Jehovah,' he is so only as imperfectly representing him who said, 'My meat is to do the will of him who sent me, and to finish his work.' If Israel is the rejected stone made the head of the corner, this is far truer of him who was indeed rejected of men, but chosen of God and precious; the corner-stone of the one great living temple of the redeemed, whether Jews or Gentiles (comp. Eph. ii. 20). See the use of the same figure in its application to our Lord by Peter, Acts iv. 11; 1 Pet. ii. 7.

"The passage which forms the connecting link between this psalm and the New Testament quotations is Is. xxviii. 16, 'Behold it is I who have laid securely in Zion a stone, a tried precious corner-stone, most securely laid, he that believeth (*i.e. resteth thereon*) shall not flee (through fear of any evil).' In this passage the Messianic reference is still more direct, even if we suppose a primary reference to the house of David. (It is interpreted as Messianic both by the Targum and, amongst the rabbinical commentators, by Rashi.) In marked contrast with this, it is said of Babylon, Jer. li. 26, 'They shall not take of thee a stone for a corner, nor a stone for a foundation.'"

PSALM CXIX.

There is no psalm in the whole collection which has more the appearance of having been exclusively designed for practical and personal improvement, without any reference to national, or even to ecclesiastical relations, than the one before us, which is wholly occupied with praises of God's Word or written revelation, as the only source of spiritual strength and comfort, and with prayers for grace to make a profitable use of it. The prominence of this one theme is sufficiently apparent from the fact to which the Masora directs attention, that there is only one verse which does not contain some title or description of the Word of God. But notwithstanding this peculiar character, the position of the psalm in the collection, and especially its juxtaposition with respect to Ps. cviii.–cxviii., its kindred tone of mingled gratitude and sadness, and a great variety of minor verbal correspondences, have led some of the best interpreters to look upon it as the conclusion of the whole series or system of psalms, supposed to have been written for the use of the returned Jews, at or near the time of the founding of the second temple. The opinion, held by some of the same writers, that the ideal speaker, throughout this psalm, is Israel, considered as the church or chosen people, will never commend itself as natural or likely to the mass of readers, and is scarcely consistent with such passages as ver. 63, 74, 79, and others, where the speaker expressly distinguishes himself as an individual from the body of the people. The same difficulty, in a less degree, attends the national interpretation of the psalms immediately preceding. Perhaps the best mode of reconciling the two views is by supposing that this psalm was intended as a manual of pious and instructive thoughts, designed for popular improvement, and especially for that of the younger generation after the return from exile, and that the person speaking is the individual believer, not as an isolated personality, but as a member of the general body, with which he identifies himself so far, that many expressions of the psalm are appropriate only to certain persons or to certain classes in the ancient Israel. To this design of popular instruction, and especially to that of constant repetition and reflection, the psalm is admirably suited by its form and structure. The alphabetical arrangement, of which it is at once the most extended and most perfect specimen, and the aphoristic character, common to all alphabetic psalms, are both adapted to assist the memory as well as to give point to the immediate impression. It follows, of course, that the psalm was rather meant to be a storehouse of materials for pious meditation than a discourse for continuous perusal. At the same time, the fact of its existence in the Psalter is presumptive proof that it was used in public worship either as a whole, or in one or more of the twenty-two stanzas into which it is divided, corresponding to the letters of the Hebrew alphabet, all the eight verses of each paragraph beginning with the same Hebrew letter. —*Alexander.*

Of the Bible acrostics, the most noteworthy, in every respect, is Ps. cxix. Its structure is exceedingly simple. The hundred and seventy-six verses of which it consists are alphabetical couplets, being eight for every letter; so that there are twenty-two alphabetical stanzas, each containing eight couplets. Here also it is easy to discover the reason that led to the adoption of the alphabetical arrangement. The psalm is a meditation on God's law—the meditation of a soul in the presence of the Lord and in communion with him. In such a psalm it is sententious wisdom rather than high poetry that we look for: and a better vehicle for the aphorisms of sententious wisdom could hardly be imagined than that which is furnished by this acrostic. If, as we believe, it dates from the age of Ezra, it affords a welcome corroboration to the conclusion we reached on other grounds, that Ezra and his contemporary scribes were men of a very different stamp from those who bore the same title at a later period. We discern in them, no doubt, the familiar features of the scribe. The jots and tittles of the law were not despicable in their eyes. Raised up to *edit* the Old Testament Scriptures, they did the work well. But they had an eye and a heart that could appreciate the weightier matters of the law. They could look up from their studies about the letter of the divine word, and ejaculate to God such prayers as these, "Open thou mine eyes that I may behold wondrous things out of thy law;" "My soul breaketh for the longing that it hath unto thy judgments at all times;" "Let my heart be sound in thy statutes, that I be not ashamed."

It is curious and not uninstructive to mark the opinions expressed regarding this psalm by the modern critics. Most of them have remarked, and very justly, that, like the rest of the sacred acrostics, it seldom rises into the region of poetry; being rather a versified meditation than a poem in the strict sense of the word. But some have gone further. Dr. Hupfeld, for example, whose *Commentary on the Psalms,* the fruit of the studies of a lifetime, is in many respects invaluable, ventures to charge it with "monotony and poverty of thought," and to contrast it disparagingly with the other psalms of the sententious or aphoristic order. An opinion like this

is worthy of being put on record, as illustrating an observation which in these days it is very important that people should lay to heart and remember. A very able man, learned, painstaking, of excellent literary taste, and honest enough in his way, may nevertheless be utterly incompetent in matters lying within the domain of spiritual religion. The criticism of the learned commentator reminds one of a remark in Augustine's preface to his homilies on the same psalm. After mentioning that a sense of the difficulty attaching to a just exposition of this particular psalm had long deterred him from publishing anything on it, as he had done upon all the rest, he goes on to say, "Doubtless there are other psalms reputed difficult, the sense of which really is wrapped in obscurity. But then, whatever else may be difficult about them, this at least is plain, that they *are* obscure. Not so here. This psalm has an air of simplicity that might lead one to suppose that what it requires is a hearer or reader, not an expositor." Our Rationalistic critics, it is plain, have not mastered the difficulty so wittily pointed out by Augustine. They have not discovered that the psalm is deep. Its scope and probable history have been admirably explained by Matthew Henry. "It seems to me," he observes, "to be a collection of (the psalmist's) pious and devout ejaculations, the short and sudden breathings and elevations of his soul to God, which he wrote down as they occurred, and, toward the latter end of his life, gathered out of his day-book where they lay scattered, added to them many like words, and digested them into this psalm, in which there is seldom any coherence between the verses, but, like Solomon's Proverbs, it is a chest of gold rings, not a chain of gold links. And we may not only learn," he adds, "by the psalmist's example, to accustom ourselves to such pious ejaculations, which are an excellent means of maintaining communion with God and keeping the heart in frame for the most solemn exercises of religion, but we must make use of the psalmist's words, both for the exciting and for the expressing of our devout affections. What some have said of this psalm is true. He that shall read it considerately, it will either warm him or shame him." Those who have visited much among the godly in affliction will not hesitate to prefer this estimate of Ps. cxix. to Dr. Hupfeld's. So far from being monotonous and jejune, it possesses quite a singular aptitude to refresh the souls of the weary; its two-and-twenty clusters yield the wine of the kingdom as copiously as any to be found in all the Bible. The remark applies, although in a somewhat lower degree, to several other alphabetical psalms — Ps. xxv. xxxiv. and xxxvii. If inferior to many others in poetical embellishment, they are inferior to none in the variety and richness of the aliment they minister to devout meditation. — *Binnie.*

Hengstenberg calls the psalm "A Children's Sermon." But it suits all classes. From its alphabetical character the Masora entitle it "The Great Alphabet;" but from its peculiar excellence many style it "The Saints' Alphabet." Bishop Cowper calls it "A Holy Alphabet, so plain that children may understand it—so rich and instructive that the wisest and most experienced may learn something from it." Clarke: "Like all other portions of divine revelation, it is elegant, important, and useful." Jebb: "It is well known that upon no portion of holy Scripture have so many practical commentaries been written. . . . It has been justly considered in all ages of the church as a storehouse of religious wisdom." One of its highest excellencies is its varied instruction on the nature of true, experimental religion. In this psalm, says Venn, "the whole inner man is delineated, and the several changing frames of our poor hearts, and the several blessed motions and inspirations of the Holy Spirit, are touched in a very affecting manner. This is the psalm I have often had recourse to when I could find no spirit of prayer in my own heart, and at length the fire was kindled and I could pray." President Edwards, in his work on *Religious Affections*, says: "I know of no other part of the Holy Scriptures where the nature and evidences of true and sincere godliness are so fully and largely insisted on and delineated."—*Plumer.*

PSALMS CXX.-CXXXIV.

Songs of Degrees. A considerable variety of opinion exists with regard to the meaning of this title, as may be seen from the author's introduction to the first in the series. The opinion that the *songs of degrees* or *ascents* were used in connection with the periodical going up of the tribes to Jerusalem, seems to be gaining ground, Mudge, Hengstenberg, Alexander, and Oehler (article "Psalms" in *Imperial Bible-Dictionary*) adopt and defend this view. It is the view adopted in a very admirable little volume on the *Pilgrim Psalms*, by Dr. M'Michael of Dunfermline, professor of ecclesiastical history to the United Presbyterian Church. We design to draw on the materials furnished by the professor in his exposition of these songs.

The objections alleged by Mr. Barnes against this view will be found ably and satisfactorily, if not conclusively, met in the following extracts from Hengstenberg and Oehler:—

Other expositors seek the origin of the appellation in the fact that *these songs were sung by the pilgrims who went up yearly to Jerusalem at the great festivals.* This explanation is undoubtedly the correct one. The עלה is the usual expression for these festival-journeys; comp. Ps. cxxii. 4; Ex. xxxiv. 24; 1 Ki. xii. 27, 28. The המעלות, *the* journeys to Jerusalem, by way of pre-eminence, can only be those ordinary journeys which were yearly repeated and prescribed in the law; comp. Ps. cxxii. 4. All other journeys to Jerusalem would have needed some expression added to define them. *Further,* the oldest to all appearance of these pilgrim-songs, that, viz., which was composed by David soon after the elevation of Zion to the sanctuary, and at the commencement of the pilgrimages to it, Ps. cxxii., contains two clauses explanatory of the מעלות, corresponding to the explanation of the משכיל in Ps. xxxii., viz., "we will go to the house of the Lord," in ver. 1, and "to which the tribes go up," עלו in ver. 4. The circumstance, moreover, that some of these psalms have, in accordance with the most manifest internal marks, been used for this purpose, is quite decisive. This is the case with Ps. cxxi., which, according to ver. 1, was designed to be sung in view of the mountains of Jerusalem, and is manifestly an evening song for the sacred band of pilgrims, to be sung in the last night-watch, the figures of which are also peculiarly suitable for a pilgrim-song; and with Ps. cxxii., which, according to the express announcement in the introduction, was sung when the sacred pilgrim trains had reached the gates of Jerusalem, and halted for the purpose of forming in order for the solemn procession into the sanctuary, Ps. cxxxiv. Besides this, we may add *finally*, that according to this interpretation, all the common peculiarities of these psalms are easily accounted for. The simplicity, the want of the parallelism, the artless way of forming a transition by a word retained from the preceding verse, the brevity, all these are peculiarities of sacred popular and pilgrim song.

The objections which have been urged against this interpretation are insignificant. Thus it has been said that it is scarcely possible to conceive that such mournful songs as are these psalms to some extent, could have been sung in the course of the joyful journeys to Jerusalem. Just as if the tone of these festival journeys would not be entirely dependent upon the then existing condition of the people! No one will deny that the nameless psalms truly emanated from the innermost feelings of the people at the time when they were originally composed; and the people could at that time find in them only a representation of their own state. Next, it is objected that several of these psalms contain no reference to such a special occasion. But such a reference was not in every case necessary; the contents might be general, and the indicating of the purpose of the psalms might be attended to only in the form and appearance which they were made to assume; and this is really the case.

The practice of travelling to Jerusalem at the festivals had already taken deep root even in the days of David and Solomon. We see this clearly from the conduct of Jeroboam in 1 Ki. xii. 28, comp. also at Ps. cxxii. It was hence very natural that David, who employed his gift of sacred song in ministering to all the wants of the people of God, should attend to this matter also, and that Solomon should continue the work. The pilgrimages suffered grievous interruption from the separation of the ten tribes; and it was only in the days of the new colony that they regained their ancient importance. In these days a third pilgrim poet arose to take his place alongside of the two ancient ones, who wrought up his own productions along with those of his predecessors into one well-arranged whole, a pilgrim-book.

The whole is grouped around Ps. cxxvii., which was composed by Solomon, who stands in middle between the first and the last of the pilgrim-poets. On both sides there stands a heptade of pilgrim-songs, consisting of two psalms composed by David, and five new ones, which have no name. The seven is divided both times by the four and the three. Each heptade contains the name of Jehovah twenty-four times; each of the connected groups, Ps. cxx.-cxxiii., cxxiv.-cxxvi., cxxviii.-cxxxi., cxxxii.-cxxxiv., twelve times; this cannot be accidental, and it renders it evident that the collector of the whole must be identical with the author of the nameless psalms.—*Hengstenberg.*

Ewald sees in the foresaid fifteen psalms, songs which were sung on the return journey of the Israelites from Babylon. The plural *ma'aloth* would have to be explained in this way, that there were several journeys of the exiles. Against this explanation it cannot be objected that Ps. cxxii. cxxiv. cxxxi. bear the name of David, Ps. cxxvii. the name of Solomon. For certainly older songs also might be assigned for the object named. But perhaps it is against Ewald's hypothesis, that the contents of the psalms are not suitable for that purpose—least of all the contents of Ps. cxxii., where Jerusalem is presupposed as a city again built with palaces. The correct view will be, that *ma'aloth* signifies the regular *pilgrimages* to Jerusalem; and we accordingly have here a collection of songs for the pilgrims of Zion. To this view several things point in these psalms. For example, Ps. cxxi. is evidently a journey-song. Ps. cxxii. begins: "I was glad when they said unto me, Let us go into the house of the Lord. Our feet shall stand within thy gates, O Jerusalem," &c. It is true some of these psalms have a more general import, inasmuch as they have for their subject Israel's distress, the consolation which Israel draws from the divine promise, and the like. But to sing of these things suited right well for those who were on their pilgrimage to Jerusalem to worship the Lord.—*Oehler.*

PSALM CXX.

3, 4. *What shall be given unto thee? or what shall be done unto thee, thou false tongue?* &c. This passage admits of two interpretations. Some scholars read the whole as an address to the slanderer: "What shall a deceitful tongue give to thee, and what shall it profit thee? No doubt your calumnies are sharp as arrows of the mighty warrior, and they burn as long as coals of juniper. Well, but what benefit do they confer upon you?" This is an excellent meaning. It is a fair question to a person who carries on such a vile trade. What will you gain by attacking the righteous? Will you increase your own happiness by cherishing malice? Will it promote your pecuniary interests? Will it make you more loved and honoured in the relations of social life? Will it prepare you for acceptance with the Judge, when all nations shall assemble before his tribunal, to give an account of their doings? Can you ever succeed in carrying out your nefarious designs against the man who is clothed from head to foot in armour of heavenly temper? No. Sharp and burning may be the arrows, strong may be the arm, and true may be the eye; but the fiery darts fall back harmless from the shield of faith, and lie cold upon the ground. The enemies of David could not deprive him of the high honours bestowed upon him by God; and humiliated and defeated, the question might be applied to them with marvellous point: What good had you from your lip of falsehood and your tongue of deceit?

We prefer, however, reading the passage as it stands in the authorized version. In this case the third verse inquires of the calumniator what penalty shall be inflicted upon him. "What shall be given unto thee? or what shall be done unto thee, false tongue?" The fourth verse supplies the answer: "Sharp arrows of the mighty, with coals of juniper." The world's sin is the world's punishment. A correspondence is frequently observed between the transgression and the retribution. The evil we had prepared for others is afterwards applied to our own lips. He who sows serpents' teeth need not look for a joyous harvest. "The heathen are sunk down in the pit that they made: in the net which they hid is their own foot taken."—*M'Michael.*

PSALM CXXI.

The idea is a very probable one, that the psalm was the evening song of the sacred pilgrim band, sung on retiring to rest upon the last evening, when the long wished-for termination of their wandering, the mountains of Jerusalem, had come into view in the distance. In this case we obtain a suitable connection with the following psalm, which would be sung *one* station further on, when the pilgrims were at the gates of Jerusalem. In this case we find an explanation of the fact, that in the middle point of the psalm there stands the Lord as the *keeper* of Israel, with reference to the declaration, "I keep thee," which was addressed to the patriarch as he slept on his pilgrimage; and in this case also "he neither slumbereth nor sleepeth," is seen in its true light.— *Hengstenberg.*

In reading this psalm one has a feeling that it is the evening song of the pilgrims as they go up to Jerusalem from their various districts, "to give thanks unto the name of the Lord." The day's journey is over, and they have reached that high land where the Holy City first bursts upon their view, with that glorious temple in the midst, its pure marble shining like a huge mountain of snow. Before the wearied pilgrims compose themselves to rest, they unite in declaring their trust in the Keeper of Israel, who neither slumbers nor sleeps. The psalm is sung, and it rises upward and upward, until it enters the ear of Him who is the hearer of prayer, and who, of all temples, prefers the humble and contrite heart. They lie down in the open air, the stars rush out one by one, as if to keep sentry over them, and soon all is still.—*M'Michael.*

3. *He that keepeth thee will not slumber.* That great eye never closes. That great eye is as bright and piercing as ever, and not for a single instant is the vigilance relaxed. A poor woman, as the eastern story has it, came to the sultan one day and asked compensation for the loss of some property. "How did you lose it?" said the monarch. "I fell asleep," was the reply, "and a robber entered my dwelling." "Why did you fall asleep?" "I fell asleep because I believed that you were awake." The sultan was so much delighted with the answer of the woman, that he ordered her loss to be made up. But what is true, only by a legal fiction, of human governments, that they never sleep, is true in the most absolute sense with reference to the divine government. We can sleep in safety because our God is ever awake. We are safe, because he never slumbers. Jacob had a beautiful picture of the ceaseless care of divine providence on the night when

he fled from his father's house. The
lonely traveller slept on the ground,
with the stones for his pillow and the
sky for his canopy. He had a wondrous vision of a ladder stretching from
earth to heaven, on which angels were
seen ascending and descending. And
he heard Jehovah saying to him, "Behold I am with thee, and will keep thee
in all places whither thou goest."—
M'Michael.

PSALM CXXII.

An introduction of two verses stands
instead of a *title*, announcing the object
of the psalm. The preceding psalm
was intended to be sung in sight of
Jerusalem, and this one at the gates of
the city, where the pilgrim train had
halted for the purpose of arranging the
solemn procession to the sanctuary. . . .
The title attributes the psalm to David
as its author; and internal evidence
confirms it. The design of the psalm
can only be explained in connection
with the times of David. Its design is
to conciliate the affections of the people
for the new capital; to procure for it
that place in their feelings which it
occupied externally. Ver. 3 takes for
granted that Jerusalem had recently,
for the first time, become a beautifully
built city; and this was the case in
David's time. At all events, the description of Jerusalem, as a city beautifully built, well compacted, adorned
with palaces, and fortified, *here* and in
ver. 7, points to a time before the captivity. . . .

The reasons which have been adduced
against the Davidic origin of the psalm
are of no force. The assertion that
ver. 2 is not applicable to David, but
only to the pilgrims who approached
the city from without, is set aside by
the remark, that David here, as he
frequently did (for example Ps. xx.
xxi.), sung from the soul of the people.
The mention of the *house of the Lord*,
in ver. 1 and 9, does not lead to the
time after the building of Solomon's
temple, for it is undeniable that even
the early sanctuary was known by this
name; comp. Ps. v. 7; xxvii. 4; lv. 14;
and at Ps. lii. 8. The assertion that
pilgrimages to Jerusalem did not come
into general use till some time after the
reign of David, when uniformity of
public worship had been completely
established, depends upon the idea,
which is not at all borne out by history,
that the directions contained in the

Pentateuch, as to there being only one
sanctuary, were not observed till a
later age. It has been proved in the
treatise on the Pentateuch and the
time of the judges, in vol. iii. of the
Beitr., that, during the whole period
of the judges, the people had only one
sanctuary, and that to it were brought
the sacrifices of the whole nation, and
that the great festivals, especially the
passover, were celebrated in accordance
with the directions of the law, Ex.
xxiii. 15-17; xxxiv. 23; Deut. xvi. 16.
That the sanctuary in Jerusalem, under
David, did in reality come exactly into
the place of the earlier one at Shiloh,
is clear from the fact, that the ark of
the covenant was there, "the heart of
the Israelitish religion," and, indeed,
the ark of the covenant rising from its
grave (comp. *Beitr.* p. 48, ss.), as intimated by the circumstance, that, as
soon as it was consecrated, sacrifices
were offered before it (2 Sam. vi. 5, 13).
The matter finally is put beyond a
doubt by the psalms of David's age, for
they speak only of *one* sanctuary, the
sanctuary at Jerusalem (comp. at Ps.
xv. 1). The old tabernacle, indeed, at
Gibeon, still continued to exist, but
only as a ruin. David did not act like
the breakers of images; he respected
externally the attachments of the
people, but with happy effect he did
everything he could to turn the regard
of the people more and more towards
Jerusalem: and the psalm before us,
along with others, served this object—
its design being to awaken love, devout
love, for Jerusalem and its sanctuary.
There are, besides, distinct traces of
solemn processions to the sanctuary in
the time of David, Ps. xlii. 4; lv. 14.—
The mention of the *house* of David
cannot seem strange. David had founded a *new house* instead of the *house of
Saul*, 2 Sam. iii. 1. Even before the
promise which he received through
Nathan, he hoped and wished that he
would continue to reign in his posterity
(comp. at Ps. xxi. 4; cxxxviii. 3), and
after that promise he always looked
upon himself as the founder of a family
which was to last for ever, for example,
Ps. xviii. 20.—Finally, the assertion
that the language is that of a *later* age
has no further foundation to rest on
than the ש occurring twice instead of
אשר. This form, however, occurs in a
much older song, that of Deborah; and
in the present instance it need occasion
very little difficulty, occurring, as it

does, in a *popular* song, which consists of the language of ordinary life, and may be expected to contain forms which would afterwards appear in written language.

As far as concerns the time of composition, the psalm takes for granted that Jerusalem had already become the ecclesiastical and civil capital. It cannot, therefore, have been composed before 2 Sam. vi.; but it must have been composed shortly after that period, as its design is to render popular the new institution, to endear to the affections of the people the city "which was the bond of sacred union."—*Hengstenberg*.

4. *Whither the tribes go up.* The church is still the centre of union. To this sacred place the tribes of God are ever going up, in accordance with the divine statute, "to give thanks unto the name of the Lord." All local peculiarities, all national distinctions, vanish in the house of God. The Asiatic and the Esquimaux, the Red Indian and the islander of the Southern Ocean, the African and the European, assemble here as one family; and throwing aside all sectional feuds and rivalries, they worship on the same holy mountain. The great bond of union is Christ, and, joined to Him who is our living Head, we are members of one another. All one in Christ. There is one Father, one Redeemer, one Holy Ghost. There is one condemnation, and there is one redemption; one cross of atonement, one throne of grace, one home in heaven. Wherever believers meet, they can sing the same psalms, and repeat the same prayers. The house of God disowns all the distinctions of earth: "The rich and poor meet together; the Lord is the maker of them all." Religion forms the great uniting principle, while sin is the source of all disorder. Love to man has its deepest roots in love to God; and we anticipate that bright millennial period when "the mountain of the house of the Lord shall be established in the top of the mountains," and all nations shall flow into it, and meet there as friends and brothers, members of the Holy Catholic Church. Pray and labour; and urge forward the chariot-wheels of the Redeemer. — *Pilgrim Psalms*.

6. *They shall prosper that love thee.* A consuming zeal for the house of God is common to all the psalms. So many of them are either lamentations over the reverses of Zion or songs of thanksgiving because of her prosperity, and so distinctly do they thus reflect her contemporary fortunes, that the careful student of the national history finds little difficulty in affixing to many of them the date at which they were composed and first sung. One consequence is, that God has thus provided songs adapted to every variety of condition in which the church can be placed. Another scarcely less important is, that the faithful are admonished to raise themselves out of that selfish isolation,—that entire absorption in the concerns of their own personal well-being,—into which even good men are apt to fall. I believe that the lesson just named is one which very many God-fearing people have sadly failed to lay to heart. They can sing that half of the Psalter which expresses the various exercises of *personal* piety; but the other half, which summons them *to remember Zion,* calls forth little of warm sympathy from their hearts. Even in the interest of personal piety itself, this is to be lamented. Job's captivity was turned when he prayed for his friends: and it has many a time been found that believers who before were troubled with weakness and perpetual fears, have been lifted up into a higher and brighter and serener region, when, looking no more on their own things only, they have become absorbed in labours and prayers in behalf of some grand Christian enterprise. The Lord will not fail to "remember his Davids and all their afflictions,"—their anxious labours for his house and kingdom. David's own faith in this matter was strong; and here he encourages God's people to pray for the peace of Jerusalem, by reminding them that "they shall prosper that love her."—*Binnie*.

A reason is here assigned why we should pray for the peace and prosperity of the church. Our own interest has an inseparable connection with it. Worldly prosperity cannot indeed be affirmed of all the true Israel; though our Saviour's declaration still preserves its value: 'But seek ye first the kingdom of God, and his righteousness; and all these things shall be added unto you." But one thing can be promised with infallible certainty, that the friends of Zion shall enjoy much spiritual prosperity. To a certain extent the benefit is theirs already. It is an excellent evidence of advancement in the divine life, when we love the house of God, pray for its peace, and labour for its welfare. And the more ardent our aspirations, and the more unremitting our exertions, the greater happiness we shall experience, and the more clearly shall we read our title to an inheritance in heaven. The best and speediest mode of promoting our own spiritual prosperity, is just to engage with heart and hand in every cause which is identified with the glory of the eternal God, and the eternal welfare of man. Indolent Christians have very little joy in the Lord. They are melancholy, moping, and discontented; and it is proper they should remain in darkness until they find out what is wrong, and take an active part in schemes of benevolence. The happy Christians are the working Christians. Make the experiment if you have not done so before; and you will soon learn how true it is, They shall prosper that love Zion.—*Pilgrim Psalms.*

PSALM CXXIII.

This psalm is either the sigh of the exile, towards the close of the captivity, looking in faith and patience for the deliverance which he had reason to hope was now nigh at hand; or it is the sigh of those who, having already returned to their native land, were still exposed to the "scorn and contempt" of the Samaritans and others, who, favoured by the Persian government, took every opportunity of harassing and insulting the Jews. Comp. Neh. ii. 19, "They laughed us to scorn, and despised us," with ver. 4 of the psalm, "The scorn of them that are at ease, the contempt of the proud."—*Perowne.*

4. *Our soul is exceedingly filled with the scorning of those that are at ease.* Be thankful that they can use no other weapons than calumny and contempt. The Jews had to contend at the same time with open violence. Were their power equal to their will, they would confiscate your property, they would confine you in dungeons, they would burn you at the stake. In Athens they would have condemned Socrates, the greatest and best philosopher of antiquity, to drink the cup of hemlock; and they would have banished Aristides, because they were tired of hearing every one call him Aristides the Just. In Jerusalem they would have goaded on the senseless rabble, and swelled the

ferocious shout, Not this man, but Barabbas! In St. Andrews they would have sat at the castle windows, and feasted their eyes when good Patrick Hamilton was consuming in the flames; and they would have gone in afterwards and dined with an unimpeachable appetite. In slave countries they would tar and feather the missionaries who proclaim to the degraded negroes the unsearchable riches of Christ. The same Satanic spirit still reigns; and can we be too grateful that these enemies of the cross are kept in chains! We live in a land of civil and religious freedom; and they cannot go beyond the boundaries of misrepresentation and scorn. They may show their teeth and growl, but they cannot bite. They may curse you, but they cannot lay a finger upon you. They may hiss at you, but what is that compared with the rattlesnake springing upon you, embracing you with his slimy folds, fastening his fangs in your flesh, and changing you in a few hours into a hideous and bloated corpse! How can we value enough the privileges of Christians in this dear land of our fathers, where Freedom has built her home! "They shall sit every man under his vine and under his fig-tree; and none shall make them afraid: for the mouth of the Lord of hosts hath spoken it."—*Pilgrim Psalms.*

PSALM CXXIV.

It is impossible for us to realize the circumstances of these persons. We know not the danger. We know not the deliverance. We know not the gratitude. Ours is indeed a blessed ignorance; but one effect of this ignorance is, that we have not a sufficient sympathy with the victims of persecution. Enjoying the blessings of religious freedom, worshipping God in our churches without distraction of spirit, how can we appreciate the condition of those pious men who were hunted as partridges on the mountains, and whose lives were placed in perpetual peril, on account of their attachment to truth! Our ancestors understood these things much better than we do. And a few months' persecution would give us a much more accurate and vivid idea of the hardships which they endured than a whole volume of eloquent description. What true men, with all their failings, were those covenanting fathers of ours! They sacrificed all that was dear to flesh and blood rather than renounce that liberty of public worship which is the inalienable birthright of the church, and which is independent of human laws, because superior to them all. Conceive them seated on a hillside in the midst of a wild moor, and just escaped from the soldiers of Claverhouse, a man ferocious as any beast of prey, and merciless as any flood of waters; and with what thrilling emotions would this psalm be sung!

> " Had not the Lord been on our side,
>   May Israel now say;
>   Had not the Lord been on our side,
>   When men rose us to slay."

—Pilgrim Psalms.

PSALM CXXV.

This psalm was composed after the Babylonish captivity. It refers to the troublous times of Nehemiah. The rebuilding of the wall of Jerusalem had commenced, but the work was carried on under most discouraging circumstances. The inveterate opposition of the Samaritans has been frequently noticed. They maligned the Jewish builders at the Persian court; and, in concert with their heathen neighbours, they had recourse to open violence. The builders were under the necessity of working with a sword at their side, so that when the trumpet sounded they might at once repair to the place where an attack was made, and with flashing weapons repel their adversaries. But with all these precautions, the poor and persecuted Hebrew colony, endeavouring to build the temple of their God and the city of their fathers, would assuredly have been destroyed had there been no gracious interposition of Heaven. Their condition may be described with singular fidelity and power in the words of the preceding psalm. If the Lord had not been on their side, their enemies would have swallowed them up alive.

The church here declares her trust in God in all time of tribulation. He would prove her friend, and that too at no distant period. And to make the divine promises visible, as it were, to the eye of sense, the illustrations are selected from the mountain scenery of Jerusalem. One may readily imagine with what thrilling sensations this sacred ode would be sung by the pious Jews. Hope fires their bosom, the blood rushes in rapid tides through their veins, fresh strength is acquired for endurance and labour, and their voices become louder and more jubilant, as, with eyes fixed upon the guardian mountains of the holy city, they sing: "They that trust in the Lord shall be as Mount Zion, which cannot be removed, but abideth for ever. As the mountains are round about Jerusalem, so the Lord is round about his people from henceforth, even for ever."—*Pilgrim Psalms.*

PSALM CXXVI.

The first colony of exiles had returned to Palestine. The permission to return had been so unexpected, the circumstances which had led to it so wonderful and so unforeseen, that when it came it could hardly be believed. To those who found themselves actually restored to the land of their fathers it seemed like a dream. It was a joy beyond all words to utter. God, their fathers' God, had indeed wrought for them, and even the heathen had recognized his hand.

It is with these thoughts that this beautiful psalm opens. But, after all, what was that little band of settlers which formed the first caravan? It was but as the trickling of a tiny rill in some desert waste. Hence the prayer bursts from the lip of the psalmist, Bring back our captives like mighty streams, which, swollen by the wintry rains, descend to fertilize the parched and desolate wilderness. Then comes the thought of the many discouragements and opposition which the first settlers had to encounter; it was a time of sowing in tears (Ezra iv. 11–24). Still faith could expect a joyful harvest. He who had restored them to the land would assuredly crown his work with blessing. —*Perowne.*

PSALM CXXVII.

Two psalms bear Solomon's name. One of these is the hundred and twenty-seventh. . . . Some recent critics throw doubt on the trustworthiness of the superscription. But most people will judge that this must be in virtue of some foregone conclusion, and will agree with Luther, Calvin, and the generality of the older commentators, in thinking that the psalm is so exactly in the manner of the wise author of the Proverbs, that we need not hesitate to attribute it to his pen. It is the lyrical expression of thoughts which run through the "dark sayings" of that book. The first part of it, for instance, is a beautiful reproduction of Prov. x. 22: "The blessing of the Lord, it maketh rich, and he addeth no sorrow with it;" and the correspondence is still closer if we translate the latter clause, as many do, "And sorrowful toil addeth nothing to it." Familiar as the proverb has become in the speech of every Christian nation, the psalm is yet more familiar. From it the pious builders of a former generation borrowed the NISI DOMINUS FRUSTRA, which may be read on the lintels of houses in our older streets. An admirable confession of faith to be made by any man who is called to be a builder in church or commonwealth! It is the Lord's blessing that builds the house and keeps the town; that fills the house with the stir of children, and peoples the town with valiant sons, who, with unabashed brow, will speak with the enemies in the gate.—*Binnie.*

2. *For so he giveth his beloved sleep.* Even so he giveth (it) to his beloved in sleep. EVEN (SO), nearly equivalent to "the very self-same thing." *He giveth (it),* i.e. bread, the necessaries of life, *in sleep.* What others obtain only with such wearing toil, such constant effort, with so much disappointment and so much sorrow, God gives to the man whom he loves, as it were *while he sleeps,* i.e. without all this anxiety and exertion. This is the interpretation now perhaps commonly adopted, but it seems to me very questionable (though I accepted it in the first edition), for the following reasons:—(1), It is necessary to supply "bread," not "bread of sorrows," in this clause; and (2), I am not satisfied that the rendering of the accusative "*in sleep*" is justifiable. . . . I am inclined, therefore, to prefer the rendering, "So he giveth his beloved sleep," though it is no doubt difficult to explain the reference of the particle "so." I suppose it refers to the principle laid down in the previous verses, there being a tacit comparison, "as all labour is vain without God's providence, so he gives the man who loves him and leaves all in his hands, calm refreshing sleep."

There is no discouragement here, it is needless to say, to honest labour. It is undue anxiety, a feverish straining, a toiling, as if toil of itself could command success, the folly of which is condemned. Compare for a similar sentiment Prov. x. 22, "The blessing of Jehovah maketh rich, and toil can add nothing thereto." The teaching is that

of our Lord in the Sermon on the Mount, Mat. vi. 25-34; see Lu. x. 41; 1 Pe. v. 7. God's beloved are not exempted from the great law of labour which lies upon all, but the sting is taken from it when they can leave all results in a Father's hand, with absolute trust in his wisdom and goodness.—*Perowne.*

The last clause of the verse may be thus rendered: He giveth his beloved in sleep. What other men are anxiously toiling for, day and night, the pious receive from God while they are sleeping. We prefer this translation. It is more in harmony with the leading principle of the psalm. And there seems, moreover, a marked allusion to Solomon himself. Solomon was called Jedidiah, which signifies the beloved of the Lord; and it was during sleep that the divine blessing was conferred. He had asked for wisdom alone, and God said, "And I have also given thee that which thou hast not asked, both riches and honour; so that there shall not be any among the kings like unto thee all thy days." The thought thus modified is extremely beautiful. God is working for his people even when they are asleep. The men of the world are toiling and struggling, labouring night and day, as if they were slaves, and with what pitiable results! But Jehovah showers rich benedictions on his beloved ones in sleep. They act to the best of their judgment; they labour without distraction of spirit; and they leave the issues in the hands of Him from whom comes down every good and every perfect gift. They lie down with a feeling of security; and while their senses are steeped in forgetfulness, and the calm slumbers are recruiting their strength for the duties of another day, God is working for them all the time, and is blessing the fruits of their honest industry. A general of Athens was uncommonly successful in several engagements. A painter who supposed that these successes were more owing to good fortune than to his abilities, represented him as sound asleep under a tree, while the goddess of liberty was twining the laurels around his brow. And so the good man sleeps: but the Shepherd of Israel sleeps not. His eye is upon him every moment; his hand is working for him all the night long as well as during the day, and crowning his efforts with success. Beyond all contradiction, he giveth his beloved in sleep.—*Pilgrim Psalms.*

3. *Lo, children are an heritage of the Lord*, &c. The psalmist's description is a very bright one (in Ps. cxxviii. namely). But there is another side to the picture. Domestic life has its share of the sorrows and anxieties that belong to this sin-stricken world. The birth of children not seldom is itself the occasion of anxiety: for how are they to be fed and clothed? Another family song has been provided to meet this case. Ps. cxxvii. is the complement of Ps. cxxviii. . . . Children are the Lord's gift; and parents may trust in him that, if they do their duty, he who sends mouths will send meat to fill them. Prudent industry ought not to be suffered to degenerate into unbelieving anxiety about the future.

These domestic psalms caused sore perplexity to the early fathers. For the notion already referred to, that conjugal life is essentially earthly in its spirit and incompatible with a high style of godliness, early came to prevail, and engendered that false and dangerous estimation of celibacy which ultimately brought forth its fruit in the monastic institutions of the Greek and Latin churches. Even Chrysostom and Augustine were not superior to this weakness. The latter divine, in expounding the psalms before us, explains away the obvious and natural sense of the words, and turns them into an allegory. The *wife* is the church;—for is not the spouse of Christ a vine from Egypt—a fruitful vine? The *olive plants* are the children of Zion: and so forth. Much can be said, no doubt, in extenuation of the error of these great men. It was an error, nevertheless, and wrought much mischief. Of the many services which the world owes to the reformers, not the least valuable was their reinstating of the family in its long-forgotten honours. Luther, in particular, vindicated the truth of God on this subject with incomparable power. His marriage was intended to be a protest against the doctrine which attributed a peculiar sanctity to single life, and a solemn declaration of his belief that the wedded life of Christians is holy; and the testimony was not thrown away. Of the four bass-reliefs that adorn the great Luther Monument just erected at Worms, one perpetuates the memory of the day on which the reformer gave his hand to Catherine von Bora, and expresses the sense entertained by the German nation of the value of the ex-

ample which he then set to his countrymen and to all Christendom. It deserves to be mentioned that Luther's high estimate of the dignity of the family was mightily fortified by the psalms, especially by the two which we have quoted. He wrote separate commentaries on them, in which he did ample justice to their natural and obvious sense. Thus men's minds were opened to perceive that the monastic idea of a religious life is a very different one indeed from that of the holy prophets and psalmists.—*Binnie.*

PSALM CXXVIII.

See under Psalm cxxvii.

PSALM CXXIX.

The psalm suits perfectly well to the time to which all the nameless pilgrim-songs belong, the period after the return from the exile. At that time the experience related in ver. 1–4 was far richer than formerly; the youth of the people, according to ver. 1 and 2, was long past and gone; and the intermediate position between the deliverance already obtained and the still existing oppression corresponds exactly to the situation of Israel at the period in question. Still it were too much to affirm that the psalm, viewed merely by itself, must of necessity belong to this period.—*Hengstenberg.*

PSALM CXXX.

When Luther, in the year 1530, was in the fortress of Coburg, on four occasions during the night there seemed to pass before his eyes burning torches, and this was followed by a severe headache. One night he saw three blazing torches come in at the window of his room, and he swooned away. His servant, coming to his assistance, poured oil of almonds into his ear, and rubbed his feet with hot napkins. As soon as he recovered he bade him read to him a portion of the Epistle to the Galatians, and during the reading fell asleep. The danger was over, and when he awoke he cried out joyfully, "Come, to spite the devil, let us sing the psalm, *De profundis*, in four parts."

Being asked on one occasion which were the best psalms, he replied, "The Pauline psalms," and being pressed to say which they were, he answered: "The 32d, the 51st, the 130th, and the 143d. For they teach us that the forgiveness of sins is vouchsafed to them that believe without the law and without works; therefore they are Pauline psalms; and when David sings, 'With thee is forgiveness, that thou mayest be feared,' so Paul likewise saith, 'God hath concluded all under sin, that he may have mercy on all.' Therefore none can boast of his own righteousness, but the words, 'That thou mayest be feared,' thrust away all self-merit, teach us to take off our hat before God and confess, *gratia est, non meritum, remissio non satisfactio*—it is all forgiveness, and no merit."—*Delitzsch in " Perowne."*

What is the great object to be accomplished by this remission of sin? It is the creation of piety. "That thou mayest be feared." This fear, being the result of pardon, cannot be the fear of punishment. . . . It is the reverence which a loving child has to a kind father: it is the reverence which is formed in the soul of the pardoned sinner as he contemplates the holy character of that God who has forgiven him, and muses upon that tremendous sacrifice through which his redemption has been achieved. . . .

The principle here laid down is a simple one. There is no true piety, there is no sacred fear of God, there is no genuine worship, there is no loving obedience until the pardon has been granted. We must ever begin with the remission of sins. The idea of the divine justice, viewed apart from the divine mercy, inspires the criminal with terror, and fills him with still deeper hatred against God. It is only when the sinner views God in Christ, reconciling the world unto himself, not imputing their trespasses unto them, that he is attracted towards him, melts in submission, and acquires a sacred fear of offending him. How, indeed, can it be otherwise? You must first convince me that God loves me before I can love him. You must first convince me that he is willing to pardon me before I can solicit his forgiveness. You must first convince me that he has removed from me this awful load of guilt, and will never place it on again, before I can serve him with a free and cheerful heart. You must first convince me that he has adopted me into his family before I can give him the affection and the obedience of a son. . . . First forgiveness, then fear: first pardon, then piety: first justification, then sanctification: first

the heart, then the life: first make the tree good, and then you will get good fruit. This is the divine plan, and nothing can be conceived more rational. But sin has introduced such disorder into the mental faculties that men do not perceive the gospel to be the manifold wisdom of God; and they turn away from it with a kind of instinctive abhorrence. Hence all perversions of the gospel reverse the divine order, and insist upon placing the effect before the cause. . . . It is just because men will not accept the simple, unencumbered, philosophical plan of God, that so many and such fatal mistakes are committed in religion. . . . "We love him, because he first loved us." "The love of Christ constraineth us; because we thus judge, that if one died for all, then were all dead: and that he died for all, that they who live should not henceforth live unto themselves but unto him who died for them, and rose again."—*Pilgrim Psalms.*

PSALM CXXXI.

This very pleasant ode is in the title ascribed to David, and furnishes one of the instances in which the testimony of the titles is summarily rejected by many recent critics. Having, first of all, made up their minds that there are no psalms of David so far on in the Psalter, they either, like Dr. Hupfeld, set aside the testimony of the title as "unworthy of refutation," or at best they explain it away as meaning no more than that this is a psalm written "after David's manner." This latter explanation is adopted by Dr. Delitzsch, who, however, admits that the sentiments of the psalm agree perfectly with all we know of David. The truth is, that the grounds on which the testimony of the inscription has, in this instance, been set aside, are fitted to confirm the impression that the scepticism with which these have come to be regarded cannot be justified. Dr. Delitzsch is undoubtedly in the right when he says that "David was a pattern of the sentiment expressed in this psalm," and that "resignation to God's guidance, submission to his dispensations, contentment with whatsoever he was pleased to mete out, were among the essential features of his noble character." By some of his many critics the royal prophet has been accused of ambition, and it is by no means unlikely that his youth showed some blossomings of that proud flower—the "last infirmity of noble minds." The sharpness with which his brothers accused him of pride, when they saw his valour roused by the disdainful challenge of the Philistine, would seem to indicate that the family at Bethlehem had observed in him aspirations and powers which looked beyond the tending of Jesse's flocks. But if ambitious thoughts found entrance into his mind, they were not cherished, or permitted to betray him into the measures characteristic of ambitious men. In all the brilliant company of gifted men who have risen from a low rank to sit amongst the mighty—the princes, statesmen, warriors of the world, it would be hard to point out a single individual who could have sung Ps. cxxxi. with such perfect truth and fitness as the son of Jesse.—*Binnie.*

2. *As a child that is weaned of his mother.* The child here introduced is a weaned child, but not one that is newly weaned. A child that has just been weaned is restless and impatient; and it still longs for its natural nourishment. But this child is quiet and contented; and it lies upon its mother's lap without any pining regrets. Thus understood, the comparison is beautiful and appropriate. David had no desire for worldly distinctions. Girt as he was with pomp and power, they had lost their attractive influence. He was as much weaned from them as a child who has no longer any relish for its former food, and is entirely resigned to the maternal care. The man of sublime genius, the victor in many a battle-field, the crowned king of Israel was meek and lowly as a little child. "My soul is even as a weaned child."

Surely this was a foreshadowing of the truth taught a thousand years afterwards by the Great Teacher himself. The child is the highest type of the Christian. "Jesus called a little child unto him, and set him in the midst of them, and said, Verily I say unto you, Except ye be converted, and become as little children, ye shall not enter into the kingdom of heaven. Whosoever therefore shall humble himself as this little child, the same is the greatest in the kingdom of heaven." It is as if he had said to the apostles: Your bosoms are panting after the high honours that await you when my kingdom is established on the earth. So eager is your craving for personal aggrandizement, that you are quarrelling even now among yourselves as to the superior places. But let me tell you, that unless this ambitious disposition be changed, and you become humble as little children, you will not get into the kingdom at all. Look at this child. Make him your pattern : be as he is : and you will be the greatest in my church. What an idea of true greatness! The child is the greatest among us all, and the greatest because unconscious of it. Heaven lies around us in our infancy. That child has but lately come from God; and, in his innocent looks and words, there beams forth a divine glory, which may put us all to shame. Pride has no existence in the bosom of a child. If there, it has been put there by its parents, who should know better. He is ignorant of all the distinctions of earth, and cares nothing about them. He has also boundless trust in a parent's love; and the thought of to-morrow leaves no dark unrest upon his soul. His is a contentment surpassing all wealth. And so, Christian parent, when that little child of yours is seated on your knees, filling your eyes with a joyous light; and when he looks up so lovingly in your face, and feels he has no want so long as he is beside you, do not be ashamed of taking from him a lesson of spiritual profit. Let the little prattler preach you a powerful sermon on the greatness of humility. May it be the chief wish of your heart to be strong in faith as he is, and to have the same confidence in your heavenly Father which he has in you.—*Pilgrim Psalms.*

PSALM CXXXII.

As Ps. xxiv. was composed by David to be sung at the bringing up of the ark to the tabernacle on Mount Zion, so Ps. cxxxii. was composed by Solomon, or by some Levitical psalmist in concert with him, to be sung when the ark was borne into its final resting-place within the golden chamber of the temple. Solomon's prayer on the occasion, as it is reported in the Chronicles, concludes with petitions that constitute the burden of the psalm, "Now therefore arise, O Lord God, into thy resting-place, thou, and the ark of thy strength : let thy priests, O Lord God, be clothed with salvation, and let thy saints rejoice in goodness. O Lord God, turn not away the face of thine anointed : remember the mercies of David thy servant," 2 Chr. vi. 41, 42. I do not forget that some, like our venerable translators, judge the psalm to have been written by David for a "prayer at the removing of the ark," and suppose that it is he who here "commendeth unto God the religious care he had for the ark;" nor do I forget that other critics connect the psalm with the consecration of the second temple. But neither supposition corresponds perfectly to the tenor of the psalm. God did not say of David's new tabernacle, "This is my rest for ever; here will I dwell:" and as for the second temple, we know indeed that its builders might well have prayed, like Solomon, "Arise, O Lord, into thy rest," but they could not have added, "Thou and the ark of thy strength;" for the ark never entered that second house. Moreover, is it not most natural to suppose that it was Solomon, and the Levites his contemporaries, the men who had been eye-witnesses of the late king's solicitude about the erection of a fit dwelling-place for the God of Jacob, that gave utterance to the affectionate reminiscence with which the psalm opens?—*Binnie.*

Some suppose that this psalm was composed by David. The arguments in favour of Solomon have more weight. "The whole tenor of this psalm," says Jebb, "is an exact epitome of the dedication prayer of Solomon (2 Chr. vi.) The topics are the same,—the building the house of the Lord—the promise to David—the inhabitation of the Almighty; and the concluding sentences of the dedication are identical with the expressions of the psalm in ver. 8-10. There can therefore be little question that this psalm was composed by Solomon." If this opinion be correct, it is almost certain that it was sung by the congregated multitudes when the ark was removed from the tabernacle in Mount Zion to the magnificent temple on Mount Moriah. It was a season of solemn joy, the greatest that had ever occurred in their national history. There was a similar use of it beyond all question at the dedication of the second temple of Ezra. The psalm is thus rich in historical associations; and frequently has it been sung by the church, when the dark clouds rolled away, and the face of God beamed again with favour, as it did in the days of old.— *Pilgrim Psalms.*

PSALM CXXXIII.

When the whole house of Israel chose David for their king, and the throne was established at Jerusalem, the new capital, he lost no time in bringing up the ark from Kirjath-jearim, and restoring the tabernacle service with more than its ancient splendour. And these great events were accompanied with a gush of sacred melody. They constituted the most memorable epoch in the history of the Hebrew church, between the exodus from Egypt and the incarnation of Christ. Accordingly the songs belonging to this period are of a peculiarly lofty and joyful character. How does the psalmist exult in the re-union of the whole house of Israel, in Ps. cxxxiii.; a song which has, times without number, enabled God's people to give tuneful utterance to the grateful feelings of their hearts when "the Lord has built up Jerusalem, and gathered together the dispersed of Israel."— *Binnie.*

PSALM CXXXIV.

The outline of the psalm may be given thus: the pilgrim-bands present themselves on the evening of their arrival at the temple, and call upon the servants of the Lord, who were there at the time of the evening sacrifice, to praise the Lord in their name and that of the people, and to pray to him. Coming with such a state of mind, they could not remain long without the blessing, therefore the priests answered them by pronouncing that. Such a psalm was most fitly appropriated as the close of the whole pilgrim-book; so that the collector of it, who was at the same time the author of all the nameless pilgrim-songs, undoubtedly placed this psalm purposely at the end, or composed it with a view to its forming the conclusion of the whole. So already Lampe: forte ille, qui fasciculum canticorum graduum collegit—hoc canticum tanquam aptum epilogum addidit.—*Heng.*

3. *The Lord . . . bless thee out of Zion.* It is God, not as the Maker of heaven and earth, but as dwelling in Zion, that informs us how sin can be pardoned, and man be recovered from the wrecks and ruins of the fall. We honour God as the Creator and Preserver of all things: we admire the power, and the wisdom, and the benevolence which are everywhere conspicuous in the work of his hands: we see his glory, as it shines forth from every flower under our feet, and sparkles from every star over our heads. But in all these manifestations of divine grandeur something is still

wanting. They cannot meet the necessities of the soul: they cannot warm into life the chilled heart, and exchange the moans of misery for the voices of joy: they cannot purge the conscience from dead works to serve the living God: they can throw no light into the darkness of the sepulchre: they cannot deliver us from the horrors of an unending perdition. In the church alone the grand problem is solved, the mighty secret is disclosed, how God can be just and the justifier of the ungodly! We turn to Calvary; and there, on that rugged cross, and amidst the rending rocks and the heaving earth, and under the blackened heavens and with these dying groans of the innocent Sufferer falling on our ears, we perceive a demonstration of divine love, and divine wisdom, and divine holiness, and divine power which transcends every illustration of the character of God that appears in the works of creation and providence. "Herein is love" (as if divine love were seen nowhere else), "not that we loved God, but that he loved us, and sent his Son to be the propitiation for our sins."

The gospel is the richest joy that ever came down from heaven to earth. The Lord who dwells in Zion reveals himself as a Father, whose children have wandered from him; but who desires, above all things, that they would return to his embrace, and possess his favour as in days of old before sin introduced discord and sorrow. We may thus approach him with perfect confidence, assured that, unworthy as we are, he will make us welcome for the sake of him whose blood cleanses from all sin. "Let us therefore come boldly unto the throne of grace, that we may obtain mercy, and find grace to help in time of need." My impenitent readers, will you not all put him to the proof and take him at his own word? He will bless you: he can bless you. And if he blesses you, who can curse you? If he justifies you, who can condemn? If he grants you grace, who can take it away? If he makes you rich, who can make you poor? If he promises you eternal life, and gives you a foretaste of it on earth, will he not redeem his pledge in heaven? Make immediate application for the bestowment of these blessings. Dream not of fitness. Talk not of preparation. They are all yours by a deed of gift, whenever you accept them for Christ's sake; and ascribe to him, as is most due, the entire merit of your redemption.

And having thus found God in Zion, and experienced the riches of his grace in Christ Jesus, then, when you walk abroad and survey the works of nature, it will seem as if they were invested with new splendour to your spiritual vision. "Acquaint thyself with God, if thou wouldst taste his works." The sun as he envelops creation in his mantle of light, and makes all things overflow with beauty, and music, and gladness, will remind you of the Sun of Righteousness, rising upon a benighted world and upon a benighted soul with healing under his wings. Each star, as it shoots out from the darkness, will remind you of the Star of Jacob, and of that fair star which directed the wise men of the East to the manger-cradle where the infant Jesus was laid. And when the deep blue heaven is studded with innumerable systems of glory, you can lift up your eyes and view them as the spirit's ladder, by which you may climb to the celestial city of our God; and you may exclaim with holy confidence, This is my home—my Father's house. I shall soon be there!

As one who, long detained on foreign shores,
Pants to return, and when he sees afar
His country's weather bleach'd and batter'd
    rocks,
From the green wave emerging, darts an eye
Radiant with joy toward the happy land;
So I with animated hopes behold,
And many an aching wish, your beamy fires,
That show like beacons in the blue abyss,
Ordain'd to guide th' embodied spirit home
From toilsome life, to never-ending rest.
Love kindles as I gaze. I feel desires,
That give assurance of their own success,
And that, infused from heaven, must thither
    tend.   o
                    Pilgrim Psalms.

PSALMS CXXXV. CXXXVI.

The late date of these two psalms may be inferred from the manner in which they are compacted of passages from the earlier portion of the Psalter. In respect of the formal arrangement, the first consists of three strophes of seven verses each, of which the historical strophe, ver. 8–14, stands out by its central position as the most important. The other psalm, although not divided into strophes, is marked by the occurrence in every verse of the well-known refrain "for his mercy endureth for ever," itself borrowed, either immediately or mediately, from Ps. cvi. 1.

The contents of the two psalms are, however, to a great extent the same; and they may therefore be conveniently treated of together. Both set forth the almighty power of God: both contain protests against idolatry: both recount the deliverance of Israel from Egypt: both make special mention of the divine overthrow of Sihon and Og, and of the assignment of their land as an heritage to Israel. A further comparison of both psalms with the solemn confession of sins contained in Neh. ix. will leave little doubt that it was in connection with the national fast therein recorded to have been observed that these psalms were composed. . . .

As the preceding fifteen psalms are historically connected with the rebuilding of the walls of *Jerusalem*, so do the two psalms now before us carry our thoughts back to the re-occupation of the Israelitish *territory*. Their historical starting-point is not indeed the first return from captivity; but rather Nehemiah's assemblage of the whole people that they might be reckoned by genealogy (Neh. vii. 5); that genealogy undoubtedly furnishing in many instances the key to the territorial inheritance to which each family was entitled. . . .

Their joy, however, was not unmingled with regret. They were indeed themselves settled again, according to the former allotment, in the land of their inheritance; but how contracted the limits of the district over which they were spread, when compared with those of the territory originally assigned to them! Samaria was occupied by a hostile race; Galilee too, for the present, was no longer theirs; and the fertile regions to the east of the Jordan, which had been so triumphantly won from Sihon the Amorite, conqueror of Moab, and from Og, the last of the old giant race, chieftains whose renown had made the story of their defeat one of the most attractive of the tales of olden Israelitish history, were now, according to all human appearance, almost irretrievably lost.

Under these circumstances the celebration of the ancient conquest of Canaan, while it furnished an appropriate theme of praise to those who were resettled in the land, contained also a stirring appeal to the people's faith. Knowing as they did that the whole land had been promised to Abraham and his seed after him, they must still believe in the perpetuity of the promise; they must look forward to the time when the blessing should be renewed in no measure of diminution; they must still believe that God would yet plead the cause of his people, and repent him concerning his servants. Samaria and Galilee, Bashan and Gilead, must not be given up for lost; the day should yet come when they that sat in darkness should see a great light. Even in former days, God, although he had given all Canaan, with Bashan, for his people's inheritance, had yet at various times suffered the Israelites to fall into the hands of their enemies for their sins; and so at the present season he was permitting the land of their inheritance to yield increase to the kings whom, because of their sins, he had set over them. Yet he had, in the days of the judges, been merciful to them on their repentance; and so even now, if they would return to him and keep his law, he would doubtless again make good to them his promise in all its fulness.

We shall not need to dwell on the spiritual manner in which God is now at last vindicating his faithfulness. To the Church Catholic, the true antitype of the ancient Israel, he has assigned for an inheritance every heathen realm throughout the world; nor ought she to rest content till every one be subjugated to her sway. We celebrate with joy the first triumphs of the gospel through the different quarters of the globe; we may exult in the career of success which in far-off lands is still being granted to it; but meanwhile, along with the Jews in Nehemiah's day, we have to bewail the provinces that we have lost; and those the very provinces, alas! over which the dominion of Christ was earliest asserted. Must the scenes of the first apostolic conquests be for ever abandoned to the darkness of superstition and the bane of misbelief? Must the regions of the East which Greece and Rome once subdued to civilize, and which Christianity in her turn subdued to enlighten, relapse into the semi-barbarism from which we hoped they had been rescued? Will God not yet repent himself concerning his servants and remember us in our low estate?—*Thrupp.*

PSALM CXXXVII.

Ver. 8, 9. *Happy shall he be that rewardeth thee*, &c. See *Appendix* on Ps. lxix. cix.

Examination shows that the imprecations are not the utterance of resentment for private injuries, or of a base desire to see personal enemies laid low. Sometimes, as in the wish expressed for the destruction of Edom and Babylon in Ps. cxxxvii., the objects of the imprecation are the nations which have cruelly wronged the people of God.—*Binnie*.

The principles so ably laid down by the author himself in his introduction and elsewhere, form a sufficient answer to the remark or concession he makes under these verses, to the effect, viz., that the language here savours more of imprecation than forgiveness, and is apparently prompted more by the spirit of revenge than by a desire of just punishment.

Calvin's view of this passage is characterized by his wonted penetration and judgment. We present the reader with it: "The psalmist discerns the coming judgment of God, though not yet apparent, by the eye of faith, as the apostle well calls faith 'the beholding of things not seen.' Incredible as it might appear that any calamity should overtake so mighty an empire as Babylon then was, and impregnable as it was generally considered to be, he sees in the glass of the Word its destruction and overthrow. He calls upon all God's people to do the same, and by faith from the elevation of Heaven's oracles, to despise the pride of that abandoned city. If the divine promises inspire us with hope and confidence, and God's Spirit attemper our afflictions to the rule of his own uprightness, we shall lift up our hands in the lowest depths of affliction to which we may be cast down, and glory in the fact that it is well with us in our worst distresses, and that our enemies are devoted to destruction. In declaring those to be happy who should *pay back vengeance upon the Babylonians*, he does not mean that the service done by the Medes and Persians, in itself, met with the approbation of God; for they were actuated in the war by ambition, insatiable covetousness, and unprincipled rivalry; but he declares that a war which was carried on in a manner under God's auspices, should be crowned with success. As God had determined to punish Babylon, he pronounced a blessing upon Cyrus and Darius, while on the other hand Jeremiah (ch. xlviii. 10) declares those cursed who should do the work of the Lord negligently, that is, fail in strenuously carrying out the work of desolation and destruction to which God had called them as his hired executioners. It may seem to savour of cruelty, that he should wish the tender and innocent infants to be dashed and mangled upon the stones, but he does not speak under the impulse of personal feeling, and only employs words which God had himself authorized, so that this is but the declaration of a just judgment, as when our Lord says, 'With what measure ye mete, it shall be measured to you again' (Mat. vii. 2). Isaiah (ch. xiii. 16) had issued a special prediction in reference to Babylon, which the psalmist has doubtless here in his eye—'Behold God has sharpened the iron, and bent the bows; he sends forth the Medes and Persians, which shall not regard silver and gold; they shall thirst for blood only,' &c."

PSALMS CXXXVIII.–CXLV.

These eight psalms form a series of Davidic psalms; and the reason assigned by our author for their insertion so near the close of the book, and far apart from the other psalms of the same author, is as probable as any other.

The titles assign the series to David; and Hengstenberg and Alexander do not hesitate to accept them as authoritative. They suppose the Psalms to have been among the last composed by David, and to have special reference to the promise in 2 Sam. vii.

We have now in Ps. cxxxviii.–cxlv. a cycle of Davidic psalms, called forth by David's reflection upon the promise in 2 Sam. vii., and by the anxiety which filled him regarding his posterity. In them he accompanies his offspring through their future history, and presents to them the anchor of safety in the storms, which he knew from his own experience certainly awaited them. We have here a prophetic legacy of David corresponding to his last words in 2 Sam. xxiii. That these psalms close the series of Davidic psalms is certainly not accidental, but is in unison with their internal character, and the time of their composition.

In Ps. cxxxviii. David sets the promise before the eyes of his family. In Ps. cxxxix. he presents to their view, for their consolation and incitement, the all-present God. In Ps. cxl. he brings still more closely to them the circumstances of danger that lay before them. In Ps. cxli. he strengthens them against the internal dangers with which the external necessity threatened them. In Ps. cxlii. cxliii. he shows them how they were to sustain themselves if matters came to an extremity with them. Ps. cxliv. forms the transition from the prayer-songs to the song of praise with which in Ps. cxlv. the whole is concluded. There manifestly exists a correspondence between Ps. cxxxviii., the rejoicing on account of the promise of the Lord, and Ps. cxlv., the rejoicing on account of its fulfilment; the lamentations and prayers are inclosed by praise and thanksgivings.

The appropriateness and connection of these psalms is acknowledged to some extent even by those who have deprived themselves of the vantage-ground of the superscriptions. Thus Ewald says of Ps. cxl.–cxliii. : " A series of songs so similar in matter, and so much of one stamp, that one can hardly doubt that they were the production of the same poet." Köster agrees and adds: " I take them for a supplement of the old Davidic songs. For in place of the liturgical expansive character of the preceding psalms, we are here at once brought back to the lively alternation of feelings which prevailed in Ps. iii. ss." Hitzig remarks on Ps. cxl. : " The three following psalms are of a quite similar kind, and appear to have been composed by one author much about the same time."

Seventy-two psalms of David have gone before. These eight bring up the entire number to eighty. We may perhaps regard Ps. cxxxviii. as the governing castle, and the remaining heptad as divided into three and four. The section would then be denoted by the extended superscription of Ps. cxlii.— *Hengstenberg.*

PSALM CXXXVIII.

This psalm belongs to that chain of Davidic psalms which were called forth by the promise in 2 Sam. vii., and which rest upon it, Ps. xviii. xxi. lxi. ci.–ciii. cx., comp. Ps. lxxii. lxxxix. cxxxii. That the promise here celebrated is no other than that is clear as day. Here, as well as there, the subject handled has respect to a promise of blessing of surpassing greatness,—the idols, which could exhibit nothing similar, must retreat before it ashamed, ver. 1; the Lord has glorified himself more by it than by all his earlier wonders, ver. 2; all kings of the earth will one day praise the Lord on account of it. Farther, here, as well as there, we have to do, not with a particular blessing, but with a chain of blessings, which reaches even to eternity, ver. 8. Finally, the promise has here the same subject as there. This is described more pointedly here in ver. 6 and 7 : God elevates the oppressed David above all height, revives him in the midst of trouble, brings down all his enemies.

If the psalm refers to the promise in 2 Sam. vii., there can be no doubt of the correctness of the superscription which ascribes it to David. For he, on whom the promise has been conferred, himself stands forth as the speaker. It is a proof also of David's authorship, the union, so characteristic of him, of bold courage (see especially ver. 3) and deep humility (ver. 6). And in proof of the same comes, finally, the near relationship in which it stands with the other psalms of David, especially those which likewise refer to the promise of the everlasting kingdom, and with David's thanksgiving in 2 Sam. vii., the conclusion of which, "And now, Lord God, the word which thou hast spoken upon thy servant and upon his house, that fulfil even to eternity, and do as thou hast spoken," remarkably agrees with the conclusion of our psalm. —*Hengstenberg.*

PSALM CXXXIX.

This psalm has often been admired for the grandeur of its sentiments, the elevation of its style, as well as the variety and beauty of its imagery. *Bishop Lowth,* in his 29th Prelection, classes it amongst the Hebrew idyls, as next to Ps. civ. in respect both to the conduct of the poem and the beauty of the style. "If it be excelled," says he, "(as perhaps it is) by the former in the plan, disposition, and arrangement of the matter, it is not in the least inferior in the dignity and elegance of its sentiments, images, and figures." "Amongst its other excellencies," says *Bishop Mant,* "it is for nothing more admirable than for the exquisite skill with which it descants on the perfections of deity. The psalmist's faith in the omnipresence and omniscience of Jehovah is in the commencement depicted with a singular and beautiful variety of the most lively expressions; nor can anything be more sublime than that accumulation of the noblest and loftiest images, in the seventh and following verses, commensurate with the limits of created nature, whereby the psalmist labours to impress upon the mind some notion of the infinity of God." If we compare this sacred poem with any hymn of classical antiquity in honour of the heathen deities, the immense superiority of the sentiments it contains must convince any reasonable person that David and the Israelites, though inferior in other respects to some other nations, surpassed thém in religious knowledge. No philosopher of ancient times ever attained to such sublime views of the perfections and moral government of God as the Hebrew prophets. How are we to account for this difference but on the supposition of the divine origin of the religion of the Hebrews? On any other supposition these psalms are a greater miracle than any of those recorded by Moses.

Bishop Horsley refers the composition of this psalm to a later age than that of David. "The frequent Chaldaisms," says he, "of the diction, argue no very high antiquity." *Dr. Adam Clarke*, on the same ground, argues that it was not written by the sweet singer of Israel, but during or after the time of the captivity. Other critics, however, maintain that the several Chaldaisms to be found in it afford no foundation for such an opinion. "How any critic," says *Jebb*, "can assign this psalm to other than David I cannot understand. Every line, every thought, every turn of expression and transition is his and his only. As for the arguments drawn from the two Chaldaisms which occur (רבעי for רבצי, and עריך for ציריך), this is really nugatory. These Chaldaisms consist merely in the substitution of one letter for another very like it in shape, and easily to be mistaken by a transcriber, particularly by one who had been used to the Chaldee idiom: but the moral arguments for David's authorship are so strong as to overwhelm any such verbal or rather *literal* criticism, were even the objections more formidable than they actually are."—*Translator's Note* in Calvin Translation Society's Edition.

As a proper pendant to Ps. viii., we name next Ps. cxxxix. Here the poet inverts his gaze from the blaze of suns to the strange atoms composing his own frame. He stands shuddering over the precipice of himself. Above is the All-encompassing Spirit, from whom the morning wings cannot save; and below, at a deep distance, appears amid the branching forest of his animal frame, so fearfully and wonderfully made, the abyss of his spiritual existence, lying like a dark lake in the midst. How between mystery and mystery his mind, his wonder, his very reason, seem to rock like a little boat between the sea and the sky. But speedily does he regain his serenity, when he throws himself, with childlike haste and confidence, into the arms of that Fatherly Spirit, and murmurs in his bosom, "How precious also are thy thoughts unto *me*, O God; how great is the sum of them;" and looking up at last in his face, cries— "Search me, O Lord. I cannot search thee; I cannot search myself; I am overwhelmed by those dreadful depths; but search me as thou only canst; see if there be any wicked way in me, and lead me in the way everlasting."—Gilfillan: *Bards of the Bible.*

7. *Whither shall I go from thy spirit.* There are in Amos certain brief and bold sublimities which class his genius with that of the best of the lesser prophets. Such, in ch. ix., is the vision of the Lord standing upon the altar, and proclaiming the inextricable dilemmas into which Israel's crimes had led them. In all Scripture occur no more powerful antitheses than the following :—"He that fleeth of them shall not flee away; and he that escapeth of them shall not escape (into safety). If they dig down into Sheol, thence shall mine hand take them. If they climb up into heaven, thence shall I bring them down. If they hide themselves in the top of Carmel, I will search for, and thence will I take them out. And if they hide themselves from mine eyes, in the bottom of the sea, thence will I command the serpent, and he shall bite them. If they go into captivity before their enemies, there will I command the sword, and it shall slay them, and I will set mine eyes upon them for evil, and not for good." How the divine omnipresence here rolls itself around the victims of the divine anger ! In Ps. cxxxix. the poet wishes to escape from the Spirit of God as from a *thought* too strange and overwhelming for him ; but here Israel would seek escape from him as he might from the centre of a forest of fire, but is doomed for ever to seek it in vain. An historian has given an animated description of the impossibility of escape which beset the steps of the fugitive from the power of the

Roman emperor. If he crossed the Alps, that power was before him; if he crossed the ocean, it was waiting for him on the shore; and the tropic or the frigid zone was equally unable to hide him from its Briarian grasp. Still, there remained for him an avenue of deliverance. He might plunge into the sea, or turn his sword against his own bowels, or pledge his oppressor in poison. But for the object of the just vengeance of Jehovah there lay no such way of escape; he could not thus set his foe at defiance. The sea would say, "It is not in me;" Sheol (or Hades) would re-echo the cry; if he dropped into the arms of death, they would but hand him into those of the king of terrors; and if he sought to mount to heaven, this were to flee into the metropolis of his foe. Other worlds were barred against him; or even were their barriers broken, this were only to take down the palisades which blocked the way of his perdition. The universe was transfigured into a menacing shape, fronting the criminal with a face of fire, and stretching out on all sides its myriad starry hands to arrest his retreat, or to shed down dismay upon his guilty soul. —Gilfillan: *Bards of the Bible.*

9. *If I take the wings of the morning,* &c. Light has been proved by many experiments to travel at the astonishing rate of 194,188 miles in one second of time! and comes from the sun to the earth, a distance of 93,513,794 miles, in 8 minutes and nearly 12 seconds! But, could I even fly upon the wings or rays of the morning light, which diffuses itself with such velocity over the globe from east to west, instead of being beyond thy reach, or by this sudden transition be able to escape thy notice, thy arm could still at pleasure prevent or arrest my progress, and I should still be encircled with the immensity of thy essence. The sentiment in this noble passage is remarkably striking, and the description truly sublime. —*Bagsters' Bible.*

14. *I am fearfully and wonderfully made.* The human frame is so admirably constructed, so delicately combined, and so much in danger of being dissolved by innumerable causes, that the more we think of it the more we tremble, and wonder at our own continued existence.

"How poor, how rich, how abject, how august,
How complicate, how wonderful is man!
How passing wonder He who made him such,
Who mingled in our make such strange extremes
Of different natures marvellously mixed!
Helpless immortal, insect infinite,
A worm, a god—I tremble at myself!"

To do justice to the subject it would be necessary to be well acquainted with anatomy. I have no doubt that a thorough examination of that "substance which God hath curiously wrought" would furnish abundant evidence of the justness of the psalmist's words; and even those things which are manifest to common observation may be sufficient for this purpose. In general, it is observable that the human frame abounds with avenues at which enter everything conducive to preservation and comfort, and everything that can excite alarm. Perhaps there is not one of these avenues but what may become an inlet to death, nor one of the blessings of life but what may be the means of accomplishing it. We live by inhalation, but we also die by it. Diseases and death, in innumerable forms, are conveyed by the very air we breathe. God hath given us a relish for divers aliments, and rendered them necessary to our subsistence; yet, from the abuse of them, what a train of disorders and premature deaths are found amongst men! And where there is no abuse, a single delicious morsel may, by the evil design of another, or even by mere accident, convey poison through all our veins, and in one hour reduce the most athletic frame to a corpse.

The elements of fire and water, without which we could not subsist, contain properties which in a few moments would be able to destroy us; nor can the utmost circumspection at all times preserve us from their destructive power. A single stroke on the head may divest us of reason or of life. A wound or a bruise of the spine may instantly deprive the lower extremities of all sensation. If the vital parts be injured so as to suspend the performance of their mysterious functions, how soon is the constitution broken up! By means of the circulation of the blood how easily and suddenly are deadly substances diffused throughout the frame! Through this fearful medium not only the taint of vice rankles in the veins of the debauchee, but virtue itself may destroy us. The putridity of a morbid subject has been imparted to the very hand stretched out to save it. The poisoned arrow, the envenomed dart, the hydrophobic saliva, derive from hence their fearful efficacy. Even the pores of the skin, necessary as they are to life, may be the means of death. Not only are poisonous substances hereby admitted, but, when obstructed by surrounding damps, the noxious humours of the body, instead of being emitted, are retained in the system, and become productive of numerous diseases, always afflictive, and often fatal to life.

From these few instances we may learn our absolute dependence upon divine preservation. So numerous are the avenues at which death may enter, that no human foresight can possibly render us secure for a single moment: and even those dangers which may in a measure be avoided require for this purpose the regular exercise of reason; but reason itself depends upon a variety of minute causes over which we have no control. Instead of wondering at the number of premature deaths that are constantly witnessed, there is far greater reason to wonder that there are no more, and that any of us survive to seventy or eighty years of age.

" Our life contains a thousand springs,
  And dies if one be gone ;
Strange that a harp of thousand strings
  Should keep in tune so long "

Assuredly it can be ascribed to nothing short of the mighty power and all-pervading providence of God. A proper sense of this truth, while it would prevent us from presumptuously exposing ourselves to unnecessary injury, would induce us to commit ourselves to the divine protection in every danger which duty calls us to encounter.—*Fuller.*

16. *Thine eyes did see my substance yet being unperfect, and in thy book all my members were written which in continuance were fashioned when as yet there were none of them.* This is one of the most obscure and doubtful verses in the book of Psalms. Its difficulty to our own translators may be gathered from the fact, that *substance being yet imperfect* answers to a single Hebrew word, and that *my members* is a gratuitous addition to the text. The first word in Hebrew occurs only here, but is clearly derived from a verb which means to *roll* or *roll up* (2 Ki. ii. 8), and may therefore be supposed itself to signify something rolled up or rolled together, and from this may be deduced the sense of something shapeless or unformed, or more specifically that of an embryo or fetus. The next difficulty

lies in the expression *all of them*, evaded in the English Bible by changing it to *all my members*, and then making this the subject of the plurals following. The best interpreters are now disposed to construe *all of them* with *days* by a grammatical prolepsis. In thy book all of them are written—namely, all my days, as they were planned, projected, or decreed, before as yet one of them had really existed. *Written* and *formed* are then parallel expressions. *All of them are written*, days are delineated or depicted. By *days* (translated in our Bible *in continuance*) we are then to understand not merely the length but the events and vicissitudes of life. See Job xiv. 5; Ps. lvi. 8. This is one of those cases in which the difficulty lies in the particular expressions, while the general import of the passage is clearly determined by the context. Instead of (לֹא) *not*, the *keri* or marginal reading in the Hebrew Bible has (לוֹ) *to him*, a variation to which no one has succeeded in attaching a coherent sense. Precisely the same difference of text exists in Ps. c. 3.—*Alexander.*

23, 24. *Search me, O God*, &c. The truly religious man is anxious to know the real state of his heart. This anxiety is very visible in the prayer before us. David had evidently been searching and trying his own heart, and it was his desire to be thoroughly acquainted with it, which led him so earnestly to beseech God to search and try it also. But the heart is a book which few of us like to study. It is one which requires close and serious thought, and thought is one of those things which our careless minds most hate. Besides, it is a book which teaches many humbling and mortifying lessons, and we do not wish to be mortified and humbled. We love the falsehood which exalts, better than we love the truth which abases us. True religion, however, begins with thoughtfulness. It turns the eyes of a man inward upon himself. It causes him to commune with his own heart, and to make "diligent search" into his own spirit. True, he may find this self-examination painful and humiliating, but this makes no matter to him. He feels that he has the salvation of an immortal soul at stake, and he is not to lose that soul for the sake of being kept easy in his follies, and proud in his sins. . . .

The sincere Christian is not conscious of having within his heart one cherished sin. This is strongly intimated in the psalmist's prayer. His words imply that if there were any wicked way in him, any evil disposition habitually indulged, he could not be walking in the way everlasting. Not that he meant to speak of himself or of any other man as wholly free from sinful thoughts and desires, for on other occasions we hear him confessing that there was much sin within him, and bitterly lamenting it. But it is one thing to have iniquity entering the breast, and another thing to harbour it and have it reigning there. St. Paul felt a sinful "law in his members," but he felt it as a "warring against the law of his mind," as opposed to the habitual frame of his soul, to that holy and heavenly principle which made him "delight in the law of God after the inward man," and enabled him to "walk not after the flesh, but after the Spirit." Every Christian also feels the same warfare within. Sin tempts and harasses him, and sometimes brings him into captivity, but it cannot hold him in bondage; it cannot make him quietly submit to its hated laws. It overcomes and degrades him for an hour, but we soon see the prisoner struggling with his vile oppressor, and bursting the bonds. Trampling his lusts underneath his feet, we hear him exclaim, "I thank God, through Jesus Christ my Lord."—Bradley's Sermons.

PSALM CXL.

To the chief musician. A psalm. By David. We find ourselves in this psalm carried back not only to the times of David but to those of the Sauline persecution, from which the images are evidently borrowed. Besides the warlike tone, the vigorous conciseness, the verbal agreements with Davidic psalms, combined with eminent originality, the very structure is Davidic, and exhibits the familiar sequence of complaint (ver. 1–5), prayer (ver. 6–8), and confident anticipation (ver. 9–13). So clearly do these features of the composition mark its origin, even independently of the inscription, that nothing can account for its position here but the hypothesis already stated, that these ancient psalms were incorporated into a series of later date and placed in the collection, not according to their individual antiquity, but according to the date of the whole set or system into which they had been made to enter. Like the psalms immediately preceding, this was probably composed by David after the reception of the great Messianic promise, and with immediate reference to it.—*Alexander.*

The old opinion, that the psalm refers to the relation between David and Saul, has a certain measure of truth for its foundation. David has here, as also in Ps. cix., borrowed the colours from this relation: in Saul, the most powerful and malignant enemy of the past, he beholds the type of the future enemies of his seed. We find, in particular, also here a strong emphasis upon calumny and false accusations, which is characteristic of the Sauline psalms. Besides, it is precisely from these psalms that this psalm more especially borrows. —*Hengstenberg.*

10. *Let burning coals fall upon them*, &c. The expressions of wrath and imprecation against the enemies of God and of his people which occur in some of the psalms . . . seem to exhibit a vindictiveness which is apt to distress the feelings of many Christian readers. In order to obviate this offence, many of our pious commentators assure us that these expressions are not maledictions or imprecations, but simply declarations of what will or may take place. But this is utterly inadmissible, for in many of the most startling passages the language of the original is plainly imperative and not indicative (see Ps. lix. 14; lxix. 25, 28; lxxix. 6). "The truth is," says the writer of an able article on the subject in the *Bibliotheca Sacra* for 1844, "that only a morbid benevolence, a mistaken philanthropy, takes offence at these psalms, for in reality they are not opposed to the spirit of the gospel, or to that love of enemies which Christ enjoined. Resentment against evil-doers is so far from being sinful, that we find it exemplified in the meek and spotless Redeemer himself (see Mark iii. 5). If the emotion and its utterance were essentially sinful, how could Paul (1 Cor. xvi. 22) wish the enemy of Christ to be accursed (ἀνάθεμα), or say of his own enemy, Alexander the coppersmith, 'The Lord reward him according to his works' (2 Tim. iv. 14); and, especially, how could the spirits of the just in heaven call on God for vengeance?" Rev. vi. 10.—*Pictorial Bible.*

PSALM CXLI.

The superscription which ascribes the psalm to David is confirmed by the close affinity it bears to the psalms of David in connection with undoubted originality. The pregnant brevity of the language extorts, even from De Wette, the confession : "I consider it, with Ps. x., to be one of the oldest." That the psalm, like the whole cycle to which it belongs, refers to greater relations than those of a private individual, is evident from the expressions, "their judges," and "our bones," in ver. 6 and 7. It is also fitly assigned to this cycle on the ground, that ver. 9 and 10 connect themselves with the preceding psalm, while ver. 6 refers to Ps. cxxxviii. 4; and lastly, on account of the predilection peculiar to this cycle for rare words and unusual forms.—*Hengstenberg.*

5. *Let the righteous smite me,* &c. *Perowne* renders—"Let a righteous man smite me, it shall be a kindness; and let him reprove me, it shall be as oil upon my head : let not my head refuse it;" and adds, "According to the rendering I have preferred of this verse, the sense will be, "I will gladly welcome even the reproofs of the good (comp. Prov. xxvii. 6; Eccl. vii. 5), and I will avail myself of prayer as the best defence against the wickedness of my persecutors." It is possible, however, that the last clause may refer not to his enemies but to the righteous, in which case it must be rendered, "For still my prayer shall be offered in their misfortunes" (so Ewald).

Again, the first two clauses have been rendered, "Let a righteous man smite me in love (accus.) and reprove me. Such oil upon the head let not my head refuse" (Delitzsch). But nothing is gained by this, and the balance of the members is not so well preserved. Others again (as Maur., Hengst.) understand by the "righteous," God, appealing to Is. xxiv. 16—where, however, the "righteous" means not God, but "the righteous nation."

In ver. 4 he had prayed that he might not be led astray by the evil he saw around him, nor allured by the blandishments and luxurious prosperity of the wicked. Now he says, on the contrary, "Let me ever be ready to welcome even reproof from the righteous," which, however harsh, is salutary. The wounds of a friend are faithful, and better than the kisses of an enemy."

7. *Our bones are scattered at the grave's mouth,* &c. These words present a strong contrast between David's treatment of his enemies and that which they adopted towards him and those who were associated with him. We are not sufficiently informed respecting the cruelties which were perpetrated against David and those who adhered to him, to enable us to point out the instances to which he here alludes; but the murder of Abimelech and of the priests who were with him furnishes a pregnant proof of the atrocities which Saul and his agents were capable of perpetrating. See 1 Sam. xxii. It appears from the language of this verse that such enormities were not confined to a few cases, but must have been numerous, to give occasion to the image which is employed to describe them. As a man who ploughs or digs the earth, scatters it in abundance and without remorse, so were the bones scattered of those who dared to show any sympathy for the sufferings of this proscribed and devoted man.—*Walford.*

PSALM CXLII.

1, 2. *I cried unto the Lord,* &c. It showed singular presence of mind in David that he was not paralyzed with fear, or that he did not in a paroxysm of fury take vengeance upon his enemy, as he easily might have done; and that he was not actuated by despair to take away his life, but composedly addressed himself to the exercise of prayer. There was good reason why the title should have been affixed to the psalm to note this circumstance, and David had good grounds for mentioning how he commended himself to God. Surrounded by the army of Saul, and hemmed in by destruction on every side, how was it possible for him to have spared so implacable an enemy, had he not been fortified against the strongest temptations by prayer? The repetition he makes use of indicates his having prayed with earnestness, so as to be impervious to every assault of temptation.

He tells us still more clearly in the next verse that he disburdened his cares unto God. To pour out one's thoughts and tell over his afflictions implies the reverse of those perplexing anxieties which men brood over inwardly to their own distress, and by which they torture themselves, and are chafed by their afflictions rather than led to God; or it implies the reverse of those frantic exclamations to which others give utterance who find no comfort in the superintending providence and care of God. In short, we are left to infer that while he did not give way before men to loud and senseless lamentations, neither did he suffer himself to be tormented with inward and suppressed cares, but made known his griefs with unsuspecting confidence to the Lord. —*Calvin.*

PSALM CXLIII.

In unison with the superscription, the psalm bears evidence throughout of David's spirit and David's mode of expression. It is almost wholly composed of the sounds of complaint, supplication, and hope, which had already been uttered in the earlier Davidic Psalms (only in such), and had sunk deep into the heart. These clear brooks were drawn from all sides into the channel of this smooth-flowing psalm, which was designed to provide quickening for the fainting souls of David's race during future times of oppression. With so much of dependence the psalm still bears throughout the character of originality, not merely where the dependence ceases, as in ver. 2, which has become of such importance for the church, and to which the psalm owes its place among those of the penitential class, though, from its predominant tendency, it does not belong to that class, but also in the dependent passages themselves, in the thoughtful and artificial manner of their collection, which could only have proceeded from the person out of whose breast the utterances originally welled forth. There is nowhere any trace of "a flat compilation;" all is feeling and life. Along with this there is the repose and self-possession of one who does not find himself immediately involved in the distress, but looks down upon it as from a high tower, and prays and intercedes for the afflicted of his seed, as Moses of old did upon the Mount.

That the psalm must not be viewed apart from those that surround it, is clear already from the connection with Ps. cxlii., comp. ver. 4 here with ver. 3 there, ver. 8 with ver. 3, and ver. 11 with ver. 7. That David calls himself so expressly at the beginning and the end the servant of God, establishes a connection with 2 Sam. vii., where, in David's thanksgiving, this appellation occurs almost in every verse.—*Hengstenberg.*

The Septuagint ascribes this psalm to the period when David was in great distress, arising from Absalom's misconduct; which is as likely an opinion as any we can form. There is probably, in ver. 2, a tacit reference to the great transgression, the consequences of which followed David all his days. As he would not fail to be reminded of it by the sorrows which had now come upon him, and as his purpose was, notwithstanding, to implore divine support and deliverance, he deprecates God's righteous judgment, since if no man could be just with God, certainly he, who had so greatly transgressed, could have no claim to such a state. The consciousness of his guilt, though he had reason to believe it was forgiven, induced him thus to abase himself before God, when he was about to offer earnest entreaties for deliverance from dangers which threatened his dignity and life; while he still maintained his hope that God looked upon him as his servant, whom he had pledged himself to protect.—*Walford.*

This is the last of the seven Penitential Psalms, as they are called. In the Hebrew it is styled a Psalm of David; in some copies of the LXX. it is further said to have been written when he had to flee from his son Absalom. It is probable that the deep tone of sorrow and anguish which pervades the psalm, and the deep sense of sin, led to the belief that it must be referred to that occasion. The spirit and the language, it is true, are not unworthy of David; yet the many passages borrowed from earlier psalms make it more probable that this psalm is the work of some later poet. Delitzsch says very truly, that if David himself did not write it —and he admits that the many expressions derived from other sources are against such a supposition—still the psalm is "an extract of the most precious balsam from the old Davidic songs."—*Perowne.*

10. *Teach me to do thy will.* He now rises to something higher, praying not merely for deliverance from outward troubles, but, what is of still greater importance, for the guidance of God's Spirit, that he might not decline to the right hand or to the left, but be kept in the path of rectitude. This is a request which should never be forgotten when temptations assail us with great severity, as it is peculiarly difficult to submit to God without resorting to unwarrantable methods of relief. As anxiety, fear, disease, languor, or pain, often tempt persons to particular steps, David's example should lead us to pray

for divine restraint, and that we may not be hurried, through impulses of feeling, into unjustifiable courses. We are to mark carefully his way of expressing himself, for what he asks is not simply to be taught what the will of God is, but to be taught and brought to the observance and doing of it. The former kind of teaching is of less avail, as upon God's showing us our duty we by no means necessarily follow it, and it is necessary that he should draw out our affections to himself. God therefore must be master and teacher to us not only in the dead letter, but by the inward motions of his Spirit; indeed there are three ways in which he acts the part of our teacher, instructing us by his Word, enlightening our minds by the Spirit, and engraving instruction upon our hearts so as to bring us to observe it with a true and cordial consent. The mere hearing of the Word would serve no purpose, nor is it enough that we understand it; there must be besides the willing obedience of the heart. Nor does he merely say, *Teach me that I may be capable of doing*, as the deluded Papists imagine that the grace of God does no more than make us flexible to what is good, but he seeks something to be actually and presently done.

He insists upon the same thing in the next clause, when he says, *Let thy good Spirit lead me*, &c., for he desires the guidance of the Spirit not merely as he enlightens our minds, but as he effectually influences the consent of our hearts, and, as it were, leads us by the hand. The passage in its connection warns us of the necessity of being sedulously on our guard against yielding to inordinate passions in any contests we may have with wicked persons, and as we have no sufficient wisdom or power of our own by which to check and restrain these passions, that we should always seek the guidance of God's Spirit, to keep them in moderation.—*Calvin.*

12. *And of thy mercy cut off*, &c. In this verse he repeats for the fifth or sixth time that he looked for life only of God's free mercy. Whatever severity may appear on the part of God when he destroys the wicked, David affirms that the vengeance taken upon them would be a proof of fatherly mercy to him. Indeed these two things often meet together—the severity and the goodness of God; for in stretching out his hand to deliver his own people, he directs the thunder of his indignation against their enemies. In short, he comes forth armed for the deliverance of his people, as he says in Isaiah, "The day of vengeance is in mine heart, and this is the year of my redemption" (Is. lxiii. 4). In calling himself *the servant of God*, he by no means boasts of his services, but rather commends the grace of God, to whom he owed this privilege. This is not an honour to be got by our own struggles or exertions—to be reckoned among God's servants; it depends upon his free choice, by which he condescends before we are born to take us into the number and rank of his followers, as David elsewhere declares still more explicitly—"I am thy servant, truly I am thy servant, and the son of thine handmaid" (Ps. cxvi. 16). This is equivalent to making himself God's client, and committing his life to his protection.—*Calvin.*

PSALM CXLIV.

In unison with the superscription, David comes forth speaking, comp. especially ver. 2, which alone suffices to dispose of the supposition, that Israel is the speaker here; and the declaration: who constrains my people under me, cannot, without great violence, be brought into accordance with that supposition. David, as the author, appropriates also from Ps. xviii. It is an arbitrary supposition, that here a transference is made to Israel of what was then said originally of David. The confirmation which the superscription here derives from the contents comes also in support of the whole cycle to which the psalm belongs. An objection has been brought against the Davidic authorship from the "traces of reading" it contains. But one would require to consider more exactly what sort of reading is here to be thought of. It is only the psalms of David which form the groundwork of this. But that it is one of David's peculiarities to derive from his earlier productions a foundation for new ones, is evident from a variety of facts (comp. Introd. to Ps. cviii.), which, if any doubt might still be entertained on the subject, would obtain a firm ground to stand upon in this psalm, which *can* only have been composed by David. Then the way and manner of the use made of such materials is to be kept in view. This is always of a spirited and feeling nature, and no trace anywhere exists of a lifeless borrowing. That we cannot think here of such a borrowing, that the appropriation of the earlier did not proceed from spiritual impotence, but rests upon deeper grounds, is manifest from the consideration of the second part, where the dependence entirely ceases, and where even the opponents of the Davidic authorship have not been able to overlook the strong poetical spirit of the time of David. They betake to the miserable shift of affirming, that the psalmist had borrowed this part from a much older poem now lost.

The situation is that of an oppression through mighty external enemies. As this psalm rests upon Ps. xviii., which was composed by David toward the end of his life, after he had obtained deliverance from all the perils of war, it cannot be referred to the personal relations of David; David rather transports himself here, as in the whole of the cycle, into the future of his race.

This psalm forms the transition from the two prayer-psalms, cxli. cxliii., to the song of praise, cxlv. The cloud of adversity begins already to disperse, and the sun of salvation is on the eve of breaking forth. Ver. 9 and 10 show that the psalmist already stands on the threshold of praise and thanksgiving. The cry from the deep has ceased; at the very commencement, the exclamation, "Let the Lord be praised," &c., breathes the spirit of victory, and leads on to the: "I will praise thy name," in Ps. cxlv.—*Hengstenberg.*

This is a kind of supplement or counterpart to Ps. xviii., in which the view there taken of David's personal experience is applied to the anticipated case of his successors. The design thus assumed accounts for the position of the psalm in the collection. That its being placed precisely here is not fortuitous, may be inferred from its furnishing a kind of link between the urgent entreaties of the preceding psalms, and the triumphant praise of those which follow. The Davidic origin of this psalm is as marked as that of any in the Psalter. The accumulation of Davidic phrases is confined to the first part, while the last is independent and original, a fact entirely inconsistent with the supposition of a later compilation. The psalmist thanks God for his protection of himself, and of mankind in general, ver. 1-4; prays for deliverance from present dangers, ver. 5-8; expresses his confident anticipation of a favourable answer, ver. 9, 10;

renews his prayer, not only for himself but for the chosen people, ver. 11–14; and felicitates them that they are such, ver. 15.—*Alexander.*

The Spirit of the Lord spake by David the words of this song when the king felt his need of the King of kings to subdue the turbulent and proud spirits who were ambitious of distinction (ver. 2), as well as to conquer the nations of idolaters who hated God's anointed (ver. 7–11). The Spirit leads him back to the day when he sang Ps. xviii. (see ver. 1, 2), the day when he was delivered from Saul and other foes; and still further back to the quiet night when the strains of Ps. viii. ascended to the ear of Jehovah (see ver. 3); but he does not fail also to lead him forward to a future day, when earth shall witness its millennial scenes, among which, not the least wonderful and refreshing shall be Israel in all the restored plenty of his last times, with the favour of Jehovah over all. In all this, David was the type of Christ.—*A. A. Bonar.*

1, 2. *Blessed be the Lord my strength which teacheth my hands to war,* &c. Let poor and humble youths to whom the future seems dark, and who yet have noble aspirations to serve God and their generation, not be cast down, but hope in the Lord. He who took David from the crook and taught him the use of the sword and the sling, and lifted up his head above all his enemies round about, is still the patron of poor and pious boys and girls, who make him their refuge and their all. It matters not how unskilful one may now be, and how wholly unprepared for a given work, if God will but take him in hand. Even parents and instructors may sometimes bring great discouragements on their most promising children and pupils. More than one of Walter Scott's teachers complained of the thickness of his skull; a number of his teachers pronounced Barrow a blockhead; while Isaac Newton was declared to be fit for nothing but to drive the team. Jesse so slighted David, as not even to call him to the sacrifice, and his brothers declared that they knew the pride and naughtiness of his heart. But God raised him above all these obstacles and oppositions. Set your hope in God, struggling youth. Never cease prayer and effort.—*Plumer.*

3. *Lord, what is man that thou takest knowledge of him!* He amplifies the goodness shown by God by instituting

a comparison. Having declared how singularly he had been dealt with, he turns his eye inward, and asks, "Who am I, that God should show me such condescension?" He speaks of man in general, only the circumstance is noticeable, that he commends the mercy of God, by considering his lowly and abject condition. In other places he mentions grounds of humiliation of a more personal or private nature,—here he confines himself to what has reference to our common nature; and though even in discussing the nature of man, there are other reasons he might have specified why he is unworthy of the regard and love of God, he briefly adverts to his being like the smoke and as a *shadow*. We are left to infer that the riches of the divine goodness are extended to objects altogether unworthy in themselves. We are warned, when apt at any time to forget ourselves, and think we are something, when we are nothing, that the simple fact of the shortness of our life should put down all arrogance and pride. The Scriptures, in speaking of the frailty of man, comprehend whatever is necessarily connected with it. And, indeed, if our life vanish in a moment, what is there stable about us? We are taught this truth also— that we cannot properly estimate the divine goodness, unless we take into consideration what we are as to our condition, as we can only ascribe to God what is due unto him, by acknowledging that his goodness is bestowed upon undeserving creatures. The reader may seek for further information upon this point in Ps. viii., where nearly the same truth is insisted upon.—*Calvin.*

7. *Send thine hand from above, rid me from the hand of strange children.* David having celebrated his victories over some of his enemies, and extolled the mercy and goodness of God, to whom he ascribeth the achievement of them, now proceedeth to request a further manifestation of the omnipotent arm in his favour against other hostile forces, which still threatened his country upon his accession to the throne; such as the Philistines, Moabites, Ammonites, &c., see 2 Sam. v. and viii. These are called, metaphorically, "great waters," threatening to overwhelm and destroy everything; and, in plainer terms, "strange children," or aliens from the covenant of Jehovah, and the commonwealth of Israel; children who "speak lies, and work wickedness," or,

as Dr. Hammond interpreteth ver. 8, "Whose mouth speaketh or maketh profession of vanity," שָׁוְא, that is, idolatry; "and their right hand," that on which they depend for support, the object of their confidence, "is a right hand of falsehood," שֶׁקֶר, and one that will fail all who rely upon it for help. Jehovah, the God of Israel, is therefore entreated once more to appear in the cause of his anointed; to go forth, as of old, to the battle against the enemies of his people, with all the tokens of his displeasure and vengeance, dismaying and putting to flight these "armies of aliens." In like manner, the church, or mystical body of Christ, is instant in prayer for the final completion of her hope. She wisheth for the glorious day when her God and Saviour shall bow the heavens and come down to judgment, causing the mountains to smoke, and flame, and dissolve, and flow down before him; when his lightnings, those arrows of his indignation, and ministers of his vengeance, shall scatter the hosts of darkness, and destroy the anti-Christian power; when we shall be delivered from every enemy, and from all that hate us, and David our king.—*Horne.*

15. *Happy is that people,* &c. He thus concludes that the divine favour had been sufficiently shown and manifested to his people. Should any object that it breathed altogether a gross and worldly spirit to estimate man's happiness by benefits of a transitory description, I would say in reply that we must read the two things in connection, that those are happy who recognize the favour of God in the abundance they enjoy, and have such a sense of it from these transitory blessings as leads them through a persuasion of his fatherly love to aspire after the true inheritance. There is no impropriety in calling those happy whom God blesses in this world, provided they do not show themselves blinded in the improvement and use which they make of their mercies, or foolishly and supinely overlook the author of them. The kind providence of God in not suffering us to want any of the means of life is surely a striking illustration of his wonderful love. What more desirable than to be the objects of God's care, especially if we have sufficient understanding to conclude from the liberality with which he supports us that he is our Father? For every-

thing is to be viewed with a reference to this point. Better it were at once to perish for want than have a mere brute satisfaction, and forget the main thing of all, that they and they only are happy whom God has chosen for his people. We are to observe this, that while God in giving us meat and drink admits us to the enjoyment of a certain measure of happiness, it does not follow that those believers are miserable who struggle through life in want and poverty, for this want, whatever it be, God can counterbalance by better consolations.—*Calvin.*

PSALM CXLV.

The well-known 45th Psalm sang of the King in his beauty; this is a hymn of praise concerning the reign of Jehovah and his kingdom. It is a Davidic and an alphabetic psalm. In regard to its alphabetic structure, it has one peculiarity, viz. the "*nun*" is omitted; the reason of which may be, that (as we have seen in some other psalms of this structure) by means of that, or some other such omission, we might be kept from putting stress on the mere form of the composition.

It is peculiar, also, in its title; indeed, quite unique—"Of David: praise." The word is תְּהִלָּה. Some render this "a hymn;" others, such as Hengstenberg, "a *praise-song*," differing in this from the תְּפִלָּה, the "*prayer-song.*" It is prayer turned into praise. Patrick remarks that the term seemed so peculiar and excellent, that it was given from this psalm to the whole book, which is entitled by the Jews the book of תְּהִלִּים. Bythner has this note on the word—"So called because it is throughout nothing but the celebration of God; so that the ancient Jews used to say, that the man was already enjoying the felicity of the age to come, who daily recited it three times with the mouth and heart." We are getting now beyond the region of former themes; all in the remaining psalms is praise, praise; and this title is an appropriate introduction to the closing group of praise-psalms. Nor is its burden less appropriate; for, being a song of the kingdom, it ushers us into the region of eternal praise.—*Bonar.*

The design of this psalm, as its contents abundantly show, is to celebrate the power, righteousness, and goodness of God. It was probably written towards the conclusion of David's reign, when the kingdom of Israel had attained its highest prosperity, and was blessed on every side with the enjoyment of perfect peace and security.

During the attention which the writer of these remarks has necessarily given to the work which is now approaching its close, he has, in several instances, felt so powerfully the excellence of these songs of Zion, as to think that that on which he had last been engaged surpassed, in interest and beauty, all that had preceded. He does not mean to pledge himself to the perfect correctness of this view; but, with regard to the psalm which is now the object of consideration, he may venture to say, that if others equal to it may be selected, none certainly can be found superior in the lucid simplicity and native grandeur of its diction, or in the affecting and engaging sentiments which it discloses. It places before us the omnipotence of the Deity, combined with such express assertions of his essential rectitude and goodness as we cannot contemplate without perceiving that, glorious as are his works, he himself is surpassing in glory and beauty; and that no object on which our thoughts can be fixed bears any comparison with him. There are, in the bosoms of all men, who are in some measure acquainted with themselves, so many memorials of weakness and of guilt that the almightiness of God, when viewed apart from the unchangeable rectitude and benignity of his character, is far more likely to produce emotions of dread and horror than any sentiments of confidence and delight. But when we behold omnipotence united with infinite love, and with wisdom and rectitude so absolutely perfect that it is the most impossible of things for him to do wrong, then, if we desire his favour and friendship to forgive and sustain us, hope extends its consoling energies to our hearts, and we learn to rejoice in knowing that He in whose hands ourselves and all creatures are and must ever be, is invested with power to effect all the purposes of his beneficent will, and to feel that we are safer in his keeping than in our own; and that though we are frail, feeble, and unworthy, he is pledged by the necessary excellence of his nature to educe good from evil, and so to direct all events, temporal and eternal, as shall demonstrate him to be the only wise and good, and to be worthy of all glory and honour from the whole intelligent universe.—*Walford.*

PSALMS CXLVI.-CL.

These are the Hallelujah psalms, so called because they begin and end with *Hallelujah.* They form a fitting close to the book of Psalms. We subjoin the eloquent words of Mr. Gilfillan:—
" Perhaps finer than all are those little bursts of irrepressible praise which we find at the close. During the course of the book you had been conducted along very diversified scenes ; now beside green pastures, now through dark glens, now by still waters, now by floods, and now by dismal swamps, now through the silent wilderness, where the sun himself was sleeping on his watch-tower—in sympathy with the sterile idleness below ; and now through the bustle and blood of battlefields, where the elements seemed to become parties in the all-absorbing fury of the fray ; but, at last, you stand beside the psalmists, upon a clear, commanding eminence, whence, looking back on the way they had been led, forward to the future, and up to their God, now no longer hiding himself from his anointed ones, they break into pæans of praise ; and, not satisfied with their own orisons, call on all objects, above, around, and below, to join the hymn, become, and are worthy of becoming, the organs of a universal devotion. The last six or seven psalms are the Beulah of the book ; there the sun shineth night and day, and the voice of the turtle is heard in the land. From a reflection of their fire have sprung the hymn which Milton ascribes to our first parents, the hymn which closes the 'Seasons,' and the great psalm which swelled from the harp of Coleridge, as he struck it to the music of the Arveiron, and in the light of the morning-star. And surely those bright gushes of song occurring at the close, unconsciously typify the time when man, saved from all his wanderings, strengthened by all his wrestlings, and recovered from his falls, shall, clothed in white robes, and standing in a regenerated earth, as in a temple, pour out floods of praise harmonizing with the old songs of heaven—when the nations, as with one voice, shall sing —

"Praise ye the Lord, God's praise within
   His sanctuary raise ;
And to him in the firmament
   Of his power give ye praise.

Because of all his mighty acts,
   With praise him magnify :
O praise him, as he doth excel
   In glorious majesty.

"Praise him with trumpet's sound; his praise
   With psaltery advance :
With timbrel, harp, string'd instruments,
   And organs, in the dance.
Praise him on cymbals loud : him praise
   On cymbals sounding high,
Let each thing breathing praise the Lord,
   Praise to the Lord give ye."
            —*Bards of the Bible.*

PSALM CXLVI.

This psalm may be divided into two equal parts, the first of which describes the happiness of those who trust in God and not in man, ver. 1-5; while the second gives the reason, drawn from the divine perfections, ver. 6-10. The psalm is distinguished from the Davidic series which precedes it (Ps. cxxxviii.-cxlv.) by its whole internal character. At the same time, its coincidences of expression with the one immediately before it, show that it was meant to be used in connection with it, and may therefore be regarded as the closing psalm of the whole series, beginning with Psalm cxxxv., and belonging to the time of Haggai and Zechariah, to which the psalm before us is expressly referred in the Septuagint version.—*Alexander.*

PSALM CXLVII.

Like the last psalm and those which follow it, this is evidently an anthem intended for the service of the second temple. It celebrates God's almighty and gracious rule over his people and over the world of nature, but mingles with this a special commemoration of his goodness in bringing back his people from their captivity and rebuilding the walls of Jerusalem. In the allusions to these events in ver. 2, 3, and ver. 13, 14, we shall probably be justified in seeing the occasion of the psalm. It may have been written for the dedication of the wall of Jerusalem, which, as we learn from Neh. xii. 27, was kept "with gladness, both with thanksgivings and with singing, with cymbals, psalteries, and with harps." It is indeed not improbable, as Hengstenberg suggests, that not this psalm only, but the rest of the psalms to the end of the book, are all anthems, originally composed for the same occasion. The wall had been built under circumstances of no ordinary difficulty and discouragement (Neh. ii. 17; iv. 23); its completion was celebrated with no common joy and thankfulness; "for God had made them rejoice with great joy; the wives also and the children rejoiced: so that the joy of Jerusalem was heard even afar off."—*Perowne*.

The Old Testament history closes,. in point of time, with the administration of Nehemiah. The great work accomplished by Nehemiah was the restoration of the walls of Jerusalem. It was by this that he was afterwards remembered: "among the elect," says the son of Sirach, "was Neemias, whose renown is great, who raised up for us the walls that were fallen, and set up the gates and the bars, and raised up our ruins again." That a memorial of that work would be preserved in the closing strains of the Psalter is no more than we might expect to find; and we may reasonably conclude both from their language and place that it was for the occasion of the thanksgiving procession after the completion of the walls that Ps. cxlviii.-cl. were written. It was evidently no ordinary assemblage. "At the dedication of the wall of Jerusalem," we read, "they sought the Levites out of all their places to bring them to Jerusalem, to keep the dedication with gladness, both with thanksgivings and with singing, with cymbals, psalteries, and with harps. And the sons of the singers gathered themselves together, both out of the plain country round about Jerusalem, and from the villages . . . ; for the singers had builded them villages round about Jerusalem." The names of the priests' sons who blew the trumpets are carefully recorded, as also those of the other Levite musicians who marched "with the musical instruments of David the man of God, and Ezra the scribe before them;" while, lastly, a sort of epilogue at the end of the chapter in which this account is contained seems to imply that every effort was on this occasion made to re-establish the sacred musical service on the basis of the rules of the original foundation of David as nearly as the circumstances of the time would permit. And in this there was an obvious fitness. The rebuilding of the walls of Jerusalem was looked upon as the return to the days of David, by whom that city had been first erected into the Israelitish capital. The trials and humiliations of the captivity seemed at length to have passed away. All was once more new; and the Israel of the restored Jerusalem was the type of the church triumphant of the last days, the glorious company of victorious saints, ransomed from the captivity of an imperious world, into whose lips this very psalm is virtually put, and whose praises a yet struggling Christendom anticipates, looking forward with the certainty of divine assurance to the season of the final exaltation of the meek, and of the final casting of the wicked down to the ground.

The psalm has its points of resemblance to Ps. xxxiii. civ.; but almost every verse in it is marked by the restoration-character which belongs to the whole. Jerusalem built up after her desolation, the bars of her gates made fast; the children of God that were scattered abroad gathered together in one, and the denizens of Zion filled with the richest of blessings within her; the wounded bound up, the heart-broken healed; these are all images, the relation of which to the general theme of the psalm can hardly be mistaken.—*Thrupp*.

4. *He telleth the number of the stars,* &c. The late celebrated astronomer, Dr. Herschel, has informed us that in the most crowded parts of the Milky Way, when exploring that region with his best glasses, he has had fields of view which contained no less than 588 stars, and these were continued for many minutes; so that "in one quarter of an hour's time there passed no less than 116,000 stars through the field of view of his telescope." It has been computed that nearly *one hundred millions of stars* might be perceived by the most perfect instruments, were all the regions of the sky thoroughly explored. And yet, all this vast assemblage of suns and worlds, when compared with what lies beyond the utmost boundaries of human vision, in the immeasurable spaces of creation, may be no more than as the smallest particle of vapour to the immense ocean. Immeasurable regions of space lie beyond the utmost limits of mortal view, into which even imagination itself can scarcely penetrate, and which are, doubtless, replenished with the operations of divine wisdom and omnipotence. . . .

In consequence of recent discoveries, we have now the strongest reason to believe, that all the stars in the universe are arranged into clusters, or groups, which astronomers distinguish by the name of *Nebulæ* or *Starry Systems*, each nebula consisting of many thousands of stars. The nearest nebula is that whitish space or zone which is known by the name of the *Milky Way*, to which our sun is supposed to belong. It consists of many hundreds of thousands of stars. When Dr. Herschel examined this region with his powerful telescopes, he found a portion of it, only fifteen degrees long and two broad, which contained 50,000 stars, large enough to be distinctly counted: and he suspected twice as many more which, for want of sufficient light in his telescope, he saw only now and then. More than 2500 nebulæ have already been observed; and if each of them contain as many stars as the Milky Way, several hundreds of millions of stars must exist, even within that portion of the heavens which lies open to our observation.—*Dick.*

17. *Who can stand before his cold?* &c. At particular times the cold in the *East* is so very intense as to kill man and beast. *Jacobus de Vitriaco*, one of the writers in the *Gesta Dei per Francos*, says, that in an expedition in which he was engaged against Mount Tabor, on the 24th of December, the cold was so intense that many of the poor people, and the beasts of burden, died by it. And *Albertus Aquensis*, another of these writers, speaking of the cold in Judea, says, that thirty of the people who attended Baldwin I. in the mountainous districts near the Dead Sea, were killed by it; and that in that expedition they had to contend with horrible hail and ice, with unheard of *snow and rain*. From this we find that the winters are often very severe in Judea; and in such cases as the above, we may well call out, "Who can stand against his cold?" —*Adam Clarke.*

PSALM CXLVIII.

It is not unlikely that this hymn of praise was composed for the great solemnity of the dedication of the second temple. It consists altogether of praise, calling upon all nature, heavenly and earthly, rational and irrational, to concur in praising him whose power, wisdom, and providence are displayed in all his works. The exhortation which is addressed to inanimate and irrational beings is the language of poetry, which indulges and delights itself in attributing to every part of nature the sentiments, emotions, and feelings by which it is itself actuated; and in the lively expression of such sentiments we behold the fervent piety of the writer, which, yielding itself up to the delightful musings of impassioned imagination, peoples the universe with intelligent natures only, on which it calls to engage with itself in celebrating the matchless excellence of the Father of all, and in whom all "live, move, and have their being."—*Walford.*

Milton's imitation of this magnificent ode in the morning hymn of Adam in *Paradise Lost* is well known (v. 153, &c.)

Isaac Taylor says:—It is but faintly and afar off that the ancient liturgies (except so far as they merely copied their originals) come up to the majesty and the wide compass of the Hebrew worship, such as it is indicated in Ps. cxlviii. Neither Ambrose, nor Gregory, nor the Greeks have reached or approached this level; and in tempering the boldness of their originals by admixtures of what is more Christian-like and spiritual, the added elements sustain an injury which is not compensated by what they bring forward of a purer or less earthly kind: feeble indeed is the tone of these anthems of the ancient church; sophisticated or artificial in their style. Nor would it be possible—it has never yet seemed so—to christianize the Hebrew anthems, retaining their power, their earth-like richness, and their manifold splendours—which are the very splendours, and the true riches, and the grandeur of God's world —and withal attempered with expressions that touch to the quick the warmest human sympathies. And as the enhancement of all these, there is the *nationality,* there is that fire which is sure to kindle fire in true human hearts—

"He showeth his word unto Jacob,
His statutes and his judgments unto Israel.
He hath not so dealt with any nation;
As for his judgments, they have not known them."

—*Perowne.*

O what a hymn of praise is here! It is a *universal chorus!* All created nature have a share, and all perform their respective parts.

All *intelligent beings* are especially called to praise him who made them in his love, and sustains them by his beneficence. *Man* particularly, in all the stages of his being—*infancy, youth, manhood,* and *old age:* all human beings have their peculiar interest in the great Father of the spirits of all flesh.

He loves *man,* wheresoever found,

of whatsoever colour, in whatever circumstances, and in all the stages of his pilgrimage, from his *cradle* to his *grave*.

Let the *lisp* of the *infant*, the *shout* of the *adult*, and the *sigh* of the *aged* ascend to the universal parent, as a gratitude offering. He guards those who *hang upon the breast;* controls and directs the headstrong and giddy, and sustains *old age* in its infirmities; and sanctifies to it the sufferings that bring on the termination of life.

Reader, this is thy God! How great, how good, how merciful, how compassionate! Breathe thy soul up to him; breathe it into him and let it be preserved in his bosom till mortality be swallowed up of life, and all that is imperfect be done away.

Jesus is thy sacrificial offering; Jesus is thy mediator. He has taken thy humanity, and placed it on the throne! He creates all things new; and faith in his blood will bring thee to his glory! Amen! Hallelujah!

The beautiful morning hymn of Adam and Eve (*Paradise Lost*, book v. line 153, &c.):—

"These are thy glorious works, Parent of good; Almighty, thine this universal frame," &c.,

has been universally admired. How many have spoken loud in its praises who have never attempted to express their feelings in a stanza of Ps. cxlviii. But to the rapturous adorers of Milton's poetry what is the song of David, or this grand music of the spheres! Know this, O forgetful man, that *Milton's* Morning Hymn is a *paraphrase of this psalm*, and is indebted to it for every excellency it possesses. It is little else than the psalmist speaking in English instead of Hebrew verse.—*Adam Clarke.*

14. *He also exalteth the horn—a people near unto him.* While all the creatures before mentioned have abundant cause to praise God for his infinite perfection and his goodness to themselves, a peculiar obligation is incumbent on his people: first, for his distinguishing favour through all periods of their history; and then, for a special mercy recently experienced, namely, the restoration from captivity, now completed by the renewal of the temple and the reconstruction of the city walls. This restoration is described, by a favourite Davidic figure, as exalting or lifting up the horn of Israel. The previous condition of the chosen people might be well represented by the opposite figure used in Job xvi. 15. *Raised a horn for*

his people seems to be only another way of saying *raised the horn of his people*. The first form of expression may have been here used for the purpose of assimilating this clause to the next, where *praise* is still dependent on the verb at the beginning, and *to raise up praise for his people* is to give them fresh occasion of still higher praise than they had ever yet been called to utter. The ancient church is here described in a fourfold manner: first, simply as *his people*; then, as *his saints*, or *gracious ones*, the objects of his mercy and the subjects of his grace; then, by their national title, as *the sons* (or *descendants*) *of Israel*; and lastly, as the *people near him*, i.e. nearer to him than all others, sustaining a more intimate relation to him. The same expression which is elsewhere applied to the priests (Lev. x. 3; Ezek. xlii. 13) is here applied to Israel as "a kingdom of priests and a holy nation" (Ex. xix. 6).—*Alexander.*

PSALM CXLIX.

7, 8. *To execute vengeance upon the heathen,* &c. This last phrase occurs also at the close of the preceding psalm. As *written* may mean written in the book of God's decrees, there is no need of supposing a reference to any part of Scripture. If there be such reference, however, it is no doubt to the threatening in Deut. xxxii. 41-43. To act as God's instruments in this great judicial process, so far from being a disgrace or hardship, is an honour reserved for all the objects of his mercy and subjects of his grace. The psalm ends as it began, with *Hallelujah!*

PSALM CL.

Composed probably by Ezra as a fitting conclusion to the Fifth Book of Psalms, and to the collection at large. This Fifth Book, unlike the preceding four books, has no formal doxology, which, as Dr. Binnie remarks, "may be due in part to the circumstance that there was no need of anything to mark the end of the last book; but it is still more satisfactorily accounted for by the character of Ps. cl. It is, in effect, a doxology from beginning to end. For not only does it begin and end with *Hallelujah*, but every one of the intermediate lines is an exhortation to *Praise the Lord.*"

Hengstenberg's beautiful remark is often quoted—"As the life and the history of the church, so also the Psalter, with all its cries from the depths, runs out in a hallelujah."

3–6. *Praise him with the sound of trumpet. . . . Let every thing that hath breath praise the Lord.* Wherewith? With every instrument—with trumpet, psaltery, harp, soft timbrel, pipe, stringed instruments, and wind-instruments; with cymbals, softly played (שָׁמַע, that do not overpower the voice of the singer); and with cymbals of jubilee (2 Sam. vi. 5). Not merely an instrument of ten strings, as at other times. but ten distinct instruments are called for; and twelve times is the call uttered, "Praise ye!" Twelve times; so that each tribe is summoned, and then all the universe besides, to use their voice.

"*Let every thing that hath breath praise Jehovah!*" All creation is summoned to take part, and angels too, for they have interest in our redemption-scenes —since he is "to reconcile all things to himself, whether they be things on earth or things in heaven" (Col. i. 20). What magnificence and majesty in this close! Praise gathered in from every creature; every instrument of joy, and gladness, and triumph, and jubilee summoned to sound loud praise;

and every heart and voice engaged to help the choir. "Every voice teems with praise; every thought is about praise; every object awakens it; every power uses itself for his service" (*Meditat. on Psalms*).

We close the book with something of the feeling with which we suppose John came away from hearing "the voice of much people in heaven saying Hallelujah!" We seem to have been brought within hearing of heavenly melody, from heavenly harps and voices. Is not the closing verse taken up in Rev. v. 13—"And every creature which is in heaven, and on earth, and under the earth, and such as are in the sea, and all that are in them, heard I saying, Blessing, and honour, and glory, and power, be unto him that sitteth upon the throne, and unto the Lamb for ever and ever!" And again, in Rev. xix. 6, 7, when the great multitude, with voice "as the voice of many waters, and as the voice of many thunderings," cry "Hallelujah! for the Lord God omnipotent reigneth. Let us be glad, and rejoice, and give honour to him; for the marriage of the Lamb is come!" —*A. A. Bonar.*

THE END.